The Chicago Guide
to Grammar, Usage, and Punctuation

Chicago Guides
to *Writing*, Editing,
and Publishing

A Manual for Writers of Research Papers, Theses, and Dissertations
Kate L. Turabian

Student's Guide to Writing College Papers
Kate L. Turabian

Writing for Social Scientists
Howard S. Becker

The Craft of Translation
John Biguenet and Rainer Schulte, editors

The Craft of Research
Wayne C. Booth, Gregory G. Colomb, and Joseph M. Williams

From Dissertation to Book
William Germano

Getting It Published
William Germano

From Notes to Narrative
Kristen Ghodsee

Writing Science in Plain English
Anne E. Greene

Storycraft
Jack Hart

How to Write a BA Thesis
Charles Lipson

Developmental Editing
Scott Norton

The Subversive Copy Editor
Carol Fisher Saller

Legal Writing in Plain English
Bryan A. Garner

The Chicago Guide to Grammar, Usage, and Punctuation

Bryan A. Garner

The University of Chicago Press
CHICAGO AND LONDON

Bryan A. Garner is president of LawProse Inc. and Distinguished Research Professor of Law at Southern Methodist University. He is the author of the grammar and usage chapter of *The Chicago Manual of Style* and editor in chief of *Black's Law Dictionary*. His many books on language and law include *Garner's Modern English Usage* and *Legal Writing in Plain English*, the latter from the University of Chicago Press.

The University of Chicago Press, Chicago 60637
The University of Chicago Press, Ltd., London
© 2016 by Bryan A. Garner
All rights reserved. Published 2016.
Printed in the United States of America

25 24 23 22 21 20 19 18   2 3 4 5

ISBN-13: 978-0-226-18885-0   (cloth)
ISBN-13: 978-0-226-19129-4   (e-book)

DOI: 10.7208/chicago/9780226191294.001.0001

Library of Congress Cataloging-in-Publication Data
Names: Garner, Bryan A., author.
Title: The Chicago guide to grammar, usage, and punctuation / Bryan A. Garner.
Other titles: Chicago guides to writing, editing, and publishing.
Description: Chicago : University of Chicago Press, 2016. | ©2016 | Series: Chicago
    guides to writing, editing, and publishing | Includes bibliographical references.
Identifiers: LCCN 2015047425 | ISBN 9780226188850 (cloth :
    alkaline paper) | ISBN 9780226191294 (e-book)
Subjects: LCSH: English language—Grammar—Handbooks, manuals, etc. |
    English language—Grammar—Study and teaching (Higher)
Classification: LCC PE1106 .G35 2016 | DDC 428.2—dc23 LC
    record available at http://lccn.loc.gov/2015047425

♾ This paper meets the requirements of ANSI/NISO Z39.48-1992 (Permanence of Paper).

To Karolyne

Other Books Written or Edited by Bryan A. Garner

Garner's Modern English Usage (Oxford Univ. Press, 2016)

"Grammar and Usage," chap. 5 in *The Chicago Manual of Style*
(Univ. of Chicago Press, 16th ed. 2010)

HBR Guide to Better Business Writing (Harvard Business Review Press, 2013)

Quack This Way: David Foster Wallace and Bryan A. Garner Talk Language and Writing
(RosePen, 2013)

Black's Law Dictionary (Thomson Reuters, 10th ed. 2014)

Garner's Dictionary of Legal Usage (Oxford Univ. Press, 3rd ed. 2011)

Guidelines for Drafting and Editing Legislation (RosePen, 2016)

Reading Law: The Interpretation of Legal Texts, with Justice Antonin Scalia
(Thomson/West, 2012)

Making Your Case: The Art of Persuading Judges, with Justice Antonin Scalia
(Thomson/West, 2008)

The Winning Brief (Oxford Univ. Press, 3rd ed. 2014)

The Redbook: A Manual on Legal Style (West, 3rd ed. 2013)

Garner on Language and Writing, with preface by Justice Ruth Bader Ginsburg (ABA, 2009)

Legal Writing in Plain English (Univ. of Chicago Press, 2nd ed. 2013)

The Elements of Legal Style, with preface by Charles Alan Wright
(Oxford Univ. Press, 2nd ed. 2002)

The Winning Oral Argument (West, 2009)

Ethical Communications for Lawyers (LawProse, 2009)

Securities Disclosure in Plain English (CCH, 1999)

The Rules of Golf in Plain English, with Jeffrey Kuhn (Univ. of Chicago Press, 4th ed. 2016)

A New Miscellany-at-Law, by Sir Robert Megarry (Hart, 2005)

Texas, Our Texas: Remembrances of the University (Eakin Press, 1984)

Basic Law Terms (West Group, 1999)

Criminal Law Terms (West Group, 2000)

Family Law Terms (West Group, 2001)

Business Law Terms (West Group, 1999)

Grammar is the cradle of all philosophy.

John of Salisbury (ca. 1120–80)

English is not a subject. *English is everything.* For us who speak English, English is everything. English is what we say and what we think.

L. A. G. Strong, *English for Pleasure* (1941)

Nobody who thinks or writes can be above grammar. It is like saying, "I'm a creative genius, I'm above concepts"—which is the attitude of modern artists. If you are "above" grammar, you are "above" concepts; and if you are "above" concepts, you are "above" thought. The fact is that then you are not above, but far below, thought. Therefore, make a religion of grammar.

Ayn Rand, *The Art of Nonfiction* (1969)

I take the candid approach because it fits my teaching situation. My students understand very well what social status means, so I simply tell them, "If you speak this way, you go in the back door; if you speak *this* way, you go in the front door." I make it very clear that I neither built the house nor did I designate the doors. In this case, I am merely an agent showing off the real estate. I have the key to the front door, and once the student has the concept of usage levels I have given him the key. The back door is always ajar.

V. Louise Higgins, "Approaching Usage in the Classroom" (1960)

Contents

Introduction. **1**
    1   The field of grammar 1
    2   Who killed grammar? 2
    3   Why study grammar? 5
    4   Overview of the book. 7

I. The Traditional Parts of Speech **13**
    5   How did we arrive at the canonical eight? 13

Nouns 19

Traditional Classifications 19
    6   Nouns generally 19
    7   Common nouns 19
    8   Proper nouns 19
    9   Count nouns 20
   10 Collective nouns. 20
   11 Expressions of multitude. 20
   12 Expressions of partition 21
   13 Mass nouns 22

Properties of Nouns 23
   14 Generally 23
   15 Case. 23
   16 Number 23
   17 Gender 24
   18 Person 24

Plurals 25
   19 Generally 25
   20 Adding "-s" or "-es" 25
   21 Plurals of proper nouns. 25
   22 Nouns ending in "-f" or "-fe" 25
   23 Nouns ending in "-o" 25
   24 Nouns ending in "-y" 26
   25 Nouns ending in "-ics" 26
   26 Compound nouns. 26
   27 Irregular plurals 27
   28 Borrowed plurals 27
   29 Plural form with singular sense 28
   30 Plural-form proper nouns 29
   31 Tricky anomalies. 29

Case 29
  32 Function. 29
  33 Common case, nominative function 29
  34 Common case, objective function. 30
  35 Genitive case 30
  36 The "of"-genitive. 31
  37 Genitives of titles and names 32
  38 Joint and separate genitives 32

Agent and Recipient Nouns 32
  39 Definitions; use 32
  40 Appositives: definition and use. 33

Conversions 33
  41 Nouns as adjectives 33
  42 Nouns as verbs 34
  43 Adverbial functions 34
  44 Other conversions. 35

Pronouns. 36

Definition and Uses 36
  45 "Pronoun" defined. 36
  46 Antecedents of pronouns 36
  47 Clarity of antecedent 37
  48 Pronouns without antecedents. 37
  49 Sentence meaning. 38

Properties of Pronouns 38
  50 Four properties. 38
  51 Number and antecedent 38
  52 Exceptions regarding number of the antecedent. 39
  53 Pronoun with multiple antecedents. 39
  54 Some traditional singular pronouns 40
  55 Gender. 40
  56 Case. 41
  57 Pronouns in apposition. 41
  58 Nominative case misused for objective 41

Classes of Pronouns 42
  59 Seven classes 42

Personal Pronouns 42
  60 Form 42
  61 Identification 43
  62 Changes in form 43

63 Agreement generally 44
64 Expressing gender 44
65 Determining gender 44
66 Special rules. 44
67 Case after linking verb 45
68 Case after "than" or "as–as" 45
69 Special uses 46
70 The singular "they" 47

Possessive Pronouns 47
71 Uses and forms. 47
72 Possessive pronouns vs. contractions. 48

Reflexive and Intensive Pronouns 48
73 Compound personal pronouns: "-self" forms. 48
74 Basic uses of reflexive and intensive pronouns 49

Demonstrative Pronouns. 49
75 Definition 49

Reciprocal Pronouns 50
76 Generally 50
77 Simple and phrasal pronouns. 50

Interrogative Pronouns. 51
78 Definition 51
79 Referent of interrogative pronouns 51

Relative Pronouns 52
80 Definition 52
81 Gender, number, and case with relative pronouns. 52
82 Positional nuances. 52
83 Antecedent 53
84 Remote relative clauses. 53
85 Omitted antecedent. 54
86 Relative pronoun and the antecedent "one". 54
87 Function of relative pronoun in clause 54
88 Genitive forms 54
89 "Whose" and "of which" 55
90 Compound relative pronouns 55
91 "Who" vs. "whom". 55

Indefinite Pronouns 56
92 Generally 56
93 The indefinite pronoun "one". 57

Adjectives 58

Types of Adjectives 58
94   Definition 58
95   Qualitative adjectives 58
96   Quantitative adjectives 58
97   Demonstrative adjectives 59
98   Possessive adjectives 59
99   Interrogative adjectives 59
100 Distributive adjectives 60
101 Indefinite adjectives 60
102 Pronominal adjectives 60
103 Proper adjectives 60
104 Compound adjectives 60
105 Relative adjectives 60

Articles as Limiting Adjectives 61
106 Definition 61
107 Definite article 61
108 Definite articles and proper names 61
109 Indefinite article 61
110 Indefinite article in specific reference 62
111 Choosing "a" or "an" 62
112 Articles with coordinate nouns 62
113 Effect on meaning 62
114 Omitted article and zero article 63
115 Article as pronoun substitute 63

Dates as Adjectives 63
116 Use and punctuation 63

Position of Adjectives 64
117 Basic rules 64
118 After possessives 64
119 Adjective modifying pronoun 64
120 Predicate adjective 64
121 Dangling participles 65
122 Distinguishing an adjective from an adverb or participle . . . 65

Degrees of Adjectives 66
123 Generally 66
124 Comparative forms 66
125 Superlative forms 66
126 Forming comparatives and superlatives 66
127 Equal and unequal comparisons 67
128 Noncomparable adjectives 67

Special Types of Adjectives. 68
 129 Participial adjectives 68
 130 Coordinate adjectives 69
 131 Phrasal adjectives 69
 132 Exceptions for hyphenating phrasal adjectives. 70

Functional Variation 70
 133 Adjectives as nouns 70
 134 Adjectives as verbs. 70
 135 Other parts of speech functioning as adjectives 70
 136 The weakening effect of injudicious adjectives 70

Verbs 71

Definitions 71
 137 Verbs generally. 71
 138 Transitive and intransitive verbs. 71
 139 Ergative verbs 72
 140 Dynamic and stative verbs 72
 141 Regular and irregular verbs 73
 142 Linking verbs. 81
 143 Phrasal verbs 82
 144 Principal and auxiliary verbs 83
 145 Verb phrases 83
 146 Contractions 84

Infinitives 84
 147 Definition 84
 148 Split infinitive. 85
 149 Uses of infinitive. 85
 150 Dangling infinitive 85

Participles and Gerunds 86
 151 Participles generally. 86
 152 Forming present participles. 86
 153 Forming past participles. 87
 154 Participial phrases. 87
 155 Gerunds 87
 156 Gerund phrases 88
 157 Distinguishing between participles and gerunds 88
 158 Fused participles. 88
 159 Dangling participles 89
 160 Dangling gerunds 90

Properties of Verbs 90
161 Five properties 90

VOICE

162 Active and passive voice 90
163 Progressive conjugation and voice 91

MOOD

164 Generally 92
165 Indicative mood 92
166 Imperative mood 92
167 Subjunctive mood 92
168 Subjunctive vs. indicative mood 92
169 Present subjunctive 93
170 Past subjunctive 93
171 Past-perfect subjunctive 94

TENSE

172 Generally 94
173 Present tense 95
174 Past indicative 95
175 Future tense 96
176 Present-perfect tense 97
177 Past-perfect tense 97
178 Future-perfect tense 97
179 Progressive tenses 97
180 Backshifting in reported speech 98

TENSES ILLUSTRATED

181 Conjugation of the regular verb "to call" 99
182 Conjugation of the irregular verb "to hide" 105
183 Conjugation of the verb "to be" 112

PERSON

184 Generally 115

NUMBER

185 Generally 115
186 Agreement in person and number 116
187 Disjunctive compound subjects 117
188 Conjunctive compound subjects 117
189 Some other nuances of number involving conjunctions 118
190 Peculiar nouns that are plural in form but singular in sense . 118
191 Agreement of indefinite pronouns 118
192 Relative pronouns as subjects 118
193 "There is"; "Here is" 119
194 False attraction to intervening matter 119

195 False attraction to predicate noun 120
196 Misleading connectives: "as well as," "along with,"
      "together with," etc. 120
197 Agreement in first and second person 121

Auxiliary Verbs 121
198 Generally 121
199 Modal auxiliaries 121
200 "Can" and "could" 121
201 "May" and "might" 122
202 "Must" 122
203 "Ought" 123
204 "Shall" 123
205 "Should" 123
206 "Will" and "would" 124
207 "Dare" and "need" 124
208 "Do" 125
209 "Have" 125

Adverbs 127

Definition and Formation 127
210 Generally 127
211 Sentence adverbs 127
212 Adverbial suffixes 128
213 Adverbs without suffixes 128
214 Distinguished from adjectives 128

Simple vs. Compound Adverbs 128
215 Standard and flat adverbs 128
216 Phrasal and compound adverbs 130

Types of Adverbs 130
217 Adverbs of manner 130
218 Adverbs of time 130
219 Adverbs of place 130
220 Adverbs of degree 131
221 Adverbs of reason 131
222 Adverbs of consequence 131
223 Adverbs of number 131
224 Interrogative adverbs 131
225 Exclamatory adverbs 132
226 Affirmative and negative adverbs 132
227 Relative adverbs 132
228 Conjunctive adverbs 133

Adverbial Degrees 133
  229 Generally 133
  230 Comparative forms 133
  231 Superlative forms 133
  232 Irregular adverbs. 134
  233 Noncomparable adverbs 134

Position of Adverbs. 134
  234 Placement as affecting meaning 134
  235 Modifying words other than verbs 134
  236 Modifying intransitive verbs 135
  237 Adverbs and linking verbs. 135
  238 Adverb within verb phrase 135
  239 Importance of placement 136
  240 Adverbial objective 136
  241 Adverbial clause 136
  242 "Only" 137

Prepositions 139

Definition and Types 139
  243 Generally 139
  244 Simple, compound 139
  245 Phrasal prepositions. 140
  246 Participial prepositions. 141

Prepositional Phrases 141
  247 Generally 141
  248 Prepositional function 141
  249 Placement 141
  250 Refinements on placement 142
  251 Preposition-stranding 142
  252 Clashing prepositions 142
  253 Elliptical phrases. 142
  254 Case of pronouns 143

Other Prepositional Issues. 143
  255 Functional variation 143
  256 Use and misuse of "like" 143

Limiting Prepositional Phrases. 144
  257 Avoiding overuse 144
  258 Cutting prepositional phrases 144
  259 Cutting unnecessary prepositions. 144
  260 Replacing with adverbs. 144
  261 Replacing with genitives. 145
  262 Using active voice 145

Conjunctions. 146

263 Definition and types 146
264 Types of conjunctions: simple and compound 146
265 Coordinating conjunctions 146
266 Correlative conjunctions 146
267 Copulative conjunctions. 147
268 Adversative conjunctions 147
269 Disjunctive conjunctions 147
270 Final conjunctions. 147
271 Subordinating conjunctions 147
272 Special uses of subordinating conjunctions. 148
273 Adverbial conjunctions. 148
274 Expletive conjunctions. 149
275 Disguised conjunctions 149
276 "With" used loosely as a conjunction. 149
277 Beginning a sentence with a conjunction 150
278 Beginning a sentence with "however" 151
279 Conjunctions and the number of a verb 151

Interjections 152

280 Definition 152
281 Usage generally. 152
282 Functional variation 152
283 Words that are exclusively interjections 152
284 Punctuating interjections 152
285 "O" and "oh" 153

II. Syntax. **155**

Sentences, Clauses, and Their Patterns 157

286 Definition 157
287 Statements. 157
288 Questions 157
289 Some exceptional types of questions 157
290 Directives 158
291 Exceptional directives 158
292 Exclamations 158

The Four Traditional Types of Sentence Structures 159

293 Simple sentence 159
294 Compound sentence 159
295 Complex sentence. 159
296 Compound-complex sentence 159

English Sentence Patterns 160
  297 Importance of word order 160
  298 The basic SVO pattern 160
  299 All seven patterns 161
  300 Variations on ordering the elements 161
  301 Constituent elements 161
  302 Identifying the subject 162
  303 Identifying the predicate 162
  304 Identifying the verb 163
  305 Identifying the object 163
  306 Identifying complements 163
  307 Inner and outer complements 164
  308 Identifying the adverbial element 164

Clauses 165
  309 In general 165
  310 Relative clauses 165
  311 Appositive clauses 166
  312 Conditional clauses 166

Ellipsis 167
  313 Generally 167
  314 Anaphoric and cataphoric ellipsis 167
  315 Whiz-deletions 168

Negation 169
  316 Negation generally 169
  317 The word "not" 169
  318 The word "no" 171
  319 Using negating pronouns and adverbs 171
  320 Using "neither" and "nor" 171
  321 Words that are negative in meaning and function 172
  322 Affix negation 172
  323 Negative interrogative and imperative statements 172
  324 Double negatives 172
  325 Other forms of negation 173
  326 "Any" and "some" in negative statements 173

Expletives 173
  327 Generally 173
  328 Expletive "it" 174
  329 Expletive "there" 174

Parallelism 175
330 Generally 175
331 Prepositions. 176
332 Paired joining terms 176
333 Auxiliary verbs. 177
334 Verbs and adverbs at the outset. 177
335 Longer elements 177

Cleft Sentences 178
336 Definition 178
337 Types 179
338 Uses. 179

Traditional Sentence Diagramming 181
339 History and description 181
340 Benefits of diagrams. 181
341 Using diagrams. 182
342 Criticisms 182
343 How diagrams work. 182
344 Baseline 183
345 Subject 184
346 Predicate. 184
347 Direct object 184
348 Objective complement 185
349 Indirect object 185
350 Subjective complement. 186
351 One-word modifiers. 186
352 Prepositional phrases. 187
353 Adjective clauses. 187
354 Adverbial clauses. 188
355 Noun clauses 188
356 Infinitives 189
357 Participles 190
358 Gerunds 191
359 Appositives 192
360 Independent elements 192
361 Conjunctions 193
362 Diagramming compound sentences 193
363 Diagramming complex sentences 194
364 Diagramming compound-complex sentences 194

Transformational Grammar 195

Overview 195
365 Definition 195
366 Scope of section 195
367 Terminology of transformational grammar. 195
368 Tools of transformational grammar. 196
369 Universal symbols in rules 196
370 Tree diagrams 196

Base Rules in Transformational Grammar 196
371 Parts of speech 196
372 Sentence basics. 196

Nouns and Noun Phrases 197
373 Functions of noun phrases 197
374 Simple noun phrases 197

Determiners 198
375 Types of determiners 198
376 Numeric and nonnumeric determiners 198
377 Multiple determiners 198
378 Determiners in noun phrases. 198
379 Prearticles. 199
380 Noun phrases with determiner and prearticle 199

Noun-Phrase Modifiers. 199
381 Modifiers 199
382 Compound nouns 199
383 Combined rules 200
384 Number, person, and possession. 200

Verb Phrases. 200
385 Introduction 200
386 Functions of verb phrase. 200
387 Principal verbs 200
388 Auxiliaries. 201
389 Auxiliary verbs. 201
390 "Have" 201
391 Multiple auxiliaries 201
392 "Be" as a principal verb. 202

Different Types of Principal Verbs. 202
393 Generally 202
394 Middle verbs 202
395 Special subtypes 203

Adverbials 203
  396 Adverbials with principal verbs 203
  397 Simple adverbs 203
  398 Functions of simple adverbs 204
  399 Prepositional phrase as adverbial 204
  400 Noun phrase as adverbial 204
  401 Adverbials of place, time, and manner 204
  402 Number and tense of verbs 204

Transformations 205
  403 Deep and surface structure 205
  404 Transformational rules 205
  405 Surface transformation 205
  406 Simple-question transformation 206
  407 Imperative transformation 206
  408 Active- to passive-voice transformation and back again 207

Spotting Ambiguities 207
  409 Identification 207
  410 Lexical ambiguity 207
  411 Surface-structure ambiguity 208
  412 Deep-structure ambiguity 209
  413 Active- and passive-voice diagrams 210

III. Word Formation 213
  414 Generally 213
  415 Criteria for morphemes 213
  416 Free and bound morphemes 214
  417 Stems and affixes 214
  418 Inflectional and derivational suffixes 215
  419 Compounding 215
  420 Conversion 216
  421 Shortened forms 216
  422 Elongations 217
  423 Reduplicative forms 218
  424 Loan translations 218
  425 Acronyms and initialisms 218
  426 Neologisms 219

IV. Word Usage 221

Introduction 223
427 Grammar vs. usage 223
428 Standard Written English 223
429 Dialect 223
430 Focus on tradition 223

Troublesome Words and Phrases 225
431 Good usage vs. common usage 225
432 Using big data to assess linguistic change 225
433 Preventive grammar 227
434 Glossary of troublesome expressions 228

Bias-Free Language 324
435 Maintaining credibility 324
436 Gender bias 324
437 Other biases 324
438 Invisible gender-neutrality 324
439 Techniques for achieving gender-neutrality 324
440 Necessary gender-specific language 326
441 Sex-specific labels as adjectives 326
442 Gender-neutral singular pronouns 327
443 Problematic suffixes 327
444 Avoiding other biased language 328
445 Unnecessary focus on personal characteristics 328
446 Unnecessary emphasis on the trait, not the person 328
447 Inappropriate labels 328

Prepositional Idioms 329
448 Idiomatic uses 329
449 Shifts in idiom 329
450 Words and the prepositions construed with them 329

V. Punctuation 345
451 Introduction 345

The Comma 347

Using Commas 347
452 With a conjunction between independent clauses 347
453 After a transitional or introductory phrase 347
454 To set off a nonrestrictive phrase or clause 348
455 To separate items in a series 348
456 To separate parallel modifiers 348

457 To distinguish indirect from direct speech 349
458 To separate the parts of full dates and addresses 349
459 To separate long numbers into three-digit chunks 349
460 To set off a name, word, or phrase used as a vocative 350
461 Before a direct question inside another sentence 350
462 To set off "etc.," "et al.," and the like at the end of a series . . . 350
463 After the salutation in an informal letter. 351

Preventing Misused Commas 351
464 Not to separate a subject and its verb. 351
465 Not to separate a verb and its object 351
466 Not to set off a quotation that blends into the sentence 352
467 Not to set off an adverb that needs emphasis 352
468 Not to separate compound predicates 352
469 Not to use alone to splice independent clauses 353
470 Not to use after a sentence-starting conjunction 354
471 Not to omit after an internal set-off word or phrase 354
472 Not to set off restrictive matter 355
473 Not around name suffixes such as Jr., III, Inc., and Ltd. . . . 356
474 Not to separate modifiers that aren't parallel 356

The Semicolon 357

Using Semicolons 357
475 To unite two short, closely connected sentences 357
476 To separate items in a complex series 358
477 In old style, to set off explanation or elaboration 358

Preventing Misused Semicolons 359
478 Not where a colon is needed, as after a formal salutation . . . 359
479 Not where a comma suffices, as in a simple list 360

The Colon 361

Using Colons 361
480 To link matter and indicate explanation or elaboration 361
481 To introduce an enumerated or otherwise itemized list 361
482 To introduce a question 362
483 Use a colon to introduce a question 363
484 After the salutation in business correspondence 363
485 To separate hours from minutes and in some citations 363
486 Without capitalizing the following matter needlessly 364

Preventing Misused Colons 364
487 Not to introduce matter that blends into your sentence 364

Parentheses 365

Using Parentheses 365
488 To set off inserted matter that you want to minimize 365
489 To clarify appositives or attributions 366
490 To introduce shorthand or familiar names 366
491 Around numbers or letters when listing items in text 366
492 To denote subparts in a citation 367
493 Correctly in relation to terminal punctuation 367
494 To enclose a brief aside 368

Preventing Misused Parentheses 368
495 Not before an opening parenthesis 368

The Em-Dash (or Long Dash) 369

Using Em-Dashes 369
496 To set off matter inserted in midsentence 369
497 To set off but emphasize parenthetical matter 369
498 To tack on an important afterthought 370
499 To introduce a specification or list 370
500 To show hesitation, faltering, or interruption 370

Preventing Misused Em-Dashes 371
501 Not using more than two in a sentence 371
502 Not after a comma, colon, semicolon, or terminal period . . 372

The En-Dash (or Short Dash) 373

Using En-Dashes 373
503 In a range, to show tension, or to join equivalents 373

Preventing Misused En-Dashes 373
504 Not in place of a hyphen or em-dash 373
505 Not with the wording it replaces 374

The Hyphen 375

Using Hyphens 375
506 To join parts of a phrasal adjective 375
507 To mark other phrasal-adjective and suffix connections . . . 376
508 In closely associated compounds according to usage 376
509 When writing out fractions and two-word numbers 376
510 To show hesitation, stammering, and the like 377
511 In proper names when appropriate 377
512 In some number groups or when spelling out a word 377
513 With "l-" suffixes (e.g., "-like") on words ending in "-ll" 377

Preventing Misused Hyphens 378
  514 Not after a prefix unless an exception applies 378
  515 Not in place of an em-dash, even when doubled ("--") 378
  516 Not with an "-ly" adverb and a participial adjective 379
  517 Not in a phrasal verb 379

The Apostrophe 380

Using Apostrophes 380
  518 To indicate the possessive case 380
  519 To mark a contraction or to signal dialectal speech 380
  520 To form plurals of letters, digits, and some abbreviations . . 381

Preventing Misused Apostrophes 381
  521 Not to form other plurals, especially of names 381
  522 Not to omit obligatory apostrophes 381

Quotation Marks 382

Using Quotation Marks 382
  523 To quote matter of 50 or fewer words 382
  524 When using a term as a term or when defining a term 382
  525 When you mean "so-called" or "but-not-really" 383
  526 For titles of short-form works, according to a style guide . . 383
  527 To show internal quotation using single marks 384
  528 To signal matter used idiomatically, not literally 384
  529 Placed correctly in relation to other punctuation 384

Preventing Misused Quotation Marks 385
  530 Not for a phrasal adjective 385
  531 Not to emphasize a word or note its informality 385

The Question Mark 386

Using Question Marks 386
  532 After a direct question 386

Preventing Misused Question Marks 386
  533 Not after an indirect question 386

The Exclamation Mark 387

Using Exclamation Marks 387
  534 After exclamatory matter, especially when quoting others . . 387

Preventing Misused Exclamation Marks 387
  535 Not to express your own surprise or amazement 387

The Period 388

Using Periods 388
536 To end a typical sentence, not a question or exclamation . . . 388
537 To indicate an abbreviated name or title 388
538 Placed properly with parentheses and brackets 389
539 To show a decimal place in a numeral 389

Preventing Misused Periods 389
540 Not with an abbreviation at sentence end 389

Brackets 390

Using Brackets 390
541 In a quotation, to enclose matter not in the original 390
542 In parenthetical matter, to enclose another parenthetical . . . 390
543 To enclose the citation of a source, as in a footnote 391

Preventing Misused Brackets 391
544 Not in place of ellipsis dots when matter is deleted 391

The Slash (Virgule) 392

Using Slashes 392
545 To separate alternatives (but never "and/or") 392
546 To separate numerical parts in a fraction 392
547 Informally, to separate elements in a date 392
548 Informally, as a shorthand signal for "per" 393
549 To separate lines of poetry or of a song 393

Preventing Misused Slashes 393
550 Not when a hyphen or en-dash would suffice 393

Bullets 394
551 To mark listed items of a more or less equal ranking 394

Ellipsis Dots 396

Using Ellipsis Dots 396
552 To show that an unfinished sentence trails off 396
553 To signal rumination, musing, or hesitation 396
554 To signal an omission of matter within a quotation 397
555 With following period, to show omission at sentence end . . . 397
556 With preceding period, to show omission after sentence . . . 397

Preventing Misused Ellipsis Dots 398
557 Omitting space or allowing a line break between dots 398
558 Beginning a quotation with ellipsis dots 399

Select Glossary   401

Sources for Inset Quotations   491

Select Bibliography   497

Acknowledgments   507

Word Index   509

General Index   543

Pronunciation Guide   583

Introduction

1 *The field of grammar.* In its usual sense, grammar is the set of rules governing how words are put together in sentences to communicate ideas—or the study of these rules. Native speakers of a language learn them unconsciously. The rules govern most constructions in any given language. The small minority of constructions that lie outside these rules fall mostly into the category of idiom and customary usage.

There are many schools of grammatical thought—and differing vocabularies for describing grammar. Grammatical theories have been in upheaval in recent years. Seemingly the more we learn, the less we know. As the illustrious editor in chief of the *Oxford English Dictionary* wrote in 1991: "An entirely adequate description of English grammar is still a distant target and at present seemingly an unreachable one, the complications being what they are."[1] In fact, the more detailed the grammar (it can run to many large volumes), the less likely it is to be of any practical use to most writers and speakers.

> It [the doctrine of usage] asserts that "Good use is the general, present-day practice of the best writers." One bone we could pick would be with that "best." How are they the best writers except by using the words in the best ways? We settle that they *are* the best writers because we find them using their words successfully. We do not settle that theirs is the right, the "good usage" of the words because *they* use them so. Never was there a crazier case of putting the cart before the horse. It is as though we were to maintain that apples are healthy because wise people eat them, instead of recognizing that it is the other way about—that it is what the food will do for us which makes us eat it, not the fact that we eat it which makes it good food.
> —I. A. Richards
> *The Philosophy of Rhetoric*

Grammar should be an attempt to describe the English language as it is actually used—beginning with the facts and not with ingrained biases about what should and should not be considered grammatical. But that's not the whole story. *Describe* English, yes—but *whose* English? The traditional view of English grammar is that it should record the linguistic habits of refined speakers and writers: the best English, or standard literary English shorn of dialect and idioms that typify the language of uneducated speakers. It is the type of English, in other words, that marks

---

1   Robert W. Burchfield, *Unlocking the English Language* (New York: Hill and Wang, 1991), 22.

its user as an educated speaker or writer. It can be found in the pages of reputable newsmagazines and nonfiction books (and much fiction, too, but less reliably so because of the utility of dialectal usage in dialogue and experimental usage within narrative).

Not everyone aspires to the standard language—and as a result our culture becomes more varied and interesting. But anyone who does aspire to it will find that it can be cultivated, partly through wide reading of serious writing and partly through close study of its techniques. Although nobody speaks or writes standard literary English infallibly—just as nobody behaves or exercises judgment infallibly—good English exists as certainly as good behavior and good judgment do.

2 *Who killed grammar?* During the 141 years from 1711 through 1851, grammars were among the most popular books published in English. There were hundreds of them. Seemingly every English-speaking household had, at a minimum, a Bible and a grammar. Lindley Murray, sometimes called "the father of English grammar,"[2] sold some 15 million copies of his *English Grammar* and other literary books from 1795 to 1840.[3] In 1851, Goold Brown's humongous *Grammar of English Grammars* appeared, occupying 1,102 pages on the subject.

For the rest of the 19th century, the teaching of grammar was fairly stable. The top names in school grammars after 1850 were John Seely Hart,[4] Allen Hayden Weld,[5] Thomas N. Harvey,[6] Simon Kerl,[7] and William H. Maxwell.[8] The dawn of the 20th century saw the rise of the first scholarly grammars and "college grammars," still along the line of traditional grammars but somewhat more elaborate and standardized. Among the leading texts through the mid-20th century were those by

---

2   Paul Harvey, *The Oxford Companion to English Literature,* 2nd ed. (Oxford: Oxford Univ. Press, 1937), 542. See also Bryan A. Garner, "Lindley Murray," in *Invisible Giants: Fifty Americans Who Shaped the Nation but Missed the History Books,* ed. Mark Carnes (New York: Oxford Univ. Press, 2002), 209–10.

3   Charles Monaghan, *The Murrays of Murray Hill* (Brooklyn: Urban History, 1998), 95.

4   John Seely Hart, *A Grammar of the English Language* (Philadelphia: Eldredge and Bro., 1882).

5   Allen Hayden Weld, *The Progressive English Grammar* (Portland, ME: Bailey and Noyes, 1863).

6   Thomas N. Harvey, *A Practical Grammar of the English Language,* rev. ed. (New York: American Book Co., 1868).

7   Simon Kerl, *A Common-School Grammar of the English Language* (New York: Ivison, Phinney, Blakeman, 1866); Kerl, *First Lessons in English Grammar* (New York: Ivison, Phinney, Blakeman, 1868).

8   William H. Maxwell, *Advanced Lessons in English Grammar* (New York: American Book Co., 1891).

Henry Sweet,[9] George Lyman Kittredge and Frank Edgar Farley,[10] Otto Jespersen,[11] Janet Rankin Aiken,[12] and George O. Curme.[13]

A campaign against traditional grammar had started by the early 20th century. In 1910 a leading commentator wrote:

> What was the meaning of the reaction against the study of formal Grammar of the Lindley Murray type? The main count against it was that it failed of practical results; failed as a communicable "art of speaking and writing the English language with propriety,"—to quote the Murray definition. The endless formalities of rule and precept were found to be wasteful burdens of knowledge unrelated to practice.[14]

What was not then known was that nothing better would replace traditional grammar—at least nothing better that might still be comprehensible to the educated public in general, and nothing related to the teaching of composition.

By the early 20th century there was a drumbeat of dissatisfaction with the doctrine of grammatical "correctness." Things like the parts of speech and sentence diagramming were criticized—mostly among expert linguists, not practical teachers. New schools of thought arose, each with its own nomenclature and classification system.[15] That trend has only continued in the years since.

Some saw growing standardization as outright dogmatism, and in 1927 Charles Carpenter

> Between charges that it was *not* being taught and *should* be taught and charges that it *was* being taught and should *not* be, grammar has had a very bad time of it for more than a quarter of a century.
> —Bertrand Evans
> "Grammar and Writing"

Fries, in his *Teaching of the English Language*, urged "the overthrow of the traditional view"[16] of correctness as determined by the rules of con-

---

9   Henry Sweet, *A New English Grammar: Logical and Historical*, 2 vols. (Oxford: Clarendon, 1891, 1898).

10 George Lyman Kittredge and Frank Edgar Farley, *An Advanced English Grammar* (Boston: Ginn, 1913).

11 Otto Jespersen, *The Philosophy of Grammar* (New York: H. Holt, 1924); Otto Jespersen, *Essentials of English Grammar* (New York: Holt, 1933).

12 Janet Rankin Aiken, *Commonsense Grammar* (New York: Thomas Y. Crowell, 1936).

13 George O. Curme, *The Grammar of the English Language*, 2 vols. (Boston: Heath and Co., 1935).

14 Percival Chubb, *The Teaching of English in the Elementary and the Secondary School* (New York: Macmillan, 1910), 205.

15 See Robert C. Pooley, *Teaching English Grammar* (New York: Appleton-Century-Crofts, 1957), 54–73.

16 Charles Carpenter Fries, *The Teaching of the English Language* (New York: Thomas Nelson and Sons, 1927), 185. The book was republished for a larger audience in 1949.

ventional school grammars. He wanted to jettison past methods: "For more than a century *good English* has been one of the major concerns of our educational system.... [Yet] we do not by any means agree as to what this *good English* is."[17] Fries was an influential voice, and over time—with the backing of the National Council of Teachers of English—the grammatical putsch succeeded.

By the mid-20th century, the structural linguists—also known as *generative grammarians*—rose with a wholly new way of describing the English language: transformational grammar. Unlike traditional grammar, this new discipline was not a didactic system to help students use "good grammar"—in fact, the linguists no longer believed in "good grammar" or in using grammar as a vehicle for teaching English composition. They came to believe that if a native speaker utters a sentence, it is necessarily appropriate to the speaker's dialect. They sought to record linguistic structures and describe syntax dispassionately and scientifically— usually with no preference for Standard Written English over regional and class dialects.

Transformational grammar was a descriptive method based on a theory first proposed by the linguist Noam Chomsky in 1957.[18] Chomsky sought to describe how people produce and understand original sentences without formally learning rules for grammatical structures. According to his original theory, native speakers assimilate the natural rules of the language and internalize them. Transformational grammar attempts to describe those internal rules by first looking at a sentence's structure and then deriving a formulalike rule or a tree diagram to show how a sentence or sentence part is formed. Sporadic, mostly unsuccessful attempts to teach grade-school children English using transformational grammar were made during the 1960s and early 1970s. Today it is taught mostly in colleges and graduate schools. Outside linguistics, transformational grammar is used mostly in computer-language-processing applications. It has an alien look and feel to traditionalists, but it can convey interesting insights into how the language works (see §§ 365–413).

In the late 20th century, it was common for the high-school and college courses that still taught grammar to treat it on dual tracks: traditional grammar plus transformational grammar.

Since then, no clear consensus has been reached, and the more advanced grammars have become so specialized and jargon-filled as to

---

17   Ibid., 1949 ed., 1–2.

18   Noam Chomsky, *Syntactic Structures* (The Hague: Mouton, 1957).

be incomprehensible to all but other specialists. In the mid-1980s, the literary critic Christopher Ricks observed that many modern grammarians express themselves in a manner "as inviting as a tall wall bottled-spiked."[19] About the same time, Robert W. Burchfield, then editor of the *Oxford English Dictionary*, said that this impenetrable grammatical gobbledygook had led to an "unrelieved intellectual apartheid" that left most educated speakers of English "disastrously uninformed and uninstructed."[20]

Small wonder that the subject is hardly studied today—given that many of these moderns call themselves *grammaticographers* who study *grammaticology*.[21] And small wonder that the grammatical heyday of the 18th and 19th centuries remains a dim memory on the literary landscape—an implausible past in which grammars were exceeded in sales only by the Bible.

In 1952 a bewildered and frustrated Harry C. Warfel, professor of English at the University of Florida, wrote *Who Killed Grammar?*, in which he detailed the demise of the subject in American secondary schools and colleges—laying blame mostly at the feet of Fries.[22] Together with other linguists, Fries had succeeded in divorcing grammatical learning from the pedagogy of English composition. The sad saga was updated and elaborated in an excellent 2003 book by David Mulroy: *The War Against Grammar*.[23]

In any event, grammar was never killed—even if it was wounded. It is very much alive, as evidenced by the interest you're showing at this very moment. Your own learning about grammar will help hasten its recovery.

3   *Why study grammar?* Perhaps the most important reason for learning about grammar is that language is basic to almost everything we do—and the more nearly you can master it, the more effectively you'll think, speak, and write. You'll be more aware of ideas and how they're expressed. You'll make finer distinctions. A knowledge of grammar is fundamental to critical thinking.

> We cannot know too much about the language we speak every day of our lives.
> —Simeon Potter
> *Our Language*

---

19   Christopher Ricks, *London Review of Books*, June 6, 1985, 9.

20   Robert W. Burchfield, *Unlocking the English Language* (London: Faber, 1989), 179.

21   See Andrew Linn, "English Grammar Writing," in *The Handbook of English Linguistics*, ed. Bas Aarts and April McMahon (Malden, MA: Blackwell, 2006), 72, 74.

22   Harry R. Warfel, *Who Killed Grammar?* (Gainesville: Univ. of Florida Press, 1952), v.

23   David Mulroy, *The War Against Grammar* (Portsmouth, NH: Boynton/Cook, 2003).

You'll also find that a knowledge of grammar and usage opens up doors for you. Without it, your opportunities in life would be limited. That's true in any culture and with every language—and it's true of English-speaking countries. If you're an ambitious speaker of English, you'll want to learn Standard Written English. You'll find a richer appreciation of English literature, and you'll benefit in ways both tangible and intangible—ways that you can't possibly appreciate until you've gained the knowledge.

An illustrative story: Many biographers of Abraham Lincoln have noted his early preoccupation with Samuel Kirkham's *English Grammar in Familiar Lectures* (1820). When he first heard about the book, Lincoln walked six miles to get a copy.[24] He burned pine shavings in a blacksmith shop so that he could read it at night.[25] He committed whole sections of the book to memory, often wheedling friends into quizzing him.[26] He wanted to learn to speak well and write well. And so he did: he is widely considered the foremost orator and writer ever to have served as president of the United States.

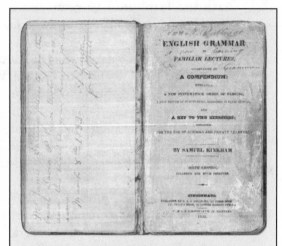

The title page of the very copy of Kirkham's *English Grammar* used by Abraham Lincoln. Mounted inside the front cover is a promissory note for $30 witnessed by Abraham Lincoln as agent.
Courtesy: Library of Congress

Another story—a little less sublime: A professor acquaintance of mine had a college student who was determined to teach Greek philosophy. But the student couldn't pass his first semester of Greek. The professor told the student what his problem was: he didn't know the first thing about English grammar. (Other profs had said he just lacked innate ability.) After taking a couple of courses in English grammar, which he

---

24 Carl Sandburg, *Abraham Lincoln, The Prairie Years* (New York: Harcourt, Brace, 1926), 139.

25 Ibid.

26 Ronald C. White Jr., *The Eloquent President* (New York: Random House, 2005), 193.

found challenging, the student tried again and succeeded with distinction. In fact, he went on to study medieval Latin as well. That competence, combined with his mastery of Greek, was decisive in getting him a good college teaching post the same year he earned his Ph.D. Today his academic career is flourishing. Both he and his advisers declare that English grammar paved the way.

Your own path will be unlike those. It will assuredly be unique. But one thing is certain: in the long term, your acquiring Standard Written English will only help you reach your most ambitious goals. Wear it lightly. Be practical, not pedantic. Seek to be astute in the way you handle language. In addition to speaking well and writing well, learn to listen well. You'll perceive more. And listen sympathetically.

4 *Overview of the book.* As traditionally understood, grammar is both a science and an art. Often, it has focused—as part I of this book does—on parts of speech (or *word classes*). Each part of speech performs a particular function in a sentence or phrase. Traditional grammar has held that there are eight parts of speech: nouns, pronouns, adjectives, verbs, adverbs, prepositions, conjunctions, and interjections.[27] Some grammars have added a ninth: articles.[28] But as you'll soon discover (see § 5), reckonings vary.

The first 285 sections of this book deal with the traditional eight; each part of speech is discussed in some detail. The purpose here is to sketch some of the main lines of English grammar using mostly traditional grammatical terms.

Part II deals with syntax: the rules governing the arrangement of words and phrases into sentences. Traditional grammarians classified sentences into four types according to their purposes (statements, questions, directives, and exclamations), as well as four structural types according to the structure of clauses (simple, compound, complex, and compound-complex). More modern grammarians have isolated seven fundamental patterns into which English sentences can be classified by word order. Part II explains these ideas along with the basics of sentence diagramming and the newer "sentence trees" of transformational grammar.

---

27 See Robert L. Allen, *English Grammars and English Grammar* (New York: Scribner, 1972), 7.

28 See, e.g., James R. Hurford, *Grammar: A Student's Guide* (Cambridge: Cambridge Univ. Press, 1994), 148–49.

In part III we take up the subject of word formation, also known as *morphology*: the study of how small word-units known as *morphemes* compose words.

The multifariously detailed questions of English usage occupy part IV. The customary forms and meanings of words and phrases are constantly and often imperceptibly shifting. Some speakers and writers push words in new directions, often unconsciously; others resist and reject these innovations, often (in the long run) to no avail. But undesirable linguistic changes needn't—and shouldn't—be immediately acquiesced in. The usage glossary here presented gives a snapshot of the language as it stands today: a compilation of editorial judgments that experienced copyeditors make routinely.

More than that, though, part IV contains an unprecedented degree of empirical evidence in the form of Google ngrams, which reflect big data as applied to Standard Written English. These ngrams show the relative frequency in print of two or more competing forms. So let's say that someone is arguing that *between him and I* should be accepted as standard—there are such people.[29] And let's say that our disputatious friend cites outlier instances in literature of *between him and I* (it should be *between him and me*, of course—each pronoun being the object of a preposition). An ngram will show relative frequencies in massive amounts of literature—more than 5.2 million books from 1500 on—to assess the truth or

---

29   See, e.g., Oliver Kamm, "The Pedant: There's Nothing Amiss with Andrew Strauss's Grammar," *Times*, May 16, 2015, http://www.thetimes.co.uk/tto/life/courtsocial/article4441761.ece (stating that it is "groundless" to insist on the objective case in such a construction and that "a pronoun within a coordinate phrase is free to take either nominative or accusative case"); Rodney D. Huddleston and Geoffrey K. Pullum, *The Cambridge Grammar of the English Language* (Cambridge: Cambridge Univ. Press, 2002), 463 (arguing that such a construction with *I* as a final coordinate is "so common in speech and used by so broad a range of speakers that it has to be recognized as a variety of Standard English").

falsity, or maybe just the plausibility, of the contention. It's also possible to calculate ratios of use through time. Here's what we find:

1820 Ratio of Frequency in Printed Books: 93:1
2008 Ratio of Frequency in Printed Books: 53:1

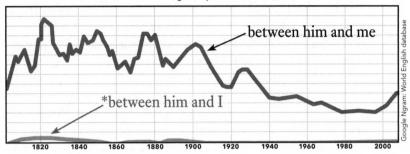

Even a ratio of 3:1 would be enough to establish serious predominance—and perhaps enough to declare (depending on the usage involved) the less-frequent form nonstandard. But anything more than 20:1 is powerful, objective evidence that the traditionally stigmatized form is in no position to be declared Standard Written English. In fact, many of the instances of its appearance in the database are probably owing to discussions of its ungrammatical nature.

Or consider a related construction—one I heard a television broadcaster use just as this book was being readied for publication—*Him and I are good friends. Because both pronouns are subjects of the plural verb *are*, they should both be in the subjective case. A few language commentators will hear such instances and opine that this phrasing has become standard. They may go so far as to say that English is gradually losing its declension of pronouns altogether—a highly indefensible position. Let's see what the ngram tells us about instances of *He and I are* (educated usage) and *Him and I are* (uneducated usage)—from 1500 to the present day:

2008 Ratio of Frequency in Printed Books: 109:1

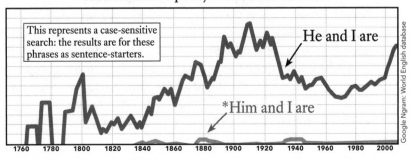

The frequency ratio of 109:1 in printed books just from the latest year we can now use, 2008, provides powerful evidence that Standard Written English is hardly on the brink of a shift toward acceptance of the nonstandard form.

This previously unavailable big-data tool allows us to gauge questions of English in a way never before possible, so that judgments about standard forms are based on something more than one person's lifetime of reading and study, however reliable that may have been. Some 67 of these ngrams appear in part IV, where they are further explained. You may well find that they make part IV compulsively browsable.

Part V consists of a full restatement of the principles of English punctuation. Each principle is illustrated with verbatim examples drawn from writers of high repute. No writer, of course, is infallible in either usage or punctuation, but these sentences illustrate sound instances of punctuation. And the illustrations' great variety contributes piquancy to what is often a dry topic.

The select glossary (see pp. 401–89) isn't to be overlooked. Learners of any subject—your author included—benefit tremendously from treating it partly as an exercise in vocabulary-building. Learning the terminology of grammar represents a huge step toward mastering the subject as a whole. Hence I have gone into more detail in the glossary than many readers might have expected. Try browsing through it from time to time as you're reading or consulting the book. You'll find that the terminology is like good wine: once you get a taste for it, you'll start picking up the nuances.

Throughout the text are inset quotations in shaded boxes. You've already encountered some. These quotations are intended to enrich the discussions with insights from writers and commentators of the past—most of them linguists and grammarians whose statements reinforce the basic message of the book: that linguistic study can be both practical and enjoyable. For the precise sources of these quotations, see pp. 491–95.

In most but not all ways, this book conforms to the recommendations found in *The Chicago Manual of Style*. I take a somewhat different stance, for example, on commas after years in month-day-year-style dates, recommending their omission when the date is used adjectivally (§ 458); on en-dashes, recommending them for expressing tension or pairing as well as for numerical ranges (§ 503); and on ellipsis dots, recommending a space before the first of four dots if the elision occurs in midsentence as opposed to after a sentence's end (§ 555). Naturally, all the grammatical discussions and usage recommendations line up closely with chapter 5 of the *Chicago Manual*—given that I am the author of that chapter.

Beware the naysayers who tell you that learning Standard Written English will stifle your creativity or cause you to write "correct" but bloodless prose. This common concern is a slight one at best. The truth is that without Standard Written English, it will be all but impossible to produce "incredibly clear, beautiful, alive, urgent, crackling-with-voltage prose."[30] That's not a bad description of what you might ultimately aim for—though the first step is straightforward and simple clarity.

Pursue your interest in words and in writing well—together with their many settled conventions. You may find that you've changed the direction of your life. As one of my multilingual friends likes to say, fall in love with language, and it will love you back.

---

30 *Quack This Way: David Foster Wallace and Bryan A. Garner Talk Language and Writing* (Dallas: RosePen, 2013), 60 (quoting David Foster Wallace).

I. The Traditional Parts of Speech

5 *How did we arrive at the canonical eight?* The traditional grammarian's approach to parts of speech is often attributed to an ancient of some renown: Dionysios Thrax, who lived in the second century B.C.[1] In *Téknē Grammatiké* (or *The Grammatical Art*), he listed eight parts of speech: noun, verb, participle, article, pronoun, preposition, adverb, conjunction. These categories were long accepted by Greek, by Roman, and later by European grammarians—and there were scores of them (hence only some highlights here).

The Roman grammarian Aelius Donatus, who lived in the fourth century A.D., wrote *Ars Grammatica*—a book that gained great popularity into the Middle Ages. His eight parts of speech were slightly different from those of Dionysios:

Dionysios	**Donatus**
noun (adjective)	noun (adjective)
verb	verb
participle	participle
article	————
pronoun	pronoun
preposition	preposition
adverb (interjection)	adverb
conjunction	conjunction
————	interjection[2]

---

1. For much of the information in the first two paragraphs, I am indebted to David Mulroy, *The War Against Grammar* (Portsmouth, NH: Boynton/Cook, 2003).

2. Rita Copeland and Ineke Sluiter, eds., *Medieval Grammar and Rhetoric: Language Arts and Literary Theory, AD 300–1475* (New York: Oxford Univ. Press, 2009), 86 (reproducing Donatus's eight parts of speech).

Both classified nouns and adjectives together—Dionysios because the two have the same kinds of inflectional endings in Greek, Donatus presumably because he was influenced by predecessors such as Dionysios. But Donatus dropped articles (Latin has none) and separated interjections from adverbs.

The Donatus model was followed by other early influential grammarians, such as Priscian, who lived in the fifth century A.D.[3] So influential was Priscian that he gave us the phrase *to break Priscian's head*, meaning "to use bad grammar." In Renaissance England, a schoolboy learning Latin might be scolded when he mistranslated a phrase from English into Latin, "No, William, you're breaking Priscian's head!"

> A zoologist who divided animals into invertebrates, mammals, and beasts of burden would not get very far before running into trouble. Yet the traditional grammar is guilty of the same error when it defines three parts of speech on the basis of meaning (noun, verb, and interjection), four more on the basis of function (adjective, adverb, pronoun, conjunction), and one partly on function and partly on form (preposition). The result is that in such an expression as "a dog's life" there can be endless futile argument about whether "dog's" is a noun or an adjective.
> —W. Nelson Francis
> "Revolution in Grammar"

So influential was Latin grammar in England that English grammars were sparse until the 18th century. But Shakespeare's main rival, Ben Jonson (1572–1637), wrote a grammar that was published in 1640,[4] three years after his death. Jonson counted "in our English speech . . . the same parts with the Latins"[5]—that is, eight. His list was that of Donatus (though Jonson's direct influence was Priscian). But then he added another: articles.[6]

When English grammars began to proliferate in the 18th and 19th centuries, there was great variability in grammarians' counts of parts of speech. In 1711, James Greenwood repeated Donatus's fourth-century roster.[7] Others of the time replicated it.[8] Still other grammarians, however,

---

3   Ibid., 169.

4   Ben Jonson, *The English Grammar* (New York: Sturgis and Walton, 1640; ed. Alice Vinton Waite, 1909).

5   Ibid., 78.

6   Ibid.

7   James Greenwood, *An Essay Towards a Practical English Grammar* (London: John Clark, 1711; 2nd ed. 1722), 54.

8   See, e.g., Daniel Duncan, *A New English Grammar* (London: Nicolas Prevost, 1731), 1; Isaac Barker, *An English Grammar Showing the Nature and Grounds of the English Language* (York: John Hildyard, 1733), 2; Thomas Dilworth, *A New Guide to the English Tongue in Five Parts* (London: Hodgson, 1740), 99.

counted only four—among these being John Entick,[9] Thomas Dyche,[10] Anne Fisher,[11] and James Harris.[12] Some had the number swell to nine (by adding articles, as Ben Jonson had done in 1640)[13] or ten (by adding adjectives).[14] There was simply no consensus.

Not until 1761 did any grammarian settle on the eight that became the canonical parts of speech in English. He was the same man who discovered oxygen: Joseph Priestley (1733–1804). In his *Rudiments of English Grammar,* he listed these:

- noun
- adjective
- pronoun
- verb
- adverb
- preposition
- conjunction
- interjection[15]

Even so, it took another 80 years or so for those eight to be firmly accepted—perhaps because the categories fluidly relate to form and function. That is, some words are called nouns because they usually function that way, but of course they can often function as adjectives and verbs as well. And any part of speech can function as an interjection. So it's not a perfect taxonomy.

9   John Entick, *A Grammatical Introduction to the English Tongue* (London: Edward and Charles Dilly, 1765), xix (names, qualities, affirmations, particles).

10   Thomas Dyche, "A Compendious English Grammar," in *A New General English Dictionary* (London: C. and R. Ware, 1765), n.p. (nouns substantive, nouns adjective, verbs, participles).

11   Anne Fisher, *A Practical New Grammar* (London: J. Brambles, A. Meggitt, and J. Waters, 1805), 49 (names, qualities, verbs, and particles).

12   James Harris, *Hermes, or A Philosophical Inquiry Concerning Universal Grammar,* 5th ed. (London: F. Wingrave, 1794), 36 (substantives or nouns, attributives or verbs, definitives or articles, connectives or conjunctions).

13   See Anonymous, *The English Accidence, Being the Grounds of Our Mother Tongue* (1833), 3; Ben Jonson, *The English Grammar* (1640; New York: Sturgis and Walton, 1909), 28.

14   See John Ash, *Grammatical Institutes: Or, An Easy Introduction to Dr. Lowth's Grammar,* rev. ed. (Philadelphia: Joseph Crukshank, 1788), 23.

15   Joseph Priestley, *The Rudiments of English Grammar* (London: R. Griffiths, 1761; rev. ed., London: T. Becket and P. A. De Hondt, 1769), 3.

The influential Robert Lowth counted nine in 1762 by adding articles;[16] John Fell followed those nine in 1784;[17] so did George Neville Ussher in 1785[18] and the highly influential Lindley Murray in 1795.[19] But more grammarians of that period counted ten by adding participles to the mix: Rowland Jones in 1771,[20] Ellin Devis in 1775,[21] Ralph Harrison in 1777,[22] Caleb Bingham in 1785,[23] E. Harrold in 1804,[24] Lady Eleanor Fenn in 1790,[25] John Hutchins in 1791,[26] Caleb Alexander in 1792,[27] Thomas Coar in 1796,[28] Duncan Mackintosh (with his two daughters) in 1797,[29] Daniel Staniford in 1797,[30] Jane Gardiner in 1799,[31] David Gurney in 1801,[32] Alexander Crombie in 1802,[33] and John Comly in 1803.[34] These

16   Robert Lowth, *A Short Introduction to English Grammar* (1762; rev. ed., London: A. Millar, T. Cadell and J. Dodsley, 1767), 8–9.

17   John Fell, *An Essay Towards an English Grammar* (London: C. Dilly, 1784), 2.

18   George Neville Ussher, *The Elements of English Grammar* (1785; 2nd ed., Gloucester: R. Raikes, 1786), 2.

19   Lindley Murray, *English Grammar Adapted to Different Classes of Learners* (York: Wilson, Spence, and Mawman, 1795), 19.

20   Rowland Jones, *The Circles of Gomer: Or, An Essay towards an Investigation and Introduction of English as a Universal Language* (London: S. Crowder, 1771), 9.

21   Ellin Devis, *The Accidence: Or, First Rudiments of English Grammar* (1775; 15th ed., London: C. Law, 1814), 2–4.

22   Ralph Harrison, *Rudiments of English Grammar* (1777; 9th Am. ed., Philadelphia: J. Bioren, 1812), 10.

23   Caleb Bingham, *The Young Lady's Accidence* (Boston: Greenleaf and Freeman, 1785; 16th ed., Boston: E. Lincoln, 1806), 3.

24   E. Harrold, *A Short Introduction to English Grammar* (1787; 6th ed., Birmingham: Knott and Lloyd, 1804), 9.

25   Lady Eleanor Fenn, *The Mother's Grammar* (London: John Marshall, 1790; 19th ed. 1833), 9.

26   John Hutchins, *An Abstract of the First Principles of English Grammar* (1791; 3rd ed., Philadelphia: J. Bioren, 1810), 14.

27   Caleb Alexander, *A Grammatical System of the English Language* (1792; 6th ed., Boston: E. T. Andrews, 1801), 5.

28   Thomas Coar, *A Grammar of the English Tongue* (London: J. Phillips, 1796), 21.

29   Duncan Mackintosh, *A Plain, Rational Essay on English Grammar* (Boston: Manning and Loring, 1797), 114.

30   Daniel Staniford, *A Short but Comprehensive Grammar* (1797; 4th ed., Boston: J. West, 1807), 6.

31   Jane Gardiner, *English Grammar: Adapted to the Different Classes of Learners* (1799; 3rd ed., London: Longman, Hurst, Rees, and Orme, 1809), 3.

32   David Gurney, *The Columbian Accidence* (Boston: Manning and Loring, 1801), 7.

33   Alexander Crombie, *The Etymology and Syntax of the English Language* (1802; 3rd ed., London: John Taylor, 1830), 20.

34   John Comly, *English Grammar Made Easy to the Teacher and Pupil* (1803; 3rd ed., Philadelphia: Kimber, Conrad, 1808), 12.

grammarians were doubtless aware of one another's work to one degree or another.

Some Americans were mavericks. In 1782, Robert Ross wrote *The American Grammar* with the help of Aaron Burr (the president of Yale College and father to the future vice president and killer of Alexander Hamilton). They counted eight parts of speech in both English and Latin but then speculated: "Since all Discourse must be about Things, their Properties, Actions, and Relations; were it not for long established Custom, we might divide Speech into four Parts, viz. Noun, Adnoun [i.e., adjective], Verb, and Participle."[35] Two years later, Noah Webster, more famous as a lexicographer than as a grammarian, counted six parts of speech.[36] But he was long-lived, and in his final grammar nearly 50 years later, he counted seven—the conventional eight minus interjections.[37] The most extreme examples were James Brown, who in his 1820 *American Grammar* counted thirty-three,[38] and William S. Balch, who in 1838 counted only two (nouns and verbs).[39]

This little survey only skims the surface. By 1801 there were 297 different listings of English parts of speech accounting for a total of 58 varieties.[40] By the 1840s, however, a consensus was gradually emerging for Priestley's eight:

- noun
- pronoun
- adjective
- verb
- adverb
- preposition
- conjunction
- interjection[41]

---

35 Robert Ross, *The American Grammar*, 7th ed. (Hartford: Nathaniel Patten, 1782), 34.

36 Noah Webster, *A Grammatical Institute of the English Language* (Hartford: Hudson and Goodwin, 1784; 4th ed. 1794), 6.

37 Noah Webster, *An Improved Grammar of the English Language* (New Haven: Hezekiah Howe, 1831; rev. ed., New Haven: Sidney Babcock, 1831; rev. ed. 1842), 10.

38 James Brown, *American Grammar* (Troy: Francis Adancourt, 1820), 1–3.

39 William S. Balch, *Lectures on Language* (Providence: B. Cranston, 1838), 20.

40 Ian Michael, *The Teaching of English from the Sixteenth Century to 1870* (Cambridge: Cambridge Univ. Press, 1987), 344.

41 See John Lindsay, *English Grammar, for Schools* (London: J. G. F. and J. Rivington, 1842), 6; Bradford Frazee, *An Improved Grammar of the English Language* (Philadelphia: Sorin and Ball, 1844), 16; Noble Butler, *A Practical Grammar of the English Language* (Louisville, KY: Morton and Griswold, 1846), 13; Allen Hayden Weld, *Weld's English Grammar*, 50th ed. (Portland, ME: Sanborn and Carter,

The variants gradually became outliers among mainstay school grammars.

Even in recent years, though, the categories aren't fully settled: modern grammarians have set the number at three,[42] four,[43] six,[44] seven,[45] eight (the traditional number),[46] nine,[47] ten,[48] eleven,[49] twelve,[50] and nineteen.[51] One says there is "no definitive answer."[52] In this way, parts of speech are rather like the biologist's species and genera: they are human constructs that aren't immutable.

In the discussion that follows, we examine the canonical eight with full knowledge that the classifications aren't airtight.

1848), 8; Samuel Stillman Greene, *A Treatise on the Structure of the English Language* (Philadelphia: Cowperthwait, 1846), 206; William Hall, *Encyclopædia of English Grammar* (Wheeling, VA: John B. Wolpf, 1849), 65; and Timothy Stone Pinneo, *Pinneo's Analytical Grammar of the English Language* (Cincinnati: Winthrop B. Smith, 1850), 20.

42 See Ernest W. Gray, *A Brief Grammar of Modern Written English* (Cleveland: World Pub., 1967), 60.

43 See Robert M. Gorrell and Charlton Laird, *Modern English Handbook*, 2nd ed. (Englewood Cliffs, NJ: Prentice-Hall, 1956), 324.

44 See Ralph Bernard Long, *The System of English Grammar* (Glenview, IL: Scott, Foresman, 1971), 168.

45 See Gordon J. Loberger and Kate Shoup Welsh, *Webster's New World English Grammar Handbook* (New York: Hungry Minds, 2001), 355.

46 See Mario Pei and Frank Gaynor, *Dictionary of Linguistics* (New York: Philosophical Library, 1954), 161; Curtis W. Hayes, *The ABC's of Languages and Linguistics*, 2nd ed. (Lincolnwood, IL: Nat'l Textbook, 1987), 30; Paul Kroeger, *Analyzing Grammar* (Cambridge: Cambridge Univ. Press, 2005), 38.

47 See Rodney D. Huddleston and Geoffrey K. Pullum, *The Cambridge Grammar of the English Language* (Cambridge: Cambridge Univ. Press, 2002), 22.

48 See Randolph Quirk and Sidney Greenbaum, *A University Grammar of English* (Harlow: Longman, 1973), 18; James Aitchison, *Dictionary of English Grammar* (London: Weidenfeld and Nicolson, 1996), 47.

49 See R. W. Burchfield, *The New Fowler's Modern English Usage* (Oxford: Clarendon, 1996), 575; Sidney Greenbaum, *The Oxford English Grammar* (Oxford: Oxford Univ. Press, 1996), 92.

50 See Randolph Quirk, *A Comprehensive Grammar of the English Language* (London: Longman, 1985), 67; Martha Kolln, *Understanding English Grammar*, 4th ed. (New York: Macmillan, 1994), 262.

51 See James Sledd, *A Short Introduction to English Grammar* (Chicago: Scott, Foresman, 1959), 110–11.

52 Laurie Bauer, *The Linguistics Student's Handbook* (Oxford: Oxford Univ. Press, 2007), 31.

Nouns

Traditional Classifications

6 *Nouns generally.* A noun is a word that names something, whether abstract (intangible) or concrete (tangible). It may be a common noun (the name of a generic class or type of person, place, thing, process, activity, or condition) or a proper noun (the name of a specific person, place, or thing—hence capitalized). A concrete noun may be a count noun (if what it names can be counted—as with *horses* or *cars*) or a mass noun (if what it names is uncountable or collective—as with *information* or *salt*). A noun-equivalent is a phrase or clause that serves the function of a noun in a sentence {to serve your country is honorable} {bring anyone you like}. Nouns and noun-equivalents are collectively called *substantives* or (especially throughout this book) *noun elements.*

7 *Common nouns.* A common noun is the generic name of one item in a class or group {a chemical} {a river} {a pineapple}. It is not capitalized unless it begins a sentence or appears in a title. A common noun is usually used with a determiner—that is, an article or other word (e.g., *some, few*) that indicates the number and definiteness of the noun element {a loaf} {the day} {some person}. Common nouns are often analyzed into three subcategories: concrete nouns, abstract nouns, and collective nouns. A concrete noun is solid or real; it indicates something perceptible to the physical senses {a building} {the wind} {honey}. An abstract noun denotes something you cannot physically see, touch, taste, hear, or smell {joy} {expectation} {neurosis}. A collective noun—which can be viewed as a concrete noun but is often separately categorized—refers to a group or collection of people or things {a crowd of people} {a flock of birds} {a herd of rhinos}. See § 10.

8 *Proper nouns.* A proper noun is the name of a specific person, place, or thing {John Doe} {Moscow} {the Hope Diamond}, or the title of a movie {*Citizen Kane*}, a play {*Death of a Salesman*}, a book {*Oliver Twist*}, a newspaper or magazine {*The New Yorker*}, a piece of music {U2's "All Because of You"}, a painting {*Mona Lisa*}, a sculpture {*The Kiss*}, or any other publication, performance, or work of art. Proper nouns may be singular

{Mary} {London} or plural {the Great Lakes} {the Twin Cities}. A proper noun is always capitalized, regardless of how it is used—unless someone is purposely flouting the rules {k.d. lang}. A common noun may become a proper noun {Old Hickory} {the Big Easy}, and sometimes a proper noun may be used figuratively and informally, as if it were a common noun {like Moriarty, he is a Napoleon of crime}. Proper nouns may be compounded when used as a unit to name something {the Waldorf-Astoria Hotel} {*Saturday Evening Post*}. Over time, some proper nouns (called *eponyms*) have developed common-noun counterparts, such as *sandwich* (from the Earl of Sandwich) and *china* (the porcelain, from the nation China). Articles and other determiners are used with proper nouns only when the last part of the noun is a common noun or the determiner provides emphasis {the Savoy Hotel} {Sam? I knew a Sam Hill once}.

9   *Count nouns.* A count noun has singular and plural forms and expresses discrete, enumerable things {dictionary–dictionaries} {hoof–hooves} {newspaper–newspapers}. As the subject of a sentence, a singular count noun takes a singular verb {the jar is full}; a plural count noun takes a plural verb {the jars are full}.

10   *Collective nouns.* A collective noun denotes an aggregate of individuals or things but is itself grammatically singular in form {group} {team} {flock} {herd}. For purposes of verb and pronoun agreement, however, collective nouns may be treated as either singular or plural, depending on whether the emphasis is on the constituent members acting as a unified whole {the committee meets on Tuesday to announce its decision} or, less commonly in American English (AmE), individually {the committee are debating their decision}. The general preference in AmE is to treat collective nouns as singular; the opposite is true in British English (BrE). But when collective nouns appear in expressions of multitude (see below), they are generally treated as plural.

11   *Expressions of multitude.* In constructions such as *a bunch of amateurs,* a collective noun expresses multitude, rather than signifying a unified group. Grammarians call collective nouns functioning this way *quantifying collectives.* (But some of the most common expressions of multitude use quantifying determiners in place of collectives: *number, lot, couple,* and *few* don't function like collective nouns in other contexts.) Such constructions place the quantifying collective or determiner between an indefinite article (*a* or *an*) and a postmodifying *of*-phrase using a plural or mass noun {a host of problems} {a group of doctors} {a set of stemware} {a lot of questions}.

As with collective nouns generally, syntax with expressions of multitude is governed by meaning and not by strict grammar—a phenomenon known as *synesis* or *notional concord*. (See § 186.) So while lone collective nouns typically signify the group as a unit and hence are treated as singular, nouns of multitude are distributive: verbs and pronouns must agree in number with the noun following *of*, not the singular noun of multitude preceding it.

If the noun following *of* is plural (as it typically is), verbs and pronouns must be too {a number of listeners always complain whenever we bring in a guest host} {a gang of kids were riding their bikes around the neighborhood}. But if the noun is a singular mass noun, use singular verbs and pronouns {a lot of this bread has mold on it}. (If the noun of multitude is plural, however, the accompanying verbs and pronouns invariably are as well {two teams of surgeons operate on their patient} {four sets of china were on sale}.)

Two caveats. First, not all constructions that place a noun between an indefinite article and a postmodifying *of*-phrase are true expressions of multitude. Constructions referring to containers or units of measurement often take this form {a jar of jellybeans} {a pound of nuts}. Here, the container or measurement noun governs meaning and therefore concord {a bushel of apples costs $60}. And a collective noun may also be followed by an *of*-phrase describing the group's composition {a school of minnows} {a herd of bison}. In those cases, the ordinary rules for collective nouns apply (i.e., the noun may be treated as singular, depending on emphasis) {a flock of geese makes its way south for the winter} {a flock of geese fly in a V formation}.

Second, when *the* (instead of *a*) precedes *number of*, the emphasis is on the number itself, not the individual things it describes, so it is treated as singular. Compare "a number of applicants *were* unqualified" with "the number of unqualified applicants *was* surprising." But not all nouns of multitude are treated this way—consider *majority* {the majority of senators vote along party lines}. As above, meaning and emphasis determine concord.

12 *Expressions of partition.* Expressions of partition, which signify a part of the group represented by the *of*-phrase (in this context termed the *partitive genitive*), follow the same rules as expressions of multitude. In place of a noun of multitude, these expressions use a partitive noun {fraction} {part} {portion}, a fraction, or a percentage {a fraction of the students raise their hands} {one-quarter of the competitors start at 10 a.m.} {only 42% of doctors report getting annual physicals}. This category includes partitive constructions using *one of those* + [plural noun] + *who/that*, which always take plural verbs and pronouns in the relative clause {she is one of those writers who wake up before dawn to start their work}. Even a fraction that is plural in form is treated as singular if it's followed by *of* and a mass noun {two-thirds of Mary's garden is planted with gladioluses}. But as with the above constructions also governed by synesis, meaning sometimes necessitates exceptions to the rule {just a fraction of those nails is all you need to do the job}. See § 186.

13 *Mass nouns.* A mass noun (sometimes called a *noncount noun*) is one that denotes something uncountable, either because it is abstract {cowardice} {evidence} or because it refers to an aggregation of people or things taken as an indeterminate whole {luggage} {the bourgeoisie}. The key difference between mass nouns and collective nouns is that unlike collective nouns (which are count nouns), mass nouns never take indefinite articles and typically do not have plural forms. (Compare *a team* to **an evidence*, or *two groups* to **two luggages*.) A mass noun can stand alone {music is more popular than ever} or with a determiner other than an indefinite article (*some* music or *the* music but not *a* music). As the subject of a sentence, a mass noun typically takes a singular verb and pronoun {the litigation is so varied that it defies simple explanation}.

Some mass nouns, however, are plural in form but are treated as grammatically singular {politics} {ethics} {physics} {news}. (See § 190.) Others are always grammatically plural {manners} {scissors} {clothes}. But just as singular mass nouns don't take an indefinite article, plural mass nouns don't combine with numbers: you'd never say **three scissors* or **six manners*. Some that refer to concrete objects, such as *scissors* or *sunglasses*, can be enumerated by adding *pair of* {a pair of scissors} {three pairs of sunglasses}. Likewise, singular concrete mass nouns can usually be enumerated by adding a unit noun such as *piece* and *of* {a piece of cutlery} {seven pieces of stationery}. Both singular and plural mass nouns can take indefinite adjectives such as *any, less, much,* and *some* that express general quantity {what you need is some courage} {he doesn't have any manners}.

Many nouns can be both mass nouns and count nouns. With concrete nouns, which tend to be countable, the countable sense refers to individual things or instances {there were white chickens beside the red wheelbarrow}; the mass sense refers to the thing viewed as a substance or material {let's have chicken for dinner}. With abstract nouns, which tend to be uncountable, the mass sense refers to the general phenomenon {the candidate's speech emphasized the importance of education}; the countable sense refers to individual instances or types {she told her son, "You'll never succeed without an education"}.

Properties of Nouns

14 *Generally.* Nouns have properties of case and number. Some traditional grammarians also consider gender and person to be properties of nouns. The change in a noun or pronoun's form to indicate these properties is called *declension*. In English, nouns change form only for number and the genitive case (see § 35); only pronouns truly decline in the traditional sense (see § 56).

15 *Case.* In English, only nouns and pronouns have case. Case denotes the relationship between a noun (or pronoun) and other words in a sentence. Grammarians disagree about the number of cases English nouns possess. Those who consider inflection (word form) the defining characteristic tend to say that there are two: common, which is the uninflected form, and genitive

> It is the business of grammar to inform the student, not how a language might have been originally constructed, but how it is constructed.
> —Noah Webster
> *A Grammatical Institute of the English Language*

(or *possessive*), which is formed by adding -'s or just an apostrophe. But others argue that it's useful to distinguish how the common-case noun is being used in the sentence, whether it is playing a nominative role {the doctor is in} or an objective role {go see the doctor}. They also argue that the label we put on nouns according to their function should match those we use for *who* and for personal pronouns, most of which do change form in the nominative and objective cases. Other grammarians even distinguish between the objective case and the dative case, the latter of which (in some languages—but not English) is inflected to signify an indirect object. But all these arguments are over a distinction without a practical difference in English word use. See §§ 32–38, 56.

16 *Number.* Number shows whether one object or more than one object is referred to, as with *clock* (singular) and *clocks* (plural). See §§ 19–31.

17   *Gender.* English nouns have no true gender, as that property is understood in many other languages. For example, whether a noun refers to a masculine or feminine person or thing does not determine the form of the accompanying article as it does in French, German, Spanish, and many other languages. Still, some English words—almost exclusively nouns denoting people or animals—are inherently masculine {uncle} {rooster} {lad} or feminine {aunt} {hen} {lass} and take the gender-appropriate pronouns. But most English nouns are common in gender and may refer to either sex {relative} {chicken} {child}. Many words once considered strictly masculine—especially words associated with jobs and professions—have been accepted as common (or *indefinite*) in gender over time {author} {executor} {proprietor}. Similarly, many forms made feminine by the addition of a suffix {aviatrix} {poetess} have been essentially abandoned. See § 443.

18   *Person.* A few grammarians attribute the property of person to nouns, distinguishing first person {I, Dan Walls, do swear that . . .}, second person {you, the professor, are key}, and third person {she, the arbiter, decides}. While those examples all use nouns in apposition to pronouns, that's not closely relevant to the question whether the nouns themselves have the property of person in any grammatical sense. But using that property in analyzing nouns does help to point out three things. First, as with grammatical case, one argument for the property of person is to keep the properties of nouns parallel to those of pronouns, even though English nouns do not change form at all in first, second, or third person as personal pronouns do. Second, person determines what form other words will take—here, the verbs. Third, the examples illustrate why attributing person to nouns requires a stretch of logic—if the pronouns were not present in the first two examples, the verb would be in the third person, even if Dan Walls were talking about himself and even if the speaker were addressing the professor.

   Although person distinction does not really occur in nouns, they do sometimes assume something approaching this function. Somebody may refer to himself or herself by using a noun or name {your Governor wishes you every happiness during this holiday season [written by the governor]} {children, your father wants you to pick up your blocks [said by the father]}. This third-person self-reference is known as *illeism*. A similar construction can be used in the second person, especially as an indication of politeness or respect {would Mother like a warm glass of milk? [the mother is being addressed]} {may I ask whether madam likes the jacket? [the woman is being spoken to by a sales clerk]}. But these instances are grammatical outliers.

Plurals

19   *Generally.* Because exceptions abound, a good dictionary or usage guide is essential for checking the standard plural form of a noun. But there are some basic rules for forming plurals.

20   *Adding "-s" or "-es."* Most plurals are formed by adding -s or -es. If a noun ends with a letter whose sound readily combines with the s sound, then use -s to form the plural {siren–sirens} {club–clubs} {toy–toys}. If the noun ends in a letter that is not euphonious with -s alone (e.g., it ends in a sibilant such as -s, -sh, -x, -z, or a soft -ch), then use -es to form the plural {box–boxes} {moss–mosses} {birch–birches}.

21   *Plurals of proper nouns.* The plural of a proper noun is formed according to the same rules as those for common nouns {the Jenkinses} {the Rabiejs [silent *j*]} {the Murrys}. Never use an apostrophe with s to form the plural of a proper noun (only the possessive, both singular and plural—see § 35).

     Pluralization confuses some families whose names end in a sibilant. *Banks* and *Flowers* look like plurals, but they're not: they're singular names. The plurals are *Bankses* and *Flowerses* {did you invite the Bankses?} {are we going to the Flowerses' party?}. Think of "keeping up with the Joneses."

22   *Nouns ending in "-f" or "-fe."* Some nouns ending in -f or -fe take an -s {reef–reefs} {dwarf–dwarfs} {safe–safes}. Other nouns change the -f to -v and add -es {hoof–hooves} {knife–knives} {wolf–wolves}. A few words have one preferred form in AmE {wharf–wharves} and historically another in BrE {wharf–wharfs [though BrE has followed the AmE model since the mid-19th century]}. Even if one knows the etymology of a word, the correct forms are unpredictable. Again, consult a reliable dictionary or usage guide.

23   *Nouns ending in "-o."* Some nouns ending in -o take an -s {avocado–avocados} {memento–mementos} {tuxedo–tuxedos}. But others take an -es {mango–mangoes} {cargo–cargoes} {volcano–volcanoes}. There is no firm rule for determining whether the plural is formed with -s or -es, but two guidelines may prove helpful: (1) Nouns used as often in the plural as in the singular usually form the plural with -es {vetoes} {heroes}. *Zeros* is an exception (and therefore hard to remember). (2) Nouns usually form the plural with -s if (a) they appear to have been borrowed from some other language {intaglio–intaglios}; (b) they are proper names {Fazio–Fazios}; (c) they are rarely used as plurals {bravado–bravados}; (d) they end in -o preceded by a vowel {portfolio–portfolios}; or (e) they are shortened words {photo–photos}. Again, keep a dictionary and a usage guide handy.

24 *Nouns ending in "-y."* Nouns ending in -y follow one of two rules: (1) If the noun is common and the -y is preceded by *qu* or by a consonant, change the -y to -i and add -es to form the plural {soliloquy–soliloquies} {berry–berries} {folly–follies}. (2) If the noun is proper or if the -y is preceded by a vowel, add -s to form the plural {Teddy–Teddys} {ploy–ploys} {buoy–buoys}. Bear in mind, there are a few exceptions {why–whys} {Ptolemy–Ptolemies}.

25 *Nouns ending in "-ics."* Nouns ending in -ics present problems because they can be singular or plural. Generally, when the word denotes the facts and principles of a particular subject, the noun is singular {metaphysics deals with abstractions}. But if the noun expresses activity or a particular manifestation, it is plural {your ethics are unimpeachable}.

26 *Compound nouns.* A compound noun, which is made of separate words (with or without hyphens), typically forms the plural by using the plural form of the noun. If the compound is solid, the word is simply pluralized in the normal way {birdcages} {toothbrushes}—though there are rare exceptions {passersby}. If the compound consists of hyphenated or separate words, only the main word (also known as the *head*) is pluralized {holes in one} {maids of honor} {courts-martial} {motion pictures}. Rarely, more than one noun in a compound will change form {woman doctor → women doctors}. This usually occurs when *man* or *woman* is used as a qualifying word but only rarely when the word isn't intended to be gender-specific. For instance, *manservant* becomes *menservants*, but *man-hour* becomes *man-hours* (not **men-hours*, because *man* refers to humans in general, not to male humans in particular). But there are exceptions: *man-of-war*, a type of ship, becomes *men-of-war*, not **man-of-wars*.

With a few words and phrases imported from Romance languages, the double plural of the source language is often kept for a time: *filet mignon* is generally recorded as *filets mignons* in dictionaries, and that was the predominant plural in print sources from about 1880 to 1980. But since 1980 the anglicized plural *filet mignons* has predominated in Standard Written English. Note that *filet* wasn't even treated as the main word or head, but instead the entire phrase took the plural *-s* at the end. But most English-speaking people have sensibly shortened the phrase to *filet* (pl. *filets*).

27 *Irregular plurals.* A few nouns have irregular plurals {child–children} {basis–bases}. With some of these words, the plural form depends on the meaning. Take the noun *louse*, for example: people may become infested with *lice* (insects), but contemptible people are *louses* (by metaphorical extension). Some nouns are ordinarily the same in both the singular and the plural {one fish, two fish} {I'd hoped to see four deer, but I saw only one deer}. And some nouns have two acceptable plurals {many Arkansans hunt duck} {we fed the ducks at the park}. The sense of a word may depend on which plural form is used. For example, a professional shrimper catches shrimp (the general name for the genus), while an ichthyologist studies shrimps (various species of shrimp).

28 *Borrowed plurals.* Many English nouns have been borrowed from other languages, especially Latin and Greek, in both their singular and plural forms:

Singular	Plural
alga	algae
alumna	alumnae
alumnus	alumni
bacillus	bacilli
bacterium	bacteria
basis	bases
cactus	cacti
cherub	cherubim
corrigendum	corrigenda
crisis	crises
criterion	criteria
datum	data
desideratum	desiderata
erratum	errata

Singular	Plural
fungus	fungi
larva	larvae
medium	media
memorandum	memoranda
phenomenon	phenomena
phylum	phyla
prolegomenon	prolegomena
seraph	seraphim
stimulus	stimuli
stratum	strata

Because these constitute irregular singulars and plurals in English, they can cause trouble: when a plural such as *alumni* or *criteria* appears much more frequently than its singular counterpart, some speakers and writers will almost inevitably begin treating the plural as a singular {*this criteria} {*I am an alumni of that school}. These nonstandard uses may never be accepted into Standard Written English—or, like *agenda*, they may (see pp. 233–34). The safest course generally is to stick to the naturalized singular and plural forms—and if the foreign plural in particular hasn't been fully naturalized in English, use a normal English plural (e.g., *apparatuses, stadiums*). In judging a word's degree of naturalization, you'll find helpful guidance in a dictionary or usage guide. For two especially tricky examples—*data* and *media*—see the following section.

29   *Plural form with singular sense.* Some nouns are plural in form but singular in use and meaning {good news is always welcome} {economics is a challenging subject} {measles is potentially deadly}. Also, a quoted plural word is treated as a singular {*mice* is the plural of *mouse*} {*sistren* is an archaic plural}.

Some traditional plurals, such as *data* and (to a lesser extent) *media*, have gradually acquired a mass-noun sense and are therefore treated as singular. Although traditionalists stick to the plural uses {the data are inconclusive} {the media are largely misreporting the event}, the new singular uses—using the terms in a collective sense rather than as count nouns—exist alongside the older ones {the data shows the hypothesis to be correct} {the media isn't infallible}. In formal contexts, the most reliable approach is to retain the plural uses unless doing so makes you feel as if you're being artificial, stuffy, and pedantic. Consider using alternative words, such as *information* and *journalists*. Or simply choose the newer usage. But make your play and be consistent—vacillating will not win the admiration of readers and listeners.

30   *Plural-form proper nouns.* A plural geographical name is often treated as singular when the name refers to a single entity {the United States is a relatively young nation} {Naples is a very beautiful city}. But there are many exceptions {the Alps have never been totally impassable}. Names of companies, institutions, and similar entities are generally treated as collective nouns—and hence singular in AmE, even when they are plural in form {General Motors reports that it will earn a profit} {American Airlines has moved its headquarters}. (For the possessive form of *General Motors* and *American Airlines*, see § 37.) In BrE, however, singular nouns that refer to individuals who work independently typically take plural verbs {Manchester United have won the FIFA Cup} {England are now leading in World Cup standings}. See § 10.

31   *Tricky anomalies.* Not all English nouns show the usual singular–plural dichotomy. For example, mass nouns such as *furniture, spaghetti,* and *wheat* have only a singular form, and *oats, scissors,* and *slacks* (= pants) exist only as plurals. Some nouns look singular but are invariably plural {the police were just around the corner} {the vermin seem impossible to eradicate}. Others look plural but are invariably singular {the news is good} {linguistics is my major}. Strangely enough, *person* forms two plurals—*persons* and *people* (see p. 303)—but *people* also forms the plural *peoples* {the peoples of the world}.

Case

32   *Function.* Case denotes the relationship between a noun or pronoun and other words in a sentence.

33   *Common case, nominative function.* The nominative (sometimes called the *subjective*) function denotes the person, place, or thing about which an assertion in a clause is made {the governor delivered a speech [*governor* is the subject]} {the shops are crowded because the holiday season has begun [*shops* and *season* are the subjects of their respective clauses]}. A noun serving a nominative function controls the verb and usually precedes it {the troops retreated in winter [*troops* is the subject]}, but through inversion it can appear almost anywhere in the sentence {high up in the tree sat a leopard [*leopard* is the subject]}. A noun or pronoun that follows a *be*-verb and refers to the same thing as the subject is called a *predicate nominative* {my show dogs are Australian shepherds [*Australian shepherds* is a predicate nominative]}. Generally, a sentence's predicate is the part that contains a verb and makes an assertion about the subject (see § 302).

34 *Common case, objective function.* The objective (sometimes called the *accusative*) function denotes either (1) the person or thing acted on by a transitive verb in the active voice {the balloon carried a pilot and a passenger [*pilot* and *passenger* are objective: the direct objects of the verb *carried*]}; or (2) the person or thing related to another element by a connective, such as a preposition {place the slide under the microscope [*microscope* is objective: the object of the preposition *under*]}. A noun in an objective function usually follows the verb {the queen consulted the prime minister [*queen* is nominative and *prime minister* is objective]}. But with an inverted construction, the object can appear elsewhere in the sentence {everything else was returned; the jewelry the thieves had already sold [*jewelry* is objective and *thieves* is nominative]}. A noun serving an objective function is never the subject of the following verb and usually does not control the number of the verb {an assembly of strangers was outside [the plural noun *strangers* is the object of the preposition *of*; the singular noun *assembly* is the subject of the sentence, so the verb *was* must also be singular]}.

Note, however, a tricky point: an object of a preposition frequently serves as the antecedent of a pronoun such as *who* {she is one of those artists who are always at the forefront of change}. *One* is not the subject of the *who*-clause (*who* is); nor is *one* the antecedent of *who* (*artists* is). Hence the verb (*are*) is plural. You can more easily see why this is so if you rearrange the sentence without changing a single word: *Of those artists who are always at the forefront of change, she is one.* See pp. 299–300.

35 *Genitive case.* The genitive case denotes (1) ownership, possession, or occupancy {the architect's drawing board} {Arnie's room}; (2) a relationship {the philanthropist's secretary}; (3) agency {the company's representative}; (4) description {a summer's day}; (5) the role of a subject {the boy's application [the boy applied]}; (6) the role of an object {the prisoner's release [someone released the prisoner]}; or (7) an idiomatic shorthand form of an *of*-phrase {one hour's delay [equal to *a delay of one hour*]}. The genitive case is also called the *possessive case*, but *possessive* is a misleadingly narrow term, given the seven different functions of this case—true possession, as ordinarily understood, being only one. For instance, the fourth function above is often called the *descriptive possessive*. This is a misnomer, however, because the form doesn't express actual possession but instead indicates that the noun is functioning as a descriptive adjective.

The genitive is formed in different ways, depending on the noun or nouns and their use in a sentence. The genitive of a singular noun is formed by adding *-'s* {driver's seat} {engineer's opinion}. The genitive of a plural noun that ends in *-s* or *-es* is formed by adding an apostrophe {parents' house} {foxes' den}. The genitive of an irregular plural noun is formed by adding *-'s* {women's rights} {mice's cage}. The genitive of a compound noun is formed by adding the appropriate ending to the last word in the compound {parents-in-law's message}. All these *-'s* and *-s'* endings are called *inflected genitives*.

Let's dwell for a moment on singular and plural possessives. They befuddle people with proper names ending in *-s*—perhaps because a famous little book by William Strunk and E. B. White, *The Elements of Style*, in all editions since the first in 1959, opens with the singular possessive but never explains how to make a plural possessive.[1] Take the case of Bob Charles, who owns a boat: you write *Bob Charles's boat*, according to most reputable style manuals (the *AP Stylebook* being to the contrary—see § 37). But what if the entire Charles family owns the boat? It's *the Charleses' boat* (no stylebook, reputable or not, being to the contrary). The rule is that you pluralize first and then add the possessive apostrophe {The Charleses' boat is having trouble keeping up with the Joneses' boat. Tom Jones's assistant just told me so.}.

36   *The "of"-genitive.* The preposition *of* may precede a noun or proper name to express relationship, agency, or possession. The choice between an inflected genitive and an *of*-construction depends mostly on style. Proper nouns and nouns denoting people or things of higher status usually take the inflected genitive {Hilda's adventures} {the lion's paw}. Compare *the perils of Penelope* with *the saucer of the chef*. Nouns denoting inanimate things can often readily take either the inflected form or the *of*-genitive {the theater's name} {the name of the theater}, but some sound right only in the *of*-genitive {the end of everything}.

---

1   See, e.g., William Strunk Jr. and E. B. White, *The Elements of Style*, 2nd ed. (New York: Macmillan, 1972), 1 ("form the possessive singular of nouns by adding *'s*"—with nary a mention of plural possessives).

The *of*-genitive is also useful when a double genitive is called for—using both *of* and a possessive form {an idea of Hill's} {a friend of my grandfather's}. The double genitive is an age-old idiom that has consistently appeared in English since the days of Geoffrey Chaucer (ca. 1343–1400). It is impossible to avoid in some constructions with personal pronouns {an acquaintance of mine} {that briefcase of hers}.

37   *Genitives of titles and names.* The genitive of a title or a name is formed by adding -'s {Lloyd's of London's records} {National Geographic Society's headquarters} {Dun & Bradstreet's rating}. This is so even when the word ends in a sibilant {Dickens's novels} {Dow Jones's money report}, unless the word itself is formed from a plural {General Motors' current production rate} {Applied Materials' financial statements}. But with a word that ends in a sibilant, it is acceptable (especially in journalism) to use a final apostrophe without the additional -*s* {Bill Gates' testimony}. See § 35.

38   *Joint and separate genitives.* If two or more nouns share possession, the last noun takes the genitive ending. (This is called the *group possessive*.) For example, *Peter and Harriet's correspondence* refers to the correspondence between Peter and Harriet. If two or more nouns possess something separately, each noun takes its own genitive ending. For example, *Peter's and Harriet's correspondence* refers to Peter's correspondence and also to Harriet's correspondence, presumably with all sorts of people. Joint possession is shown by a single apostrophe plus -*s* only when two nouns are used. If a noun and a pronoun are used to express joint possession, the noun must take an apostrophe plus -*s*. For example, *Hilda and Eddie's vacation* becomes (when Eddie has already been mentioned) *Hilda's and his vacation* or (if Eddie is speaking in first person) *Hilda's and my vacation.*

Agent and Recipient Nouns

39   *Definitions; use.* An agent noun denotes a person who performs some action. It is usually indicated by the suffix -*er* {adviser} or -*or* {donor}. The most common agent nouns end in -*er*; generally, -*or* appears in words that were brought into English directly from Latin. Consult a good dictionary or usage guide. A recipient noun denotes a person who receives something or action, or one for whom something is done. It is usually indicated by the suffix -*ee*, signaling a passive sense. For example, an *honoree* is one who is honored. In legal usage, a recipient noun often means "one to whom"; for example, a *lessee* is one to whom property is leased. In recent years there has been a fad in coining new *-ee* words, and sometimes the meaning is not at all passive; for example, an *attendee* is one who attends. If these words unnecessarily displace their active-voice equivalents and can be ambiguous (what's the difference between an *attender* and an *attendee?*), they should be avoided.

40 *Appositives: definition and use.* An appositive is a noun element that immediately follows another noun element in order to define or further identify it {George Washington, our first president, was born in Virginia [*our first president* is an appositive of the proper noun *George Washington*]}. An appositive is said to be "in apposition" with the word or phrase to which it refers. Commas frame an appositive unless it is restrictive— e.g., compare *Robert Burns, the poet, wrote many songs about women named Mary* (*poet* being a nonrestrictive appositive noun) with *the poet Robert Burns wrote many songs about women named Mary* (*Robert Burns* restricting *poet* by precisely identifying which poet). A restrictive appositive cannot be removed from a sentence without obscuring the identity of the word or phrase that the appositive relates to. The type of appositive you use can substantially affect a sentence's meaning. For example, compare *My dog Skippy is a Norwegian elkhound* with *My dog, Skippy, is a Norwegian elkhound.* Except for the commas surrounding the appositive in the second sentence, the two sentences are identical. The restrictive appositive in the first sentence may suggest that the writer has more than one dog—hence the reader needs to know which one is being spoken of. The nonrestrictive appositive suggests that there is only one dog because it is not critical to know the dog's name to understand just what the writer is referring to.

Conversions

41 *Nouns as adjectives.* Words that are ordinarily nouns sometimes function as other parts of speech, such as adjectives or verbs. A noun-to-adjective transition takes place when a noun modifies another noun {the morning newspaper} {a state legislature} {a varsity sport} (*morning, state,* and *varsity* function as adjectives). These are also termed *attributive nouns.* Occasionally, the use of a noun as an adjective can produce ambiguity. For example, the phrase *fast results* can be read as meaning either "rapid results" or (less probably but possibly) "the outcome of a fast." Sometimes the noun and its adjectival form can be used interchangeably—e.g., *prostate cancer* and *prostatic cancer* both refer to cancer of the prostate gland. But sometimes the use of the noun instead of the adjective may alter the meaning—e.g., *a study group* is not necessarily *a studious group*. A preposition may be needed to indicate a noun's relationship to other sentence elements. But if the noun functions as an adjective, the preposition must be omitted; at times this can result in a vague phrase—e.g., *voter awareness* (awareness *of* voters or *by* them?). Context might suggest what preposition is implied, but a reader may have to deduce the writer's meaning.

42   *Nouns as verbs.* English nouns commonly pass into use as verbs; it always has been so. (The resulting verbs are called *denominal verbs*.) For example, in 1220 the noun *husband* meant "one who tills and cultivates the earth" {the husband has worked hard to produce this crop}. It became a verb meaning "to till, cultivate, and tend crops" around 1420 {you must husband your land thoughtfully}. New noun-to-verb transitions often occur in dialect or jargon. For example, the noun *mainstream* is used as a verb in passages such as *more school districts are mainstreaming pupils with special needs*. In formal prose, such recently transformed words should be used cautiously if at all.

43   *Adverbial functions.* Words that are ordinarily nouns occasionally function as adverbs {we rode single file} {Sam walked home}. This shift usually happens when a preposition is omitted {we rode in a single file} {Sam walked to his home}.

   Traditional grammarians have typically called such nouns-as-adverbs *adverbial objectives*. Often they modify verbs:

> We arrived Saturday.
> He went home.
> She jogged miles and miles.
> Each cover costs $4.

Often, too, an adverbial objective modifies an adjective {the team is four members strong} {the proposal is worth considering}.

44   *Other conversions.* Words that ordinarily function as other parts of speech, as well as various types of phrases, may function as nouns. Aside from the obvious instance of pronouns (see § 45), these include:

- adjectives such as *poor* {the poor are always with us} (see § 133);
- adverbs such as *here* and *now* {we cannot avoid the here and now};
- participles (gerunds) such as *swimming* {swimming in that lake can be dangerous} (see § 155);
- infinitives such as *to discover* {to discover the truth is our goal} (see §§ 147–50);
- phrases such as those denoting monetary amounts {six million dollars went toward restoring the arena}; and
- clauses such as *what the people want* {what the people want is justice}.

Pronouns

Definition and Uses

45 *"Pronoun" defined.* A pronoun is a word used as a substitute for a noun or, sometimes, another pronoun. It is used in one of two ways. (1) A pronoun may substitute for an expressed noun or pronoun, especially to avoid needless repetition. For example, most of the nouns in the sentence *The father told the father's daughter that the father wanted the father's daughter to do some chores* can be replaced with pronouns: *The father told his daughter that he wanted her to do some chores.* (2) A pronoun may also stand in the place of an understood noun. For example, if the person addressed has been identified elsewhere, the question *Susan, are you bringing your boots?* can be more simply stated as *Are you bringing your boots?* And in the sentence *It is too hot,* the indefinite *it* is understood to mean *the temperature* (*of something*).

> When a tiny word gives you a big headache, it's probably a pronoun.
> —Patricia T. O'Conner
> *Woe Is I*

There are also a few word pairs, such as *each other, one another,* and *no one,* that function as pronouns. These are called *phrasal pronouns.*

46 *Antecedents of pronouns.* A pronoun typically refers to an antecedent— that is, an earlier noun, pronoun, phrase, or clause in the same or in a previous sentence. Pronouns with antecedents are called *anaphoric pronouns.* (*Anaphora* refers to the use of a word or phrase to refer to or replace one used earlier.) An antecedent may be explicit or implicit, but it should be clear. Miscues and ambiguity commonly arise from (1) a missing antecedent {the clown's act with his dog made it a pleasure to watch [where *it* is intended to refer to the circus, which is not explicitly mentioned in the context]}; (2) multiple possible antecedents {Scott visited Eric after his discharge from the army [where it is unclear who was discharged— Scott or Eric]}; and (3) multiple pronouns and antecedents in the same sentence {when the bottle is empty or the baby stops drinking, it must be sterilized with hot water because if it drinks from a dirty bottle, it could become ill [where one hopes that the hot-water sterilization is for the bottle]}.

47 *Clarity of antecedent.* Writers sometimes engage in what is called *broad reference* by allowing a pronoun to refer to an entire idea instead of to an identifiable noun element {she consistently returned his letters unread; this caused him much dismay}. The demonstrative pronouns *this* and *that*, as well as the pronoun *it*, are most often used in this way. If the idea to which such a pronoun refers is reasonably clear, broad reference is acceptable in informal writing. But often it is considered a faulty construction {He had to deliver newspapers early each morning on Wednesdays. This annoyed him no end. [What is *this*? The fact that he was delivering newspapers? That the mornings were so early? That the responsibility fell on Wednesdays?]}.

The mere fact that a noun element precedes a pronoun does not necessarily mean that the noun element is an antecedent. Sometimes, as we see in the next section, a pronoun does not have an antecedent {Mr. Allen borrowed my golf clubs} {Mrs. Wallace gave us good advice}.

Occasionally, too, the pronoun precedes its referent—a figure of speech termed *cataphora*, or anticipatory reference {if she wants our help, Sarah will call us}. As a matter of Standard Written English, editors often prefer to swap the positions of cataphoric pronouns and their referents so that readers won't be needlessly in suspense about who or what is being referred to, especially in a long sentence {if it is something you decide you really need, then your mother and I will consider getting a car for you}. Cataphora often permissibly occurs in constructions involving *like, as, do,* or *have* {like his colleagues, Mr. Thomas hopes to win reelection}.

One more point: A pronoun normally requires a noun or another pronoun as its antecedent. And because possessives function as adjectives rather than nouns, some writers have argued that possessives should not serve as antecedents of pronouns used in the nominative or objective case. But compare *Mr. Blain's background qualified him for the job* with *Mr. Blain had a background that qualified him for the job.* Not only is the identity of *him* perfectly clear in either construction, but the possessive in the first—a usage blessed by respected authorities—makes for a more economical sentence.

48 *Pronouns without antecedents.* Some pronouns do not require antecedents. The first-person pronouns *I* and *we* (as well as *us*) stand for the speaker or a group that includes the speaker, so they almost never have an antecedent. Similarly, the second-person pronoun *you* usually needs no antecedent {are you leaving?}, although one is sometimes supplied in direct address {Katrina, do you need something?}. Expletives such as *there* and *it* (some of which are pronouns) have no antecedents {it is time to go} {this is a fine mess} (see § 327–29). And the relative pronoun *what* and the interrogative pronouns (*who, which, what*) never take an antecedent {who cares what I think?}. In colloquial usage, *they* often appears without an antecedent {they say she's a good golfer}, though skeptical listeners and readers may want to know who "they" are.

49 *Sentence meaning.* The presence or absence of a pronoun may affect the meaning of a sentence. For example, if a noun is used as an appositive of a first-person pronoun, the sense is much different from that of a purely third-person reference. Compare *I, Claudius, once ruled the Roman Empire* with *Claudius once ruled the Roman Empire.* Or *talk to me, your physician, about the symptoms* with *talk to your physician about the symptoms.* As an imperative, the second-person pronoun *you* may usually be either used or omitted without changing the meaning: *You, come here!* is much the same as *Come here!* although the pronoun adds an aggressive tone. When it is not used imperatively, however, *you* cannot be omitted without shifting the sentence to the third person—e.g., *You children rake the yard* (speaking to the children) with *Children rake the yard* (speaking about the children—but in second-person direct address: *Children, rake the yard*).

Properties of Pronouns

50 *Four properties.* A pronoun has four properties: number, person, gender, and case. A pronoun must agree with its antecedent in number, person, and gender. (This is called *pronoun–antecedent agreement.*) But only the third-person singular (*he, she, it*) is capable of indicating all three. Some pronouns can show only number—first-person singular and plural (*I, we*) and third-person plural. The second-person pronoun (*you*) indicates person only: it is no longer capable of showing singular or plural, since the form is the same for both in Modern English. First- and third-person personal pronouns (except *it*), *who*, and *whoever* can show nominative and objective case (*I, me; we, us; he, him; she, her; they, them; who, whom; whoever, whomever*); possessive pronouns represent the genitive case.

51 *Number and antecedent.* A pronoun's number is guided by that of its antecedent or referent—that is, a singular antecedent takes a singular pronoun of the same person as the antecedent, and a plural antecedent takes a plural pronoun of the same person as the antecedent {a book and its cover} {the dogs and their owner}. A collective noun takes a singular pronoun if the members are treated as a unit {the audience showed its appreciation} but a plural if they act individually {the audience rushed back to their seats}. (See § 10.) A singular noun that is modified by two or more adjectives to denote different varieties, uses, or aspects of the object may take a plural pronoun {British and American writing differ in more ways than just their spelling [here, *writing* may be thought of as an elided noun after *British*]}. Two or more singular nouns or pronouns that are joined by *and* are taken jointly and referred to by a plural pronoun {the boy and girl left their bicycles outside}.

52 *Exceptions regarding number of the antecedent.* There are several refinements to the rules just stated: (1) When two or more singular antecedents denote the same thing and are connected by *and*, the pronoun referring to the antecedents is singular {a lawyer and role model received her richly deserved recognition today}. (2) When two or more singular antecedents are connected by *and* and modified by *each*, *every*, or *no*, the pronoun referring to the antecedents is singular {every college and university encourages its students to succeed}. (3) When two or more singular antecedents are connected by *or*, *nor*, *either–or*, or *neither–nor*, they are treated separately and referred to by a singular pronoun {neither the orange nor the peach smells as sweet as it should}. (4) When two or more antecedents of different numbers are connected by *or* or *nor*, the pronoun's number agrees with that of the nearest (usually the last) antecedent. If possible, cast the sentence so that the plural antecedent comes last {neither the singer nor the dancers have asked for their paychecks}. (5) When two or more antecedents of different numbers are connected by *and*, they are referred to by a plural pronoun regardless of the antecedents' order {the horses and the mule kicked over their water trough}.

53 *Pronoun with multiple antecedents.* When a pronoun has two or more antecedents that differ from the pronoun in person, and the antecedents are connected by *and*, *or*, or *nor*, the pronoun must take the person of only one antecedent. The first person is preferred to the second, and the second person to the third {you or I should get to work on our experiment}. In that example, the antecedents are in the second and first person. The following pronoun *our* is in the first person, as is the antecedent *I*. {You and she can settle your dispute.} Here, the antecedents are in the second and third person, so the following pronoun *your* takes the second person. If the pronoun refers to only one of the connected nouns or pronouns, it takes the person of that noun {you and Marian have discussed her trip report}. At times, the pronoun may refer to an antecedent that is not expressed in the same sentence; it takes the number of that antecedent, not of any connected noun or pronoun that precedes it {neither they nor I could do his work [*his* is referring to someone named in a preceding sentence]}.

54 *Some traditional singular pronouns.* The antecedents *anybody, anyone, each, either, everybody, everyone, neither, nobody, no one, one, somebody,* and *someone* have traditionally been treated as singulars that require a singular pronoun:

> Is anyone taking his parents?
> Everybody tried his best.
> Someone should bring his car.

But if a sentence patently refers only to females, the pronoun is traditionally feminine {each of the alumnae was responsible for her own gift} {every one of the sorority members had her say}.

Increasingly in Modern English, the possessive plural pronoun *their* replaces *his* in constructions such as these—to the consternation of traditionalists, to the relief of women's-rights proponents, and to the indifference of most other people. The shift, which originated hundreds of years ago,[2] did not become predominant in edited English until the 1980s. *Everybody did his best* still contends with *Everybody did their best,* but it appears to be losing the battle. Many experienced writers and editors simply avoid the problem with a little "preventive grammar" (see § 435). Tread carefully.

55 *Gender.* If the antecedents are of different genders and are joined by *and,* a plural pronoun is normally used to refer to them {the sister and brother are visiting their aunt}. But if a pronoun refers to only one of the antecedent nouns connected by *and,* the pronoun's gender is that of the noun referred to {the uncle and niece rode in his car}. A special problem arises when the antecedent nouns are singular, are of different genders or an indeterminate gender, and are joined by *or* or *nor.* Using *he, his,* and *him* as a common-gender pronoun is now widely considered sexist, and picking the gender of the nearest antecedent may be misleading (e.g., {some boy or girl left her lunch box on the bus}). A good writer can usually recast

---

2   See Robert D. Eagleson, "A Singular Use of *They,*" *Scribes J. Legal Writing* 5 (1994–95): 87, 89.

the sentence to eliminate the need for any personal pronoun at all {some child left a lunch box on the bus}. See §§ 49, 439.

56   *Case.* Sets of word forms by which a language differentiates the functions that a word performs in a sentence are called the word's *cases.* A pronoun that functions as the subject of a finite verb is in the nominative case {they went to town}. A personal pronoun in the possessive case is governed by the name of the thing possessed {President Barack Obama took his advisers with him to Hawaii}. A pronoun that functions as the object of a verb or preposition is in the objective case {they gave her a farewell party} {they gave it to him}. A pronoun put after an intransitive verb or participle agrees in case with the preceding noun or pronoun referring to the same thing. A pronoun used in an absolute construction is in the nominative: its case depends on no other word {she being disqualified, our best hope is gone}.

57   *Pronouns in apposition.* The case of a pronoun used in an appositive con- struction (see § 311) is determined by the function (subject or object) of the words with which it is in apposition {we three—Bruce, Brad, and I— traveled to Augusta} {she asked us—Barbara, Sarah, and me—to move our cars}.

58   *Nominative case misused for objective.* The objective case governs per- sonal pronouns used as direct objects of verbs {call me tomorrow}, indi- rect objects of verbs {write me a letter}, or objects of prepositions {makes sense to me}. One of the most persistent slips in English is to misuse the nominative case of a personal pronoun in a compound object:

> **Poor:**   *The test would be simple for you or I.
> **Better:** The test would be simple for you or me.
>
> **Poor:**   *Read this and tell Laura and I what you think.
> **Better:** Read this and tell Laura and me what you think.

The mistake may arise from overcorrecting a common error that young children are prone to—using the objective case for a personal pronoun in a compound subject, as in *Jim and me want to go swimming.* Such prob- lems arise in compounds so exclusively that the foolproof way to check for them is to read the sentence with the personal pronoun alone: no one would mistake *The test would be simple for I* or *Read this and tell I what you think* for correct grammar. See § 58.

A few language commentators in recent years have taken the radical position that *between you and I* and other such phrases are now "standard" because the object of the preposition isn't the pair of pronouns but instead the "coordinate phrase" with an invariable *and I*.[3] The better view is that these mistaken nominatives are Stage 3 misusages—common but widely rejected as nonstandard among well-read, highly literate people. They are no longer Stage 1—universally rejected—but neither are they Stage 5 (universally accepted apart from pedantic, eccentric outliers), and they may never become Standard Written English (see pp. 8–9, §§ 428–30). For more on the five stages in the Language-Change Index, see *Garner's Modern English Usage*, 4th ed. (New York: Oxford Univ. Press, 2016), xxxi, l, li.

Classes of Pronouns

59 *Seven classes.* There are seven classes of pronouns:

> personal (*I, you, he, she, it, we,* and *they*);
> demonstrative (*that* and *this*);
> reciprocal (*each other* and *one another*);
> interrogative (*what, which,* and *who*);
> relative (*that, what, which,* and *who*);
> indefinite (e.g., *another, any, each, either,* and *none*); and
> adjective (e.g., *any, each, that, this, what,* and *which*).

Many pronouns, except personal pronouns, may function as more than one type—e.g., *that* may be a demonstrative, relative, or adjective pronoun—depending on its use in a particular sentence.

Personal Pronouns

60 *Form.* A personal pronoun shows by its form whether it is referring to the speaker (first person), the person or thing spoken to (second person), or the person or thing spoken of (third person). Personal pronouns, in other words, convey the source, goal, and topic of an utterance. By their form, they also display number, gender, and case.

---

3   See Oliver Kamm, *Accidence Will Happen* (London: Weidenfeld and Nicolson, 2015), 141–42: "*Between you and I* is permissible. . . . Almost all style manuals disagree with me on this, but I modestly submit that they're wrong. . . . The convention about the cases of conjoined pronouns is required by any rule of English grammar."

61 *Identification.* The first person is the speaker or speakers {I need some tea} {we heard the news}. The second person shows who is spoken to {you should write that essay tonight}. And the third person shows who or what is spoken of {she is at work} {it is in the glove compartment}.

> In all the ranks, degrees, and situations of life, a knowledge of the principles and rules of grammar must be useful; in some situations it must be necessary to the avoiding of really injurious errors.
> —William Cobbett
> *A Grammar of the English Language*

The first-person-singular pronoun *I* is always capitalized no matter where it appears in the sentence {if possible, I will send you an answer today}. All other pronouns are capitalized only at the beginning of a sentence, unless they are part of an honorific title {Her Majesty, the Queen of England}.

62 *Changes in form.* Personal pronouns change form (or *decline*) according to person, number, and case. Apart from the second person, all personal pronouns show number by taking a singular and plural form. Although the second-person pronoun *you* is both singular and plural, it always takes a plural verb, even if only a single person or thing is addressed.

The Forms of Personal Pronouns

Singular pronouns	NOMINATIVE	OBJECTIVE	GENITIVE	REFLEXIVE
First person	I	me	my, mine	myself
Second person	you	you	your, yours	yourself
Third person	he	him	his	himself
	she	her	her, hers	herself
	it	it	its	itself

Plural pronouns	NOMINATIVE	OBJECTIVE	GENITIVE	REFLEXIVE
First person	we	us	our, ours	ourselves
Second person	you	you	your, yours	yourselves
Third person	they	them	their, theirs	themselves

There are four essential rules about the nominative and objective cases. (1) If the pronoun is the subject of a clause, it is in the nominative case {he is vice president}. (2) If the pronoun is the object of a verb, it is objective {she thanked him}. (3) If a pronoun is the object of a preposition, it is objective {please keep this between you and me}. (4) If the pronoun is the subject of an infinitive, it is objective {Jim wanted her to sing}.

63   *Agreement generally.* A personal pronoun agrees with the noun for which it stands in both gender and number {John writes, and he will soon write well} {Sheila was there, but she couldn't hear what was said}.

64   *Expressing gender.* Only the third-person-singular pronouns directly express gender. In the nominative or objective case, the pronoun takes the antecedent noun's gender {the president is not in her office today; she's at a seminar}. In the genitive case, the pronoun always takes the gender of the possessor, not of the person or thing possessed {the woman loves her husband} {Thomas is visiting his sister} {the kitten pounced on its mother}. Some nouns may acquire gender through personification, a figure of speech that refers to a nonliving thing as if it were a person. Pronouns enhance personification when a feminine or masculine pronoun is used as if the antecedent represented a female or male person (as was traditionally done, for example, when a ship or other vessel was referred to with the pronoun *she* or *her*).

65   *Determining gender.* Most English nouns do not have grammatical gender unless they have a specific meaning. (See § 17.) So choosing the appropriate personal pronoun may depend on whether the person's or animal's sex is known or important enough to be worth mentioning. For instance, you may declare *That singer is awful. I hope she'll stop soon!* (the speaker knows the person's sex) or *That's my neighbor's pet pig: its name is Rasher* (the animal's sex is not known to the speaker or not important to understanding). Usually a word referring to a human requires a gender-specific pronoun. You can say *I hear a baby crying somewhere; it must be wet* (the baby's sex is not known to the speaker and not important to understanding) (see § 69). But you don't say *The bank manager got into its car.* When you must use a masculine or feminine pronoun but don't know the person's sex, you'll probably want to cast the sentence so that a pronoun isn't necessary. Avoid using sex-specific pronouns "generically." See § 439.

66   *Special rules.* Some special rules apply to personal pronouns. (1) If a pronoun is the subject of a clause, or follows a conjunction but precedes the verb, it must be in the nominative case {she owns a tan briefcase} {although Delia would like to travel, she can't afford to}. (2) If a pronoun is the object of a verb or preposition, it must be in the objective case {the rustic setting helped him relax} {that's a matter between him and her}. (3) If a prepositional phrase contains more than one object, all the objects must be in the objective case {will you send an invitation to him and me?}. (4) If a pronoun is the subject of an infinitive, it must be in the objective case {does Tina want me to leave?}.

67 *Case after linking verb.* Strictly speaking, a pronoun serving as the complement of a *be*-verb or other linking verb should be in the nominative case {it was she who asked for a meeting}. In that construction, *she* functions as a predicate nominative; when a pronoun does this, it is termed an *attribute pronoun*. The same construction occurs when someone who answers a telephone call is asked, "May I speak to [answerer's name]?" The refined response is *This is he*, not **This is him*.

But in many sentences, the result can sound pedantic or eccentric to the modern ear {was that he on the phone?}. In formal writing, some fastidious readers will consider the objective case to be incorrect in every instance. But the colloquial objective is widely considered to be acceptable:

> **Informal:** The most qualified candidate was her.
> **Formal:**　The most qualified candidate was she.

See p. 287.

The position is somewhat different with first-person pronouns as predicate nominatives. *It's me!* is widely considered perfectly acceptable—even preferable to the priggish-sounding *It's I!* Answering to the French *C'est moi*, the phrasing *It's me* gradually became established beginning in the late 18th century and is now unimpeachable.

68 *Case after "than" or "as–as."* The case of a pronoun following a comparative construction, typically at the end of a sentence, depends on who or what is being compared. In *My sister looks more like our father than I* [or *me*], for example, the proper pronoun depends on the meaning. If the question is whether the sister or the speaker looks more like their father, the pronoun should be nominative because it is the subject of an understood verb {my sister looks more like our father than I do}. But if the question is whether the father or the speaker looks more like the sister, the pronoun should be objective because it is the object of a preposition in an understood clause {my sister looks more like my father than she looks like me}. Whatever the writer's intent with the original sentence, the listener or reader can't be entirely certain about the meaning. It would be better to reword the sentence and avoid the elliptical construction. See § 314.

69 *Special uses.* Some personal pronouns have special uses.

(1) *He, him,* and *his* have traditionally been used as pronouns of inde-terminate gender equally applicable to a male or female person {if the finder returns my watch, he will receive a reward}. Because these pronouns are also masculine-specific, they have in recent years been regarded as sexist when used generically, and their indeterminate-gender use is declining. (See §§ 65, 436.)

(2) *It* eliminates gender even if the noun's sex could be identified. Using *it* does not mean that the noun has no sex—only that the sex is unknown or unimportant {the baby is smiling at its mother} {the mockingbird is building its nest}.

(3) *We, you,* and *they* can be used indefinitely, i.e., without an antecedent, in the sense of "persons," "one," or "people in general." *We* is some-times used by an individual who is speaking for a group {the council's representative declared, "We appreciate your concern"} {the maga-zine's editor wrote, "In our last issue, we covered the archaeological survey of Peru"}. This latter use is called "the editorial *we.*" Some writ-ers also use *we* to make their prose appear less personal and to draw in the reader or listener {from these results we can draw only one conclusion}. *You* can apply indefinitely to any person or all persons {if you read this book, you will learn how to influence people [*you* is indefinite—anyone who reads the book will learn]}. The same is true of *they* {they say that Stonehenge may have been a primitive calendar [those denoted by *they* are unidentified and perhaps unimportant]}.

(4) *It* also has several uses as an indefinite pronoun: (a) *it* may refer to a phrase, clause, sentence, or implied thought {he said that the web-site is down, but I don't believe it [without the pronoun *it*, the clause might be rewritten *I don't believe what he said*]}; (b) *it* can be the sub-ject of a verb (usually a *be*-verb) without an antecedent noun {it was too far}, or an introductory word or expletive for a phrase or clause that follows the verb {it is possible that Jerry Paul is on vacation}; (c) *it* can be the grammatical subject in an expression about time, weather, distance, or the like {it is almost midnight} {it is beginning to snow}; and (d) *it* may be an expletive that anticipates the true grammatical subject or object {I find it hard to accept this situation}. Using the indefinite *it* carelessly may result in obscurity {Paul asked about my cough again; it is starting to annoy me [what is annoying, Paul's ask-ing or the cough itself?]} {my cousin is a doctor; it is an interesting

profession [there is no noun naming the profession (medicine), so *it* lacks a necessary antecedent]}.

70   *The singular "they."* Normally, a singular antecedent requires a singular pronoun. But because *he* is no longer universally accepted as a generic pronoun referring to a person of unspecified gender, people commonly (in speech and in informal writing) substitute the third-person-plural pronouns *they, them, their,* and *themselves,* and the nonstandard singular **themself.* While this usage is accepted in those spheres, it is still considered nonstandard in formal writing. Avoiding the plural form by alternating masculine and feminine pronouns is awkward and only emphasizes the inherent problem of not having a generic third-person pronoun. Employing an artificial form such as **s/he* is distracting at best, and ridiculous to many readers. There are several ways to avoid the problem. For example, use the traditional, formal *he or she, him or her, his or her, himself or herself.* Stylistically, this device can be awkward or even stilted, but if used sparingly it can be functional. For other devices, see § 439.

Possessive Pronouns

71   *Uses and forms.* The possessive pronouns, *my, our, your, his, her, its,* and *their,* are used as limiting adjectives to qualify nouns {my dictionary} {your cabin} {his diploma}. Despite their name, possessive pronouns function in a much broader series of relationships than mere possession {my professor} {your argument}. Each form has a corresponding absolute possessive pronoun (also called an *independent possessive*) that can stand alone without a noun: *mine, ours, yours, his, hers, its,* and *theirs.* The independent form does not require an explicit object: the thing possessed may be either an antecedent or something understood {this dictionary is mine} {this cabin of yours is nice} {where is hers?}. An independent possessive pronoun can also stand alone and be treated as a noun: it can be the subject or object of a verb {hers is on the table} {pass me yours}, or the object of a preposition {put your coat with theirs}. When used with the preposition *of,* a double possessive is produced: *that letter of Sheila's* becomes *that letter of hers.* Such a construction is unobjectionable. Note that none of the possessive personal pronouns is spelled with an apostrophe.

72 *Possessive pronouns vs. contractions.* The possessive forms of personal pronouns are *my, mine, our, ours, your, yours, his, her, hers, its,* and *their.* Again, none of them takes an apostrophe. Nor does the possessive form of *who* (*whose*). Apart from these exceptions, the apostrophe is a universal signal of the possessive in English, so it is a natural tendency (and a common error) to overlook the exceptions and insert an apostrophe in the forms that end in *-s* (or the sibilant *-se*). Aggravating that tendency is the fact that some of the words have homophones that are contractions—another form that is also signaled by apostrophes. The pronouns that don't sound like legitimate contractions seldom present problems, even if they do end in *-s* (*hers, yours, ours*). But several do require special attention, specifically *its* (the possessive of *it*) and *it's* ("it is"); *your* (the possessive of *you*) and *you're* ("you are"); *whose* (the possessive of *who*) and *who's* ("who is"); and the three homophones *their* (the possessive of *they*), *there* ("in that place" or "in that way"), and *they're* ("they are").

Poor: *Its rare for my dog not to eat all it's food.
Better: It's rare for my dog not to eat all its food.

Poor: *Your not going to believe you're eyes.
Better: You're not going to believe your eyes.

Poor: *Whose to say who's fault the accident was?
Better: Who's to say whose fault the accident was?

Poor: *They're bags were over their, but now there not.
Better: Their bags were over there, but now they're not.

See § 146.

Reflexive and Intensive Pronouns

73 *Compound personal pronouns: "-self" forms.* Several personal pronouns form compounds by taking the suffix *-self* or *-selves*. These are *my–myself; our–ourselves; your–yourself; your–yourselves; him–himself; her–herself; it–itself;* and *them–themselves*. The indefinite pronoun *one* forms the compound pronoun *oneself.* All these compound personal pronouns are the same in both the nominative case and the objective case. They have no possessive forms. They are used for four purposes: (1) for emphasis (in which case they are termed *intensive pronouns*) {I saw Queen Beatrice herself} {I'll do it myself}; (2) to refer to the subject of the verb (in which case they are termed *reflexive pronouns*) {he saved himself the trouble of asking} {we support ourselves}; (3) to complement a verb that requires a reflexive pronoun {she availed herself of the privilege} {we need to acquaint ourselves with Beethoven's string quartets}; and (4) to substitute for a simple personal pronoun {this getaway weekend is just for myself}. This fourth use is the least well established in Standard Written English. If a simple personal pronoun will suffice (e.g., *I* or *me*), use that instead.

74 *Basic uses of reflexive and intensive pronouns.* The words *myself, ourselves, yourself, yourselves, himself, herself, itself,* and *themselves* are used in two ways, and it's useful to distinguish between their functions as reflexive and intensive personal pronouns. Compare the intensive pronoun in *I burned the papers myself* (in which the object of *burned* is *papers*) with the reflexive pronoun in *I burned myself* (in which the object of *burned* is *myself*).

Reflexive pronouns serve as objects that usually look back to the subject of a sentence or clause {the cat scared itself} {Gayla took it on herself to make the first move} {Ayoka dressed herself today} {don't repeat yourself [the subject of this imperative sentence is understood to be *You*]}.

Intensive pronouns repeat the antecedent noun or pronoun to add emphasis {I myself don't care} {did you speak with the manager herself?} {Kate herself has won several writing awards} {did you knit that yourself?}. An intensive pronoun is used in apposition to its referent, so it's in the nominative case.

A common problem occurs when the *-self* form does not serve either of those functions. For example, the first-person pronoun in a compound might be used as a subject:

Poor: The staff and myself thank you for your contribution.
Better: The staff and I thank you for your contribution.

Or it might be used as an object that does not refer to the subject:

Poor: Deliver the equipment to my partner or myself.
Better: Deliver the equipment to my partner or me.

Demonstrative Pronouns

75 *Definition.* A demonstrative pronoun (or, as it is sometimes called, a *deictic pronoun*) is one that points directly to its antecedent in the text: *this* or *that* for a singular antecedent {this is your desk} {that is my office}, and *these* or *those* for a plural antecedent {these have just arrived} {those need to be answered}. *This* and *these* point to objects that are near in space, time, or thought, while *that* and *those* point to objects that are somewhat remote in space, time, or thought. The antecedent of a demonstrative pronoun can be a noun, phrase, clause, sentence, or implied thought, as long as the antecedent is clear. *Kind* and *sort*, each referring to "one class," are often used with an adjectival *this* or *that* {this kind of magazine} {that sort of school}. The plural forms *kinds* and *sorts* are preferred in Standard Written English with the plural demonstratives {these kinds of magazines} {those sorts of schools}. A demonstrative pronoun standing alone cannot refer to a human antecedent; it must be followed by a word denoting a person. For example: *I heard Mike's son playing. That child is talented.* In the second sentence, it would be erroneous to omit *child* or some such noun after *that*.

Reciprocal Pronouns

76 **Generally.** *Each other* and *one another* are called *reciprocal pronouns* because they express a mutual relationship between elements {after much discussion, the two finally understood each other} {it's true that we love one another}. Compare the nuances of meaning that a reciprocal or plural reflexive pronoun creates in the same sentence: {after our hike, we all checked ourselves for ticks [each person inspected him- or herself]} {after our hike, we checked one another for ticks [each member inspected one or more of the others]}. Reciprocal pronouns can also take the inflected genitive *-'s* to express possession {we admired each other's watches}.

In traditional usage, *each other* is reserved for two {she and I protected each other} and *one another* for more than two {all five of us watched out for one another}. See p. 267.

77 **Simple and phrasal pronouns.** Because the reciprocal pronouns (along with *no one*) consist of two separate words operating as a single pronoun, they are sometimes termed *phrasal pronouns*. Contrast the simple pronouns *I, me, we, he, she,* and *they,* which have always been written as one word. (Pronouns such as *myself, everyone, whoever,* and *another* were originally open compounds that became closed over time. Only *no one* remains open, most likely because the repeated *o* would cause pronunciation miscues in a closed compound. In BrE it's often hyphenated.)

Interrogative Pronouns

78 *Definition.* An interrogative pronoun asks a question. The three inter-
rogatives are *who, what,* and *which.* Only one, *who,* declines: *who* (nominative), *whom* (objective), *whose* (possessive) {who starred in *Casablanca*?}
{to whom am I speaking?} {whose cologne smells so nice?}. In the nominative case, *who* is used in two ways: (1) as the subject of a verb {who
washed the dishes today?}; and (2) as a predicate nominative after a linking verb {it was who?}. In the objective case, *whom* is used in two ways:
(1) as the object of a verb {whom did you see?}; and (2) as the object of a
preposition {for whom is this building named?}. Yet *who* is often used for
whom as the object of a verb:

> **Informal:** Who did you want?
> **Stuffy:** Whom did you want?

The same is true of *who* when it begins a clause as the object of a stranded
preposition:

> **Informal:** Who are you talking about?
> **Stuffy:** Whom are you talking about?

79 *Referent of interrogative pronouns.* To refer to a person, *who, what,* or
which can be used. But they are not interchangeable. *Who* is universal or
general: it asks for any one or more persons among a universe of people.
The answer may potentially include any person, living or dead, present or
absent {who wants to see that movie?} {who were your greatest inspira-
tions?}. *Who* also asks for a particular person's identity {who is that person standing near the Emerald Buddha?}. *Which* and *what,* when followed
by a noun denoting a person or persons, are usually selective or limited;
they ask for a particular member of a group, and the answer is limited
only to the group addressed or referred to {which explorers visited China
in the 16th century?} {what ice-skater is your favorite?}. To refer to a person, animal, or thing, either *which* or *what* may be used {which one of you
did this?} {what kind of bird is that?}. When applied to a person, *what*
often asks for the person's character, occupation, qualities, and the like
{what do you think of our governor?}. When applied to a thing, *what* is
broad and asks for any one thing, especially of a set {what is your quest?}
{what is your favorite color?}.

Relative Pronouns

80 *Definition.* A relative pronoun is one that introduces a dependent (or *relative*) clause and relates it to the independent clause. Relative pronouns in common use are *who, which, what,* and *that. Who* is the only relative pronoun that declines: *who* (nominative), *whom* (objective), *whose* (possessive) {the woman who presented the award} {a source whom he declined to name} {the writer whose book was a best seller}. *Who* refers only to a person, but it can be used in the first, second, or third person. *Which* refers only to an animal or a thing. *What* refers only to a nonliving thing. *Which* and *what* are used only in the second and third person. *That* refers to a person, animal, or thing, and it can be used in the first, second, or third person. When a relative pronoun qualifies a noun element in the clause it introduces, it is sometimes called a *relative adjective.* See § 105.

81 *Gender, number, and case with relative pronouns.* A relative pronoun agrees with its antecedent in gender, person, and number. If a personal pronoun follows a relative pronoun, and both refer to the same antecedent in the independent clause, the personal pronoun takes the gender and number of that antecedent {I saw a farmer who was plowing his fields with his mule}. If the personal pronoun refers to a different antecedent from that of the relative pronoun, it takes the gender and number of that antecedent {I saw the boy and also the girl who pushed him down}. (See §§ 62–64.) A personal pronoun does not govern the case of a relative pronoun. Hence an objective pronoun such as *me* may be the antecedent of the nominative pronoun *who,* although a construction formed in this way sounds increasingly archaic or even incorrect {she was referring to me, who never graduated from college} {it was we whom they objected to}.

When a construction may be technically correct but sounds awkward or artificial {I, who am wronged, have a grievance}, the best course may be to use preventive grammar and find a different construction {I have been wronged; I have a grievance} {having been wronged, I have a grievance}. See § 433.

82 *Positional nuances.* A relative pronoun is in the nominative case when no subject comes between it and the verb {the professor who lectured was brilliant}. When one or more words intervene between the relative pronoun and the verb, the relative is governed by the following verb or by a verb or a preposition within the intervening clause {the person whom I called is no longer there} {it was John who they thought was in the bleachers}. When a relative pronoun is interrogative, it refers to the word or phrase containing the answer to the question for its consequent, which agrees in case with the interrogative {whose book is that? Joseph's}.

83   *Antecedent.* Usually a relative pronoun's antecedent is a noun or pronoun in the independent clause on which the relative clause depends. For clarity, it should immediately precede the pronoun {the diadem that I told you about is in this gallery}. The antecedent may also be a noun phrase or a clause, but the result can sometimes be ambiguous: in *the bedroom of the villa, which was painted pink,* does the *which*-clause refer to the bedroom or to the villa? See the following section.

84   *Remote relative clauses.* For clarity, pronouns must have unambiguous antecedents. A common problem with the relative pronouns *that, which,* and *who* arises if you separate the relative clause from the noun to which it refers. The longer the separation, the more pronounced the problem—especially when one or more unrelated nouns fall between the true antecedent and the clause. Consider *the guy down the street that runs through our neighborhood*: if the intent is for *that runs through our neighborhood* to refer to *the guy* rather than *the street*, the writer should reword the phrase to make that instantly clear to the reader.

> **Poor:** Stress caused her to lose the freedom from fear of the future, which she once enjoyed.
>
> **Better:** Stress caused her to lose what she once enjoyed: freedom from fear of the future.

> **Poor:** After the news came out, the CEO fired the aide, a friend of the chairman, who was the target of the investigation.
>
> **Better:** After the news came out, the CEO fired the aide, who was the target of the investigation and also a friend of the chairman.

> **Poor:** There are plenty of applicants with the right skills that wouldn't fit in with our staff.
>
> **Better:** There are plenty of applicants who have the right skills but who still wouldn't fit in with our staff.

> **Poor:** The benefits to clients that the new policy has brought are enormous.
>
> **Better:** The benefits that the new policy has brought to clients are enormous.

Poor: The question is whether a member of a gang that is arrested at the scene continues to be "present" and therefore accountable for any crime occurring after the arrest. (The relative pronoun *that* might refer either to *gang* or to *member*.)

Better: The question is whether a gang member who is arrested at the scene continues to be "present" and therefore accountable for any crime occurring after the arrest.

See § 310.

85 *Omitted antecedent.* If no antecedent noun is expressed, *what* can be used to mean *that which* {is this what you were looking for?}. But if there is an antecedent, use a different relative pronoun: *who* {where is the man who spoke?}, *that* (if the relative clause is restrictive, i.e., essential to the sentence's basic meaning) {where are the books that Jones told us about?}, or *which* (if the relative clause is nonrestrictive, i.e., could be deleted without affecting the sentence's basic meaning) {the sun, which is shining brightly, feels warm on my face}.

86 *Relative pronoun and the antecedent "one."* A relative pronoun takes its number from its antecedent. That's easy enough when the antecedent is simply *one*. But if *one* is part of a noun phrase with a plural noun such as *one of the few* or *one of those*, the relative pronoun following takes the plural word as its antecedent—not *one*. Treat the pronoun as a plural and use a plural verb. For example, in *Lily is one of those people who are famous for being famous*, the plural verb *are* links a quality belonging to *those people*. See § 34.

87 *Function of relative pronoun in clause.* A relative pronoun may function as the subject or object of a clause, or it may be adverbial. Using relative clauses makes it possible to condense several thoughts and eliminate repetitive elements. For instance, in *the driver who parked this car went into the store*, the pronoun *who* in the relative clause *who parked this car* identifies the driver and the previous action {the driver parked this car; the driver went into the store}.

88 *Genitive forms.* The forms *of whom* and *of which* are genitives {the child, the mother of whom we talked about, is in kindergarten} {this foal, the sire of which Belle owns, will be trained as a hunter-jumper}. These forms have an old-fashioned sound and can often be rephrased more naturally {the child *whose* mother we talked about is in kindergarten}. The relative *what* forms the genitive *of what* {a list *of what* we need}. The relative *that* forms the genitive *of that* (the preposition being placed at the end of the phrase) {no legend *that* we know *of*} or *of which* {no legend *of which* we know}. On ending a sentence with a preposition, see § 251.

89   *"Whose" and "of which."* The relatives *who* and *which* can both take *whose* as a possessive form (*whose* substitutes for *of which*) {a movie the conclusion *of which* is unforgettable} {a movie *whose* conclusion is unforgettable}. Some writers object to using *whose* as a replacement for *of which*, especially when the subject is not human, but the usage is centuries old and is widely accepted as preventing unnecessary awkwardness. Compare *the company whose stock rose faster* with *the company the stock of which rose faster*. Either form is acceptable, but the possessive *whose* is far smoother.

90   *Compound relative pronouns.* *Who, whom, what,* and *which* form compound relative pronouns by adding the suffix *-ever.* The compound relatives *whoever, whomever, whichever,* and *whatever* apply universally to any or all persons or things {whatever you do, let me know} {whoever needs to write a report about this book may borrow it}. The compounds *whoever* and *whomever* are distinguished in Standard Written English. *Whoever* is nominative and equivalent to *anyone who.* It is used for the subject of a clause, as in *we will give a prize to whoever finds the hidden egg* (although the entire *whoever*-clause is the object of the preposition *to,* the word *whoever* is the subject of that clause and therefore must be in the nominative case). *Whomever* is objective and equivalent to *anyone* (or *anyone whom*). It is an object, never the subject of a clause {give the key to whomever I point to}.

91   *"Who" vs. "whom."* *Who* and *whoever* are nominative pronouns. Each can be used as a subject {whoever said that?} or as a predicate nominative {it was who?}. *Whom* and *whomever* are the objective forms, used as the object of a verb {you called whom?} or of a preposition {to whom are you referring?}.

Three problems arise with determining the correct case. First, because the words are so often found in the inverted syntax of an interrogative sentence, their true function in the sentence can be hard to see without sorting the words into standard subject–verb–object syntax. In the following example, sorting the incorrect "I should say whom is calling" makes the case easier to determine:

Poor: *Whom should I say is calling?
Better: Who should I say is calling?

Second, determining the proper case can be confusing when the pronoun serves a function (say, nominative) in a clause that itself serves a different function (say, objective) in the main sentence. The pronoun's function in its clause determines its case.

Poor: *I'll talk to whomever will listen.
Better: I'll talk to whoever will listen.

Okay: Whoever you choose will suit me.
Better: Whomever you choose will suit me.

In the first example, the entire clause *whoever will listen* is the object of the preposition *to*. But in the clause itself, *whoever* serves as the subject, and that function determines its case. Similarly, in the second example *whomever* is the object of *choose* in the clause, so it must be in the objective case even though the clause itself serves as the subject of the sentence.

Third, as the second example above shows, a further distraction can arise when the *who*-clause itself contains a nested clause, typically of attribution or identification (here, *you choose*). See § 309.

Indefinite Pronouns

92   *Generally.* An indefinite pronoun is one that generally or indefinitely represents an object, usually one that has already been identified or doesn't need exact identification. The most common examples are *another, any, both, each, either, neither, none, one, other, some,* and *such.* There are also compound indefinite pronouns such as *anybody, anything, anyone, everybody, everyone, everything, nobody, no one, oneself, somebody,* and *someone. Each, either,* and *neither* are also called *distributive pronouns* because they separate the objects referred to from others referred to nearby. Indefinite pronouns have number.

When an indefinite pronoun is the subject of a verb, it is usually singular {everyone is enjoying the dinner} {everybody takes notes during the first week}. But sometimes an indefinite pronoun carries a plural sense in informal prose {nobody could describe the music; they hadn't been listening to it} {everyone understood the risk, but they were lured by promises of big returns}.

The forms of indefinite pronouns are not affected by gender or person, and the nominative and objective forms are the same. To form the possessive, the indefinite pronoun may take -'s {that is no one's fault} {is this anyone's jacket?} or the adverb *else* plus -'s {don't interfere with anybody else's business} {no one else's cups were broken}.

93   *The indefinite pronoun "one."* As a pronoun, *one* has two primary uses: (1) as a substitute for a count noun that has already been mentioned or is readily inferable {a leather book requires more care than a cloth one} {where's your better half? she's a good one!}; and (2) as a generic pronoun referring to people in general {one prefers not receiving this kind of news in public} {one might thank oneself for keeping mum}. The second use is more typical of BrE than of AmE. One might easily verify that for oneself.

Adjectives

Types of Adjectives

94 *Definition.* An adjective is a word (more particularly, a type of word sometimes called an *adjunct*) modifying a noun or pronoun; it is often called a *describing word*. An adjective tells you what sort, how many, how large or small, whose, etc. It may modify an understood as well as an expressed noun {he is a good as well as a wise man [*man* is understood after *good*]}. An adjective may add a new idea to a noun or pronoun by describing it more definitely or fully {red wagon} {human error}. Or it may be limiting {three pigs} {this time}. Most adjectives derive from nouns, as *plentiful* derives from *plenty* or as *stylish* derives from *style*; some derive from verbs, roots, or other adjectives.

Often a suffix creates the adjective. Among the suffixes that often distinguish adjectives are -*able* {manageable}, -*al* {mystical}, -*ary* {elementary}, -*ed* {hammered}, -*en* {wooden}, -*esque* {statuesque}, -*ful* {harmful}, -*ible* {inaccessible}, -*ic* {artistic}, -*ish* {foolish}, -*ive* {demonstrative}, -*less* {helpless}, -*like* {childlike}, -*ly* {ghostly} -*ous* {perilous}, -*some* {lonesome}, and -*y* {sunny}. But many adjectives do not have distinctive endings and are recognizable only by their function {old} {tall} {brilliant}.

Depending on its syntactic position, an adjective is either attributive or predicative. An attributive adjective precedes the noun element it modifies {good sportsmanship} {fine writing}. A predicative adjective (also termed a *predicate adjective*) occurs after a linking verb {the sky is blue} or after an object, as a complement {she found him scintillating} {they considered the problem difficult}.

95 *Qualitative adjectives.* The largest class of adjectives is the qualitative (or *descriptive*) type: they tell you what type or kind or class or feature. They denote characteristics {gray} {young} {wizened} {plump}.

96 *Quantitative adjectives.* A quantitative adjective limits the meaning of a noun by defining quantity or the order in which things should be considered. Number-related adjectives may denote an exact or definite number {fourteen} {sixth} or denote number generally {many} {few}. Nonnumeric adjectives follow cardinal numbers {one giant leap}, but if both ordinal and cardinal numbers appear in a phrase, the ordinal usually precedes the cardinal number {the first nine episodes}. An adjective denoting a position in a series is also treated like an ordinal number {the first three copies} unless it denotes a quality of the noun itself; then a cardinal number may precede the ordinal {the three first editions of Johnson's *Dictionary* [meaning three copies of the first edition, not editions 1–3]}.

97 *Demonstrative adjectives.* A demonstrative adjective is one that can point to things, persons, or ideas—usually *this, that, these, those, the,* and *such* {this nurse saw that doctor administer the medicine}. Some demonstrative adjectives must agree in number with the nouns they modify—as a matter of what is called *adjective–noun agreement.* In particular, the singular forms *this* and *that* modify singular nouns {this book} {that enterprise}; the plural forms *these* and *those* modify plural nouns {these photographs are colorful} {those etchings will be hard to clean}. Normally, *this* and *these* refer to things close at hand (either literally or figuratively); *that* and *those* refer to things more distant.

Such (= of this or that kind) is typical of literary English {because several ruffians lurked on the fringes of the crowd, she preferred to stay away completely to avoid such people}. Lawyers frequently use *such* synonymously with one of the other demonstrative adjectives—that is, not to mean "of this or that type" but instead to displace *this* or *that* {although she considered buying 100 Maple Avenue, my client decided not to pursue such property}. But this usage is considered poor legal style because it occasionally introduces ambiguities (has the client decided not to buy property of that kind? or just the previously identified property?).

98 *Possessive adjectives.* The main possessive pronouns—namely *my, our, your, his, her, its,* and *their*—are often called *possessive adjectives* since their function is to qualify nouns {my hat} {our house} {their magnanimity}. See § 71.

99 *Interrogative adjectives.* An interrogative adjective asks a question {which train will you be taking?} {what good is it to argue?}, whether direct or indirect, while modifying a noun element in the question. An interrogative adjective, which qualifies a noun {what drink do you want?}, is distinguishable from an interrogative pronoun (see §§ 78–79), which itself stands for a noun {what do you want?}.

100 *Distributive adjectives.* Just as there are distributive pronouns (see § 92), there are distributive adjectives: *any, no, each, every, either, neither,* etc. when qualifying a noun {any car} {each member} {neither argument}.

101 *Indefinite adjectives.* Indefinite adjectives correspond to indefinite pronouns (see §§ 92–93), except that they modify nouns. The most common are *all, another, any, both, each, either, few, less, many, much, neither, one, other, several,* and *some*—when followed by a noun.

102 *Pronominal adjectives.* A pronominal adjective functions as a noun modifier. It must agree in number with the noun to which it belongs {all people} {these sorts of favors} {those kinds of indulgences}. All pronouns other than personal pronouns, *who,* and *none* may serve as adjectives {those windows} {some coyotes}. The adjective *no* is used instead of *none* {no one astronaut} {no other paradise}.

103 *Proper adjectives.* A proper adjective is one that, being or deriving from a proper name, always begins with a capital letter {a New York minute} {a Cuban cigar} {a Canadian dollar}. A proper name used attributively is still capitalized, but it does not cause the noun it modifies to be capitalized. A place-name containing a comma—such as *Toronto, Ontario,* or *New Delhi, India*—should generally not be used as an adjective because a second comma may be considered obligatory {we met in a Toronto, Ontario, restaurant} The comma after *Ontario* in that sentence is awkward. Compare the readability of *a New Delhi, India, marketplace* with *a New Delhi marketplace* or *a marketplace in New Delhi, India* (substituting a prepositional phrase for the proper adjective).

104 *Compound adjectives.* A compound adjective is composed of two or more words operating as a single adjective. It can be a closed compound {a straitlaced disciplinarian}, an open compound {the West Virginia miners}, or a hyphenated phrasal adjective {well-bred children}.

105 *Relative adjectives.* A relative adjective is a relative pronoun functioning as an adjective by modifying a noun element in the dependent adjectival or noun clause it introduces {he is an author whose books become richer with every reading} {take whichever path will get you there quickest}.

Articles as Limiting Adjectives

106   *Definition.* Articles are function words that are more important for the role they play in a sentence's structure than for their semantic content. An article is a limiting adjective that precedes a noun or noun phrase and determines its use to indicate something definite (*the*) or indefinite (*a* or *an*). An article might stand alone or be used with other adjectives {a road} {an elaborate design} {the yellow-brick road}.

107   *Definite article.* A definite article points to a definite object that (1) is so well understood that it does not need description (e.g., *the package is here* is a shortened form of *the package that you expected is here*); (2) is a thing that is about to be described {the sights of Chicago}; or (3) is important {the grand prize}. The definite article belongs to nouns in the singular {the star} or the plural number {the stars}.

108   *Definite articles and proper names.* Generally, the definite article is used for proper names {the Majestic Theatre} and is usually lowercase even when it is a part of the name {the Beatles}. But there are exceptions {The Hague}. An indefinite article may be used in some circumstances, as when referring to one of several things or people that have the same proper name {I know a Timothy Benbow who lives in Oxfordshire and another in Gloucestershire} {one of Janice's ancestors was an Earl or Duke of Northumberland in the 15th or 16th century}.

If a proper name is reduced to an abbreviation, the definite article is often retained when the acronym stands alone. For example, *the National Football League* is usually written as *the NFL* {the Dallas Cowboys joined the NFL in 1960}. But if the proper name doesn't usually take the definite article, the abbreviation won't take it. So *the Columbia Broadcasting System* is abbreviated and written *CBS* {do you watch CBS?}. The definite article is absorbed into the acronym when it acts as an adjective {FCC standards allow the media to police themselves} {the TV listings [the definite article is associated with *listings*, not *TV*]}.

109   *Indefinite article.* An indefinite article points to a nonspecific object, thing, or person that is not distinguished from the other members of a class. The thing may be singular {a student at Princeton}, or uncountable {a multitude}, or generalized {an idea inspired by Milton's *Paradise Lost*}.

110 *Indefinite article in specific reference.* In a few usages, the indefinite article provides a specific reference {I saw a great movie last night} and the definite article a generic reference {the Scots are talking about independence [generalizing by nationality]}.

111 *Choosing "a" or "an."* With the indefinite article, the choice of *a* or *an* depends on the sound of the word it precedes. *A* precedes words with a consonant sound, including /y/, /h/, and /w/, no matter how the word is spelled {a eulogy} {a historic occasion} {a onetime pass}. *An* comes before words with a vowel sound {an FBI agent} {an *X-Files* episode} {an hour ago}.

The same is true for abbreviations. If the first letter or syllable is sounded as a consonant, use *a* {a BTU calculation} {a GB of memory}. If the first sound is a vowel, then use *an* {an MBA degree} {an ATM}. Some abbreviations are commonly used as whole words—and are technically called *acronyms* (the term *initialisms* being reserved for abbreviations in which each character is sounded separately, as with *NBA*). With an acronym, the sound of the first syllable controls {an AIDS epidemic} {a MEDEVAC helicopter}. Some have variant pronunciations and may be sounded out letter by letter or as whole words: for example, a local-area network may be an LAN (/el-ay-en/) or a LAN (/lan/), and a radio-operated car is an ROC (/ahr-oh-see/) or a ROC (/rok/). Choose *a* or *an* according to whether the abbreviation's first sound is more often spoken as a vowel or as a consonant. A dictionary may help. See p. 228.

112 *Articles with coordinate nouns.* With a series of coordinate nouns, an article may appear before each noun, but it is not necessary {the rosebush and hedge need trimming}. If the things named make up a single idea, it's especially unnecessary to repeat the article {in the highest degree of dressage, the horse and rider appear to be one entity}. And if the named things are covered by one plural noun, the definite article should not be repeated {in the first and second years of college}. But if you want to distinguish concepts or add emphasis, then do repeat the article {the time, the money, and the effort were all wasted}.

113 *Effect on meaning.* Because articles have a demonstrative value, the meaning of a phrase may shift depending on the article used. For example, *an officer and gentleman escorted Princess Grace to her car* suggests (though ambiguously) that the escort was one man with two descriptive characteristics. But *an officer and a friend escorted Princess Grace to her car* suggests that two people acted as escorts. Similarly, *do you like the red and blue cloth?* suggests that the cloth contains both red and blue threads. But *do you like the red and the blue cloth?* suggests that two different fabrics are being discussed. The clearest way to express the idea that the cloth contains both red and blue is to hyphenate the phrase as a compound modifier: *red-and-blue cloth*; and with two kinds of cloth, the clear expression is either to repeat the word *cloth* (*the red cloth and the blue cloth*) or to use *cloth* with the first adjective rather than the second (*the red cloth and the blue*).

114 *Omitted article and zero article.* The absence of an article may alter a sentence's meaning—e.g., the meaning of *the news brought us little comfort* (we weren't comforted) changes if *a* is inserted before *little*: *the news brought us a little comfort* (we felt somewhat comforted). An article that is implied but omitted is called a *zero article*, common in idiomatic usage. For example, in the morning you may *make the bed*, but at night you *go to bed* (not *the bed*)—and notice *in the morning* vs. *at night*). The zero article usually occurs in idiomatic references to time, illness, transportation, personal routines, and meals {by sunset} {has cancer} {travel by train} {go to bed} {make breakfast}.

115 *Article as pronoun substitute.* An article may sometimes substitute for a pronoun. For example, the blanks in *a patient who develops the described rash on ____ hands should inform ____ doctor* may be filled in with either a possessive pronoun or the definite article (*the*).

Dates as Adjectives

116 *Use and punctuation.* Dates are often used as descriptive adjectives, more often today than in years past. If a month-year or month-day date is used as an adjective, no hyphen or comma is needed {October 31 festivities} {December 2014 financial statement}. If a full month-day-year date is used, then a comma is sometimes considered necessary both before and after the year {the May 27, 2016, ceremonies}. But this construction is awkward because the adjective (which is forward-looking) contains two commas (which are backward-looking); the construction is therefore best avoided {ceremonies on May 27, 2016}. When the full date is used adjectivally, some writers omit the second comma {the May 27, 2016 ceremonies}.

Position of Adjectives

117 *Basic rules.* An adjective that modifies a noun element usually precedes it {perfect storm} {spectacular view} {a good bowl of soup}. Such an adjective is called an *attributive adjective*. An adjective may follow the noun element if the adjective (1) expresses special emphasis {reasons innumerable} {captains courageous}; (2) occurs in this position in standard usage {court-martial} {notary public}; (3) is a predicate adjective following a linking verb {I am ready}; (4) functions as an appositive set off by commas or dashes {the man, tall and thin, stood in the corner}; or (5) modifies a pronoun of a type usually followed by an adjective {anything good} {everything yellow} {nothing important} {something wicked}. (An adjective that follows its noun is termed a *postpositive adjective* because it appears after the noun it modifies.) Some adjectives are always in the predicate and never appear before what they modify {the city is asleep} {the door was ajar}. Others appear uniformly before the nouns they modify {utter nonsense} {a mere child}. Phrasal adjectives may precede or follow what they modify. When a modifying phrase follows the noun element it modifies, it is traditionally called an *adjective phrase*. See §§ 131–32.

118 *After possessives.* When a noun phrase includes a possessive noun, as in *children's shoes* or *the company's president*, the adjective follows the possessive {children's athletic shoes} {the company's former president} (unless the reference is to athletic children or a former company). The same is true of possessive pronouns {her red dress}.

119 *Adjective modifying pronoun.* When modifying a pronoun, an adjective usually follows the pronoun {the searchers found him unconscious} {some like it hot}, sometimes as a predicate adjective {it was insensitive} {who was so jealous?}.

120 *Predicate adjective.* A predicate adjective is an adjective that follows a linking verb (see §§ 142, 183) but modifies the subject {the child is afraid} {the night became colder} {this tastes delicious} {I feel bad}. If an adjective in the predicate modifies a noun or pronoun in the predicate, it is not a predicate adjective. For example, in *the train will be late*, the adjective *late* modifies the subject *train*. But in *the train will be here at a late hour*, the adjective *late* modifies the noun *hour*, not the subject *train*.

So even though it occurs in the predicate, it is not known as a *predicate adjective*, which by definition follows a linking verb.

121   *Dangling participles.* A participial adjective often appears before an independent clause {watching constantly, the lioness protected her cubs from danger}. Such a participial phrase is said to "dangle" when the participle lacks grammatical connection to a noun that performs the action denoted by the participle. This grammatical problem occurs when a participial form is not immediately followed by the noun it modifies {before receiving the medal, the general congratulated the soldier [*receiving* is meant to attach to *soldier*, not *general*]}.

> **Poor:**   Bounding through the woods, we saw a herd of deer.
> **Better:**   We saw a herd of deer bounding through the woods.
>
> **Poor:**   Elated by the letter from a long-lost friend, life took a turn for the better for Doris.
> **Better:**   Elated by the letter from a long-lost friend, Doris found her life taking a turn for the better.

The same problem arises when a possessive follows the participial phrase {dodging the traffic, his cellphone got dropped in the street [the cellphone wasn't dodging traffic]}. If you recast the sentence to eliminate the dangler, you'll improve the style {the general congratulated the soldier before awarding the medal} {dodging the traffic, he dropped his cellphone in the street}. For certain participles functioning as prepositions (or subordinating conjunctions) and therefore exempt from the rule against dangling, see § 246.

122   *Distinguishing an adjective from an adverb or participle.* Some adjectives have an *-ly* ending and therefore resemble adverbs {friendly} {goodly}. Others end with *-ed* or *-ing* and resemble participial verbs {insulting} {tired}. Placement usually distinguishes whether a word is an adjective. Compare *a calculated risk* (*calculated* is an adjective) with *the risk has been calculated* (*calculated* is a participle), and compare *his lectures are boring* (*boring* is an adjective) with *he is boring the class* (*boring* is a participle). Also, *Eddie did a fine job* (*fine* is an adjective) with *the camera works fine* (*fine* is an adverb). See § 214.

Degrees of Adjectives

123 *Generally.* An adjective is gradable into three degrees: the positive or absolute {hard}, the comparative {harder}, and the superlative {hardest}. A positive adjective simply expresses an object's quality without reference to any other thing {a big balloon} {bad news}.

124 *Comparative forms.* A comparative adjective expresses the relationship between a specified quality shared by two things, often to determine which has more or less of that quality {a cheaper ticket} {a happier ending}. The suffix *-er* usually signals the comparative form of a common adjective having one or two syllables {light–lighter} {merry–merrier}. These forms are called *synthetic comparatives.* A positive adjective with three or more syllables typically takes *more* (or *greater, less, fewer,* and so forth) instead of a suffix to form the comparative {intelligent–more intelligent} {purposeful–more purposeful}. These forms are called *periphrastic comparatives.* Among the exceptional three-syllable positive forms that make synthetic comparatives are *unlucky* {*unluckier*} and *unsteady* {*unsteadier*}. Yet *more unlucky* and *more unsteady* are available as periphrastic alternatives.

Some adjectives with two syllables take the *-er* suffix {lazy–lazier} {narrow–narrower}, but most two-syllable adjectives take *more* {more hostile} {more careless}. A two-syllable adjective ending in *-er, -le, -ow, -ure,* or *-y* can typically use either the *-er* suffix or *more*—unless it is prefixed with *un-* {unluckier} {unsteadier}.

125 *Superlative forms.* A superlative adjective expresses the relationship between at least three things and denotes an extreme of intensity or amount in a particular shared quality {the biggest house on the block} {the bitterest pill of all}. The suffix *-est* usually signals the superlative form of a common adjective having one or two syllables {lighter–lightest}. These forms are called *synthetic superlatives.* An adjective with three or more syllables takes *most* instead of a suffix to form the superlative {quarrelsome–most quarrelsome} {humorous–most humorous}. These forms are called *periphrastic superlatives.* Some adjectives with two syllables take the *-est* suffix {holy–holiest} {noble–noblest}, but most two-syllable adjectives take *most* {most fruitful} {most reckless}.

126 *Forming comparatives and superlatives.* A few rules govern the forming of a short regular adjective's comparative and superlative forms. (1) If the adjective is a monosyllable ending in a single vowel followed by a single consonant, the final consonant is doubled before the suffix is attached {red–redder–reddest}. (2) If the adjective ends in a silent -*e*, the -*e* is dropped before adding the suffix {polite–politer–politest}. (3) A participle used as an adjective requires *more* or *most* before the participle; no suffix is added to form the comparative or the superlative {this teleplay is more boring than the first one} {I am most tired on Fridays}. (4) A few one-syllable adjectives—*real, right,* and *wrong*—can take only *more* and *most*. Even then, these combinations occur only in informal speech. (5) *Eager, proper,* and *somber,* unlike many other two-syllable adjectives, also take only *more* and *most*; none can take a suffix. (6) A two-syllable adjective to which the negative prefix *un-* has been added can usually either take a suffix or take *more* or *most,* even if the total number of syllables is three {unhappiest} {most unhappy}. (7) Participles that function as adjectives never take suffixes; they use only *more* and *most* {a more appealing outfit} {the most stunning smile}. (8) Many adjectives are irregular—there is no rule that guides their comparative and superlative forms {good–better–best} {less–lesser–least}. A good dictionary will show the forms of an irregular adjective. (9) An adjective can never take both a suffix and *more* or *most* (or *less, least,* etc.). This is a grammatical fault known as a *double comparative* {*more wronger} or a *double superlative* {*least wrongest}. It is stigmatized as nonstandard.

127 *Equal and unequal comparisons.* A higher degree of comparison is signaled by a suffix (-*er* or -*est*), or by *more* or *most*. (See §§ 124–26.) A lower degree is shown by *less* (comparative) or *least* (superlative) {cold–less cold} {less cold–least cold}. Equivalence is shown by the use of the *as–as* construction {this is as old as that} and sometimes by *so* {that test was not so hard as the last one}.

128 *Noncomparable adjectives.* An adjective that, by definition, describes an absolute state or condition—e.g., *entire, impossible, pregnant, unique*—is called *noncomparable*. It cannot take a comparative suffix and cannot be coupled with a comparative term (*more, most, less, least*). Nor can it be intensified by a word such as *very, largely,* or *quite*. But on the rare occasion when a particular emphasis is needed, a good writer may depart from this rule and use a phrase such as *more perfect,* as the framers of the United States Constitution did in composing its preamble {We the

People of the United States, in order to form a more perfect Union . . .}. Among the adjectives generally considered noncomparable are these:

absolute	inevitable	singular
adequate	infinite	stationary
chief	irrevocable	sufficient
complete	main	ultimate
devoid	manifest	unanimous
entire	only	unavoidable
false	paramount	unbroken
fatal	perfect	uniform
favorite	perpetual	unique
final	possible	universal
ideal	preferable	void
impossible	principal	whole

Special Types of Adjectives

129 *Participial adjectives.* A participial adjective is simply a verb's participle (see §§ 151–54, 157–59) that modifies a noun or pronoun. It can be a present participle (verb ending in -*ing*) {the dining room} {a walking stick} {a rising star} or a past participle (usually a verb ending in -*ed*) {an endangered species} {a completed assignment} {a proven need}. Some past-participial adjectives have only this adjectival function, the past-participial verb having taken a different form {a shaven face} {a graven image}. When a past participle (see § 151) functioning as an adjective has its own modifier, that modifier may itself be modified with an adverb such as *quite* {a quite fatigued traveler}, *barely* {a barely concealed wince}, *little* {a little-known fact}, or an adverbial phrase such as *very much* {a very much distrusted public official}. If the past participle has gained a strong adjectival quality, *very* will do the job alone without the quantitative *much* {very tired} {very drunk}. But if the participial form seems more like a verb, *very* needs *much* to help it do the job {very much appreciated} {very much delayed}. A few past participles (such as *bored, interested, pleased, satisfied*) are in the middle of the spectrum between those having mostly adjectival qualities and those having mostly verbal qualities. With these few, the more stringent editorial position is to include the quantitative *much*.

130 *Coordinate adjectives.* A coordinate adjective is one that appears in a sequence with one or more related adjectives to modify the same noun. Coordinate adjectives should be separated by commas or by *and* {skilled, experienced chess player} {nurturing and loving parent}. If one adjective modifies the noun and another adjective modifies the idea expressed by the combination of the first adjective and the noun, the adjectives are not considered coordinate and should not be separated by a comma. For example, *a lethargic soccer player* describes a soccer player who is lethargic. Likewise, phrases such as *white brick house* and *wrinkled canvas jacket* are unpunctuated because the adjectives are not coordinate: they have no logical connection in sense (a white house could be made of many different materials; so could a wrinkled jacket). The most useful test is this: if *and* would fit between the two adjectives, a comma is necessary.

131 *Phrasal adjectives.* A phrasal adjective (also called a *compound modifier*) is a phrase that functions as a unit to modify a noun. A phrasal adjective follows these basic rules: (1) Generally, if placed before a noun, the phrase should be hyphenated to avoid misdirecting the reader {dog-eat-dog competition}. There may be a considerable difference between the hyphenated and the unhyphenated forms: compare *small animal hospital* with *small-animal hospital*. (2) If a compound noun is an element of a phrasal adjective, the entire compound noun must be hyphenated to clarify the relationship among the words {video-game-magazine dispute} {college-football-halftime controversy}. (3) If more than one phrasal adjective modifies a single noun, hyphenation becomes especially important {19th-century song-and-dance numbers} {state-inspected assisted-living facility}. (4) If two phrasal adjectives end in a common element, the ending element should appear only with the second phrase, and a suspension hyphen should follow the unattached words to show that they are related to the ending element {the choral- and instrumental-music programs}. (5) If the phrasal adjective denotes an amount or a duration, the plural should be dropped. For instance, *pregnancy lasts nine months* but is *a nine-month pregnancy*, and a shop *open 24 hours a day* has *a 24-hour-a-day schedule*. The plural is retained only for fractions {a two-thirds majority}. (6) If a phrasal adjective becomes awkward, the sentence should probably be recast. For example, *The news about the lower-than-expected third-quarter earnings disappointed investors* could become *The news about the third-quarter earnings, which were lower than expected, disappointed investors*. Or perhaps this: *Investors were disappointed by the third-quarter earnings, which were lower than expected.*

132 *Exceptions for hyphenating phrasal adjectives.* There are exceptions to hyphenating phrasal adjectives: (1) If a phrasal adjective follows a linking verb, it is often unhyphenated—e.g., compare *a well-trained athlete* with *an athlete who is well trained.* (2) When a proper name begins a phrasal adjective, the name is not hyphenated {the Monty Python school of comedy}. (3) A two-word phrasal adjective that begins with an adverb ending in *-ly* is not hyphenated {a sharply worded reprimand} (but *a not-so-sharply-worded reprimand*).

Functional Variation

133 *Adjectives as nouns.* An adjective-to-noun shift (sometimes called an *adnoun*) is relatively common in English. Some adjectives are well established as nouns and are perfectly suitable for most contexts. For example, *a postmortem examination* is often called *a postmortem*; *collectible objects* are *collectibles*; and *French people* are *the French*. Any but the most established among such nouns should be used only after careful consideration. If there's an alternative, it will almost certainly be better. For example, there is probably no good reason to use the adjective *collaborative* as a noun (i.e., as a shortened form of *collaborative enterprise*) when the perfectly good *collaboration* is available. See § 44.

134 *Adjectives as verbs.* Adjective-to-verb shifts are uncommon in English but occur once in a while, usually as jargon or slang {the cargo tanks were inerted by introducing carbon dioxide into them} {it would be silly to low-key the credit for this achievement}. They generally don't fit comfortably into formal prose.

135 *Other parts of speech functioning as adjectives.* Words that ordinarily function as other parts of speech, but sometimes as adjectives, include nouns (see § 41), pronouns (see § 102), and verbs (see § 151).

136 *The weakening effect of injudicious adjectives.* Use care in handling adjectives. In the best style, they don't bolster nondescript nouns when a stronger alternative is available. For example, *famous people* has less force than *celebrities*. An adjective may also diminish the impact of a statement by drawing emphasis away from the noun. Compare *it is the undeniable truth* with *it is the truth*. Some adjectives are so close in meaning that one swallows the other or creates a redundancy. You'll often find that omitting one will make the noun—and the sentence—stronger.

Verbs

Definitions

137 *Verbs generally.* A verb shows the performance or occurrence of an action or the existence of a condition or a state of being, such as an emotion. A verb is the most essential part of speech—the only one that can express a full thought by itself (with the subject understood) {Run!} {Enjoy!} {Think!}. (One-word sentences such as *Why?* or *Yes* alone can express complete thoughts, but these are in fact elliptical sentences omitting a clause implied by context. {Why [did she do that]?} {Yes[, you may borrow that book].}. See § 313.)

> Verbs act. Verbs move. Verbs do. Verbs strike, soothe, grin, cry, exasperate, decline, fly, hurt, and heal. Verbs make writing go, and they matter more to our language than any other part of speech.
>
> —Donald Hall
> *Writing Well*

138 *Transitive and intransitive verbs.* Depending on the presence or absence of an object, a verb is classified as transitive or intransitive. A transitive verb requires an object to express a complete thought; the verb indicates what action the subject exerts on the object. For example, *the cyclist hit a curb* states what the subject *cyclist* did to the object *curb*. (A few transitive verbs have what are called *cognate objects*, which are closely related etymologically to the verb {drink a drink} {build a building} {see the sights}.) An intransitive verb does not require an object to express a complete thought {the rescuer jumped}, although it may be followed by a prepositional phrase serving an adverbial function {the rescuer jumped to the ground}. Many verbs may be either transitive or intransitive, the different usages often distinguishing their meanings. For example, when used transitively, as in *the king's heir will succeed him*, the verb *succeed* means "to follow and take the place of"; when used intransitively, as in *the chemist will succeed in identifying the toxin*, it means "to accomplish a task." With some verbs, no such distinction is possible. For example, in *I will walk; you ride*, the verb *ride* is intransitive. In *I will walk; you ride your bike*, the verb *ride* is transitive, but its meaning is unchanged. A verb that is normally used transitively may sometimes be used intransitively to emphasize the verb and leave the object undefined or unknown {the patient eats poorly [*how well* the patient eats is more important than *what* the patient eats]}.The test for whether a given verb is transitive is to try it with various possible objects. For each sentence in which an object is plausible, the verb is being used transitively. If an object doesn't work idiomatically, the verb is being used intransitively.

Common Transitive Verbs		Common Intransitive Verbs	
attach	lift	appear	happen
block	make	arrive	laugh
borrow	move	belong	nap
buy	name	collapse	occur
close	offer	come	remain
cut	punch	cough	rise
file	reject	cry	sleep
fix	smash	disappear	smile
give	staple	exist	sneeze
hit	take	fall	stay
kick	use	gallop	vanish

139 *Ergative verbs.* Some verbs, called *ergative* or *ambitransitive verbs,* can be used transitively or intransitively {the impact shattered the windshield} {the windshield shattered}. The noun that serves as the object when the verb's use is transitive becomes the subject when the verb's use is intransitive. For example, with the noun *door* and the verb *open,* one can say *I opened the door* (transitive) or *the door opened* (intransitive). Many verbs can undergo ergative shifts {the torpedo sank the boat} {the boat sank}. For example, the verb *ship* was once exclusively transitive {the company shipped the books on January 16}, but in commercial usage it is now often intransitive {the books shipped on January 16}. Likewise, *grow* (generally an intransitive verb) was transitive only in horticultural contexts {the family grew several types of crops}, but commercial usage now makes it transitive in many other contexts {how to grow your business}. Careful writers and editors employ such usages cautiously if at all, preferring well-established idioms.

140 *Dynamic and stative verbs.* Verbs can be classified as either dynamic (or *action*) or stative (or *nonaction*). Dynamic verbs express actions that a subject can carry out {Jim wrote an article} {Maria bought a car}. Stative verbs, by contrast, express a state or condition, not an action {Jim has the article} {Maria owns a car}. Examples:

Dynamic Verbs	Stative Verbs
argue	be
call	consider
drink	doubt
drive	dread
fly	enjoy
jump	exist
lift	hate
push	imagine
sew	imply
shout	know
sketch	need
taste	prefer
walk	seem
wash	suffer
watch	understand

Only dynamic verbs can appear in the present-progressive tense {Jim is writing a book} and the past-progressive tense {Maria was buying a car}. Stative verbs simply don't function idiomatically in those contexts.

141 *Regular and irregular verbs.* The past-tense and past-participial forms of most English words are formed by appending *-ed* to the basic form {draft–drafted–drafted}. If the verb ends in *-e*, only a *-d* is appended {charge–charged–charged}. (Sometimes a final consonant is doubled: for the spelling rules of these regular forms, see § 174.) These verbs are classified as *regular*, or *weak* (the latter is a term used in philology to classify forms of conjugation).

But a few common verbs have maintained forms derived mostly from Old English roots {begin–began–begun} {bet–bet–bet} {bind–bound–bound} {bite–bit–bitten}. These verbs are called *irregular* or *strong verbs*. The various inflections of strong verbs defy simple classifications, but many past-tense and past-participial forms (1) change the vowel in the base verb (as *begin*), (2) keep the same form as the base verb (as *bet*), (3) share an irregular form (as *bind*), or (4) change endings (as *bite*). (The vowel change between cognate forms in category 1 is called an *ablaut*.) The verb *be* is highly irregular, with eight forms (*is, are, was, were, been, being, be,* and *am*). Because no system of useful classification is possible for irregular verbs, a reliable memory and a general dictionary are essential tools for using the correct forms consistently. Further complicating the spelling of irregular verbs is the fact that the form may vary according to the sense of the word. When used to mean "to offer a price," for example, *bid* keeps the same form in the past tense and past participle, but when it means "to offer a greeting," it forms *bade* (traditionally rhyming with *glad*) and *bidden*. The form may also depend on whether the verb is being used literally {wove a rug} or figuratively {weaved in traffic}. Finally, a few verbs that are considered regular have an alternative past tense and past participle that is formed by adding *-t* to the simple verb form {dream–dreamed} {dream–dreamt}. When these alternatives are available, AmE tends to prefer the forms ending in *-ed* (e.g., *dreamed, learned, spelled*), while BrE often prefers the forms ending in *-t* (*dreamt, learnt, spelt*).

The table below should be understood with those complications in mind. It lists only the irregular forms that are commonly used in Standard Written English. Words that may also take regular forms are italicized as a signal that the forms shown here may be incorrect in some usages. Irregular verbs are a closed word class, meaning that there is a finite number that can be exhaustively listed. (Other closed word classes include pronouns, articles, and auxiliary verbs. Regular verbs, on the other hand, are an example of an open word class—along with nouns, adjectives, and adverbs.) The list below, however, includes only the most common of the 270 or so irregular verbs. It also omits many words recently coined on the pattern of an old one (for instance, *cablecast* and *simulcast*, both formed on the analogy of *broadcast*). Those words almost always maintain the same inflections as the words they are built on.

It's useful to read over this list with an eye to memorizing the inflections. Try the past-tense and past-participial forms in sentences that you can devise {I mistook your meaning}. Some may sound stuffy {I forbore attending the optional meeting}, but on the whole you'll probably find it pleasing to be reminded of the standard inflections. Knowing them builds confidence in a speaker or writer.

Irregular Verbs

PRESENT TENSE	PAST TENSE	PAST PARTICIPLE
abide	*abode*	*abode*
alight	*alit*	*alit*
arise	arose	arisen
awake	awoke	awaked (or awoken)
be	was	been
bear	bore	borne
beat	beat	beaten

Irregular Verbs cont'd

PRESENT TENSE	PAST TENSE	PAST PARTICIPLE
become	became	become
befall	befell	befallen
beget	begot	begotten
begin	began	begun
behold	beheld	beheld
bend	bent	bent
bereave	*bereft*	*bereft*
beseech	*besought*	*besought*
beset	beset	beset
bespeak	bespoke	bespoken (or bespoke)
bet	bet	bet
bid (= to express)	bade	bidden
bid (= to offer)	bid	bid
bind	bound	bound
bite	bit	bitten
bleed	bled	bled
blow	blew	blown
break	broke	broken
breed	bred	bred
bring	brought	brought
broadcast	broadcast	broadcast
browbeat	browbeat	browbeaten
build	built	built
burn	burnt (BrE)	burnt (BrE)
burst	burst	burst
buy	bought	bought
cast	cast	cast
catch	caught	caught
choose	chose	chosen
cleave (= to split)	cleft (or clove)	cleft (or cloven)
cling	clung	clung
clothe	*clad*	*clad*
come	came	come
cost	cost	cost
creep	crept	crept
crow	*crow*	crowed
cut	cut	cut
deal	dealt	dealt
dig	dug	dug
dive	*dove* (AmE)	dived
do	did	done

Irregular Verbs cont'd

PRESENT TENSE	PAST TENSE	PAST PARTICIPLE
draw	drew	drawn
dream	*dreamt* (BrE)	*dreamt* (BrE)
drink	drank	drunk
drive	drove	driven
dwell	*dwelt*	*dwelt*
eat	ate	eaten
fall	fell	fallen
feed	fed	fed
feel	felt	felt
fight	fought	fought
find	found	found
fit	*fit* (AmE)	*fit* (AmE)
flee	fled	fled
fling	flung	flung
floodlight	floodlit	floodlit
fly	flew	flown
forbear	forbore	forborne
forbid	forbade	forbidden
forecast	forecast	forecast
foresee	foresaw	foreseen
foretell	foretold	foretold
forget	forgot	forgotten
forgive	forgave	forgiven
forsake	forsook	forsaken
forswear	forswore	forsworn
freeze	froze	frozen
gainsay	gainsaid	gainsaid
get	got	gotten (AmE), got (BrE)
give	gave	given
go	went	gone
grind	ground	ground
grow	grew	grown
hamstring	hamstrung	hamstrung
hang (a picture)	hung	hung
have	had	had
hear	heard	heard
heave	*hove*	*hove*
hew	hewed	*hewn*
hide	hid	hidden
hit	hit	hit

Irregular Verbs cont'd

PRESENT TENSE	PAST TENSE	PAST PARTICIPLE
hold	held	held
hurt	hurt	hurt
inlay	inlaid	inlaid
input	input	input
inset	inset	inset
interweave	interwove	interwoven
keep	kept	kept
kneel	knelt	knelt
know	knew	known
lay (= to place)	laid	laid
lead	led	led
leap	*leapt* (mostly BrE)	*leapt* (mostly BrE)
learn	*learnt* (BrE)	*learnt* (BrE)
leave	left	left
lend	lent	lent
let	let	let
lie (= to rest)	lay	lain
light	*lit*	*lit*
lose	lost	lost
make	made	made
mean	meant	meant
meet	met	met
miscast	miscast	miscast
misdeal	misdealt	misdealt
mishear	misheard	misheard
mislay	mislaid	mislaid
mislead	misled	misled
misread	misread	misread
misspell	*misspelt* (BrE)	*misspelt* (BrE)
misspend	misspent	misspent
mistake	mistook	mistaken
misunderstand	misunderstood	misunderstood
mow	mowed	*mown*
outbid	outbid	outbid (BrE)
outdo	outdid	outdid
outgrow	outgrew	outgrown
output	output	output
outrun	outran	outrun
outsell	outsold	outsold
outshine	outshone	outshone

Irregular Verbs cont'd

PRESENT TENSE	PAST TENSE	PAST PARTICIPLE
overbid	overbid	overbid
overcome	overcame	overcome
overdo	overdid	overdid
overdraw	overdrew	overdrawn
overeat	overate	overeaten
overfly	overflew	overflown
overhang	overhung	overhung
overhear	overheard	overheard
overlay	overlaid	overlaid
overlie	overlay	overlain
overpay	overpaid	overpaid
override	overrode	overridden
overrun	overran	overrun
oversee	oversaw	overseen
overshoot	overshot	overshot
oversleep	overslept	overslept
overtake	overtook	overtaken
overthrow	overthrew	overthrown
partake	partook	partaken
pay	paid	paid
put	put	put
quit	*quit*	*quit*
read	read	read
rebuild	rebuilt	rebuilt
recast	recast	recast
redo	redid	redone
rehear	reheard	reheard
remake	remade	remade
rend	rent	rent
repay	repaid	repaid
reread	reread	reread
rerun	reran	rerun
resell	resold	resold
reset	reset	reset
resit	resat	resat
retake	retook	retaken
retell	retold	retold
rewrite	rewrote	rewritten
rid	rid	rid
ride	rode	ridden

Irregular Verbs cont'd

PRESENT TENSE	PAST TENSE	PAST PARTICIPLE
ring	rang	rung
rise	rose	risen
run	ran	run
saw	sawed	*sawn* (BrE)
say	said	said
see	saw	seen
seek	sought	sought
sell	sold	sold
send	sent	sent
set	set	set
sew	sewed	sewn
shake	shook	shaken
shear	sheared	*shorn*
shed	shed	shed
shine	*shone*	*shone*
shoe	*shod*	*shod*
shoot	shot	shot
show	showed	shown
shrink	shrank	shrunk
shrive	*shrove*	*shriven*
shut	shut	shut
sing	sang	sung
sink	sank	sunk
sit	sat	sat
slay	slew	slain
sleep	slept	slept
slide	slid	slid
sling	slung	slung
slink	slunk	slunk
slit	slit	slit
smell	*smelt* (BrE)	*smelt* (BrE)
smite	smote	smitten
sow	sowed	sown
speak	spoke	spoken
speed	sped	sped
spell	*spelt* (BrE)	*spelt* (BrE)
spend	spent	spent
spill	*spilt* (BrE)	*spilt* (BrE)
spin	spun	spun
spit	spat	spat

Irregular Verbs cont'd

PRESENT TENSE	PAST TENSE	PAST PARTICIPLE
split	split	split
spoil	*spoilt* (BrE)	*spoilt* (BrE)
spread	spread	spread
spring	sprang	sprung
stand	stood	stood
stave	*stove*	*stove*
steal	stole	stolen
stick	stuck	stuck
sting	stung	stung
stink	stank	stunk
strew	strewed	strewn
stride	strode	strode
strike	struck	struck
string	strung	strung
strive	strove	striven
sublet	sublet	sublet
swear	swore	sworn
sweep	swept	swept
swim	swam	swum
swing	swung	swung
take	took	taken
teach	taught	taught
tear	tore	torn
tell	told	told
think	thought	thought
throw	threw	thrown
thrust	thrust	thrust
tread	*trod*	*trodden*
underbid	underbid	underbid
undercut	undercut	undercut
undergo	underwent	undergone
underlie	underlay	underlain
underpay	underpaid	underpaid
undersell	undersold	undersold
understand	understood	understood
undertake	undertook	undertaken
underwrite	underwrote	underwritten
undo	undid	undone
unfreeze	unfroze	unfrozen
unwind	unwound	unwound
uphold	upheld	upheld

Irregular Verbs cont'd

PRESENT TENSE	PAST TENSE	PAST PARTICIPLE
upset	upset	upset
wake	*woke*	*woken*
wear	wore	worn
weave	wove	woven
wed	*wed*	*wed*
weep	wept	wept
wet	*wet*	*wet*
win	won	won
wind	wound	wound
withdraw	withdrew	withdrawn
withhold	withheld	withheld
withstand	withstood	withstood
wring	wrung	wrung
write	wrote	written

142   *Linking verbs.* A linking verb (also called a *copula* or *connecting verb*) is one that links the subject to a closely related word in the predicate—a subjective complement. The linking verb itself does not take an object because it expresses a state of being instead of an action {Mr. Block is the chief executive officer} {that snake is venomous} {his heart's desire is to see his sister again}. There are two kinds of linking verbs: *be*-verbs and intransitive verbs that are used in a weakened sense, such as *appear, become, feel, look, seem, smell,* and *taste.* The weakened intransitive verbs often have a figurative sense akin to that of *become,* as in *He fell heir to a large fortune* (he didn't physically fall on or into anything) or *The river ran dry* (a waterless river doesn't run—it has dried up).

Some verbs only occasionally function as linking verbs—among them *act* {act weird}, *get* {get fat}, *go* {go bald}, *grow* {grow weary}, *lie* {lie fallow}, *prove* {prove untenable}, *remain* {remain quiet}, *sit* {sit still}, *stay* {stay trim}, *turn* {turn gray}, and *wax* {wax eloquent}. Also, some passive-voice constructions contain linking verbs {this band was judged best in the contest} {she was made sales-force manager}.

If a verb doesn't have a subjective complement, then it doesn't qualify as a linking verb in that particular construction. For instance, when a *be*-verb conveys the sense "to be situated" or "to exist," it is not a linking verb {Kansas City, Kansas, is across the river} {there is an unfilled receptionist position}. Likewise, if a verb such as *appear, feel, smell, sound,* or *taste* is followed by an adverbial modifier instead of a subjective complement {he appeared in court} or a direct object {the dog smelled the scent}, it isn't a linking verb.

143 *Phrasal verbs.* A phrasal verb is usually a verb plus a preposition (or particle) {settle down} {act up} {phase out}. A phrasal verb is not hyphenated, even though its equivalent noun or phrasal adjective might be—e.g., compare *to flare up* with *a flare-up*, and compare *to step up the pace* with *a stepped-up pace.* Three rules apply: (1) if the phrasal verb has a sense distinct from the component words, use the entire phrase—e.g., *hold up* means "to rob" or "to delay," and *get rid of* and *do away with* mean "to eliminate"; (2) avoid the phrasal verb if the verb alone conveys essentially the same meaning—e.g., *rest up* is equivalent to *rest*; and (3) don't compress the phrase into a one-word verb, especially if it has a corresponding one-word noun form—e.g., one *burns out* (phrasal verb) and suffers *burnout* (noun).

> Present-day phrasal verbs remain equally protean. A student who has had the maximum number of loans has "loaned out," not the same as older "lend out" or more recent "max out" meaning "reach and pass one's maximum performance"; cf. "veg [vej] out," "become torpid as though in a vegetative state," and "hulk out," "go into a frenzy like the title character in the television series *The Incredible Hulk.*" A shampoo that "lathers in extra body and manageability" also exemplifies conversion ("lather" as verb) and phrasal verb. Phrasal verbs remain idiomatic, too: "in" and "out" are antonyms, but "fill in" and "fill out" (a blank or form) are virtually synonyms; while to be "all set up" is the opposite of "all upset." Older "fall down" gives "downfall" but newer "melt down" and "fall out" give "meltdown" and "fallout"; likewise "breakthrough" and "kickback." The verb/noun is "shoot out" but "shoot off" gives "offshoot." The verb "take out" gives two nouns, "takeout" if it is food but "outtake" if it is edited film.
>
> —W. F. Bolton
> *The Language of 1984*

In a phrasal verb, the preposition is an integral part of the verb, serving as an adverb but often with a figurative, idiomatic sense:

- She turned up four new witnesses.
- Put out the candles.
- The interviewer took down everything she said verbatim.

Although you might think at first that a preposition starts a prepositional phrase—that *witnesses, candles,* and *everything* are the objects of prepositions—that is not so. Grammatically, the nouns are direct objects of the verbs shaded in the above examples: in each sentence, the words *up, out,* and *down* could come after instead of before the noun:

- She turned four new witnesses up.
- Put the candles out.
- The interviewer took everything she said down verbatim.

Except in questions, prepositions can't be switched around in this way. But in the following sentences, the preposition doesn't function as part of the phrasal verb:

- She ran up the stairs.
- Several reporters walked out this door.
- He tumbled down the stairs.

Although an entire prepositional phrase can conceivably be moved {down the stairs he tumbled}, the single preposition can't be moved in the way demonstrated above with phrasal verbs.

Although most phrasal verbs consist of two words {look over} {take up [= to begin as a hobby]}, many consist of three {get away with} {look up to} {put up with}.

144   *Principal and auxiliary verbs.* Depending on its uses, a verb is classified as principal or auxiliary. A principal verb is one that can stand alone to express an act or state {he jogs} {I dreamed about Xanadu}. If combined with another verb, it expresses the combination's leading thought {a tiger may roar}. An auxiliary verb is used with a principal verb to form a verb phrase that indicates mood, tense, or voice {you must study for the exam!} {I will go to the store} {the show was interrupted}. The most commonly used auxiliaries are *be, can, do, have, may, must, ought, shall,* and *will.* For more on auxiliary verbs, see §§ 198–209.

145   *Verb phrases.* The combination of an auxiliary verb with a principal verb is a verb phrase, such as *could happen, must go,* or *will be leaving.* When a verb phrase is modified by an adverb, the modifier typically goes directly after the first auxiliary verb, as in *could certainly happen, must always go,* and *will soon be leaving.* The idea that verb phrases should not be "split" in this way is quite mistaken (see § 238). A verb phrase is negated by placing the negative adverb *not* after the first auxiliary {we have not called him}. In an interrogative sentence, the first auxiliary begins the sentence and is followed by the subject {must I repeat that?} {do you want more?}. An interrogative can be negated by placing *not* after the subject {do you not want more?}, but a contraction is often more natural {don't you want more?}. Most negative forms can be contracted {we do not–we don't} {I will not–I won't} {he has not–he hasn't} {she does not–she doesn't}, but *I am not* is contracted to *I'm not* (never *I amn't*). The corresponding interrogative form is *aren't I?* Sometimes the negative is emphasized if the auxiliary is contracted with the pronoun and the negative is left standing alone {he is not–he isn't–he's not} {we are not–we aren't–we're not} {they have not–they haven't–they've not}.

Verb phrases are sometimes also called *complete verbs*. But this term can be ambiguous, since some grammarians use it instead for only the principal verb in a phrase. So in the sentence "We have not thanked him for working so hard," *complete verb* could refer to *have thanked* or simply *thanked*. To further confuse the issue, others call any nonlinking finite verb a *complete verb*—meaning that *working* could also be a complete verb. Combine this ambiguity with the potential for conflating *complete verb* and *complete predicate* (see § 303), and it's easy to see why this term is best avoided.

146 *Contractions.* Most types of writing benefit from the use of contractions. If used thoughtfully, contractions in prose sound natural and relaxed, and make reading more enjoyable. *Be*-verbs and most of the auxiliary verbs are contracted when followed by *not*: *are not–aren't*; *was not–wasn't*; *cannot–can't*; *could not–couldn't*; *do not–don't*; and so on. A few, such as *ought not–oughtn't*, look or sound awkward and are best avoided. Pronouns can be contracted with auxiliaries, with forms of *have*, and with some *be*-verbs. Think before using one of the less common contractions, which often don't work well in prose, except perhaps in dialogue or quotations. Some examples are *I'd've* (I would have), *she'd've* (she would have) *it'd* (it would), *should've* (should have), *there're* (there are; there were), *who're* (who are; who were), and *would've* (would have). Also, some contracted forms can have more than one meaning. For instance, *there's* may be *there is* or *there has*, and *I'd* may be *I had* or *I would*. The particular meaning may not always be clear from the context.

Nouns can also form contractions with auxiliaries, *have*-verbs, and some *be*-verbs, but they often look and sound clumsy {you'd think the train'd be on time for once} {the stores're sold out of fondue sets} {the DVDs've melted in the heat}. And nouns contracted with *is* may initially resemble possessives {Robin's falling out of the tree} {Amalie's firing the head chef right now}. Consider using a pronoun instead.

Infinitives

147 *Definition.* An infinitive verb, also called the verb's *root* or *stem*, is a verb that in its principal uninflected form may be preceded by *to* {to dance} {to dive}. It is the basic form of the verb, the one listed in dictionary entries. The preposition *to* is sometimes called the "sign" of the infinitive {he tried to open the door}, and it is sometimes classed as an adverb (see § 210). In the active voice, *to* is generally dropped when the infinitive follows an auxiliary verb {you must flee} and can be dropped after several verbs, such as *bid, dare, feel, hear, help, let, make, need,* and *see* {you dare say that to me?}. But when the infinitive follows one of these verbs in the passive voice, *to* should be retained {he cannot be heard to deny it} {they cannot be made to listen}. The *to* should also be retained after *ought* and *ought not* (see § 203).

148   *Split infinitive.* Although from about 1850 to 1925 many grammarians stated otherwise, it is now widely acknowledged that adverbs sometimes justifiably separate the *to* from the principal verb {they expect to more than double their income next year}. See § 238.

149   *Uses of infinitive.* The infinitive has great versatility. It is sometimes called a *verbal noun* because it can function as part of a verb phrase {someone has to tell her} or a noun {to walk away now seems rash}. The infinitive also has limited uses as an adjective or an adverb. As a verb, it can take (1) a subject {we wanted the lesson to end}, (2) an object {try to throw the javelin higher}, (3) a predicate complement {want to race home?}, or (4) an adverbial modifier {you need to think quickly in chess}.

An infinitive takes on the role of principal verb when used with a finite verb whose sense doesn't express a full thought; as often happens with *dare, ought, am able,* etc. {you ought to apologize to her} {I am finally able to laugh again}. Without the infinitive to express the specific obligation, ability, etc., such sentences make little sense. That's why this use is termed the *complementary infinitive*: it completes the meaning of the finite verb, which takes on a modal quality {I am going to wash my hair tonight}. (This usage should not be confused with an infinitive operating as a subjective or objective complement, which is a noun or adjectival function.)

As a noun, the infinitive can perform as (1) the subject of a finite verb {to fly is a lofty goal} or (2) the object of a transitive verb or participle {I want to hire a new assistant}. An infinitive may be governed by a verb {cease to do evil}, a noun {we all have talents to be improved}, an adjective {she is eager to learn}, a participle {they are preparing to go}, or a pronoun {let him do it}.

150   *Dangling infinitive.* An infinitive phrase can be used, often loosely, to modify a verb—in which case the sentence must have a grammatical subject (or an unexpressed subject of an imperative) that could logically perform the action of the infinitive. If there is none, then the sentence may be confusing. For example, in *To repair your car properly, it must be sent to a mechanic,* the infinitive *repair* does not have a logical subject; the infinitive phrase *to repair your car* is left dangling. But if the sentence is rewritten as *To repair your car properly, you must take it to a mechanic,* the logical subject is *you.*

Participles and Gerunds

151   *Participles generally.* A participle is a nonfinite verb that is not limited by person, number, or mood, but does have tense. Two participles are formed from the verb stem: the present participle invariably ends in *-ing,* and the past participle usually ends in *-ed.* See § 174.

    The present participle consists of the present stem of the verb plus *-ing* {ask–asking}, sometimes with the final consonant of the stem doubled {spin–spinning}. It denotes the verb's action as being in progress or incomplete at the time expressed by the sentence's principal verb {watching intently for a mouse, the cat settled in to wait} {hearing his name, Jon turned to answer}.

    The past participle is the third principal part of a verb. For a regular verb, it is formed by adding *-d, -ed,* or *-t* to the present stem and is identical with the past tense {call–called–called}. For irregular verbs, there are several patterns: the principal parts of the verb may be identical {slit–slit–slit}, the first and third parts may be identical {run–ran–run}, the second and third parts may be identical {spin–spun–spun}, or all three parts may be different {sing–sang–sung}. The past participle denotes the verb's action as being completed {planted in the spring} {written last year}.

    There are other types of participles as well. All verbs have a perfect participle {having called} and a perfect-progressive participle {having been calling}. Transitive verbs have passive forms of the present participle {being called} and of the perfect participle {having been called}.

    Participles occur in many types of verb phrases. The past participle appears in the active-voice versions of the present perfect {have called}, the past perfect {had called}, and the future perfect {will have called}. It also appears in all tenses with the passive voice {was called} {were called} {am called}. See § 181 (verb conjugations with *call*).

152   *Forming present participles.* The present participle is formed by adding *-ing* to the stem of the verb {reaping} {wandering}. If the stem ends in

-ie, the *-ie* usually changes to *-y* before the *-ing* is added {die–dying} {tie–tying}. If the stem ends in a silent *-e*, that *-e* is usually dropped before the *-ing* is added {giving} {leaving}. There are two exceptions to this rule. The silent *-e* is retained when (1) the word ends with *-oe* {toe–toeing} {hoe–hoeing} {shoe–shoeing}, or (2) the verb has a participle that would resemble another word but for the distinguishing *-e* (e.g., *dyeing* means something different from *dying*, and *singeing* means something different from *singing*). The spelling rules for inflecting words that end in *-y* and for doubling final single consonants are the same as those given in § 174. Regular and irregular verbs both form the present participle in the same way. The present participle is the same for all persons and numbers.

153 *Forming past participles.* With regular verbs, the past participle is formed in the same way as the past indicative—that is, the past-indicative and past-participial forms are always identical {stated–stated} {pulled–pulled}. For irregular verbs, the forms are sometimes the same {paid–paid} {sat–sat} and sometimes different {forsook–forsaken} {shrank–shrunk}. See § 141.

154 *Participial phrases.* A participial phrase is made up of a participle plus any closely associated word or words, such as modifiers or complements. It can be used (1) as an adjective to modify a noun or pronoun {nailed to the roof, the slate stopped the leaks} {she pointed to the clerk drooping behind the counter}, or (2) as an absolute phrase {generally speaking, I prefer spicy dishes} {they having arrived, we went out on the lawn for our picnic}. For more on participial adjectives, see §§ 121–22, 129.

155 *Gerunds.* A gerund is a present participle used as a noun. It is not limited by person, number, or mood, but it does have tense. Being a noun, the gerund can be used as (1) the subject of a verb {complaining about it won't help}; (2) the object of a verb {I don't like your cooking}; (3) a predicate nominative or complement {his favorite pastime is sleeping}; or (4) the object of a preposition {reduce erosion by terracing the fields}. In some sentences, a gerund may substitute for an infinitive. Compare the use of the infinitive *to lie* as a noun {to lie is wrong} with the gerund *lying* {lying is wrong}.

Even though a gerund is always used as a noun, it retains some characteristics of a verb. Specifically, it can take an object {mailing letters kept her busy all day} and it can be modified by an adverb {preparing assiduously enabled him to succeed}.

156   *Gerund phrases.* A gerund phrase consists of a gerund, its object, and any modifiers that may be present {winning the bid amid so much competition made her proud}. The phrase in that example consists of the gerund *winning*, its object *bid*, the article (or adjective) *the* modifying *bid*, and the adverbial phrase *amid so much competition*. In addition to serving as the subject of a clause, a gerund phrase may function as:

- a direct object of a verb {we worried about his believing that idea};
- a subjective complement {that is throwing the baby out with the bathwater};
- an objective complement {we call this soldiering on};
- an adverbial objective {the offer is worth considering closely};
- the object of a preposition {they were amply rewarded for working overtime};
- an appositive {his strategy, being silent when there was no significant news, made everyone even more anxious}; or
- part of an absolute construction {her being honest about unpleasant facts having established trust with her opposite number, the two were able to proceed cooperatively}.

The same words may function as either a gerund phrase {knowing his own shortcomings made him more fearless as a competitor} or a participial phrase {knowing his own shortcomings, he decided to play it safe}.

157   *Distinguishing between participles and gerunds.* Because participles and gerunds both derive from verbs, the difference between them depends on their function. A participle is used as a modifier {the running water} or as part of a verb phrase {the meter is running}; it can be modified only by an adverb {the swiftly running water}. A gerund is used as a noun {running is great exercise}; it can be modified only by an adjective {sporadic running and walking makes for a great workout}.

Along with infinitives, which can function as nouns {to lie is immoral} or modifiers {the decision to leave is always hard}, participles and gerunds are collectively called *verbals*. A phrase comprising more than one verbal is called a *group verbal* {hoping to change her mind was futile}.

158   *Fused participles.* As nouns, gerunds are modified by adjectives {double-parking is prohibited}, including possessive nouns and pronouns {Critt's parking can be hazardous to pedestrians}. By contrast, a present participle is always modified (if at all) by an adverb, whether the participle serves as a verb {she's parking the car now}, an adjective {I'll be looking for a parking place}, or an adverb {finally parking, we saw that the store had already closed}. It is traditionally considered a linguistic fault (a *fused participle*) to use a nonpossessive noun or pronoun with a gerund:

Poor: *Me painting your fence depends on *you paying me first.
Better: My painting your fence depends on your paying me first.

In the poor example, *me* looks like the subject of the sentence, but it doesn't agree with the verb *depends*. Instead, the subject is *painting*—a gerund, here seeming to be "modified" by *me*, a pronoun. In the predicate, *you* looks like the object of the preposition *on*, but the true object is the gerund *paying*.

There are times, however, when the possessive is unidiomatic. You usually have no choice but to use a fused participle with a nonpersonal noun {we're not responsible for the jewelry having been mislaid}, a nonpersonal pronoun {we all insisted on something being done}, or a group of pronouns {the settlement depends on some of them agreeing to compromise}.

159 *Dangling participles.* Both participles and gerunds are subject to dangling. A participle that has no syntactic relationship with the nearest subject is called a *dangling participle* or just a *dangler*. In effect, the participle ceases to function as a modifier and functions as a kind of preposition. Often the sentence is illogical, ambiguous, or even incoherent {*frequently used in early America, experts suggest that shaming is an effective punishment [*used* does not modify the closest noun, *experts*; it modifies *shaming*]} {*being a thoughtful mother, I believe Meg gives her children good advice [the writer at first seems to be attesting to his or her own thoughtfulness rather than Meg's]}. Recasting the sentence so that the misplaced modifier is associated with the correct noun is the only effective cure {experts suggest that shaming, often used in early America, is an effective punishment} {I believe that because Meg is a thoughtful mother, she gives her children good advice}. Using passive voice in an independent clause can also produce a dangler. In *Finding that the questions were not ambiguous, the exam grades were not changed*, the participle *finding* "dangles" because there is no logical subject to do the finding. The sentence can be corrected by using active voice instead of passive, so that the participle precedes the noun it modifies {finding that the questions were not ambiguous, the teacher did not change the exam grades}. Quite often writers will use *it* or *there* as the subject of the independent clause after a participial phrase, thereby producing a dangler without a logical subject {*reviewing the suggestions, it is clear that no consensus exists [a possible revision: *Our review of the suggestions shows that no consensus exists*]}.

160   *Dangling gerunds.* When the participle in a dangling gerund is the object of a preposition, it functions as a noun rather than as a modifier. For example, *After finishing the research, the screenplay was easy to write* (who did the research and who wrote the screenplay?). The best way to correct a dangling gerund is to revise the sentence. The example above could be revised as *After Gero finished the research, the screenplay was easy to write*, or *After finishing the research, Gero found the screenplay easy to write*. Dangling gerunds can result in improbable statements. Consider **while driving to San Antonio, my phone ran out of power*. The phone wasn't at the wheel, so *driving* is a dangling gerund that shouldn't refer to *my phone*. Clarifying the subject of the gerund improves the sentence {while I was driving to San Antonio, my phone ran out of power}.

Properties of Verbs

161   *Five properties.* A verb has five properties: voice, mood, tense, person, and number. Verbs are conjugated (inflected) to show these properties.

VOICE

162   *Active and passive voice.* Voice shows whether the subject acts (active voice) or is acted on (passive voice)—that is, whether the subject performs or receives the action of the verb. Only transitive verbs are said to have voice. The clause *the judge levied a $50 fine* is in the active voice because the subject *judge* is acting. But *the tree's branch was broken by the storm* is in the passive voice because the subject *branch* does not break itself—it is acted on by the object *storm*. The passive voice is always formed by joining an inflected form of *to be* (or, in colloquial usage, *get*) with the verb's past participle. Compare *the ox pulls the cart* (active voice) with *the cart is pulled by the ox* (passive voice). A passive-voice verb in a dependent clause

> Passive voice will always have certain important uses, but remember that you must keep your eye on it at all times or it will drop its *o* and change swiftly from passive voice to passive vice.
> —Lucille Vaughan Payne
> *The Lively Art of Writing*

often has an implied *be*-verb: in *the advice given by the novelist*, the implied words *that was*—omitted by what is known as a *whiz-deletion* (see § 315)—are understood to come before *given*; so the passive construction is *was given*. Although the *be*-verb is sometimes implied, the past participle must always be expressed. Sometimes the agent isn't named {his tires were slashed}.

As a matter of style, passive voice {the matter will be given careful consideration} is typically, though not always, inferior to active voice {we will consider the matter carefully}. The choice between active and passive voice may depend on which point of view is desired. For instance, *the mouse was caught by the cat* describes the mouse's experience, whereas *the cat caught the mouse* describes the cat's.

What is important is to be able to identify passive voice reliably. Remember that *be*-verbs alone are not passive—hence *he is thinking about his finances* isn't in the passive voice. It's just a *be*-verb plus a present participle. To make it passive voice, you'd have to write *his finances are thought about by him* (an awkward sentence, to say the least). The two necessary elements are a *be*-verb (occasionally understood contextually) and a past participle:

Passive Voice

is	misled
are	written
was	sent
were	demolished
been	built
being	completed
be	confirmed
am	bothered

If the passive-voice verb is followed by the preposition *by* (plus the noun that performs the action), it is a long-passive construction. If the *by*-phrase is omitted, it is known as a *short passive*:

Long passive:	Mistakes were made by our office.
Short passive:	Mistakes were made.

Because of its vagueness, the short passive is sometimes (by no means always) used to evade or to deflect responsibility.

163 *Progressive conjugation and voice.* If an inflected form of *be* is joined with a verb's present participle, a progressive conjugation results {the ox is pulling the cart}. If the verb is transitive, the progressive conjugation is in active voice because the subject is performing the action, not being acted on. (See § 162.) But if both the principal verb and the auxiliary are *be*-verbs followed by a past participle {the cart is being pulled}, the result is a passive-voice construction.

MOOD

164 *Generally.* Mood (or *mode*) indicates the manner in which the verb expresses an action or state of being. The three moods are indicative, imperative, and subjunctive.

165 *Indicative mood.* The indicative mood is the most common in English. It is used to express facts and opinions and to ask questions {amethysts cost very little} {the botanist lives in a garden cottage} {does that bush produce yellow roses?}.

166 *Imperative mood.* The imperative mood expresses commands {go away!}, direct requests {bring the tray in here}, and, sometimes, permission {come in!}. It is simply the verb's stem used to make a command, a request, an exclamation, or the like {put it here!} {give me a clue} {help!}. The subject of the verb, *you*, is understood even though the sentence might include a direct address {give me the magazine} {Cindy, take good care of yourself [*Cindy* is a direct address, not the subject]}. Use the imperative mood cautiously: in some contexts it could be too blunt or unintentionally rude. You can soften the imperative by using a word such as *please* {please stop at the store}. If that isn't satisfactory, you might recast the sentence in the indicative {will you stop at the store, please?}.

167 *Subjunctive mood.* Although the subjunctive mood no longer appears with much frequency, it is useful when you want to express an action or a state not as a reality but as a mental conception. Typically, the subjunctive expresses an action or state as doubtful, imagined, desired, conditional, hypothetical, or otherwise contrary to fact. Despite its decline, the subjunctive mood persists in stock expressions such as *perish the thought, heaven help us*, or *be that as it may*. For particulars about subjunctive constructions, see the sections that follow.

168 *Subjunctive vs. indicative mood.* The subjunctive mood signals a statement contrary to fact {if I were you}, including wishes {if I were a rich man}, conjectures {oh, were it so}, demands {the landlord insists that the dog go}, and suggestions {I recommend that she take a vacation}. Three errors often crop up with these constructions. First, writers sometimes use an indicative verb form when the subjunctive form is needed:

Poor: If it wasn't for your help, I never would have found the place.

Better: If it weren't for your help, I never would have found the place.

Second, indicative-mood sentences sometimes resemble these subjunctive constructions but aren't statements contrary to fact:

Poor: I called to see whether she were in.

Better: I called to see whether she was in.

Third, one often sees *If I would have gone, I would . . .*, with two conditionals, instead of *If I had gone, I would . . . .*

Although the subjunctive mood is often signaled by *if*, not every *if* takes a subjunctive verb. When the action or state might be true but the writer does not know, the indicative is called for instead of the subjunctive {if I am right about this, please call} {if Napoleon was in fact poisoned with arsenic, historians will need to reevaluate his associates}.

169   *Present subjunctive.* The present-tense subjunctive mood is formed by using the base form of the verb, such as *be*. This form of subjunctive often appears in suggestions or requirements {he recommended that we be ready at a moment's notice} {we insist that he retain control of the accounting department}. The present-tense subjunctive is also expressed by using either *be* plus the simple-past form of the verb or a past-form auxiliary plus an infinitive {the chair proposed that the company be acquired by the employees through a stock-ownership plan} {today would be convenient for me to search for that missing file} {might he take down the decorations this afternoon?}.

170   *Past subjunctive.* Despite its label, the past-tense subjunctive mood refers to something in the present or future but contrary to fact. It is formed using the verb's simple-past tense, except for *be*, which becomes *were* regardless of the subject's number. For example, the declaration *if only I had a chance* expresses that the speaker has little or no chance. Similarly, *I wish I were safe at home* almost certainly means that the speaker is not at home and perhaps not safe—though it could also mean that the speaker is at home but quite unsafe.

This past-tense-but-present-sense subjunctive typically appears in the form *if I (he, she, it) were* {if I were king} {if she were any different}. That is, the subjunctive mood ordinarily uses a past-tense verb (e.g., *were*) to connote uncertainty, impossibility, or unreality where the present or future indicative would otherwise be used. Compare *If I am threatened, I will quit* (indicative) with *If I were threatened, I would quit* (subjunctive), or *If the canary sings, I smile* (indicative) with *If the canary sang* (or *should sing*, or *were to sing*), *I would smile* (subjunctive).

171 *Past-perfect subjunctive.* Just as the past subjunctive uses a verb's simple-past-tense form to refer to the present or future, the past-perfect subjunctive uses a verb's past-perfect form to refer to the past. The past-perfect subjunctive typically appears in the form *if I (he, she, it) had been* {if he had been there} {if I had gone}. That is, the subjunctive mood ordinarily uses a past-perfect verb (e.g., *had been*) to connote uncertainty or impossibility where the past or past-perfect indicative would otherwise be used. Compare *If it arrived, it was not properly filed* (indicative) with *If it had arrived, it could have changed the course of history* (subjunctive). The past-perfect subjunctive is identical in form to the past-perfect indicative, so the two can be distinguished only by context: if a past-perfect clause is followed by a conditional clause, the first clause is usually subjunctive as well. Compare *If it had snowed the night before, then the children always made a snowman* (indicative) with *If it had snowed the night before, school would have been canceled* (subjunctive).

TENSE

172 *Generally.* Tense shows the time in which an act, state, or condition occurs or occurred. The three major divisions of time are present, past, and future. (Most modern grammarians hold that English has no future tense; see § 175.) Each division of time breaks down further into a perfect tense denoting a comparatively more remote time by indicating that the action has been completed: present perfect, past perfect, and future perfect. And all six of these tenses can be further divided into a progressive tense (also called *imperfect* or *continuous*), in which the action continues. (Rather than treating these as twelve distinct tenses, many modern grammarians classify the perfect and progressive as *aspects*, optional forms relating an action's status—completed or ongoing—to the time expressed by one of the three main tenses.)

173 *Present tense.* The present tense is the infinitive verb's stem, also called the *present indicative* {walk} {drink}. It primarily denotes acts, conditions, or states that occur in the present {the dog howls} {the air is cold} {the water runs}. It is also used (1) to express a habitual action or general truth {cats prowl nightly} {polluted water is a health threat}; (2) to refer to timeless facts, such as memorable persons and works of the past that are still extant or enduring {Julius Caesar describes his strategies in *The Gallic War*} {the Pompeiian mosaics are exquisite}; and (3) to narrate a fictional work's plot {the scene takes place aboard the *Titanic*}. The latter two uses are collectively referred to as the *historical-present tense,* and the third is especially important for those who write about literature. Characters in books, plays, and films *do* things—not *did* them. If you want to distinguish between present action and past action in literature, the present-perfect tense is helpful {Hamlet, who has spoken with his father's ghost, reveals what he has learned to no one but Horatio}.

The present indicative is the verb stem for all persons, singular and plural, in the present tense—except for the third-person singular, which adds an -*s* to the stem {takes} {strolls} {says}. If the verb ends in -*o*, an -*es* is added {goes} {does} {torpedoes}. If the verb ends in a consonant followed by -*y*, the -*y* is changed to -*i* and then an -*es* is added {carry–carries} {identify–identifies} {multiply–multiplies}.

174 *Past indicative.* The past indicative denotes an act, state, or condition that occurred or existed at some explicit or implicit point in the past {the auction ended yesterday} {we returned the shawl}. For a regular verb, it is formed by adding -*ed* to its base form {jump–jumped} {spill–spilled}. If the verb ends in a silent -*e*, only a -*d* is added to form the past tense and past participle {bounce–bounced}. If it ends in -*y* preceded by a consonant, the -*y* changes to an -*i* before forming the past tense and past participle with -*ed* {hurry–hurried}. If it ends in a double consonant {block}, two vowels and a consonant {cook}, or a vowel other than -*e* {veto}, a regular verb forms the past tense and past participle by adding -*ed* to its simple form {block–blocked–blocked} {cook–cooked–cooked} {veto–vetoed–vetoed}.

If the verb ends in a single vowel before a consonant, several rules apply in determining whether the consonant is doubled. It is always doubled in one-syllable words {pat–patted–patted}. In words of more than one syllable, the final consonant is doubled if it is part of the syllable that is stressed both before and after the inflection {prefer–preferred–preferred}, but not otherwise {travel–traveled–traveled}. In BrE, there is no such distinction: all such consonants are doubled.

Irregular verbs form the past tense and past participle in various ways {give–gave–given} {hide–hid–hidden} {read–read–read}. See § 141.

175   *Future tense.* What is traditionally known as the *future tense* is formed by using *will* with the verb's stem form {will walk} {will drink}. It refers to an expected act, state, or condition {the artist will design a wall mural} {the restaurant will open soon}. *Shall* may be used instead of *will*, but in AmE it typically appears only in first-person questions {shall we go?} and in legal requirements {the debtor shall pay within 30 days}. In most contexts, *will* is preferred—or *must* with legal requirements.

Two further points deserve mention here.

First, modern grammarians and linguists have generally repudiated the paradigm formerly taught in English grammar classes.

The Outmoded *Shall–Will* Paradigm

Simple Futurity

	SINGULAR	PLURAL
First person	I shall	we shall
Second person	you will	you will
Third person	he will	they will

Determination, Promise, or Command

	SINGULAR	PLURAL
First person	I will	we will
Second person	you shall	you shall
Third person	she shall	they shall

It was an artificial concoction that never reflected the actual English usage of any appreciable segment of English-speaking people.

Second, much more radically, most linguists are now convinced that, technically speaking, English has no future tense at all—that *will* is simply a modal verb that should be treated with all the others.[4] Yet the future tense remains a part of traditional grammar and is discussed here in the familiar way.

---

4   See, e.g., R. L. Trask, *Language: The Basics* (London: Routledge, 1995), 58.

176 *Present-perfect tense.* The present-perfect tense is formed by using *have* or *has* with the principal verb's past participle {have walked} {has drunk}. (Because all three perfect tenses use a form of *have* plus a past participle, they are called *compound tenses*.) It is formed the same way in both the indicative and subjunctive moods (see §§ 167–68), and in both it denotes an act, state, or condition that is now completed or continues up to the present {I have put away the clothes} {it has been a

> The present-perfect tense is often used with the adverb *always*. "I have always hoped that he would behave better." "I have always believed that good may come out of evil." "I have always hoped that one day I may become rich."
> —W. P. Jowett
> *Chatting About English*

long day} {I will apologize, even if I have done nothing wrong}. The present perfect is distinguished from the past tense because it refers to (1) a time in the indefinite past {I have played golf there before} or (2) a past action that comes up to and touches the present {I have played cards for the last 18 hours}. The past tense, by contrast, indicates a more specific or a more remote time in the past.

177 *Past-perfect tense.* The past-perfect (or *pluperfect*) tense is formed by using *had* with the principal verb's past participle {had walked} {had drunk}. It refers to an act, state, or condition that was completed before another specified or implicit past time or past action {the engineer had driven the train to the roundhouse before we arrived} {by the time we stopped to check the map, the rain had begun falling} {the movie had already ended}.

178 *Future-perfect tense.* The future-perfect tense is formed by using *will have* with the verb's past participle {will have walked} {will have drunk}. It refers to an act, state, or condition that is expected to be completed before some other future act or time {the entomologist will have collected 60 more specimens before the semester ends} {the court will have adjourned by five o'clock}. *Shall* can also form the future perfect, but usually only for the first person, and in very few parts of the English-speaking world is it prevalent {I shall have finished by tomorrow} {we shall have written before we embark}.

179 *Progressive tenses.* The progressive tenses, also known as *continuous tenses*, show action that progresses or continues. With active-voice verbs, all six basic tenses can be made progressive by using the appropriate *be*-verb and the present participle of the main verb, as so:

- present progressive {he is playing tennis};
- present-perfect progressive {he has been playing tennis};
- past progressive {he was playing tennis};
- past-perfect progressive {he had been playing tennis};
- future progressive {he will be playing tennis}; and
- future-perfect progressive {he will have been playing tennis}.

Any such tense requiring additional words for its expression is considered an *expanded tense*.

With the passive voice, the present- and past-progressive tenses are made by using the appropriate *be*-verb with the present participle *being*, plus the past participle of the main verb, as so:

- present {I am being dealt the cards}; and
- past {I was being dealt the cards}.

Progressive tenses frequently appear in the posing and answering of questions {Are you studying? No, I'm answering e-mails}.

180   *Backshifting in reported speech.* When one speaker or writer conveys the words of another, grammarians call the result *reported speech*. There are two types of reported speech: direct and indirect speech (also called *direct* and *indirect discourse*). Direct speech repeats another's words verbatim (or at least purports to), usually in the form of a quotation {he said, "I've never come here by this route"}. Indirect speech, on the other hand, conveys the content but not the form—that is, it paraphrases the original utterance without quoting the exact words {he said he had never gone there by that route}.

Notice that in the second example, several words from the original statement have changed. That's because indirect discourse reflects the reporting speaker's deixis—the reporter's perspective on identity, time, and place. So pointing elements in the original utterance shift accordingly: verbs and pronouns shift in person (*I* becomes *he*), and references to location shift in relation to distance (*here* becomes *there*; *this* becomes *that*; even *come* becomes *go*)—unless the identity or location of the reporter and the original speaker are the same. References to time usually become more remote (*now* becomes *then*)—unless the original utterance was a future reference to the time when something will be reported {"I'll call you then" → she said she'd call me now} or the original speaking and the reporting happen in the same window of time {"I am here now" → he says he is here now}.

This shift in time is particularly important for verb tense. Indirect speech typically involves backshifting—the changing of present-tense to past-tense verbs when currently relating what someone earlier said in the present tense. Since the reporting clause uses the past tense (*he said*), the verbs in the original utterance must become more remote in the reported clause (the present-perfect *have come* becomes the past-perfect *had gone*). Grammarians call this relationship, in which the verb tense of the reporting clause governs that of the reported clause, the *sequence of tenses*. Exactly what tense a reported verb backshifts to is dictated by context. When the reporting clause is in the present tense, backshifting is unnecessary {"we want to leave" → they say they want to leave}. And sometimes the backshift is either impossible (past-perfect verbs cannot become any more remote) or optional. For instance, *I have walked 12 miles today* becomes (at a later time) *he said he had walked 12 miles that day.* But *I have tried a thousand times* could become either *he said he had tried a thousand times* or *he said he has tried a thousand times.* Backshifting also occurs in sentences with hypothetical conditional clauses (see § 312).

TENSES ILLUSTRATED

181   *Conjugation of the regular verb "to call."*

Principal parts: call, called, called

INFINITIVES	*Active*	*Passive*
Present	to call	to be called
Present progressive	to be calling	——
Perfect (present perfect)	to have called	to have been called
Perfect progressive	to have been calling	——

PARTICIPLES	*Active*	*Passive*
Present	calling	being called
Perfect (present perfect)	having called	having been called
Perfect progressive	having been calling	——
Past	——	called

GERUNDS	*Active*	*Passive*
Present	calling	being called
Perfect (present perfect)	having called	having been called
Perfect progressive	having been calling	——

Indicative Mood, Active Voice

Singular	*Plural*
PRESENT TENSE	
I call	we call
you call	you call
he calls	they call
PRESENT-PROGRESSIVE TENSE	
I am calling	we are calling
you are calling	you are calling
he is calling	they are calling
PRESENT-EMPHATIC TENSE	
I do call	we do call
you do call	you do call
he does call	they do call
PRESENT-PERFECT TENSE	
I have called	we have called
you have called	you have called
he has called	they have called
PRESENT-PERFECT-PROGRESSIVE TENSE	
I have been calling	we have been calling
you have been calling	you have been calling
he has been calling	they have been calling
PAST TENSE	
I called	we called
you called	you called
he called	they called
PAST-PROGRESSIVE TENSE	
I was calling	we were calling
you were calling	you were calling
he was calling	they were calling
PAST-EMPHATIC TENSE	
I did call	we did call
you did call	you did call
he did call	they did call
PAST-PERFECT TENSE	
I had called	we had called
you had called	you had called
he had called	they had called

Singular   *Plural*

PAST-PERFECT-PROGRESSIVE TENSE

I had been calling	we had been calling
you had been calling	you had been calling
he had been calling	they had been calling

FUTURE TENSE

I will call	we will call
you will call	you will call
he will call	they will call

FUTURE-PROGRESSIVE TENSE

I will be calling	we will be calling
you will be calling	you will be calling
he will be calling	they will be calling

FUTURE-PERFECT TENSE

I will have called	we will have called
you will have called	you will have called
he will have called	they will have called

FUTURE-PERFECT-PROGRESSIVE TENSE

I will have been calling	we will have been calling
you will have been calling	you will have been calling
he will have been calling	they will have been calling

Indicative Mood, Passive Voice

PRESENT TENSE

I am called	we are called
you are called	you are called
he is called	they are called

PRESENT-PROGRESSIVE TENSE

I am being called	we are being called
you are being called	you are being called
he is being called	they are being called

PRESENT-PERFECT TENSE

I have been called	we have been called
you have been called	you have been called
he has been called	they have been called

Singular	*Plural*

PAST TENSE

I was called	we were called
you were called	you were called
he was called	they were called

PAST-PROGRESSIVE TENSE

I was being called	we were being called
you were being called	you were being called
he was being called	they were being called

PAST-PERFECT TENSE

I had been called	we had been called
you had been called	you had been called
he had been called	they had been called

FUTURE TENSE

I will be called	we will be called
you will be called	you will be called
he will be called	they will be called

FUTURE-PERFECT TENSE

I will have been called	we will have been called
you will have been called	you will have been called
he will have been called	they will have been called

Imperative Mood, Active Voice

PRESENT TENSE

| call | call |

PRESENT-PROGRESSIVE TENSE

| be calling | be calling |

PRESENT-EMPHATIC TENSE

| do call | do call |

Imperative Mood, Passive Voice

PRESENT TENSE

| be called | be called |

Subjunctive Mood, Active Voice

Singular	*Plural*

PRESENT TENSE

I call	we call
you call	you call
he call	they call

PRESENT-PROGRESSIVE TENSE

I be calling	we be calling
you be calling	you be calling
he be calling	they be calling

PRESENT-EMPHATIC TENSE

I do call	we do call
you do call	you do call
he do call	they do call

PRESENT-PERFECT TENSE

I have called	we have called
you have called	you have called
he have called	they have called

PRESENT-PERFECT-PROGRESSIVE TENSE

I have been calling	we have been calling
you have been calling	you have been calling
he have been calling	they have been calling

PAST TENSE

I called	we called
you called	you called
he called	they called

PAST-PROGRESSIVE TENSE

I were calling	we were calling
you were calling	you were calling
he were calling	they were calling

PAST-EMPHATIC TENSE

I did call	we did call
you did call	you did call
he did call	they did call

PAST-PERFECT TENSE

I had called	we had called
you had called	you had called
he had called	they had called

Singular	*Plural*

PAST-PERFECT-PROGRESSIVE TENSE

I had been calling	we had been calling
you had been calling	you had been calling
he had been calling	they had been calling

PAST-CONDITIONAL TENSE

had I called	had we called
had you called	had you called
had he called	had they called

FUTURE TENSE

I should call	we should call
you should call	you should call
he should call	they should call

FUTURE-PROGRESSIVE TENSE

I should be calling	we should be calling
you should be calling	you should be calling
he should be calling	they should be calling

FUTURE-PERFECT TENSE

I should have called	we should have called
you should have called	you should have called
he should have called	they should have called

FUTURE-PERFECT-PROGRESSIVE TENSE

I should have been calling	we should have been calling
you should have been calling	you should have been calling
he should have been calling	they should have been calling

Subjunctive Mood, Passive Voice

PRESENT TENSE

I be called	we be called
you be called	you be called
he be called	they be called

PRESENT-PERFECT TENSE

I have been called	we have been called
you have been called	you have been called
he have been called	they have been called

	Singular	*Plural*

PAST TENSE

I were called — we were called
you were called — you were called
he were called — they were called

PAST-PROGRESSIVE TENSE

I were being called — we were being called
you were being called — you were being called
he were being called — they were being called

PAST-PERFECT TENSE

I had been called — we had been called
you had been called — you had been called
he had been called — they had been called

PAST-CONDITIONAL TENSE

had I been called — had we been called
had you been called — had you been called
had he been called — had they been called

FUTURE TENSE

I should be called — we should be called
you should be called — you should be called
he should be called — they should be called

FUTURE-PERFECT TENSE

I should have been called — we should have been called
you should have been called — you should have been called
he should have been called — they should have been called

182 *Conjugation of the irregular verb "to hide."*

Principal parts: hide, hid, hidden

INFINITIVES	*Active*	*Passive*
Present	to hide	to be hidden
Present progressive	to be hiding	——
Perfect (present perfect)	to have hidden	to have been hidden
Perfect progressive	to have been hiding	——
PARTICIPLES	*Active*	*Passive*
Present	hiding	being hidden
Perfect (present perfect)	having hidden	having been hidden
Perfect progressive	having been hiding	——
Past	——	hidden

GERUNDS	*Active*	*Passive*
Present	hiding	being hidden
Perfect (present perfect)	having hidden	having been hidden
Perfect progressive	having been hiding	——

Indicative Mood, Active Voice

Singular	*Plural*

PRESENT TENSE

I hide	we hide
you hide	you hide
he hides	they hide

PRESENT-PROGRESSIVE TENSE

I am hiding	we are hiding
you are hiding	you are hiding
he is hiding	they are hiding

PRESENT-EMPHATIC TENSE

I do hide	we do hide
you do hide	you do hide
he does hide	they do hide

PRESENT-PERFECT TENSE

I have hidden	we have hidden
you have hidden	you have hidden
he has hidden	they have hidden

PRESENT-PERFECT-PROGRESSIVE TENSE

I have been hiding	we have been hiding
you have been hiding	you have been hiding
he has been hiding	they have been hiding

PAST TENSE

I hid	we hid
you hid	you hid
he hid	they hid

PAST-PROGRESSIVE TENSE

I was hiding	we were hiding
you were hiding	you were hiding
he was hiding	they were hiding

Singular	*Plural*

PAST-EMPHATIC TENSE

I did hide	we did hide
you did hide	you did hide
he did hide	they did hide

PAST-PERFECT TENSE

I had hidden	we had hidden
you had hidden	you had hidden
he had hidden	they had hidden

PAST-PERFECT-PROGRESSIVE TENSE

I had been hiding	we had been hiding
you had been hiding	you had been hiding
he had been hiding	they had been hiding

FUTURE TENSE

I will hide	we will hide
you will hide	you will hide
he will hide	they will hide

FUTURE-PROGRESSIVE TENSE

I will be hiding	we will be hiding
you will be hiding	you will be hiding
he will be hiding	they will be hiding

FUTURE-PERFECT TENSE

I will have hidden	we will have hidden
you will have hidden	you will have hidden
he will have hidden	they will have hidden

FUTURE-PERFECT-PROGRESSIVE TENSE

I will have been hiding	we will have been hiding
you will have been hiding	you will have been hiding
he will have been hiding	they will have been hiding

Indicative Mood, Passive Voice

PRESENT TENSE

I am hidden	we are hidden
you are hidden	you are hidden
he is hidden	they are hidden

Singular	*Plural*

PRESENT-PROGRESSIVE TENSE

I am being hidden	we are being hidden
you are being hidden	you are being hidden
he is being hidden	they are being hidden

PRESENT-PERFECT TENSE

I have been hidden	we have been hidden
you have been hidden	you have been hidden
he has been hidden	they have been hidden

PAST TENSE

I was hidden	we were hidden
you were hidden	you were hidden
he was hidden	they were hidden

PAST-PROGRESSIVE TENSE

I was being hidden	we were being hidden
you were being hidden	you were being hidden
he was being hidden	they were being hidden

PAST-PERFECT TENSE

I had been hidden	we had been hidden
you had been hidden	you had been hidden
he had been hidden	they had been hidden

FUTURE TENSE

I will be hidden	we will be hidden
you will be hidden	you will be hidden
he will be hidden	they will be hidden

FUTURE-PERFECT TENSE

I will have been hidden	we will have been hidden
you will have been hidden	you will have been hidden
he will have been hidden	they will have been hidden

Imperative Mood, Active Voice

PRESENT TENSE

hide	hide

PRESENT-PROGRESSIVE TENSE

be hiding	be hiding

PRESENT-EMPHATIC TENSE

do hide	do hide

Imperative Mood, Passive Voice

Singular   *Plural*

PRESENT TENSE

be hidden   be hidden

Subjunctive Mood, Active Voice

PRESENT TENSE

I hide   we hide
you hide   you hide
he hide   they hide

PRESENT-PROGRESSIVE TENSE

I be hiding   we be hiding
you be hiding   you be hiding
he be hiding   they be hiding

PRESENT-EMPHATIC TENSE

I do hide   we do hide
you do hide   you do hide
he do hide   they do hide

PRESENT-PERFECT TENSE

I have hidden   we have hidden
you have hidden   you have hidden
he have hidden   they have hidden

PRESENT-PERFECT-PROGRESSIVE TENSE

I have been hiding   we have been hiding
you have been hiding   you have been hiding
he have been hiding   they have been hiding

PAST TENSE

I hid   we hid
you hid   you hid
he hid   they hid

PAST-PROGRESSIVE TENSE

I were hiding   we were hiding
you were hiding   you were hiding
he were hiding   they were hiding

Singular	*Plural*

PAST-EMPHATIC TENSE

I did hide	we did hide
you did hide	you did hide
he did hide	they did hide

PAST-PERFECT TENSE

I had hidden	we had hidden
you had hidden	you had hidden
he had hidden	they had hidden

PAST-PERFECT-PROGRESSIVE TENSE

I had been hiding	we had been hiding
you had been hiding	you had been hiding
he had been hiding	they had been hiding

PAST-CONDITIONAL TENSE

had I hidden	had we hidden
had you hidden	had you hidden
had he hidden	had they hidden

FUTURE TENSE

I should hide	we should hide
you should hide	you should hide
he should hide	they should hide

FUTURE-PROGRESSIVE TENSE

I should be hiding	we should be hiding
you should be hiding	you should be hiding
he should be hiding	they should be hiding

FUTURE-PERFECT TENSE

I should have hidden	we should have hidden
you should have hidden	you should have hidden
he should have hidden	they should have hidden

FUTURE-PERFECT-PROGRESSIVE TENSE

I should have been hiding	we should have been hiding
you should have been hiding	you should have been hiding
he should have been hiding	they should have been hiding

Subjunctive Mood, Passive Voice

Singular	*Plural*

PRESENT TENSE

I be hidden

you be hidden

he be hidden

we be hidden

you be hidden

they be hidden

PRESENT-PERFECT TENSE

I have been hidden

you have been hidden

he have been hidden

we have been hidden

you have been hidden

they have been hidden

PAST TENSE

I were hidden

you were hidden

he were hidden

we were hidden

you were hidden

they were hidden

PAST-PROGRESSIVE TENSE

I were being hidden

you were being hidden

he were being hidden

we were being hidden

you were being hidden

they were being hidden

PAST-PERFECT TENSE

I had been hidden

you had been hidden

he had been hidden

we had been hidden

you had been hidden

they had been hidden

PAST-CONDITIONAL TENSE

had I been hidden

had you been hidden

had he been hidden

had we been hidden

had you been hidden

had they been hidden

FUTURE TENSE

I should be hidden

you should be hidden

he should be hidden

we should be hidden

you should be hidden

they should be hidden

FUTURE-PERFECT TENSE

I should have been hidden

you should have been hidden

he should have been hidden

we should have been hidden

you should have been hidden

they should have been hidden

183   *Conjugation of the verb "to be."*

The verb *be* has eight forms (*be, is, are, was, were, been, being,* and *am*) and has several special uses. First, it is sometimes a sentence's principal verb meaning "exist" {I think, therefore I am}. Second, it is more often used as an auxiliary verb {I was born in Lubbock}. When joined with a verb's present participle, it denotes continuing or progressive action {the train is coming} {the passenger was waiting}. When joined with a past participle, the verb becomes passive {a signal was given} {an earring was dropped} (see § 162). Often this type of construction can be advantageously changed to active voice {he gave the signal} {she dropped her earring}. Third, *be* is the most common linking verb that connects the subject with something affirmed of the subject {truth is beauty} {we are the champions}. Occasionally a *be*-verb is used as part of an adjective {a wannabe rock star [want to be]} {a would-be hero} or noun {a has-been}.

Be has some nuances in the way it's conjugated. (1) The stem is not used in the present-indicative form. Instead, *be* has three forms: for the first-person singular, *am*; for the third-person singular, *is*; and for all other persons, *are*. (2) The present participle is formed by adding *-ing* to the root *be* {being}. It is the same for all persons, but the present progressive requires also using *am, is,* or *are* {I am being} {it is being} {you are being}. (3) The past indicative has two forms: the first- and third-person singular use *was*; all other persons use *were* {she was} {we were}. (4) The past participle for all persons is *been* {I have been} {they have been}. (5) The imperative is the verb's stem {be yourself!}.

Principal parts: be, been, been

INFINITIVES
Present	to be
Perfect (present perfect)	to have been

PARTICIPLES
Present	being
Perfect (present perfect)	having been
Past	been

GERUNDS
Present	being
Perfect (present perfect)	having been

Indicative Mood

Singular   *Plural*

PRESENT TENSE

I am   we are
you are   you are
he is   they are

PRESENT-PROGRESSIVE TENSE

I am being   we are being
you are being   you are being
he is being   they are being

PRESENT-PERFECT TENSE

I have been   we have been
you have been   you have been
he has been   they have been

PRESENT-PERFECT-PROGRESSIVE TENSE

I have been being   we have been being
you have been being   you have been being
he has been being   they have been being

PAST TENSE

I was   we were
you were   you were
he was   they were

PAST-PROGRESSIVE TENSE

I was being   we were being
you were being   you were being
he was being   they were being

PAST-PERFECT TENSE

I had been   we had been
you had been   you had been
he had been   they had been

PAST-PERFECT-PROGRESSIVE TENSE

I had been being   we had been being
you had been being   you had been being
he had been being   they had been being

Singular	*Plural*

FUTURE TENSE

I will be	we will be
you will be	you will be
he will be	they will be

FUTURE-PERFECT TENSE

I will have been	we will have been
you will have been	you will have been
he will have been	they will have been

Imperative Mood

PRESENT TENSE

be	be

Subjunctive Mood

PRESENT TENSE

I be	we be
you be	you be
he be	they be

PRESENT-PERFECT TENSE

I have been	we have been
you have been	you have been
he have been	they have been

PRESENT-PERFECT-PROGRESSIVE TENSE

I have been being	we have been being
you have been being	you have been being
he have been being	they have been being

PAST TENSE

I were	we were
you were	you were
he were	they were

PAST-PROGRESSIVE TENSE

I were being	we were being
you were being	you were being
he were being	they were being

Singular	Plural

PAST-PERFECT TENSE

I had been	we had been
you had been	you had been
he had been	they had been

PAST-PERFECT-PROGRESSIVE TENSE

I had been being	we had been being
you had been being	you had been being
he had been being	they had been being

FUTURE-PERFECT TENSE

I should have been	we should have been
you should have been	you should have been
he should have been	they should have been

FUTURE TENSE

I should be	we should be
you should be	you should be
he should be	they should be

CONDITIONAL TENSE

had I been	had we been
had you been	had you been
had he been	had they been

PERSON

184 *Generally.* A verb's person shows whether the act, state, or condition is that of (1) the person speaking (first person), (2) the person spoken to (second person), or (3) the person or thing spoken of (third person).

NUMBER

185 *Generally.* The number of a verb must agree with the number of the noun or pronoun used with it. In other words, the verb must be singular or plural. Only the third-person present-indicative singular changes form to indicate number and person {I sketch} {you sketch} {she sketches} {they sketch}. (*Be* changes form in a few other contexts, however [see § 183]. And most modal auxiliaries lack a distinct third-person-singular form.) The second-person verb is always plural in form, whether one person or more than one person is spoken to {you are a wonderful person} {you are wonderful people}.

186 *Agreement in person and number.* A finite verb agrees with its subject in person and number—which is to say that a singular subject takes a singular verb {the solution works}, while a plural subject takes a plural verb {the solutions work}. When a verb has two or more subjects connected by *and*, it agrees with them jointly and is plural {Socrates and Plato were wise}. When a verb has two or more subjects connected by *or* or *nor*, the verb agrees with the last-named subject {Bob or his friends have your key} {neither the twins nor Jon is prepared to leave}. When the subject is a collective noun conveying the idea of unity or multitude, the verb is singular {the nation is powerful}. When the subject is a collective noun conveying the idea of plurality, the verb is plural {the faculty were divided in their sentiments}.

This last type of construction, in which meaning rather than strict grammar governs syntax, is called *synesis* or *notional concord*. In English, synesis occurs when a grammatically singular subject takes a plural verb. (Synesis applies to pronouns, too: note the use of *their* to refer to *faculty* above and to *team, total*, and *bulk* below.) This is more common in BrE than AmE, but it appears in all varieties of the language—most often with collective nouns {the team were honing their skills}. But many other nouns such as *number, total, lot, multitude, myriad*, and *majority* can also function as plural when followed by an *of*-phrase using a plural noun {a majority of senators support the bill} {a number of people were there} {a total of 37 students have voiced their concerns}. These nouns of multitude are usually treated as singular when they are preceded by the definite article, when the *of*-phrase uses a singular mass noun, or when they appear without an *of*-phrase {the number of people was staggering} {a lot of this chicken has gone bad} {a majority is more than we can hope for}.

But there are exceptions: sometimes the *of*-phrase is implied or displaced {over a hundred demonstrators turned out; a lot [of the demonstrators] were carrying signs} {of those present, only a minority were against the proposition}. And sometimes the sense is plural even when *the* precedes the noun {the bulk of librarians say their work is fulfilling}. The deciding factor is whether the focus is on the subject as a single cohesive entity or as a group of individual elements (though sometimes either option is appropriate {a multitude of options confront the customer [focusing on the individual options]} {a multitude of options confronts the customer [focusing on the total number of options]}). See §§ 10–13.

Likewise, a plural subject indicating a quantity of something considered as a unit takes a singular verb {three hundred dollars is a reasonable price} {six weeks is a long time to wait} {three-quarters of the grain was infested}. But if the plural subject represents a number of individual items, then the verb is plural {three hundred tourists were enrolled in the excursion} {six weeks have passed since the accident} {two-thirds of the flowers were destroyed}.

A book or film title incorporating a plural, or a plural word referred to as a word, is considered singular and takes a singular verb {*The Replacements* is her favorite movie} {*errata* is the plural of *erratum*}.

A gerund, an infinitive, or a clause used as a subject ordinarily requires a singular verb {her negotiating wins over many a client} {to succeed is to thrive} {what this house needs is a new coat of paint}. Some gerunds, however, have well-accepted plural forms that take plural verbs {beginnings always present a challenge} {her musings were a delight to everyone}.

187 *Disjunctive compound subjects.* When two or more discrete subjects of mixed number (i.e., not all singular or plural) are joined with a disjunctive such as *or, either–or,* or *neither–nor,* the verb should agree with the nearest subject:

> **Poor:** Either the teachers or the school board have the authority to act.
>
> **Better:** Either the teachers or the school board has the authority to act.
>
> **Better:** Either the school board or the teachers have the authority to act.

As the second "better" example shows, placing the plural subject closest to the verb makes the sentence sound more natural.

188 *Conjunctive compound subjects.* When two singular subjects are joined by a conjunctive such as *and,* the verb should be plural. The common error here is to ignore the compound nature of the subject:

> **Poor:** Public relations and recruiting is a big part of the coach's job.
>
> **Better:** Public relations and recruiting are a big part of the coach's job.

Notice that the plural subject (*public relations and recruiting*) determines the number of the verb—not the singular complement (*a big part*).

Two exceptions. First, if the subjects are not discrete but instead refer to a single thing, use a singular verb {corned beef and cabbage is the traditional St. Patrick's Day fare} {spaghetti and meatballs is her favorite dish}. A singular verb may also be appropriate when the subjects are rhetorically close {fame and fortune was her goal}. But this is often a matter of idiom {time and tide wait for no one}. Second, if *each* or *every* modifies singular subjects joined by *and*, the verb is singular {each box, suitcase, and handbag is inspected}.

189 *Some other nuances of number involving conjunctions.* If a compound subject contains both singular and plural nouns, how do you choose the controlling noun? When the nouns are linked by *and*, they form a plural subject and take a plural verb {the children and their nanny are going to the park}. If the subject contains a prepositional phrase, only the nouns that are not part of the phrase control the verb {Maxine together with her friend was laughing}. When the nouns or noun phrases are linked with a disjunctive conjunction, then the noun closest to the verb controls it {Bill or Mary was responsible} {neither the dogs nor the mailman is to blame}. In a few constructions, *or* may be only weakly disjunctive so that either a singular or plural verb may be used {a word or two is needed} {a word or two are needed}. A mass-noun phrase may take a singular verb {the nation's military might and power was not enough}.

190 *Peculiar nouns that are plural in form but singular in sense.* A few nouns ending in -*s* are plural in form but take a singular verb {the news comes on at 7:00}. Some plural forms can go either way as singular {politics is nasty business} {ethics is worthy of study} or plural {his politics are troubling the voters} {her ethics are irreproachable}—singular for *politics* and *ethics* when referring to the art or science. See § 13.

191 *Agreement of indefinite pronouns.* An indefinite pronoun (see § 92) such as *anybody, anyone, everybody, everyone, nobody, no one, somebody,* and *someone* routinely takes a singular verb {everyone receives credits for this course} {somebody knows where the car is}.

192 *Relative pronouns as subjects.* A relative pronoun used as the subject of a clause can be either singular or plural, depending on the pronoun's antecedent {a woman who likes skydiving} {people who collect books}.

Perhaps one of the trickiest constructions involves *one of those who* or *one of those that*:

> **Poor:**   She is one of those employees who works tirelessly.
> **Better:**   She is one of those employees who work tirelessly.

In this construction, the subject of the verb *work* is *who*, and the antecedent of *who* is *employees*, not *one*. You can see this easily if you reorder the syntax (without adding or subtracting a word): *Of those employees who work tirelessly, she is one.*

193   *"There is"; "Here is."* When appearing at the beginning of a sentence, the word *there* is typically an expletive standing in for the subject—sometimes called a *dummy subject*. It is not the subject itself. Instead, it causes an inversion of the subject and the verb—so that the verb precedes. The actual subject in such a construction is sometimes termed an *anticipatory* or *delayed subject*. The fact that the sentence order is inverted from the usual subject–predicate order does not change the rule that the number of the subject determines the number of the verb {there is nothing to fear} {there are two options}. It is a common error to mistake *There* for the subject and use a singular verb (especially with the contraction *There's*) when the true subject is plural:

> **Poor:**   There's snacks on the table.
> **Better:**   There are snacks on the table.

A similar error often occurs with the adverbs *Here* and *Where:*

> **Poor:**   Here's your options.
> **Better:**   Here are your options.

> **Poor:**   Where's my keys?
> **Better:**   Where are my keys?

194   *False attraction to intervening matter.* When words separate the subject and verb, writers may be misled to use a verb that agrees in number with a nearby noun instead of the more distant subject. While this error sometimes results in a singular verb with a plural subject, the more common mistake is to be tempted toward a plural verb with a singular subject. The most common troublemaker is the object or objects of an intervening prepositional phrase:

> **Poor:** The idea underlying all these arguments are that Shakespeare must have been apprenticed in a law office as a young adult.
>
> **Better:** The idea underlying all these arguments is that Shakespeare must have been apprenticed in a law office as a young adult.

Sometimes, however, a lack of strict agreement is appropriate—a type of construction called *synesis*. For more on subject–verb agreement, see § 186.

195 *False attraction to predicate noun.* When the subject and a predicate noun differ in number, the subject governs the number of the verb {mediocrity and complacency are the source of his ire} {the source of his ire is mediocrity and complacency}. A plural predicate noun after a singular subject may mislead a writer into error by suggesting a plural verb. When this occurs, the simple correction of changing the number of the verb may make the sentence awkward, and the better approach then is to rework the sentence:

> **Poor:** My downfall are sweets.
> **Better:** My downfall is sweets.
> **Better:** Sweets are my downfall.

196 *Misleading connectives: "as well as," "along with," "together with," etc.* Adding to a singular subject by using a phrasal connective such as *along with, as well as, in addition to, together with,* and the like does not make the subject plural. This type of distraction can be doubly misleading because the intervening material seems to create a compound subject, and the modifying prepositional phrase may itself contain one or more plural objects. If the singular verb sounds awkward in such a sentence, try the conjunction *and* instead:

> **Poor:** The bride as well as her bridesmaids were dressed in mauve.
> **Better:** The bride as well as her bridesmaids was dressed in mauve.
> **Better:** The bride and her bridesmaids were dressed in mauve.

197 *Agreement in first and second person.* A personal pronoun used as a subject requires the appropriate verb form according to the person of the pronoun:

I am	he is	I go	he goes
you are	she is	you go	she goes
we are	it is	we go	it goes
they are		they go	

Here comes the tricky point: pronouns joined by *or*, *either–or*, or *neither–nor* are traditionally said to take the verb form that agrees with the nearer subject {either he or I am in for a surprise} {either you or he is right} {*neither you nor I am a plumber}. Because these constructions are admittedly awkward, speakers and writers typically find another way to express the thought {one of us is in for a surprise} {one of you is right} {neither of us is a plumber}.

But the empirical evidence undercuts **neither you nor I am*, **neither they nor I am*, **neither she nor I am*, etc. When the second element is the first-person singular, *are* predominates over *am* in post-1800 print sources by an average ratio of 5:1. *Either you or I am* is closest, but even that loses in frequency to *either you or I are* by a 2:1 margin.

Yet all such constructions are uncommon. The lesson here is to avoid having the first-person singular as the second subject element with a correlative conjunction: use a little preventive grammar.

Auxiliary Verbs

198 *Generally.* An auxiliary verb (sometimes termed a *helping verb*) is a highly irregular verb used with one or more other verbs to form voice, tense, and mood. It always precedes the principal verb. The most common auxiliary verbs are explained in the following sections.

199 *Modal auxiliaries.* A subset of auxiliary verbs, called *modal auxiliaries* or *modals*, are used to express ability, necessity, possibility, willingness, obligation, and the like {they might be there} {she could be leaving at this very moment}. They are so called because they indicate the principal verb's mood. (See §§ 164–71.) All the verbs described below are modal auxiliaries except the last two: *do* and *have*.

200 *"Can" and "could."* *Can* uses only its stem form in the present indicative {I can} {it can} {they can}. In the past indicative, *can* becomes *could* for all persons {he could see better with glasses}. *Can* does not have an infinitive form (*to be able to* is substituted), or a present or past participle. (Such words lacking one or more inflected forms normal for their word class are traditionally called *defective*. Most modal auxiliaries are defective verbs.) When it denotes ability, capacity, or permission, *can* is always followed by an explicit or implicit bare infinitive as the principal verb {you can carry this trunk}. When used in the sense of permission, *can* is colloquial for *may* {can I go to the movies?}. *Can* also connotes actual possibility or common experience {storms can be severe in spring} {days can pass before a decision is announced}.

Could is often used to talk about the past {she could hum a tune at six months of age} or to discuss someone's general ability at a given time {when he was 11, he could drive a golf ball 250 yards}. But *could* is also used as a softer, less definite equivalent of *can* in reference to future events {we could travel to Cancun if you wanted to}. In this use, the meaning is close to "would be able to" {you could be promoted within six months if you'd just apply yourself!}.

201   *"May" and "might."* *May* denotes either permission {you may go to the movies} or possibility {I may go to the movies}. In negating permission, *may not* is sometimes displaced by the more intensive *must not*. Compare *You may not climb that tree* with *You must not climb that tree*.

May most commonly connotes an uncertain possibility {you may find that assignment too difficult}, and it often becomes *might* {you might find that assignment too difficult}. Is there a connotative difference? Yes: *may* tends to express likelihood {we may get there on time}, while *might* expresses a stronger sense of doubt {we might still get there on time—if the traffic clears}. *Might* can also express a contrary-to-fact hypothetical {we might have been able to make it if the traffic had been better}.

This verb has only its stem form in the present indicative {I may} {it may} {they may}. In the past indicative, *may* often becomes *might*, especially to connote uncertainty {the jeweler might have forgotten to call} {they might be delayed}. *May* does not have an infinitive form, or a present or past participle. As an auxiliary denoting wishfulness or purpose, *may* forms a subjunctive equivalent {may you always be happy} {give so that others may live}.

202   *"Must."* *Must* denotes a necessity that arises from someone's will {we must obey the rules}, from circumstances {you must ask what the next step is}, or from rule or obligation {all applications must be received by

May 31 to be valid}. *Must* also connotes a logical conclusion {that must be the right answer} {that must be the house we're looking for} {it must have been Donna who phoned}. This auxiliary verb does not vary its form in either the present or past indicative. It does not have an infinitive form (*to have to* is substituted), or a present or past participle. Denoting obligation, necessity, or inference, *must* is always used with a bare infinitive {we must finish this design} {everyone must eat} {the movie must be over by now}.

203 *"Ought."* Ought denotes either what is reasonably expected of a person as a matter of duty {they ought to fix the fence} or what we guess or conclude is probable {they left at dawn, so they ought to be here soon}. It is more emphatic than *should* but less strong than *must*. This verb does not vary its form in either the present or past indicative. It has no infinitive form, or present or past participle. Denoting a duty or obligation, *ought* is always used with an infinitive, even in the negative {we ought to invite some friends} {the driver ought not to have ignored the signal}. *To* is occasionally omitted after *not* {you ought not worry}, but the better usage is to include it {you ought not to worry}. See also § 147.

204 *"Shall."* This verb uses only its stem form in the present indicative. It is a relatively rare word in present-day AmE, except in first-person jocular uses {shall we dance?} {shall I fetch you some coffee?}. *Shall* traditionally connotes necessity or compulsion, often, but not always, in the form of a promise or a legal obligation {each applicant shall be present at the meeting}. It may reflect the intent of the speaker {I shall return} {you shall never see me again} or another person {you shall have your money soon}. *Shall* also conveys a sense of potential or probability {the coupon shall expire soon}. In almost all senses, *shall* is archaic and replaceable with *will* or *must*. But *should* is still current.

205 *"Should."* Should, the past-indicative form of *shall*, is used for all persons, and always with a principal verb {they should be at home} {should you read that newspaper?}. *Should* does not have an infinitive form, or a present or past participle. *Should* often carries a sense of duty, compulsion, or expectation {I should review those financial-planning tips} {you should clean the garage today} {it should be ready by now}. Sometimes it carries a sense of inference {the package should have been delivered today}. And sometimes it conveys the speaker's attitude {how should I know?} {you shouldn't have to deal with that}. *Should* and *ought* are quite similar and often interchangeable in discussions of what is required, what is advisable, or what we think it is right for people either to do or to have done. *Should* is slightly less emphatic than *ought*, but it appears with greater frequency.

206 *"Will" and "would."* In its auxiliary uses, *will* uses only its stem form in the present indicative {she will} {they will}. In the past indicative, the only form for all persons is *would* {we would go fishing on Saturdays} {she would say that!}. *Will* often carries a sense of the future {she will be at her desk tomorrow} or, in the past form *would*, expresses a conditional statement {I would recognize the house if I saw it again}. It can also express certainty {I'm sure you will understand}; decisions and other types of volition {I really will work out more}; requests, orders, and offers {will you stop that!} {will you take $5 for it?}; or typical behavior {she will read for hours on end}.

Would is often a softer, less definite equivalent of *will* {would you please stop that?}. It is used for reported speech (see § 180) {the porter said that he would be here in five minutes}; to talk about a past action that had not yet occurred at the time we are now discussing {within the two years after his 19th birthday, he would win four championships on the PGA Tour}; to make polite requests and offers {would you reshelve your books, please?} {would you prefer coffee or tea?}; to talk about typical behavior in the past {I remember that she would make weekly treks to the public library, hauling bagfuls of books}.

207 *"Dare" and "need."* These two words are more commonly used as full verbs. Because they sound rather quaint as auxiliaries, they should be used sparingly and carefully. But their auxiliary uses haven't completely atrophied. As an auxiliary, *dare* is used in interrogative and negative sentences, and in sentences containing uncertainty. *Dare* expresses the speaker's attitude toward the action {she dare not tell me a lie} {dare he spend a night in that graveyard?}. Because the sound is somewhat archaic, the preference is to use *dare* as a full verb. Compare *he dare not come back alone* (*dare* is an auxiliary) with *he does not dare to come back alone* (*dare* is a full verb).

As a full verb, *need* expresses something that the subject requires {the zoo needs a new giraffe}. As an auxiliary verb, *need* states an immediate necessity {I need to leave now}. As in that example, *need* is usually followed by an infinitive—sometimes a bare infinitive {I needn't be reminded [i.e., I'm already aware of something]} {we needn't rush [i.e., there's no reason to hurry]}. As with *dare*, the auxiliary *need* may sound old-fashioned. It is often replaced with *have to* or *don't have to*.

208   *"Do."* The auxiliary verb *do* (sometimes called a *dummy auxiliary*) frequently creates emphatic verbs. It has two forms in the present indicative: *does* for the third-person singular, and *do* for all other persons. In the past indicative, the only form for all persons is *did*. The past participle is *done*. As an auxiliary verb, *do* is used only in the present indicative {we do plan some charity work} and past indicative {did you speak?}. When the verb in an imperative statement is coupled with *not*, *do* also appears {do not touch!} {don't be an idiot!}.

Examples:

Present indicative:	I do think I can do it.
Past indicative:	I did think I could do it.
Imperative:	Do be in touch!

But *do* doesn't always create emphasis: it is idiomatically required in negative statements and in some types of yes–no questions and their answers:

He did not want to go.
Do you really want to participate?
I don't believe it for a moment.
Does Helen like Beethoven's symphonies?
Don't you intend to edit this manuscript?

When used in these ways, the verb *do* is separated from the principal verb by the adverb *not*, by the subject of the sentence, or by both.

When denoting performance, *do* can also act as a principal verb {he does well in school} {they do good work}. *Do* can sometimes substitute for a verb, thereby avoiding repetition {Marion dances well, and so do you} {he caught fewer mistakes than you did}.

209   *"Have."* This verb has two forms in the present indicative: *has* for the third-person singular, and *have* for all other persons. In the past indicative, the only form for all persons is *had*; the past participle is also *had*.

When *have* functions as an auxiliary verb, the present or past indicative of *have* precedes the past participle of a verb to form that verb's present-perfect or past-perfect indicative mood {I have looked everywhere} {he had looked for a better rate}. When preceding an infinitive, *have* denotes obligation or necessity {I have to finish this paper tonight!}. *Had* plus *to* and an infinitive expresses the past form of *must* {I had to leave yesterday afternoon}.

When denoting possession, action, or experience, *have* functions as a sentence's principal verb {she has a car and a boat} {you have a mosquito on your neck} {we'll have a party next week}. *Have* may also be used with *do* to express actual or figurative possession {do you have the time?} {do we have room?} {Vicky did not have her coat}.

Colloquially, *have got* is used to mean *acquired* or *possess* {I have got a new car} {she has got blue eyes}. But when *have got* precedes *to* plus an infinitive, it means *must* {I have got to pass this test!}. *Have got to* is somewhat more emphatic and more informal than *have to*.

Adverbs

Definition and Formation

210 *Generally.* An adverb is a word (more particularly, an *adjunct*) that qualifies, limits, describes, or modifies a verb, an adjective, or another adverb {she studied constantly [*constantly* qualifies the verb *studied*]} {the juggler's act was really unusual [*really* qualifies the adjective *unusual*]} {the cyclist pedaled very

> The right adverb, fresh and adroitly placed, is one of life's finest small pleasures.
> —John R. Trimble
> *Writing with Style*

swiftly [*very* qualifies the adverb *swiftly*]}. An adverb may also qualify a preposition, a conjunction, or an entire independent clause {the birds flew right over the lake [*right* qualifies the preposition *over*]} {this is exactly where I found it [*exactly* qualifies the conjunction *where*]} {apparently you forgot to check your references [*apparently* qualifies the rest of the clause]}. Some intensifying adverbs may modify an adjective {the bids differ by a very small amount} or an adverb {he moved along very quickly}, but not a verb. You can't say *He spoke very* or *She played very*. Other adverbs of this sort—often called *intensifiers*—are *more, most, much, quite, rather, really, somewhat,* and *too.* Grammarians have also traditionally used the term *adverb* as a catchall category to sweep in words that aren't readily put into other categories (such as *not, please,* and the infinitival *to* [see § 147] and the particle in a phrasal verb [see § 143]).

211 *Sentence adverbs.* An adverb that modifies an entire sentence is called a *sentence adverb* {fortunately, we've had rain this week} {undoubtedly he drove his car to the depot}. Sentence adverbs most commonly indicate doubt or emphasize a statement's certainty. Some common examples are *maybe, possibly,* and *however.* They are sometimes called *modal adverbs.* They usually appear at the beginning of the sentence {still, I think you should leave} {anyway, the test is finished} {luckily, the car stopped in time}, but they can also appear within the sentence {you must realize, however, that his story was a lie}. On the use of *hopefully* and *doubtfully* as sentence adverbs, see pp. 266, 280.

212   *Adverbial suffixes.* Many adjectives have corresponding adverbs distinguished by the suffix *-ly* or, after most words ending in *-ic, -ally* {slow–slowly} {careful–carefully} {public–publicly} {pedantic–pedantically}. Most adjectives ending in *-y* preceded by a consonant change the *-y* to *-i* when the suffix is added, but some don't {happy–happily} {shy–shyly}. A few adjectives ending in *-e* drop the vowel {true–truly} {whole–wholly}. If an adjective ends in an *-le* that is sounded as part of a syllable, it is replaced with *-ly* {terrible–terribly} {simple–simply}. An adjective that ends in a double *-l* takes only a *-y* suffix {dull–dully}. Many adjectives ending in *-le* or *-ly* do not make appealing adverbs {juvenile–juvenilely} {silly–sillily}. If an *-ly* adverb looks clumsy {ghastlily} {uglily}, either rephrase the sentence or use a phrase {in a ghastly manner} {in an ugly way}. A few other suffixes are used for adverbs, especially in informal speech {he rides cowboy-style} {park your cars curbside}. A few nouns form adverbs by taking the ending *-ways* {side–sideways}, *-ward* {sky–skyward}, or *-wise* {clock–clockwise}. And adverbial suffixes are sometimes added to phrases {she replied matter-of-factly}.

Finally, not every word ending in *-ly* is an adverb—some are adjectives {lovely} {curly}.

213   *Adverbs without suffixes.* Many common adverbs don't have an identifying suffix {almost} {never} {here} {now} {just} {seldom} {late} {near} {too}. See § 215.

214   *Distinguished from adjectives.* Unlike an adjective, an adverb doesn't modify a noun or pronoun {we made an early start and arrived at the airport early [the first *early* is an adjective modifying the noun *start*; the second is an adverb modifying *arrived*]}. Some adverbs are identical to prepositions (e.g., *up* and *off*) but are distinguishable because they are not attached to a following noun {he ran up a large bill} {let's cast off}. These prepositional adverbs (sometimes called *particles* or *particle adverbs*) are typically parts of phrasal verbs. See § 143.

Simple vs. Compound Adverbs

215   *Standard and flat adverbs.* A simple adverb is a single word that qualifies a single part of speech {hardly} {now} {deep}. There are two types. A standard adverb has the ending *-ly* {quickly} {broadly}. A flat or bare adverb has no *-ly* ending {doubtless} {fast}. Some flat adverbs have an *-ly* form but may work equally well or even better without the *-ly*, especially when used with an imperative in an informal context {drive slow} {hold on tight} {tell me quick}. Some flat adverbs are always used in their flat form {work fast} because the *-ly* has become obsolete (although it may linger in other words—e.g., *steadfast* and *steadfastly*). And the flat adverb may have a different meaning from the *-ly* adverb. Compare *I am working hard* with *I am hardly working*.

Because flat adverbs are less numerous than standard adverbs—some of them appearing only in literary usages {I was taken unawares} {I must needs go}—there is a tendency to add *-ly* to many of them as well, as with **doubtlessly* and **thusly*. These "double adverbs" are normally considered poor usage.

Among the more common flat adverbs are these:

about	high	slow
across	how	so
after	ill	somehow
afterward	in	somewhat
alike	indeed	somewhere
almost	just	soon
also	late	still
altogether	less	straight
always	little	then
anywhere	long	there
around	loud	through
away	low	thus
below	much	too
beyond	near	unawares
by	never	under
close	not	up
deep	now	very
doubtless	nowhere	well
down	off	when
even	out	whenever
far	perhaps	where
farther	quick	wherever
fast	quite	why
further	rather	wide
hard	right	worse
here	sharp	wrong
hereafter	since	yet

216 *Phrasal and compound adverbs.* A phrasal adverb consists of two or more words that function together as an adverb {in the meantime} {for a while} {here and there}. A compound adverb appears to be a single word but is a compound of several words {notwithstanding} {heretofore} {thereupon}. Compound adverbs should be used cautiously and sparingly because they tend to make the tone stuffy.

Types of Adverbs

217 *Adverbs of manner.* Some adverbs, called *manner adverbs* or *adverbs of manner,* describe "how," "in what way," or "by what method" an action or condition occurs {Ollie stubbornly refused to say where he'd been} {this novelist writes well} {the onlookers shouted with all their might} {Swadsi works unnecessarily hard [the two adverbs of manner work differently here: *unnecessarily* modifies *hard,* which in turn modifies the verb *works*]} {the battle raged fiercely}. More examples of manner adverbs are *foolishly, quickly, otherwise,* and *namely.* A manner adverb may replace a prepositional phrase that functions adverbially—e.g., *the customer shouted in an angry manner* becomes *the customer shouted angrily.*

218 *Adverbs of time.* An adverb of time indicates duration {they walked two hours without stopping}, repetition {that picture has rarely fallen off the wall}, date {I met Martin when I was in Wales}, and frequency {deliveries are made weekly}. Some present-time adverbs are *immediately, now, today,* and *tonight.* Future-time adverbs include *soon* and *tomorrow.* Adverbs showing repetition or duration include *always, often, rarely,* and *seldom.* Some adverbs such as *after, before, early, late,* and *soon* indicate temporal relationships among periods or events. An adverb of time may replace a prepositional phrase—e.g., *no one is available at this point in time* is better rendered *no one is now available.*

219 *Adverbs of place.* An adverb of place or location (also called a *locative adverb*), or of direction, shows the place at which the action of the verb occurs or the direction that it takes. It often answers the question "where" or "in (at) what place" {we'll be driving north in the morning} {the vicar traveled here through the woods} {they threw the sack over the fence} {walk around to the back door} {lying there by the roadside}. Some commonly used adverbs of place are *about, anywhere, everywhere, here, inside, on, upon, within, in back, in front, in here, above, below, in, on,* and *forward.*

A manner adverb may replace a locative adverbial phrase—e.g., *put your toys away in a proper place* becomes *put your toys away properly.*

220 *Adverbs of degree.* An adverb of degree describes the intensity or quality of an action in terms of "how much," "how little," or "in what degree" {the work was not so easy} {we were treated quite fairly} {he lectured very enthusiastically}. Adverbs of degree generally modify adjectives {the movie was rather dull} {the room is too bright} or other adverbs {you type much faster than I do} {don't drink so deep}. Examples of adverbs of degree are *highly, too,* and *very.*

221 *Adverbs of reason.* An adverb of reason or cause answers the questions "why" or "for what purpose" {you can't take that pen because it belongs to me} {he found out what the problem was; accordingly, we now know its source}. Several adverbs of reason are conjunctive {you didn't turn in your term paper, so I think you might be penalized}. See § 228.

222 *Adverbs of consequence.* An adverb of consequence (sometimes called a *consequential adverb*) introduces a clause that states an inference {the governor named his erstwhile rival to a judgeship so that no serious competition would be around come reelection time}, conclusion {dogs eat steak, and a steak is missing; therefore the dog must have eaten the steak}, or result {there were no signs warning of danger; thus it seemed safe to go inside}. Examples of consequential adverbs are *so that, such that, therefore,* and *thus.*

223 *Adverbs of number.* An adverb of number (also called a *numeric adverb*) indicates order or position. Adverbs of number are traditionally formed by adding the *-ly* suffix to ordinal numbers {secondly} {thirdly}, but such forms are now generally considered less editorially desirable: the ordinal numbers alone can function adverbially {first, choose a subject; second, decide what to write about that subject}.

224 *Interrogative adverbs.* Interrogative adverbs are used to ask questions; they include words like *how, when, where,* and *why.* Such an adverb can be used to ask a direct question {how did you find it?} or an indirect question {I don't know why Ken went to Italy}. It can also modify some word or phrase in the sentence. For instance, in *Where did you leave the keys?*, the adverb *where* asks the question and also modifies *did leave.* And in *When did the mail arrive?*, the adverb *when* asks a question and also modifies *did* *arrive.* Interrogative adverbs often present a question about manner {how did you get here?}, time {when does the seminar begin?}, place {where are you going for the holidays?}, degree {how accurate were those calculations?}, reason {why do you have an umbrella?}, and number {how many golf tournaments have you won?}.

225 *Exclamatory adverbs.* Many of the same words that function as interrogative adverbs can be used to introduce exclamations as well {how thoughtful of you!} {why, you're a darling!}. When used in this way, these words are called *exclamatory adverbs.*

226 *Affirmative and negative adverbs.* Affirmative adverbs indicate assent or approval. They can be single words {certainly} {really} {absolutely} or expressions {by all means} {as you say}. *Yes* may be used as an affirmative adverb {yes, I will go with you}. Negative adverbs indicate disapproval or denial {not at all} {never}. *No, not,* and *never* are the most common negative adverbs {never repeat this to anyone} {your request will not be granted}. *Yes* and *no* are also independent adverbs and can stand alone; the rest of the answer is implied {Will you go with me? Yes [*I will go with you* is implied]} {Do we have enough sugar? No [*We do not have enough sugar* is implied]}. *Not* is never used as part of the verb even though it may be part of the verb phrase; it reverses the usual meaning of the verb—e.g., *not going* means *staying.* Some adverbs, such as *hardly, scarcely,* and *barely,* have negative meanings; if they appear with *not* or *never,* an ungrammatical double negative occurs—e.g., *they could never hardly expect it; *we didn't meet scarcely anybody; *he hasn't barely begun.* These constructions, of course, are nonstandard. In Standard English, two negatives cancel each other out and are generally equivalent to a weak affirmative {such things are not uncommon} {it's not invisible to the naked eye}.

227 *Relative adverbs.* A relative adverb joins a dependent (subordinate) clause to an independent (main) clause while modifying the clause of which it is a part:

- The team came to a point where any further progress depended on their leader. (adjective clause)
- The tournament begins when the gong is rung. (adverbial clause)
- We cannot tell why the business has lost so much money. (noun clause)

228 **Conjunctive adverbs.** A conjunctive adverb (sometimes called a *connective adverb*) is used as a conjunction to connect a dependent clause to an independent clause {Robin arrived after we had eaten dinner}. A conjunctive adverb may appear to modify the verbs in the introduced clauses, but its primary function is to connect the clauses; ordinary subordinate conjunctions merely introduce dependent clauses. Conjunctive adverbs may denote time {Jay returned before we could find the vitamin E}, place {I know the river where the largest trout can be caught}, or reason {he ran out of the theater because an emergency arose}, and can be used to introduce clauses that are used as nouns. Conjunctive adverbs also introduce noun clauses {why Simon skipped school today is a mystery [*why Simon skipped school* is the subject of the verb *is*]}; {I don't see how I could possibly finish on time [*how I could possibly finish* is the direct object of *don't see*]}. Conjunctive adverbs include *as, as if* (manner), *where, whence, whither* (place), *after, as, before, ere, since, till, until, when,* and *while* (time).

Adverbial Degrees

229 **Generally.** Like adjectives (see § 123), adverbs have three degrees: the positive, the comparative, and the superlative. A positive adverb simply expresses a quality without reference to any other thing {the nurse spoke softly} {the choir sang merrily}.

230 **Comparative forms.** A comparative adverb compares the quality of a specified action shared by two things {Bitey worked longer than Arachne} {Rachel studied more industriously than Edith}. Most one-syllable adverbs that do not end in *-ly* form the comparative by taking the suffix *-er* {sooner} {harder}. These forms are called *synthetic comparatives*. Multisyllable adverbs usually form the comparative with *more* or *less* {the Shakespearean villain fenced more ineptly than the hero} {the patient is walking less painfully today}. These forms are called *periphrastic comparatives*. But there are exceptions for adverbs that end in *-ly* if the *-ly* is not a suffix {early–earlier}.

231 **Superlative forms.** A superlative adverb compares the quality of a specified action shared by at least three things {Sullie bowled fastest of all the cricketers} {of the three doctoral candidates, Dunya defended her dissertation the most adamantly}. In a loose sense, the superlative is sometimes used for emphasis rather than comparison {the pianist played most skillfully}. Most one-syllable adverbs that do not end in -ly form the superlative by taking the suffix -est {soonest} {hardest}. These forms are called *synthetic superlatives*. Multisyllable adverbs usually form the superlative with *most* or *least* {everyone's eyesight was acute, but I could see most acutely} {of all the people making choices, he chose least wisely}. These forms are called *periphrastic superlatives*. There are exceptions for adverbs that end in -ly if the -ly is not a suffix {early–earliest}.

232 *Irregular adverbs.* A few adverbs have irregular comparative and superlative forms {badly–worse–worst} {little–less–least}. A good dictionary is the best resource for finding an irregular adverb's forms of comparison.

233 *Noncomparable adverbs.* Many adverbs are noncomparable. Some, by their definitions, are absolute and cannot be compared {eternally} {never} {singly} {uniquely} {universally}. Most adverbs indicating time {now} {then}, position {on}, number {first} {finally}, or place {here} are also noncomparable.

Position of Adverbs

234 *Placement as affecting meaning.* To avoid miscues, an adverb should generally be placed as near as possible to the word it is intended to modify. For example, in *the marathoners submitted their applications to compete immediately,* what does *immediately* modify—*compete* or *submitted*? Placing the adverb with the word it modifies makes the meaning clear—e.g., *the marathoners immediately submitted their applications to compete.* A misplaced adverb can completely change a sentence's meaning. For example, *we nearly lost all our camping equipment* states that the equipment was saved; *we lost nearly all our camping equipment* states that almost everything was lost.

235 *Modifying words other than verbs.* If an adverb qualifies an adjective, an adverb, a preposition, or a conjunction, it should immediately precede the word qualified {our vacation was very short} {the flight took too long} {your fence is partly over the property line} {leave only when the bell rings}. The adverb or adverbs modifying a single adjective, grouped with that adjective, are called an *adjective cluster* {a classically trained pianist}.

236 *Modifying intransitive verbs.* If an adverb qualifies an intransitive verb, it should immediately follow the verb {the students sighed gloomily when homework was assigned} {the owl perched precariously on a thin branch}. Some exceptions are *always, never, often, generally, rarely,* and *seldom,* which may precede the verb {mountaineers seldom succeed in climbing K2}.

237 *Adverbs and linking verbs.* Adverbs do not generally follow linking verbs (see § 142), such as *be*-verbs, *appear, become, feel, hear, look, seem, smell,* and *taste.* These verbs connect a descriptive word with the clause's subject; the descriptive word applies to the subject, not the verb {he seems honest}. To determine whether a verb is a linking verb, consider whether the descriptive word describes the action or condition, or the subject. For example, **the sculptor feels badly* literally describes an impaired tactile sense (though that couldn't conceivably be the intended meaning). But *the sculptor feels bad* describes the sculptor as unwell or perhaps experiencing guilt (*bad* being not an adverb but a predicate adjective).

238 *Adverb within verb phrase.* When an adverb qualifies a verb phrase, the normal place for the adverb is between the auxiliary verb and the principal verb {the administration has consistently repudiated this view} {the reports will soon generate controversy} {public opinion is sharply divided}. (See § 145.) Some adverbs may follow the principal verb {you must go quietly} {are you asking rhetorically?}. There has never been a rule against placing an adverbial modifier between the auxiliary verb and the principal verb in a verb phrase. In fact, it's typically preferable to put the adverb there {the heckler was abruptly expelled} {the bus had been seriously damaged in the crash}. Sometimes it is perfectly appropriate to split an infinitive with an adverb to add emphasis, clarify meaning, or produce a natural sound. (See § 148.) A verb's infinitive or *to* form is split when an intervening word immediately follows *to* {to bravely assert}. If the adverb bears the emphasis in a phrase {to boldly go} {to strongly favor}, the split infinitive is justified and often even necessary. But if moving the adverb to the end of the phrase doesn't suggest a different meaning or impair the sound, then you have an acceptable way to avoid splitting the infinitive. Recasting a sentence just to eliminate a split infinitive or to avoid splitting the

> When there is a compound verb form, it is usual to put the adverb between the auxiliary and the main verb. "I have always wanted to do so." "He has rarely failed us."
>
> —W. P. Jowett
> *Chatting About English*

infinitive can alter the nuance or meaning of the sentence. For example, *it's best to always get up early* (*always* modifies *get up*) is not quite the same as *it's always best to get up early* (*always* modifies *best*). It can also make the phrasing sound unnatural—e.g., *it's best to get up early always.*

239 ***Importance of placement.*** An adverb's placement is also important because adverbs show time {we'll meet again}, place or source {put the flowers here} {where did you get that idea?}, manner {speak softly}, degree or extent {sales are very good} {how far is it to the British pub?}, reason {I don't know why Pat couldn't find the right answer}, consequence {we should therefore hasten to support her candidacy}, and number {first, we need to get our facts straight}. Adverbs can also express comments or observations {Vic was undoubtedly late} {Imani clearly recalled everything}.

240 ***Adverbial objective.*** Sometimes a noun element functions as an adverb or adverbial phrase that completes a predicate: this is called an *adverbial objective.* The most frequently cited example is *home* in *He went home.* But other noun elements commonly have this function {we did it the new way} {she learned her lesson the hard way}.

241 ***Adverbial clause.*** A dependent clause that modifies a verb, an adjective, or an adverb in the independent clause is called an *adverbial clause.* Essentially, it is a subordinate clause that functions as an adverb {I will call you when I'm ready} {she marked the manuscript as clearly as she could}. Although the placement of an adverbial clause is variable, generally it follows the word it modifies if it expresses place, manner, result, or comparison.

Adverbial clauses may indicate any of several things:

Place
Can you say where you have been?

Time or circumstance
He won the race at a time when most of his rivals were abroad.

Manner
She nodded her head in a way that suggested full understanding.

Cause
We stayed behind because we wanted to be sure that the house would be safe.

Result

He stayed behind, so he missed the opportunity.

Purpose

He hit the ball to the middle of the green so as to avoid the hazards both left and right.

Condition

Call if you're going to be late.

Concession

Although the plane was delayed by 12 hours, we still made it back home for the party.

Comparison

Jane is not as tall as you are.

242 *"Only."* The word *only* can function as an adverb {I'll come by only if you call}, an adjective {the only equipment we have}, or a conjunction {I wanted to see you, only I had an-other appointment}—and it can modify any part of speech. In its adverbial uses, it is sometimes called a *focusing adverb*. When re-ferring to the subject of a sentence, *only* usually precedes the subject {only Maritza could get away with that!} {only my father remembers that incident}. When referring to

> *Only.* This universally misplaced word, which is capable as an adjective or an adverb of modifying almost any part of speech, or, as an adversative con-junction, of introducing a clause, can be sure of its proper modification only by being rigorously placed next to its principal.
> —George Frederick Genung
> *The Working Principles of Grammar*

other parts of a sentence, *only* can be placed either fastidiously (and un-ambiguously) before what it logically modifies or else in "midposition" (maybe ambiguously) in a position that to many speakers of English feels more comfortably idiomatic.

Precise

He reads only nonfiction.

Midposition

He only reads nonfiction. (He does nothing else?)

Precise

She has traveled to Asia only once.

Midposition

She has only traveled to Asia once. (No real argument about meaning—but the fastidious editor will be bothered.)

The midposition *only* can cause ambiguities more frequently than its users suspect—which is why professional editors tend to think of *only* as being poorly placed more often than any other word in English. Consider: *I only talked to your daughter last night.* Does that mean that I did nothing else with her? That I talked with no one else? That it was (remarkably) just last night that we talked?

The midposition *only* may be acceptable in speech because the speaker can use intonation to make the meaning clear. But there is no guidance from intonation in writing, so the more words there are between *only* and the word it truly modifies, the greater the chance that the sentence will be genuinely ambiguous.

Speakers and writers of BrE tend to be less concerned or uptight about the fastidious placement of *only* than speakers and writers of AmE. And they tend to think that a precisely placed *only* is fussy and formal. If you're working cross-culturally, you might want to be aware of this difference.

Prepositions

Definition and Types

243 *Generally.* A preposition is an uninflected function word or phrase linking a noun element (the preposition's object) with another part of the sentence to show the relationship between them. Prepositions express such notions as position (*about, above, below, on, under*), direction (*in, into, to, toward*), time (*after, before, during, until*), and source (*from, of, out of*).

A preposition's object (sometimes termed an *oblique object*) is usually a noun, or else a pronoun in the objective case {between me and them}. Usually a preposition comes before its object, but there are exceptions. For example, the preposition can end a clause, especially a relative clause, or sentence {this isn't the pen that Steve writes with} {I'd like to see the problem through}. And a preposition used with the relative pronoun *that* (or with *that* understood) always follows the object {this is the moment (that) I've been waiting for}. It also frequently, but not always, follows the relative pronouns *which* {which alternative is your decision based on?} {this is the alternative on which my decision is based} and *whom* {there is a banker (whom) I must speak with} {I can't tell you to whom you should apply}.

244 *Simple, compound.* Many prepositions are relatively straightforward. A simple preposition consists of a single monosyllabic word {as} {at} {by}. A compound preposition has two or more syllables; it may be made up of two or more words {into} {outside} {upon}.

Simple Prepositions	Compound Prepositions
as	about
at	above
by	across
down	after
for	against
from	alongside
in	around
like	before
of	below
off	beneath

Simple Prepositions	Compound Prepositions
on	between
plus	despite
since	except
through	inside
to	onto
toward	opposite
up	throughout
with	underneath
	until
	without

245 *Phrasal prepositions.* A phrasal preposition, sometimes called a *complex preposition*, is two or more separate words used as a prepositional unit. Many of these phrasal prepositions are symptoms of officialese, bureaucratese, or other types of verbose style. If a single-word preposition will do in context, use it. For example, if *about* will replace *with regard to* or *in connection with*, a judicious editor will inevitably prefer to use the simpler expression.

Phrasal Prepositions

according to	at the point of	in case of
alongside of	at the risk of	in comparison with
along with	because of	in connection with
apart from	by contrast with	in consideration of
as against	by means of	in contrast to
as between	by reason of	in contrast with
as compared with	by way of	in front of
as distinct from	contrary to	in place of
as distinguished from	exclusive of	in regard to
as far as	for fear of	in relation to
aside from	for purposes of	in respect of
as opposed to	for the sake of	in respect to
as regards	from among	insofar as
as to	from between	in spite of
as touching	in accordance with	instead of
at the cost of	in addition to	in terms of
at the hands of	in apposition with, to	
at the instance of		

Phrasal Prepositions cont'd

in the case of	on behalf of	up to
in the interest of	on the part of	with a view to
in the matter of	out of	without regard to
in the way of	out of regard for	with reference to
in view of	out of respect for	with regard to
irrespective of	prior to	with respect to
next to	regardless of	with the view of
on account of	subsequent to	

246 *Participial prepositions.* A participial preposition is a participial form that functions as a preposition (or sometimes as a subordinating conjunction). Examples are *assuming, barring, concerning, considering, during, notwithstanding, owing to, provided, regarding, respecting,* and *speaking of.* Unlike other participles, these words do not create danglers when they have no subject {considering the road conditions, the trip went quickly} {regarding Watergate, he had nothing to say}. See § 159.

Prepositional Phrases

247 *Generally.* A prepositional phrase consists of a preposition, its object, and any words that modify the object. A prepositional phrase can be used as a noun {for James to change his mind would be a miracle}, an adverb (also called an *adverbial phrase*) {we strolled through the glade}, or an adjective (also called an *adjectival phrase*) {we'd love to see the cathedrals of Paris}.

248 *Prepositional function.* Prepositions signal many kinds of relationships. For example, a preposition may express a spatial relationship {to} {from} {out of} {into}; time {at} {for} {throughout} {until}; cause {because of} {on account of}; means {like} {with} {by}; possession {without} {of}; exceptions {but for} {besides} {except}; support {with} {for}; opposition {against}; or concession {despite} {for all} {notwithstanding}.

249 *Placement.* A prepositional phrase with an adverbial or adjectival function should be as close as possible to the word it modifies to avoid awkwardness, ambiguity, or unintended meanings {is there a person with a small dog named Sandy here?} {the woman with the Popular Front circulates petitions}.

250   *Refinements on placement.* If a prepositional phrase equally modifies all the elements of a compound construction, the phrase follows the last element in the compound {the date, the place, and the budget for the wedding have been decided}. If the subject is singular and followed by a plural prepositional phrase, the predicate is singular—e.g., compare the predicate in *the man and his two daughters have arrived* with that in *the man with two daughters has arrived* and in *the man has arrived with his two daughters*.

251   *Preposition-stranding.* The traditional caveat of yesteryear against ending sentences or clauses with prepositions is an unnecessary and pedantic restriction. And it is wrong. As Winston Churchill is often said to have put it sarcastically, "That is the type of arrant pedantry up with which I shall not put." A sentence that ends in a preposition may sound more natural than a sentence carefully constructed to avoid a final preposition. Compare, for example, *This is the case I told you about* with *This is the case about which I told you.* The "rule" prohibiting terminal prepositions was an ill-founded superstition based on a false analogy to Latin grammar. Today many grammarians use the dismissive term *pied-piping* for this phenomenon.

> "The man I am talking about" is infinitely better English than "The man about whom I am talking," as should be apparent to all familiar with good speech, listening to the two forms. Yet legions of our young folk will leave school having firmly implanted in their heads, and alas their use, that for reasons beyond their ken, the more elegant, dressy, scholar-like way of saying it is, "The man of whom I am talking"—no matter how strongly their instincts, bless them, tell them it is unnatural and forced.
>
> —Richard Burton
> *Why Do You Talk like That?*

252   *Clashing prepositions.* If a phrasal verb {give in} precedes a prepositional phrase {in every argument}, the back-to-back prepositions will clash {he gives in in every argument}. Recast the sentence when possible to avoid juxtaposed prepositions—e.g., *rather than continue arguing, he always gives in,* or *in every argument, he gives in.* For more on phrasal verbs, see § 143.

253   *Elliptical phrases.* Sometimes a prepositional phrase is elliptical, being an independent expression without an antecedent. It often starts a clause and is normally detachable from the statement without affecting the meaning. Elliptical prepositional phrases include *for example, for instance, in any event, in a word, in the last analysis,* and *in the long run* {in any event, call me when you arrive}.

254 *Case of pronouns.* If a pronoun appears in a prepositional phrase, the pronoun is usually in the objective case {with me} {alongside her} {between them}. (See §§ 56, 66.) But note that *than* may function as either a conjunction or a preposition {he's taller than I [am]} {he's taller than me}. In edited English, *taller than I* has predominated over *taller than me* in AmE from its very beginnings, and in BrE it predominated until the 1990s. Throughout the literary history of Modern English, *than me, than her,* etc. have been regarded as less polished (to say the least) than *than I, than she,* etc. That is to say, in formal registers *than* (like *as*) is considered a conjunction, not a preposition. But in spoken English, *than* and *as* are often treated as prepositions that take a pronoun in the objective case {you're better than me} {you're as well known as me}.

A possessive pronoun may be used before the preposition's object {to my house}.

Other Prepositional Issues

255 *Functional variation.* Some words that function as prepositions may also function as other parts of speech. The distinguishing feature of a preposition is that it always has an object. A word such as *above, behind, below, by, down, in, off, on,* or *up* can be used as either an adverb or a preposition. When used as a preposition, it takes an object {let's slide down the hill}. When used as an adverb, it does not {we sat down}. Some conjunctions may serve as prepositions (e.g., *than* and *but*). The conjunction joins a clause containing an explicit or implied separate action. Compare the prepositional *but* in *everyone but Fuzzy traveled abroad last summer* (*but* is used to mean "except") with the conjunctive *but* in *I like the cut but not the color* (*but* joins a clause containing an implied separate action: *I don't like the color*).

256 *Use and misuse of "like."* *Like* is probably the least widely understood preposition. Its traditional function is adjectival, not adverbial, so that *like* governs nouns and noun phrases {teens often see themselves as star-crossed lovers like Romeo and Juliet}. As a preposition, *like* is followed by a noun or by a pronoun in the objective case {the person in that old portrait looks like me}.

Increasingly today in ordinary speech, *like* displaces *as* or *as if* as a conjunction to connect clauses. For example, in *it happened just like I said it would happen,* traditional grammarians would want to replace *like* with *as;* and in *you're looking around like you've misplaced something, like* with *as if.* Because *as* and *as if* are conjunctions, they are followed by pronouns in the nominative case {do you work too hard, as I do?}.

Although *like* as a conjunction has been considered nonstandard since the 17th century, today it is common in dialectal and colloquial usage {he ran like he was really scared}.

Limiting Prepositional Phrases

257 *Avoiding overuse.* Prepositions can easily be overused. Stylistically, a good ratio to strive for is one preposition for every ten to fifteen words. Five editorial methods can reduce the number of prepositions in a sentence.

258 *Cutting prepositional phrases.* If the surrounding prose's context permits, a prepositional phrase can be eliminated—e.g., *the most important ingredient in this recipe* could be reduced to *the most important ingredient* when it appears within a passage focused on a particular recipe.

259 *Cutting unnecessary prepositions.* A noun ending in *-ance, -ence, -ity, -ment, -sion,* or *-tion* is often formed from a verb {qualification–qualify} {performance–perform}. These nouns are sometimes called *nominalizations* or *zombie nouns,* and they often require additional words, especially prepositions (that is, *during her performance of the concerto* is essentially equivalent to *while she performed the concerto,* but it is somewhat more abstract and requires the preposition *of*).

> The overuse of prepositions is a severe and extremely common fault. Indeed, if I wanted to offer a single rule for improving the quality of writing, I would unhesitatingly say, Reduce the number of prepositions.
> —Lester S. King
> *Why Not Say It Clearly:*
> *A Guide to Scientific Writing*

Using a verb instead of a nominalization often eliminates one or two prepositions. For example, *toward maximization of* becomes simply *to maximize,* so that *our efforts toward maximization of profits failed* might be edited down to *our efforts to maximize profits failed.*

260 *Replacing with adverbs.* A strong adverb may replace a weaker prepositional phrase. For example, *the president spoke with force* is weak compared with *the president spoke forcefully.*

261   *Replacing with genitives.* A genitive may replace a prepositional phrase, especially an *of*-genitive. For example, *I was dismayed by the complexity of the street map* essentially equals *The street map's complexity dismayed me.* See § 36.

262   *Using active voice.* Changing from the long passive voice (with *by* after the verb) to an active-voice construction always eliminates a preposition. For example, *the ship was sailed by an experienced crew* equals *an experienced crew sailed the ship.*

Conjunctions

263 **_Definition and types._** A conjunction is a function word that connects sentences, clauses, or words within a clause {my daughter graduated from college in December, and my son will graduate from high school in May [*and* connects two sentences]} {I said hello, but no one answered [*but* connects two clauses]} {we're making progress slowly but surely [*but* joins two adverbs within an adverbial clause]}. In Standard English, conjunctions connect pronouns in the same case {he and she are colleagues} {the teacher encouraged her and me}. A pronoun following the conjunction *than* or *as* is normally in the nominative case even when the clause that follows is understood {you are wiser than I [am]} {you seem as pleased as she [does]}—except in informal or colloquial English {you are wiser than me}. In the latter instance, *than* can be read as a preposition.

264 **_Types of conjunctions: simple and compound._** A conjunction may be simple, a single word such as *and, but, if, or,* or *though.* Most are derived from prepositions. Compound conjunctions are single words formed by combining two or more words. Most are relatively modern formations and include words such as *although, because, nevertheless, notwithstanding,* and *unless.* Phrasal conjunctions are connectives made up of two or more separate words. Examples are *as though, inasmuch as, in case, provided that, so that,* and *supposing that.* The two main classes of conjunctions are coordinating and subordinating.

265 **_Coordinating conjunctions._** Coordinating conjunctions join words or groups of words of equal grammatical rank, i.e., elements of independent and equal rank, such as two nouns, two verbs, two phrases, or two clauses {are you speaking to him or to me?} {the results are disappointing but not discouraging}. Coordinating conjunctions are further broken down into copulative, adversative, disjunctive, and final. A coordinating conjunction may be either a single word or a correlative conjunction.

266 **_Correlative conjunctions._** Correlative conjunctions are conjunctions used in pairs, often to join successive clauses that depend on each other to form a complete thought. Correlative conjunctions must frame structurally identical or matching sentence parts {she wanted both to win the gold medal and to set a new record}; in other words, each member of the pair should immediately precede the same part of speech {they not only read the book but also saw the movie} {if the first claim is true, then the second claim must be false}. Some examples of correlative conjunctions are *as–as; if–then; either–or, neither–nor; both–and; where–there; so–as;* and *not only–but also.* For more on parallelism with correlative conjunctions, see § 332.

267   *Copulative conjunctions.* Copulative or additive coordinating conjunctions denote addition. The second clause states an additional fact that is related to the first clause. These conjunctions include *and, also, moreover,* and *no less than* {one associate received a raise, and the other was promoted} {the jockeys' postrace party was no less exciting than the race itself}.

268   *Adversative conjunctions.* Adversative or contrasting coordinating conjunctions denote contrasts or comparisons. The second clause, sometimes called an *adversative clause,* usually qualifies the first clause in some way. These conjunctions include *but, still, yet,* and *nevertheless* {the message is sad but inspiring} {she's earned her doctorate, yet she's still not satisfied with herself}.

269   *Disjunctive conjunctions.* Disjunctive or separative coordinating conjunctions denote separation or alternatives. Only one of the statements joined by the conjunction may be true; both may be false. These conjunctions include *either, or, else, but, nor, neither, otherwise,* and *other* {that bird is either a heron or a crane} {you can wear the blue coat or the green one}.

270   *Final conjunctions.* Final or illative coordinating conjunctions denote inferences or consequences. The second clause gives a reason for the first clause's statement, or it shows what has been or ought to be done in view of the first clause's expression. These conjunctions include *consequently, for, hence, so, thus, therefore, as a consequence, as a result, so that,* and *so then* {he had betrayed the king; therefore, he was banished} {it's time to leave, so let's go}.

271   *Subordinating conjunctions.* A subordinating conjunction connects clauses of unequal grammatical rank. The conjunction introduces a clause that is dependent on the independent clause {follow this road until you reach the highway} {that squirrel is friendly because people feed it} {Marcus promised that he would help}. A pure subordinating conjunction has no antecedent and is not a pronoun or an adverb {take a message if someone calls}.

272 *Special uses of subordinating conjunctions.* Subordinating conjunctions or conjunctive phrases often denote the following relationships:

1. *Comparison or degree*—e.g., *than* (if it follows comparative adverbs or adjectives, or if it follows *else, rather, other,* or *otherwise*), *as, else, otherwise, rather, as much as, as far as,* and *as well as* {is a raven less clever than a magpie?} {these amateur musicians play as well as professionals} {it's not true as far as I can discover}.

2. *Time*—e.g., *since, until, as long as, before, after, when, as,* and *while* {while we waited, it began to snow} {the tire went flat as we were turning the corner} {we'll start the game as soon as everyone understands the rules} {the audience returned to the auditorium after the concert's resumption was announced}.

3. *Condition or assumption*—e.g., *if, though, unless, except, without,* and *once* {once you sign the agreement, we can begin remodeling the house} {your thesis must be presented next week unless you have a good reason to postpone it} {I'll go on this business trip if I can fly first class}.

4. *Reason or concession*—e.g., *as, inasmuch as, why, because, for, since, though, although,* and *albeit* {since you won't share the information, I can't help you} {Sir John decided to purchase the painting although it was very expensive} {she deserves credit because it was her idea}.

5. *Purpose or result*—e.g., *that, so that, in order that,* and *such that* {we dug up the yard so that a new water garden could be laid out} {he sang so loudly that he became hoarse}.

6. *Place*—e.g., *where* {I found a great restaurant where I didn't expect one to be}.

7. *Manner*—e.g., *as if* and *as though* {he swaggers around the office as if he were an executive}.

8. *Appositions*—e.g., *and, or, what,* and *that* {the buffalo, or American bison, was once nearly extinct}.

9. *Indirect questions*—e.g., *whether, why,* and *when* {he could not say whether we were going the right way}.

273 *Adverbial conjunctions.* An adverbial conjunction connects two clauses and also qualifies a verb {the valet has forgotten where Alvaro's car is parked [*where* qualifies the verb *is parked*]}. There are two types of adverbial conjunctions: relative and interrogative. A relative adverbial conjunction does the same job as any other adverbial conjunction, but it has an antecedent {do you recall that cafe where we first met? [*cafe* is the antecedent of *where*]}. An interrogative adverbial conjunction indirectly states a question {Barbara asked when we are supposed to leave [*when* poses the indirect question]}. Some common examples of conjunctive relative adverbs are *after, as, before, until, as, now, since, so, when,* and *where.* Interrogative adverbs are used to ask direct and indirect questions; the most common are *why, how, when, where,* and *what* {I don't see how you reached that conclusion}.

274   *Expletive conjunctions.* An expletive conjunction is a conjunction that connects two thoughts that are not expressed in the same sentence. The conjunction refers to a preceding sentence and often, but not always, begins the sentence {but then the professor pointed out the flaws in their reasoning} {survival is thus the most important motivation}.

275   *Disguised conjunctions.* So-called disguised conjunctions are participles that have long been used as conjunctions—e.g., *barring, considering, provided, regarding, speaking,* and *supposing.* A disguised conjunction does not have a subject, while a verb does {considering the poor road conditions, we traveled swiftly [*considering* as a preposition]} {we traveled swiftly, considering the poor road conditions [*considering* as a disguised conjunction]} {the committee is considering a budget increase [*considering* as a verb]}. The key distinction between a conjunction and a participial preposition is that a conjunction does not take an object but a preposition does. (See §§ 243, 246.) Compare *the steak and eggs were perfectly cooked* (*eggs* is part of the subject, not the object of *and*) with *the steak comes with eggs* (*eggs* is the object of the preposition *with*). The key distinction between a conjunction and an adverb is that a conjunction does not qualify any part of speech. Compare the use of *before* in *I've seen this movie before* (adverb) with *the cart is standing before the horse* (preposition) and *it began raining before we left* (conjunction).

276   *"With" used loosely as a conjunction.* The word *with* is sometimes used as a quasi-conjunction meaning "and." This construction is nonstandard: the *with*-clause appears to be tacked on as an afterthought. For example, the sentence *Everyone else grabbed the easy jobs with me being left to scrub the oven* could be revised as *Since everyone else grabbed the easy jobs, I had to scrub the oven.* Or it could also be split into two independent clauses joined by a semicolon—e.g., *Everyone else grabbed the easy jobs; I had to scrub the oven.* Instead of *with*, find the connecting word, phrase, or punctuation that best shows the relationship between the final thought and the first, and recast the sentence.

277   *Beginning a sentence with a conjunction.* There is a widespread belief— one with no historical or grammatical foundation—that it is an error to begin a sentence with a conjunction such as *and, but,* or *so.* In fact, a substantial percentage (often as many as 10%) of the sentences in first-rate writing begin with conjunctions. It has been so for centuries, and even the most conservative grammarians have followed this practice. Charles Allen Lloyd's 1938 words fairly sum up the situation as it stands even today:

> Next to the groundless notion that it is incorrect to end an English sentence with a preposition, perhaps the most widespread of the many false beliefs about the use of our language is the equally groundless notion that it is incorrect to begin one with "but" or "and." As in the case of the superstition about the prepositional ending, no textbook supports it, but apparently about half of our teachers of English go out of their way to handicap their pupils by inculcating it. One cannot help wondering whether those who teach such a monstrous doctrine ever read any English themselves.[5]

Still, *but* as an adversative conjunction can occasionally be unclear at the beginning of a sentence. Evaluate the contrasting force of the *but* in question, and see whether the needed word is really *and*; if *and* can be substituted, then *but* is almost certainly the wrong word. Consider this example: *He went to school this morning. But he left his lunch box on the kitchen table.* Between those sentences is an elliptical idea, since the two actions are in no way contradictory. What is implied is something like this: *He went to school, intending to have lunch there, but he left his lunch behind.* Because *and* would have made sense in the passage as originally stated, *but* is not the right word—the idea for the contrastive *but* should be explicit.

To sum up, then, *but* is a perfectly proper way to open a sentence, but only if the idea it introduces truly contrasts with what precedes. For that matter, *but* is often an effective way of introducing a paragraph that develops an idea contrary to the one preceding it.

---

5   Charles Allen Lloyd, *We Who Speak English: And Our Ignorance of Our Mother Tongue* (New York: Thomas Y. Crowell, 1938), 19.

278 *Beginning a sentence with "however."* *However* has been used as a conjunctive adverb since the 14th century. Like other adverbs, it can be used at the beginning of a sentence. But *however* is more ponderous and has less impact than the simple *but*. As a matter of style, *however* is more effectively used within a sentence to emphasize the word or phrase that precedes it {The job seemed exciting at first. Soon, however, it turned out to be exceedingly dull}. For purposes of euphony and flow, not of grammar, many highly accomplished writers shun the sentence-starting *however* as a contrasting word. Yet the word is fine in that position in the sense "in whatever way" (not followed by a comma) {however that may be, we've now made our decision}.

279 *Conjunctions and the number of a verb.* Coordinating and disjunctive conjunctions affect whether a verb should be plural or singular. Conjunctions such as *and* and *through* indicate that group sentence elements impart plurality, so a plural verb is correct {the best vacation and the worst vacation of my life were on cruises} {the first through seventh innings were scoreless}. But conjunctions such as *or* and *either–or* distinguish the elements and do not impart plurality, so the singular verb is used if the elements are singular {a squirrel or a chipmunk raids the bird feeder every day} {either William or Henry dances with Lady Hill}. Other types of conjunctions have no effect on the verb's number; for example, if *and* is used as a copulative conjunction, the verb that follows may be singular {Andrés's bicycle was new, and so was his helmet}.

Interjections

280 **Definition.** An interjection or exclamation is a word, phrase, or clause that denotes strong feeling {never again!} {you don't say!}. An interjection has little or no grammatical function in a sentence; it is used absolutely {really, I can't understand why you put up with the situation} {oh no, how am I going to fix the damage?} {hey, it's my turn next!}. It is frequently allowed to stand as a sentence by itself {Oh! I've lost my wallet!} {Ouch! I think my ankle is sprained!} {Get out!} {Whoa!}. Introductory words like *well* and *why* may also act as interjections when they are meaningless utterances {well, I tried my best} {why, I would never do that}. The punctuation offsetting the interjections distinguishes them. Compare the different meanings of *Well, I didn't know him* with *I didn't know him well*, and *Why, here you are!* with *I have no idea why you are here* and *Why? I have no idea.*

281 **Usage generally.** Interjections are natural in speech {your order should be shipped, oh, in eight to ten days} and frequently used in dialogue (and formerly in poetry). As a midsentence interrupter, an interjection may direct attention to one's phrasing or reflect the writer's or speaker's attitude toward the subject, especially with informal and colloquial tone {because our business proposal was, ahem, poorly presented, our budget will not be increased this year}.

282 **Functional variation.** Because interjections are usually grammatically independent of the rest of the sentence, all other parts of speech may be used as interjections. A word that is classified as some other part of speech but used with the force of an interjection is called an *exclamatory noun, exclamatory adjective*, etc. Some examples are *good!* (adjective); *idiot!* (noun); *help!* (verb); *indeed!* (adverb); *me!* (pronoun); *and!* (conjunction); *quickly!* (adverb).

283 **Words that are exclusively interjections.** Some words are used only as interjections—for example, *ouch, whew, ugh, psst*, and *oops*.

284 **Punctuating interjections.** An exclamation mark usually follows an interjection {oh no!} or the point where the strong feeling ends {oh no, I've forgotten the assignment!}. But as with other interrupters, when an interjection appears midsentence, it is typically set off by commas, parentheses, or dashes {he's a nice enough lad, but his manners are—forgive me—somewhat lacking}.

285 *"O" and "oh."* The interjections *O* and *oh* are similar in appearance but distinguished in meaning and use. *O* is always capitalized and is typically unpunctuated as a form of classically stylized direct address {O Jerusalem!}. It most often appears in poetry (especially pre-20th-century poetry). *Oh* takes the place of other interjections to express an emotion such as pain {ow!}, surprise {what!}, wonder {strange!}, or aversion {ugh!}. It is lowercase if it doesn't start the sentence, and it is typically followed by a comma {oh, why did I have to ask?} {the scenery is so beautiful, but oh, I can't describe it!}. *Oh* is more common in prose than in poetry.

II. Syntax

Sentences, Clauses, and Their Patterns

286   *Definition. Syntax* is the collective term we use to denote all the rules governing how words are arranged into sentences. In an analytic language like English—one that, unlike a synthetic language, uses word order to show word relations (as opposed to inflections of various kinds)—syntax is particularly important in expressing meaning. (See § 297.) Through syntax, we can make four types of utterances: statements, questions, directives, and exclamations.

287   *Statements.* Most sentences are statements having a declarative structure in which (1) the clause contains a subject and (2) the subject precedes the verb. Sometimes in speech and informal writing, the subject is merely implied {[he] missed the ball} {[I] think I'll go to the store}. In a few negative idioms, the subject may follow part of the verb phrase {scarcely had we arrived when we had to return}.

288   *Questions.* Sentences that seek to elicit information are known as *questions*. They have an interrogative structure, which typically begins with a question word. There are three main types: (1) yes–no questions, which are intended to prompt an affirmative or negative response {will we be gone long?}; (2) *wh-* questions, so called because they characteristically start with *who, what, when, where, why, which,* or *how* (not quite a *wh-* word, but it counts) {which apples do you want?}; and (3) alternative questions, which prompt a response relating to options mentioned in the sentence {would you rather play golf or tennis?}.

289   *Some exceptional types of questions.* Four types of interrogative utterances aren't classifiable under the three categories given just above. Two are yes–no questions. The first is the spoken sentence in which one's pitch rises at the end, in a questioning way—but the structure is that of a declarative sentence {he's going to Corpus Christi?}. To show vexation in such a question, the question marked may be paired with an exclamation mark {she's going to Padre Island?!}. The second special type of yes–no question is the tag question, in which the interrogative inversion appears at the end of a statement {he has arrived, hasn't he?} {it's good, isn't it?}. A few tag questions are signaled by particular words without the interrogative inversion {it's raining, right?} {you're tired, eh?} {you want to go, yes?}. A third special type is the exclamatory question, in which the interrogative structure appears, but when the statement is spoken, one's tone normally falls at the end {isn't it nice out here!} {how great is this!}. Finally, a rhetorical question is phrased in the interrogative structure but is meant as an emphatic or evocative statement—without the expectation of an answer {why should I care?} {who knows how long it might take?}

290 *Directives.* A directive or imperative is a sentence that instructs somebody to do or not to do something. The word *command* is sometimes used as a synonym, but most grammarians consider the term *command* more appropriate for one of the eight main types of directives, all of which are in the imperative mood of the verb:

- command {come here now!};
- prohibition {don't do that!};
- invitation {join us for dinner!};
- warning {watch out for rattlesnakes!};
- plea {stay here} {help!};
- request {put your book away};
- well-wishing {play well} {have a good time!}; and
- advice {put on some insect repellent}.

291 *Exceptional directives.* Several directives depart from these common patterns, as when the subject is expressed {sit you down} {you stay there}; they begin with *let* {let's have a picnic} {let us wait}; or they begin with *do* {do help yourself}.

292 *Exclamations.* An exclamation expresses the extent to which a speaker is moved, aroused, impressed, or disgusted by something. It can take the form of a simple interjection (see § 280) {by golly!} {pishposh!}. Or it can follow a sentence structure consisting of *what* or *how* followed by a subject and verb {what an extraordinary novel this is!} {how well she writes!}. Exclamations are sometimes elliptically expressed {what finery!} {how pretty!} {how ugly!}. In formal, literary English, exclamations can be signaled by inverted word order {little did I expect such unfair treatment}.

The Four Traditional Types of Sentence Structures

293 *Simple sentence.* A simple sentence consists of a single independent clause with no dependent clause {no man is an island}. A sentence can be simple despite having internal compound constructions such as subjects, main verbs, objects of prepositions, and others {time and tide wait for no man}.

294 *Compound sentence.* A compound sentence contains two independent clauses (called *coordinate clauses*) with no dependent clause {the rain was heavy, and my umbrella was not much help}. Grammarians are divided on the question whether one type of sentence should be labeled compound or simple: *She arrived early and stayed late.* Traditional grammarians have tended to call this a simple sentence with a compound predicate (where *arrived* and *stayed* are coordinate verbs). Transformational grammarians have tended to call it a compound sentence with an elided subject in the second clause {she arrived early[,] and [she] stayed late}.

> Good sentences do not spring into existence by a lucky accident, any more than does good architecture, or good painting, or a well-designed machine, or a properly-fitted suit of clothes. Why indeed should any rational person expect a good sentence to come by chance? Yet the person who writes an utterly makeshift sentence, the end of which is not even vaguely planned when he writes the beginning, will often fail to see anything wrong with what he has written.
> —Louis Foley
> *Beneath the Crust of Words*

295 *Complex sentence.* A complex sentence contains a single independent clause with one or more dependent clauses {I'll be home after I finish work}. Such a sentence may have only one dependent clause {she won because she practiced so hard}, or it may contain a variety of dependent clauses {the books that were nominated argued that most behavioral differences among people aren't genetic in origin [containing two dependent clauses: the adjective clause *that were nominated* and the noun clause *that most behavioral differences among people aren't genetic in origin*]}.

296 *Compound-complex sentence.* A compound-complex sentence contains two independent clauses and at least one dependent clause {it was a beautiful evening, so after we left work we went for a walk [*after we left work* is a dependent clause between two independent clauses]}. It differs from a complex sentence only because it contains more than one independent clause. Like the independent clauses of a compound sentence, those of a compound-complex sentence are called *coordinate clauses*.

English Sentence Patterns

297 *Importance of word order.* English is known as an *analytic language*— one that depends largely on word order. (A *synthetic language*, such as Latin, depends largely on inflectional forms of words.) In the transition from Old English (A.D. 450–1100) to Middle English (1100–1500), the language lost most of its inflected forms—except those for pronouns (*I– me–mine*, etc.). Nouns no longer have nominative and accusative cases. Instead, word order governs meaning.

Consider this example: *Michael likes crystal. Michael* is the subject, *likes* the verb, and *crystal* the object. It's the basic subject–verb–object (SVO) pattern. We deduce the meaning from the position of the words: Michael is an admirer and perhaps a collector of fine glass. If we change it to *Crystal likes Michael*, the meaning is transformed because of the SVO order. We now infer that someone named Crystal thinks fondly about someone named Michael. The SVO pattern is highly significant: it governs the meaning of most English statements. Departures from it typically signal either unusual emphasis or the posing of a question (as opposed to the making of a statement).

298 *The basic SVO pattern.* Despite the seeming potential for monotony in having sentence after sentence using the same fundamental word order, English offers enough variety in vocabulary and in sentence elements that can function as subjects, verbs, and objects to keep things interesting. Consider these examples, all of which use the pattern but with interesting levels of sophistication:

- Mary likes pomegranates.
  S   V   O

- The man we were talking about objected to our arguments.
    S   V   O

- The woman down the street is selling loaves of bread.
    S   V   O

- The obstacles that we face create opportunities.
    S   V   O

- How you think of yourself affects both the way you approach
  <u>How you think of yourself</u> <u>affects</u> both <u>the way you approach</u>
          S   V   O
  <u>the problems of everyday life</u> and <u>the degree to which you're</u>
           O   O
  <u>perceived as being well-adjusted.</u>
          O

299   *All seven patterns.* Syntactic patterns other than the SVO pattern are available, but they are limited to specific types that range from two to four of these elements: subject (S), verb (V), [direct] object (O), indirect object (IO), complement (C), adverbial (A). Here are all seven basic clause patterns:

- S + V   Sandy smiled.
- S + V + O   Sandy hit the ball.
- S + V + C   Sandy is eager.
- S + V + A   Sandy plays well.
- S + V + IO + O   Sandy gave Jerry the ball.
- S + V + O + C   Sandy got her bag wet.
- S + V + O + A   Sandy wrote her score on the card.

300   *Variations on ordering the elements.* When clause elements appear in a different order, the inversion may indicate either a question {is Sandy all right? [V–S–C]} or a special kind of emphasis:

- <u>Sandy Winn</u> <u>my name</u> <u>is!</u>
        C   S   V
- <u>Bully</u> <u>you</u> <u>say!</u>
    O   S   V

Inversions of this type achieve a special emphasis precisely because they depart from the normal sequence of sentence elements.

301   *Constituent elements.* Grammarians use the term *constituent* to denote a word or phrase constituting part of a larger grammatical construction. As the fundamental building blocks of a grammatical sentence, the subject and predicate are the two broadest constituents. Unless the sentence comprises only a simple subject and a simple predicate {Bill runs}, one or both of these constituents will have constituents of their own, called *immediate constituents.*

    In the sentence *People who exercise regularly are healthier than those who don't*, both subject and predicate have immediate constituents.

The complete subject is *People who exercise regularly*, and its immediate constituents are the simple subject, *People*, and the adjective clause *who exercise regularly*. That clause's immediate constituents are the relative pronoun *who* and the verb phrase *exercise regularly*, which itself breaks down into the verb *exercise* and the adverb *regularly*.

Likewise, the predicate, *are healthier than those who don't*, divides into the simple predicate *are* and the subjective complement *healthier than those who don't*. That clause's immediate constituents are the adjective *healthier* and the adverbial clause *than those who don't*, which comprises the subordinating conjunction *than* and the noun clause *those who don't*. The noun clause contains its subject, *those*, and the relative clause *who don't*, itself composed of the relative pronoun *who* and *don't*, a contraction of the verb phrase *do not*. This verb phrase finally breaks down into its immediate constituents, the finite verb *do* and the negative particle *not*.

As you can see, each individual word is the constituent of a larger grammatical element. But for a group of words to be a constituent, it must form a discrete grammatical unit. So *People who, are healthier than,* and *regularly are*, for instance, are not valid constituents. Understanding constituent elements is essential to sentence diagramming, discussed at length in the next chapter.

302   *Identifying the subject.* Only a noun, noun phrase, or noun clause (any of these three being a *noun element*) can function as the subject of a clause. It normally appears before the verb in a statement {the crowd cheered constantly} and after the first verb in a question {are you planning to attend?}. The subject governs whether the verb is singular or plural {a golf pro was present} {several golf pros were present}. The subject also governs the form of certain objects and complements {Malik is my friend} {Malik and I are friends} {I helped myself} {you helped yourself} {they helped themselves}. The noun element is called the *simple subject*, and it along with any modifying elements constitutes the *complete subject*.

303   *Identifying the predicate.* The predicate of a sentence consists of everything but the subject—namely, the finite verb together with all its modifiers, objects, and complements. (This is sometimes called the *complete predicate*, and the finite verb alone the *simple predicate*.) It may be one word {the birds flew} or it may be many {I once saw a book that was printed in Venice in 1491}. The arrangement of component parts of the predicate accounts for variations in the seven patterns listed in § 299. Let us consider them in turn.

304 *Identifying the verb.* The verb is the most crucial part of a predicate—and indeed of the clause structure generally. Other elements can be more readily omitted than the verb. For example, each of the shaded words could potentially be omitted here: *That guy shouts on his cellphone.* True, when using the verb alone you'd have to be pointing to or nodding at the man to say merely "Shouts." But it's conceivable. Without the verb, though, the rest of the sentence is probably incoherent.

305 *Identifying the object.* An object element in a sentence typically follows the subject and verb. It must be a noun element, and it may be either a direct object {please pay cash} or an indirect object {please pay me cash} of a transitive verb. Remember that a transitive verb is one that requires a direct object to give the sentence a sense of completeness. Note that when both a direct and an indirect object are present, the indirect object comes first {he did us a favor}.

To identify a direct object, simply ask a "what" or "who" question using the verb in the sentence.

> *The child lost her bracelet.*

The child lost what? *Her bracelet.* That's the direct object of the verb *lost*. In particular, the noun *bracelet* is the object, *her* being a modifier (a possessive pronoun used adjectivally).

To identify an indirect object, ask: *To whom?* or *For whom?* But first understand that it will appear only in a sentence that has a direct object. An indirect object typically appears only in a sentence whose verb suggests giving, communicating, or transacting (common examples being *bring, buy, get, give, send, teach, tell,* and *write*). Start by identifying the direct object:

> *The boy gave his friend a present.*

What did he give? A *present.* That's the direct object (we asked a "what" question with the verb). To whom? To *his friend.* That's the indirect object (we asked a "to whom" question).

306 *Identifying complements.* A complement is an adjunct expressing meaning that adds to that of the subject or object. A subjective complement normally follows a linking verb, most commonly a *be*-verb {she is a podiatrist} {the announcer looked angry}. An objective complement normally follows a direct object, and its meaning relates to that object {they called her Mitzi} {she made everyone cheerful}.

When the subjective complement is a pronoun, it most traditionally appears in the nominative case {this is he} {it is I}. But in informal contexts, native speakers of English have long said *That's him* and *It's me*. These usages are now considered unimpeachable in all but the most elevated prose.

307 *Inner and outer complements.* When a transitive verb is followed by two complements, they are typically either an indirect and a direct object {his actions earned him a medal} or a direct object and an objective complement {Susan's friends all think her trustworthy}. In either case, the first complement is called the *inner complement* (e.g., *him* in the first example, *her* in the second); the second is called the *outer complement* (e.g., *medal* in the first example, *trustworthy* in the second).

A verb that can take both a direct object and an objective complement (such as *think* in the second example above) is called a *factitive verb*. Some grammarians limit this term to only those verbs that effect a change in the object, such as *appoint, choose, elect, make,* and *render* {the board elected William its new chair} {her response rendered him speechless}. (Under this narrower definition, *think,* for instance, does not qualify because it doesn't change its object.)

308 *Identifying the adverbial element.* The adverbial element in a sentence may consist of a single adverb {they left suddenly}, a prepositional phrase {they left in a hurry}, a noun used adverbially {they went home}, or an entire clause {they left as soon as the band started playing hard rock}. Adverbials are distinctive clause elements because (1) several may occur in a single sentence {we called Thursday to talk about her needs}; (2) they can be used in several positions within a sentence {[once] he [once] suggested [once] that we start a band [once]}; (3) they have a broad range of semantic purposes, such as manner {we gushed exuberantly}, space {he stayed within his bounds}, and time {we rested all day}; and (4) they perform several functions in the construction of sentences, from modifying the verb {he quickly left} to linking clauses {he could tell when I needed help} to commenting on entire statements {obviously, he doesn't care}.

Although most adverbials are purely optional, a few are required to complete the verb's meaning {Laredo lies on the Texas–Mexico border} {we lived within our means} {I put the lobsters on the platter} {the baby's croup lasted six months}.

Clauses

309 *In general.* A *clause* is a grammatical unit that contains a subject, a finite verb, and any complements that the verb requires. An *independent clause* can stand alone as a sentence {José saw a squirrel}, while a *dependent clause* cannot stand alone because of the presence of a word by which it would normally be linked to an independent clause {because he was hungry, he sat down for a meal}. A dependent clause is usually introduced either by a relative pronoun (making them relative clauses) or by a subordinating conjunction, which establishes the semantic relationship between the independent clause and the dependent one. Combining related ideas by linking one or more dependent clauses to an independent one is called *subordination*, and the result is a complex sentence. See § 295.

> When it comes to language, nothing is more satisfying than to write a good sentence. It is no fun to write lumpishly, dully, in prose the reader must plod through like wet sand. But it is a pleasure to achieve, if one can, a clear running prose that is simple yet full of surprises. This does not just happen. It requires skill, hard work, a good ear, and continued practice, as much as it takes Heifetz to play the violin. The goals . . . are clarity, interest, and aesthetic pleasure.
> —Barbara Tuchman
> *Practicing History:
> Selected Essays*

Because a dependent clause is always subordinate to an independent clause for contextual meaning, it is also called a *subordinate clause*. A dependent clause commonly serves one of several functions, as:

- the direct object of a verb {everyone believed that the note was genuine [the *that*-clause is the direct object of *believed*]};
- an adjectival clause modifying a noun element {he who hesitates is lost [*who hesitates* adjectivally modifies *he*]}; or
- an adverbial clause modifying a verb or verb phrase {I bought the car despite my father's warning not to [the *despite*-clause modifies the verb *bought*]}.

310 *Relative clauses.* A relative clause is a subordinate clause that is introduced by a relative pronoun and modifies the noun element (or sentence or clause) it follows {the car that you own} {those who follow his progress} {they were ten minutes late to the opera, which meant they couldn't enter until the end of the first act}.

In some relative clauses, called *contact clauses*, the relative pronoun is merely implied {all the people you mention have already registered [the relative pronoun *who* is implied in *people* [*whom*] *you mention*]}. Because the necessary connective is omitted, contact clauses are a type of elliptical clause—one often involving what is known as a *whiz-deletion* (so called because it so often amounts to the omission of *who is*). See § 315.

311 *Appositive clauses.* A clause used in apposition to a noun element in the sentence is called an *appositive clause.* Though these are often (but not always) introduced with the same words that introduce relative clauses (*that, which, who*), the two differ in that a relative clause functions only within the sentence, while an appositive clause is self-contained: with its introductory relative pronoun removed, it could stand on its own as a grammatical sentence {we all heard the report that the beloved broadcaster had died [without *that*, the remaining appositive clause is grammatically complete: *the beloved broadcaster had died*]}.

312 *Conditional clauses.* A conditional clause (also called a *protasis*) is an adverbial clause, typically introduced by *if* or *unless* (or *should, although, though, despite,* or others), establishing the condition in a conditional sentence. Usually this is a direct condition, indicating that the main clause (also called the *apodosis*) is dependent on the condition being fulfilled. Sometimes, however, the clause may express an indirect condition {if I recall correctly, his assistant's name is Miljana}, alternative conditions {the party will be a success whether or not it rains}, or an open range of possibilities {whatever you're doing, it's working}.

Most often, though, a conditional clause expresses a direct condition, which may be open (real or factual) or hypothetical (closed or unreal). An open condition leaves unanswered the question whether the condition will be fulfilled {if you don't finish the work on time, we'll have to reevaluate our arrangement}. A hypothetical condition, on the other hand, assumes that the condition has not been, is not, or is unlikely to be fulfilled {if he had only remembered to wear a raincoat, he wouldn't have ruined his new suit} {if I had a hammer, I could fix this creaky stair} {the transition would be much harder if she left without giving notice}.

In the last three examples above, the hypothetical nature of the direct condition is conveyed by backshifting the verb tense. In the first sentence, the past hypothetical condition is expressed by the verb's taking the past perfect in the conditional clause (*had . . . remembered*) and the modal past perfect in the main clause (*would . . . have ruined*). In the second and third sentences (present and future hypothetical conditions, respectively), the verb takes the past tense in the conditional clause (*had/left*) and the past modal in the main clause (*could fix/would be*).

Ellipsis

313   *Generally.* A grammatical ellipsis (sometimes called an *omission*) occurs when part of a clause is left understood and the reader or listener is able to supply the missing words. This "recovery" of omitted words is possible because of shared idiomatic knowledge, context, and what's called the *principle of recoverability* {he preferred chocolate, she vanilla [*preferred* is understood in the second clause]}. A sentence containing such an ellipsis is called an *elliptical sentence.*

In colloquial speech, an ellipsis is useful to avoid repetition, shorten the message, and make it easier to understand. It's particularly appropriate for commands and exclamations, and especially when asking or answering a question whose complete answer would essentially repeat the question. For example:

> *Thank you.* (I thank you.)
>
> *One lump or two?* (Would you like one lump of sugar or two?)
>
> *Glad you like it!* (I'm glad that you like it!)
>
> *Which is better and why?* (Which choice is better, and why is it better?)
>
> [Can you tell me who built this house?] *The Tucker family.* (Yes, I can tell you. The Tucker family built this house.)

314   *Anaphoric and cataphoric ellipsis.* When an ellipsis refers to something already mentioned, it's called an *anaphoric ellipsis* {I thought we had ordered more printer paper, but we didn't [order more printer paper]}. When the elided information appears later in the sentence, the ellipsis is called a *cataphoric ellipsis* {unless you have no other choice [but to drink it], it's best to avoid drinking the well water here}.

Ellipsis is often desirable when sentence elements are parallel and repetition is unnecessary. For example:

> *Not only classical but rock music is seriously studied by scholars now.* (Classical music is seriously studied by scholars now; rock music is also seriously studied by scholars now.)
>
> *We will drive to Louisville on Saturday and to Chicago next week.* (We will drive to Louisville on Saturday, and we will drive to Chicago next week.)

When a subordinate clause and main clause have the same subject, the subordinate clause may be elided:

> When *you are* late for work, you are expected to call and explain why.
> When late for work, you are expected to call and explain why.

> While *he was* sailing, William encountered a pod of blue whales.
> While sailing, William encountered a pod of blue whales.

But when the subject of the subordinate clause is an object (as of a preposition) in the main clause, an ellipsis leads to an illogical sentence:

> If *bread is* kept too long in hot weather, mold will grow on it.
> *If kept too long in hot weather, mold will grow on the bread.

In the second sentence, the writer or speaker creates a stumble for the reader or listener, who won't at first see that it's the *bread* that should not be kept too long. Avoid creating this type of misplaced modifier. See § 159.

If an ellipsis creates an ambiguity, restore the omitted words or recast the sentence to make the meaning clear. For example, the meaning of this sentence pair is unclear: *Penguins consume huge amounts of fish. Seals, too.* Does it mean that penguins eat seals? Or that seals eat fish? The meaning is clarified by restating the thought: *Penguins consume huge amounts of fish. So do seals.*

315 ***Whiz-deletions.*** A relative or subordinate clause is often introduced by a relative pronoun (*who, which,* or *that*) plus a linking verb. Although these introductory phrases can sometimes make it easier for a reader or listener to understand how the subordinate clause relates to the rest of the sentence, they can often be omitted {the man [who is] down the hall is my cousin}. This type of ellipsis is called a *whiz-deletion* or *relative-clause reduction* (*whiz* is the grammarian's shorthand for "who is"). For example:

> The man *who is planning* the ceremony wants to postpone the date.

> The man *planning* the ceremony wants to postpone the date.

When it's a natural idiomatic choice, the whiz-deletion can create a more economical expression. But it can also create ambiguity or change the meaning. Compare the sentences below before and after the whiz-deletion of *that was.*

> The president needs the report *that was written by* the accountant.
> The president needs the report *written by* the accountant.

In the first sentence, it's clear that the report exists. In the second, the report might or might not yet exist: has the accountant written it already, or does the president want the accountant to write it? That is, might it be that the ellipsis consists of the infinitive *to be* after *report*?

The president needs the report [to be] *written by* the company's accountant.

Negation

316 *Negation generally.* A statement may be expressed in positive or negative terms. Negation is the grammatical process of reversing the expression in a sentence. There are four common types: (1) using the negative particle *not* or *no*; (2) using negating pronouns such as *nobody, none, no one, nothing*, or negating adverbs such as *nowhere, never, neither*; (3) using the coordinating conjunctions *neither* and *nor* (or both of them as correlative conjunctions); (4) using words that are negative in meaning and function, such as *hardly* (= almost not), *scarcely* (= almost not), *barely* (= almost not), *few* (= not many; not much), *little* (= not much), *rarely* (= almost never), and *seldom* (= almost never)—or words having negative affixes such as *a-* {atypical}, *dis-* {disrobe}, *in-* {inimitable} (together with the assimilated forms *im-, il-,* and *ir-*), *non-* {nonemployee}, *un-* {untidy}, *-less* {careless}, and *-free* {hassle-free}.

317 *The word "not."* The simplest and most common form of negation involves using the particle *not*. Used with ordinary verbs and with auxiliary verbs, *not* typically negates a verb, an object, a phrase, or a clause. *Not* typically precedes whatever sentence element is being negated.

To negate an ordinary verb in the present- or past-tense indicative mood (see §§ 173–74), the verb is replaced by a compound of *do* or *did* plus *not* and a bare infinitive.

They sell newspapers in the hotel.
They do not sell newspapers in the hotel.

Kerri sings at the opera today.
Kerri does not sing at the opera today.

The waiter returned with our order.
The waiter did not return with our order.

Not usually immediately follows the principal verb or an auxiliary. If there are two or more verbs in the negative expression, *not* always follows the first of them.

> I am happy.
> I am not happy.
>
> I should leave for work.
> I should not leave for work.
>
> I should leave for work, but I cannot find my glasses.

With participles, *not* precedes the participle {not given any warning, Tim nonchalantly opened the door} {not coming to any conclusions, the jury decided to suspend deliberations} {not having heard the news, Brett innocently asked how Tara was doing in school}. The subject is normally elided from the participial phrase.

Not doesn't have to negate everything that follows it. It may be limited to the element immediately following {I discovered not a scientific breakthrough but a monstrous development}.

A sentence containing *not* may be qualified by another element that limits the extent of the negation. The word's or clause's placement may significantly alter the scope of negation. For example:

> He definitely did not accept the job offer.
> [It is final: he rejected the job offer.]
>
> He did not definitely accept the job offer.
> [It is uncertain: he might still reject the offer.]
>
> We have not eaten yet.
> [We have not eaten, but we expect to eat at some time.]

Not can be contracted to -*n't* and appended to most auxiliary verbs without changing the form of the verb (e.g., *are not* → *aren't*, *would not* → *wouldn't*, *has not* → *hasn't*). The exceptions, involving *am, can, do, will,* and *shall,* are well known to native speakers of the language:

> am → am not → [no contraction with negative: use *I'm not*, etc.]
> can → cannot → can't
> will → will not → won't
> shall → shall not → shan't

Shan't isn't used in AmE except in jest;[1] it still sometimes appears in BrE.

---

1   For an illuminating anecdote about this word, see *Garner on Language and Writing* (Chicago: American Bar Ass'n, 2009), xix–xx.

318 *The word "no."* Unlike *not,* which can negate any element of a sentence, *no* negates only adjectives and nouns. When used with an adjective phrase, it might produce ambiguity. For example, in *we found no eggs for sale,* it's clear that the speaker found nothing. But in *we found no fresh eggs for sale,* does the speaker mean they found no eggs at all, only eggs that weren't fresh, or eggs that were fresh but not for sale?

319 *Using negating pronouns and adverbs.* Pronouns such as *nobody, none, no one,* and *nothing* or adverbs such as *nowhere* and *never* also result in negation. These words make it unnecessary to use *not.* They can help reduce the number of words and improve the flow of a sentence.

> We did not see anyone in the audience.
> We saw no one in the audience.

> The children do not have anything to do.
> The children have nothing to do.

> You do not ever listen!
> You never listen!

> I cannot put the groceries anywhere.
> There's nowhere to put the groceries.

320 *Using "neither" and "nor."* The correlative conjunctions *neither* and *nor* negate alternatives simultaneously. Traditionally, only pairs are framed by *neither–nor,* but writers and speakers sometimes use a *neither–nor–nor* construction, as in the third example below.

> The dog and the cat are not friendly.
> Neither pet is friendly.
> Neither the dog nor the cat is friendly.

> The radiator does not leak, and the water pump also does not leak.
> Neither the radiator nor the water pump leaks.

> Neither John nor Sally nor Brenda can attend the meeting.

In that last example, some writers include only the last *nor.* But again, a simple *neither–nor* construction isn't recommended with three or more elements, the sequence *neither–nor–nor* being preferable.

321 *Words that are negative in meaning and function.* Some words diminish or restrict the truth of a statement rather than entirely negating it. Words such as *few* and *little* convey the senses "not many" and "not much"; *barely, hardly,* and *scarcely* connote "almost not"; and *rarely* and *seldom* are equivalent to "not often" {there's little doubt that the perpetrator will be identified} {it's scarcely worth the trouble to finish} {I've seldom gotten enough sleep since the baby was born}.

322 *Affix negation.* Words that are inherently negative or opposite to other words, especially those with negative prefixes or suffixes, do not change the syntax of the sentence. While syntactical negation denies or negates a statement, it does not necessarily do any more than that. Negating by affix may produce a subtle semantic difference. For example, *I am unhappy* clearly conveys that the speaker is dissatisfied. But *I am not happy* conveys only that the speaker is experiencing some emotion other than happiness. Is the speaker sad? Angry? Confused? Stoically contented? The sentence doesn't give an answer. Common negative prefixes include *dis-* {disrespectful}, *im-* {impolite}, *in-* {indecent}, *ir-* {irrelevant}, and *un-* {unplanned}. The most common negative suffixes are *-less* {hopeless} {useless} and *-free* {smoke-free} {trouble-free}. Such affixes expressing the loss, lack, or negation of some quality are also called *privative* (a word related to *deprive*).

323 *Negative interrogative and imperative statements.* In a negative interrogative statement, the first auxiliary verb may be contracted with *not*: *Aren't you doing your homework tonight?* If it is not contracted, then *not* or *no* precedes the negated element {are you not doing your homework tonight?} {is there no satisfying you?}. Questions phrased with a negating word are called (unsurprisingly) *negative questions*; those without negation are *positive questions*.

   In an imperative statement, the negative particle always follows the imperative verb or is contracted with it {come no closer!} {don't talk back!}.

324 *Double negatives.* When a sentence contains two negatives, in Standard English they are usually thought to cancel each other out to make a mild positive {he didn't not say anything [he did say something]} {this isn't an uncommon problem [it's more or less common]}. In dialect, by contrast, the sentence is often meant to express an emphatic negative {he didn't say nothing [he said nothing at all]} {we're not going nowhere special [we're going somewhere, but it isn't special]}. This linguistic trait has its roots in Old and Middle English, in which the use of multiple negatives (whether in odd or even numbers) served as emphasis.

Yet in Standard English today, one negative conveys the denial. Multiple negatives often lead to ambiguity. For example, in *I wouldn't be surprised if Dan doesn't find the hammer*, does the speaker expect Dan to find the hammer or not to find it? In general, though, multiple negation results in a cancellation of other negatives {we didn't say the children couldn't come along [we didn't say anything about whether the children could come]}.

325 *Other forms of negation.* A sentence can express negation even though it doesn't contain any plainly negative elements. Two common means of achieving this effect are using *but* in the sense "if not" and *except* in the sense "but not" {what is a pampered dog *but* [= if not] a child in a fur suit?} {you may borrow the car *except* [= but not] when it is raining}.

Then there's the old joke about a grammar teacher who asserted that two positives could never make a negative. A student responded: "Yeah, right."

326 *"Any" and "some" in negative statements.* When the negating particle is *not*, then *any-* words must be used with it, not *some-* words. *Any-* words include *any, anyone, anybody, anything,* and *anywhere. Some-* words include *some, someone, somebody, something,* and *somewhere.*

> **Not this:** I don't want to see somebody. [Unless the meaning is one particular person I'm not naming.]
> **But this:** I don't want to see anybody.

> **Not this:** There aren't some seats left.
> **But this:** There aren't any seats left.

Expletives

327 *Generally.* Though *expletive* commonly denotes a swearword {expletive deleted}, in grammar *expletive* signifies a word that has no lexical meaning but serves a merely structural role in a sentence—as a noun element. The two most common expletives are *it* {it is true!} and *there* {there must be an answer}. An expletive *it* or *there* may be in the subject position, especially when the subject of a sentence is a clause {it is a rule that children must raise their hands to speak during class [the rule is that children must raise their hands to speak during class]} {it is better to stay here than to go there [to stay here is better than to go there]}. In this position, the expletive shifts the emphasis to the predicate containing the true subject. The sentence implies a "who" or "what" question that is answered by the subject. For example, *It is foolish to ignore facts* tells the reader "what" it is foolish to ignore and emphasizes "facts."

An expletive *it* may also take the position of a direct object, especially when the real object is a clause or noun phrase {some people don't like it that stores are open for business on Thanksgiving [some people don't like stores' being open for business on Thanksgiving]}. Using an expletive in this way can tighten a verb phrase and emphasize the object. Compare *it was taken for granted that our team would win* with *we took for granted that our team would win*.

328   *Expletive "it."* Whereas the pronoun *it* adds meaning to a sentence because it has an antecedent or else is the formal subject of a *be*-verb in the sense of "a person" or "a thing," an expletive *it* adds no meaning and takes the subject's or object's place when the subject or object shifts to the predicate: *It is not known what happened* → *What happened is not known.*

Usually readers have no difficulty intuitively understanding whether they're encountering a pronoun *it* or an expletive *it*. But when the expletive and the pronoun appear close together, they may cause the reader to stumble {The much-anticipated feast was a disappointment; it was poorly cooked and presented. It is hard to believe that such a famous chef thought it would be edible, let alone delight gourmands}. Avoid having several *its* in a passage clash in this way.

Some other names for the expletive *it* are *ambient it, anticipatory it, dummy it, empty it, introductory it, nonreferential it,* and *prop it*.

329   *Expletive "there."* The word *there* is also frequently used as an expletive with *be* or an intransitive verb (especially a linking verb) followed by the subject {there are many different viewpoints presented in the students' essays} {there were several hundred members present at the conference}. An expletive *there* shouldn't be confused with *there* as an adverb of place.

There seemed to be someone outside. (*There* is an expletive.)
Someone seemed to be there. (*There* refers to a place.)

There appear to be at least 50 people. (*There* is an expletive.)
At least 50 people appear to be there. (*There* refers to a place.)

There once reigned a king called Frederick the Great. (*There* is an expletive.)

A king called Frederick the Great once reigned there. (*There* refers to a place.)

As in those illustrations, the expletive *there* appears before the verb; the adverbial *there* normally appears in the predicate.

Parallelism

330   *Generally.* Parallel constructions—series of like sentence elements—are common in good writing. Compound structures may link words {win, lose, or draw}, phrases {government of the people, by the people, for the people}, dependent clauses {that all men are created equal; that they are endowed by their Creator with certain unalienable rights; that among these are life, liberty, and the pursuit of happiness}, or sentences {I came; I saw; I conquered}. Every element of a parallel series must be a functional match (word, phrase, clause, sentence) and serve the same grammatical function in the sentence (e.g., noun, verb, adjective, adverb). This syntactic linking of matching elements is called *coordination.* But when linked items do not match, the syntax of the uncoordinated sentence breaks down:

> No long complex sentence will hold up without parallel construction. Paralleling can be very simple. Any word will seek its own kind, noun to noun, adjective to adjective, infinitive to infinitive.
> —Sheridan Baker
> *The Practical Stylist*

Poor: She did volunteer work in the community kitchen, the homeless shelter, and taught free ESL classes offered by her church.

Better: She did volunteer work in the community kitchen, the homeless shelter, and her church, where she taught free ESL classes.

Poor: The candidate is a former county judge, state senator, and served two terms as attorney general.

Better: The candidate is a former county judge, state senator, and two-term attorney general.

The examples illustrate how the syntax breaks down when a series is not parallel. In the second one, for instance, the subject, predicate, and modifier (*the candidate is a former*) fit with the noun phrases *county judge* and *state senator*, but the third item in the series renders nonsense: **The candidate is a former served two terms as attorney general.* The first two elements in the series are nouns, while the third is a separate predicate. The corrected version makes each item in the series a noun element.

331 *Prepositions.* In a parallel series of prepositional phrases, repeat the preposition with every element unless they all use the same preposition. A common error occurs when a writer lets two or more of the phrases share a single preposition but inserts a different one with another element:

> **Poor:** I looked for my lost keys in the sock drawer, the laundry hamper, the restroom, and under the bed.
> **Better:** I looked for my lost keys in the sock drawer, in the laundry hamper, in the restroom, and under the bed.

If the series had not included *under the bed*, the preposition could have been used once to apply to all the objects:

> **Better:** I looked for my lost keys in the sock drawer, the laundry hamper, and the restroom.

332 *Paired joining terms.* Correlative conjunctions such as *either–or, neither–nor, both–and,* and *not only–but also* and some adverb pairs such as *where–there, as–so,* and *if–then* must join grammatically parallel sentence elements. It is a common error to mismatch elements framed by correlatives.

> **Poor:** I'd like to either go into business for myself or else to write freelance travel articles.
> **Better:** I'd like either to go into business for myself or else to write freelance travel articles.

> **Poor:** Our guests not only ate all the turkey and dressing but both pumpkin pies as well.
> **Better:** Our guests ate not only all the turkey and dressing but both pumpkin pies as well.

In the second example, the verb *ate*, when placed after the first correlative, attaches grammatically to *all the turkey* but not to *both pumpkin pies as well*. When moved outside the two phrases containing its direct objects, it attaches to both—and the phrasing becomes parallel.

333 *Auxiliary verbs.* If an auxiliary verb appears before a series of verb phrases, it must apply to all of them. A common error is to include one phrase that takes a different auxiliary verb:

> **Poor:** The proposal would streamline the application process, speed up admission decisions, and has proved to save money when implemented by other schools.
> **Better:** The proposal would streamline the application process, speed up admission decisions, and save money.
> **Better:** The proposal would streamline the application process and speed up admission decisions. It has proved to save money when implemented by other schools.

The auxiliary verb *would* in that example renders the nonsensical *would has proved* when parsed with the third element of the predicate series. The first solution resolves that grammatical conflict, while the second breaks out the third into a separate sentence—which also avoids shifting from future tense to past tense in midsentence.

334 *Verbs and adverbs at the outset.* A listing of dos and don'ts, for example, may be directives, each item being a complete clause. Most items in the list may begin with verbs in the imperative mood. Note that it does not destroy parallelism to have some of those verbs preceded by an adverb (e.g., *never*)—as in the third and fifth items here:

> If you sometimes ignore care labels, you will minimize risks if you know that some care labels should never or rarely be disregarded:
> - Obey care labels on expensive garments that you cannot afford to damage or replace.
> - Obey care labels that are carefully written or provide a lot of detail.
> - Never ignore "Dry-clean" or "Dry-clean only" instructions.
> - Beware of defying dry-cleaning instructions on any crisp, tailored, or heavily sized linen or cotton garments.
> - Never ignore instructions to use mild soap or detergent or cool water, especially with silk or wool.

335 *Longer elements.* Even with a longer list, such as one involving bullets, the individual elements must have parity. In the next example, what follows the colon within each item must be a verb (given the first two elements), but the parallelism breaks down in the third and in the sixth through eighth elements with their noun strings. Also, the third and eighth elements are introduced by adjectives, not nouns.

> **Poor:** Maslow boiled down volumes of existing research to a list of needs and desires that people try to fulfill:
> - transcendence: help others realize their potential;
> - self-actualization: realize our own potential, self-fulfillment, peak experiences;
> - aesthetic: symmetry, order, beauty, balance;
> - learning: know, understand, mentally connect;
> - esteem: achieve, be competent, gain approval, independence, or status;
> - belonging: love, family, friends, affection;
> - security: protection, safety, stability; and
> - physical: hunger, thirst, bodily comfort.

With minor adjustments, the structures are made fully parallel:

> **Better:** Maslow boiled down volumes of existing research to a list of needs and desires that people try to fulfill:
> - transcendence: help others realize their potential;
> - self-actualization: realize our own potential, self-fulfillment, peak experiences;
> - aesthetics: achieve symmetry, order, beauty, balance;
> - learning: know, understand, mentally connect;
> - esteem: achieve, be competent, gain approval, independence, or status;
> - belonging: give and receive love and affection from family and friends;
> - security: gain protection, safety, stability; and
> - physicality: relieve hunger and thirst, achieve bodily comfort.

Cleft Sentences

336 *Definition.* A cleft sentence opens with a special type of subject clause (an *it*-clause, a *what*-clause, or a similar clause) that changes the focus by adding two or three words (such as *it*, *was*, and *who*; *there*, *are*, and *that*; or *what* and *was*) {it was the manager who handled the customer's complaint} {there are still some missing items that have to be accounted for} {what the campaign lacked was a vibrant slogan}. Most often the sentence begins with an expletive *it* and a *be*-verb (the *it*-clause). The subject clause emphasizes new information that identifies a person, a place, a time, an object, a cause, etc. For example:

> It was Manuel who met Adam in college. (The focus is on the actor.)
>
> It was Adam whom Manuel met in college. (The focus is on the person that the actor met.)
>
> It was in college that Manuel met Adam. (The focus is on the time or place when they met.)

The part of a cleft sentence beginning with the relative pronoun usually refers to information already given. Hence it may be reduced when the information that would be in the final clause is understood:

> When did Manuel and Adam become acquainted?
> It was in college (that they met).

337   *Types.* A cleft sentence may be declarative {it is the quality of the work that concerns me} {there was an incident that led to the concert's postponement}. Or it may be interrogative {is it the quality of the work that you're concerned about?} {what was the incident that led to the concert's postponement?}.

It may also be positive or negative. A positive cleft sentence states a truth. A negative cleft sentence uses simple negation (*not, no*) to state the contrary. Often the relative pronoun is elided in a whiz-deletion (as with the bracketed words below—see § 315)—e.g.:

> **Positive:** There are many movies [that are] worth seeing this weekend.
>
> **Negative:** There are not many movies [that are] worth seeing this weekend.
>
> **Negative:** There are no movies [that are] worth seeing this weekend.

338   *Uses.* A cleft sentence is sometimes used for dramatic effect to signal a shift or a beginning, especially to create a more interesting lead-in for a topic:

> It was hours later that Burns discovered he'd left his wallet on the counter.
>
> It was in 1912 that shipbuilders and legislators learned the cost of not providing ocean liners with adequate numbers of lifeboats.

In some contexts, a cleft sentence may imply a contrast or mistake. For instance, *It's not Joan who wants to be a social activist* implies that Joan is being distinguished from another person or that someone else has been mistakenly identified.

Traditional Sentence Diagramming

339 **History and description.** The traditional system of sentence diagramming bears the names of its developers, Alonzo Reed and Brainerd Kellogg, who in 1878 introduced it in two grammar texts: *Graded Lessons in English* and *Higher Lessons in English*. Reed–Kellogg diagrams show each word in a sentence placed according to its function. The subject and the main verb—along with any predicate nominative, predicate adjective, direct object, or indirect object—occupy the main horizontal line and show the

> I really do not know that anything has ever been more exciting than diagramming sentences. I suppose other things may be more exciting to others when they are at school but to me undoubtedly when I was at school the really completely exciting thing was diagramming sentences and that has been to me ever since the one thing that has been completely exciting and completely completing.
> —Gertrude Stein
> "Poetry and Grammar"

core thought communicated by the sentence (the kernel sentence). Adjectives and adverbs are attached to the words they modify on descending diagonal lines. Reed and Kellogg were not the first to develop such a scheme: predecessors date back to the first half of the 19th century, using rectangles or balloons to hold the words instead of lines. But Reed and Kellogg's grammars were widely adopted, and Reed–Kellogg diagrams—with some refinements—were standard teaching tools for much of the 20th century. They fell out of favor in elementary and secondary schools in the 1960s, along with formal classroom units in grammar generally.

340 **Benefits of diagrams.** Diagrams help you recognize sentence patterns (e.g., a predicate nominative or predicate adjective with a linking verb, a direct object with a transitive verb, subordinate clauses, prepositional phrases). By showing the primary parts of the sentence on the baseline, diagrams can help you sort out how all the other words fit into the syntax. By separating the words according to their functions, diagrams can help you spot some common grammatical errors—such as disagreement in number and case, or lack of parallelism in compound constructions. With an especially complex sentence, a diagram can help reveal the writer's meaning.

341   *Using diagrams.* A sentence does not have to be diagrammed fully and rigorously for the exercise to be useful. An informal sketch of just a discrete syntactical unit can also help you decide whether a singular or plural verb is needed or whether a pronoun in a certain position should be in the nominative or objective case. An adept can diagram mentally rather than by physically drawing it on paper.

> Churchill reports that the most valuable training he ever received in rhetoric was in the diagramming of sentences. Think of it! Yet the diagramming of a sentence, regardless of the grammatical system, can be a live subject as soon as one asks not simply "How is this sentence put together?" but rather "Why is it put together in this way?" or "Could the rhetorical balance and hence the desired persuasion be better achieved by writing it differently?"
> —Wayne C. Booth
> "The Rhetorical Stance"

342   *Criticisms.* Critics of diagramming say that it does not reflect modern concepts of grammar and that by abandoning the flow of prose in favor of a logical reordering, a diagram can make understanding the meaning harder, not easier. The attack on the classroom use of diagrams was part of a larger assault on traditional grammar generally. More specifically, some curriculum reformers thought grammar lessons took away class time that could be better spent on other pursuits, such as literature. But many other teachers and students have found diagramming to be an extremely useful pedagogical device.

343   *How diagrams work.* While there are variations on the Reed–Kellogg forms for representing some grammatical functions, with each of these the core structure and the arrangement of related words, phrases, and clauses are largely unchanged. The alterations in style reflect such details as representing the two constituents of correlative conjunctions (e.g., *not only–but also*) together on a dotted line, or separating them so that each correlative appears close to the words it introduces.

344 *Baseline.* The main baseline of a sentence (or independent clause) is central to the sentence's diagram, containing its nucleus of meaning—the subject and verb, plus any direct object or subjective complement. It consists of a horizontal line divided by a vertical line running through it. On the left of the line is the subject, on the right the predicate. It can be as simple as a noun or pronoun and a verb:

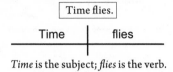

Time is the subject; *flies* is the verb.

With the imperative mood, a diagram may consist of the verb alone (the noun or pronoun being implied):

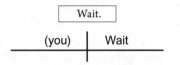

Wait is the verb. The subject is understood as *you*.

Connected to the horizontal line is every other element of the sentence—usually modifiers (e.g., adjectives, adverbs, prepositional phrases, relative clauses) but sometimes also appositives, absolute constructions, expletives, and more. Some attach above the line, some below. Similar lines are used for other clauses, whether independent or subordinate, so it's helpful to indicate the priority of the main baseline of the sentence (or of each independent clause in a compound sentence) in some way, such as by using a thicker line or by starting the line a little farther to the left than other elements on the diagram.

345 ***Subject.*** The subject of a clause may be a single word, a noun phrase, or a noun clause. It is in the nominative case. In the active voice, the subject is the agent or actor causing the verb's action or state; in the passive voice, the subject is the recipient of the verb's action or state.

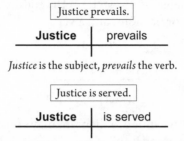

Justice is the subject, *prevails* the verb.

Justice is the subject of this passive-voice sentence.
It is the recipient of the action of the verb *is served*.

346 ***Predicate.*** The predicate always contains the main verb and any auxiliary verbs and particles (idiomatic prepositions that are essential to the nonliteral meaning of a phrasal verb, as with *out* in *I'll check it out*). Most predicates also include either a direct object or a subjective complement, and some also include a complement associated with the direct object.

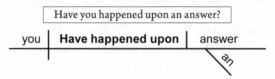

Happened upon (= to discover) is a phrasal verb. *Have* is capitalized because it begins the sentence; *upon*, usually a preposition, is an idiomatic particle that is part of the phrasal verb.

347 ***Direct object.*** A direct object is a noun or pronoun representing the recipient of the verb's action or state. If it's a pronoun, it's in the objective case. A direct object appears on the predicate side of the baseline, next to the verb but separated from it by a vertical line above the baseline.

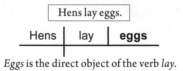

Eggs is the direct object of the verb *lay*.

348 *Objective complement.* An objective complement functions as a noun or adjective and names or describes the outcome of some change the verb makes to the direct object (e.g., *king* in *Who made you king?* or *wet* in *The rain got us wet*). In other words, it completes the action of the verb. In a diagram, the objective complement appears to the right of the direct object and separated from it by a back-slanted line (pointing toward the direct object).

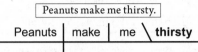

Thirsty is an objective complement. Here it is an adjective completing the action that the verb, *make*, has on the direct object, *me*.

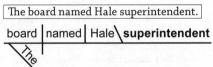

Superintendent is an objective complement. Here it is a noun referring to the direct object, *Hale*, and completing the action of the verb, *named*.

349 *Indirect object.* An indirect object names the recipient of the verb's action on the direct object (e.g., *me* in *Hand me the pliers*). It is the functional equivalent of a *to*-prepositional phrase after the direct object (*to me* in *Hand the pliers to me*)—except that the indirect object is preposed and the *to* is dropped. On a diagram, the indirect object is placed on a horizontal line below the verb and connected to it by a diagonal line.

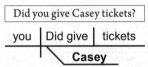

Casey is the indirect object of the verb *did give*; *tickets* is its direct object.

350   *Subjective complement.* A subjective complement is either a predicate nominative (e.g., *accountant* in *Merrill is an accountant*) or a predicate adjective (e.g., *great* in *Indian food sounds great*). It is separated from the verb by a back-slanted line above the baseline (pointing toward the subject). It may accompany either a *be*-verb or a linking verb such as *seem, become, grow,* or *taste.*

| Something smells delicious. |

Something | smells \ **delicious**

Delicious is a subjective complement in the form of a predicate adjective.
It describes the subject, *something.*

| Allen Konigsberg became Woody Allen. |

Allen Konigsberg | became \ **Woody Allen**

Woody Allen is a subjective complement
in the form of a predicate nominative.
It refers directly to the subject, *Allen Konigsberg.*

351   *One-word modifiers.* A modifier adds information about a noun (in the case of an adjective) or a verb, adjective, or adverb (in the case of an adverb). It may be a one-word adjective, adverb, or article, or it may be a phrase (most frequently a prepositional phrase) or a subordinate clause. The function it plays in the sentence determines its placement in a diagram. A one-word modifier is placed on a diagonal line below the word it modifies.

| Our first crop survived the long drought fairly well. |

crop | survived | drought
Our *first* — *well* *fairly* — *the* *long*

Our is a possessive pronoun and *first* is an adjective; both independently modify
the noun *crop.* The adverb *well* modifies the verb *survived*
and is itself modified by the adverb *fairly.* The article *the* and the
adjective *long* independently modify the noun *drought.*

352   *Prepositional phrases.* A prepositional phrase couples a preposition (e.g., *at, before, of*) with a noun or pronoun as its object. It may function as an adjective or an adverb. In a diagram, a prepositional phrase appears under the word it modifies, on a branch consisting of a diagonal line holding the preposition and a horizontal line holding its object.

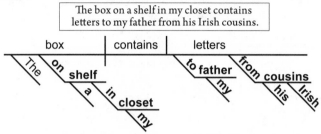

This sentence contains four prepositional phrases: *on a shelf* modifies the subject, *box*; *in my closet* modifies the object of that preposition, *shelf*; *to my father* modifies the direct object, *letters*, as does *from his Irish cousins.*

353   *Adjective clauses.* An adjective clause is a subordinate clause that modifies a noun in another clause, either further defining it (a restrictive clause) or adding supplementary but nonessential information about it (a nonrestrictive clause). It may be introduced by a relative pronoun (*that, whichever, who, whom,* or *whose*) or a subordinating conjunction (e.g., *when, where, whatever, why, how*). (See §§ 271–73.) The clause is put on a separate diagram below the diagram holding the word it modifies, and connected to it by a dashed line from the modified word to the relative pronoun or adverb that introduces the adjective clause.

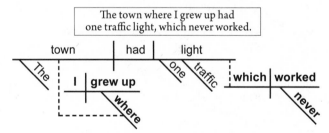

This sentence contains two adjective clauses: *where I grew up,* which modifies the subject, *town*; and *which never worked,* which modifies the direct object, *light.*

354 *Adverbial clauses.* An adverbial clause is a subordinate clause that modifies a verb, adjective, or adverb in another clause by specifying its time, place, duration, amount, cause, purpose, or condition. It is introduced by a subordinating conjunction (e.g., *when, whenever, where, if, as soon as, although, once, before*). In a diagram, an adverbial clause is much like an adjective clause, but the modified word in the independent clause is connected to the verb in the subordinate clause with a dashed line. The subordinating conjunction appears on the dashed line.

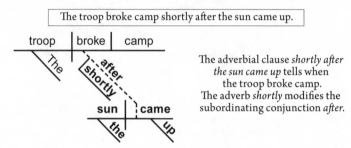

The adverbial clause *shortly after the sun came up* tells when the troop broke camp. The adverb *shortly* modifies the subordinating conjunction *after*.

355 *Noun clauses.* A noun clause is a subordinate clause that functions as the subject or object of another clause. A noun clause is diagrammed on a separate baseline above the clause and connected to it by a "pedestal" (a vertical line atop a delta of two short diagonal lines). Its placement in the diagram depends on its function in the sentence.

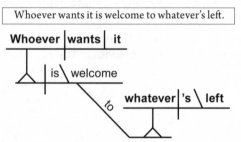

The subordinate noun clause *Whoever wants it* is the subject of the sentence; the subordinate noun clause *whatever's left* is the object of the preposition *to*.

A noun clause may be introduced by a conjunction (e.g., *that*) or an adverb (e.g., *where* or *if*). Some writers tend to omit *that* in a noun clause, but doing so can sometimes cause a brief miscue.

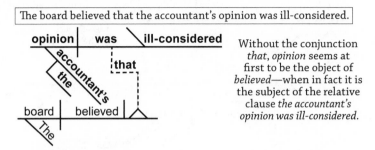

The board believed that the accountant's opinion was ill-considered.

Without the conjunction *that*, *opinion* seems at first to be the object of *believed*—when in fact it is the subject of the relative clause *the accountant's opinion was ill-considered*.

A noun clause may also be introduced by an interrogative pronoun (e.g., *why, when, where*), an adjective (e.g., *which, whose, what*), or an adverb (e.g., *when, how, why*).

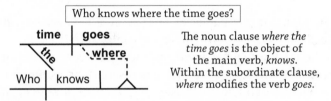

Who knows where the time goes?

The noun clause *where the time goes* is the object of the main verb, *knows*. Within the subordinate clause, *where* modifies the verb *goes*.

356 **Infinitives.** An infinitive is a verb typically introduced by *to* (e.g., *to fish* in *I like to fish*)—see § 147. With a bare infinitive, the *to* is omitted (e.g., before *laugh* in *Don't make me laugh*). When an infinitive is part of the main verb, it is diagrammed (with *to* unless it's a bare infinitive) on the baseline like any other verb. An infinitive phrase may take an object (e.g., *a secret* in *Do you want to know a secret?*) and may function as a noun, an adjective, or an adverb. The phrase is diagrammed on a branch just as a prepositional phrase is, with *to* on the diagonal line. If it serves as a noun, its diagram appears on a pedestal. If it serves as an adjective or adverb, it goes below the word it modifies.

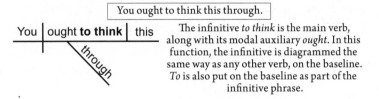

You ought to think this through.

The infinitive *to think* is the main verb, along with its modal auxiliary *ought*. In this function, the infinitive is diagrammed the same way as any other verb, on the baseline. *To* is also put on the baseline as part of the infinitive phrase.

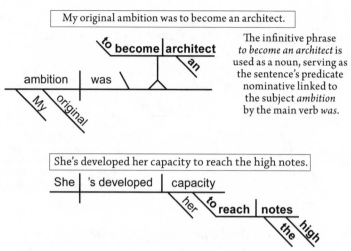

My original ambition was to become an architect.

The infinitive phrase *to become an architect* is used as a noun, serving as the sentence's predicate nominative linked to the subject *ambition* by the main verb *was*.

She's developed her capacity to reach the high notes.

The infinitive phrase *to reach the high notes* is used as an adjective modifying *capacity*. Its diagram is placed below the modified word.

357 *Participles.* The participles of a verb (see § 151) are its inflected forms typically ending in *-ed* (the past participle) and *-ing* (the present participle), though the past participle of an irregular verb may be unpredictable (e.g., *told, written*). With auxiliary verbs, participles function as verbs in the progressive and perfect tenses (e.g., *is missing* or *has missed*). The past tense is also used with a *be*-verb to form the passive voice (e.g., *is missed* in *He is sorely missed*, or *was missed* in *The deadline was missed*). A participle may also function without an auxiliary as an adjective (e.g., *the missing link, a missed opportunity*). Like a verb, it can take an object. As an adverb, a participle is diagrammed under the word it modifies, curved around a diagonal line connected to a horizontal line. Its object goes on the horizontal line, separated from the participle by a vertical line above the line.

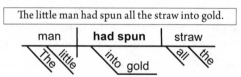

The little man had spun all the straw into gold.

The main verb, *spun*, is the past participle of the irregular verb *spin*, used in this sentence to form the past-perfect tense. As a verb, it is diagrammed on the baseline with its auxiliary verb, *had*.

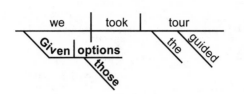

Given those options is a participial phrase modifying the subject, *we. Guided* is a participle standing alone and modifying the direct object, *tour.*

358 *Gerunds.* A gerund is the present participle of a verb (with its *-ing* ending) functioning as a noun in the sentence {I enjoy reading and painting} (see § 155). It's distinguished from the present participle when used as a verb in the progressive tenses {I have been reading all morning; this afternoon I'll be painting}. A gerund may take an object and modifiers {I enjoy reading biographies and painting landscapes of the mountains}. It is diagrammed as a present participle just as any other verb is. A gerund phrase appears on a separate baseline above the main baseline on a pedestal, with the gerund draped around a line with a vertical offset. Like other nouns, a gerund may also be used attributively and function as an adjective. When that is so, it is diagrammed the same way as any other adjective, on a straight diagonal line below the word it modifies.

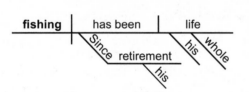

The gerund *fishing* is a noun functioning as the subject of the sentence. Because it is not part of a phrase, it needs no special formatting here.

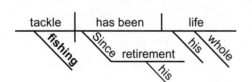

Here, the gerund *fishing* (still a noun) is used adjectivally to modify the subject *tackle.* Because it is not part of a phrase, it needs no special formatting.

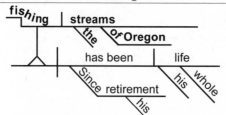

Since his retirement, fishing the streams of Oregon has been his whole life.

Here, the subject is the gerund phrase *fishing the streams of Oregon*. The phrase is diagrammed with a separate main axis atop a pedestal linked to its place in the main sentence.

359 *Appositives.* An appositive is a noun, pronoun, or phrase standing beside a noun element and further identifying it or adding information about it (see § 40). An appositive usually follows the word with which it is associated, but it may also precede that word. An appositive is diagrammed in parentheses beside the word to which it refers (and atop a pedestal if it is a clause). Any modifiers in an appositive phrase are placed on the baseline below the main appositive and inside the parentheses.

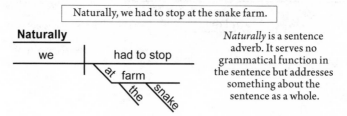

Mrs. Roush, my fifth-grade teacher, taught me sentence diagramming.

My fifth-grade teacher is an appositive, identifying *Mrs. Roush*.

360 *Independent elements.* Several types of constructions use words that serve no grammatical function in the sentence: vocatives (words of direct address), interjections (see § 280), expletives that stand in for the subject in an inverted sentence (see § 193), absolute constructions (see p. 401), and sentence adverbs (see § 211). They are all diagrammed on a separate line or lines above or beside the baseline but not connected to it.

Naturally, we had to stop at the snake farm.

Naturally is a sentence adverb. It serves no grammatical function in the sentence but addresses something about the sentence as a whole.

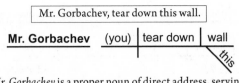

Mr. Gorbachev is a proper noun of direct address, serving
no grammatical function in the sentence.

361 *Conjunctions.* A conjunction joins two or more sentence parts, whether
words, phrases, or clauses. It is diagrammed on a dashed line connecting the things it joins. An internal compound structure is diagrammed
on a branch that splits into as many separate but parallel structures as
there are items in the compound, with the parallel structures connected
by a dashed line holding the conjunction that joins them. Correlative
conjunctions (e.g., *either–or, not only–but also*) go together on the connecting line, with each part close to the item with which it is associated
in the sentence.

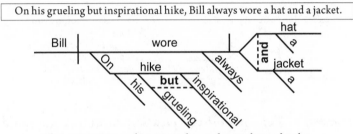

The conjunction *and* joins two direct objects, *hat* and *jacket*.
The conjunction *but* joins the adjectives *grueling* and
inspirational, both of which modify *hike*.

362 *Diagramming compound sentences.* A compound sentence consists of
two or more independent clauses, usually (but not always) joined by a
conjunction. (See § 293.) The clauses are joined by a dashed line with
a short horizontal section holding the conjunction. The dashed line
attaches to the baselines at the main verbs.

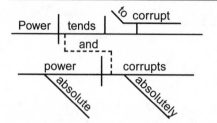

Power tends to corrupt, and absolute power corrupts absolutely.

The independent clauses *power tends to corrupt* and *absolute power corrupts absolutely* could stand alone as complete sentences. *And* is a coordinating conjunction.

363 *Diagramming complex sentences.* A complex sentence consists of an independent clause and at least one dependent clause linked by a relative pronoun (e.g., *that, which, who*), an adverb (e.g., *where, when, why*), or a subordinating conjunction (e.g., *if, after, because*). (See § 295.) The clauses are joined by a slanting dashed line connecting the two linked elements.

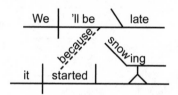

We'll be late because it started snowing.

The independent clause *we'll be late* could stand alone. The subordinate clause *because it started snowing* could not, but serves as an adverbial modifier explaining why.

364 *Diagramming compound-complex sentences.* A compound-complex sentence contains two independent clauses and at least one dependent clause. (See § 296.) The independent clauses are joined by a dashed line with a short horizontal section holding a conjunction (as with a compound sentence), and the dependent clause is joined by a slanting dashed line connecting it to one of the independent clauses (as with a complex sentence).

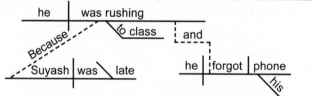

Because Suyash was late, he was rushing to class, and he forgot his phone.

The independent clauses are *he was rushing to class* and *he forgot his phone.* The dependent clause *because Suyash was late* attaches to the first.

Transformational Grammar

Overview

365   *Definition.* Transformational grammar is a descriptive approach that does not provide normative rules but instead seeks to derive and explain the rules of a language by showing how native speakers generate sentences. It is based on a theory first proposed by the linguist Noam Chomsky in 1957. Chomsky sought to describe how people produce and understand original sentences without formally learning rules for grammatical structures. Native speakers assimilate the natural rules of a language and internalize them.

> Compared to the standard grammars, the transformational descriptions are only fragments.
> —James Sledd
> "Syntactic Strictures"

Transformational grammar derives those internal rules by examining sentence structures and producing a formulalike rule or a tree diagram to show how a sentence or a sentence part is formed. Widespread, mostly unsuccessful attempts to teach grade-school children transformational grammar were made during the 1960s and early 1970s. Today it is taught mostly in colleges and graduate schools. Outside linguistics, transformational grammar is used primarily in computer-language-processing applications. Although it has an alien look and feel to traditionalists, it can convey interesting insights into how the language works.

366   *Scope of section.* Entire books are devoted to deriving rules from sentences of increasing complexity and attempting to explain sentences that deviate from previously derived rules. This section will focus on the established transformational-grammar rules for fairly simple sentences. A list of further readings is provided in the bibliography.

367   *Terminology of transformational grammar.* Many aspects of transformational grammar have several different names, depending on the source consulted. For example, transformational grammar itself is also termed *transformational-generative grammar, generative grammar, generative-transformational grammar,* and *generative-transformational theory.* For the sake of simplicity, this section uses only the one name (with a few exceptions).

Likewise, because the abbreviations used in the rules vary depending on the source, this section uses only basic abbreviations.

368 *Tools of transformational grammar.* Because transformational grammar is a descriptive grammar, it uses tools that illustrate, rather than dictate, sentence structures. The tools include universal symbols, formulalike statements, and treelike diagrams. Symbols and formulas are useful because they are precise and apply to all sentences, not just particular ones or only sentences that have already been created.

369 *Universal symbols in rules.* In a rule, the first element is a symbol for the sentence part being defined, placed at the far left. Next is a right-pointing arrow ($\rightarrow$), which means "rewrite as." The elements are set out to the right of the arrow in the order of their appearance in a sentence. Parentheses ( ) around a component show that it is optional; not every sentence or sentence part will have that component. Curly brackets { } around a list of components mean that any of the components may be included but not necessarily all.

370 *Tree diagrams.* Besides the formula-style rules, diagrams can be helpful to show the structure of a sentence. Because the diagrams are branching and treelike, they are called *tree diagrams*. Every tree diagram begins with a sentence (S) consisting of a subject, or noun phrase (NP), plus a predicate, or verb phrase (VP):

That is the starting point.

Base Rules in Transformational Grammar

371 *Parts of speech.* Transformational grammarians use most of the same names for the individual parts of speech as traditional grammarians. These are used in formulating the rules for sentence structure, as discussed below.

372 *Sentence basics.* A sentence (S) consists of two components: a noun phrase (or *subject*) (NP) and a verb phrase (or *predicate*) (VP). A kernel sentence (K) is a basic statement that can't be derived from another sentence. In appearance, it is the simple subject plus the simplest verb phrase or predicate. Anything after the verb phrase is called a *sentence modifier* (SM). So the two most basic rules of transformational grammar can be expressed this way:

K $\rightarrow$ NP + VP   We play.
                            We play soccer.

S $\rightarrow$ K + (SM)   We play soccer on Saturday night in Rialto.

In a diagram, these rules would be expressed this way:

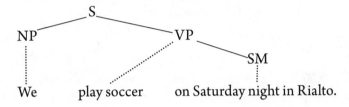

Nouns and Noun Phrases

373   *Functions of noun phrases.* In a kernel sentence, the subject is a noun phrase—so called even if it's a simple noun. Anywhere in a sentence, a noun phrase can function in all the same ways as a noun.

374   *Simple noun phrases.* There are four types of simple noun phrases: (1) a proper noun, (2) a personal pronoun, (3) an indefinite pronoun, and (4) a common noun with or without a determiner (Det). These are rules of what constitutes a noun phrase:

$$NP \rightarrow \begin{cases} \text{proper noun} \\ \text{personal pronoun} \\ \text{indefinite pronoun} \\ \text{(Det) + N} \end{cases}$$

For each type of noun, the symbol is "N." So the rule can be reduced further to:

NP $\rightarrow$ N

Determiners

375 *Types of determiners.* Nouns, especially singular common nouns, may require some kind of determiner, shown by the symbol "Det." (If such nouns in the singular typically need a preceding determiner [*ball, hat, shelf, house*], they are called *bounded nouns*.) Determiners are definite and indefinite articles, demonstrative pronouns, indefinite pronouns, and numbers. The rule is expressed this way:

$$\text{Det} \rightarrow \begin{cases} \text{definite article} \\ \text{indefinite article} \\ \text{demonstrative pronoun} \\ \text{indefinite pronoun} \\ \text{number} \end{cases}$$

376 *Numeric and nonnumeric determiners.* There are two types of determiners. A number, whether cardinal or ordinal, is a numeric determiner (numDet). All other determiners are nonnumeric (nonDet). Given this information, we can write out each rule defining each kind of determiner:

$$\text{numDet} \rightarrow \begin{cases} \text{cardinal number} \\ \text{ordinal number} \end{cases}$$

$$\text{nonDet} \rightarrow \begin{cases} \text{definite article (nonDet:def)} \\ \text{indefinite article (nonDet:indef)} \\ \text{demonstrative pronoun (nonDet:demon)} \\ \text{indefinite pronoun (nonDet:pro)} \end{cases}$$

377 *Multiple determiners.* A noun phrase may have more than one determiner, of the same or of different types. A numeric determiner may follow a nonnumeric determiner {a second strike}, or it may stand alone {seven samurai}. With this information, we can refine the rule for a determiner:

$$\text{Det} \rightarrow \begin{cases} \text{nonDet} + (\text{numDet}) \\ \text{nonDet} + \text{numDet} \\ (\text{nonDet}) + \text{numDet} \end{cases}$$

378 *Determiners in noun phrases.* The use of a determiner in a noun phrase is illustrated by these rules:

nonDet + NP	some weekdays; each fish
numDet + NP	three mice; two hundred soldiers
nonDet + numDet + NP	the twelfth man; those four geese

379   *Prearticles.* A prearticle (preArt) is a modifying phrase ending in *of*—such as *a lot of, some of, nine of*—that may precede a determiner. Hence we can rewrite the final rule for a determiner:

Det → (pre-Art) + Det

380   *Noun phrases with determiner and prearticle.* The following phrases show how a prearticle may be used with a determiner and a noun phrase:

NP	onlookers
numDet + NP	nine onlookers
nonDet:def + numDet + NP	the nine onlookers
preArt + nonDet:def + numDet + NP	some of the nine onlookers
preArt + nonDet:demon + numDet + NP	some of those nine onlookers

Noun-Phrase Modifiers

381   *Modifiers.* In Standard English, a one-word modifier (Mod) may precede the noun phrase and follow a determiner. There can also be multiple modifiers. The basic rule is as follows:

NP → (Det) + (Mod) + N	
NP → N	sky
NP → nonDet:def + N	the sky
NP → Mod + N	blue sky
NP → nonDet:def + Mod + N	the blue sky
NP → nonDet:def + Mod + Mod + N	the endless blue sky

382   *Compound nouns.* In an open compound noun, which is composed of a noun immediately followed by a modifier, such as *body politic* or *battle royal*, the modifier is part of the noun, not a separate element, so there is no separate rule for it. (In traditional grammar, the adjectives here—*politic* and *royal*—are termed *postpositive adjectives* because they are placed after the nouns.)

383   *Combined rules.* When all the rules are combined, a noun phrase is more fully defined.

$$NP \rightarrow (preArt) + (Det) + (Mod) + N$$

NP $\rightarrow$ N	sugar
NP $\rightarrow$ Mod + N	brown sugar
NP $\rightarrow$ nonDet:demon + Mod + N	this brown sugar
NP $\rightarrow$ preArt + nonDet:demon + Mod + N	part of this brown sugar

384   *Number, person, and possession.* The basic rules covered to this point don't reflect certain qualities in the noun phrase, such as number, person, and possession. In transformational grammar, these are shown in a tree diagram so that the sentence's developmental structure is clear. The simplest way to show a noun's number and whether it is possessive is to use an indicator in parentheses. For example:

child (PLURAL) $\rightarrow$ children
pronoun (SINGULAR) (FIRST PERSON) $\rightarrow$ I
I (POSSESSIVE) $\rightarrow$ my

Verb Phrases

385   *Introduction.* Verb phrases are much more complex than noun phrases. Different types of verbs behave differently and have different effects on other parts of the phrase. Hence verb phrases generate many more rules. This section surveys only the basic rules and reveals how quickly they become complicated.

386   *Functions of verb phrase.* The verb phrase (VP) consists of the verb or verbs plus other elements and functions as the sentence's predicate. The simplest predicate is a principal verb standing alone or a principal verb plus an object (consisting of a noun phrase). The simple predicate is also termed a *verbal* (V). Not every kernel sentence will have an object, so the rule looks like this:

$$VP \rightarrow V + (NP)$$

387   *Principal verbs.* A principal verb (e.g., *leave, practice, swim, write*) is the simplest verb phrase (VP).

$$VP \rightarrow V$$

388　*Auxiliaries.* In transformational grammar, *auxiliary* refers to any verb in addition to the principal verb when that verb's form is controlled by the subject and may cause a change in the verbal. There are three types: (1) auxiliary verbs, (2) *be*-verbs, and (3) *have*. The auxiliary always precedes the principal verb. For each type, the symbol "Aux" is used in the rewritten formula for a verb phrase:

$$VP \rightarrow (Aux) + V$$

389　*Auxiliary verbs.* An ordinary auxiliary verb (Aux:a)—such as *must, would, may*—has no effect on the principal verb's infinitive form.

$$VP \rightarrow V \qquad\qquad go$$
$$VP \rightarrow Aux:a + V \qquad must\ go$$

But *be*-verbs (Aux:be) cause the principal verb to take an *-ing* ending.

$$VP \rightarrow V \qquad\qquad go$$
$$VP \rightarrow Aux:be + Ving \quad be\ going$$

390　*"Have."* Although *have* (Aux:have) is classified as an auxiliary verb, it causes the principal verb to take the form of its past participle. The change in the verb is indicated by showing the verb's tense.

$$VP \rightarrow (Aux:have) + V(\text{PRESENT PERFECT}) \quad go$$
$$VP \rightarrow Aux:have + V(\text{PRESENT PERFECT}) \quad have\ gone$$

391　*Multiple auxiliaries.* Auxiliary verbs and either *have* or *be* may be used in the same sentence. The principal verb is still affected by the *have* or *be*.

$VP \rightarrow V$	(We) go.
$VP \rightarrow Aux:a + V$	(We) must go.
$VP \rightarrow Aux:be + Ving$	(We) are going.
$VP \rightarrow Aux:have +$	
$\qquad V(\text{PRESENT PERFECT})$	(We) have gone.
$VP \rightarrow Aux:a + Aux:be + Ving$	(We) must be going.
$VP \rightarrow Aux:a + Aux:have +$	
$\qquad V(\text{PRESENT PERFECT})$	(We) must have gone.

392   *"Be" as a principal verb.* A *be*-verb is not always an auxiliary. When there is no other principal verb, the *be*-verb functions as the principal verb and behaves like any other principal when coupled with auxiliaries:

$$VP \rightarrow V \qquad\qquad\quad \text{(I) am (a dancer.)}$$
$$VP \rightarrow Aux{:}a + V \qquad \text{(I) will be (a dancer.)}$$
$$VP \rightarrow Aux{:}have + V \quad \text{(I) have been (a dancer.)}$$

Different Types of Principal Verbs

393   *Generally.* Principal verbs generally fall into one of three categories: *transitive* (Vt), which must have a direct object, *intransitive* (Vi), which never takes an object, and *linking* (Vlk), which takes a predicate nominative, such as a noun phrase, or a predicate adjective (Adj). (Some verbs can be transitive or intransitive. See § 139.) You can distinguish between a transitive verb and a linking principal verb by seeing whether the sentence can be rewritten in passive voice. Only transitive verbs can be grammatically expressed in the passive voice. For example, *Maribel caught the mistake* bears essentially the same meaning as the passive-voice sentence *the mistake was caught by Maribel*. Both sentences are grammatical. But in *Nancy became a real-estate agent*, the phrase *real-estate agent* is a predicate nominative (*Nancy* and *real-estate agent* refer to the same person), and **a real-estate agent was become by Nancy* isn't idiomatically possible. So *catch* is a transitive verb and *become* is a linking verb. The rule for a principal verb, then, is:

$$V \rightarrow \begin{cases} Vt \\ Vi \\ Vlk \end{cases}$$

And in the verbal:

$$VP \rightarrow \begin{cases} Vi & \text{(Ted) swims.} \\ Vlk + NP & \text{(Sue) is a conductor.} \\ Vlk + Adj & \text{(She) seems tired.} \\ Vt + NP & \text{(He) builds a house.} \end{cases}$$

394   *Middle verbs.* Some verbs, such as *cost, fit, have, resemble, suit,* and *weigh,* must have a direct object but can't be grammatically rewritten in the passive voice. A native speaker will produce a sentence like *I have a head cold* but never *A head cold is had by me*. So these are not true transitive verbs. But they also never take a predicate nominative, so neither are they linking verbs. Because they fall somewhere between the two types, we call them *middle verbs* (Vmid).

VP → Vmid + NP   (It) cost a fortune.

395 *Special subtypes.* Some transitive verbs can take either one object (a direct object) or two objects (one indirect, one direct). These verbs have two subtypes. When a verb has two objects and they are not appositives, then when the phrasing is in the passive voice, the direct object exchanges roles with the subject. It's also possible for the indirect object to become the subject, although the sentence may sound archaic. We label this subtype *Vt:do*. When a verb has two objects that are not appositives, a passive-voice phrasing has the indirect object become the subject. This verb subtype is *Vt:ido*.

K → NP + Vt:do + NP + NP
Active: My best friend sold me the painting.
Passive: The painting was sold to me by my best friend.
Passive: I was sold the painting by my best friend.

K → NP + Vt:ido + NP + NP
Active: The voters elected Green mayor.
Passive: Green was elected mayor by the voters.

Adverbials

396 *Adverbials with principal verbs.* Adverbials may be adverbs or other parts of speech functioning as adverbs, including prepositional phrases and noun phrases. The placement of an adverbial depends on the adverbial's function and the type of verb. Not every verb has an adverbial, so this element is optional in kernel sentences.

397 *Simple adverbs.* A one-word adverb (Adv) may immediately follow or precede a principal verb or may appear after a noun phrase that follows the principal verb or immediately after the first auxiliary in the verb phrase. Sometimes, too, the adverb may appear between the *to* and the infinitive (V:inf). When an infinitive is split, the *to* becomes a particle (Part). So we can further define a verbal this way:

V → Adv + V	(you) hesitantly refuse
V → V + Adv	(you) drive carefully
V → Part + V:inf + Adv	(I tried) to ask politely
V → Part + Adv + V:inf	(I tried) to politely ask
V → V + NP + Adv	(you) see your doctor alone
V → Aux:a + Adv + V	(it) will not rain
V → Aux:have + Adv + V	(it) has not rained
V → Aux:be + Adv + V	(it) is not raining
V → Aux:a + Adv + Aux:be + V	(it) must not be raining

398 *Functions of simple adverbs.* One-word adverbs can be more narrowly identified as adverbs of manner (Adv:man), time (Adv:time), place (Adv:place), and so on.

399 *Prepositional phrase as adverbial.* A prepositional phrase (PP) is any phrase that begins with a preposition and contains a noun phrase, which is the object of the preposition. As an adverbial (PP:adv), it usually follows the principal verb.

VP → (Aux) + V + (PP:adv)

400 *Noun phrase as adverbial.* A noun phrase may function as an adverbial when it is the object of a prepositional phrase from which the preposition has been dropped. A noun-phrase adverbial usually indicates manner (NPAdv:man), or especially time (NPAdv:time). A noun-phrase adverbial of time may be a noun phrase coupled with an adverb {last Monday} or a noun phrase followed by an adverb such as *ago* {a long time ago}.

Ving + NPAdv:man	(We're) going *step by step.*
Aux:a + V + NPAdv:time	(The package) will arrive *later tomorrow.*
V(PAST) + NPAdv:time	(We) finished *an hour ago.*

401 *Adverbials of place, time, and manner.* Three types of adverbials—manner (Adv:man), place (Adv:place), and time (Adv:time)—occur with transitive and intransitive verbs.

402 *Number and tense of verbs.* The general rules cover all possible sentences in present tense, but verbs must also be conjugated for number and for tense. The quality of the verb is stated in parentheses beside the affected word. For example, the basic rule for a sentence is expressed as NP + VP, but the underlying structure might be expressed as nonDet:def + numDet + N(PLURAL) + V(PAST) + nonDet:indef + Mod + N.

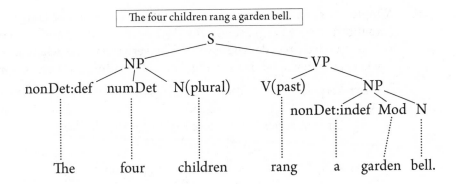

Transformations

403 ***Deep and surface structure.*** When we talk about what a speaker intends a sentence to mean, we are referring to the sentence's *deep structure.* The sentence actually produced by the speaker and the meaning perceived by others is the *surface structure.*

404 ***Transformational rules.*** The rules of grammar that govern how words are inflected and their placement in sentences are transformational rules. For example, in English grammar, kernel sentences must consist of a noun phrase (NP) and a verb phrase (VP). The rule is K → NP + VP.

> All I know about grammar is its infinite power. To shift the structure of a sentence alters the meaning of the sentence, as definitely and inflexibly as the position of a camera alters the meaning of the object photographed. Many people know about camera angles now, but not so many know about sentences.
> —Joan Didion
> "Why I Write"

405 ***Surface transformation.*** Once a sentence is formed, it may need an additional transformation to make it a question or a command, or to change its form from active to passive or vice versa. In the process of surface transformation, sentences are transformed from one form into another by rearranging, adding, or deleting small sentence elements.

406 **_Simple-question transformation._** Kernel sentences can be transformed into interrogative kernel sentences (IK) by rearranging the word order so that a verbal precedes the subject. The verbal remains where it was in the kernel sentence but may change form depending on the auxiliary.

Ex: kernel: There are snacks for the children.
                   (K → NP + VP)
   interrogative: Are there snacks for the children?
                   (IK → VP + NP)

Ex: kernel: Al should paint the room.
                   (K → NP + VP)
   interrogative: Should Al paint the room?
                   (IK → Aux:modal + NP + VP)

Ex: kernel: Al paints the walls.
                   (K → NP + VP)
   interrogative: Does Al paint the walls?
                   (IK → Aux:do + NP + VP)

Ex: kernel: Al paints the room.
                   (K → NP + VP)
   interrogative: Is Al painting the room?
                   (IK → Aux:be + NP + VP)

Ex: kernel: Al painted the room.
                   (K → NP + VP)
   interrogative: Has Al painted the room?
                   (IK → Aux:have + NP + VP)

407 **_Imperative transformation._** Kernel sentences can be transformed into imperative statements by deleting the subject and any auxiliary attached to the verbal.

Ex: kernel: You must file this.
               (NP + VP)

   imperative: File this.
               (VP)

408 *Active- to passive-voice transformation and back again.* You form the passive voice by transposing the noun phrases (subject and direct object), putting a preposition (usually *by*) before the former subject, and coupling the past-participial form of the verbal with the appropriate *be*-verb.

active: Gordon prepared a gourmet dinner.
(NP:subj + V + NP:obj)

passive: The gourmet dinner was prepared by Gordon.
(NP:obj + be V(PAST) + V(PAST) + prep + NP:subj)

passive: The winning goal was kicked by Beckham.
(NP:obj + be V(PAST) + V(PAST) + prep + NP:subj)

active: Beckham kicked the winning goal.
(NP:subj + V + NP:obj)

For more on these transformations—and on the curious uses of *subject* and *object* in the depictions above—see § 413.

Spotting Ambiguities

409 *Identification.* Ambiguity is difficult or impossible to see in traditional Reed–Kellogg diagrams. As you will see in the next few sections, tree diagrams can help make ambiguity apparent because ambiguous sentences often have at least two logical diagrams.

410 *Lexical ambiguity.* Lexical or semantic ambiguity occurs when a word (or phrase) may have more than one meaning. A diagram won't reveal the source of the problem if the word or phrase that is ambiguous serves the same function in both meanings.

For instance, in *We stopped at the bank,* the noun *bank* could refer to a financial institution or the land beside a river. A diagram can't distinguish between them, since this is a problem not of grammar or syntax but of diction, or word choice, and so is beyond the scope of sentence diagramming.

But if the word that causes the ambiguity has different functions, then the sentence can be usefully diagrammed. For example, in *They are baking pots,* we can't readily determine what function *baking* is serving: is it a verb or an adjective? We also can't tell who or what *they* refers to. Should the sentence be read as "They (people) are baking the pots (in a kiln)" or "They (the pots) are pots for baking (food)"? The diagrams reveal the ambiguity:

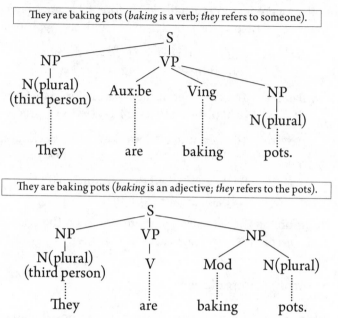

411 **Surface-structure ambiguity.** In surface-structure ambiguity, a sentence has all the necessary elements but has two possible diagrams that reflect different interpretations. For example, in *The treasurer could not approve the budget,* does the sentence mean that the treasurer was unable to approve the budget or might yet disapprove it? The diagrams show the ambiguity:

The word *not* might modify *could*:

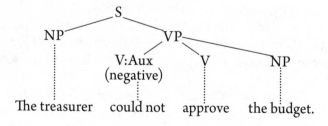

But with a different sense, the word *not* might modify *approve*:

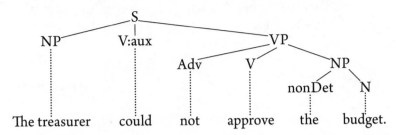

412   *Deep-structure ambiguity.* When a sentence is being formed mentally, a deep-structure ambiguity may occur because elements have been omitted or are not grouped in a way that shows the intended meaning. For example, the statement *The chicken is ready to eat* could mean that *the chicken is ready to be eaten by someone* (it's been cooked) or that *the chicken is ready to eat something* (it's hungry). The sentence has three possible tree diagrams. The diagrams have the same branches, but in the first, the surface-structure diagram, it's hard to say what function some of the words are serving or what their meaning is. The deep structures reveal the source of the ambiguities. In those, you can see that minor edits would clarify the sentence's meaning.

Surface structure: *The chicken is ready to eat.* It isn't clear what the meaning of *to eat* is or how it is related to *the chicken.* It could be a prepositional phrase or an infinitive principal verb.

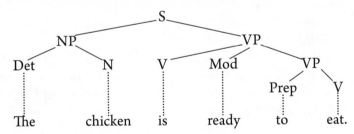

Deep structure 1: *The chicken is ready to be eaten (by somebody).* This possible meaning is in passive voice. The actor is not named. The *be*-verb is an auxiliary, and *to be eaten* is an infinitive.

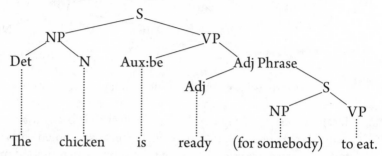

Deep structure 2: *The chicken is ready to eat (something).* This possible meaning is in active voice. *The chicken* is the actor. The *be*-verb is the principal verb, and *to* is a preposition heading the adverbial phrase *to eat (something).*

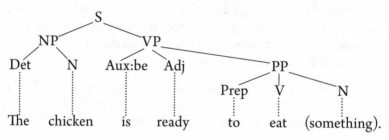

413 *Active- and passive-voice diagrams.* Passive-voice sentences are more complicated than those in active voice. When both the actor and recipient of the action are identified, the emphasis may shift slightly to whichever is named first. But unless you have a good reason to emphasize the object instead of the actor, the active voice is preferable. Diagrams show how much easier it is to understand an active-voice sentence and how much more work is required to produce a passive-voice sentence:

Active voice: *Daisy stopped Willard.*
Active-voice rules:
   Actor is subject.
   Direct object receives or is affected by the action.

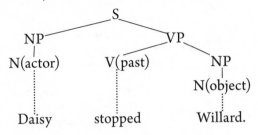

Passive voice: *Willard was stopped by Daisy.*
Passive-voice rules:
   Object receiving or affected by the action is the subject.
   Principal verb must have a *be*-verb auxiliary.
   Actor is object of a preposition.
   Prepositional phrase follows verb and acts as adverb.

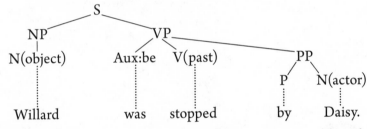

Both diagrams have the same key elements in common, although they are arranged differently: *stop* (V)(PAST), *Willard* (N)(OBJECT), and *Daisy* (N)(ACTOR).

One confusing aspect of many transformational approaches is that the word *object* is used for the recipient of the action—and in a passive-voice construction, it is actually the subject of the sentence. *Object*, then, bears a counterintuitive sense to anyone familiar with traditional grammatical approaches. In the sentence above, *Willard* is conventionally termed the *grammatical subject* and *Daisy* is the *object of a preposition*.

So be wary of the terminological transformations that occur in studying one grammatical approach as opposed to another. Again, the extensive glossary at the back of this book should prove useful to you.

III. Word Formation

414   *Generally.* Word formation, also known as *morphology*, has already come up in the discussions about the parts of speech. The inflections of verbs, the special suffixes of nouns and verbs, and the *-ly* suffix for most adverbs are all matters of word formation. It is the study of morphemes—the component parts of words. For example, *un-mis-giv-ing-ly* contains five morphemes: two prefixes, a base word or stem (*give*), and two suffixes. One of morphology's major aims is studying how specific morphemes, and changes in morphemes, express grammatical categories and relationships, such as part of speech, case, number, and tense. This subfield is called *inflectional morphology*, or *accidence*.

415   *Criteria for morphemes.* A morpheme is a short word segment that meets three tests: (1) it's a word or word part that conveys meaning; (2) it can't be divided into smaller meaningful segments without losing its meaning or leaving meaningless remainders; and (3) it retains a fairly stable meaning regardless of the context in which it appears.

Consider as an example the word *strength*. First, it's a word that is listed in every English-language dictionary. Second, it can't be divided into smaller units that would have independent meanings. Third, it has a fairly stable meaning whether in reference to someone's physical prowess, someone's moral fiber or courage, the sturdiness of a metal, or the volume of a sound. Literally or metaphorically, the word conveys a fairly consistent set of analogous senses.

Take another example: the differences between *cheap, cheapen,* and *cheapened*. *Cheap* is one morpheme; *cheapen* consists of two (*cheap* + *-en*); *cheapened* consists of three (*cheap* + *-en* + *-ed*). To *cheapen* is to make something cheap: *-en* carries the sense "to make." This morpheme occurs also in such words as *brighten, darken, enlighten, soften,* and *stiffen*. Hence

-en is a morpheme. So is *-ed*, the past-tense morpheme for countless regular verbs.

416 *Free and bound morphemes.* Morphemes are either free or bound. A free morpheme can be uttered meaningfully by itself. Simple words such as *itch* and *look* and *speak* are free morphemes. But a bound morpheme cannot be uttered by itself: it must be attached to one or more other morphemes to form a word. You would never say *-er, -ly, -non, pre-, re-,* or *un-* in isolation. Some words consist entirely of bound morphemes, examples being *combine, eject, internal, manual, modify, semblance, tenacious,* and *uxorial.*

417 *Stems and affixes.* Morphemes can also be classed as either stems or affixes. A *stem*, essentially, is the morpheme that carries the central meaning within a word {likable} {relist} {readability} {unmistakable}. Although most stems in English are free morphemes, some are not (e.g., the *dent-* in *dental, dentist, denture,* and *dentition*). These are called *bound stems.*

An affix is a bound morpheme appearing before or after a stem. English uses two types of affixes: prefixes, which occur before the stem {abnormal} {antithesis} {consent} {impersonate} {preview}; and suffixes, which occur after the stem {spillage} {licensure} {threads} {immortalize} {viewed}. Although prefixes are normally single or double in a given word—double especially when *un-* is one of the two {unexpected} {undissolved}—suffixes may come in threes and fours {atomizers [3]} {personalities [3]} {normalizers [4]}. The long word *antidisestablishmentarianism* has three prefixes (*anti-, dis-, es-*) and three suffixes (*-ment, -arian, -ism*). Forming a word by adding an affix to another word is called *derivation.*

Some languages, such as Austronesian languages, use infixes, a third type of affix inserted within a stem itself. (Prefixes and suffixes, which attach before or after a stem, are collectively called *adfixes* by contrast.) Rare examples of English infixes do occur in slang. For example, *-ma-* can imply ironic pseudosophistication {edu*ma*cation}, and *-iz-* appears in hip-hop slang {h*iz*ouse} (though this doesn't affect the word's meaning). Some technical terminology, such as chemical nomenclature, also uses infixes.

A similar process, called *tmesis*, sometimes occurs in colloquial English, whereby a speaker inserts a word (typically profanity) between the parts of a compound or other polysyllabic word for emphasis {fan-*freaking*-tastic} {when-*the-hell*-ever} {a-*whole*-nother}. But since these are whole words, not bound morphemes, they aren't true infixes. And though some grammarians consider all but the last suffix in a string to be infixes (e.g., -*ify* and -*er* in *pacifiers* or -*ize* in *colonization*), a true infix must appear within a word stem. Hence true infixes in Standard English are virtually nonexistent.

418 *Inflectional and derivational suffixes.* An inflectional suffix attaches to a word to mark it as a particular part of speech. There are eight of them:

    (1) the noun plural -*s* {cats};
    (2) the noun possessive -'*s* {cat's};
    (3) the present-tense verb's third-person-singular -*s* {permeates};
    (4) the present-participial -*ing* {permeating};
    (5) the past-tense verb's -*ed* {permeated};
    (6) the past-participial -*en* {eaten};
    (7) the comparative -*er* {smarter}; and
    (8) the superlative -*est* {smartest}.

All others are derivational suffixes, and they typically have three characteristics. First, they don't close off a word—hence you can often add another derivational suffix, so that *pole* becomes *polar* becomes *polarize* becomes *polarization*. Second, a derivational suffix usually changes the part of speech of the word to which it's added (note how this happened in the example of *pole* just given). Third, the derivational affixes that get added to specific words are known to competent users of the language but are often unpredictable. To make a noun from the verb *to establish*, we use -*ment*; for *to fail*, we use -*ure*; for *to act*, we use -*ion*; and so on.

> A *compound* differs from a *complex* word in that it is composed entirely of free forms: *bookcase, bookshelf, bookshop, bookstall*. These are *primary compounds* since each consists of two simple free forms. Such primary compounds differ from *word-groups* or *phrases* in (a) phonemic qualities of components; (b) juncture; or (c) stress; or by a combination of two or more of these. Thus the primary compound *blackbird* differs from the phrase *black bird* in (c); *already* from *all ready* in (b) and (c); and *gentleman* from *gentle man* in (a), (b) and (c). In describing the structure of a compound the investigator should examine (1) the relation of the members to each other; and (2) the relation of the whole compound to its members.
> —Simeon Potter
> *Modern Linguistics*

419 *Compounding.* When two stems are combined to form a new word, they are said to be compounded. The stems may but don't have to be the same part of speech. For example:

    adjective–adjective: bitter + sweet → bittersweet
    adjective–noun: black + board → blackboard

adjective–verb: white + wash → whitewash
noun–noun: basket + ball → basketball
noun–verb: tooth + pick → toothpick (though *pick* can also be a noun)
preposition–preposition: in + to → into
preposition–verb: out + run → outrun
verb–adverb: stand + still → standstill
verb–noun: work + room → workroom
verb–preposition: run + down → rundown
verb–verb: stir + fry → stirfry

A compositional compound is one whose meaning comes from the meanings of its parts. For example, *redbird* denotes a bird that is red, and *lawbook* denotes a book about law. (The process of making such compounds is called *agglutination*.) A noncompositional compound has a meaning that is different from those of its parts. For example, *breakdown* has never meant "a fracture in a downward direction."

420 *Conversion.* The process of conversion occurs whenever a word is changed from one part of speech to another {we watched tomatoes being canned} {we pickled some pears} {that was a fine throw}. There are two types of conversion: complete and partial. In complete conversion, the word can take all the prefixes and suffixes used for a particular part of speech. A completely converted word has all the characteristics of the part of speech that it functions as and none of any other. For example, when *slow* is used as a verb, it can take suffixes to change the tense: *slow–slowed–slowed*. And when it's an adjective, it can take suffixes to show comparison: *slow–slower–slowest*. In partial conversion, a word functioning as a different part of speech won't take some characteristics (such as affixes) or function as only one part of speech. For instance, *boy* may be an adjective or a noun at the same time {boy king [the king is very young; the boy is a king]}.

For more on noun conversions, see §§ 41–44; for more on adjective conversions, see §§ 133–36.

421 *Shortened forms.* Many words are truncated forms of longer words. Speakers of English are notoriously parsimonious with their syllables—hence they will lop off the beginning of a word (*bus* comes from *omnibus, copter* from *helicopter, plane* from *airplane*); the end of a word or phrase (*coed* comes from *coeducational student, co-op* from *cooperative, comp* from *composition, math* from *mathematics*); and sometimes both the beginning and the end of a word (*flu* comes from *influenza, fridge* from *refrigerator*).

There are technical terms denoting the processes resulting in clipped forms. If the initial syllable or syllables are dropped {phone}, it's called *aphaeresis*. If the middle of a word is dropped {ne'er} {apothegm [from *apophthegm*—an epigram or aphorism]}, it's called *syncope* or *hyphaeresis*. If the end of a word is dropped {ad} {oft}, it's called *apocope*. The sounds are typically lost because they are unstressed in speech. Compounds may also have clipped forms (compound-clipping). Part of one or each word may be dropped (*pop music* from *popular music*), and the result may form one word (*navicert* from *navigation certificate*, *sitcom* from *situation comedy*).

Clippings typically begin as slang within special groups that are so familiar with a word that hearing only part of it is sufficient to get the whole meaning. For example, a business plans to run an *ad* {advertisement}, a doctor performs a physical *exam* {examination}, and a paratrooper packs a *chute* {parachute}. If clippings are adopted by the general public, they become part of standard language; otherwise, they remain group-specific slang.

422 *Elongations.* Sometimes words get lengthened, usually unnecessarily. Hence *preventive* often becomes **preventative*—the addition of the extra syllable in the middle of a word being called *epenthesis*. There are many common forms of epenthesis in dialectal English. One is the addition of a consonant, such as *r*, to separate vowel sounds in adjacent syllables {*drawing* becomes /draw-ring/ or to lengthen a sound {*wash* becomes /warsh/}. Another is the addition of a consonant with a labial sound, such as *p* or *b*, before one with an alveolar {*something* becomes /somepthing/} {*family* becomes /fambly/}. Or a vowel may be inserted between consonants {*athlete* becomes /athalete/} {*realtor* becomes /realator/}.

Another type of elongation occurs with back-formed words, in which a longer form of a verb is created from a cognate noun. Hence **administrate* is a back-formation (or *denominal verb*) from the noun *administration*—the verb *administer* being standard. Other examples are **cohabitate*, **delimitate*, **filtrate*, **interpretate*, **revolute*, **solicitate*.

Still another type of elongation occurs with slangy infixes—discussed previously as *tmesis* in § 417.

423   *Reduplicative forms.* Many two-part words consist of repeated syllables, rhyming syllables, or syllables that sound like an earlier one but with a change in vowel or in an initial consonant. Many are solid:

> boohoo
> flimflam
> froufrou
> hobnob
> hodgepodge
> humdrum
> knickknack
> kowtow
> powwow
> riffraff
> zigzag

Others are treated as hyphenated compounds or even unhyphenated phrases:

> boo-boo
> boogie-woogie
> helter-skelter
> hocus pocus
> hurly-burly
> jiggery-pokery
> pooh-pooh
> willy-nilly

424   *Loan translations.* A loan translation, or *calque*, is a word formed by translating the elements of a foreign word to produce a word consisting of native elements—the word's meaning generally corresponding closely to that of the foreign word. Hence *masterpiece* seems to have been formed in the 18th century to correspond either to the Dutch word *meesterstuk* or to the German word *Meisterstück*, both meaning "a piece of work so good as to qualify a worker as a master craftsman." Other examples are *standpoint* from the German *Standpunkt* and *homesickness* from *Heimweh*.

425   *Acronyms and initialisms.* The two types of abbreviations known as *acronyms* and *initialisms* are similar but distinct. An acronym consists of the first letters of parts of a compound term and is treated as a single word {scuba = self-contained underwater breathing apparatus} {NATO = North Atlantic Treaty Organization}. Some acronyms, such as *scuba*, *laser,* and *radar,* eventually become words. An initialism is also made of the first letters, but each letter is sounded separately {DNA = deoxyribonucleic acid} {rpm = revolutions per minute}.

426 *Neologisms.* Neologisms, or newly coined words, may be introduced into the language in many ways. They may be made from people's names {the special interests are trying to bork our nominee}, they may be portmanteau words {this family uses *hangry* for someone who is angry because of hunger}, they may be colorfully metaphorical {they're all a bunch of couch potatoes}, they may take nontraditional affixes {he's become an online shopaholic}, they may denote new technological phenomena {Dad took a selfie!}, or they may be nontraditional collocations newly taken to form a lexical unit {he's doing some online training}. There are others. Because lexicographers monitor new entrants into the language, it's always a good idea to consult an up-to-date, reputable dictionary. Often it can take a long time for neologisms to settle into the language and lose their newfangled feel. That is less true of technological innovations that become an everyday part of people's lives {cellphone} {handheld device} {podcast} {webinar}.

Launching neologisms is no easy matter: reputable lexicographers won't admit a term into their dictionaries until it has proved itself by gaining a significant degree of currency. How and why words take root in the language—or fail to—remains something of a mystery. A successful word somehow fills a need. Speakers of a language hear it and read it. If enough of them find it serviceable—and "enough" is really not very many, in real numbers—then it will be recorded in various writings, including transcripts of the spoken word. Ultimately it will be enshrined in a dictionary. But it's a word, assuredly, long before that.

IV. Word Usage

Introduction

427   *Grammar vs. usage.* The great mass of linguistic issues that writers and editors wrestle with don't really concern grammar at all—they concern usage: the collective habits of a language's native speakers. It's an arbitrary fact, but ultimately an important one, that *corollary* means one thing and *correlation* something else. Yet there seems to be an irresistible law of language that two words so similar in sound will inevitably be confounded by otherwise literate users of language—a type of mistake called *catachresis*. Some confusions, such as the one just cited, are relatively new. Others, such as *lay* vs. *lie* and *infer* vs. *imply*, are much older.

428   *Standard Written English.* In any age, careful users of language will make distinctions; careless users of language will blur them. We can tell, by the words that someone uses and the way they go together, something about the education and background of that person. We know whether people speak educated English and write what is commonly referred to as Standard Written English.

     Just as the best-written English reads as if it were spoken—it is speakable—the best-spoken English is refined enough that it could be transcribed with minimal editing. But few speakers approach that ideal—and no sensible person would want to at all moments. Even so, polished writers and speakers tend to narrow the gap between the written word and the spoken word.

429   *Dialect.* Of course, some writers and speakers prefer to use dialect, and use it to good effect. Will Rogers is a good example. He had power as a speaker of dialect, as when he said: "Liberty don't work near as good in practice as it does in speeches." And fiction writers often use dialect in dialogue. They may even decide to put the speaker's voice in dialect. Such decisions fall outside the scope of this book.

430   *Focus on tradition.* In the short space of this chapter, only the basics of Standard Written English can be covered. Because no language stands still—because the standards of good usage change, however slowly—no guide could ever be written to the satisfaction of all professional editors.

What is intended here is a guide that steers writers and editors toward the unimpeachable uses of language—hence it takes a fairly traditional view of usage. For the writer or editor of most prose intended for a general audience, the goal is to stay within the mainstream of literate language as it stands today.

Troublesome Words and Phrases

431   *Good usage vs. common usage.* Several first-rate American desktop dictionaries are now available. The best dictionary-makers are signaled by the imprints of Merriam-Webster, Webster's New World, American Heritage, Oxford University Press, and Random House.

> One justification sometimes heard for freedom in breaking the rules of the language game is that languages change with time anyway. But that argument is beside the point. Even though the rules may change tomorrow, they are still binding while they are in force today.
>
> —Peter Farb
> *Word Play*

But one must use care and judgment in consulting *any* dictionary. The mere presence of a word in the dictionary's pages does not mean that the word is in all respects fit for print as Standard Written English. The dictionary merely describes how speakers of English have used the language; despite occasional usage notes, lexicographers generally disclaim any intent to guide writers and editors on the thorny points of English usage—apart from collecting evidence of what others do. So *infer* is recorded as meaning, in one of its senses, *imply*; **irregardless* as meaning *regardless*; **restauranteur* as meaning *restaurateur*; and on and on. That is why, in the publishing world, it is generally necessary to consult a style or usage guide, such as *Fowler's Modern English Usage* or my own *Garner's Modern English Usage*.

The standards of good usage make demands on writers and editors, whereas common usage can excuse any number of slipshod expressions. Even so, good usage should make only reasonable demands—not setting outlandishly high standards. The purpose of the following glossary is to set out the reasonable demands of good usage as it stands today, with the benefit of longtime empirical study of the subject together with new tools that rely on big data.

432   *Using big data to assess linguistic change.* Since the late 20th century, so-called corpus linguistics has allowed researchers to assess the relative prevalence of words, phrases, and linguistic constructions within a huge sampling of texts. Many vast corpora have been assembled and used, but in recent years they have all been dwarfed by the Google ngram, which reflects a corpus of almost all the books published in the English language—about 5.2 million of them—from 1500 to (at present) 2008. The Google ngram allows you to search for a string of up to five words; to limit the temporal range as you wish, as long as the years occur from 1500 to 2008; and to define the corpus as World English, American English, British English, and even subsets such as English fiction. (To use ngrams yourself, simply search "ngram viewer" and start tinkering with searches: it's extraordinarily easy to use. For comparative searches, separate the terms you're searching for with a comma.) What is especially useful for our purposes is that the word-frequency data reflect the considered choices of published authors and professional editors. Because the type-faces used since 1700 or so are more reliably susceptible of optical-char-acter-recognition (OCR) technology, the ngrams reproduced throughout the following glossary display mostly post-1700 results.

The numbers to the left of an online ngram are relatively unimportant for understanding the significance of the graph: they indicate the fre-quency of a given search term in relation to the entire corpus and are expressed in infinitesimal per-centages. Although these numbers are omitted from the ngrams here reproduced, their data have been translated into word-frequency ratios—typically using the most recent data available (from 2008). What is important is the graph line over time, indicating the emergence of a search term and its frequency in comparison with another search term. Here you can see which of two expressions has

> There are, of course, degrees of cor-rectness, and there is no such thing as speaking a language perfectly. There must always be room, on the frontiers, as it were, even among the best author-ities on usage. But a certain minimal conformity to rules of pronunciation, syntax, and meaning is a necessary condition for speaking a language even "badly" or "incorrectly." The idea of somebody "getting everything wrong" while speaking English makes no more sense than that of somebody playing the Moonlight Sonata but never hitting a right note. We recognize "error" by its presence against a background of rule conformity.
> —Max Black
> *The Labyrinth of Language*

preponderated in printed works over what period of time. From that information about word frequency, it is possible to draw certain conclu-sions—circumspectly, one hopes. You can certainly imagine how a rash partisan might use ngrams to urge fallacious conclusions, as by arguing that *any* evidence of use in print is enough to say that a given wording is standard. Statistics are *always* subject to abuse and distortion. With pru-dent use, however, ngrams introduce a healthy dose of empiricism to dis-cussions of English usage.

The effect is to base linguistic judgments about word frequency, and therefore about many elements of Standard Written English, on solid empirical evidence. It is now possible, through big data, to know with some certainty which usages are mainstream in Standard Written English and which ones are linguistic outliers, variants, and anomalies—and to chart changes over time. Up to now, pronouncements of this kind were necessarily based on linguistic guesswork and extrapolation.

Note that some degree of savvy is necessary in framing ngram searches. You can't get reliable results if you simply search for "home in, hone in" because of the innumerable false hits you'll receive: every instance of *her home in Malibu* (or *Katmandu*, etc.) will skew the results. And the vast literature may contain instances of such constructions as *he preferred to hone in his shed* (hone his tools, that is). So the search terms must give enough context to retrieve useful results. Hence "home in on, hone in on"—or even the past-tense forms "homed in on, honed in on"—will yield reliable results. For past participles, the contextualizing auxiliaries are critically important: one can't simply search for "swam, swum" to know whether *swum* is the predominant past participle, but instead "had swam, had swum." Variations with *has* and *have* will yield similar results, as you can test for yourself.

433   *Preventive grammar.* If a technically correct form of words might sound pretentious, awkward, or untrue to your voice, try another phrasing that sounds more natural. Sentences like these may be strictly "correct," but they're odd:

> It is I to whom thanks are due.
> He gave it to me, who am grateful.
> Neither they nor he is responsible.
> Would it were she had been there!

Instead of trying to defend those sentences against someone who suggests they might be "wrong," you're better off not having the question arise at all, as by writing:

> They owe me a thank-you.
> He gave it to me—and I'm grateful.
> They're not responsible, and neither is he.
> If only she had been there!

It is hardly good to use "defensible" language that sounds alien, creaky, or artificial to ordinary readers—that is, to ordinary educated readers. The best course is to find an alternative expression.

434 *Glossary of troublesome expressions.*

> **a; an.** Use the indefinite article *a* before any word beginning with a consonant sound {a euphonious phrase} {a utopian dream}. Use *an* before any word beginning with a vowel sound {an officer} {an honorary degree}. The word *historical* and its variations cause missteps, but if the *h*- in these words is pronounced, it takes an *a* {an hour-long talk at a historical society}. The accompanying illustration shows this to be the strong trend since the early 20th century.
>
> Likewise, an initialism (whose letters are sounded out) may be paired with one article, while an acronym (which is pronounced as a word) beginning with the same letter is paired with the other {an HTML website for a HUD program}. See § 111.

2008 Ratio of Frequency in Printed Books: 4:1

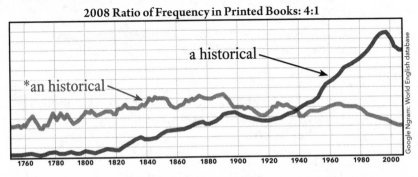

> **ability; capability; capacity.** *Ability* refers to a person's physical or mental power or skill to do something {the ability to ride a bicycle}. *Capability* refers more generally to power or ability to do something challenging {she has the capability to play soccer professionally} or to the quality of being able to use or be used in a certain way {a jet with long-distance-flight capability}. *Capacity* refers especially to a vessel's ability to hold or contain something {a high-capacity fuel tank}. Used figuratively, *capacity* refers especially to a person's physical or mental power to learn {an astounding capacity for mathematics}. It can also be used as a synonym for *ability* {capacity for love}, as a formal word for someone's job, position, or role {in an advisory capacity}, as a word denoting an amount that can be produced or dealt with {full capacity}, or as a means of denoting size or power {engine capacity}.
>
> **abjure; adjure.** To *abjure* is to deny or renounce publicly, esp. under oath {the defendant abjured the charge of murder} or to declare one's permanent abandonment of a place {abjure the realm}. To *adjure* is to charge someone to do something as if under oath {I adjure you to keep this

secret} or to try earnestly to persuade {the executive committee adjured all the members to approve the plan}. Some writers misuse *adjure* for either *abhor* (= to detest) or *require* (= to mandate).

about; approximately. When idiomatically possible, use the adverb *about* instead of *approximately*. In the sciences, however, *approximately* is preferred {approximately 32 coding-sequence differences were identified}. Avoid coupling either word with another word of approximation, such as *guess* or *estimate*.

abridgment. So spelled in AmE. In BrE, the medial *-e-* is preferred (except in law).

abrogate; arrogate. To *abrogate* something is to repeal or disregard it {abrogate a treaty} {abrogate one's duties}. To *arrogate* something is to take it (usu. an office or a responsibility) for oneself without the authority or right to do so {once in office, the former general arrogated full control of the military} or, less often, to give responsibility to someone else {arrogate the decision to a subcommittee}.

abstruse. See **obtuse.**

accept; except. To *accept* something is to receive it {accept this gift} or regard it as proper {accept the idea}. To *except* something is to exclude it or leave it out {club members will be excepted from the admission charge}, and to *except to* something is to object to it.

acceptance; acceptation. *Acceptance* is the general term, referring to approval, toleration, or admission {acceptance into law school}. *Acceptation* is a highly specialized term referring to the common (or "accepted") meaning, usage, or pronunciation of a word {*hopefully* in its oldest acceptation denotes "in a hopeful manner"}.

access, *vb.* The conversion of nouns to verbs has long been one of the most common ways that word-usage changes happen in English. Today, few people quibble with using *contact, debut,* or *host,* for example, as a verb. *Access* can be safely used as a verb when referring to computing {access a computer} {access the Internet} {access a database}. Outside the digital world, though, it can be jarring and is best avoided. Cf. **impact.**

The ngram illustration is intended not to show whether a given usage is standard, but only the relative frequency of wholly unrelated terms—and the precipitate rise of *access* as a verb.

1960 Ratio of Frequency in Printed Books (*accessed* vs. *contacted*): 1:98
2008 Ratio of Frequency in Printed Books: 3:1

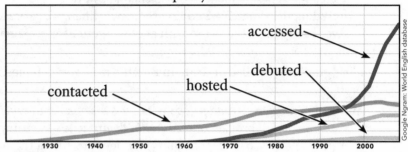

accord; accordance. The first word means "agreement" {we are in accord on the treaty's meaning} {we have reached an accord}. The second word means "conformity" {the book was printed in accordance with modern industry standards}.

accuse; charge. A person is *accused of* or *charged with* a misdeed. *Accused* is less formal than *charged* (which suggests official action). Compare *Jill accused Jack of eating her chocolate bar* with *Maynard was charged with theft.*

acknowledgment. So spelled in AmE. In BrE, the *-dgem-* spelling is preferred (except in law).

acquiesce. To *acquiesce* is to do what someone else wants or to passively allow something to happen. The connotation is usually acceptance without enthusiasm or even with opposition that is not acted on. The word traditionally takes the preposition *in* {the minority party acquiesced in the nomination}, although *to* is also accepted. *With* is not standard.

actual fact, in. Redundant. Try *actually* instead, or simply omit.

acuity; acumen. What is *acute* is sharp, and these two words apply to mental sharpness. *Acuity* most often refers to sharpness of perception—the ability to think, see, or hear clearly {visual acuity}. *Acumen* always refers to mental prowess, esp. the ability to think quickly and make good judgments.

adapt. See **adopt.**

addenda (= [1] additional items, or [2] a list of additional items) is a plural {the addenda are in order}. The singular is *addendum* {we have a single addendum}.

addicted; dependent. In the best usage, one is physically *addicted* to something but psychologically *dependent* on something.

adduce; deduce; induce. To *adduce* is to give as a reason, offer as a proof, or cite as an example in order to prove that something is true {as evidence of reliability, she adduced her four years of steady volunteer work as a nurse's aide}. *Deduce* and *induce* are opposite processes. To *deduce* is to reason from general principles to specific conclusions, or to draw a specific conclusion from general knowledge {from these clues about who committed the crime, one deduces that the butler did it}. In a related logical sense, to *induce* is to form a general principle based on specific observations {after years of studying ravens, the researchers induced a few of their social habits}. In its mere common uses, however, to *induce* is (1) to persuade someone to do something, esp. something unwise {nothing could induce me to try that again}; (2) to make a woman give birth to her baby, as by administering a drug {induce labor}; or (3) to cause a particular physical condition {induce vomiting}.

adequate; sufficient; enough. *Adequate* refers to the suitability of something in a particular circumstance {an adequate explanation} {adequate provisions}. *Sufficient* refers to an amount that is enough to meet a particular need (always with an abstract concept, a mass noun, or a plural) {sufficient water} {sufficient information} {sufficient cause} {sufficient resources}. *Enough*, the best word for everyday purposes, meaning "as much or as many as are needed or wanted," modifies both count nouns {enough people} and mass nouns {enough oil}.

adherence; adhesion. With a few exceptions, the first term is figurative, the second literal. Your *adherence* to the transportation code requires the *adhesion* of an inspection sticker to your windshield.

adjure. See **abjure.**

administrator. See **executor.**

admission; admittance. *Admission* is generally figurative, suggesting particularly the rights and privileges granted with permission to enter {the student won admission to a first-rate university} or

> People really do judge one another according to their use of language. Constantly. . . . "Correct" English usage is, as a practical matter, a function of whom you're talking to and of how you want that person to respond—not just to your utterance but also to *you*.
> —David Foster Wallace
> "Authority and American Usage"

the price paid for entry {admission is $10}. *Admittance* is more limited and more a matter of physical entry, but it too is tinged with the idea of permission {no admittance beyond this point}.

adopt; adapt. To *adopt* something is to take it as your own, most often a child but also a belief, cause, name, hobby, pet, and so forth. To *adapt* something is to apply it to a new use or to change it to make it suitable for a different purpose {adapting the car to run on ethanol}; the word is often used reflexively {adapt herself to a new job}.

adopted; adoptive. *Adopted* applies to a child or dependent {adopted son}. It is incorrect when applied to the ones who do the adopting; instead, use *adoptive*, the more general adjective corresponding to *adopt* {adoptive parents}.

adverse; averse. Though etymologically related, these words have undergone differentiation. *Adverse* means either "strongly opposed" or "unfavorable" and typically refers to things (not people) {adverse relations between the nations complicated matters} {an adverse wind blew the ship off course}. *Averse* means "feeling negatively about" or "having a strong dislike or unwillingness," and it refers to people {he's averse to asking for directions}.

advise; advice. To *advise* is to give *advice*. Some writers have trouble with words whose noun form ends in *-ice* and verb form in *-ise*. It might help to remember the pronunciation of *-ice*; if that doesn't fit the word you're writing, you know to make it *-ise*. Avoid using *advise* as a pretentious substitute for *tell*—save it for times when actual advice is given.

adviser; advisor. The first spelling has long been editorially preferred. Yet *-or* now rivals it in frequency, perhaps through the influence of the adjective *advisory*.

1960 Ratio of Frequency in Printed Books: 4:1

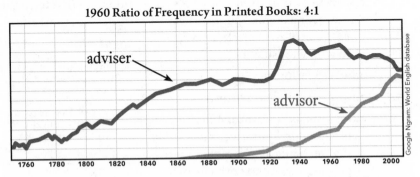

affect; effect. *Affect*, almost always a verb, means "to influence or do something that produces a change; to have an effect on" {the adverse publicity affected the election}. To *affect* can also mean "to pretend to have a particular feeling or manner" {affecting a Scottish accent}. (The noun *affect* has a specialized meaning in psychology: emotional expressiveness. Consult your dictionary.) *Effect*, usually a noun, means "an outcome, result" {the candidate's attempted explanations had no effect} or "a change caused by an event, action, occurrence, etc." {harmful effects of smoking}. But it may also be a verb meaning "to make happen, produce" {the goal had been to effect a major change in campus politics}.

affirmative, in the; in the negative. These are slightly pompous ways of saying *yes* and *no*. They result in part because people are unsure how to punctuate *yes* and *no*. The ordinary way is this: *he said yes* (without quotation marks around *yes*, and without a capital); *she said no* (ditto).

afflict. See **inflict.**

affront. See **effrontery.**

*after having [+ **past participle**]. Though common, this phrasing is redundant. Try instead *after* [+ present participle]: change *after having passed the audition, she . . .* to *after passing the audition, she . . . .* Or this: *having passed the audition, she . . . .*

2008 Ratio of Frequency in Printed Books: 11:1

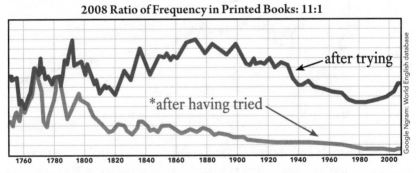

afterward, *adv.;* **afterword,** *n.* The first means "later"; the second means "an epilogue." On *afterward(s)*, see **toward.**

*aged (four) years old. Redundant. Write *aged four years, four years old,* or *four years of age.*

agenda. Though the Latin etymon is plural—and although even the singular *agendum* sometimes appears in English—the noun *agenda* has taken on singular senses in Modern English: either "a list of subjects or problems to be dealt with" {high on the agenda} or, "collectively, the ideas, esp. social or political ideas, that a person or group hopes to promote" {hidden agenda}. Even though some hard-core Latinists object to it, *agendas* is the plural in English.

aggravate. Traditionally, *aggravate* most properly means "to intensify (something bad)" {aggravate an injury} {an aggravated crime}. If the sense is "to bother," try *annoy* or *irritate* or *exasperate* instead.

aid; aide. *Aid* can be a verb (= to help) or a noun (= assistance). *Aide* is a noun (= helper), as in *teacher's aide*; in military parlance, it denotes someone assigned to help a superior officer {general's aide}.

*ain't. This contraction is famously dialectal—a word not to be used except either in the dialogue of a nonstandard speaker or in jest.

alibi. Avoid this as a synonym for *excuse*. The traditional sense is "the defense of having been elsewhere when a crime was committed."

all (of). Delete the *of* whenever possible {all the houses} {all my children}. The most common exception occurs when *all of* precedes a nonpossessive pronoun {all of us} {all of them}.

1803 Ratio of Frequency in Printed Books: 210:1
2008 Ratio of Frequency in Printed Books: 8:1

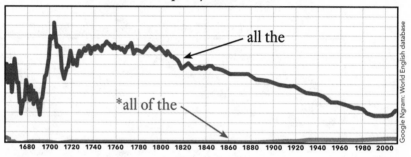

alleged. Traditional usage applies this participial adjective to things, esp. acts {alleged burglary}, not to the actors accused of doing them {alleged burglar}. That distinction is still observed by some publications, but it has largely been abandoned. Although *allegedly* /ə-**lej**-əd-lee/ has four syllables, *alleged* has only two: /ə-**lejd**/.

all ready. See **already**.

all right. Two words. Avoid *alright*—which has long been regarded as nonstandard.

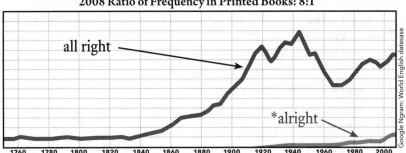

2008 Ratio of Frequency in Printed Books: 8:1

all together. See **altogether.**

allude; elude; illude. To *allude* is to hint at something indirectly {he alluded to the war by mentioning "our recent national unpleasantness"}. It's often loosely used where *refer* or *quote* would be better—that is, where there is a direct mention or quotation. To *elude* is to avoid capture {the fox eluded the hunters}. To *illude* (quite rare) is to deceive {your imagination might illude you}.

allusion; reference. An *allusion* is an indirect or casual mention or suggestion of something {the cockroach in this story is an allusion to Kafka}. A *reference* is a direct or formal mention {the references in this scholarly article have been meticulously documented}. See **reference.**

alongside. This term, meaning "at the side of," should not be followed by *of.*

a lot. Two words, not one.

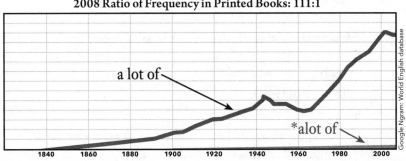

2008 Ratio of Frequency in Printed Books: 111:1

already; all ready. The first refers to time {the movie has already started}; the second refers to people's preparation {are the actors all ready?}.

*alright. See **all right.**

altar, *n.;* **alter,** *vb.* An *altar* is a table or similar object used for sacramental purposes. To *alter* is to change.

alternate, *adj. & n.;* **alternative,** *adj. & n. Alternate* implies (1) a substitute for another {we took the alternate route} or (2) every other or every second {alternate Saturdays}. *Alternative* implies availability as another, usu. sounder choice or possibility {alternative fuel sources}. The noun uses are analogous {the awards committee named her as alternate} {we have no alternative}.

although; though. Euphony governs the choice. *Although* is somewhat more formal.

altogether; all together. *Altogether* means "wholly" or "entirely" {that story is altogether false}. *All together* refers to a unity of time or place {the family will be all together at Thanksgiving}.

alumnus; alumna; alumni; alumnae. Traditionally male, *alumnus* has in recent decades been considered unmarked or gender-neutral. The casualism *alum* is more obviously unmarked. *Alumna* is marked as feminine, as is its plural *alumnae*; both are used primarily at girls' schools and women's colleges and universities. The plural *alumni* is unmarked for sex, esp. where the people referred to are males and females. Using *alumni* as a singular {*I'm an alumni of that school!} is poor usage.

amend; emend. The first is the general term, meaning "to change or add to something written or spoken" {the city amended its charter to abolish at-large council districts} or "to make better" {amend your behavior!}. The second means "to remove one or more mistakes from (a text, etc.)" {for the second printing, the author emended several typos that had reached print in the first}. The noun corresponding to *amend* is *amendment*; the one corresponding to *emend* is *emendation*.

amiable; amicable. Both mean "friendly," but *amiable* refers to people who are easy to like {an amiable waiter} and *amicable* to relationships that involve goodwill and a lack of quarreling {an amicable divorce}.

amid. See **between.**

among. See **between.**

amount; number. *Amount* is used with mass nouns {a decrease in the amount of pollution} {a small amount of money}. *Number* is used with count nouns {a growing number of dissidents} {the number of coins in your pocket}.

an. See **a.**

and. Popular belief to the contrary, this conjunction usefully begins sentences, typically outperforming *moreover, additionally, in addition, further,* and *furthermore.* (See § 277.) Yet it does not occur as a sentence-starter as often as *but.* See **but.**

2008 Ratio of Frequency in Printed Books (*And* vs. *Further*): 19:1

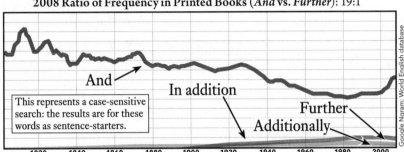

and/or. Avoid this Janus-faced term. It can often be replaced by *and* or *or* with no loss in meaning. Where it seems needed {take a sleeping pill and/or a warm drink}, try ... *or* ..., *or both* {take a sleeping pill or a warm drink, or both}. But think of other possibilities {take a sleeping pill, perhaps with a warm drink}.

anecdotal. This adjective corresponds to *anecdote,* but in one sense the words have opposite connotations. An anecdote is a story that is thought (but not known) to be true. But *anecdotal evidence* refers to accounts that are suspect because they are not objectively verified.

anecdote; antidote. An *anecdote* is a story, usu. illustrative of a situation or of a person's character. An *antidote* counteracts poison or, by extension, a problem or a bad situation.

angry. See **mad.**

anticipate. Avoid this word as a loose synonym for *expect.* Strictly, it means either "to foresee, take care of in advance, or forestall" {a good writer anticipates a reader's queries as they arise} or "to do something before someone else" {ancient rhetoricians anticipated the findings of modern reader-expectation theorists}.

anxious. Avoid it as a synonym for *eager.* The standard sense is "worried, nervous, distressed."

anyone; any one. The one-word *anyone* is a singular indefinite pronoun used in reference to no one in particular {anyone would know that}. The two-word phrase *any one* is a more emphatic form of *any,* referring to a single person or thing in a group {do you recognize any one of those boys?} {I don't know any one of those stories}.

anyplace. See **anywhere.**

anyway; *anyways. The former is standard; the latter, traditionally considered dialectal, has made inroads into the speech of many otherwise educated people born since about 1980. But it remains nonstandard.

2008 Ratio of Frequency in Printed Books: 84:1

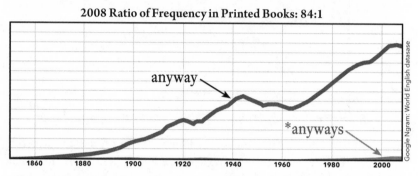

anywhere; any place. The first is preferred for an indefinite location {my keys could be anywhere}. But *any place* (two words) is narrower when you mean "any location" {they couldn't find any place to sit down and rest}. Avoid the informal one-word **anyplace.*

apparatus. Pl. *apparatuses*—not **apparati* (false Latin). The correct Latin plural, *apparatus* (unchanged in form as a fourth-declension noun), is sometimes used in technical contexts. The false Latin **apparati* typifies a common form of hypercorrection.

2008 Ratio of Frequency in Printed Books: 21:1

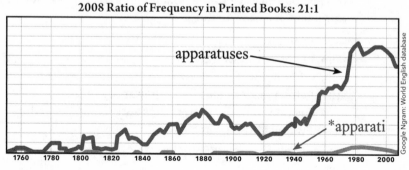

appendix. Pl. *appendixes* or *appendices.*

appertain. See **pertain.**

appraise; apprise. To *appraise* is to assess or put a value on something {the jeweler appraised the necklace}. To *apprise* is to inform or notify someone about something {keep me apprised of any developments}.

appreciate. Three senses: (1) to understand fully; (2) to increase in value; (3) to be grateful for (something). Sense 3 often results in verbose constructions; instead of *I would appreciate it if you would let me know*, try *I would appreciate your letting me know* or, more simply, *please let me know*.

apprise. See **appraise.**

approve; endorse. *Approve* implies positive thought or a positive attitude rather than action apart from consent. *Endorse* implies both a positive attitude and active support.

approve (of). *Approve* alone connotes official sanction or acceptance {the finance committee approved the proposed budget}. *Approve of* suggests thinking favorably about {she approved of her sister's new hairstyle}.

approximately. See **about.**

apt; likely. Both mean "fit, suitable," but *apt* is used for general tendencies or habits {the quarterback is apt to drop the football}. *Likely* expresses probability {because he didn't study, it's likely that he'll do poorly on the exam}. Although *likely* is traditional as a synonym of *probable*, many writers and editors object to its use as a synonym of *probably*.

    Apt has two other senses: (1) "exactly right for a given situation or purpose" {an apt remark}, and (2) "quick to learn" {an apt pupil}.

area. Often a nearly meaningless filler word, as in *the area of partnering skills*. Try deleting *the area of*. In the sciences, however, its more literal meaning is often important and should be retained. Cf. **space.**

arrogate. See **abrogate.**

as far as. Almost always wordy. Avoid the nonstandard phrasing that uses *as far as* in place of *as for*—that is, avoid using *as far as* without the completing verb *is concerned* or *goes*. Compare *as far as change is concerned, it's welcome* with *as for change, it's welcome*.

> It cannot . . . be laid down too emphatically that it is not the business of grammarians or scholars to decide what is good usage. Their function is limited to ascertaining and recording it. This can only be done by the prolonged and careful study of the language, as it has been employed by its best authors.
> —Thomas R. Lounsbury
> *History of the English Language*

as is. In reference to an acquisition, *as is* is framed in quotation marks and refers to the acceptance of something without guarantees or representations of quality {purchased "as is"}. The phrase *on an "as is" basis* is verbose.

***as of yet.** See *as yet.

***as per.** This phrase, though common in the commercial world, has long been considered nonstandard. Instead of **as per your request*, write *as you requested* or (less good) *per your request.* The recent innovation **as per usual* for *as usual* is an illiteracy.

assault; battery. These are popularly given the same meaning. But in law *assault* refers to a threat that causes someone to reasonably fear physical violence, and *battery* refers to a violent or repugnant intentional physical contact with another person. In the strict legal sense, an assault doesn't involve touching; a battery does.

assemblage; assembly. An *assemblage* is an informal collection of people or things. An *assembly* is a group of people, esp. decision-makers, organized for a purpose {a national assembly}, a meeting {regular public assemblies}, or the process of putting together the parts of something {instructions for assembly}.

assent; consent. The meanings are similar, but *assent* connotes a more affirmative agreement after careful consideration; *consent* connotes mere allowance, or sometimes grudging acquiescence.

as such. This pronominal phrase always requires an antecedent for *such* {satellite TV is a luxury and, as such, has a limited market}. The phrase is now often loosely used as a synonym for *therefore.* Avoid this misusage.

> **Poor:** Science seeks out truth in an organized way and, as such, must be looked upon as an end in itself.
>
> **Better:** Science is the organized search for truth and, as such, must be looked upon as an end in itself.

assumption; presumption. An *assumption* is not drawn from strong evidence; typically, it is a hypothesis that one accepts as true without definite proof {your assumption can be tested by looking at the public records}. A *presumption* implies a basis in evidence or at least experience; if uncontradicted, a *presumption* may support a decision {the legal presumption of innocence}.

assure. See **ensure.**

as to. This two-word preposition is best used only to begin a sentence that could begin with *on the question of* or *with regard to* {as to those checks, she didn't know where they came from}. Otherwise, use *about* or some other preposition.

as well as. If a singular noun or pronoun precedes *as well as*, the verb following the phrase should be singular {Juan, as well as Eleanor, is eager to hear the recital}. That is, the phrase *as well as* introduces an aside. It doesn't function like the coordinating conjunction *and* to create a compound subject.

*****as yet; *as of yet.** Stilted and redundant. Use *yet, still, so far,* or some other equivalent.

attain; obtain. To *attain* something is either to accomplish it through effort (e.g., a goal) {she soon attained a position of power}, or to reach a particular age, size, level, etc. {the stock market attained a new high this morning}. To *obtain* something is to get it or gain possession of it {obtaining information}. In best usage, you *attain* a degree and *obtain* a diploma. It can be a fine distinction, and in common usage the words are often treated as synonyms.

at the present time; at this time; at present. These are turgid substitutes for *now, today, currently,* or even *nowadays* (a word of perfectly good literary standing). Of the two-word versions, *at present* is least suggestive of bureaucratese.

at the time that; at the time when. Use the plain and simple *when* instead.

auger; augur. The spellings of these words can be tricky because they are pronounced the same \aw-gər\. The tool for boring is an *auger. Augur* means "a clairvoyant or seer" (noun) or "to foretell" (verb). *Augurs well* is an idiomatic equivalent of *bodes well.* The related noun *augury* refers to an indication of what will happen in the future.

avenge, *vb.;* **revenge,** *vb.* & *n. Avenge* connotes a just exaction for a wrong {historically, family grudges were privately avenged}. The corresponding noun is *vengeance. Revenge* connotes the infliction of harm on another out of anger or resentment {the team is determined to revenge its humiliating loss in last year's championship game}. *Revenge* is much more commonly a noun {they didn't want justice—they wanted revenge}.

averse. See **adverse.**

avocation; vocation. An *avocation* is a hobby or pleasant pastime {stamp-collecting is my weekend avocation}. A *vocation* is one's profession or, especially in a religious sense, one's calling {she had a true vocation and became a nun}.

awhile; a while. The one-word version is adverbial; it means "for a short time" {let's stop here awhile}. The two-word version is a noun phrase that follows the preposition *for* or *in* {she worked for a while before beginning graduate studies}.

backward(s). See **toward**.

bacteria. This term is plural {the bacteria are no longer present}, the less-well-known singular being *bacterium* {a new bacterium has been discovered}. Avoid **this bacteria is* for *these bacteria are.*

bale; bail. The more common term is *bale* (= a bundle or to form into a bundle, as of hay or cotton). *Bail* is most often a verb (= to drain by scooping, as of getting water out of a boat using a pail); it is also a noun and verb regarding the posting of security to get out of jail pending further proceedings. *Bail* is also used informally to denote leaving quickly or escaping {the couple bailed from the party}. To *bail out* someone (a phrasal verb) is to get the person out of trouble.

barbecue. Preferably so spelled—not **barbeque* or **Bar-B-Q.*

based on. This phrase has two legitimate and two illegitimate uses. It may unimpeachably have verbal force (*base* being a transitive verb, as in *they based their position on military precedent*) or, in a passive sense, adjectival force (*based* being read as a past-participial adjective, as in *a sophisticated thriller based on a John le Carré novel*). Two uses, however, are traditionally considered slipshod. *Based on* should not have adverbial force {rates are adjusted annually, based on the 91-day Treasury bill} or prepositional force (as a dangling participle) {based on this information, we decided to stay}. Try other constructions {rates are adjusted annually on the basis of the 91-day Treasury bill} {with this information, we decided to stay}.

basis. Much overworked, this word most properly means "foundation; the facts, things, or ideas from which something can be developed." It often appears in the phrase *on a . . . basis* or some similar

> To those who have power or aspire to power, it is not enough that language should be intelligible: it must also be correct. For most nonlinguists, correctness is not to be determined by majority usage or by majority vote. It is assumed to be somehow immanent in language and known by those who speak with authority on the language. Correct performance marks the user as a responsible member of society; incorrect performance is viewed as contributing to the decay of the language. It therefore matters greatly to many that we spell *all right* as two words, that we preserve the distinction between *who* and *whom* (at least in formal writing), that we avoid dangling participles, that we do not use *flaunt* in place of *flout*. These are minor in themselves, but they represent social values: an ordered, hierarchical society where distinctions are maintained. For those who know what is right, the wrong choices evoke silent reproach, ridicule, or passionate objections.
> —Sidney Greenbaum
> *Good English and
> the Grammarian*

construction. When possible, substitute adverbs (*personally*, not *on a personal basis*) or simply state the time (*daily*, not *on a daily basis*). The plural is *bases* {the legislative bases are complicated}.

bated breath. So spelled—not **baited breath*. Someone who waits with *bated breath* is anxious or excited (literally "holding [abating] one's breath").

battery. See **assault.**

because. This word is normally a subordinating conjunction that introduces a dependent clause that expresses cause, reason, or motive {the grass is soggy because it's been raining} {I re-sent the message because it kept getting bounced back}. When *because* follows a negative, it is preceded by a comma if the *because*-clause explains the negative {I didn't call yesterday, because I was traveling all day [without the comma, the suggestion might be that I didn't call for a different reason]}.

Some uses of *because* are casualisms best avoided in Standard Written English {he seemed drunk because he kept slurring his words} {just because I was late is no reason to be angry!} On **reason is because*, see **reason.**

beggar, *vb.* Literally "to make very poor (i.e., to make into a beggar)," this verb commonly appears in such phrases as *to beggar description* (meaning "to be impossible to describe") {her beauty beggars description} or *to beggar belief* {his lack of common sense beggars belief}. Avoid such distortions as **begs description* and **begs belief.*

begging the question. This phrase traditionally denotes a logical fallacy of assuming as true what has yet to be proved—or adducing as proof for some proposition something that's every bit as much in need of proof as the first proposition. For example, someone might try to "prove" the validity of a certain religion by quoting from that religion's holy text. But the phrase gets misused in many ways—as (erroneously) meaning "prompting a question," "inviting an obvious question," "evading a question," and "ignoring a question."

behalf. *In behalf of* means "in the interest or for the benefit of" {the decision is in behalf of the patient}. *On behalf of* means "acting as agent or representative of" {on behalf of Mr. Scott, I would like to express heartfelt thanks}.

bemused. This word means "bewildered, distracted, or confused." It is not a synonym of "amused."

benevolence; beneficence. *Benevolence* is the attribute of being disposed to kindness or capable of doing good {the priest's benevolence was plainly evident}. It applies most often to people but may also apply to things that are beneficial. *Beneficence* is a major act of kindness or the performance of good deeds generally {the villagers thanked him for his beneficence}. The first term denotes a quality, the second conduct.

beside; besides. *Beside* is a preposition of position, whether literal {beside the road} or figurative {beside the point}. *Besides* may be a preposition meaning "other than" {who's going besides us?} or an adverb meaning "also" or "anyway" {besides, who wants to know?}.

better. In the idiomatic verb phrase *had better* [+ verb], don't drop the auxiliary verb *had*—though you may reduce it by contraction {I'd better go now}.

between; among; amid. *Between* indicates one-to-one relationships {between you and me}. *Among* indicates undefined or collective relationships {honor among thieves}. *Between* has long been recognized as being perfectly appropriate for more than two objects if multiple one-to-one relationships are understood from the context {trade between members of the European Union}. The ngram below may surprise you.

Amid is often used with mass nouns {amid talk of war}—though it can often be used with abstract nouns in the plural {resigned amid rumors of misconduct} {the investigation comes amid growing concerns}. *Among* is invariably used with plurals of count nouns {among the children}. Avoid *amidst* and *amongst*, especially in AmE.

1813 Ratio of Frequency in Printed Books: 15:1
2008 Ratio of Frequency in Printed Books: 3:1

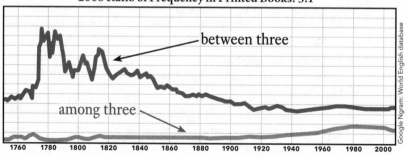

between three

among three

Google Ngram: World English database

1760 1780 1800 1820 1840 1860 1880 1900 1920 1940 1960 1980 2000

between you and me. This is the correct phrasing—not *between you and I*, which is a classic example of hypercorrection. Both pronouns function as objects of the preposition *between*. See **I**. See also § 58.

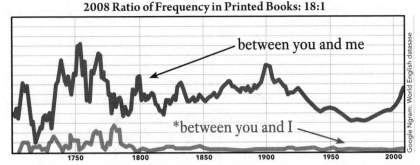

2008 Ratio of Frequency in Printed Books: 18:1

between you and me

*between you and I

Google Ngram: World English datasase

1750 · 1800 · 1850 · 1900 · 1950 · 2000

This point, however, requires some elaboration. Corpus linguistics shows that when coordinated pronouns form the complement of a preposition, "hypercorrect nominative forms are generally rare."[1] The ratio of 18:1 in printed books confirms this conclusion. But in recent years some grammarians who have become apologists for the hypercorrect *between you and I* have gone so far as to call it "standard" and to disclaim labeling the usage *hypercorrect*.[2] The idea is that with coordinated pronouns, both cases—nominative and objective—are so common as to make either choice "standard" variety. This lax evaluation underdescribes the three-fold linguistic reality that (1) the traditional objective case of pronouns functioning as objects of a preposition continues to predominate in Standard Written English—and vastly so; (2) the most knowledgeable, refined speakers and writers choose the correct objective pronouns as objects; and (3) although the hypercorrect forms may be spreading, they continue to bespeak linguistic insecurity, which perhaps is also spreading as a result of maleducation.

True, Shakespeare put the phrase '*tween you and I* in a character's mouth, but that was at a time when English grammar was much less settled than it came to be in the 18th century. And in any event, that usage was an outlier even in the Elizabethan era. Further, the socio-linguistic point that Shakespeare might have been making by having a character mouth that phrase may well be lost in the mists of time. But just as Shakespeare used many locutions that would have been considered nonstandard by the 18th century, his use of '*tween you and I* cannot be considered a significant datum in the modern argument.

bi-; semi-. Generally, *bi-* means "two" (*biweekly* means "every two weeks"), while *semi-* means "half" (*semiweekly* means "twice a week"). Because

---

1   Douglas Biber et al., *Longman Grammar of Spoken and Written English* (Harlow: Pearson, 1999), 339.
2   See Rodney Huddleston and Geoffrey K. Pullum, *The Cambridge Grammar of the English Language* (Cambridge: Cambridge Univ. Press, 2002), 463.

these prefixes are often confounded, writers should be explicit about the meaning.

biannual; semiannual; biennial. *Biannual* and *semiannual* both mean "twice a year" {these roses bloom biannually}. But *biennial* means "once every two years" or "every other year" {our legislature meets biennially}. To avoid confusion, write *semiannual* instead of *biannual*, and consider writing *once every two years* instead of *biennial*.

biceps. Although *biceps* was traditionally a singular noun, the word is now regarded as plural (the more traditional plural being *bicepses* [anglicized] or *bicipites* [Latin]). The standard terms are now *bicep* as the singular and *biceps* as the plural.

billion; trillion. The meanings can vary in different countries. In the United States, a *billion* is 1,000,000,000. In Great Britain, Canada, and Germany, a *billion* is traditionally a thousand times more than that (a million millions, or what Americans call a *trillion*)—though the AmE sense now predominates even in BrE. Further, in Great Britain a trillion is traditionally a million million millions, what Americans would call a quintillion (1,000,000,000,000,000,000). Although the American definitions are gaining acceptance, writers need to remember the historical geographic distinctions.

blatant; flagrant. An act that is *blatant* is both bad and plain for all to see {a blatant error}. One that is *flagrant* is done brazenly as well as openly, often with a stronger suggestion of shocking illegality or immorality {a flagrant violation of the law}.

bombastic. A *bombastic* speech or essay is pompously long-winded and self-important but essentially empty of real substance. The word has nothing to do with temper.

bona fide; bona fides. The first is the adjective meaning "good-faith" {that's a bona fide contention—not disingenuous in the slightest} or "genuine" {that's a bona fide first edition}. It's pronounced /**boh**-nə fɪd/. *Bona fides*, a noun pronounced /**boh**-nə fɪ-deez/, means "sincerity and honesty of purpose" {he has thoroughly established his conservative bona fides}.

born; borne. *Born* is used only as an adjective {a born ruler} or in the fixed passive-voice verb *to be born* {the child was born into poverty}. *Borne* is the general past participle of *bear* {this donkey has borne many heavy loads} {she has borne three children}. It is also used as a suffix {foodborne} {vectorborne}.

both–and. These correlative conjunctions should frame matching syntactic parts. Hence don't write *She is both a writer and she skis professionally*, but instead *She is both a writer and a professional skier*. See §§ 266, 332.

breach, *n.* & *vb.*; **breech,** *n.* A *breach* is a gap in or violation of something {a breach of contract}, or a serious disagreement {healing the breach between the nations}. To *breach* is to break, break open, or break through {breach the castle walls}. *Breech* refers to the lower or back part of something, especially the buttocks {a breech birth} or the part of a modern firearm where bullets are inserted {the rifle's breech}.

bring; take. The distinction may seem obvious, but the error is common. The simple question is, where is the action directed? If it's toward you, use *bring* {bring home the bacon}. If it's away from you, use *take* {take out the trash}. You *take* (not *bring*) your car to the mechanic.

broadcast. It's an irregular verb that doesn't change its form in the past tense or past participle. **Broadcasted* is a solecism.

burn. Inflect this verb *burn–burned–burned* in AmE (*burnt* being the usual past form only in BrE). But in AmE and BrE alike, *burnt* is the past-participial adjective {burnt toast}.

but. Popular belief to the contrary, this conjunction usefully begins contrasting sentences, typically with greater strength and speed than *however*. Avoid putting a comma after it. As the following ngram shows, the sentence-starting *but* has been prevalent throughout literary history. It is an exceedingly useful device that one finds throughout the work of the best writers. Note, too, that the ngram numbers for *however* also reflect the unimpeachable uses of the word to mean "in whatever way" or "to whatever degree" {however trivial you may think the issue is, most people care about it}. See § 277. Cf. **and.**

1900 Ratio of Frequency in Printed Books: 24:1
2008 Ratio of Frequency in Printed Books: 3:1

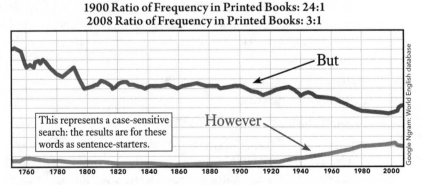

But

However

This represents a case-sensitive search: the results are for these words as sentence-starters.

Google Ngram: World English database

1760 1780 1800 1820 1840 1860 1880 1900 1920 1940 1960 1980 2000

by means of. Often verbose. Use *by* or *with* if either one suffices.

by reason of. Use *because* or *because of* unless *by reason of* is part of an established phrase {by reason of insanity}.

cache; cachet. *Cache*, a count noun, refers either to a quantity of goods or valuables that have been stashed away or to a storage buffer within a computer. *Cachet*, generally a mass noun, refers most commonly to prestige or fetching appeal—or else a seal on a document or a commemorative design.

cactus. Pl. *cacti* or *cactuses*.

can; could. *Can* means "to be able to" and expresses certainty {I can be there in five minutes}. *Could* is better for a sense of uncertainty or a conditional statement {could you stop at the cleaners today?} {if you send a deposit, we could hold your reservation}. See § 200.

can; may. *Can* most traditionally applies to physical or mental ability {she can do calculations in her head} {the dog can leap over a six-foot fence}. In colloquial English, *can* also expresses a request for permission {can I go to the movies?}, but this usage is not recommended in formal contexts. *May* suggests possibility {the class may have a pop quiz tomorrow} or permission {you may borrow my car}. A denial of permission is properly phrased formally with *may not* {you may not borrow my credit card} or, less formally, with *cannot* or *can't* {you can't use the computer tonight}. See §§ 200–201.

candelabra. This is the plural, the singular being *candelabrum*, meaning "a decorative object that holds several lamps or candles." The double plural **candelabras* is a solecism.

cannon; canon. A *cannon* is an artillery weapon that fires metal balls or other missiles. A *canon* is (1) a general rule or principle, (2) an established criterion, (3) the sum of a writer or composer's work, (4) the collective literature accepted by a scholastic discipline, (5) a piece of music in which a tune is started by one performer and is mimicked by each of the others, or (6) a Christian priest having special duties within a church or cathedral.

cannot. One word, except in expressions such as *can not only . . . but also*.

capability. See **ability.**

capacity. See **ability.**

capital; capitol. A *capital* is a seat of government (usually a city) {Jefferson City is the capital of Missouri}. A *capitol* is a building in which a legislature meets {the legislature opened its new session in the capitol today}.

carat; karat; caret. *Carat* measures the weight of a gemstone; *karat* measures the purity of gold. To remember the difference, think of *24K gold*. (In BrE, the spelling *carat* serves in both senses.) *Caret* is a mark on a manuscript indicating where matter is to be inserted; borrowed from Latin in the 17th century, it literally means "(something) is lacking."

career; careen. The word *career*'s career as a verb meaning "to go full speed" may be about over—except in BrE (in which the two verbs contend in what is still a tight race). In AmE, its duties have been assumed by *careen* (traditionally, "to tip to one side while moving"), even though nothing in that verb's time-honored definition denotes high speed. So today in AmE it's typically *careened down the hill* but in BrE *careered down the hill.*

2008 Ratio of Frequency in Printed Books: 7:1

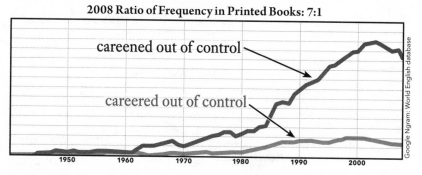

caret. See **carat.**

case. This multifaceted word is often a sign of verbal inflation, especially in its uses as a near-synonym of *situation*. For example, *in case* means "if"; *in most cases* means "usually"; *in every case* means "always." The word is justifiably used in law (in which a *case* is a lawsuit or judicial opinion) and in medicine (in which the word refers to an instance of a disease or disorder). Of course, the word can also denote a box or container {briefcase}, an argument or set of reasons {state your case}, or a grammatical word form of the type you studied in § 15.

cause célèbre. This word most strictly denotes a legal case, esp. a prosecution, that draws great public interest. By extension, it refers to a notorious episode, event, or even person. It does not properly denote a person's pet cause. Though it retains its acute and grave accents, the phrase is now considered naturalized enough not to be italicized (except when called out as a phrase, as in the next sentence). Yet the plural retains its French form: *causes célèbres.*

censer; censor, *n.*; sensor. The correct spellings can be elusive. A *censer* is either a person who carries a container of burning incense or the container itself. A *censor* is a person who suppresses objectionable subject matter. A *sensor* is a mechanical or electronic device for discovering light, heat, movement, etc.

censor, *vb.*; **censure,** *vb.* To *censor* is to review books, films, letters, etc. to remove objectionable material—that is, to suppress {soldiers' letters are often censored in wartime}. To *censure* is to criticize strongly or disapprove, or to officially reprimand {the House of Representatives censured the president for the invasion} {in some countries the government *censors* the press; in the United States the press often *censures* the government}.

*center around. Although this illogical phrasing does have apologists, stylists tend to use either *center on* or *revolve around.*

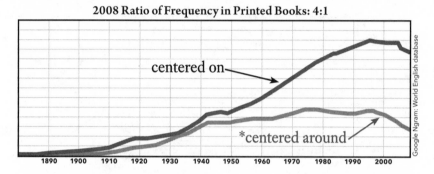

2008 Ratio of Frequency in Printed Books: 4:1

certainty; certitude. If you are absolutely sure about something, you display both *certainty* (firm conviction) and *certitude* (cocksureness). That fact you are sure about, however, is a *certainty* but not a *certitude*—the latter is a trait applied to people only.

chair; chairman; chairwoman; chairperson. *Chair* is widely regarded as the best gender-neutral choice. Since the mid-17th century, *chair* has referred to an office of authority. See § 439.

chaise longue. So written—not **chaise lounge*, the product of metathesis resulting from folk etymology. Pl. *chaises longues* (/shayz **long**/).

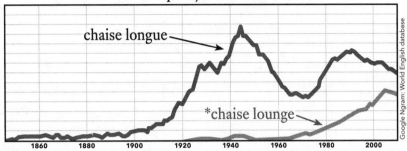

1945 Ratio of Frequency in Printed Books: 20:1
2008 Ratio of Frequency in Printed Books: 1.4:1

chaise longue

*chaise lounge

Google Ngram: World English database

1860 1880 1900 1920 1940 1960 1980 2000

charge. See **accuse**.

chastise. So spelled—not **chastize*.

cherub. The plural is *cherubs* when referring to adorable children but *cherubim* (a naturalized Hebrew phrase) when referring to angelic beings.

childish; childlike. *Childlike* is used positively to connote innocence, eagerness, and freshness {a childlike smile}. *Childish* is pejorative; it connotes immaturity, silliness, and unreasonableness {childish ranting}.

chord; cord. *Chord* denotes (1) a group of harmonically consonant notes {major chords} {minor chords} or (2) a straight line joining the ends of an arc (sense 2 being a technical term in mathematics and engineering). *Cord* is the word denoting a thick string or rope {spinal cord} {umbilical cord} {vocal cord}, an electrical wire that supplies electricity to an appliance or other equipment, or a quantity of firewood.

> The study of common errors in the construction of sentences and the use of words serves much the same purpose to the student of "English" as the study of pathology does to the student of medicine. And it has the not negligible advantage that it appeals to a primitive instinct. No one can deny that the discovery of other people's mistakes gives us profound satisfaction.
> —Adam Gowans Whyte
> *An Anthology of Errors*

circumstances. Both *in the circumstances* and *under the circumstances* are acceptable, but *under* is now much more common in AmE. *In* predominates in BrE.

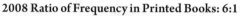

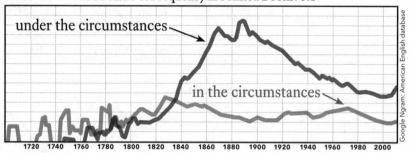

cite, *n.;* **site.** As a noun, *cite* is colloquial for *citation*, which refers to a source of information {a cite to *Encyclopaedia Britannica*}. A *site* is a place or location used for a particular purpose {building site} {website}. Cf. **sight.**

citizen; subject. In a governmental sense, these are near-synonyms that should be distinguished. A *citizen* owes allegiance to a nation whose sovereignty is a collective function of the people {a citizen of Germany}. A *subject* owes allegiance to an individual sovereign because the form of government is monarchical {a subject of the queen}.

class. This word denotes a category or group of things that are considered together because of their similarities {the class of woodwind instruments}. Properly, a *class* is never one type {the oboe is a type of woodwind} or one kind of thing {a drum is one kind of percussion instrument}.

classic; classical. *Classic* means "important, authoritative, outstanding" {*The Naked Night* is one of Ingmar Bergman's classic films}. *Classical* applies to a traditional set of values in literature, music, design, etc. {classical Greek} {a classical composer} or to the definitive or earliest-characterized form {classical EEC syndrome}.

clean; cleanse. Although various cleaning agents are called "cleansers," *clean* displaced *cleanse* long ago in most of the word's literal senses. *Cleanse* retains the Old English root meaning "pure": its use today usually refers to spiritual or moral purification.

cleave. This verb was originally two different words, and that difference is reflected in the opposite meanings that *cleave* has: (1) to cut apart {to cleave meat} and (2) to cling together {standing in the rain, his clothes cleaving to his body}. The conjugations are (1) *cleave, cleft* (or *clove*), *cleft* (or *cloven*); and (2) *cleave, cleaved, cleaved.*

clench; clinch. *Clench*, which connotes a physical action, normally involves a person's hands, teeth, jaw, or stomach {he clenched his hand into a fist}. *Clinch*, the more common term, has mostly figurative uses about finally achieving something after a struggle {clinched the title} {clinched the victory}. But there is an exception to the nonphysical uses of *clinch*: if two people *clinch*, they hold each other's arms tightly, as in boxing.

climactic; climatic. *Climactic* is the adjective corresponding to *climax* {during the movie's climactic scene, the projector broke}. *Climatic* corresponds to *climate* {the climatic conditions of northern New Mexico}.

clinch. See **clench.**

***close proximity.** Redundant. Write either *close* or *in proximity*.

closure; cloture. *Closure* denotes the temporary or permanent closing or final resolution of something. *Cloture* denotes the parliamentary procedure of closing debate and taking a vote on a legislative bill or other measure.

cohabit; *cohabitate. *Cohabit* is the traditional verb for living with another person in a sexual relationship without being married. **Cohabitate*, a back-formation from *cohabitation*, is best avoided.

2008 Ratio of Frequency in Printed Books: 6:1

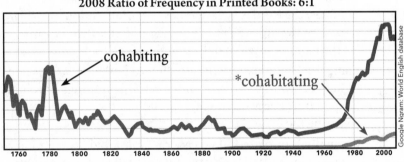

cohort. From the name for a division in the Roman army, *cohort* is traditionally a collective noun denoting a large group that is either undergoing a similar experience or being studied, as by sociologists or psychologists. But the accepted senses of the term have broadened substantially. Today it most often appears in AmE in a sense that was first recorded in 1952: as a count noun denoting a single colleague or friend, sometimes in a mildly disapproving way.

coin a phrase; coin a word. To *coin* something is to make it, as a mint stamps a coin. So to *coin a phrase* or a word is to create it, not merely repeat it.

coleslaw. So spelled—not *coldslaw.

collaborate; corroborate. To *collaborate* is to cooperate on some undertaking, esp. in the arts or sciences {the participants are collaborators}. To *corroborate* something is to back up its reliability with proof or evidence {the expert corroborated the witness's testimony}.

collegial; collegiate. *Collegial* answers to *colleague* {a healthy collegial work environment}; *collegiate* answers to *college* {collegiate sports}.

commendable; commendatory. What is done for a worthy cause is *commendable* {commendable dedication to helping the poor}. What expresses praise is *commendatory* {commendatory plaque}.

common; mutual. What is *common* is shared by two or more people {borne by different mothers but having a common father}. What is *mutual* is reciprocal or directly exchanged by and toward each other {mutual obligations}. Strictly, *friend in common* is better than *mutual friend* in reference to a third person who is a friend of two others.

commonweal; commonwealth. The *commonweal* is the public welfare. Traditionally, a *commonwealth* was a state established by public compact or by the consent of the people to promote the general good (commonweal), and where the people reserved supreme authority. In the United States, the word is synonymous with *state*, four of which are still called commonwealths: Kentucky, Massachusetts, Pennsylvania, and Virginia. The Commonwealth of Puerto Rico is also a U.S. territory.

compare. To *compare with* is to discern both similarities and differences between things. To *compare to* is to liken things or to note primarily similarities between them, especially in the active voice {Are you comparing me to *him*? I hope not!}.

compelled; impelled. If you are *compelled* to do something, you have no choice in the matter {Nixon was compelled by the unanimous Supreme Court decision to turn over the tapes}. If you are *impelled* to do something, you still may not like it, but you are convinced that it must be done {the voter disliked some candidates but was impelled by the income-tax issue to vote a straight-party ticket}. Whereas *compel* connotes an outside force, *impel* connotes an inner drive.

compendious; voluminous. These are not synonyms, as many apparently believe. *Compendious* means "concise, abridged." *Voluminous*, literally "occupying many volumes," most commonly means "vast" or "extremely lengthy."

complacent; complaisant; compliant. To be *complacent* is to be content with oneself and one's life—with the suggestion that one may be smugly unwilling to improve or unprepared for future trouble. To be *complaisant* is to be easygoing and eager to please others. To be *compliant* is to be amenable to orders or to a regimen imposed by others.

compliment; complement. A *compliment* is a flattering or praising remark {a compliment on your skill}. A *complement* is something that completes or brings to perfection {the lace tablecloth was a complement to the antique silver}. The words are also verbs: to *compliment* is to praise, while to *complement* is to supplement adequately or to complete. In the grammatical sense, a *complement* is a word or phrase that follows the verb to complete the predicate.

The corresponding adjectives are *complimentary,* meaning (1) "expressing praise," or (2) "given to someone free of charge"; and *complementary,* meaning (1) "going well together, despite differences," or (2) "consisting of two geometric angles that, added together, take up 90 degrees."

comprise; compose. Use with care. To *comprise* is "to consist of, to include" {the whole comprises the parts}. To *compose* is "to make up, to form the substance of something" {the parts compose the whole}. The phrase **is comprised of,* though increasingly common, remains nonstandard. Instead, try *is composed of* or *consists of.* See **include.**

2008 Ratio of Frequency in Printed Books: 5:1

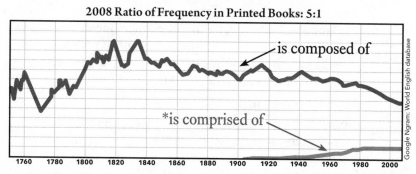

concept; conception. Both words may refer to an abstract thought, but *conception* also means "the act of forming an abstract thought." Avoid using either word as a high-sounding equivalent of *idea, design, thought,* or *program.*

concerned. See **as far as.**

condole, *vb.;* **console,** *vb.* These are closely related but not identical. To *condole with* is to express sympathy to {community leaders condoled with the victims' families}. The corresponding noun is *condolence* {they expressed their condolences at the funeral}. To *console* is to comfort in a time of distress or disappointment {the players consoled their humiliated coach}. The corresponding noun is *consolation* {their kind words were small consolation}.

confidant; confidante; confident. A *confidant* is a close companion, someone (male or female) you confide in. *Confidante*, a feminine form, is a fading alternative spelling of *confidant* (used only in reference to a female confidant). It reflects French gender spellings. *Confident* is the adjective meaning "sure that something will happen in the way one wants or expects" or "sure that something is true."

> All through the life-long process of learning one's "mother-tongue," one is liable to apprehend wrongly and to reproduce inexactly.
> —William Dwight Whitney
> *The Life and Growth of Language*

congruous; congruent. Both terms mean "in harmony, in agreement." The first is seen most often in its negative form, *incongruous*, meaning "strange, unexpected, or unsuitable in a particular situation" {the modern house looks incongruous in this old neighborhood}. The second is used in math to describe triangles that are identical in their angles as well as in the length of their sides {congruent angles}.

connote; denote. To *connote* (in reference to language) is to convey a meaning beyond the basic one, especially through emotive nuance {the new gerund *parenting* and all that it connotes}. To *denote* (again in reference to language) is to specify the literal meaning of something {the phrase *freezing point* denotes 32 degrees Fahrenheit or 0 degrees Celsius}. Both words have figurative uses {all the joy that parenthood connotes} {a smile may not denote happiness}.

consent. See **assent.**

consequent; subsequent. The first denotes causation; the second does not. A *consequent* event always happens after the event that caused it, as does a *subsequent* event. But a *subsequent* event does not necessarily occur as a result of the first: it could be wholly unrelated but merely later in time.

consider. Add *as* only when you mean "to examine or discuss for a particular purpose" {handshaking considered as a means of spreading disease}. Otherwise, omit *as* {we consider him qualified}.

consist. There are two distinct phrases: *consist of* and *consist in*. The first, by far the more common one, applies to the physical components that make up a tangible thing {the computer-system package consists of software, the CPU, the monitor, and a printer}. The second refers to the essence of a thing, especially in abstract terms {moral government consists in rewarding the righteous and punishing the wicked}.

console. See **condole.**

contact, *vb.* If you mean *write* or *call* or *e-mail*, say so. But *contact* is undeniably a brief way of referring to communication without specifying the means.

contagious; infectious. Both broadly describe a disease that is communicable. But a *contagious* disease spreads by direct contact with an infected person or animal {rabies is a contagious disease}. An *infectious* disease is spread by germs on a contaminated object or element, such as earth or water {tetanus is infectious but not contagious}.

> The existence of different manners of speech for persons in various ranks is a familiar fact. We are constantly sorting and classifying people according to them. A variation of any national language according to social levels is called *class dialect.* . . . When we talk, then, we tell much more about ourselves than the factual statements we are making. The sum total of small nuances will indicate much about our training, environment, economic position, and even profession. In conversation we are unconsciously providing a rich commentary about ourselves which supplements the clothing and outward possessions we gather.
> —Margaret Schlauch
> *The Gift of Tongues*

contemporary; contemporaneous. Both express coinciding time, but *contemporary* usually applies to people, and *contemporaneous* applies to things or actions. Because *contemporary* has the additional sense "modern," it is unsuitable for contexts involving multiple times. That is, a reference to *Roman, Byzantine, and contemporary belief systems* is ambiguous; change *contemporary* to *modern*.

contemptuous; contemptible. If you are *contemptuous*, you are feeling and showing that you think someone or something deserves no respect. If you are *contemptible*, others will have that attitude toward you.

content; contents. *Content* applies to the ideas, facts, or opinions in a written or oral presentation {the lecture's content was offensive to some who were present}. *Contents* usually denotes physical ingredients: the things that are inside a box, bag, room, etc. {the package's contents were difficult to discern by X-ray}. If the usage suggests many items, material or nonmaterial, *contents* is correct {table of contents} {the investigative report's contents}.

continual; continuous. What is *continual* may go on for a long time, but always there are brief interruptions, so that it can be characterized as intermittent or frequently repeated {continual nagging}. What is *continuous* never stops—it remains constant or uninterrupted {continuous flow of water}. A line that is continuous has no gaps or holes in it.

contravene; controvert. To *contravene* is to conflict with or violate (the law, a rule, etc.) {the higher speed limit contravenes our policy of encouraging fuel conservation}. To *controvert* is to challenge or contradict {the testimony controverts the witness's prior statement}.

convince. See **persuade.**

copyright, *vb.* This verb, meaning "to obtain the legal right to be the only producer or seller of a book, play, film, or other creative work for a specific length of time," is conjugated *copyright–copyrighted–copyrighted.* Note the spelling, which has nothing to do with *write.*

cord. See **chord.**

corollary; correlation. A *corollary* is either (1) a subsidiary proposition that follows from a proven mathematical proposition, often without requiring additional evidence to support it, or (2) a natural or incidental result of some action or occurrence. A *correlation* is a positive connection between things or phenomena. If used in the context of physics or statistics, it denotes the degree to which the observed interactions and variances are not attributable to chance alone.

> People should not be sharply corrected for bad grammar, provincialisms, or mispronunciation; it is better to suggest the proper expression by tactfully introducing it oneself in, say, one's reply to a question or one's acquiescence in their sentiments, or into a friendly discussion of the topic itself (not of the diction), or by some other suitable form of reminder.
> —Marcus Aurelius
> *Meditations*

corporal; corporeal. What is *corporal* relates in some way to the body {corporal punishment}; what is *corporeal* has a physical form that can be touched {not our spiritual but our corporeal existence}.

corps; core. A *corps* is a body of like workers, as in an army, with special duties and responsibilities {Marine Corps} {press corps}. It is often misspelled like its homophone, *core*, which denotes the central or most important part of something {the core of the problem} {the earth's core}.

correlation. See **corollary.**

corroborate. See **collaborate.**

could. See **can.**

could have. This phrase is often contracted to *could've*—but the homophone **could of* is an illiteracy.

couldn't care less. This is the standard phrasing. Avoid the illogical form **could care less*—which, though never understood in its literal sense, is a badge of linguistic carelessness. Try adding the word *possibly* after *couldn't*. The less-than-overwhelming ratio in the ngram is doubtless attributable to the phrase's being a colloquialism—one that rarely occurs in Standard Written English. Please care about even your oral phrasing. And if you habitually use the exclamation *Whatever!*, try replacing it with *I couldn't possibly care less!*

2008 Ratio of Frequency in Printed Books: 2:1

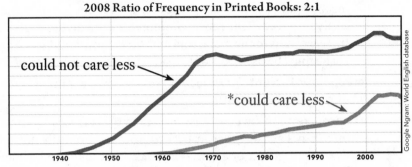

councillor; counselor. A *councillor* is one who sits on a council {city councillor}. A *counselor* is one whose job is to help and advise people with problems {personal counselor}. In BrE, the spelling is *counsellor*.

couple. Using *couple* as an adjective has traditionally been regarded as non-standard phrasing—though it is increasingly common as a casualism. Add *of* {we watched a couple of movies}.

2008 Ratio of Frequency in Printed Books: 8:1

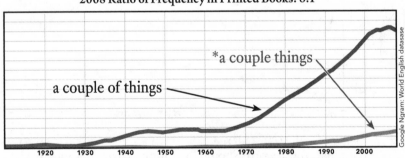

When referring to two people as a unit {married couple}, the noun *couple* takes either a singular or a plural verb {the couple is happy} {the couple are honeymooning in Ravello}. When the pronoun *they* follows *couple*—if a pronoun is used at all, it is normally plural—the plural verb is preferable {the couple were delighted by their friends' responses}.

court-martial. Two words joined by a hyphen, whether the phrase functions as a noun or as a verb. Because *martial* acts as an adjective meaning "military," the plural of the noun is *courts-martial.* The third-person-singular verb is *court-martials* {if the general court-martials him, he'll have much to answer for}. In AmE, the inflected spellings of the verb are *court-martialed, court-martialing*; in BrE, the spellings are *court-martialled, court-martialling*.

credible; creditable; credulous. *Credible* means "believable; deserving trust"; *creditable* means "praiseworthy; deserving approval"; *credulous* means "gullible; tending to believe whatever one is told—and therefore easily deceived." The most common error involving cognate forms of these words is in the malapropism **strains credulity*. If some form of that cliché must be used, it should read *strains credibility*.

creep–crept–crept. So inflected—except in the phrase *creep out* {that movie creeped me out!}.

crevice; crevasse. Size matters. A crack in the sidewalk is a *crevice* (accent on the first syllable) because it's narrow and typically not very deep; a fissure in a glacier or a dam is a *crevasse* (accent on the second syllable) because it's a deep open crack.

criminal. See **unlawful**.

criteria. This is the plural form of *criterion* (= a standard for judging): one *criterion*, two *criteria*. The double plural **criterias* is a solecism.

2008 Ratio of Frequency in Printed Books: 16:1

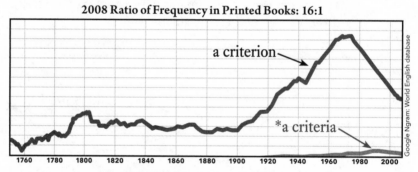

current, *adj.*; **currently,** *adv.* Often redundant when used with the present tense, these words should be omitted when possible {CMA is ~~currently~~ preparing to publish its membership directory} {he is ~~currently~~ working on a book about the world's largest unsolved art heist}.

damp, *vb.*; **dampen.** Both words convey the sense "to moisten." *Damp* also means "to reduce with moisture" {damp the fire} or "to diminish vibration or oscillation of (a wire or voltage)" {damp the voltage}. In a figurative sense, *dampen* means "to make [a feeling, mood, activity, etc.] less intense or enjoyable" {dampen one's hopes}.

data. Though originally this word was a plural of *datum*, it is now commonly treated as a mass noun and coupled with a singular verb. In formal writing (and always in the sciences), use *data* as a plural. Whatever you do, though, use the term consistently within a single writing—either singular or (more formally) plural.

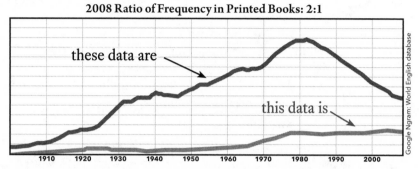

2008 Ratio of Frequency in Printed Books: 2:1

these data are

this data is

Google Ngram: World English database

1910 1920 1930 1940 1950 1960 1970 1980 1990 2000

deadly; deathly. *Deadly* means "capable of causing death" {deadly snake venom} or "likely to cause as much harm as possible {deadly enemies}. *Deathly* means "arousing thoughts of death or a dead body" {deathly silence}.

deceptively. This word is famously ambiguous. Consider: *The towns are deceptively far apart from each other.* Does this statement mean that they seem far apart but in fact are close? Or that they seem close but are in fact far apart? Avoid the word whenever it might cause confusion. Sometimes, admittedly, the word is clear {he answered the questions deceptively time after time}.

decide whether; decide if. See **determine whether.**

decimate. This word literally means "to kill every tenth person," a means of repression that goes back to Roman times. But the word has come to mean "to inflict heavy damage or destroy a large part of something," and this use has long been predominant. Avoid *decimate* when you are referring to complete destruction. That is, don't say that a city was **completely decimated.*

deduce. See **adduce.**

defamation; libel; slander. *Defamation* is the communication of a falsehood that damages someone's reputation. If it is recorded, especially in writing, it is *libel*, otherwise, it is *slander.*

definite; definitive. *Definite* means "clear, exact" {a definite yes}. *Definitive* means either "not subject to further revision in the near future" {we have a definitive agreement} or "of such high quality as to be unimprovable for a long time" {the definitive guide}.

defuse; diffuse. The first means "to reduce the danger or tension in (a situation, etc.)" {they defused a ticking time bomb}. The second means "to spread or disperse" {books diffuse knowledge}.

delegate. See **relegate.**

deliberate, *adj.;* **deliberative.** As an adjective, *deliberate* means either "planned; carefully thought out" {a deliberate response} or "slow and steady" {deliberate progress}. *Deliberative* means "of, characterized by, or involving debate"; the word most often applies to an assembly {deliberative body} or a process {deliberative meetings}.

denote. See **connote.**

denounce; renounce. To *denounce* is either to criticize harshly, especially in public {they denounced the prisoner swap}, or to accuse, as by giving incriminating information about someone's illegal political activities to the authorities {denounced him to the police}. To *renounce* is either to relinquish or reject {renounced her citizenship} or to declare publicly that one no longer believes something or will no longer behave in some way {renounce violence}.

dependant, *n.;* **dependent,** *adj. & n.* In BrE, the first is the preferable noun {he claimed three dependants on his tax return}; the second is the adjective {the family has become dependent on welfare}. But in AmE, *dependent* is the usual form as both noun and adjective.

dependent, *adj.* See **addicted.**

depend on. Although *upon* is best reduced to *on* in this phrase, no further reduction is idiomatic: *depend* demands an *on.* Hence don't write **That depends how we approach the problem,* but rather *That depends on how we approach the problem.*

> Use the right word, not its second cousin.
> —Mark Twain
> "Fenimore Cooper's Literary Offenses"

deprecate. In general, to *deprecate* is to strongly disapprove or criticize. But in the phrase *self-deprecating*—which began as a mistaken form of *self-depreciating* but is now standard—the sense of *deprecate* is "to belittle." In the computer-software world, *deprecate* serves as a warning: a *deprecated* feature or function is one that will be phased out of future release of software, so that users should quickly begin looking for alternatives.

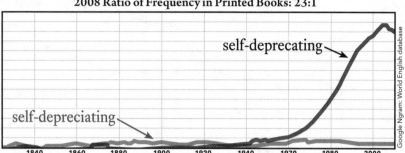

2008 Ratio of Frequency in Printed Books: 23:1

derisive; derisory. What is *derisive* ridicules as stupid or silly {derisive laughter}. What is *derisory* invites or deserves ridicule {that derisory "banana" hat}, especially when a laughably small amount of money is offered or given {my derisory paychecks}.

deserts; desserts. The first are deserved {he got his just deserts}, the second eaten {the many desserts on the menu}. *Just desserts* is a common misspelling (unless the meaning is "only postprandial sweets").

despite; in spite of. For brevity, prefer *despite*.

determine whether; determine if. The first phrasing is irreproachable style; the second is acceptable as a colloquialism. The same is true of *decide whether* vs. *decide if.*

detract. See **distract.**

device; devise. Like other *-ice* and *-ise* words, the *-c-* marks the noun {mechanical device} and *-s-* the verb {devise a plan}. For a possible tip on keeping them straight, see **advise.**

dice. This word is plural: one *die,* two *dice* {the dice we were using weren't legitimate}.

different. The phrasing *different from* is generally considered preferable to *different than* {this company is different from that one},

> The question "Is this correct written English?" can be more specifically phrased: "Would a copy editor pass this?" "Does this accord with the style books of the publishing houses?"
> —Paul Roberts
> "The Relation of Linguistics to the Teaching of English"

but sometimes the adverbial phrase *differently than* is all but required {she described the scene differently than he did}. In BrE, *different to* is not uncommon—but it is distinctively BrE, whereas *different from* is standard everywhere.

2008 Ratio of Frequency in Printed Books (*from* vs. *than*): 11:1

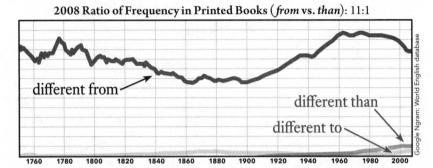

differ from; differ with. *Differ from* is the usual construction denoting a contrast {the two species differ from each other in subtle ways}. *Differ with* regards differences of opinion {the state's senators differ with each other on many issues}.

diffuse. See **defuse.**

diphtheria; diphthong; ophthalmology. Don't forget that these words have a *ph-* before the *th-*, both orthographically and in speech.

disburse; disperse. To *disburse* is to distribute money, especially from a large sum available for some specific purpose. To *disperse* is (1) to spread in various directions over a wide area {the clouds dispersed} or (2) to cause to go away in different directions {police dispersed the unruly crowd}.

disc. See **disk.**

discomfort; discomfit. *Discomfort* is a noun meaning "ill at ease." It can also be used as a verb meaning "to put ill at ease." But doing so often invites confusion with *discomfit*, which originally meant "to defeat utterly." Today it means "to thwart, confuse, annoy, or embarrass" {the ploy discomfited the opponent}. The distinction has become a fine one, since a *discomfited* person is also uncomfortable. *Discomfiture* is the corresponding noun.

discreet; discrete. *Discreet* means either "careful about not divulging secrets or upsetting others" {a discreet silence} or "showing modest taste; nonostentatious" {discreet jewelry}. *Discrete* means "separate, distinct, unconnected" {six discrete parts}.

discriminating, *adj.*; **discriminatory.** The word *discrimination* can be used in either a negative or a positive sense, and these adjectives reflect that ambivalence. *Discriminatory* means "reflecting a biased, unfair treatment" {discriminatory employment policy}. *Discriminating* means "analytically refined, discerning, tasteful" {a discriminating palate}.

disinterested. This word should be reserved for the sense "not having a financial personal interest at stake and therefore able to judge a situation fairly; impartial." Avoid it as a replacement for *uninterested* (which means "unconcerned, bored").

disk; disc. *Disk* is the usual spelling {floppy disk} {disk drive}. But *disc* is preferred in a few specialized applications {compact disc} {disc brakes} {disc harrow}.

disorganized; unorganized. Both mean "not organized," but *disorganized* suggests (1) a group in disarray, either thrown into confusion or inherently unable to work together {the disorganized 1968 Democratic National Convention in Chicago}, or (2) a person who is exceedingly bad at arranging or planning things {disorganized students}.

disperse. See **disburse.**

dissociate. So written—preferably not **disassociate.*

distinctive; distinguished; distinguishable. A *distinctive* feature is something that makes a person (or place or thing) easy to recognize {U2's distinctive sound}. But it does not necessarily make that person *distinguished* (respected and admired) {the distinguished professor wears a distinctive red bow tie}. It does, however, make the person *distinguishable* (easy to see as being different from something else)—a term that does not carry the positive connotation of *distinguished.*

> Fatalism about language cannot be the philosophy of those who care about language; it is the illogical philosophy of their opponents. Surely the notion that, because usage is ultimately what everybody does to words, nobody can or should do anything about them is self-contradictory. Somebody, by definition, does something; and this something is best done by those with convictions and a stake in the outcome, whether the stake of private pleasure or of professional duty does not matter. Resistance always begins with individuals.
>
> —Wilson Follett
> *Modern American Usage*

distract; detract. *Distract* (= to turn [something] away) is always transitive {distract attention}. *Detract* can be transitive (= to take [something] away) {grief detracts something from the buoyancy of life} but is more often intransitive (= to diminish) with *from* {detracts from the value}.

dive, *vb.* The preferred conjugation has traditionally been *dive–dived–dived.* The irregular form *dove,* though, has become the slightly predominant past-tense form in AmE and should be accepted as standard: *dive–dove–dived*. Traditionalists will stick to the older inflection.

1911 Ratio of Frequency in Printed Books: 6:1
2008 Ratio of Frequency in Printed Books: 1.1:1

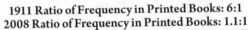

he dove into

he dived into

Google Ngram: American English database

1840 1860 1880 1900 1920 1940 1960 1980 2000

doctrinal; doctrinaire. *Doctrinal* means "of, relating to, or constituting a doctrine"; it is neutral in connotation {doctrinal differences}. *Doctrinaire* means "dogmatic," suggesting that the person described is stubborn and narrow-minded {a doctrinaire ideologue}.

doubtfully, *adv.* In recent years, this term has come into use as a sentence adverb (see § 211) functioning as a correlative of *hopefully* and as an antonym of *undoubtedly* {Will you be attending the party? Hopefully—but doubtfully [That is, I hope I'll be able to go, but I doubt it]}. Should you abstain from this usage in Standard Written English? No doubt.

doubtless, *adv.* Use this form (it's called a *flat adverb* [see § 215])—not *doubtlessly.

doubt that; doubt whether; doubt if. *Doubt that* conveys a negative sense of strong skepticism or questioning {I doubt that you'll ever get your money back}. *Doubt whether* also conveys a sense of skepticism, though less strong {the official says that he doubts whether the company could survive}. *Doubt if* is a casual phrasing for *doubt that*.

downward, *adj. & adv.* Preferably so written in AmE—not *downwards* (normal in BrE). See **toward**.

drag. Conjugated *drag–dragged–dragged*. The past form *drug* is dialectal.

dream. Either *dreamed* (more typical in both AmE and BrE) or *dreamt* is acceptable for the past-tense and past-participial forms.

drink, *vb.* Correctly conjugated *drink–drank–drunk* {they had not drunk any fruit juice that day}.

drown, *vb.* Conjugated *drown–drowned–drowned*.

drunk, *adj.*; **drunken.** *Drunk* describes a current state of intoxication {drunk driver}. (By contrast, a *drunk*—like a *drunkard*—is someone who is habitually intoxicated.) *Drunken* describes either a trait of habitual intoxication {drunken sot} or intoxicated people's behavior {a drunken brawl}.

dual; duel. *Dual* is an adjective meaning "having two parts or two of something" {dual exhaust}. A *duel* is a fight between two people, esp. a formal and often deadly combat with pistols or swords.

due to. In strict traditional usage, *due to* should be interchangeable with *attributable to* {the erratic driving was due to some prescription drugs that the driver had taken} or *owed to* {thanks are due to all who helped}. When used adverbially, *due to* is often considered inferior to *because of* or *owing to*. So in the sentence *Due to the parents' negligence, the entire family suffered,* the better phrasing would be *Because of* [or *Owing to*] *the parents' negligence, the entire family suffered.*

> To treat the sick, you must have a good knowledge of the healthy. But it is even better to know something about the disease. If the writer means to fight for the best possible use of language, he must be forever on his guard against the elements that words are prone to.
> —Konstantin Fedin
> "Notebook"

due to the fact that. Use *because* instead.

dumb. This word means either "stupid" or "unable to speak." In the second sense, the adjective *mute* is clearer (and less offensive) for most modern readers. But on the noun use of *mute*, see **moot.**

dwarf. Pl. *dwarfs*, not **dwarves*.

dying; dyeing. *Dying* is the present participle of *die* (= to cease living); *dyeing* is the present participle of *dye* (= to color with a liquid).

each. As a noun serving as the subject of a clause, *each* takes a singular verb {each of them was present that day}. But when it serves as an emphatic appositive for a plural noun, the verb is plural {they each have their virtues} {the newspapers each sell for $3}.

each other; one another. Traditionalists use *each other* when two things or people are involved, *one another* when more than two are involved. See § 76.

eatable. See **edible.**

economic; economical. *Economic* means "of, relating to, or involving large-scale finances" {federal economic policy} or "profitable enough to persist" {the business is no longer economic}. *Economical* means "thrifty; financially efficient; cheap and not wasteful" {an economical purchase}.

edible; eatable. What is *edible* is fit for human consumption {edible flowers}. What is *eatable* is at least minimally palatable {the cake is slightly burned but still eatable}.

effect. See **affect.**

effete. Traditionally, it has meant "worn out, sterile" or "lacking power, character, or vitality." Today it is often used to mean "snobbish," "effeminate," or "unduly pampered." Because of its ambiguity, the word is best avoided altogether.

effrontery; affront. *Effrontery* is an act of shameless impudence or shocking audacity. An *affront* is a deliberate insult.

e.g. See **i.e.**

either. Like *neither,* this word takes a singular verb when it functions as subject {is either of the spouses present today?}. For *either–or* constructions, see § 266.

either–or. For these correlative conjunctions, see §§ 266, 332.

elemental; elementary. Something that is *elemental* is an essential constituent {elemental ingredients} or a power of nature {elemental force}. Something that is *elementary* is basic, introductory, or easy {an elementary math problem}.

elicit; illicit. To *elicit* information or a reaction is to get it from someone, especially in challenging circumstances {to elicit responses}. Something *illicit* is disallowed by law or rule and usually also condemned generally by society {an illicit scheme}. Writers often mistakenly use the adjective *illicit* when they need the verb *elicit.*

elude. See **allude.**

embarrass. See **harass.**

emend. See **amend.**

emigrate. See **immigrate.**

eminent; imminent. What is *eminent* is famous, important, and respected {the eminent professor} or derives from high standing or authority {eminent domain}. What is *imminent* is looming, likely to happen soon, and almost always bad {imminent disaster}.

emotive; emotional. The first means "arousing intense feeling" {emotive language calculated to persuade the jury}; the second means "of, relating to, or involving intense feelings" {an emotional response}.

empathy; sympathy. *Empathy* is the ability to understand other people's feelings and problems {tremendous empathy with others}. *Sympathy* is generally compassion and sorrow one feels for another's misfortunes, especially on a particular occasion {our sympathies are with you}—but it can also be support for a plan or idea {right-wing sympathies} or a mutual understanding and warmth arising from compatibility {there was no personal sympathy between them}.

endemic. See **epidemic.**

endorse. See **approve.**

enervate; innervate. These words are antonyms. To *enervate* is to weaken or drain of energy. To *innervate* is to stimulate or provide with energy.

enormity; enormousness. *Enormity* means "monstrousness, moral outrageousness, atrociousness" {the enormity of the Khmer Rouge's killings}. *Enormousness* means "hugeness" or "immensity" {the enormousness of Alaska}.

enough. See **adequate.**

enquire. See **inquire.**

ensure; insure; assure. *Ensure* is the general term meaning "to make sure that something will (or won't) happen." In best usage, *insure* is reserved for underwriting financial risk. So we *ensure* that we can get time off for a vacation, and *insure* our car against an accident on the trip. We *ensure* events and *insure* things. But we *assure* people of things by telling them what's what, so that they won't worry. The important thing to remember is that we ensure occurrences and assure people.

2008 Ratio of Frequency in Printed Books (*ensure* vs. *insure*): 37:1

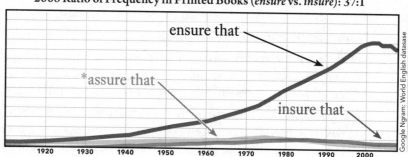

*enthused, *adj.* Use *enthusiastic* instead.

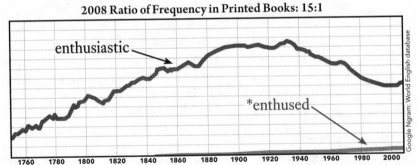

2008 Ratio of Frequency in Printed Books: 15:1

enumerable; innumerable. What's *enumerable* is countable and listable {the enumerable issues that we need on the agenda}. What's *innumerable* can't be counted, at least not practically {innumerable stars in the sky}. The second word is far more common. Because the two are pronounced so similarly, be wary of using them in speech.

envy. See **jealousy.**

epidemic; endemic; pandemic. An *epidemic* disease breaks out, spreads through a limited area (such as a state), and then subsides {an epidemic outbreak of measles}. (The word is frequently used as a noun {a measles epidemic}.) An *endemic* disease is perennially present within a region or population {malaria is endemic in parts of Africa}. (Note that *endemic* describes a disease and not a region: it is incorrect to say **this region is endemic for* [a disease].) A *pandemic* disease is prevalent over a large area, such as a nation or continent, or the entire world {the 1918–19 flu pandemic}.

*equally as. This is typically faulty phrasing. Delete *as.*

espresso. So spelled—not **expresso.*

et al. This is the abbreviated form of *et alii* ("and others")—the *others* being people, not things. Since *al.* is an abbreviation, the period is required—but note that no period follows the *et* (Latin for "and"). Cf. **etc.**

etc. This is the abbreviated form of *et cetera* ("and other things"); it should never be used in reference to people. *Etc.* implies that a list of things is too extensive to recite. But often writers seem to run out of thoughts and tack on *etc.* for no real purpose. Also, two redundancies often appear with this abbreviation: (1) **and etc.,* which is poor style because *et* means "and," and (2) *etc.* at the end of a list that begins with *for example, such as, e.g.,* and the like. Those terms properly introduce a short list of examples. Cf. **et al.**

event. The phrase *in the event that* is a verbose and formal way of saying *if*.

eventuality. This term often needlessly displaces more specific everyday words such as *event, result,* and *possibility*.

every day, *adv.;* **everyday,** *adj.* The first is adverbial, the second adjectival. You may wear your *everyday* clothes *every day*.

every one; everyone. The two-word version is an emphatic way of saying "each" {every one of them was there}; the second is a pronoun equivalent to *everybody* {everyone was there}.

everywhere. This is the preferable word—not **everyplace*.

evoke; invoke. To *evoke* something is to bring it out {evoke laughter} or bring it to mind {evoke childhood memories}. *Invoke* has a number of senses, including to assert (something) as authority {invoke the Monroe Doctrine}, to appeal (to someone or a higher power) for help {invoke an ally to intervene}, and to conjure up {invoke spirits of the past}.

exceptional; exceptionable. What is *exceptional* is uncommon, superior, rare, or extraordinary {an exceptional talent}. What is *exceptionable* is objectionable or offensive {an exceptionable slur}.

executor; administrator. In a will, a person designates an *executor* to distribute the estate after death. When a person dies without a will or without specifying an executor, the court will appoint an *administrator* to do the same. The feminine forms *administratrix* and *executrix* are unnecessary and should be avoided. See § 443.

explicit; implicit. If something is *explicit*, it is deliberately and clearly spelled out, as in the text of a well-drafted statute. If it is *implicit*, it is not specifically stated but is either suggested in the wording or necessary to effectuate the purpose. Avoid *implicit* to mean "complete, unmitigated."

fact that, the. This much-maligned phrase is not always avoidable. But hunt for a substitute before deciding to use it. Sometimes *that* alone suffices.

farther; further. The traditional distinction is to use *farther* for a physical distance {we drove farther north to see the autumn foliage} and *further* for a figurative distance {let's examine this further} {look no further}. Although it's a refinement of slight importance, connoisseurs will appreciate it.

fax, *n. & vb.* Derived from *facsimile transmission*, the shortened *fax* is almost universally preferred for convenience. The plural is *faxes*. Note that the word is governed by the same rules of capitalization as other nouns. *FAX* is incorrect: the word is not an acronym.

2008 Ratio of Frequency in Printed Books: 19:1

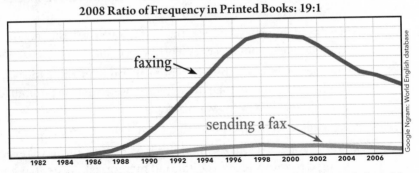

faze; phase, *vb.* To *faze* is to disturb or disconcert {Jones isn't fazed by insults}. To *phase* (usually *phase in* or *phase out*) is to schedule or perform a plan, task, or the like in stages {phase in new procedures} {phase out the product lines that don't sell}. The negative adjective for "unaffected" is *unfazed,* not **unphased.*

feel. This verb is weak when used as a substitute for *think* or *believe.*

feel bad. Invariably, the needed phrase is *feel bad* (not **feel badly*). See § 237.

fewer. See **less.**

fictional; fictitious; fictive. *Fictional* (from *fiction* as a literary genre) means "of, relating to, or involving imagination" {a fictional story}. *Fictitious* means "imaginary; counterfeit; false" {a fictitious name}. *Fictive* means "possessing the talent for imaginative creation" {fictive gift}; although it can also be a synonym for *fictional,* in that sense it is a needless variant. Also, anthropologists use *fictive* to describe relationships in which people are treated as family members despite having no bond of blood or marriage {fictive kin}.

finalize. Meaning "to bring to an end or finish the last part of," this word has often been associated with inflated jargon. Although its compactness may recommend it in some contexts, use *finish* when possible.

first. In enumerations, use *first, second, third,* etc. Avoid the *-ly* forms.

fish. The usual plural is *fish* {thousands of fish}—although the older plural is sometimes used for different varieties {the indigenous fishes of the Mississippi} or for small groups {look at the three fishes!}.

fit. This verb is undergoing a shift. It has traditionally been conjugated *fit–fitted–fitted,* but today *fit–fit–fit* is prevalent in AmE {when she tried on the dress, it fit quite well}. In the passive voice, however, *fitted* is still normal {the horse was fitted with a new harness}.

flagrant. See **blatant.**

flair. See **flare.**

flammable; inflammable. *Flammable* was invented in the early 20th century as an alternative to the synonymous word *inflammable*, which some people misunderstood—dangerously—as meaning "not combustible." Today *flammable* is the standard term. Its antonym is *nonflammable.*

1940 Ratio of Frequency in Printed Books: 1:12
2008 Ratio of Frequency in Printed Books: 2:1

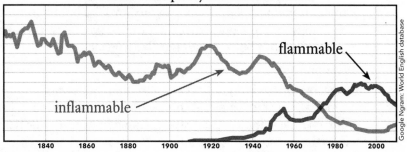

flare; flair. A *flare* is an unsteady and glaring light {an emergency flare} or a sudden outburst {a flare-up of fighting}. A *flair* is an outstanding talent {a flair for mathematics} or originality and stylishness {performed with flair}.

flaunt; flout. The first means "to show off ostentatiously" {they flaunted their wealth}. The second means "to openly disobey" {they flouted the rules}.

fleshy; fleshly. The first is literal and physical—usually meaning "plump" {fleshy arms} {fleshy peaches}. The second is metaphorical and abstract—usually meaning "carnal, sexual" {fleshly desires} {fleshly dreams}.

flounder; founder. Although the figurative sense of both verbs is "to go wrong," the literal senses evoke different images. To *flounder* is to struggle awkwardly, as though walking through deep mud {the professor glared while the unprepared student floundered around for an answer}. To *founder* (usually in reference to a boat or ship) is to sink or run aground {the ship foundered on the rocks}.

flout. See **flaunt.**

following. Avoid this word as an equivalent of *after.* Consider the possible miscue in *Following the presentation, there was a question-and-answer session. After* is both simpler and clearer.

forbear, *vb.;* **forebear,** *n.* The terms are unrelated, but the spellings are frequently confused. To *forbear* is to refrain {he wanted to speak but decided to forbear [the conjugation is *forbear–forbore–forborne*]}. A *forebear* is an ancestor {the house was built by Murray's distant forebears}.

forego; forgo. To *forego* is to go before {the foregoing paragraph}. The word appears most commonly in the phrase *foregone conclusion.* To *forgo,* by contrast, is to do without or renounce {they decided to forgo that opportunity}.

foreword; preface. A *foreword* (not *forward*) is a book's introduction that is written by someone other than the book's author. An introduction written by the book's author is called a *preface.*

forgo. See **forego.**

formally; formerly. What is done *formally* is done according to custom {formally attired} or by rule or law {formally sworn in}. What was done *formerly* was done previously or at an earlier time {formerly living in North Attleboro}.

former; latter. In the best usage, these words apply only to pairs. The *former* is the first of two, the *latter* the second of two.

fortuitous; fortunate. *Fortuitous* means "happening by chance," usually (but not always) with a good result {the rotten tree could have fallen at any time; it was just fortuitous that the victims drove by when they did}. *Fortunate* means "lucky" {we were fortunate to win the raffle}. Today, unfortunately, *fortuitous* is poaching on the semantic turf of *fortunate.*

forward(s). See **toward.**

founder. See **flounder.**

free rein. So written—not **free reign.*

fulsome, *adj.* This word does not preferably mean "very full" but "too much, excessive to the point of being repulsive." Traditionally, a "fulsome speech" is one that is so overpacked with thanks or hyperbole as to sound insincere. The word's slipshod use arises most often in the cliché *fulsome praise,* which can suggest the opposite of what the writer probably intends.

fun. Use this word as a noun {that was good fun}. Except as a purposeful casualism, avoid using it as an adjective meaning "enjoyable" or "amusing" (as in **a fun time)*—and avoid **funner* and **funnest.*

further. See **farther.**

future, in the near. Use *soon* or *shortly* instead.

gauntlet; gantlet. Lexicographers and usage critics—especially American ones—have sought since the 19th century to make a distinction. Etymologically, the two words have different histories: throwing down the *gauntlet* (= glove) and running the *gantlope* (= ordeal). But *gauntlet* has taken over both meanings. The standard phrases have been *run the gauntlet* and *throw down the gauntlet* since about 1800—the former phrase by a 10-to-1 margin over the competing form *run the gantlet*. Efforts to separate the terms have run their grueling course.

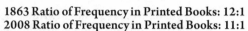

1863 Ratio of Frequency in Printed Books: 12:1
2008 Ratio of Frequency in Printed Books: 11:1

gentleman. This word is a vulgarism when used as a synonym for *man*. When used in reference to a cultured, refined man, it is susceptible to some of the same objections as those leveled against *lady*. Use it cautiously. Cf. **lady.**

get. Though shunned by many writers as too casual, *get* often sounds more natural than *obtain* or *procure* {get a divorce}. It can also substitute for a stuffy *become* {get hurt}. The verb is conjugated *get–got–gotten* in AmE and *get–got–got* in BrE.

    Get is the only verb apart from *be*-verbs that, when coupled with a past participle, can create a passive-voice construction {get stolen} {get waylaid}. See § 162.

gibe; jibe; jive. A *gibe* is a biting insult or taunt: *gibes* are figuratively thrown at their target {the angry crowd hurled gibes at the miscreant}. To *jibe* is to be in accord or to agree {the verdict didn't jibe with the judge's own view of the facts}. *Jive* can be either a noun (referring to swing music or to misleading talk that is transparently untrue) or a verb (meaning "to dance to such music" or "to try to mislead with lies").

gild. See **guild.**

go. This verb is conjugated *go–went–gone*. *Went* appears as a past participle only in dialect.

gourmet; gourmand. Both are aficionados of good food and drink. But a *gourmet* knows and appreciates the fine points of food and drink, whereas a *gourmand* tends toward gluttony.

graduate, *vb.* Whereas *graduate* means "to grant a diploma to or confer a degree on," *graduate from* means "to receive a diploma or degree from (a school, university, or other institution)." A school can *graduate* a student or a student can *graduate from* a school, but a student does not *graduate* a school—at least not in good usage.

1900 Ratio of Frequency in Printed Books: 1:1
2008 Ratio of Frequency in Printed Books: 29:1

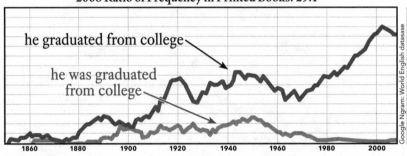

2008 Ratio of Frequency in Printed Books: 9:1

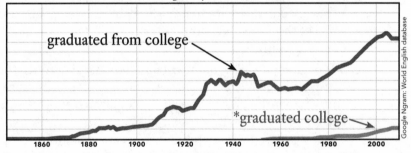

graffiti. Borrowed as an Italian plural—the singular being *graffito*—*graffiti* is now regarded as a mass noun taking a singular verb {graffiti was all over the wall}. *Graffiti were* suggests preciosity in modern usage.

grateful; gratified. To be *grateful* is to be thankful or appreciative. To be *gratified* is to be pleased, satisfied, or indulged.

grievous. So spelled {a grievous misdeed}—not **grievious.*

grisly; grizzly. What is *grisly* is gruesome or horrible {grisly details}. What is *grizzly* is grayish {grizzly hair} or bearish {the North American grizzly bear}.

guild, *n.;* **gild,** *vb.* A *guild* is an organization of persons with a common interest or profession {a guild of goldsmiths}. To *gild* is to put a thin layer of gold on something {gild a picture frame}, sometimes in a figurative sense {gilding the lily}.

had better. See **better.**

hail; hale. To *hail* is to salute or greet {hail, Caesar!}, to acclaim enthusiastically {hailed as the greatest novelist of her time}, or to shout as an attention-getter {hail a taxi}. To *hale* is to compel to go {haled into court}.

    Hail is also a noun denoting ice-pellet precipitation, or something like it {a hail of insults}. *Hale* is also an adjective describing someone who is physically sound and free from infirmities.

half (of). Delete the *of* whenever possible {half the furniture}. When *half* is followed by a singular noun, the verb is singular {half the state is solidly Democratic}; when it is followed by a plural noun, the verb is plural {half the people are Republicans}.

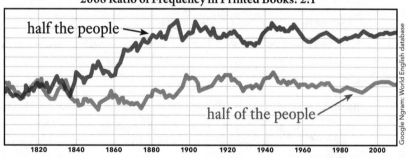

2008 Ratio of Frequency in Printed Books: 2:1

handful. If *handful* applies to a mass noun, use a singular verb {a handful of trouble is ahead}. But if *handful* applies to a plural count noun, use a plural verb {only a handful of walnut trees still line Main Street}.

hangar; hanger. One finds *hangars* (large buildings where aircraft are kept) at an airport {airplane hangars}. Everywhere else, one finds *hangers* {clothes hangers} {picture hangers}.

hanged; hung. *Hanged* is used as the past participle of *hang* only in its transitive form when referring to the killing (just or unjust) of a human being by suspending the person by the neck {criminals were hanged at Tyburn Hill}. But if death is not intended or likely, or if the person is suspended by a body part other than the neck, *hung* is correct {he was hung upside down as a cruel prank}. In most senses, of course, *hung* is the past form of *hang* {Abdul hung up his clothes}.

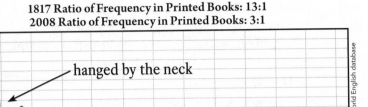

Google Ngram: World English database

1817 Ratio of Frequency in Printed Books: 13:1
2008 Ratio of Frequency in Printed Books: 3:1

hanger. See **hangar.**

harass; embarrass. The first word has one -*r*-; the second has two. The pronunciation of *harass* also causes confusion. The dominant American pronunciation stresses the second syllable, while BrE stresses the first.

hardly; scarcely. These words are often treated as negatives. Beware that using them with negative constructions often typifies uneducated speech, as in **I can't hardly listen to that!*

harebrained. So spelled (after the timid, easily startled animal)—not **hairbrained.*

hark back. So written—preferably not **harken back* or **hearken back.*

have; have got. In formal prose, prefer *have* {I have four nickels} and *do not* (or *don't*) *have* {I don't have any such books}. In informal contexts—especially in BrE—*have got* {I've got four pence} and *have not* (or *haven't*) *got* {I haven't got any such books} are common.

he. 1. For the use of *he* as a generic pronoun referring to either sex, see §§ 436, 442. **2.** For a discussion of *than he* (vs. *him*), see § 68.

healthy; healthful. Traditionally, a living thing that is *healthy* enjoys good health; something that is *healthful* promotes health {a healthful diet will keep you healthy}. But gradually *healthy* is taking over both senses.

help (to). Omit the *to* when possible {talking will help resolve the problem}.

he or she. To avoid sexist language, many writers use this alternative phrasing (in place of the generic *he*). Use it sparingly—preferably after exhausting all other, less obtrusive methods of achieving gender-neutrality. In any event, *he or she* is much preferable to **he/she*, **s/he*, **(s)he*, and the like. See §§ 436, 438–39.

her. For a discussion of *than she* (vs. *her*), see § 68.

hers. So written—not *her's.

him. For a discussion of *than he* (vs. *him*), see § 68.

historic; historical. The shorter word refers to what is momentous in history {January 16, 1991, was a historic day in Kuwait}. *Historical*, meanwhile, refers simply to anything that pertains to or occurred in history {the historical record}.

On the question whether to use *a* or *an* before *historic* and *historical*, see **a; an** (p. 228).

hoard; horde. A *hoard* is a supply, usually secret and sometimes valuable. *Hoard* is also a verb meaning "to amass such a supply," especially when there is no need to do so. A *horde* was originally a tribe of Asian nomads; today a *horde* is a large crowd, esp. one that moves in a noisy, uncontrolled way.

Hobson's choice. Today this clichéd idiom is usually taken to mean "a choice between two bad options." But the original sense referred to Thomas Hobson (1544–1631), a stable keeper in Cambridge, England, whose customers could take the horse closest to the door or nothing. Hobson's choice, then, was no choice at all. Use of the new sense may irk some purists. It is a blunder to make the first word in this phrase *Hobbesian*, as if the reference were to the English philosopher Thomas Hobbes (1588–1679).

> There is a general standard. Its criteria may not be official. They may not even be recognized and accepted by the majority of the people. By no power can they conceivably be enforced in common usage. They are in constant dispute by so-called authorities. This standard occupies a region hazily defined as to boundary, a battleground for theories and the rivalry of rulemakers. The sciences of grammar and rhetoric are not exact; but actually the disputes over one principle or rule and another do but emphasize the existence of an irrepressible desire for standardisation.
> —Edward N. Teall
> *Putting Words to Work*

hoi polloi. This is a mildly disparaging phrase for "common people." It does not refer to elites, though some writers and speakers misuse it in this way (perhaps from false association with *hoity-toity*). It is a plural. Although *hoi* is Greek for "the," the phrase is commonly rendered *the hoi polloi* and has been at least since it was used by John Dryden in 1668.

1940 Ratio of Frequency in Printed Books: 3:1
2008 Ratio of Frequency in Printed Books: 1:1

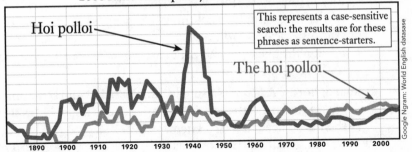

Hoi polloi

The hoi polloi

This represents a case-sensitive search: the results are for these phrases as sentence-starters.

Google Ngram: World English datasase

holocaust. When capitalized, this word refers to the Nazi genocide of European Jews in World War II. When not capitalized, it refers (literally or figuratively) to extensive devastation caused by fire or to the systematic and malicious killings of human beings on a vast scale. Avoid any light or hyperbolic use of this word.

home in. This phrase is frequently misrendered **hone in.* (*Hone* means "to sharpen.") *Home in* refers to what homing pigeons and aerial bombs do; the meaning is "to come closer and closer to a target."

1974 Ratio of Frequency in Printed Books: 16:1
2008 Ratio of Frequency in Printed Books: 2:1

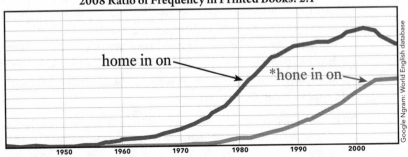

home in on

*hone in on

Google Ngram: World English database

homicide. See **murder.**

homogeneous. So written, in five syllables—preferably not **homogenous.*

hopefully. The old meaning of the word ("in a hopeful manner") seems unsustainable; the newer meaning ("I hope" or "it is to be hoped that"), as a sentence adverb (see § 211), spread in the 1960s and 1970s and seems here to stay. But many careful writers still deplore the new meaning.

horde. See **hoard.**

however. 1. On using this word to start a sentence, see § 278. **2.** On the problem of creating a comma splice with *however,* see § 469.

humanitarian. This word means "involving the promotion of human welfare" {humanitarian philanthropy}. Avoid using it in a phrase such as *the worst humanitarian disaster in decades,* where it really means just "human."

hung. See **hanged.**

I; me. When you need a first-person pronoun, use one. It's not immodest to do so; it's superstitious not to. But be sure you get the right one {Sally and I are planning to go} {give John or me a call} {keep this between you and me}. For more on the case of pronouns, see § 56. See **between you and me.**

idyllic. An *idyll* is a short pastoral poem, and by extension *idyllic* means charming or picturesque. It is not synonymous with *ideal* (perfect).

i.e.; e.g. The first is the abbreviation for *id est* ("that is"); the second is the abbreviation for *exempli gratia* ("for example"). The English equivalents are preferable in formal prose, though sometimes the compactness of these two-character abbreviations makes them desirable. Always put a comma after either one.

if; whether. While *if* is conditional, *whether* introduces an alternative, often in the context of an indirect question. Use *whether* in two circumstances: (1) to introduce a noun clause: *he asked whether his tie was straight* (the alternatives are *yes* and *no*), and (2) when using *if* produces ambiguity. In the sentence *he asked if his tie was straight,* the literal meaning is "whenever his tie was straight, he asked"; the popular meaning "he wanted someone to tell him whether his tie did or didn't need straightening" may not be understood by all readers. More tellingly, *Call me to let me know if you can come* means that you should call only if you're coming. *Call to let me know whether you can come* means that you should call regardless of whether the answer is yes or no. Avoid substituting *if* for *whether* unless your tone is intentionally informal or you are quoting someone. See **determine whether** & **whether.**

> There is no such thing as THE dictionary. There are many English dictionaries, and these differ widely in their accuracy and reliability as a record of English words and usages. Even among the good ones there are differences in the treatment of individual entries.
> —Wallace L. Anderson
> and Norman C. Stageberg
> *Introductory Readings on Language*

ignoramus. Pl. *ignoramuses*—not **ignorami* (though some might argue that it's fitting). The word is a verb in Latin meaning "we do not know"—not a first-declension noun.

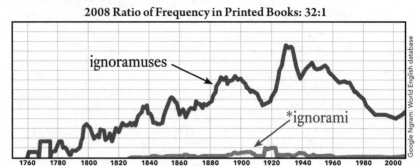

2008 Ratio of Frequency in Printed Books: 32:1

Google Ngram: World English database

ilk. This noun commonly means "type" or "sort" in modern usage, and unobjectionably so today {of his ilk} {of that ilk}. The Scottish phrase *of that ilk* means "of the same name or place."

illegal. See **unlawful.**

illegible; unreadable. Handwriting or printing that is *illegible* is not clear enough to be read {illegible scrawlings}. Writing that is *unreadable* is so poorly composed as to be either incomprehensible or intolerably dull.

illicit. See **elicit** & **unlawful.**

illude. See **allude.**

immigrate; emigrate. To *immigrate* is to enter a country to live permanently, leaving a past home. To *emigrate* is to leave one country to live in another one. The cognate forms also demand attention. Someone who moves from Ireland to the United States is an *immigrant* here and an *emigrant* there. An *émigré* is also an *emigrant*, but especially one in political exile.

imminent. See **eminent.**

impact. Resist using this word as a verb. Try *affect* or *influence* instead. Besides being hyperbolic, *impact* is still considered a solecism by traditionalists (though it is gaining ground). Cf. **access.**

impeachment. *Impeachment* is the legislative equivalent of an indictment, not a conviction. In the U.S. federal system, the House of Representatives votes on impeachment, and the Senate votes on removal from office.

impelled. See **compelled.**

implicit. See **explicit.**

imply; infer. The writer or speaker *implies* (hints, suggests); the reader or listener *infers* (deduces). Writers and speakers often use *infer* as if it were synonymous with *imply*, but careful writers always distinguish between the two words. See **inference.**

important; importantly. In the phrase *more important(ly)*—usually at the outset of a sentence—traditionalists prefer the shorter form as an ellipsis of *what is more important*, normally with a comma following. But *more importantly* is now established as a sentence adverb—and it's unobjectionable.

impractical; impracticable. The first is the more general adjective, meaning "not sensible" or "unrealistic" {impractical planning that doesn't account for travel expenses}. The second means "impossible to carry out" {landing aircraft on that hole-ridden runway proved impracticable}.

in actual fact. See **actual fact, in.**

inasmuch as. *Because* or *since* is almost always a better choice. See **because** & **since.**

in behalf of. See **behalf.**

incidence; incident; instance. Be careful with the first of these words: it has to do with relative rates and ranges {the incidence of albinism within a given society}. Perhaps leave it to scientists and actuaries. An *incident* (= an event, occurrence, or happening) should be distinguished from an *instance* (= a case, example).

include; comprise. The basic difference between these near-synonyms is that *include* implies nonexclusivity {the collection includes 126 portraits [suggesting that there is much else in the collection]}, while *comprise* implies exclusivity {the collection comprises 126 silver spoons [suggesting that nothing else is part of the collection]}. Oddly, in patent law—and there alone—*comprise* carries a nonexclusive sense. See **comprise.**

> It has been maintained by some scholars that in the evolution of the language everything happens for the best, and that English in particular has lost nothing, at least so far as its grammar is concerned, that would have been worth keeping. But this extreme optimistic view can hardly be sustained.
> —Henry Bradley
> *The Making of English*

in connection with. This is a vague, fuzzy phrase {she explained the financial consequences in connection with the transaction} {Ray liked everything in connection with golf} {Phipson was compensated in connection with its report}. Try replacing the phrase with *of, related to,* or *associated with* {she explained the financial consequences of the transaction}, *about*

{Ray liked everything about golf}, or *for* {Phipson was compensated for its report}.

incredible; incredulous. *Incredible* properly means "too strange to be believed; difficult to believe." Colloquially, it is used to mean "astonishingly good" {it was an incredible trip}. *Incredulous* means "disbelieving, skeptical" {people are incredulous about the rising gas costs}.

inculcate; indoctrinate. One *inculcates* values *into* a child but *indoctrinates* the child *with* values. That is, *inculcate* always takes the preposition *into* and a value or values as its object {inculcate courage into soldiers}. *Indoctrinate* takes a person as its object {indoctrinate children with the habit of telling the truth}.

> When you encounter someone else's English, you can almost always draw some important conclusions about what kind of person you are dealing with.
>
> —R. L. Trask
> *Language: The Basics*

indicate. Often vague. When possible, use a more direct verb such as *state, comment, show, suggest,* or *say.*

individual. Use this word to distinguish a single person from a group. When possible, use a more specific term, such as *person, adult, child, man,* or *woman.*

indoctrinate. See **inculcate.**

induce. See **adduce.**

in excess of. Try replacing this verbose phrase with *more than* or *over.* See **over.**

infected; infested. Something that is *infected* is contaminated, specifically by disease or metaphorically by corruption. Something that is *infested* is overrun by something negative such as vermin, predatory animals, or crime.

infectious. See **contagious.**

infer. See **imply.**

inference. Use the verb *draw,* not *make,* with *inference* {they drew the wrong inferences}. Otherwise, readers may confuse *inference* with *implication.* See **imply.**

infested. See **infected.**

inflammable. See **flammable.**

inflict; afflict. Events, illnesses, punishments, etc. are *inflicted on* living things or entities {an abuser inflicts cruelty}. The sufferers are *afflicted with* or *by* disease, troubles, etc. {agricultural communities are afflicted with drought}.

ingenious; ingenuous. These words are similar in form but not in meaning. *Ingenious* describes what is intelligent, clever, and original {an ingenious invention}. *Ingenuous* describes a person who is candid, naive, and without dissimulation, or an action or statement with those qualities {a hurtful but ingenuous observation}.

innate; inherent. An *innate* characteristic is one that a living thing has from birth; it should be distinguished, then, from a talent or disposition that one acquires from training or experience. An *inherent* characteristic is also part of a thing's nature, but life is not implied. A rock, for example, has an inherent hardness.

innervate. See **enervate.**

innocent; not guilty. If you are *innocent*, you are without blame. If you are *not guilty*, you have been exonerated by a jury. Newspapers avoid the *not guilty* phrase, though, because the consequences of accidentally leaving off the *not* could be serious. See **pleaded.**

innumerable. See **enumerable.**

in order to; in order for. Often these expressions can be reduced to *to* and *for*. When that is so, and rhythm and euphony are preserved or even heightened, use *to* or *for*.

in proximity. See *close proximity.

input. As a noun, this word—meaning "contributions and suggestions"—seems less and less jargonistic by the year {did you have any input into the design?}. When it's used as a verb meaning "to put in," the jargonistic odor attached to the word is stronger {did you input the data?}. The verb is preferably inflected *input–input–input*—not *inputted. Cf. **output.**

> It is not surprising that most of us choose and use our words with no more thought than we give to respiration, fondly supposing that it is as easy and natural to speak the English language as it is to breathe the English air. But I, though I have no particular title nor aptitude for the affair and am in error as frequently as you, exhort you boldly in the nation's name to worry about words, to have an affection and respect and a curiosity for words, to keep a dictionary in the home and ask yourself often: "Now, why do I say that?" I am not urging you to be always right: for few can hope for that. But we can all worry; and that is the beginning of virtue.
>
> —A. P. Herbert
> *What a Word!*

inquire. The normal spellings in AmE and BrE alike are *inquire* and *inquiry*. *Enquire* and *enquiry* are primarily BrE variants.

in regard to. This is the phrase, not the nonstandard **in regards to*. But try a single-word substitute instead: *about*, *regarding*, *concerning*, etc.

1867 Ratio of Frequency in Printed Books: 6,419:1
2008 Ratio of Frequency in Printed Books: 13:1

insidious; invidious. What is *insidious* spreads gradually to cause damage—at first without being noticed {an insidious conspiracy}; what is *invidious* involves moral offensiveness and serious unpleasantness {invidious discrimination}.

in spite of. See **despite**.

instance. See **incidence**.

insure. See **ensure**.

intense; intensive. *Intense* means (1) "having a strong effect" {intense pressures}, (2) "involving a great deal of effort during a very short time" {intense concentration}, or (3) "having unduly strong feelings or a demeanor of exaggerated seriousness" {he's a bit too intense}. *Intense* is always preferred outside philosophical and scientific usages. But *intensive* should be retained in customary phrases such as *labor-intensive* and *intensive care*.

intently; intensely. An act done *intently* is done purposefully and with concentration and determination. One that is done *intensely* is done with great power, passion, or emotion, but not necessarily with deliberate intent.

inter; intern. *Inter* is a verb meaning "to bury (a dead person)"; the corresponding noun is *interment*. An *intern* is a student working temporarily to gain experience, esp. in a profession. *Intern* is also a verb with two senses. As an intransitive verb, it means "to work as an intern" {interning at the U.S. Senate}; the corresponding noun is *internship*. As a transitive verb, it means "to confine (a civilian) to a certain place or district without a criminal charge, esp. in wartime or for political reasons"; the corresponding noun is *internment*.

internecine. The accepted meaning of this word has shifted far from its origin, which described a war of slaughter, and from its more modern sense, regarding warfare that is mutually destructive. In American usage today, *internecine* also describes any internal controversy or power struggle. Some traditionalists object to that use as being too far removed from the word's traditional senses.

in the affirmative. See **affirmative, in the.**

in the event that. See **event.**

in the near future. See **future, in the near.**

in the negative. See **affirmative, in the.**

inveigh; inveigle. To *inveigh* is to protest, usu. against something {picketers inveighed against annexation}. To *inveigle* is to cajole or ensnare, esp. by misleading {inveigling a friend to attend the party}.

invidious. See **insidious.**

invoke. See **evoke.**

***irregardless.** An error. Use *regardless* (or possibly *irrespective*).

2008 Ratio of Frequency in Printed Books: 572:1

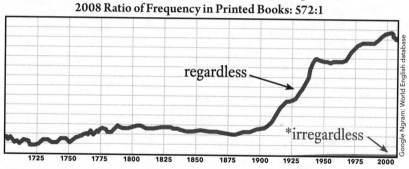

it is I; it is me. Both are correct and acceptable. The first phrase, using the first-person predicate nominative, is strictly grammatical (and a little stuffy); the second is idiomatic (and relaxed), and it is often contracted to *it's me.* In third-person constructions, however, a greater stringency holds sway in good English {this is he} {it isn't she who has caused such misery}. See § 67.

its; it's. *Its* is the possessive form of *it*; *it's* is the contraction for *it is* {it's a sad dog that scratches its fleas}.

jealousy; envy. *Jealousy* connotes feelings of resentment toward another, particularly in matters relating to an intimate relationship {sexual jealousy}. *Envy* refers to covetousness of another's advantages, possessions, or abilities {his transparent envy of others' successes}.

jibe; jive. See **gibe.**

judgment. So spelled in AmE. In BrE, the spelling *-dgem-* is preferred (except in law).

karat. See **carat.**

kind. Use *this kind of question* or *these kinds of questions*—not **these kind of questions.*

kudos. Preferably pronounced /k[y]oo-dos/ (not /-dohz/), this word means "praise and admiration." It is singular, not plural. Hence avoid **kudo is* or **kudos are.*

lady. When used as a synonym for *woman*—indeed, when used anywhere but in the phrase *ladies and gentlemen*—this word will be considered objectionable by some readers who think that it refers to a patronizing stereotype. This is especially true when it is used for unprestigious jobs {cleaning lady} or as a condescending adjective {lady lawyer}. Some will insist on using it to describe a refined woman. If they've consulted this entry, they've been forewarned. Cf. **gentleman.** See § 441.

> I'm tired of television announcers, hosts, newscasters, and commentators, nibbling away at the English language, making obvious and ignorant mistakes.
> —George Carlin
> *Brain Droppings*

last; lastly. As with *first, second,* etc., prefer *last* when introducing a final point of discussion—or (of course) *finally.*

latter. See **former.**

laudable; laudatory. *Laudable* means "praiseworthy, even if not fully successful" {a laudable effort}. *Laudatory* means "expressing praise" {laudatory phone calls}.

lay; lie. Admittedly, the traditional conjugations are more blurred than ever. Mastering them has proved difficult for people. Nevertheless, here goes.

Lay is a transitive verb—that is, it demands a direct object {lay your pencils down}. It is inflected *lay–laid–laid* {I laid the book there yesterday} {these rumors have been laid to rest}. (The children's prayer *Now I lay me down to sleep* is a good mnemonic device for the transitive *lay.*)

Lie is an intransitive verb—that is, it never takes a direct object {lie down and rest}. It is inflected *lie–lay–lain* {she lay down and rested} {he hasn't yet lain down in 23 hours}. In a doctor's office, you should be asked to *lie back* or *lie down*.

2008 Ratio of Frequency in Printed Books: 10:1

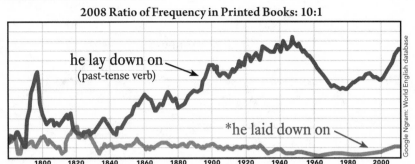

leach; leech. To *leach* is to percolate or to separate out solids in solution by percolation. A *leech* is a bloodsucker (whether literal or figurative). By extension of that noun, to *leech* is either to attach oneself to another as a leech does or to drain the resources of something.

lead. See **led.**

lean. This verb is inflected *lean–leaned–leaned*—not, preferably, **leant.*

leap. This verb is inflected *leap–leaped–leaped* in AmE (that's been so since the 18th century) and *leap–leapt–leapt* in BrE.

learn. The predominant inflection is *learn–learned–learned*, though *learnt* is an acceptable variant in BrE.

lease; let. Many Americans seem to think that *let* is colloquial and of modern origin. In fact, the word is 300 years older than *lease* and just as proper. One distinction between the two words is that either the owner or the tenant can be said to *lease* property, but only the owner can be said to *let* it.

led. This is the correct spelling of the past tense and past participle of the verb *lead*. It is often misspelled *lead*, maybe in part because of the pronunciation of the metal *lead* or the past tense and past participle *read*, which rhymes with *led*.

leech. See **leach.**

lend, *vb.*; **loan,** *vb. & n. Lend* is the correct term for letting someone use something with the understanding that it (or its equivalent) will be returned. The verb *loan* is standard esp. when money is the subject of the transaction—but even then, *lend* appears somewhat more frequently in

> The teacher and the printing-press are the great supporters of linguistic tradition.
> —Henry Alexander
> *The Story of Our Language*

edited English. *Loan* is the noun corresponding to both *lend* and *loan, vb.* The past-tense and past-participial form of *lend* is *lent.*

2008 Ratio of Frequency in Printed Books: 2:1

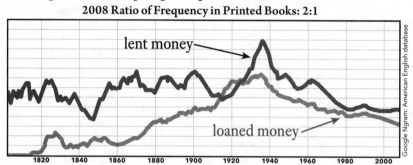

less; fewer. Reserve *less* for mass nouns or amounts {less salt} {less soil} {less water}. Reserve *fewer* for count nouns {fewer calories} {fewer people} {fewer suggestions}. One easy guideline is to use *less* with singular nouns and *fewer* with plural nouns.

2008 Ratio of Frequency in Printed Books: 7:1

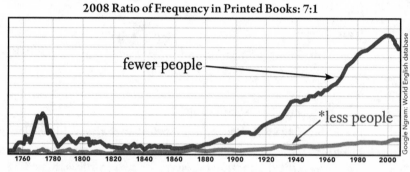

lest. This is one of the few English words that invariably call for a verb in the subjunctive mood {he didn't want to drive lest he take a wrong turn} {he has turned down the volume lest he disturb his roommates}. The conjunction is somewhat more common in BrE than in AmE.

let. See **lease.**

libel. See **defamation.**

license, *n.* & *vb.* So spelled in AmE and BrE alike—though in BrE *licence* is a variant spelling for the noun.

lie. See **lay.**

life-and-death; *life-or-death. The problem of logic aside (life and death being mutually exclusive), the first phrase is the standard idiom {a life-and-death decision}. Note the spikes in frequency of use during World War I and World War II.

2008 Ratio of Frequency in Printed Books: 2:1

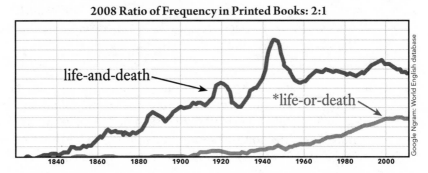

light, *vb.* This verb can be inflected either *light–lit–lit* or *light–lighted–lighted*—and irreproachably so. The past-participial adjective tends to be *lighted* when not modified by an *-ly* adverb {a lighted building} {a well-lighted hall}, but *lit* if an *-ly* adverb precedes {brightly lit sconces} {a nicely lit walkway}.

lightning. So spelled {lightning strike}—unless the sense is "making or becoming lighter" {lightening your load}.

like; as. The use of *like* as a conjunction (as in the old jingle "tastes good like a cigarette should") has long been a contentious issue. Traditionally speaking, *like* is a preposition, not a conjunction equivalent to *as* {you're much like me [*me* is the object of the preposition *like*]} {do as I say [the conjunction *as* connects the imperative *do* with the independent clause *I say*]}. As a casualism, however, the conjunctive *like* has become especially common since the mid-20th century {nobody cares like I do} {it tastes good like a fine chocolate should}. In Standard Written English, a conjunctive *like* will still provoke frowns among some readers. But the objections are slowly dwindling. If you want your prose to be unimpeachable and heightened, stick to *as* and *as if* for conjunctive senses {as we've observed, man is a social animal} {it looks as if it might rain}.

like; such as. Is it permissible to say *Universities like MIT and Stanford help set the government's policies in technical fields*? That is, should it be *such as*? Are the exemplars actually listed to be included in the genus denoted by the noun preceding *like*? Literalists say that only colleges *similar* to MIT and Stanford—but not those schools themselves—are included, so if MIT and Stanford *are* meant to be included, the reference should be to *Universities such as MIT and Stanford*. This hard-nosed literalism may be hard to shake, but it's hardly impossible for writers like you and me.

likely. See **apt.**

literally. This word means "actually; without exaggeration." It should not be used loosely in figurative senses, as in *they were literally glued to their seats* (unless glue had in fact been applied). Wherever guides have accepted this usage, they should be disregarded.

loan. See **lend.**

loathe, *vb.;* **loath,** *adj.* To *loathe* (/loh<u>th</u>/)something is to detest it intensely or to regard it with disgust {I loathe tabloid television}. Someone who is *loath* (/lohth/) is reluctant or unwilling {Tracy seems loath to admit mistakes}. The soft *-th-* sound in *loathsome* (/loh<u>th</u>-səm/), meaning "abhorrent," prompts many to misspell it **loathesome.*

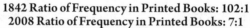

1842 Ratio of Frequency in Printed Books: 102:1
2008 Ratio of Frequency in Printed Books: 7:1

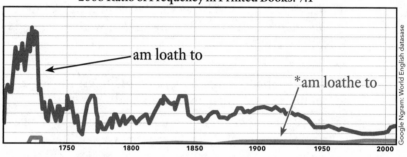

am loath to

*am loathe to

Google Ngram: World English datasase

lose; loose, *vb.;* **loosen.** To *lose* something is to be deprived of it. To *loose* something is to release it from fastenings or restraints. To *loosen* is to make less tight or to ease a restraint. *Loose* conveys the idea of complete release, whereas *loosen* refers to only a partial release.

lot. See **a lot.**

luxuriant; luxurious. The two terms are fairly often confused (an example of catachresis). What is *luxuriant* is lush and grows abundantly {a luxuri-ant head of hair}. What is *luxurious* is lavish, extravagant, and comfort-able {a luxurious resort}.

mad; angry. Some people object to using *mad* to mean "angry" and would reserve it to mean "insane." But the first sense dates back 700 years and isn't likely to disappear. As common as it is in everyday use, though, it has been so stigmatized that most people avoid it in formal writing.

majority. This noun preferably denotes countable things {a majority of votes cast}, not uncountable ones {the majority of the time}. Use *most* whenever it fits.

When referring to a preponderance of votes cast, *majority* takes a singular verb {her majority was 7%}. But referring to a predominant group of people or things, it can take either a singular verb {the majority in the House was soon swept away} or a plural one {the majority of the voters were against the proposal}. Typically, if a genitive with a plural object follows *majority*, the verb should be plural {a majority of music teachers prefer using the metronome}.

malevolent; maleficent. *Malevolent* describes an evil mind that wishes to harm others {with malevolent intent}. *Maleficent* is similar but describes desire by the miscreant for accomplishing evil {maleficent bullying}.

malodorous. See **odious.**

maltreatment. See **mistreatment.**

mankind. Consider *humankind* instead.

manslaughter. See **murder.**

mantle; mantel. A *mantle* is a long, loose garment like a cloak—almost always today being used in a metaphorical sense {assuming the mantle of a martyr}. A *mantel* is a wood or stone structure around a fireplace {family pictures on the mantel}.

> It is right to be concerned about the proliferation of mistakes in language, about changes that obliterate useful distinctions, about obscure or clumsy writing, about unethical abuses through language.
> —Sidney Greenbaum
> *Good English and the Grammarian*

many. See **numerous.**

marriage; wedding. *Marriage* best refers to the legal status of two people united by vows or a marriage contract. Figuratively, it refers to the merger of two entities or the blending or juxtaposition of two things {a marriage of gospel and bluegrass}. *Wedding* refers to the ceremony or act of joining in marriage.

masterful; masterly. *Masterful* describes a person who is dominating and imperious. *Masterly* describes a person who has mastered a craft, trade, or profession; the word often means "authoritative" {a masterly analysis}. Because *masterly* does not readily make an adverb (**masterlily* being extremely awkward [see § 212]), try *in a masterly way.*

may; can. See **can.**

may; might. *May* expresses what is possible, is factual, or could be factual {I may have turned off the stove, but I can't recall doing it}. *Might* suggests something that is uncertain, hypothetical, or contrary to fact {I might have won the marathon if I had entered}. See § 201.

me. See **I.**

medal; meddle; metal; mettle. A *medal* is an award for merit; a *metal* is a type of substance, usually hard and heavy. To *meddle* is to interfere. And *mettle* is a person's character, courage, and determination to do something no matter how difficult.

media; mediums. In scientific contexts and in reference to mass communications, the plural of *medium* is predominantly *media* {some bacteria flourish in several types of media} {the media are reporting more medical news}. Although one frequently sees *media is*, the plural use is recommended instead. If *medium* refers to a spiritualist, the plural is *mediums* {several mediums have held séances here}.

memoranda; memorandums. Although both plural forms are correct, *memoranda* has predominated since the early 19th century. Don't use *memoranda* as if it were singular—the word is *memorandum* {this memorandum is} {these memoranda are}.

2008 Ratio of Frequency in Printed Books: 8:1

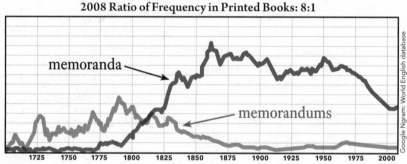

metal; mettle. See **medal**.

mete out. The phrase meaning "to distribute" or "to assign" is so spelled {mete out punishment}. **Meet out* is a common error, esp. in the erroneous past tense **meeted out*.

meter. So spelled in both AmE and BrE in reference to an instrument that measures or records {water meter}. It is also so spelled in AmE in reference to the unit of length and to poetic rhythms—in which senses BrE prefers *metre*.

might. See **may**.

militate. See **mitigate**.

minuscule. Something that is minuscule is "very small." Probably because of the spelling of the modern word *mini* (and the prefix of the same spelling, which is recorded only from 1936), it is often misspelled **miniscule*. In printing, *minuscules* are lowercase letters and *majuscules* are capital (uppercase) letters.

mischievous. This three-syllable word is so spelled—not **mischievious* (a bit of misspelling mischief).

misspell, *vb.* So spelled. It's inflected *misspell–misspelled–misspelled,* although *misspelt* often occurs in BrE.

mistreatment; maltreatment. *Mistreatment* is the more general term. *Maltreatment* denotes a harsh form of mistreatment, involving abuse by rough or cruel handling.

mitigate; militate. To *mitigate* is to lessen or soften the effects of something unpleasant, harmful, or serious; *mitigating circumstances* lessen the seriousness of a crime. To *militate,* by contrast, is to have a marked effect on; the word is usually followed by *against* {his nearsightedness militated against his ambition to become a commercial pilot}. Avoid the mistaken phrase **mitigate against* for the correct *militate against.*

1860 Ratio of Frequency in Printed Books: 2,528:1
2008 Ratio of Frequency in Printed Books: 4:1

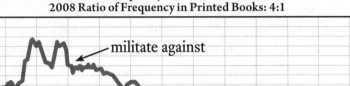

moot; mute. *Moot* (/moot/) means (traditionally) "debatable" {a moot point worth our attention} or (by modern extension) "having no practical significance" {a moot question that is of no account}. *Mute* (/m[y]oot/) means "silent, speechless"—and is often considered offensive when used as a noun {deaf-mute}.

more important(ly). See **important.**

more than. See **over.**

much; very. *Much* generally intensifies past-participial adjectives {much obliged} {much encouraged} and some comparatives {much more} {much worse} {much too soon}. *Very* intensifies adverbs and most adjectives {very carefully} {very bad}, including past-participial adjectives that have more adjectival than verbal force {very bored}. See § 129.

murder; manslaughter; homicide. All three words denote the killing of one person by another. *Murder* and *manslaughter* are both unlawful killings, but *murder* is done maliciously and intentionally. *Homicide* includes killings that are not unlawful, such as by a police officer acting properly in the line of duty. *Homicide* also refers to a person who kills another.

mute. See **moot.**

mutual. See **common.**

myself. Avoid using *myself* as a pronoun in place of *I* or *me*—a quirk that arises most often after an *and* or *or.* Instead, use it reflexively {I did myself a favor} or emphatically {I myself have tried to get through that book!}. See §§ 73–74.

naturalist; naturist. *Naturalist* most often denotes a person who studies natural history, esp. a field biologist or an amateur who observes and usually photographs, sketches, or writes about nature. *Naturist* denotes a nature-worshipper or a nudist.

> The most important part of our everyday English has not to do with grammar, or with spelling, or with pronunciation. It has to do with the right use of words as to their meaning and their logical connection; and this may be learned by study and by care at almost any time of life.
> —Richard Grant White
> *Every-Day English*

nauseous; nauseated. Whatever is *nauseous*, traditionally speaking, induces a feeling of nausea—it makes us feel sick to our stomachs. To feel sick is to be *nauseated*. Although the use of *nauseous* to mean *nauseated* may be too common to be called an error anymore, strictly speaking it is poor usage. Because of the ambiguity in *nauseous*, the wisest course may be to stick to the participial adjectives *nauseated* and *nauseating.*

necessary; necessitous. *Necessary* means "required under the circumstances" {the necessary arrangements}. *Necessitous* means "impoverished" {living in necessitous circumstances}.

neither. Four points. First, like *either,* this word when functioning as subject of a clause takes a singular verb {neither of the subjects was given that medicine}. Second, a *neither–nor* construction should frame grammatically parallel expressions {neither the room's being too cold nor the heater's malfunction could justify his boorish reaction} (both noun elements). (See §§ 266, 332.) Third, a simple *neither–nor* construction should have only two elements {neither bricks nor stones}—though it's perfectly permissible to multiply *nors* for emphasis {neither snow nor rain nor heat nor gloom of night}. Fourth, the word is acceptably pronounced either /**nee**-thər/ or /**nı**-thər/.

nerve-racking; *nerve-wracking. Use the former. See **rack.**

1920 Ratio of Frequency in Printed Books: 14:1
2008 Ratio of Frequency in Printed Books: 2:1

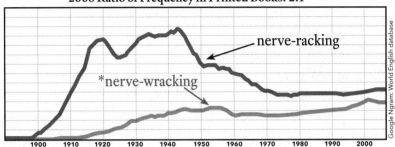

nevertheless. One word.

no. See **affirmative, in the.**

noisome. This word has nothing to do with *noise.* It means noxious, offensive, or foul-smelling {a noisome landfill}.

none. This word may take either a singular or a plural verb. A guideline: if it is followed by a singular noun, treat it as a singular {none of the building was painted}; if by a plural noun, treat it as a plural {none of the guests were here when I arrived}. But for special emphasis, it is quite proper (though possibly stilted) to use a singular verb when a plural noun follows {none of my suggestions was accepted}.

nonetheless. One word.

nonplussed. Traditionally meaning "surprised and confused" {she was nonplussed when he took off the mask}, this word is now frequently misused to mean "unfazed"—almost the opposite of its literary sense. Avoid this newer usage, and avoid the variant spelling *nonplused.* See **faze.**

normality. Prefer this word over *normalcy.*

2008 Ratio of Frequency in Printed Books: 2:1

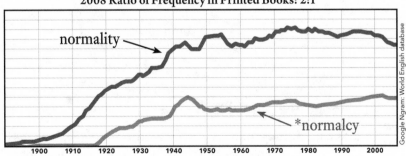

notable; noticeable; noteworthy. *Notable* (= readily noticed) applies both to physical things and to qualities {notable sense of humor}. *Noticeable* means "detectable with the physical senses" {a noticeable limp}. *Noteworthy* means "remarkable; deserving attention" {a noteworthy act of kindness}.

not guilty. See **innocent.**

not only–but also. For these correlative conjunctions, see §§ 266, 332.

notwithstanding. One word. Less formal alternatives include *despite, although,* and *in spite of.* The word *notwithstanding* may precede or follow a noun {notwithstanding her bad health, she decided to run for office} {her bad health notwithstanding, she decided to run for office}.

number. See **amount.**

numerous. This is typically a bloated word for *many.*

observance; observation. *Observance* means "obedience to a rule or custom" {the family's observance of Passover}. *Observation* means either "the watching of something" or "a remark based on watching or studying something" {a keen observation about the defense strategy}. Each term is sometimes used when the other would be the better word.

obtain. See **attain.**

obtuse; abstruse. *Obtuse* describes a person who can't understand; *abstruse* describes an idea that is hard to understand. A person who is *obtuse* is dull and, by extension, dull-witted. What is *abstruse* is incomprehensible or nearly so.

octopus. Pl. *octopuses*—not **octopi* (which is false Latin).

1960 Ratio of Frequency in Printed Books: 4:1
2008 Ratio of Frequency in Printed Books: 3:1

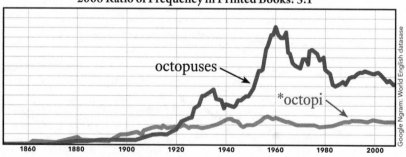

odious; odorous; odoriferous; malodorous. *Odious* means "hateful" or "extremely unpleasant" {odious Jim Crow laws}. It is not related to the other terms, but it is sometimes misused as if it were. *Odorous* means "detectable by smell (for better or worse)" {odorous gases}. *Odoriferous* means essentially the same thing: it has meant "fragrant" as often as it has meant "foul." *Malodorous* means "smelling quite bad." The mistaken form **odiferous* is often used as a jocular equivalent of *smelly*—but most dictionaries don't record it.

of. Avoid using this word needlessly after *all, off, inside,* and *outside.* Also, prefer *June 2015* over *June of 2015.* To improve your style, try removing every *of*-phrase that you reasonably can.

> I have waged a private war against *of.*
> —William H. C. Propp
> *Exodus 1–18* (Introduction)

off. Never put *of* after this word {we got off the bus}.

2008 Ratio of Frequency in Printed Books: 42:1

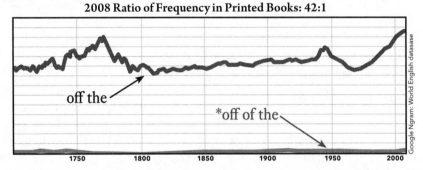

off the

*off of the

1750   1800   1850   1900   1950   2000

Google Ngram: World English datasase

officious. A person who is *officious* is aggressively nosy and meddlesome— and overeager to tell people what to do. The word has nothing to do with *officer* and should not be confused with *official.*

oftentimes. Prefer the shorter *often.*

on; upon. Prefer *on* to *upon* unless introducing an event or condition {put that on the shelf, please} {upon the job's completion, you'll get paid}. For more about *on,* see **onto.**

on behalf of. See **behalf.**

one another. See **each other.**

one ... his. Prefer *one ... one's* or *you ... your.*

one of those who; one of those that. These constructions require a plural verb in the *who*-clause because the antecedent of *who* is the plural immediately preceding—not *one* {she's one of those performers who are always in high demand}. See §§ 34, 86.

1900 Ratio of Frequency in Printed Books: 17:1
2008 Ratio of Frequency in Printed Books: 9:1

oneself. One word—not **one's self.*

onto; on to; on. When is *on* a preposition, and when an adverb? The sense of the sentence should tell, but the distinction can be subtle. *Onto* implies a movement, so it has an adverbial flavor even though it is a preposition {the gymnast jumped onto the bars}. When *on* is part of the verb phrase, it is an adverb and *to* is the preposition {the gymnast held on to the bars}. One trick is to mentally say "up" before *on*: if the sentence still makes sense, then *onto* is probably the right choice {she leaped onto the cap-stone}. Alone, *on* does not imply motion {the gymnast is good on the parallel bars}.

oppress; repress. *Oppress*, meaning "to persecute or tyrannize," is more negative than *repress*, meaning "to restrain or subordinate."

or. If this conjunction joins singular nouns functioning as subjects, the verb should be singular {cash or online payment is acceptable}.

oral. See **verbal.**

oration. See **peroration.**

ordinance; ordnance. An *ordinance* is a municipal regulation or an authoritative decree. *Ordnance* is military armament, especially artillery but also weapons and ammunition generally.

orient; orientate. To *orient* is to get one's bearings (literally, "to find east") {it took the new employee a few days to get oriented to the firm's suite}.

Unless used in the sense "to face or turn to the east," *orientate* is a poor variation to be avoided.

2008 Ratio of Frequency in Printed Books: 21:1

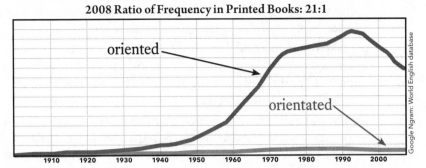

ought; should. Both express a sense of duty, but *ought* is stronger. Unlike *should, ought* requires a fully expressed infinitive, even in the negative {you ought not to see the movie}. Don't omit the *to*—as many otherwise well-educated speakers and writers have begun doing in recent years. See §§ 203, 205.

ours. So spelled—not *our's*.

ourselves. This is the word—not *ourself*.

output. This word is more commonly a noun than a verb, but when used as a verb it should be inflected *output–output–output*. Cf. **input.**

outside. In spatial references, no *of* is necessary—or desirable—after this word. But *outside of* is acceptable as a colloquialism meaning "except for" or "aside from."

over. As an equivalent of *more than*, this word is perfectly good idiomatic English. Cf. **in excess of.**

***overly.** Avoid this word, which is not considered the best usage. Try *over-* as a prefix {overprotective} or *unduly* {unduly protective}.

pair. This is a singular form, the plural being *pairs* {three pairs of shoes}. Yet *pair* may take either a singular verb {this pair of sunglasses was on the table} or a plural one {the pair were inseparable from the moment they met}.

palette; palate; pallet. An artist's *palette* is either the board that an artist uses for mixing colors or (collectively) the colors used by a particular artist or available in a computer program. Your *palate* is the roof of your mouth specifically or your taste in food generally. A *pallet* is a low, usually wooden platform for storing and transporting goods in commerce, or a crude bed consisting of a bag filled with straw.

pandemic. See **epidemic.**

parameters. Though it may sound elegant or scientific, this word is usually just pretentious when it is used in nontechnical contexts. Stick to *boundaries, limits, guidelines, grounds, elements,* or some other word.

partake in; partake of. To *partake in* is to participate in {the new student refused to partake in class discussions}. To *partake of* is either to get a part of {partake of the banquet} or to have a quality, at least to some extent {this assault partakes of revenge}.

partly; partially. Both words convey the sense "to some extent; in part" {partly responsible}. *Partly* is preferred in that sense. But *partially* has the additional senses of "incomplete" {partially cooked} and "unfairly; in a way that shows bias toward one side" {he treats his friends partially}.

> Words are tricky things, and it is only by careful study that you will learn to appreciate their subtle shades of meaning and to distinguish peculiarities of usage.
> —M. Alderton Pink
> *Craftsmanship in Writing*

past; passed. *Past* can be an adjective {past events} (often postpositive {times past}), a noun {remember the past}, a preposition {go past the school}, or an adverb {time flew past}. *Passed* is the past tense and past participle of the verb *pass* {we passed the school} {as time passed}.

pastime. This word combines *pass* (not *past*) and *time*. It is spelled with a single *s* and a single *t*.

peaceable; peaceful. A *peaceable* person or nation is inclined to avoid strife {peaceable kingdom}. A *peaceful* person, place, or event is serene, tranquil, and calm {a peaceful day free from demands}.

peak; peek; pique. These three sometimes get switched through writerly blunders. A *peak* is an apex, a *peek* is a quick or illicit glance, and a fit of *pique* is an episode of peevishness and wounded vanity. To *pique* is to annoy or arouse: an article *piques* (not *peaks*) one's interest.

pedal; peddle. *Pedal* is a noun, verb, or adjective relating to the pedal extremity, or foot. As a noun, it denotes a machine device that is operated by the foot and does some work, such as powering a bicycle or changing the sound of a piano. As a verb, it means to use such a device. As an adjective, it means "of or concerning such a device or its use." *Peddle* is a verb meaning either "to try to sell goods to people by traveling from place to place" or "to sell questionable goods to people"—questionable because they may be illegal, harmful, or low-quality {peddling magazine subscriptions door to door}.

peek. See **peak.**

pendant, *n.;* **pendent,** *adj.* A *pendant* is an item of dangling jewelry, especially one worn around the neck. What is *pendent* is hanging or suspended from something.

peninsula. This is the noun denoting a piece of land almost entirely surrounded by water but joined to a large area of land {they sailed around the Florida Peninsula}. The adjective is *peninsular* {the peninsular arm of Florida}. The adjective is often misused for the noun.

penultimate. This adjective means "next to last" {the penultimate paragraph in the précis}. Many people have started misusing it as a fancy equivalent of *ultimate.* The word *antepenultimate* means "the next to the next-to-last."

people; persons. The traditional view is that *persons* is used for smaller numbers {three persons}, and *people* with larger ones {millions of people}. But today most people use *people* even for small groups {only three people were there}. Note from the ngram that since 1980 *people* has actually become more common for small groups.

1839 Ratio of Frequency in Printed Books: 1:24
2008 Ratio of Frequency in Printed Books: 3:1

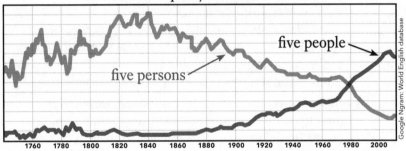

period of time; time period. Avoid these phrases. Try *period* or *time* instead.

peroration; oration. A *peroration,* strictly speaking, is the conclusion of an *oration* (speech). Careful writers avoid using *peroration* to refer to a long, rousing, or bombastic speech or piece of writing.

perpetuate; perpetrate. To *perpetuate* something is to sustain it or prolong it indefinitely {perpetuate the species}. To *perpetrate* is to commit or perform an act, esp. one that is illegal or morally wrong {perpetrate a crime}.

personally. Three points. First, use this word only when an actor does something that would normally be done through an agent {the president personally signed this invitation} or to limit other considerations

{Jean was affected by the decision but was not personally involved in it}. Second, *personally* is redundant when combined with an activity that necessarily requires the actor's presence {the senator personally shook hands with the constituents}. Third, *personally* shouldn't appear with *I* when stating an opinion; it weakens the statement and doesn't reduce the speaker's liability for the opinion. The only exception arises if a person is required to advance someone else's view but holds a different personal opinion {in the chamber I voted to lower taxes because of the constituencies I represented; but I personally believed that taxes should have been increased}.

persons. See **people.**

perspective, *n.* This is the word meaning "point of view" {from our perspective}—not *prospective* (an adjective meaning "expected to be something in the future") {a prospective CEO}.

persuade; convince. *Persuade* is associated with actions {persuade him to buy a suit}. *Convince* is associated with beliefs or understandings {she convinced the auditor of her honesty}. The phrase *persuade to (do)* has traditionally been considered better than *convince to (do)*—the latter having become common in AmE in the 1950s. But either verb will take a *that*-clause {the committee was persuaded that an all-night session was necessary} {my three-year-old is convinced that Santa Claus exists}.

> We ought to resist any perversion of the meaning of a word as long as we can.
> —Henry Bett
> *Some Secrets of Style*

pertain; appertain. *Pertain to,* the more common term, means "to relate directly to" {the clause pertains to assignment of risk}. *Appertain to* means "to belong to or concern something as a matter of form or function" {the defendant's rights appertain to the Fifth Amendment}.

phase. See **faze.**

phenomenon. This is the singular {the phenomenon of texting}, the plural being *phenomena* {cultural phenomena}.

pique. See **peak.**

pitiable; pitiful. To be *pitiable* is to be worthy of pity. To be *pitiful* is either to be very poor in quality or to be so sad or unfortunate as to make people feel sympathy.

pleaded; *pled. The first is the standard past-tense and past-participial form {he pleaded guilty} {they have pleaded with their families}. Avoid **pled*.

1826 Ratio of Frequency in Printed Books: 19:1
2008 Ratio of Frequency in Printed Books: 2:1

plethora. This noun denotes an excess, surfeit, or overabundance. Avoid it as a mere equivalent of "abundance."

pompom. So written, as a reduplicative word, even though the French loan-word was *pompon*. The French spelling is now a variant form in English.

populace; populous. The *populace* is the population of a country as a whole. A *populous* place is densely populated.

pore. To *pore over* something written is to read it intently {they pored over every word in the report}. Some writers confuse this word with *pour*.

practicable; possible; practical. These terms differ in shading. What is *practicable* is capable of being done; it's feasible. What is *possible* might be capable of happening or being done, but there is some doubt. What is *practical* is fit for actual use or in a particular situation.

precede; proceed. To *precede* is to happen before or to go before in some sequence, usually time. It also means "to outrank" or "to surpass" in some measure such as importance, but this sense is usually conveyed with the noun *precedence* {the board's vote takes precedence over the staff's recommendation}. The word is often misspelled **preceed*. To *proceed* is to go on, whether beginning, continuing, or resuming.

precipitate, *adj.;* **precipitous.** What is *precipitate* occurs suddenly or rashly, without proper consideration; it describes demands, actions, or movements. What is *precipitous* is dangerously steep; it describes cliffs and inclines.

precondition. Try *condition* or *prerequisite* instead.

predominant, *adj.;* **predominate,** *vb.* Like *dominant, predominant* is an adjective {a predominant point of view}. Like *dominate, predominate* is a verb {a point of view that predominates throughout the state}. Using *predominate* as an adjective is nonstandard.

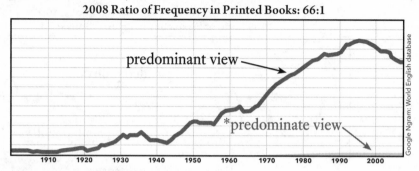

2008 Ratio of Frequency in Printed Books: 66:1

predominant view

*predominate view

preface. See **foreword.**

prejudice, *vb.* Although *prejudice* is a perfectly normal English noun to denote an all-too-common trait, the corresponding verb is a legalism. For a plain-English equivalent, use *harm* or *hurt.*

preliminary to. Make it *before, in preparing for,* or some other natural phrasing.

prerogative. A *prerogative* is a right or privilege afforded by one's office or class. It is often misspelled and mispronounced as if the first syllable were *per.*

prescribe. See **proscribe.**

presently. This word is ambiguous. Write *now* or *soon,* whichever you really mean.

presumption. See **assumption.**

preventive. Although the corrupt form **preventative* is fairly common, the strictly correct form is *preventive.*

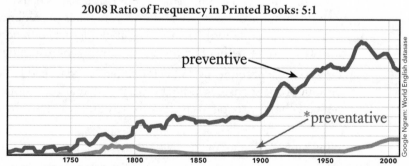

2008 Ratio of Frequency in Printed Books: 5:1

preventive

*preventative

*previous to. Make it *before.*

principle; principal. A *principle* is a natural, moral, or legal rule {the principle of free speech}. The corresponding adjective is *principled* {a principled decision}. A *principal* is a person of high authority or prominence {a school principal} or an initial deposit of money {principal and interest}. *Principal* is also an adjective meaning "most important." Hence a *principal* role is a primary one.

*****prior to.** Make it *before* or *until.*

proceed. See **precede.**

process of, in the. You can almost always delete this phrase without affecting the meaning. Cf. **current.**

propaganda. This is a singular noun denoting information that, being false or misleading, is used by a government or political group to influence people {propaganda was everywhere}. The plural is *propagandas.*

prophesy; prophecy. *Prophesy* is the verb meaning "to say what will happen in the future, esp. by using supernatural or magical knowledge" {the doomsayers prophesied a market boom despite the bad news}. *Prophecy* is the noun denoting a prediction made esp. by someone claiming to have supernatural or magical powers {their prophecies did not materialize}. **Prophesize* is an erroneous form sometimes encountered.

> To realize fully the difference between words and what they stand for is to be ready for differences as well as similarities in the world.
> —S. I. Hayakawa
> *Symbol, Status, and Personality*

proscribe; prescribe. To *proscribe* something is to prohibit it {legislation that proscribes drinking while driving}. To *prescribe* is to say officially what must be done in a particular situation {Henry VIII prescribed the order of succession to include three of his children} or to specify a medical remedy {the doctor prescribed anti-inflammatory pills and certain exercises}.

prospective. See **perspective.**

prostrate; prostate. One *prostrates* oneself by lying facedown on the ground in submission or worship, or from weakness. The *prostate* is a gland in the reproductive systems of male mammals.

protuberance. So spelled. Perhaps because *protrude* means "to stick out," writers want to spell *protuberance* (= something that bulges out) with an extra *r* (after the *t*). But the words are from different roots.

proved; proven. *Proved* is the preferred past participle for the verb *prove* {it was proved to be true}. Use *proven* only as an adjective {a proven success}.

1820 Ratio of Frequency in Printed Books: 275:1
2008 Ratio of Frequency in Printed Books: 2:1

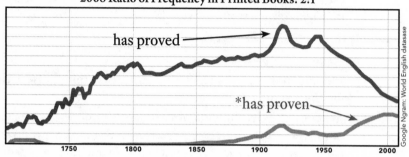

proximity. See *close proximity.

purposely; purposefully. What is done *purposely* is done deliberately or intentionally, or "on purpose." What is done *purposefully* is done with a certain goal or a clear aim in mind. An action may be done *purposely* without any particular interest in a specific result—that is, not *purposefully*.

question whether; question of whether; question as to whether. The first phrasing is traditionally considered best. The others are phraseologically inferior. See **as to.**

2008 Ratio of Frequency in Printed Books (two main forms): 1:1

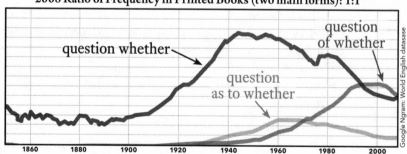

quick(ly). *Quickly* is the general adverb. But *quick* is properly used as an adverb in the idiomatic phrases *get rich quick* and *come quick*. See § 215.

quote; quotation. Traditionally a verb, *quote* is often used as an equivalent of *quotation* in speech and informal writing. Also, there is a tendency for writers (especially journalists) to think of *quotes* as contemporary remarks usable in their writing and of *quotations* as being wisdom of the ages expressed pithily.

rack; wrack. The spelling *rack* is complex: it accounts for nine different nouns and seven different verbs. As between *rack* and *wrack*, the former is standard in all familiar senses {racking his brains} {racked with guilt} {nerve-racking} {rack and ruin}. *Wrack* is the standard spelling only for the noun meaning "seaweed, kelp." See **nerve-racking.**

raise; raze. To *raise* is to elevate, move upward, enhance, bring up, etc. {we raised some money}. To *raze* is to demolish, level to the ground, remove, etc. {they razed the building}.

reason. Two points. First, as to *reason why*, although some object to the supposed redundancy of this phrase, it is centuries old and perfectly acceptable English. *Reason that* is not always an adequate substitute {can you give reasons why *that* is preferable to *which* as a restrictive relative pronoun?}. Second, **reason . . . is because* is not good usage—*reason . . . is that* being preferred {the reason we returned on July 2 is that we wanted to avoid hordes of tourists}.

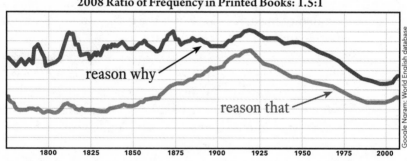

2008 Ratio of Frequency in Printed Books: 1.5:1

recur; reoccur. To *recur* is to happen again and again {his knee problems recurred throughout the rest of the year}, to return to in one's attention or memory {she recurred to her war experiences throughout our visit}, or to come back to one's attention or memory {the idea recurred to him throughout the night}. To *reoccur* is merely to happen again {the leak reoccurred during the second big rain}.

reek. See **wreak.**

reference; referral. A *reference* is a source of information, a person to provide information, an authority for some assertion, or a strong allusion to something. It's also an attributive adjective {reference book}. It's not universally accepted as a transitive verb. *Referral* is a narrower term denoting the practice or an instance of (1) directing someone to another person who can help, esp. a professional or a specialist, or (2) relegating some matter to another body for a recommendation or resolution.

refrain; restrain. To *refrain* is to restrain yourself or to keep from doing something; it is typically an act of self-discipline. Other people *restrain* you by stopping you from doing something, especially by using physical force {if you don't refrain from the disorderly conduct, the police will restrain you}. Yet it is possible to restrain oneself by controlling one's own emotions or behavior—and doing so is known as *self-restraint*.

refute, *vb.* To *refute* is to prove that a statement or an idea is wrong—not merely to deny or rebut.

regardless. See *irregardless.

regrettable; regretful. What is *regrettable* is unfortunate or unpleasant enough to make one wish that things were otherwise. A person who is *regretful* feels sorry or disappointed about something done or lost. The adverb *regrettably*, not *regretfully*, is the synonym of *unfortunately*.

rein; reign. A *rein* (usu. plural) controls a horse; it is the right word in idioms such as *take the reins*, *give free rein*, and, as a verb, *rein in*. A *reign* is a state of or term of dominion, esp. that of a monarch but by extension dominance in some field. This is the right word in idioms such as *reign of terror* and, as a verb, *reign supreme*.

relegate; delegate. To *relegate* is to assign a lesser position than before {the officer was relegated to desk duty pending an investigation}. To *delegate* is to authorize a subordinate to act in one's behalf {Congress delegated environmental regulation to the EPA} or to choose someone to do a particular job or to represent an organization or group {she was delegated to find a suitable hotel for the event}.

reluctant. See **reticent.**

renounce. See **denounce.**

reoccur. See **recur.**

repellent; repulsive. *Repellent* and *repulsive* both denote the character of driving others away. But *repulsive* has strong connotations of being so disgusting as to make one feel sick.

repetitive; repetitious. Both mean "occurring over and over." But whereas *repetitive* is fairly neutral in connotation, *repetitious* has taken on the nuance of tediousness that induces boredom.

replace. See **substitute.**

repress. See **oppress.**

repulsive. See **repellent.**

restaurateur. So spelled—not **restauranteur.*

2008 Ratio of Frequency in Printed Books: 188:1

restive; restful. *Restive* means "so dissatisfied or bored with a situation as to be impatient for change." *Restful* means "peaceful, quiet, and conducive to relaxation."

restrain. See **refrain.**

reticent. Avoid using this word as a synonym for *reluctant.* It means "unwilling to talk about what one feels or knows; taciturn" {when asked about the incident, the congressional representative became uncharacteristically reticent}.

revenge. See **avenge.**

rob; steal. Both verbs mean "to wrongfully take (something from another person)." But *rob* also includes a threat or act of harming, usu. but not always to the person being robbed.

role; roll. A *role* is an acting part {the role of Hamlet} or the way in which someone or something is involved in an activity or situation, esp. in reference to influence {the role that money plays as an incentive}. *Roll* has many meanings, including a roster {guest roll}; something made or done by rolling {roll of the dice}; and something in the shape of a cylinder or sphere, whether literally {dinner roll} or figuratively {bankroll}. *Roll* can also be a verb meaning to rotate {roll over!}, to wrap [something] {roll up the leftovers}, or to move forward {the cart rolled down the hill}.

run the gauntlet. See **gauntlet.**

sacrilegious. This is the correct spelling. There is a tendency by some to switch the *-i-* and *-e-* on either side of the *-l-*, but in fact the word is related to *sacrilege*, not *religion* or *religious.*

scarcely. See **hardly.**

seasonal; seasonable. *Seasonal* means either "happening as expected or needed during a particular time of year" {snow-skiing is a seasonal hobby} or "relating to the seasons or a season" {the seasonal aisle stays stocked most of the year, starting with Valentine's Day gifts in January}. *Seasonable* means "timely" {seasonable motions for continuance} or "fitting the time of year" {it was unseasonably cold for July}.

self-deprecating. See **deprecate.**

semi-. See **bi-.**

semiannual. See **biannual.**

sensor. See **censor.**

sensual; sensuous. What is *sensual* involves indulgence of the physical senses—especially sexual gratification. What is *sensuous* usually applies to aesthetic enjoyment; it is primarily hack writers who imbue the word with salacious connotations.

sewer; sewage; sewerage. *Sewer* denotes a wastewater pipe or passage. *Sewage* denotes the waste carried through such a pipe or passage. *Sewerage* denotes the sewer system as a whole, including treatment plants and other facilities, and the function of the disposal of sewage and wastewater in general.

shall. This word is complicated. For the traditional *will–shall* paradigm that modern grammarians have long repudiated, see § 175. The reality is that *shall* is little used in everyday contexts outside BrE—not in North America but also not in Australia, Ireland, or Scotland. In legal contexts, it frequently appears in statutes, rules, and contracts, supposedly in a mandatory sense but actually quite ambiguously. It is perhaps the most widely litigated word in the law—with wildly varying results in its multifarious interpretations. Legal drafters are therefore often advised to avoid it altogether in favor of *must, is, will, may,* and other phrases among which *shall*'s various meanings can be allocated.[3]

shear; sheer. *Shear* is the noun or verb relating to (1) the cutting tool, or (2) a force affecting movement, such as a crosswind or the slipping of plates in an earthquake. *Sheer* is most often an adjective meaning (1) "semitransparent" {a sheer curtain}, (2) "nothing but" {sheer madness}, or (3) "almost vertical" {a sheer cliff}.

sherbet. So spelled—not the erroneous reduplicative form **sherbert.*

---

3   See Garner, *Legal Writing in Plain English,* 2nd ed. (Chicago: Univ. of Chicago Press, 2013), 125–28; *Garner's Dictionary of Legal Usage,* 3rd ed. (New York: Oxford Univ. Press, 2011), 952–55 (collecting many authorities).

shine. When this verb is intransitive, it means "to give or make light"; the past tense is *shone* {the stars shone dimly}. When it is transitive, it means "to cause to shine"; the past tense is *shined* {the caterer shined the silver}.

should. See **ought**.

sight; site. A *sight* may be something worth seeing {the sights of London} or a device to aid the eye {the sight of a gun}, among other things. A *site* is a place, whether physical {a mall will be built on this site} or electronic {website}. The figurative expression meaning "to focus on a goal" is *to set one's sights*. Cf. **cite**.

simplistic. This word, meaning "oversimplified," has derogatory connotations. Don't confuse it with *simple*.

since. This word may relate either to time {since last winter} or to causation {since I'm a golfer, I know what "double bogey" means}. Some writers erroneously believe that the word relates exclusively to time. But the causal *since* was a part of the English language before Chaucer wrote in the fourteenth century, and it is useful as a slightly milder way of expressing causation than *because*. But if there is any possibility of confusion with the temporal sense, use *because*. See **because** & **inasmuch as**.

sink. Inflected *sink–sank–sunk*. Avoid using *sunk* as a simple past, as in *the ship sunk.

site. See **cite; sight**.

skulduggery. Traditionally so spelled—not (through folk etymology) *skullduggery*. The Scottish derivation has nothing to do with skulls. But *skullduggery* has been the slightly predominant spelling in AmE since the mid-1990s.

slander. See **defamation**.

slew; slough; *slue. As a noun, *slew* (/sloo/) is an informal word equivalent to *many* or *lots* {you have a slew of cattle}. It is sometimes misspelled *slough* (a legitimate noun meaning "a grimy swamp" [pronounced either /sloo/ or /slow/]). The phrase *slough of despond* (from Bunyan's *Pilgrim's Progress* [1678]) means "a state of depression or sadness from which one cannot easily lift oneself." This term is etymologically different from *slough* (/sləf/), meaning "to discard" {slough off dry skin}.

> Nobody learns his mother tongue so perfectly as never to make any grammatical mistake.
> —Henry Bradley
> *The Making of English*

As a present-tense verb, to *slew* is to turn or slide violently or suddenly in a different direction—or to make a vehicle do so {the car keeps slewing sideways}. In AmE, a variant spelling of this verb is *slue. As a

313

past-tense verb, *slew* corresponds to the present-tense *slay* {Cain slew Abel}.

slow. This word, like *slowly*, may be an adverb. Generally, prefer *slowly* {go slowly}. But when used after the verb in a pithy statement, especially an injunction, *slow* often appears in colloquial usage {go slow!} {take it slow}. See § 215.

*slue. See **slew.**

smell. Inflected *smell–smelled–smelled*, although *smelt* is almost as frequent a past form in BrE. The same was true in AmE until about 1930, when the past form *smelled* acquired ascendancy.

sneak. This verb is conjugated as a regular verb: *sneak–sneaked–sneaked.* Reserve **snuck* for dialect and tongue-in-cheek usages.

1943 Ratio of Frequency in Printed Books: 39:1
2008 Ratio of Frequency in Printed Books: 1.3:1

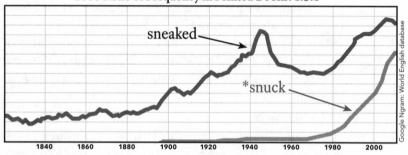

sort. Use *this sort of* or *these sorts of*—never **these sort of.*

space. As a figurative noun, this word has become a voguish equivalent of *area* {though not initially interested in journalism, he has decided to move into that space}. Although (or perhaps because) this usage is au courant, avoid it. Cf. **area.**

spell, *vb.* Inflected *spell–spelled–spelled*, although the variant past form *spelt* is common in BrE. The same was true in AmE until about 1870, when the past form *spelled* became the predominant spelling.

> No language is logical in every respect, and we must not expect usage to be guided always by strictly logical principles. It was a frequent error with the older grammarians that whenever the actual grammar of a language did not seem conformable to the rules of abstract logic they blamed the language and wanted to correct it.
> —Otto Jespersen
> *Growth and Structure of the English Language*

spill. Inflected *spill–spilled–spilled*—or *spilt* in the set phrase *spilt milk* and in many BrE contexts.

spit. If used to mean "to expectorate," the verb is inflected *spit–spat–spit* {he spat a curse} {he has spit many a curse}. But if used to mean "to skewer," it's *spit–spitted–spitted* {the hens have been spitted for broiling}.

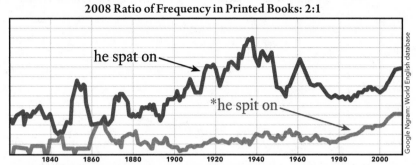

2008 Ratio of Frequency in Printed Books: 2:1

spoil. Inflected *spoil–spoiled–spoiled*, although the variant past form *spoilt* is common in BrE.

spring. Inflected *spring–sprang–sprung*. Avoid *sprung* as a simple-past form.

stanch. See **staunch.**

stationary; stationery. *Stationary* describes a state of immobility or of staying in one place {if it's stationary, paint it}. *Stationery* denotes writing materials, especially paper for writing letters, usually with matching envelopes {love letters written on perfumed stationery}. To remember the two, try associating the *-er* in *stationery* with the *-er* in *paper*; or remember that a *stationer* is someone who sells the stuff.

staunch; stanch. *Staunch* is an adjective meaning "ardent and faithful" {a staunch Red Sox supporter}. *Stanch* is the AmE verb meaning "to stop the flow"; it is almost always used in regard to bleeding, literally and metaphorically {after New Hampshire the campaign hemorrhaged; only a big win in South Carolina could stanch the bleeding}. In BrE, however, *staunching the flow* is the standard wording.

> Words sometimes change their proper historical meaning, and when the change is sanctioned by a general and established usage it must be accepted. On the other hand, we ought to resist any perversion of the meaning of a word as long as we can.
> —Henry Bett
> *Some Secrets of Style*

steal. See **rob.**

strait; straight. A *strait* (often pl.) is (1) literally, a narrow channel connecting two large bodies of water separated by two areas of land {Strait of Magellan}, or (2) figuratively, a difficult position {dire straits}. This is the word used in compound terms with the sense of constriction {straitlaced} {straitjacket}. *Straight* is most often an adjective meaning unbent, steady, sober, candid, honest, or heterosexual.

2008 Ratio of Frequency in Printed Books: 3:1

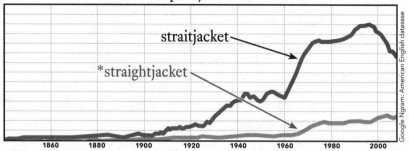

strata, *n.* This is the plural for *stratum.* Keep it plural {Fussell identified nine discrete strata in American society}. Avoid the double plural **stratas.*

strategy; tactics. A *strategy* is a long-term plan for achieving a goal. A *tactic* is a shorter-term method for achieving an immediate but limited success. A strategy might involve several tactics. By the way, although *strategy* is so spelled, *stratagem* has an -*a*- in the middle syllable.

subject. See **citizen.**

subsequent. See **consequent.**

subsequently. Try *later.*

*subsequent to. Make it *after.*

substitute; replace. To *substitute* is to put someone or something in place of another {he substituted a replica for the original}. To *replace* is to insert something in the place of someone or something else {he replaced the original with a replica}. It's sloppy usage to let *substitute* appear in the place of *replace.*

such. This word, when used to replace *this* or *that*—as in "such building was later condemned"—is symptomatic of legalese. *Such* is actually no more precise than *the, this, that, these,* or *those.* It's perfectly acceptable, however, to use *such* with a mass noun or plural noun when the meaning is "of that type" or "of this kind" {such impudence galled the rest of the family} {such vitriolic exchanges became commonplace in the following years}. For the misuse of *as such,* see **as such.**

such as. See **like.**

sufficient. See **adequate.**

supersede. The root of this word derives from *sedeo*, the Latin word for "to sit, to be established," not *cedo*, meaning "to yield." Hence the spelling varies from the root in words such as *concede*, *recede*, and *secede*.

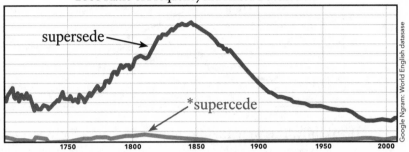

1880 Ratio of Frequency in Printed Books: 89:1
2008 Ratio of Frequency in Printed Books: 12:1

swim. Inflected *swim–swam–swum*. Avoid using *swam* as a past participle.

sympathy. See **empathy.**

systematic; systemic. *Systematic* means "according to a plan or system, organized methodically, or arranged in a system." *Systemic*, meaning "affecting the whole of something," is limited in use to physiological systems {a systemic disease affecting several organs} or, by extension, other systems that may be likened to the body {systemic problems within the corporate hierarchy}.

tactics. See **strategy.**

take. See **bring.**

tantalizing; titillating. A *tantalizing* thing torments us because we want it badly, yet it is always just out of reach. A *titillating* thing tickles us pleasantly, literally or figuratively—and the word often carries sexual connotations.

> The dictionary invites a playful reading. It challenges anyone to sit down with it in an idle moment only to find an hour gone by without being bored.
> —Mortimer Adler
> "How to Read a Dictionary"

text, *vb*. Inflected *text–texted–texted*, as a regular verb. Avoid using the uninflected *text* for the past-tense forms.

than. 1. For *different than* vs. *different from*, see **different. 2.** For a discussion of *than I* (vs. *me*), see § 68.

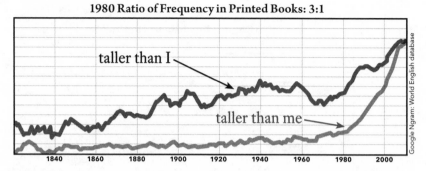

1980 Ratio of Frequency in Printed Books: 3:1

taller than I

taller than me

Google Ngram: World English database

1840 1860 1880 1900 1920 1940 1960 1980 2000

thankfully. This word traditionally means "appreciatively; gratefully." It is not in good use as a substitute for *thank goodness* or *fortunately*.

that; which. These are both relative pronouns (see §§ 80–91). In polished American prose, *that* is used restrictively to narrow a category or identify a particular item being talked about {any building that is taller must be outside the state}; *which* is used nonrestrictively—not to narrow a class or identify a particular item but to add something about an item already identified {alongside the officer trotted a toy poodle, which is hardly a typical police dog}. *Which* is best used restrictively only when it is preceded by a preposition {the situation in which we find ourselves}. Otherwise, it is almost always preceded by a comma, a parenthesis, or a dash. In BrE, writers and editors seldom observe the distinction between the two words.

Is it a useful distinction? Yes. At least one commentator has tried to dismiss it as the "daydream" of H. W. Fowler, the renowned usage expert who in 1926 wrote *A Dictionary of Modern English Usage*. But as I have shown elsewhere, the distinction long predates Fowler[4]—and the language inarguably benefits from having a terminological as well as a punctuational means of telling a restrictive from a nonrestrictive relative pronoun, punctuation often being ill-heeded. Apologists for the restrictive *which*—again, the recommendation here is to make it nonrestrictive unless it follows a preposition—urge that *which* can sometimes be more euphonious than *that*. If that is ever so, it is an extreme rarity.

One final point. Is it acceptable to use *that* in reference to people? Is *friends that arrive early* an acceptable alternative to *friends who arrive early*? The answer is yes. *Person that* has long been considered good

---

4   See *Garner's Modern English Usage*, 4th ed. (New York: Oxford Univ. Press, 2016), 901–2.

idiomatic English. Even so, *person who* is nearly three times as common as *person that* in edited English.

thaw. This is the word meaning "to unfreeze." Avoid **unthaw.*

theirs. So written {the book is theirs}—not **their's.*

themselves. This is the standard reflexive pronoun—never **themself.*

there; their; they're. *There* denotes a place or direction {stay there}. *Their* is the possessive pronoun {all their good wishes}. *They're* is a contraction of *they are* {they're calling now}.

therefore; therefor. The words have different senses. *Therefore*, the common word, means "as a result; for that reason" {the evidence of guilt was slight; therefore, the jury acquitted the defendant}. *Therefor*, a legalism, means "for it" or "for them" {he took the unworn shirt back to the store and received a refund therefor}.

though. See **although.**

threshold; withhold. The first word has one -*h*-, the second two. In fact, *threshold* does not derive from *hold* at all. *Withhold* does, of course, and retains the -*h*- in both parts of the compound.

thus. This is the adverb—not **thusly.* Use *thus* (it's called a *flat adverb*—see § 215).

till. This is a perfectly good preposition and conjunction {open till 10 p.m.}. It is not a contraction of *until* and should not be written '*til.* Some will argue that they want to contract *until* instead of using *till.* They might as well argue that they want to contract *unto* and write *I plan on giving a present 'to you.*

2008 Ratio of Frequency in Printed Books: 33:1

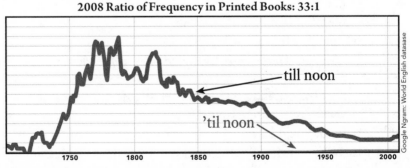

timbre; timber. *Timbre* is a musical term meaning "tonal quality of the sound made by a particular musical instrument or voice." *Timber* is the correct spelling in all other uses, which relate to trees or wood.

time period. See **period of time.**

titillating. See **tantalizing.**

tolerance; toleration. *Tolerance* is the habitual quality of being *tolerant* —that is, willing to allow people to say, believe, or do what they want without criticism or punishment. *Toleration* is a particular instance of being *tolerant.*

torpid. See **turbid.**

tortious; tortuous; torturous. What is *tortious* relates to torts (civil wrongs) or to acts that give rise to legal claims for torts {tortious interference with a contract}. What is *tortuous* is full of twists and turns and therefore makes travel difficult {a tortuous path through the woods}. What is *torturous* involves severe physical and mental suffering {a torturous exam}.

toward; towards. The preferred form in AmE is *toward*: this has been so since about 1900. In BrE, *towards* predominates. The same is true for other directional words, such as *upward, downward, forward,* and *backward,* as well as *afterward.* The use of *afterwards* and *backwards* as adverbs is neither rare nor incorrect (and is preferred in BrE). For the sake of consistency, many American editors prefer the shorter forms without the final *-s.*

transcript; transcription. A *transcript* is either a written record, as of a trial or a radio program, or an official record of a student's classes and grades. *Transcription* is the act or process of creating a transcript.

transpire, *vb.* Although its traditional sense is "to come to be known" {it transpired that he had paid bribes}, *transpire* more commonly today means "happen" or "occur" {what transpired when I was away?}. In that newer sense, *transpire* still carries a vague odor of jargon and pretentiousness. But that is disappearing.

trillion. See **billion.**

triumphal; triumphant. Things are *triumphal* (done or made to celebrate a victory) {a triumphal arch}. But only people feel *triumphant* (displaying pleasure and pride as a result of a victory or success) {a triumphant Caesar returned to Rome}.

try and. Prefer *try to.*

turbid; turgid; torpid. *Turbid* water or liquid is thick and opaque from churned-up mud or detritus {a turbid pond}; by extension, *turbid* means "unclear, confused, or disturbed" {a turbid argument}. *Turgid* means "swollen," and by extension "pompous and bombastic" {turgid prose}. *Torpid* means "idle, lazy, and sleepy" {a torpid economy}.

ultimate. See **penultimate.**

unexceptional; unexceptionable. The first means "not very good; no better than average." The second means "not open to objection."

uninterested. See **disinterested.**

unique. Reserve this word for the sense "one of a kind." Avoid it in the sense "special, unusual." Phrases such as *very unique, *more unique, *somewhat unique, and so on—in which a degree is attributed to *unique*—aren't the best usage.

unlawful; illegal; illicit; criminal. This list is in ascending order of negative connotation. An *unlawful* act may even be morally innocent (for example, letting a parking meter expire). But an *illegal* act is something that society formally condemns, and an *illicit* act calls to mind moral degeneracy {illicit drug use}. Unlike *criminal*, the first three terms can apply to civil wrongs.

unorganized. See **disorganized.**

unreadable. See **illegible.**

upon. See **on.**

upward(s). See **toward.**

use; utilize. *Use* is usually the best choice for simplicity. *Utilize* is usually an overblown alternative of *use*, but it is occasionally the better choice when the distinct sense is "to use to best effect" {how to utilize our staff most effectively}.

utmost. This is the word {do your utmost!}, never *upmost.

venal; venial. A person who is *venal* is mercenary or open to bribery—willing to use power and influence dishonestly in return for money {a venal government official}; a thing that is *venal* is purchasable {venal livestock}. A *venial* fault or sin is trivial enough to be pardonable or excusable {a venial offense} {a venial error}.

verbal; oral. If something is put into words, it is *verbal*. Technically, *verbal* covers both written and spoken utterance. If you wish to specify that something was conveyed by word of mouth, use *oral*.

very. See **much.**

vocation. See **avocation.**

voluminous. See **compendious.**

waive; wave. To *waive* is to relinquish claim to or not to insist on enforcing. To *wave* is to move to and fro.

wangle. See **wrangle.**

wedding. See **marriage.**

whether. Generally, use *whether* alone—not with the words *or not* tacked on {they didn't know whether to go}. The *or not* is necessary only when you mean to convey the idea "regardless of whether" {we'll finish on time whether or not it rains}. On the distinction between *whether* and *if*, see **if.**

which. See **that.**

while. *While* may substitute for *although* or *whereas*, especially if a conversational tone is desired {while many readers may disagree, the scientific community has overwhelmingly adopted the conclusions here presented}. Yet because *while* can denote either time or contrast, the word is occasionally ambiguous; when a real ambiguity exists, *although* or *whereas* is the better choice.

who; whom. Here are the traditional rules: *who* is a nominative pronoun used as (1) the subject of a finite verb {it was Jim who bought the coffee today} or (2) a predicate nominative when it follows a linking verb {that's who}. *Whom* is an objective pronoun that may appear as (1) the object of a verb {I learned nothing about the man whom I saw} or (2) the object of a preposition {the woman to whom I owe my life}. Today there are two countervailing trends: first, there's a decided tendency to use *who* colloquially in most contexts; second, among those insecure about their grammar, there's a tendency to overcorrect oneself and use *whom* when *who* would be correct. Writers and editors of formal prose often resist the first of these; everyone should resist the second. See § 91.

whoever; whomever. Avoid the second unless you are certain of your grammar {give this book to whoever wants it} {I cook for whomever I love}. If you are uncertain why these examples are correct, use *anyone who* or (as in the second example) *anyone.*

who's; whose. The first is a contraction {who's on first?}, the second a possessive {whose life is it, anyway?}. Unlike *who* and *whom*, *whose* may refer to things as well as people {the Commerce Department, whose bailiwick includes intellectual property}. See § 89.

whosever; whoever's. The first is correct (though increasingly rare) in formal writing {whosever bag that is, it needs to be moved out of the way}; the second is acceptable in casual usage {whoever's dog got into our garbage can, the owner should clean up the mess}.

withhold. See **threshold.**

workers' compensation. This is the preferred name for workplace accident-insurance plans, not *workmen's compensation*. Notice that *workers* is always plural. When used as a phrasal adjective (see § 131), it is hyphenated {workers'-compensation system}.

wrack. See **rack.**

wrangle; wangle. To *wrangle* is to argue, esp. angrily over a long period {still wrangling over their parents' estate}. To *wangle* is to get something or arrange for something to happen by cleverness, manipulation, or trickery {wangle a couple of last-minute tickets}.

> The writer's obsessive love of words is a source of suffering, but of suffering that he will never regret.
> —Konstantin Fedin
> "Notebook"

wreak; reek. *Wreak* means (1) "to cause a great deal of harm or many problems" {to wreak havoc on the administration}, or (2) "to punish someone in revenge" {to wreak vengeance on his erstwhile friends}. The past tense is *wreaked*, not *wrought*. (The latter is an archaic form of the past tense and past participle of *work*.) *Reek* can be a verb meaning "to stink" or a noun meaning "stench."

wrong; wrongful. These terms are not interchangeable. *Wrong* has two senses: (1) "immoral, unlawful" {it's wrong to bully smaller children}, and (2) "improper, incorrect, unsatisfactory" {many of the math answers are wrong}. *Wrongful* likewise has two senses: (1) "unjust, unfair" {wrongful conduct}, and (2) "unsanctioned by law; having no legal right" {it was a wrongful demand on the estate}.

yes. See **affirmative, in the.**

your; you're. *Your* is the possessive form of *you* {your class}. *You're* is the contraction for *you are* {you're welcome}.

Bias-Free Language

435 *Maintaining credibility.* Discussions of bias-free language—language that is neither sexist nor suggestive of other conscious or subconscious prejudices—have a way of descending quickly into politics. But there is a way to avoid the political quagmire: if we focus solely on maintaining credibility with a wide readership, the argument for eliminating bias from your writing becomes much simpler. Biased language that is not central to the meaning of the work distracts readers, and in their eyes the work is less credible. Few texts warrant the deliberate display of linguistic biases. Nor is it ideal, however, to call attention to a supposed absence of linguistic biases, since this will also distract readers and weaken credibility.

436 *Gender bias.* Consider the issue of gender-neutral language. On the one hand, a great many reasonable readers find it unacceptable to use the generic masculine pronoun (*he* in reference to no one in particular). On the other hand, it is unacceptable to a great many readers (often different readers) either to resort to nontraditional gimmicks to avoid the generic masculine (by using *he/she* or *s/he, for example) or to use *they* as a kind of singular pronoun. Either approach sacrifices credibility with some readers.

437 *Other biases.* The same is true of other types of biases, such as slighting allusions or stereotypes based on characteristics such as race, ethnicity, disability, religion, sexual orientation, transgender status, or birth or family status. Careful writers avoid language that reasonable readers might find offensive or distracting—unless the biased language is central to the meaning of the writing. See § 296.

438 *Invisible gender-neutrality.* What is wanted is a kind of invisible gender-neutrality. There are many ways to achieve this invisibly gender-neutral language, but it takes some thought and often some hard work.

439 *Techniques for achieving gender-neutrality.* Nine methods are suggested below because no single method will work for every writer or in every context. Choose the combination of methods that works best in the context you've created.

1. **Omit the pronoun.** Sometimes a personal pronoun is not really necessary. For instance, in *the programmer should update the records when data is transferred to her by the head office*, if there is only one programmer, the pronoun phrase *to her* can be omitted: *the programmer should update the records when data is transferred by the head office*. Note that the shorter sentence is tighter as well as gender-free.

2. **Repeat the noun.** If a noun and its pronoun are separated by many words, try repeating the noun. For instance, *a writer should be careful not to needlessly antagonize readers, because her credibility would otherwise suffer* becomes *a writer should be careful not to needlessly antagonize readers, because the writer's credibility would otherwise suffer*. Take care not to overuse this technique. Repeating a noun too frequently will irritate readers. If you have to repeat a noun more than twice in a sentence or repeat it too closely, you should probably rewrite the sentence.

3. **Use a plural antecedent.** By using a plural antecedent, you eliminate the need for a singular pronoun. For instance, *a contestant must conduct himself with dignity at all times* becomes *contestants must conduct themselves with dignity at all times*. The method may cause a slight change in connotation. In the example, a duty becomes a collective responsibility rather than an individual one.

4. **Use an article instead of a pronoun.** Try replacing the singular personal pronoun with a definite or indefinite article. Quite often you'll find that the effect on the sentence's meaning is negligible. For instance, *A student accused of cheating must actively waive his right to have his guidance counselor present* becomes *A student accused of cheating must actively waive the right to have a guidance counselor present*.

5. **Use the neutral singular pronoun *one*.** Try replacing the gender-specific personal pronoun with the gender-neutral singular pronoun *one*. For instance, *an actor in New York is likely to earn more than he is in Paducah* becomes *an actor in New York is likely to earn more than one in Paducah*.

6. **Use the relative pronoun *who*.** This technique works best when it replaces a personal pronoun that follows *if*. It also requires revising the sentence slightly. For instance, *employers presume that if an applicant can't write well, he won't be a good employee* becomes *employers presume that an applicant who can't write well won't be a good employee*.

7. **Use the imperative mood.** The imperative eliminates the need for an explicit pronoun. Although its usefulness is limited in some types of writing, you may find that it avoids prolixity and more forcefully addresses the target audience. For instance, *a lifeguard must keep a*

close watch over children while he is monitoring the pool becomes *keep a close watch over children while monitoring the pool.*

8. **In moderation, use *he or she*.** Although it is an easy fix, the phrase *he or she* should be used sparingly, preferably only when no other technique is satisfactory. For instance, *if a complainant is not satisfied with the board's decision, then he can ask for a rehearing* becomes *if a complainant is not satisfied with the board's decision, then he or she can ask for a rehearing.* If you find you need to repeat the pronouns in the same sentence, don't. Revise the sentence instead.

9. **Revise the sentence.** If no other technique produces a sentence that reads well, rewrite the sentence so that personal pronouns aren't needed. The amount of revision will vary. For instance, *if a boy or girl misbehaves, his or her privileges will be revoked* becomes *if someone misbehaves, that person's privileges will be revoked.* And *a person who decides not to admit he lied will be considered honest until someone exposes his lie* becomes *a person who denies lying will be considered honest until the lie is exposed.*

440 *Necessary gender-specific language.* It isn't always necessary or desirable to use gender-neutral terms and phrasings. If you're writing about something that clearly concerns only one sex (e.g., *women's studies; men's golf championship*) or an inherently single-sex institution (e.g., a sorority; a Masonic lodge), trying to use gender-neutral language may lead to absurd prose {be solicitous of a pregnant friend's comfort; he or she will need your support}.

441 *Sex-specific labels as adjectives.* It's acceptable to use the noun *woman* as a modifier {woman judge}. In recent decades, *woman* has been rapidly replacing *lady* in such constructions. The adjective *female* is also used often but may be less acceptable to some readers who feel that it is somehow dismissive or derogatory (perhaps because it's a biological term used for animals as well as humans). *Female* is also relatively common in some phrasings (e.g., *female police officer*).

But be careful to use such modifiers only when the subject's gender is relevant. Referring to a "woman judge" when her sex isn't germane to the discussion risks offending many readers by implying that there is something unusual or remarkable about a woman in that profession. As a rule, don't use such a modifier—or a gendered suffix (see § 443)—unless you would also do so for a male in the same context.

442 *Gender-neutral singular pronouns.* The only gender-neutral singular pronoun in English is *it*, which doesn't refer to humans (with very limited exceptions). Clumsy artifices such as **s/he* and **(wo)man* or artificial genderless pronouns have all been tried—for many years—with no success. They won't succeed. And those who use them invite credibility problems. Indefinite pronouns such as *anybody* and *someone* don't always satisfy the need for a gender-neutral alternative because they are traditionally regarded as singular antecedents that call for a third-person-singular pronoun. Many people substitute the plural *they, them,* and *their* for the singular *he, she, him, his,* or *her.* Although *they* and *their* have become common in informal usage, these are not considered fully acceptable in formal AmE—though BrE is much more accepting of them.[5] Yet they are steadily gaining ground. For now, unless you are given guidelines to the contrary, be wary of using them in a singular sense.

443 *Problematic suffixes.* The trend in AmE is toward eliminating sex-specific suffixes. Words with feminine suffixes such as *-ess* and *-ette* are easily replaced with the suffix-free forms, which are increasingly accepted as applying to both men and women. For example, *author* and *testator* are preferable to *authoress* and *testatrix.* The suffix *-man* is more problematic. The word *person* rarely functions well as a suffix. It tends to make words such as *chairperson* and *anchorperson* sound more pompous or wooden than the simpler (and correct) *chair* or *anchor.* Also, an unfortunate tendency (or suspicion) is that the *-person* suffix is being used only for women. So unless a *-person* word is well established (such as *salesperson*, which dates from 1901), don't automatically substitute *-person* for *-man.* English has many alternatives that

> There are other, subtler forms of sexist language. One is to refer to prominent men by their title or last name but to prominent women by their full name or married name: for instance, designating the United States president as "President Reagan" but the British prime minister as "Mrs. Thatcher" or referring to the American male writer as "Hemingway" but the American female writer as "Eudora Welty." Another is to mention specifically the appearance or marital status of women but not of men. For instance, it would be sexist to mention in a report that a woman employee is "an attractive blonde" or "a divorcee" but not to indicate whether a man employee is married or divorced or whether he is attractive or homely.
> —Maxine Hairston
> *Successful Writing*

---

5   See Bas Aarts, *Oxford Modern English Grammar* (Oxford: Oxford Univ. Press, 2010), 5 ("the use of the plural pronoun *they* with a non-specific singular antecedent [is] sanctioned by widespread current usage").

are not necessarily newly coined, including *police officer* (first recorded in 1797), *firefighter* (1903), and *mail carrier* (1788).

444 *Avoiding other biased language.* Comments that betray a writer's conscious or unconscious biases or ignorance may cause readers to lose respect for the writer and interpret the words in unintended ways. Below are some things to watch for.

445 *Unnecessary focus on personal characteristics.* As a matter of style, it's wise to avoid irrelevant references to personal characteristics such as sex, race, ethnicity, disability, age, religion, sexual orientation, and social standing. Such pointless references may affect a reader's perception of you or the person you are writing about or both. They may also invoke a reader's biases and cloud your meaning. When it is important to mention a characteristic because doing so will help the reader develop a picture of the person you are writing about, use care. For instance, in the sentence *Shirley Chisholm was probably the finest black woman member of the House of Representatives that New York has ever had,* the phrase *black woman* might imply to some readers that (1) Chisholm was a great representative "for a woman" but may have been surpassed by many or even all men, (2) she stands out only among black women who have served in Congress, or (3) it is unusual for a woman or an African American to hold high office. But in *Shirley Chisholm was the first black woman to be elected to Congress and one of New York's all-time best representatives,* the purpose of the phrase *black woman* is not likely to be misunderstood.

446 *Unnecessary emphasis on the trait, not the person.* A characteristic is best not made into a label. It should preferably be used as an adjective, not as a noun. Instead of referring to someone as, for instance, *a Catholic* or *a deaf-mute,* put the person first by writing *a Catholic man* or *he is Catholic,* and *a deaf-and-mute child* or *the child is deaf and mute.*

447 *Inappropriate labels.* People are sensitive to labels, especially those that describe them or the group they identify with. Labels change, sometimes rapidly, so that what is acceptable at one point in time is not at another. More than one acceptable label may be widely used at the same time. Or a particular label may be preferred in one geographic area but objectionable in another. Some labels may have subtle differences. And some are suitable for things but not people. Your best guide for choosing which term to use is the affected individual's or group's preference. Be aware of what's current and appropriate.

Prepositional Idioms

448 *Idiomatic uses.* Among the most persistent word-choice issues are those concerning prepositions. Which prepositions go with which words? You *fill* A *with* B but *instill* B *into* A; you *replace* A *with* B but *substitute* B *for* A; you *prefix* A *to* B but *preface* B *with* A; you *force* A *into* B but *enforce* B *on* A; finally, A *implies* B, so you *infer* B *from* A. And that's only the beginning of it.

449 *Shifts in idiom.* While prepositional idioms often give nonnative speakers of English nightmares, even native speakers of English often need to double-check them. Often the language undergoes some shifting. There may be a difference between traditional literary usage (*oblivious of*) and prevailing contemporary usage (*oblivious to*). Sometimes the writer may choose one or the other preposition for reasons of euphony. (Is it better, in a given context, to *ruminate on, about,* or *over* a specified problem?) Sometimes, too, the denotative and connotative differences can be striking: it's one thing to be *smitten with* another and quite a different thing to be *smitten by* another.

450 *Words and the prepositions construed with them.* Words generally have certain prepositions associated with them, and these prepositions show the relationships with other words. It's often a matter of idiom. The list below hardly exhausts the possible combinations, but it contains the pairings that most often give writers trouble. For any such words, Google's ngrams can be invaluable.

aberration (*n.*): from, of
abhorrence (*n.*): of
abhorrent (*adj.*): to
abide (*vb.*): with [stay], by [obey]
abound (*vb.*): in, with
absolve (*vb.*): from [guilt], of [obligation]
absolved (*adj.*): from, of, by
abstain (*vb.*): from
abut (*vb.*): on, against
accede (*vb.*): to
accommodate (*vb.*): by, for, in, with, to
accompanied (*vb.*): to, by, [not *with*]

accompany (*vb.*): to, by, with
accord (*n.*): with, between, over, about
accord (*vb.*): in, to, with
accordance (*n.*): with
account (*n.*): of, for, to, about, with
account (*vb.*): to [a person], for [a thing or a person]
accountable (*adj.*): to, for
accuse (*vb.*): of
acquainted (*adj.*): with
acquiesce (*vb.*): in, to [preferably not *with*]
acquit (*vb.*): of

act (*vb.*): on, for, to, against
adapt (*vb.*): to, from, for
addicted (*adj.*): to
adept (*vb.*): at, in
adequate (*adj.*): for, to
adhere (*vb.*): to
adherence (*n.*): to
adhesion (*n.*): of, to {the adhesion of
   one polymer to another}
adjacent (*adj.*): to
adjust (*vb.*): to, for
admit (*vb.*): to, into, of
adverse (*adj.*): to
advert (*vb.*): to
affiliate (*vb.*): with, to
afflict (*vb.*): with
agree (*vb.*): to, on, upon [terms],
   about [concur], with [a person],
   in [a specified manner, e.g., in
   general or in principle]
allow (*vb.*): to, for, of
alternate (*vb.*): between
analogous (*adj.*): to [preferably not
   with]
angry (*adj.*): at, about, with
answer (*vb.*): to, for
antagonism (*n.*): toward, to, between
antagonistic (*adj.*): toward, to
antipathy (*n.*): toward, to, against, for
anxious (*adj.*): about [preferably not
   to]
apply (*vb.*): for, to, toward
apprise (*vb.*): of
apropos (*adj.*): of
argue (*vb.*): with [a person], over,
   about [a situation or thing], for,
   against [a position]
ask (*vb.*): about, for, to, of, after
attend (*vb.*): to
attribute (*vb.*): to
averse (*adj.*): to
badge (*n.*): of
badger (*vb.*): into, about
balance (*n.*): of, between, against

ban (*n.*): on, from
ban (*vb.*): from
banish (*vb.*): from, to
bank (*vb.*): on [rely], off [carom], at,
   with [a financial institution]
bar (*n.*): to, of
bargain (*vb.*): for, on, with
barge (*vb.*): in, into
barter (*vb.*): for, with, between
base (*n.*): of, for
based (*adj.*): on [preferably not
   upon], in
because (*conj.*): of
beckon (*vb.*): to, at, for
becoming (*adj.*): on, of, to
beeline (*n.*): for, to, toward
beg (*vb.*): for, to, of
beguile (*vb.*): with, into
behalf (*n.*): of
behave (*vb.*): toward, for
beholden (*adj.*): to, for
belong (*vb.*): to, in
benefit (*n.*): of, from, to, for
benefit (*vb.*): from, by
bereft (*adj.*): of
beset (*vb.*): by, with
bestow (*vb.*): on [preferably not *upon*]
betray (*vb.*): to, by
betrayed (*adj.*): to, by
bias (*n.*): against, for, toward
biased (*adj.*): against, for, toward
bid (*n.* or *vb.*): on, for, to
bigoted (*adj.*): against
bigotry (*n.*): against
binding (*adj.*): on [preferably not
   upon]
blame (*vb.*): for, on
blaspheme (*vb.*): against
blasphemy (*n.*): against
bleed (*vb.*): from, for
blend (*vb.*): in, together, with, into,
   through, throughout
blossom (*vb.*): into
blunder (*vb.*): on, upon, into, out

bond (*n.*): of, with, between

border (*n.*): of, between, with, at

border (*vb.*): on [preferably not *upon*], against

bored (*adj.*): by, with [preferably not *of*]

born (*adj.*): to, of, in, into

borne (*vb.*): by

boycott (*n.*): of, on

brace (*vb.*): for, against

break (*n.*): in, for, from, with

break (*vb.*): with, in, into, through, out

bristle (*vb.*): at, with

browse (*vb.*): around, through, for

brush (*vb.*): by, past, against, in, out

budget (*vb.*): for

butt (*vb.*): into

buy (*vb.*): from, into, for, out

cahoots (*n.*): with

cajoled (*adj.*): into

capable (*adj.*): of

capacity (*n.*): of, to, as, for

capitalize (*vb.*): on, for

capitulate (*vb.*): to

care (*n.*): of

care (*vb.*): for, about

careful (*adj.*): about, with, of, in, to

careless (*adj.*): about, with, of, in

cause (*n.*): of, for

caused (*vb.*): by, with, to

caution (*vb.*): about, against

cautious (*adj.*): about, of, in, with

celebrated (*adj.*): for, as

censure (*vb.*): for, over, as

center (*vb.*): on, upon [not *around*]

chafe (*vb.*): at, under

chagrined (*adj.*): at

chance (*n.*): of, at, for, against, to, on

characteristic (*n.* & *adj.*): of

characterize (*vb.*): as

characterized (*adj.*): by

charge (*vb.*): for, at, to, with, in, into, out

chase (*vb.*): out, from, after

cheat (*vb.*): at, on

check (*vb.*): into, on, over, out, through, to

chide (*vb.*): for

chortle (*vb.*): about, over

claim (*n.*): to, against, for, on, of, about, over

clamor (*n.* & *vb.*): about, against, over, for

cling (*vb.*): to

cluster (*vb.*): around

coalesce (*vb.*): into

coax (*vb.*): into, out, over

coequal (*adj.*): with

coerce (*vb.*): into

cognizant (*adj.*): of

cohesion (*n.*): between, among

coincide (*vb.*): with

coincidental (*adj.*): with [at the same time], to

collaborate (*vb.*): on, with

collide (*vb.*): with

collude (*vb.*): with

collusion (*n.*): between, among, over, to

comfort (*n.*): to, for, in

commensurate (*adj.*): with, to

comment (*n.*): on [a thing], about [a person], to

commiserate (*vb.*): with

commit (*vb.*): to

commune (*vb.*): with

communion (*n.*): with

compare (*vb.*): with [literal], to [metaphorical]

compatible (*adj.*): with

compete (*vb.*): in, against, with, for, to, over

competitive (*adj.*): with, in

complacent (*adj.*): about, toward, over

complement (*n.*): of

complementary (*adj.*): to

compliment (*n.*): on

complimentary (*adj.*): of

comply (*vb.*): with [not *to*]

comport (*vb.*): with

composed (*adj.*): of

compress (*vb.*): into

compromise (*n. & vb.*): on, with

conceive (*vb.*): of

concord (*vb.*): with

concur (*vb.*): in, with

concurrence (*n.*): in, with, of

condemn (*vb.*): to, for, as

conducive (*adj.*): to

confer (*vb.*): on, upon, with, about, over

conference (*n.*): about, between, among, on

confide (*vb.*): to, in

confidence (*n.*): in, to

conflict (*n.*): over, about, of, with

conflict (*vb.*): with

conform (*vb.*): to, with

conformance (*n.*): with

confuse (*vb.*): with

confusion (*n.*): over, about, between, among

congruence (*n.*): with

congruent (*adj.*): with

connected (*adj.*): with, by, at, for, through, to

connivance (*n.*): of, with

connive (*vb.*): at, to, with, in

consider (*vb.*): as {considered as a possible replacement}, for {considered for the job opening}

considerate (*adj.*): of, toward

consideration (*n.*): of, to, for

consist (*vb.*): of [components or ingredients] {a year consists of 12 months}, in [qualities] {efficient production consists in accurately predicting demand}

consistent (*adj.*): with

consonant (*adj.*): with

conspire (*vb.*): to, with, against

constrain (*vb.*): from

constraint (*n.*): on, upon, of, in

construe (*vb.*): as

construed (*adj.*): as, by

consult (*vb.*): with, on, about

consultant (*n.*): to, on, for, in

contaminate (*vb.*): with, by

contemporaneous (*adj.*): with

contemporary (*adj.*): with

contemporary (*n.*): of [people]

contempt (*n.*): for, of

contend (*vb.*): with, against, for

contiguous (*adj.*): to

contingent (*adj.*): on [preferably not *upon*]

contract (*n.*): to, for, with

contrary (*adj.*): to

contrast (*n.*): with, to, between, among

contrast (*vb.*): with, to

contribute (*vb.*): to, for

control (*n.*): of, over

convenient (*adj.*): for, to

conversant (*adj.*): with, in

convict (*vb.*): of, for [not *in*]

convince (*vb.*): of

coordinate (*vb.*): with

coordination (*n.*): with, between, among

correlate (*vb.*): with, to

correlation (*n.*): to, between, among

correspond (*vb.*): with, about [communications], to [relationships]

correspondence (*n.*): with, about, between, among

count (*vb.*): on, against, for

couple (*n.*): of

couple (*vb.*): to, with

credit (*n.*): for, to, on

credit (*vb.*): to, with

crusade (*n. & vb.*): against, for

culminate (*vb.*): in

cure (*n.*): for

cure (*vb.*): of

dabble (*vb.*): in, at

dally (*vb.*): with, over, at

dawdle (*vb.*): over

deal (*n. & vb.*): with, in, for, over, about

debar (*vb.*): from

debate (*n. & vb.*): about, with

decide (*vb.*): on, between, among, against, for

deduce (*vb.*): from

deduct (*vb.*): from

deduction (*n.*): from, for

default (*vb.*): on

defer (*vb.*): to

deference (*n.*): to

deferential (*adj.*): to

defiant (*adj.*): toward

defrauded (*vb.*): of

degenerate (*vb.*): into, from

deliberate (*adj.*): in [cautious]

deliberate (*vb.*): about, over, on [discuss]

delight (*n.*): at, about, over

delight (*vb.*): in

delighted (*adj.*): about, with, by, over, at, for

delve (*vb.*): into

demonstrate (*vb.*): against, for

depend (*vb.*): on [preferably not *upon*]

dependent (*adj.*): on

depict (*vb.*): as

deprive (*vb.*): of

derive (*vb.*): from

derogate (*vb.*): from

derogatory (*adj.*): about, of, toward

described (*vb.*): as

designated (*vb.*): as

designation (*n.*): as

desist (*vb.*): from

despair (*vb.*): of

desperate (*adj.*): for, about

despondent (*adj.*): about, over, at

destitute (*adj.*): of

destructive (*adj.*): to, of

detract (*vb.*): from

detriment (*n.*): to, for, of

deviate (*vb.*): from

devoid (*adj.*): of

devolve (*vb.*): on, upon

devoted (*adj.*): to

devotee (*n.*): of

devotion (*n.*): to, of

dictate (*vb.*): to

die (*vb.*): of, from, by, with, for, in

differ (*vb.*): from [a thing or quality], with [a person], about, over, on [an aspect]

difference (*n.*): between, among, of, to

different (*adj.*): from [but when an independent clause follows *different*, the conjunction *than* is better {movies are different today than they were in the fifties}]

differentiate (*vb.*): from, between, among

differently (*adv.*): from, than

digress (*vb.*): from

digression (*n.*): from, on

disabuse (*vb.*): of

disbar (*vb.*): from

discourage (*vb.*): from

discouraged (*adj.*): about, over, by

discredit (*n.*): to, on

discriminate (*vb.*): against, between, among, from

disdain (*n.*): for, of

disdainful (*adj.*): of

disgruntled (*adj.*): over, about, at, with

disloyal (*adj.*): to

disloyalty (*n.*): to, toward

dispense (*vb.*): with

displaced (*adj.*): by

displeased (*adj.*): at, about, by, over [a thing], with [a person] dispose (*vb.*): of

disposition (*n.*): to, toward

dispossessed (*adj.*): of, from

dispute (*n.*): over, about, with

disqualify (*vb.*): from, for

disregard (*n.*): for

dissent (*n. & vb.*): from, against [preferably not *to* or *with*]

dissimilar (*adj.*): to [not *from*]

dissociate (*vb.*): from

distaste (*n.*): for

distinguish (*vb.*): from, between, among

distinguished (*adj.*): for, by

distraught (*adj.*): over, about, at

distressed (*adj.*): about, by, at, over

diverge (*vb.*): from

diverted (*vb.*): from, to, for, by

divested (*vb.*): of

divide (*vb.*): between, among, into, by

divided (*adj.*): over, about, on

dominant (*adj.*): over, in

dominate (*vb.*): over

dominion (*n.*): over

doom (*vb.*): to

doomed (*adj.*): to, for

dote (*vb.*): on, upon

dovetail (*vb.*): into

drip (*vb.*): from, with

due (*adj.*): to, for

dun (*vb.*): for

ear (*n.*): for {an ear for music}, to {lend an ear to this music}

earmark (*n.*): of {all the earmarks of a great race}

earmark (*vb.*): for {funds earmarked for defense}

ecstatic (*adj.*): over, about, at

educate (*vb.*): to, for, about, against

education (*n.*): in, about

effective (*adj.*): for, against, in

elated (*adj.*): at, about, over

eligible (*adj.*): for

embark (*vb.*): on, for

embody (*vb.*): in

emerge (*vb.*): from, as

emigrate (*vb.*): from, to

émigré (*n.*): from

empathize (*vb.*): with

emphatic (*adj.*): about, in

employ (*vb.*): as, in

enamored (*adj.*): of [not *with*]

encouraged (*adj.*): by, at, about, over

encroach (*vb.*): on, upon

encumbered (*adj.*): with, by

endow (*vb.*): with

endowed (*adj.*): by, with

enforce (*vb.*): on, upon

enjoin (*vb.*): from, to, upon

enlarge (*vb.*): upon, on

ensure (*vb.*): against

enter (*vb.*): into

enthusiastic (*adj.*): about, over, at

entice (*vb.*): with, into

entitle (*vb.*): to

entrap (*vb.*): in, into

entrapment (*n.*): into

entrust (*vb.*): to, with

envious (*adj.*): of, toward

envision (*vb.*): as

equal (*adj.*): to, in

equate (*vb.*): with

equidistant (*adj.*): from [preferably not *between*]

equivalent (*adj.*): to, in [preferably not *with*]

equivalent (*n.*): of

equivocal (*adj.*): about

escalate (*vb.*): into

escape (*vb.*): from

estrange (*vb.*): from

estrangement (*n.*): from, between, over

etch (*vb.*): into

evolve (*vb.*): into, from

exasperated (*adj.*): by, at, about, over

excerpt (*n.*): from [not *of*]

exclusive (*adj.*): of

exile (*n. & vb.*): to, from

exonerate (*vb.*): from

expand (*vb.*): into, on

export (*vb.*): from, into

expropriate (*vb.*): from, for

expunge (*vb.*): from

extolled (*adj.*): as

extradite (*vb.*): from, to

facility (*n.*): for, with, at, in

famous (*adj.*): for, as

fascinated (*adj.*): by, with, at

fascination (*n.*): for, about

fashion (*vb.*): into, from

fasten (*vb.*): to, onto, in, on

fault (*vb.*): for

favor (*vb.*): with

feud (*n.*): between, among, with, about, over, against

feud (*vb.*): with, about, over

fidget (*vb.*): with

filch (*vb.*): from

fill (*vb.*): with, in

find (*vb.*): for, against

finicky (*adj.*): about

fixation (*n.*): on

flair (*n.*): for

flee (*vb.*): from, to, for

flinch (*vb.*): at, from

flirt (*vb.*): with, at

fond (*adj.*): of

fondness (*n.*): for

forage (*vb.*): for

forbid (*vb.*): to [formal], from [informal]

force (*n.*): of, by, against, for, in

force (*vb.*): into, onto, from

foreclose (*vb.*): on

fortify (*vb.*): with, against

fortunate (*adj.*): in

fraternize (*vb.*): with

fraught (*adj.*): with

free (*adj.*): from, of

fret (*vb.*): over, about

frugal (*adj.*): with, of

fulminate (*vb.*): against

fume (*vb.*): over, about

furious (*vb.*): about, at, over

furnish (*vb.*): with

gamut (*n.*): from . . . to

gasp (*n. & vb.*): for, at

generous (*adj.*): with, to, toward, in

genial (*adj.*): toward, with

gentle (*adj.*): with, about

gibe (*n.*): at, about

gibe (*vb.*): at

given (*adj.*): to

glare (*n.*): of

glare (*vb.*): at

glisten (*vb.*): in, with, from, from, off

glitter (*n.*): of

glitter (*vb.*): in, with

gloat (*vb.*): over, about

graduate (*n.*): of, in

graduate (*vb.*): from

grapple (*vb.*): with, for, onto

grateful (*adj.*): for, to

gratified (*adj.*): by, with, at

gravitate (*vb.*): toward, to, around

grieve (*vb.*): over, for, after, with, at

gripe (*n.*): about

gripe (*vb.*): at, about

grounded (*adj.*): in, from

grudge (*n.*): against, over, about

guard (*vb.*): against, from

guarded (*adj.*): about, from, by

habit (*n.*): of

hack (*vb.*): down, through, at

haggle (*vb.*): over, about, for, with

hail (*vb.*): as, from

hale (*vb.*): into

hammer (*vb.*): on, into, at

handy (*adj.*): with, at

hanker (*vb.*): for, after

happen (*vb.*): upon, on, to

hardened (*adj.*): to

harp (*vb.*): on, about

hassle (*n. & vb.*): with, over, about

hedge (*n.*): against
heedful (*adj.*): of
heedless (*adj.*): of
hegemony (*n.*): over
hesitate (*vb.*): over
hesitation (*n.*): in, on, about, over
hinder (*vb.*): from, in
hindrance (*n.*): to
hinge (*vb.*): upon, on
hobnob (*vb.*): with
holdover (*n.*): from
hostile (*adj.*): toward, to, about, over
hostility (*n.*): against, toward, to, about, over
hover (*vb.*): around, over, near, between, above
huddle (*vb.*): in, with, around
hunger (*vb.*): for, after
hurtle (*vb.*): toward, through, past, down, at
identical (*adj.*): with, to
identify (*vb.*): to, as, by, with
idolize (*vb.*): as
ignorance (*n.*): of
ignorant (*adj.*): of [not *to*], in
imbued (*adj.*): with
immigrant (*n.*): from [not *to*]
immigrate (*vb.*): to, into [not *from*]
immune (*adj.*): to, from
immunize (*vb.*): against
impatience (*n.*): with [esp. people], at, about
impinge (*vb.*): on, upon
implicit (*adj.*): in
import (*vb.*): from, into
importune (*vb.*): for
impose (*vb.*): on, upon
impregnate (*vb.*): with
impress (*vb.*): upon [people], as, on, into, with
impressed (*adj.*): with, by
impression (*n.*): of, on [preferably not *upon*], in, as, with
impute (*vb.*): to

inaugurate (*vb.*): as, into
incidental (*adj.*): to
include (*vb.*): in, among
inclusive (*adj.*): of
incompatible (*adj.*): with
incompetence (*n.*): of, in, by, on [the part of], at, among
incongruent (*adj.*): with
incongruous (*adj.*): with
inconsistent (*adj.*): with
incorporate (*vb.*): into, with
inculcate (*vb.*): into, in
incumbent (*adj.*): on, upon
independence (*n.*): from
independent (*adj.*): of [not *from*]
indifferent (*adj.*): to
indigenous (*adj.*): to
indignant (*adj.*): about, at, over, with, toward
induct (*vb.*): into
indulge (*vb.*): in
indulgent (*n.*): of, toward
infatuation (*n.*): with
infer (*vb.*): from
infiltrate (*vb.*): into
infiltration (*n.*): into, of, by
inflict (*vb.*): on
influence (*n.*): of, over, upon, for
influence (*vb.*): to, by, for
inform (*vb.*): on, about, of
informed (*adj.*): about
infringe (*vb.*): on, upon
infringement (*n.*): of, on
infuse (*vb.*): into
ingratiate (*vb.*): with
inhere (*vb.*): in [not *within*]
inherent (*adj.*): in, to
inimical (*adj.*): to
initiate (*vb.*): into
inject (*vb.*): into
innate (*adj.*): in
inoculate (*vb.*): against
input (*n.*): into

inquire (*vb.*): into [situations], of [people], after [people]

inquisitive (*adj.*): about

inroad (*n.*): into

inseparable (*adj.*): from

insight (*n.*): into

insist (*vb.*): on

instill (*vb.*): in, into [not *with*]

insulate (*vb.*): from, against

insure (*vb.*): against, for

intent (*adj.*): on, upon

intention (*n.*): of, to

intercede (*vb.*): in, with, for

interest (*n.*): in

interject (*vb.*): into

interlace (*vb.*): with

intrude (*vb.*): on, upon, into

inveigh (*vb.*): against

inveigle (*vb.*): into, from

jealous (*adj.*): of [not *about* or *with*]

jibe (*vb.*): with

join (*vb.*): in, into, with

jump (*vb.*): at, to, for, with, into, over, through

junior (*adj.*): to, in

jurisdiction (*n.*): over

justified (*adj.*): in

juxtaposed (*adj.*): with

kid (*vb.*): about

kindness (*n.*): toward, to, of

knack (*n.*): for, of, to

knowledgeable (*adj.*): about

known (*adj.*): for, to, by, as

kudos (*n.*): to, for

label (*vb.*): with, as

lacking (*adj.*): in

laden (*vb.*): with

lament (*n.*): for, of, to, on, over

lament (*vb.*): over

languish (*vb.*): in

lap (*vb.*): against

lapse (*n.*): in

lapse (*vb.*): in, into

lash (*vb.*): into, at, against

latch (*vb.*): onto

lavish (*vb.*): with, on

lax (*adj.*): in, about, on, toward

leaf (*vb.*): through

leer (*vb.*): at

leery (*adj.*): of

lenient (*adj.*): with, in, toward, on

level (*vb.*): to [raze], with [confide], against [accuse]

liable (*adj.*): for, to

liaison (*n.*): between, with

liberate (*vb.*): from

liberties (*n.*): with

liken (*vb.*): to

likeness (*n.*): to, between

limited (*adj.*): to, in

linger (*vb.*): over

lock (*vb.*): on, onto

lull (*n.*): in [lapse]

lull (*vb.*): into [trick], to [sleep]

lure (*vb.*): into

lurk (*vb.*): in

mad (*adj.*): at, about

made (*adj.*): from, of, with, without, into

magnanimous (*adj.*): toward, of

malice (*n.*): toward, against

maneuver (*vb.*): into, for

marred (*adj.*): by

marriage (*n.*): to, into, of

married (*adj.*): to

marry (*vb.*): into

martyr (*n.*): to

martyred (*adj.*): for

marvel (*vb.*): at

mastery (*n.*): of [a skill], over [people]

meant (*vb.*): as [intent], for [destination], by [action]

meddle (*vb.*): in, with

merge (*vb.*): with, into

mesh (*vb.*): with

meticulous (*adj.*): in, about

migrate (*vb.*): to, from, between

militate (*vb.*): against

mill (*vb.*): around, about

mindful (*adj.*): of

minister (*vb.*): to

mitigate (*vb.*): (none)

mulct (*vb.*): of

muse (*vb.*): over, about, upon, on

mutiny (*vb.*): against

nail (*vb.*): to, into

naive (*adj.*): about, of

necessary (*adj.*): for, to, in

necessity (*n.*): of, for

need (*n.*): of, for

neglectful (*adj.*): of

negligent (*adj.*): about, in, of

negotiate (*vb.*): with, for, over, about, from [a position of —]

nestle (*vb.*): into, against

newcomer (*n.*): to

niggardly (*adj.*): about, in, with, toward, to

niggle (*vb.*): about, over

nominate (*vb.*): for, as, to

notorious (*adj.*): for, as

object (*n.*): of

object (*vb.*): to, about

obligation (*n.*): to

obligatory (*adj.*): on, upon, for

oblivious (*adj.*): of [preferred], to

observance (*n.*): of

observant (*adj.*): of

observation (*n.*): about, of, for

obsessed (*adj.*): with, by

obsession (*n.*): with, for

obstinate (*adj.*): about, in

obtrude (*vb.*): on, upon, into

odds (*n.*): against, of [possibility], with, over [conflict]

odious (*adj.*): to

off (*prep. & adv.*): none [not *of*]

offend (*vb.*): against

offended (*adj.*): by, about, at, with [a person]

offensive (*adj.*): to

offer (*vb.*): as

omen (*n.*): for, of

open (*adj.*): for, to

open (*vb.*): to, for, with, by, onto

operate (*vb.*): on, for, against

opposite (*adj.*): to

opposite (*n.*): of, to

opposition (*n.*): to

ordeal (*n.*): by

oscillate (*vb.*): between

oust (*vb.*): from

outlet (*adj.*): for, to

overcome (*adj.*): by, with

overgrown (*adj.*): with, by

owing (*adj.*): to

pale (*vb.*): in, beside, at

pall (*n.*): over

panacea (*n.*): for

pander (*vb.*): to

panic (*vb.*): at, over, about

parallel (*adj.*): to, with

parallel (*n.*): between, among, with

paramount (*adj.*): over

paranoid (*adj.*): about, over

parity (*n.*): between, among, of, in

parlay (*vb.*): into

parley (*n. & vb.*): with

part (*vb.*): from [a person], with

partake (*vb.*): of

partial (*adj.*): to

patterned (*adj.*): after, on, upon

peculiar (*adj.*): to

penchant (*n.*): for

perceive (*vb.*): as

perceptible (*adj.*): to

perceptive (*adj.*): of

peripheral (*adj.*): to

periphery (*n.*): of

permeate (*vb.*): through, into, with

permeated (*adj.*): by, with

permit (*n.*): for

permit (*vb.*): of

perpendicular (*adj.*): to

persecution (*n.*): for

persevere (*vb.*): in, at, against

persist (*vb.*): in [an action], against [obstacles]

persuade (*vb.*): by

persuaded (*adj.*): of, by

pertaining (*adj.*): to

pertinent (*adj.*): to

perturbed (*adj.*): at, by, about, over

pervaded (*adj.*): with

pilfer (*vb.*): from

pine (*vb.*): for, after

piqued (*adj.*): by, at

plot (*vb.*): against

plow (*vb.*): into, through

plunge (*vb.*): to, into, from

ponder (*vb.*): over, about, on, upon

pore (*vb.*): over, through

posture (*vb.*): as

pox (*n.*): on

preach (*vb.*): to, about, against, at

precedence (*n.*): of, over

precedent (*adj.*): to

precedent (*n.*): for, of

precise (*adj.*): about

preclude (*vb.*): from

precursor (*n.*): to, of

predestined (*adj.*): to

predicate (*vb.*): on, upon

predilection (*n.*): for

predisposed (*adj.*): to

predominate (*vb.*): over

preeminent (*adj.*): in

preface (*n.*): to, of

preface (*vb.*): with

preferable (*adj.*): to [not *than*]

preference (*n.*): for, to

prefix (*vb.*): to

pregnant (*adj.*): with [the child], by [the father]

prejudice (*n.*): against, for, to

prejudice (*vb.*): by, against, for

prejudiced (*adj.*): by, against, for

prejudicial (*adj.*): to

preoccupied (*adj.*): with

preparatory (*adj.*): to

prepare (*vb.*): for

prerequisite (*adj.*): to, for, of

prerequisite (*n.*): for, to

present (*adj.*): at

present (*vb.*): to, with

preside (*vb.*): at, over

pretext (*n.*): for

prevail (*vb.*): over, against, on, upon

prevent (*vb.*): from

proceeds (*n.*): from, of

proclivity (*n.*): for, to [not *toward*]

prod (*vb.*): into, to

prodigal (*adj.*): with

proficient (*adj.*): at, in

profit (*vb.*): by, from

prohibit (*vb.*): from, by

prohibition (*n.*): against, on

prologue (*n.*): of [a book], to [an event]

propensity (*n.*): for

propinquity (*n.*): to

propitious (*adj.*): for, to, of

protect (*vb.*): from, against

protective (*adj.*): of, toward, over, about

protest (*n. & vb.*): against, for

provide (*vb.*): with, for, against

provoke (*vb.*): into, to

punctilious (*adj.*): in, about, to [a fault]

punish (*vb.*): for

punishable (*adj.*): by

purge (*n.*): of

purge (*vb.*): from, of

puzzle (*vb.*): over

puzzling (*adj.*): to

quake (*vb.*): with

qualified (*adj.*): for, by, as

qualify (*vb.*): for, as

qualms (*n.*): about

quandary (*n.*): over, about

quarrel (*n.*): between, with, over, about

quarrel (*vb.*): over, about, with

quibble (*vb.*): over, about, with

quiver (*vb.*): with

radiant (*adj.*): with, in

rage (*n.*): against, at [anger], with [fad]

rage (*vb.*): against, at

rail (*vb.*): against, at

railroad (*vb.*): through

raise (*vb.*): from, for, with, to

raised (*adj.*): for, in, from, to, with

rally (*vb.*): around, to, for

ram (*vb.*): into

rant (*vb.*): at, about

rate (*vb.*): as, among, with, for, in

rationalization (*n.*): for

rave (*vb.*): about, over

react (*vb.*): to, against

reason (*n.*): for, to, behind, against

reason (*vb.*): with, about, on

reasonable (*adj.*): about

recede (*vb.*): from

receptive (*adj.*): to

reciprocate (*vb.*): by, for, with

reciprocity (*n.*): between, with, to

reckon (*vb.*): on, with

recoil (*n.* & *vb.*): from, at

recompense (*n.* & *vb.*): for

reconcile (*vb.*): with [a person], to [a situation]

reconciliation (*n.*): with

recourse (*n.*): to

redeem (*vb.*): from, with, for, at

redolent (*adj.*): of, with

redound (*vb.*): to

refer (*vb.*): to, for

regale (*vb.*): with

regard (*n.*): for, to

regard (*vb.*): as, with

regardless (*adj.*): of

regret (*n.*): over, about, for

rejoice (*vb.*): in, over, at, with

relation (*n.*): to, between, among

relations (*n.*): with, between, among

relationship (*n.*): to, between, with, to

relegate (*adj.*): to

relieve (*vb.*): of

relieved (*adj.*): at, of

remarkable (*adj.*): for

remember (*vb.*): of, about, from, as

remembrance (*n.*): of

reminisce (*vb.*): about

reminiscent (*n.*): of

rend (*vb.*): into

renege (*vb.*): on

renowned (*adj.*): for, as, by, among

repent (*vb.*): of

repentance (*n.*): for

replace (*vb.*): with

replaced (*adj.*): by, with

replacement (*n.*): for

replete (*adj.*): with

representative (*adj.*): of

representative (*n.*): of, from, to, for

reprisal (*n.*): against, on, upon, for

reprove (*vb.*): for

repugnance (*n.*): between [contradiction]

repugnant (*adj.*): to

request (*n.*): for, to, of

request (*vb.*): from, of

resemblance (*n.*): between, among, to, of

resentment (*adj.*): of, at, against, toward, about, over

reservations (*n.*): for [accommodations], about [reluctance]

resign (*vb.*): from [a position], to [a situation]

resolute (*adj.*): in

respect (*n.*): for, to, of, from, as

respite (*n.*): from

restrain (*vb.*): from

restraint (*n.*): of, in, by

result (*n.*): of, from

result (*vb.*): in, from

resulting (*adj.*): in, from

reticent (*adj.*): about
retire (*vb.*): from, to
retroactive (*adj.*): to
revel (*vb.*): in
revelation (*n.*): of, about, to
revenge (*n.*): on, upon, for
revolve (*vb.*): around, about
revulsion (*n.*): at, toward, against, for
reward (*vb.*): for, with, by
rifle (*vb.*): through
ripe (*adj.*): for
ripen (*adj.*): into
roam (*vb.*): around
rob (*vb.*): of
ruminate (*vb.*): on, about, over
safe (*adj.*): for, from
sanction (*n.*): for [punishment], of [approval], to
sanction (*vb.*): by, for, against
sanctuary (*n.*): to, from, for
satiate (*vb.*): with
satisfaction (*n.*): to, in, for, with, about, over
satisfied (*adj.*): with
scared (*adj.*): by, at, about, for
scavenge (*vb.*): for
schism (*n.*): between, in
schooled (*adj.*): in
scoff (*vb.*): at
scourge (*n.*): of, to
scream (*vb.*): at, for, in, with, after
screen (*n.*): between
screen (*vb.*): from
secede (*vb.*): from
secure (*adj.*): against, from, in, of, about
secure (*vb.*): against, from, by
segregate (*vb.*): from, into, by
sensible (*adj.*): about, of
sensitive (*adj.*): to
sentimental (*adj.*): about, over
separate (*vb. & adj.*): from
serve (*vb.*): on, for, with
settle (*vb.*): on, with, for, in, into

shame (*n.*): on, to, about, for
shame (*vb.*): into
share (*vb.*): with, in, among, between
shield (*n. & vb.*): from, against
shiver (*vb.*): from [cold], at, with [fear]
shriek (*vb.*): in, with, at
shrink (*vb.*): from
shrug (*vb.*): at
shudder (*vb.*): at, from
shuttle (*vb.*): between, among
shy (*adj.*): about, of
sift (*vb.*): through, from
significance (*n.*): of
significant (*adj.*): to, for, about
similar (*adj.*): to [not *as*]
similarity (*n.*): to, of, in, between, among
simultaneous (*adj.*): with
skeptical (*adj.*): of, about
skillful (*adj.*): at, in [an activity], with [tools]
slanted (*adj.*): against, toward
slave (*n.*): of, to
slave (*vb.*): over
sleep (*n.*): over, about
sleep (*vb.*): on, in, with
smell (*n.*): of
smell (*vb.*): like, of
smile (*vb.*): at, about, on
smitten (*adj.*): with, by
snuggle (*vb.*): into, against
solicitous (*adj.*): of, toward
solicitude (*n.*): for, to, about, toward
solidarity (*n.*): with
sore (*adj.*): from, over, about, at
sorry (*adj.*): for, about
sought (*adj.*): for, after
spat (*n. & vb.*): with
speculate (*vb.*): about, on, in
speculator (*n.*): in
spy (*vb.*): on, upon, for
squeeze (*vb.*): through, into, out
standing (*n.*): with, among, in, as

started (*adj.*): by, at
stern (*adj.*): with, toward
stigma (*n.*): to, about, over, from
stigmatize (*vb.*): as
stint (*n.*): as, in
stir (*n.*): over, about, at, in, through-out, among, around
stir (*vb.*): into, in
stock (*n.*): of, in
stoical (*adj.*): about, toward
storm (*vb.*): into, through
stray (*vb.*): from, onto, into
streak (*n.*): of
streak (*vb.*): through, across, past, into, down, on, off, toward
streaked (*adj.*): with
stream (*vb.*): into, through, toward
strewn (*adj.*): with
stricken (*adj.*): with
strict (*adj.*): about, with
strife (*n.*): among, between, in, over, about, throughout
strike (*vb.*): against, for, over, at, as
strive (*vb.*): for, against
struggle (*n. & vb.*): for, against, with, over, through
study (*vb.*): for, at, under
stumble (*vb.*): upon, across, onto, on, into, over, around
submit (*vb.*): to
subordinate (*n.*): of
subordinate (*vb. & adj.*): to
subscribe (*vb.*): to [a periodical or an opinion], for [stock]
subsidiary (*adj.*): to
subsidiary (*n.*): of
subsidy (*n.*): to, for
subsist (*vb.*): on
substitute (*n. & vb.*): for
succeed (*vb.*): in [an endeavor], to [an estate], as [a position]
suffer (*vb.*): from, with
suitable (*adj.*): for
suited (*adj.*): for, to

summon (*vb.*): to, into, for, before
superstitious (*adj.*): about
supervision (*n.*): of, over
supplement (*n.*): to
supplement (*vb.*): with, by
supplementary (*adj.*): to
supply (*n.*): of, for
supply (*vb.*): with, for, to
susceptible (*adj.*): to [problem], of [meaning]
suspect (*n.*): in
suspect (*vb.*): of, in, as
suspicion (*n.*): of, about, on
suspicious (*adj.*): of, about, at, over
swing (*n. & vb.*): at [try to hit], to, toward, from [trend]
sympathetic (*adj.*): to, toward, with
sympathize (*vb.*): with, in
sympathy (*n.*): for, with, to
synchronize (*vb.*): with
synchronous (*adj.*): to
synonymous (*adj.*): to, with
taken (*adj.*): by, with
tally (*vb.*): up [compute], with [agree]
tantamount (*adj.*): to
tap (*vb.*): on, against, at, into, for
taste (*n.*): of, for, in
taunt (*vb.*): for, with, about, into
tear (*vb.*): off, into, at, after, from, to
tease (*vb.*): for, with, about, into
teem (*vb.*): with
tend (*adj.*): to, toward
tendency (*n.*): to, toward
tender (*adj.*): to, with, toward [gentle]
tender (*n.*): for [offer]
tender (*vb.*): to [give]
terms (*n.*): of [an agreement], with [a situation]
testify (*vb.*): about, against, for, to, at, in
thankful (*adj.*): for, to, about, in
thirst (*n.*): for
thirst (*vb.*): after, for

timid (*adj.*): about, around, with

tinge (*n.*): of

tinge (*vb.*): with, in

tinged (*adj.*): with, in

tinker (*vb.*): at, with

toast (*n.*): of [fame], to [salute]

tolerance (*n.*): for, toward, of, with

tough (*adj.*): on, with, about, for

tout (*vb.*): for, as

toy (*vb.*): with

trade (*n.*): with, among, between, in, for

trade (*vb.*): for [swap], in [sell], with [do business with], at [patronize], on [buy and sell at]

traffic (*n.* & *vb.*): in

treat (*vb.*): for, with, like, to, as, of

tremble (*vb.*): in, with, from, at

trouble (*n.*): with, from, over, about

trouble (*vb.*): with, about

trust (*n.*): in [faith], for [beneficial trust]

trust (*vb.*): in, with, to

umbrage (*n.*): at, to

unbeatable (*adj.*): at, in, against

unbecoming (*adj.*): of, to, in

unbiased (*adj.*): toward, about

unburden (*vb.*): of

uncomfortable (*adj.*): with, about

uncooperative (*adj.*): toward, with, about

undaunted (*adj.*): in [a task], by [obstacles]

unequal (*adj.*): to [a challenge], in [attributes]

unfaithful (*adj.*): to, in

unfamiliar (*adj.*): with, to

unfeeling (*adj.*): toward, about

uniform (*adj.*): in, with, to

uniformity (*n.*): of, in

unify (*vb.*): with, into, around, against

unique (*adj.*): to, in, about

unjustified (*adj.*): in

unmindful (*adj.*): of

unpalatable (*adj.*): to

unpopular (*adj.*): with, for, among

unsparing (*adj.*): of

unstinting (*adj.*): in

unsuitable (*adj.*): for

unsuited (*adj.*): to

unused (*adj.*): to

upbraid (*vb.*): for, over

upset (*adj.*): with, at, about, over

used (*adj.*): to [accustomed], for [applied]

vacillate (*vb.*): between, on, within

value (*vb.*): for, as, at, over, above, below, beyond

vanish (*vb.*): from, into

variance (*n.*): with

variation (*n.*): in, from

variety (*n.*): of, to

vary (*vb.*): between, among, with, in, from

verge (*vb.*): on, upon

versatile (*adj.*): at, in, with, around

vest (*vb.*): in, with

vested (*adj.*): in, with

vexed (*adj.*): with [someone], about, at [something]

vie (*vb.*): for, in, with, against, over

visualize (*vb.*): as

void (*adj.*): of

wade (*vb.*): into, across, in, through

wage (*vb.*): against, over

wait (*vb.*): for, on, upon, by, at

waiver (*n.*): of

want (*n.*): of

want (*vb.*): for

wanted (*adj.*): by, for, in

wanting (*adj.*): in

war (*vb.*): against, with, over

watch (*vb.*): over, for

waver (*vb.*): between, over, about

weak (*n.*): in, at, from, with

weakened (*adj.*): by, from

weakness (*n.*): for, against, from, toward

wean (*vb.*): from

weep (*vb.*): for, over, about, at

weigh (*vb.*): against, on, upon

wince (*vb.*): at, in

wizard (*n.*): at, of

wonder (*vb.*): about, at

worm (*vb.*): into

worthy (*adj.*): of

wrangle (*vb.*): over, with, about

wrest (*vb.*): from

yearn (*vb.*): for, about

yield (*vb.*): to, against

zeal (*n.*): for

zealous (*adj.*): about, in, for

V. Punctuation

451   ***Introduction.*** Punctuation is an elaborate cuing system by which writers signal to their readers how to move smoothly through the prose. Used properly, punctuation helps writers achieve clarity and emphasis. Used improperly, it does just the opposite. Often, though, punctuation problems are a symptom of bad writing. As one authority observes, "Most errors of punctuation arise from ill-designed, badly shaped sentences, and from the attempt to make them work by means of violent tricks with commas and colons."[1] So learning punctuation is closely allied with learning to write solid, sophisticated sentences. You can't have one skill without the other. Hence the guidance that follows.

> Punctuation is the notation in the sheet music of our words, telling us when to rest, or when to raise our voices; it acknowledges that the meaning of our discourse, as of any symphonic composition, lies not in the units but in the pauses, the pacing and the phrasing.
> —Pico Iyer
> "In Praise of the Humble Comma"

    All the illustrative sentences below—the good ones, that is—appear in the work of the writers named. If you haven't heard of the writers, don't despair: if you're curious, research them a little. See whether you might like to read their work. The short passages here excerpted give only the most minuscule sampling of their prose, which merits closer study. For now, though, focus on each point at hand as you study the examples. But relish the fact that the illustrations aren't fabricated for purposes of this book: they are the work of some of the language's most adept wordsmiths.

---

1   Hugh Sykes Davies, *Grammar Without Tears* (New York: Day, 1951), 167.

The Comma

12 Uses, 11 Misuses

> *The comma (,) marks the slightest possible separation in ideas or grammatical construction—especially between words, phrases, and clauses.*

Using Commas

452 *Use a comma when you join two independent clauses with a coordinating conjunction (such as "and," "but," "nor," "or," "so," or "yet").*

- Two or three of the spectators were sniffling, and one was weeping loudly. (Stephen Crane)
- Dirk was going home to dinner, and I proposed to find a doctor. (W. Somerset Maugham)
- It was an unscheduled stop, and the platform of the small station was crowded with people. (Ayn Rand)
- It is true that the exact historical connections are often hard to establish, but a social context must always be presumed. (F. W. Bateson)

453 *Use a comma after a transitional word or phrase (though not "and," "but," "for," "so," or "yet"), an introductory phrase (especially a long one), or a subordinate clause that precedes an independent clause.*

- Nevertheless, the conditions behind the kitchen door were suitable for a pigsty. (George Orwell)
- Aside from that remark, all our conversation was about personalities. (Theodore H. White)
- Taking out the crumpled paper, I looked at the telephone number. (Ralph Ellison)
- For the most part, we come to works of art when the labels have already been pasted on. (Roger Shattuck)

454 *Use a pair of commas to mark the beginning and end of a nonrestrictive phrase or clause—that is, either an appositive or a phrase or clause that gives incidental or descriptive information that isn't essential to the meaning of the sentence.*

- A sensitive person is one who, because he has corns himself, always treads on other people's toes. (Oscar Wilde)
- He is, as we say, a creature of circumstance. (A. R. Orage)
- The indecencies and the double meanings of Sterne, if anything, intensify the solitude. (V. S. Pritchett)
- If, when he rose, the bench did not rise with him, the ale was understrength. (Frank Muir)

455 *Use a comma to separate items in a series—including the next-to-last and last (but never before an ampersand).*

- Archer was not such a simpleton as to be unaware that some women are vulgar, violent, and immodest according to Victorian conceptions of modesty. (George Bernard Shaw)
- I noticed that Wilde, Baudelaire, and Swinburne are stacked up beside Joyce as rivals in decadence and intellect. (Hart Crane)
- A steady stream of articles, letters, communications, documents, and committee reports flowed from his facile pen. (Henry Steele Commager)
- The air was foul with the stench of bilge, the reek of the untrimmed lamps, the exhalation of so many breaths, and the stale smell of warm bedding. (Frank Norris)

456 *Use a comma to separate adjectives that each qualify a noun (or adverbs that each qualify an adjective) in parallel fashion—that is, when "and" could appear between the modifiers without changing the meaning of the sentence, or when you could reverse the modifiers' order without affecting the meaning.*

- The Brite brothers were ingenious, self-reliant men. (Erle Stanley Gardner)
- Every year I have stupid, lazy greenhorns to deal with. (Eugene O'Neill)
- No writer seems more hopelessly, inexpugnably preppy than Salinger. (Wilfrid Sheed)
- It was blindingly, glaringly hot. (Margaret Mitchell)

457 *Use a comma to distinguish indirect from direct speech.*

- And she said, "Please never look at me like that." (Ernest Hemingway)
- "Tell me again," she begged, moving over to one end of her boulder. (Dashiell Hammett)
- He took a breath and let it out and at last said, "No, I don't mean that." (Ray Bradbury)
- "There, sir," said the butcher, "that's how we do it in Leadenhall Market, asking your pardon." (Patrick O'Brian)

458 *Use commas to separate the parts of full dates and addresses, but (1) omit any comma before a zip code; (2) when writing just the month and the year, don't separate them with a comma (July 2005); and (3) when writing the month, day, and year, omit the comma after the year if you're using the date as an adjective (the November 20, 2006 meeting).*

- Exactly fifty-two B-17s were available for service as late as May 1940. (David M. Kennedy)
- Lamon gained access to Pinkerton's February 23, 1861 report, in which the detective recounted the name-leaking episode. (Michael J. Kline)
- The Wilsons managed to live and ride in comparative peace for about four years, until February 2, 1872, when the boys rode into Trinidad, and George Wilson began gambling at the Exchange Saloon. (J. Evetts Haley)

459 *Use commas to separate thousands written numerically—but not strings of numbers that are not considered in thousands.*

- Mostly out of laziness, I decide to start my low-wage life in the town nearest to where I actually live, Key West, Florida, which with a population of about 25,000 is elbowing its way up to the status of a genuine city. (Barbara Ehrenreich)
- The median net worth of black households in this country is $4,604, or just one-tenth the median net worth of white families—$44,408. The comparable figure for Hispanics is $5,345. (Carl T. Rowan)
- Here you'd find yourself on the wrong side—it's they who stand for the individual and we just stand for Private 23987. (Graham Greene)

460 *Use a comma to set off a name, word, or phrase used as a vocative.*

- Mother, I have nothing particular to write about. (Walt Whitman to his mother)
- Look to your daughter, Archie. (Carl Sandburg to Archibald MacLeish)
- Are you well, dear Victoria? (Aldous Huxley to Victoria Ocampo)
- Listen, you contumacious rat, don't throw your dreary tomes at me. (Alexander Woollcott to Ira Gershwin)

461 *Use a comma before a direct question contained within another sentence.*

- You begin to ask the question, Why is it that people have to pay water bills in a world that is two-thirds water? (Martin Luther King Jr.)
- As some of the children ask, we must ask, Why do people no longer suffice? (Sherry Turkle)
- We can pose the question, Where did these attitudes and behavior originate? (Cathy J. Cohen)
- The answer I like best to the query, What is ethology? is the charge given in Tinbergen's questions: What is the function and history of each behavior pattern? How does it develop? What is the mechanism? (Peter H. Klopfer)

462 *Use a comma before "etc." and "et al."—and equivalent phrases, such as "and so forth" and "and the like"—when they are the final items in a list, unless they follow only a single item.*

- Foods rich in soluble fiber like oats, beans, barley, and many fruits and vegetables (apples, oranges, carrots, etc.) should make up one-quarter of your total fiber intake for the day. (Bonnie Taub-Dix)
- An analysis of the dramas of Ibsen, Shaw, Oscar Wilde, et al. wouldn't necessarily lead one to suspect the fact. (William Morgan Hannon)
- The continent has been overrun by imposters of celebrities, writers, actors, and so forth. (Tennessee Williams)
- Jones et al. were of the opinion that the epidermal damage appeared more consistent with mechanical rather than chemical action. (Graham C. Kearn)

463   *For informal letters, use a comma after the salutation.*

- Dear Sir, . . . (Thomas Babington Macaulay to Henry S. Randall)
- Dear Noel, . . . (Alexander Woollcott to Noel Coward)
- Dear Ian, . . . (Raymond Chandler to Ian Fleming)

Preventing Misused Commas

464   *Don't use a comma between a subject and its verb, except to set off a nonrestrictive phrase or clause.*

Not this: Everything else on the farm, was destroyed.
But this: Everything else on the farm was destroyed.

Not this: The bowers and arbors in these villa gardens, are among the loveliest we've seen.
But this: The bowers and arbors in these villa gardens are among the loveliest we've seen.

Okay: The Vespa, somehow, was far more stable than I had expected and wonderfully easy to ride.
Better: The Vespa was somehow far more stable than I had expected and wonderfully easy to ride.
Or this: Somehow, the Vespa was far more stable than I had expected and wonderfully easy to ride.

465   *Don't use a comma between a verb and its object, except to set off a nonrestrictive phrase or clause.*

Not this: Not wanting to make a scene, she released, grudgingly, her hold on the necklace.
But this: Not wanting to make a scene, she grudgingly released her hold on the necklace.

Not this: Just before he hit, at full speed, the rough stone wall of the pool, the All-American freestyler tucked his chin, swung his legs over his head, and flipped over.

> An errant, or superfluous, or omitted comma may work great havoc.
> —G. H. Vallins
> *Good English: How to Write It*

But this: Just before he hit the rough stone wall of the pool at full speed, the All-American freestyler tucked his chin, swung his legs over his head, and flipped over.

Not this: Nobody thought it possible to thread, so perfectly, the needle the way Stockton could.

But this: Nobody thought it possible to so perfectly thread the needle the way Stockton could.

466 *Don't use a comma to set off a quotation that blends into the rest of the sentence.*

Not this: Later on I would learn that my wife referred to me in public as, "a king-sized botfly."

But this: Later on I would learn that my wife referred to me in public as "a king-sized botfly."

Not this: A good invention in Canada and the northern part of the States is, "the picnic area."

But this: A good invention in Canada and the northern part of the States is "the picnic area."

Not this: Waving her rolling pin angrily, the baker chased the young boys down the alley, screaming at them to, "get lost."

But this: Waving her rolling pin angrily, the baker chased the young boys down the alley, screaming at them to "get lost."

467 *Don't use commas to set off an adverb thought to need emphasis.*

Not this: Meanwhile, he worked, entirely, by himself.

But this: Meanwhile, he worked entirely by himself.

Not this: There was nothing else to do but release, squirming and thrashing, the cat cradled in her arms.

But this: There was nothing else to do but release the squirming and thrashing cat cradled in her arms.

468 *Don't use a comma in the second part of a compound predicate—that is, when a second verb has the same subject as an earlier one.*

Not this: He hated sitting in the armchairs, but felt much more at ease in the kitchen chairs.

But this: He hated sitting in the armchairs but felt much more at ease in the kitchen chairs.

Not this: Mrs. Phancey insisted that the motel was defenseless, and said that we should screw down everything that could be screwed down.

But this: Mrs. Phancey insisted that the motel was defenseless and said that we should screw down everything that could be screwed down.

Not this: Then I felt afraid again, and resumed paddling furiously.

But this: Then I felt afraid again and resumed paddling furiously.

469 *Don't use a comma as if it were a strong mark—a period, a semicolon, a colon, or an em-dash—to splice together independent clauses.*

Not this: It all came about in the most ordinary way, one evening, after the customary men's meeting, the old man came home with a sorrowful countenance.

But this: It all came about in the most ordinary way. One evening, after the customary men's meeting, the old man came home with a sorrowful countenance.

Or this: It all came about in the most ordinary way: one evening, after the customary men's meeting, the old man came home with a sorrowful countenance.

Not this: He was trumpeting away with euphoria, however, there was little cause for it.

But this: He was trumpeting away with euphoria; however, there was little cause for it.

Or this: He was trumpeting away with euphoria; but there was little cause for it.

Or this: He was trumpeting away with euphoria—but there was little cause for it.

470   *Generally, don't use a comma after a sentence-starting conjunction.*

Not this: But, too often, the people who talk this way go on to churn out the ancient formulas we have been listening to for a whole lifetime.

> Misleading punctuation . . . introduces uncertainty as to an author's meaning. And any oddities in punctuation divert the reader's attention from the subject matter.
>
> —Reginald O. Kapp
> *The Presentation of Technical Information*

But this: But too often, the people who talk this way go on to churn out the ancient formulas we have been listening to for a whole lifetime.

Not this: And, you mustn't think that he was a cold and unemotional man.

But this: And you mustn't think that he was a cold and unemotional man.

471   *Don't omit a second comma after a word or phrase set off from the rest of the sentence by a preceding comma (unless the word or phrase ends the sentence).*

Not this: In the autumn of 1540, six months after Coronado left Compostela several fragments of his little army were widely scattered throughout the interior of North America.

But this: In the autumn of 1540, six months after Coronado left Compostela, several fragments of his little army were widely scattered throughout the interior of North America.

Not this: A university, in a burst of ecumenism appoints a voodoo priest-in-residence.

But this: A university, in a burst of ecumenism, appoints a voodoo priest-in-residence.

Not this: In many industries, large and small development of new products has been severely slowed.

But this: In many industries, large and small, development of new products has been severely slowed.

472 *Don't use commas to set off a restrictive phrase, clause, or appositive—one that is essential to the meaning of the sentence.*

> *Not this:* Each of us agreed to give $50, to finance the first issue.
> *But this:* Each of us agreed to give $50 to finance the first issue.

> *Not this:* He briefly plunged into city affairs, with ardor and courage.
> *But this:* He briefly plunged into city affairs with ardor and courage.

> *Not this:* He told the truth in a powerful book, that was so true no publisher would take it.
> *But this:* He told the truth in a powerful book that was so true no publisher would take it.

> *Not this:* My daughter, Beulah, is more theatrical than her sisters.
> *But this:* My daughter Beulah is more theatrical than her sisters.

> *Not this:* To have characters tell their own story, on a stage, raises problems distinct from those involved in putting the story between the covers of a novel.
> *But this:* To have characters tell their own story on a stage raises problems distinct from those involved in putting the story between the covers of a novel.

> *Not this:* The words, that determine the subject matter of modern discussions of art, emerge fairly clearly in these statements.
> *But this:* The words that determine the subject matter of modern discussions of art emerge fairly clearly in these statements.

> *Not this:* The century, that gave us Shakespeare, witnessed some of the greatest epics in world history.
> *But this:* The century that gave us Shakespeare witnessed some of the greatest epics in world history.

473   *Don't use commas around suffixes following names, such as Jr., Sr., III, Inc., and Ltd.*

>   *Not this:* Sammy Davis, Jr.
>   *But this:* Sammy Davis Jr.
>
>   *Not this:* Oliver Wendell Holmes, Sr.
>   *But this:* Oliver Wendell Holmes Sr.
>
>   *Not this:* Davis Love, III
>   *But this:* Davis Love III
>
>   *Not this:* Penrose Books, Ltd.
>   *But this:* Penrose Books Ltd.
>
>   *Not this:* Forever 21, Inc.
>   *But this:* Forever 21 Inc.

474   *Don't use a comma to separate adjectives that are not coordinate—that is, when one or more of the adjectives form a unit with the noun they modify.*

>   *Not this:* He wore a brown, fishing hat.
>   *But this:* He wore a brown fishing hat.
>
>   *Not this:* They lived in a brown, brick house.
>   *But this:* They lived in a brown brick house.
>
>   *Not this:* Hayden stayed in their upstairs, guest bedroom.
>   *But this:* Hayden stayed in their upstairs guest bedroom.

The Semicolon

3 Uses, 2 Misuses

> *The semicolon (;) marks a grammatical separation in the relations of a thought to a degree greater than that expressed by a comma. Between clauses, it especially shows coordination.*

Using Semicolons

475 *Use a semicolon to unite two closely connected sentences. This convention is proper even if the second or final independent clause begins with a conjunction.*

- The subtle beauties of the heath were lost to Eustacia; she only caught its vapors. (Thomas Hardy)
- The miasma spreads to dramatists and dramatic critics; the former drift into charlatanry and the latter into a cowardly and disgusting dishonesty. (H. L. Mencken)
- He was determined now; it might just make the difference to him in the struggle for power, and besides, it contained the element of revenge. (Winston Churchill)
- Pride and brute tenacity are useful allies in war or any difficult time; but they have their weaknesses. (Sir Richard Livingstone)
- Sand-grouse and flocks of the blue bee-eater will scatter at your approach; a great eagle may rise and soar away; you will see herds of gazelle cantering across the plain. (V. Sackville-West)
- It was begun in February 1811 and finished soon after June 1813; that is to say, it took Jane Austen about twenty-eight months to complete a novel containing some 160 thousand words divided into forty-eight chapters. (Vladimir Nabokov)

476 *Use a semicolon to separate items in a list or series when (1) any single element contains an internal comma, (2) the enumeration follows a colon, or (3) the items are broken into subparagraphs.*

- The drawing-room began to look empty: the baccarat was discontinued for lack of a banker; more than one person said goodnight of his own accord, and was suffered to depart without expostulation; and in the meanwhile Mr. Morris redoubled in agreeable attentions to those who stayed behind. (Robert Louis Stevenson)
- A syllogism consists of three parts: major premise, minor premise, and conclusion, and for the rhetorician the three appeals are to pathos, ethos, and logos; the color wheel suggests that all colors come from the basic trio of red, yellow, and blue; matter divides into solid, liquid, and gas; that basic building block of matter, the atom, is made up of electron, neutron, and proton. (Brooks Landon)
- Appearing with General Recoil on "Town Meeting of the Upper Air" were to be Mrs. Florence Gill, president of the Women's Auxiliary of the Sons of Original Matrons; Amory Buxton, head of the Economics and Withholding Council of the United Nations; and a young man named Tollip, representing one of the small, ineffectual groups that advocated world federation. (E. B. White)
- She would have given anything to have him tell her that it would be easier to measure the intentions of the wind or the patience of the waves on the shore than the intensity of his love; that there was no winter night cold enough to damp the ever burning fires of his passion; that he spent the days dreaming and nights awake, assailed by the madness of memories and counting, with the anguish of a condemned man, the hours until he would hold her again. (Isabel Allende)

477 *In old-fashioned style, it is permissible to use a semicolon where one would normally use a dash today or perhaps a comma—to set off a dependent clause or a phrase by way of explanation or elaboration.*

- Golf is a great game and a great art; like a kind of moving outdoor chess. (Patric Dickinson)
- Families live in rooms, one side of which is open; a bed, a table, a baby's cot set on the floor above a precipice. (Dame Laura Knight)

- His tomb of Wilde could be called the first work of sculpture of our century; while the Rock Drill is more extraordinary still and foreshadows the appalling future to which a major part of the human race is binding itself with vows and catchwords. (Sacheverell Sitwell in reference to Jacob Epstein)

Preventing Misused Semicolons

478 *Don't use a semicolon where a colon is needed—especially after a salutation.*

Not this: Dear Gordon; . . .
But this: Dear Gordon: . . .

Not this: Daddy and I worked late every afternoon of the war, picking vegetables from our Victory garden; carrots, tomatoes, potatoes, and squash.
But this: Daddy and I worked late every afternoon of the war, picking vegetables from our Victory garden: carrots, tomatoes, potatoes, and squash.

Not this: In fact his ruling was totally unnecessary; for the court found that the People had failed to take reasonable care to ascertain the facts. [A comma would be fine here in place of the semicolon.]
But this: In fact his ruling was totally unnecessary: the court found that the People had failed to take reasonable care to ascertain the facts.

479 *Avoid the semicolon where a comma suffices—especially in a list with no internal commas.*

> *Not this:* The most exemplary of modern comedians; Charlie Chaplin; managed to incorporate a class struggle within his fragile figure.
>
> *But this:* The most exemplary of modern comedians, Charlie Chaplin, managed to incorporate a class struggle within his fragile figure.

> *Not this:* Some experts; even among American foreign policy's sternest critics; accept that self-description.
>
> *But this:* Some experts, even among American foreign policy's sternest critics, accept that self-description.

> *Not this:* Our panelists hail from San Francisco; Los Angeles; and Seattle.
>
> *But this:* Our panelists hail from San Francisco, Los Angeles, and Seattle.

The Colon

7 Uses, 1 Misuse

> *The colon (:) most commonly either marks an introduction or enumeration or signals apposition or equality to connect one clause with another one that explains the first. It is also used sometimes as the equivalent of an em-dash, and it has some specialized uses as a notation after a formal salutation and in certain types of citations.*

Using Colons

480 *Use a colon to link two separate clauses or phrases when you need to indicate a step forward from the first to the second—as when the second part explains the first part or provides an example.*

- It was nothing, he said: only a little accident. (James Joyce)
- Whichever way she turned, an ironical implication confronted her: she had the exasperated sense of having walked into the trap of some stupid practical joke. (Edith Wharton)
- Einstein was utterly reticent about his personal life: a "puritanical reserve" was necessary, he said, to a scientist seeking truth. (C. P. Snow)
- Once you admit that you can change the object of a strongly felt affection, you undermine the whole structure of love and marriage, the whole philosophy of Shakespeare's sonnet: this had been the approved, though unspoken, opinion of the rectory and its mental acres of upper air. (Muriel Spark)
- Every generation takes it for granted that development will continue in a straight line: the stupider the human being, the more does he take it for granted. (Hilaire Belloc)

481 *Use a colon to introduce a list—especially one that is enumerated or broken down into subparagraphs.* [The fourth bulleted item exemplifies legal style only.]

- The passage holds two of her stately passions: a sympathy for animals and a pleasure in history's glacial movement, with its cumulative shifts of sensibility. (John Updike)
- It is all there: the pity, the pride, the just contempt, the righteous but controlled anger, the infinite compassion. (John Simon)

- Inevitably, liberalism tries to meet the challenge of communism by means of the approved procedures that follow from liberal principles: plenty of talk and free speech—negotiations, as talk between nations is called; the appeal to man's better side, his rationality and supposed common interests in peace, disarmament, and a lift in the general standard of living; reduction of tensions; avoidance of risky confrontations; exchange and Truth programs to prove to the communists the goodness of our intentions; reform and economic improvement for everybody in the world; in short, peaceful coexistence phasing into appeasement and collaboration. (James Burnham)

- **4.1** *Preparation for implementation of plain-writing requirements.*
    (A) In general. No later than 9 months after the date of enactment of this Act, the head of each agency must:
    (1) designate one or more senior officials within the agency to oversee the agency implementation of this Act;
    (2) communicate the requirements of this Act to the employees of the agency;
    (3) train employees of the agency in plain writing;
    (4) establish a process for overseeing the ongoing compliance of the agency with the requirements of this Act;
    (5) create and maintain a plain-writing section of the agency's website as required under § 4.1(B) that is accessible from the homepage of the agency's website; and
    (6) designate one or more agency points-of-contact to receive and respond to public input on:
    (a) agency implementation of this Act; and
    (b) the agency reports required under § 5.
    (Plain Writing Act of 2010 [as presented in Garner, *The Redbook: A Manual on Legal Style*, 3rd ed. (St. Paul: West, 2013), 548, 549])

482 *Use a colon to introduce a wholly self-contained quotation, especially a long one.* (A comma is often proper as well in this context. [See § 457.])

- His wife said: "If the rumors I hear are true, enough Tlingits have filtered in to wipe us out." (James Michener)

- An aged Halberdier, much decorated for long years of good conduct, said: "I'll get Captain McKinney." (Evelyn Waugh)
- At her own death, when the locked box she always kept on her bedside table was finally opened, all it contained was a letter from Rob with the notation in Elizabeth's hand: "The last letter he ever wrote." (Helene Hanff)
- Dr. Armstrong said warmly: "This speeding's all wrong—all wrong! Young men like you are a danger to the community." (Agatha Christie)

483 *Use a colon to introduce a question. (Capitalization is optional after this colon.)*

- That is quite true, and out of it arises another question: may the writer take the reader into his confidence about his characters? (E. M. Forster)
- The matter at issue is: What kind of people like Jane Austen? (Lionel Trilling) (A comma would be proper here as well. [See § 461.])
- Well, then let me ask you short and sweet: is Mrs. Linde getting a job in the bank? (Henrik Ibsen)

484 *Use a colon after the salutation in formal correspondence. (A comma is acceptable in informal letters.)*

- Dear Sir: .... (Samuel Johnson to James Boswell)
- Dear Mrs. Meloney: .... (Theodore Roosevelt to Mrs. William Brown Meloney)
- Dear Dr. Canby: .... (E. B. White to Henry Seidel Canby)

485 *Use a colon to separate hours from minutes and certain parts of citations in which its use is traditional.*

- At 5:10 a.m., the el train from the Morse stop in Chicago to the Davis stop in Evanston is surprisingly safe for young white women. (Tina Fey)
- The torments of hell are expressed sometimes by weeping and gnashing of teeth (as Matt. 8:12), sometimes by the worm of conscience (as Isa. 66:24, and Mark 9:44, 46, 48). (Thomas Hobbes)
- *Century Magazine* 32 (1886): 934. (James I. Robertson Jr.)

486 *Use a lowercase letter after a colon (unless the first word is a proper noun) when the colon is used within a sentence, even if it introduces your own independent clause. Capitalize the first word after a colon when the colon introduces more than one sentence, a direct question, or speech in dialogue.*

- My next thought concerned the choice of an impression, or effect, to be conveyed: and here I may as well observe that, throughout the construction, I kept steadily in view the design of rendering the work *universally* appreciable. (Edgar Allan Poe)
- Justice Brennan added a further element to the test he laid down in the *Roth* case: that, to be bannable, material must be "utterly without redeeming social value." (Anthony Lewis)
- This at least I know to be a mistake: an instance of the pathetic fallacy (angry cloud, proud mountain, presumptuous little Beaujolais) by which we ascribe animate qualities to inanimate phenomena. (Christopher Hitchens)
- The "nationalization of slavery" rested on an assumption shared with the abolitionists: the survival of the South's slave-labor system required the active collaboration of the federal government. (Bruce Levine)

Preventing Misused Colons

487 *Don't use a colon to introduce a quotation or list that blends into the syntax of your sentence.*

Not this: I recall quite clearly—she told him to: "bring the child straight home."
But this: I recall quite clearly—she told him to "bring the child straight home."

Not this: These boys possess what Jane calls: "a one-track mind."
But this: These boys possess what Jane calls "a one-track mind."

Not this: Overwhelmed and unprepared, local officials asked the federal government for: "all the help they could get."
But this: Overwhelmed and unprepared, local officials asked the federal government for "all the help they could get."

Parentheses

7 Uses, 1 Misuse

Parentheses [( )] are pairs of upright curves that indicate a word, phrase, or clause that has been interjected by way of explanation or qualification.

Using Parentheses

488 *Use parentheses to set off an inserted phrase, clause, or sentence that you want to minimize.*

- David Jones learned the Russian cuisine under a dour cook named Ivan (a name easily Welshified into Ifan), who had himself served on merchant ships plying the Baltic. (Anthony Burgess)
- A later type of rulers, explicitly and increasingly the servants of Whitehall, and serving only for a limited period (after which they returned to their native country, either to retirement or to some other activity) aimed rather to bring to India the benefits of Western civilization. (T. S. Eliot)
- Sometimes, in the morning, if her feet ached more than usual, Mrs. Harris felt a little low. (Nobody did anything about broken arches in those days, and the common endurance test of old age was to keep going after every step cost something.) She would hang up her towel with a sigh and go into the kitchen, feeling that it was hard to make a start. (Willa Cather)
- Though I have no belief in the power of education to turn public school boys into Newtons (it being quite obvious that, whatever opportunity may be offered, it is only those rare beings desirous of learning and possessing a certain amount of native ability who ever do learn anything), yet I must insist, in my own defense, that the system of mathematical instruction of which, at Eton, I was the unfortunate victim, was calculated not merely to turn my desire into stubborn passive resistance, but also to stifle whatever rudimentary aptitude in this direction I might have possessed. (Aldous Huxley)

489 *Use parentheses for clarifying appositives or attributions.*

- Outside we have a soprano (Gilda) and a baritone (Rigoletto); inside are a mezzo-soprano (Maddalena) and a tenor (the Duke). (Fred Plotkin)
- I was fortunate to hear the enormously successful novelist Chuck Hogan (*The Standoff*) talk about his novel *Prince of Thieves*, which was set in Charlestown, Massachusetts. (Andrew McAleer)

490 *Use parentheses to introduce shorthand or familiar names.*

- In the young people's section the benches were placed close together, and when a child's legs no longer comfortably fitted in the narrow space, it was an indication to the elders that that person could now move into the intermediate area (center church). (Maya Angelou)
- The Russians tracked the U-2 with their radar and made a number of attempts to knock it down with their surface-to-air missiles (SAMs), but the flight was a success. (Stephen Ambrose)
- The Assizes of London are held at the Central Criminal Court (the Old Bailey). (Henry Cecil)
- Around 2002, Stone Yamashita was approached by Hewlett-Packard (HP). (Chip Heath and Dan Heath)

491 *Use parentheses around numbers or letters when you're listing complex items in text. (Note that they should come in pairs: preferably "(A)," not "A).")* [*The Chicago Manual of Style* recommends periods, not parentheses, for vertical lists—as in the third bulleted example.]

- The two motive forces can be represented for the present purpose by two almost axiomatic statements, thus: (1) "An official wants to multiply subordinates, not rivals," and (2) "Officials make work for each other." (C. Northcote Parkinson)
- Mill's *Principles* carefully distinguished three cases of value determination: (1) with perpendicular supply curves, (2) with horizontal supply curves, and (3) with upward-sloping supply curves. (Thomas Sowell)
- Now for your questions.
    - (1) Life for me is real as I believe it to be a spark of the Divine.

(2) Religion not in the conventional but in the broadest sense helps me to have a glimpse of the Divine essence. This glimpse is impossible without full development of the moral sense. Hence religion and morality are, for me, synonymous terms.

(3) Striving for full realization keeps me going.

(4) This striving is the source of whatever inspiration and energy I possess.

(5) My treasure lies in battling against darkness and all forces of evil.

(Mohandas K. Gandhi)

492 *Use parentheses to denote subparts in a citation.*

- The License and Agreement requires the publication of various programmes; for instance, Clause 15(2) orders the broadcast of "an impartial account day by day prepared by professional reporters of the proceedings in both Houses of the United Kingdom Parliament." (Harry Street)
- The Government reads § 1089(e) simply to shore up § 1089(a)'s immunization of medical personnel against tort liability. (Justice Ruth Bader Ginsburg)

493 *Place parentheses correctly in relation to other punctuation, so that terminal punctuation goes outside the closing parentheses unless (1) the entire sentence is parenthetical or (2) the parenthetical matter requires a question mark or an exclamation mark.*

- Married couples split up with dismaying consequences (Truman Van Brunt abandons Christina, and their son Walker betrays and loses his Jessica). (Mark C. Carnes)
- Lying on the lawn beneath the tree in both pictures are three barely distinguishable figures. (They are thought to be Camille, Monet's first wife, Sisley, and Sisley's wife.) (John Berger)

- One great mistake made by many of the scholarly poets of the Renaissance was their thinking that the ancients were all alike and equally valuable, the mistake of not seeing that the ancient poets differed as individuals, and had different ideals, which they followed in different ways. (On the other hand, there are many examples of censure of the ancients, leading later to the dispute of ancients and moderns, where the upholders of the moderns held the ancients were not classical enough, and that the moderns could beat them at their own game.) (W. P. Ker)
- A speech can be similarly X-rayed or photographed and its structure revealed. If one examined such a speechgraph (what else could it be called?), there would be seen symbols such as squares, circles, and lines. (Louis Nizer)

494 *Use parentheses to enclose a brief aside, even as short as a single exclamation mark or question mark.*

- James E. Robinson, in a recent study, considers that the marriage (!) of Bottom and Titania translates the comprehension of the relation of nature and experience into comic myth. (Hallett Smith)

Preventing Misused Parentheses

495 *Never use a comma before an opening parenthesis.*

Not this: Some of the college players find match play, (which produced Travers, Jones, Little, Littler, Palmer, Nicklaus, et al., as national champions) intolerable.

But this: Some of the college players find match play (which produced Travers, Jones, Little, Littler, Palmer, Nicklaus, et al., as national champions) intolerable.

Not this: Macduff's grief, (as Malcolm has urged) is converted to expedient anger.

But this: Macduff's grief (as Malcolm has urged) is converted to expedient anger.

The Em-Dash (or Long Dash)

5 Uses, 2 Misuses

> *An em-dash (—) is a horizontal line that marks an emphatic insertion, an informal introduction, or a sharp break in thought. It is not so called because it runs the width of a capital M (a common misconception). Rather, it takes its name from a unit of typographic measurement: an* em *was the height of a traditional metal piece of type (about the width of a capital H). Copyeditors signal it by the mark [ⓜ].*

Using Em-Dashes

496 *Use a pair of em-dashes to set off an inserted phrase that, because of what it modifies, needs to go in the middle of a sentence.*

- I think you behave—and write—nicely, nobly even, if you like to be told so. (Algernon Charles Swinburne)
- In America—as elsewhere—free speech is confined to the dead. (Mark Twain)
- A curious machinery of effort is the best—even the simplest—imitation of the laws of nature. (Garry Wills)
- It is doubtful that public support will be forthcoming unless the libraries—public and university both—do a better job of presenting their case to the public than has been done until now. (Norman Cousins)

497 *Use an em-dash to set off a parenthetical phrase that you want to highlight.*

- He was not exactly a mathematician, but he had the true architect's love for the perfect figures of solid geometry—the cube, the sphere, the cylinder, the cone—and the things that happen when these figures intersect each other. (John Summerson in reference to Sir Edward Lutyens)
- We have lately been making difficulties about passports—not merely keeping foreigners out but even forbidding our own citizens to travel in foreign countries—very much in the Russian fashion. (Edmund Wilson)
- They say—the astrologers, I mean—that it will get better and better for me as I go on. (Henry Miller)

- I suppose we all—even nuns—dream of a life other than the one we actually live on this indifferent earth. (Larry McMurtry)

498 *Use an em-dash to tack on an important afterthought.*

- Livia was in the Box, too—a peculiar honor paid her as my father's mother. (Robert Graves)
- He just liked the early morning to himself, quiet, no voices—especially not Marion's voice. (Raymond Chandler)
- They might call him a watchman but he was a pimp—a dirty pimp, the lowest thing in the world. (John Steinbeck)
- It was June when we buried him—the summer solstice. (Susan Cheever)

499 *Use an em-dash to introduce a specification or a list when more of a pause is suggested than a colon might convey.*

- They sold everything here—fruit, vegetables, dairy, geese, fish. (Isaac Bashevis Singer)
- The great Russian writers are like men deprived by an earthquake or a railway accident not only of their clothes, but also of something subtler and more important—their manners, the idiosyncrasies of their characters. (Virginia Woolf)
- This rule fulfills three purposes—it expresses snobbish feeling, it measures competitive power, and it passes on to the degree-granting institution the task of judging intellectual and scholarly aptitudes. (Jacques Barzun)

500 *Use an em-dash to show hesitation, faltering, or interruption.*

- "I—I—don't know, sir," replied Oliver. (Charles Dickens)
- "Ralph, wow, I—I feel better already." (Thomas Pynchon)
- "You are just what I—what I wanted," he said. (Frances Hodgson Burnett)
- The thing that made Will laugh most was that the very fellow who did it got his trousers burnt trying to put out the fire, and he asked the—is it Faculty or President? (Louisa May Alcott)
- "After that"—his voice faltered—"that—machine, for duplicating the glass. Well, the machine did its work." (William F. Buckley)

- CARROLL. Come, come! But she—?
  STEPHEN. She was fine. She insisted that we should fight it together. (J. M. Barrie)
- "No tricks now or—." "Oh, you can trust me, you can trust me!" (Sir Arthur Conan Doyle)

Preventing Misused Em-Dashes

501 *Don't use more than two em-dashes in a sentence.*

Not this: The circumstances of this death are completely distorted by the professor, a fateful follower of the gentlemen of the daily press who—perhaps for political reasons—had falsified the culprit's motives and intentions without awaiting his trial—which unfortunately was not to take place in this world.

> It's not wise to violate the rules until you know how to observe them.
> —T. S. Eliot
> quoted in *Good Advice on Writing*, William Safire and Leonard Safir, eds.

But this: The circumstances of this death are completely distorted by the professor, a fateful follower of the gentlemen of the daily press who—perhaps for political reasons—had falsified the culprit's motives and intentions without awaiting his trial, which unfortunately was not to take place in this world.

Not this: It had added some editorial pages that dealt only with local problems—the hideous new lamp standards, infrequent buses on the Number 11 route, the theft of milk bottles—things that really interested only one group of people—housewives.

But this: It had added some editorial pages that dealt only with local problems—the hideous new lamp standards, infrequent buses on the Number 11 route, the theft of milk bottles—things that really interested only one group of people: housewives.

502 *Don't use a comma, colon, semicolon, or terminal period before an em-dash. A question mark or exclamation point is acceptable in that position.*

Not this: They were waiting for her outside the warehouse;—Bill, hands in pockets, was leaning against the railing and watching as the hoodlums stalked around their smashed bikes, cursing and swearing.

But this: They were waiting for her outside the warehouse; Bill, hands in pockets, was leaning against the railing and watching as the hoodlums stalked around their smashed bikes, cursing and swearing.

Not this: She remembered the girl in the coffee shop who had been staring at David. There was something about her face:—girls always gave that certain move when they thought someone was cute.

But this: She remembered the girl in the coffee shop who had been staring at David. There was something about her face—girls always gave that certain move when they thought someone was cute.

Not this: Herbert flinched.—Violet turned away from him and walked back toward the shimmering curtain of air that he had come through.

But this: Herbert flinched. Violet turned away from him and walked back toward the shimmering curtain of air that he had come through.

The En-Dash (or Short Dash)

1 Use, 2 Misuses

> *An en-dash (–) is a horizontal line that marks a span, a tension, or a pairing of equals. As with the em-dash, the name refers not to the letter N but to the en, a typographical measurement equivalent to half an em. Copyeditors signal it by the mark [⊕].*

Using En-Dashes

503   *Use an en-dash as an equivalent of "to" (as when showing a span of pages), to express tension or difference, or to denote a pairing in which the elements carry equal weight.*

- Victor Hugo (1802–1885) stands by himself, an exuberant, bold, florid, and sometimes rather tawdry mind, erupting plays, poems, novels, and political disquisitions. (H. G. Wells)
- The more extreme barbarities of the 1929–1953 period have been abolished and seem unlikely to return. (Dwight Macdonald)
- He hadn't eaten on the Dallas–San Francisco flight and was hungry. (Margaret Truman)
- Evaluation on the GOOD–BAD dimension is an automatic operation of System 1, and you formed a crude impression of the ranking of the dolphin among the species that came to mind. (Daniel Kahneman)
- We took the tube, which is now £2 per person, or about $4–8 for two, probably not much less than a taxi. (Thomas B. Lemann)

Preventing Misused En-Dashes

504   *Don't use an en-dash in place of a hyphen or an em-dash.*

Not this: Betting circulars cannot be sent to those under twenty–one years of age.

But this: Betting circulars cannot be sent to those under twenty-one years of age.

Not this: He held his breath until they hit the city-limits sign –
then Jeremy exhaled.

But this: He held his breath until they hit the city-limits sign—
then Jeremy exhaled.

Not this: It is lamentable that newspaper editors feel constrained –
as many do – by fear of contempt proceedings from
publishing articles on the subject.

But this: It is lamentable that newspaper editors feel constrained—
as many do—by fear of contempt proceedings from
publishing articles on the subject.

505 *Don't use an en-dash in a "from–to" construction, the en-dash purporting
to replace "to." Instead, use both "from" and "to."*

Not this: The meeting will run from 5:00–6:30 p.m.
But this: The meeting will run from 5:00 to 6:30 p.m.

Not this: We flew from Chicago–Glasgow last night.
But this: We flew from Chicago to Glasgow last night.

The Hyphen

8 Uses, 4 Misuses

> *The hyphen (-) is a short horizontal mark indicating the joining of word-elements (as there), the division of syllabic elements at the end of a line, or elongation in the sounding of a spoken word.*

Using Hyphens

506 ***Use a hyphen to connect the parts of a phrasal adjective—that is, a phrase whose words function together to modify a noun.***

- A chaise drew up in front of the parsonage, the horse pricking his ears at the bell-drum-fife noise. (Carl Sandburg)
- The whole piece was kind of a go-figure story. (David Foster Wallace)
- Fox Renick suddenly became engaged in a sort of coddle-and-feed operation, with Rory Cade as the target. (Sheila Bosworth)
- A half-grown boy wearing a wagon-wheel-size hat crouched awkwardly on the posts. (Annie Proulx)
- Being competitive, risk-taking, status-conscious, dedicated, single-minded, persevering—it can make all the difference to success. (Helena Cronin)
- It may even be that I unconsciously assume the famous it's-a-nice-place-to-visit-but-I'd-hate-to-live-here look. (Joseph Wood Krutch)

> However frenzied or disarrayed or complicated your thoughts might be, punctuation tempers them and sends signals to your reader about how to take them in. We rarely give these symbols a second glance: they're like invisible servants in fairy tales—the ones who bring glasses of water and pillows, not storms of weather or love. . . . Their presence is more felt than seen. It's the words that will capture your eyes, enticing them to dally and glisten. One quick blink and you've caught the comma's or slash's or hyphen's message, huddled in a parenthetical clasp. The accomplishments are no less astonishing for occurring in a flash.
> —Karen Elizabeth Gordon
> *The New Well-Tempered Sentence*

507 *Use a suspensive hyphen to indicate the idea that the final word of a second phrasal adjective goes also with the elliptically stated first phrasal adjective, or that a suffix could be joined with another (especially an earlier) affix.*

- Interval training, in which you alternate from low- to high-impact aerobic activity, has also been shown to be quite effective. (Sanjay Jain)
- These are short, two- or three-minute searches. (Natalie Goldberg)
- In Minnesota, you'll find an awful lot of Toms and Marys and pages on pages of Johnsons, Andersens, and other -sons and -sens. (David Haynes)

508 *Use a hyphen in certain compound nouns and noun phrases when the words are particularly closely associated (check a good current dictionary, though nonce phrases won't be listed).* [The first three bulleted examples are admittedly old-fashioned.]

- He always liked to get visitors alone in the billiard-room and tell them stories about a mysterious lady, a foreign royalty, with whom he had driven about in London. (C. S. Lewis)
- Her pantomime of his action suggests a man pursuing something on the ground before him and striking at it ever and again with his walking-stick. (H. G. Wells)
- There was not a sound in the room, except the ticking of a floor-clock in a corner. (Ellery Queen)
- "They all cheered," said my great-grandfather. (Norman Mailer)
- In his *Innocents Abroad*, he struck an attitude—*let's-have-no-more-of-this-European-nonsense*—and though inwardly he must have grown out of it, he did his best to maintain it. (J. B. Priestley)

509 *Use a hyphen when writing out fractions and two-word numbers under 100.*

- To scout out new mining properties, they hired a man named John Hays Hammond for $250,000 a year plus a one-fourth share in all new mines he discovered—and he proved to be a bargain at the price. (Joseph Epstein)
- Ninety-eight percent of Agassi Prep's students are minority. (Bill Clinton)
- Nine and three-quarters. (J. K. Rowling)

510 *Use a hyphen to show hesitation within a word, stammering, stuttering, lengthening of a sound, or accentuating syllables.*

- "I'm sorry, Ezra. I didn't mean—I-I'm nervous tonight." (Eugene O'Neill)
- "I wonder if I love him" became a song the way she said it, and she would sing over and over to herself: "I won-der, I won-der." (John O'Hara)
- "If we had the g-guts! I could go outside to-today, if I had the guts. My m-m-mother is a good friend of M-Miss Ratched, and I could get an AMA signed this afternoon, if I had the guts!" (Ken Kesey)
- He strikes a great-man pose and yells at no one in particular, "Isn't it *fun* to be the cho-re-o-gra-*pheur*?" (Terry Teachout)

511 *Use a hyphen in proper names when appropriate.*

- Al-Farabi's doctrine of emanation became generally accepted by the Faylasufs. (Karen Armstrong)
- The Home Guards were making their first attack from the police-headquarters building on Schneidermühlen-Gasse. (Günter Grass)
- An outfit out of Denver called Holloway Brothers has offered to buy Koker-Hanks. (John Grisham)

512 *Use a hyphen to separate groups of numbers that are not ranges (such as telephone numbers and social-security numbers) or when spelling out a word letter by letter.*

Not this: #3517–6 (en-dash)
But this: #3517-6 (hyphen)

Not this: SSN 315—37—1982 (em-dashes)
But this: SSN 315-37-1982 (hyphens)

Not this: B–A–R–B–A–R–A H–I–N–E–S (en-dashes)
But this: B-A-R-B-A-R-A H-I-N-E-S (hyphens)

513 *Use a hyphen with the suffixes "-less" and "-like" when the root word ends with "-ll."*

Not this: callless
But this: call-less

Not this: thrillless
But this: thrill-less

Not this: shelllike
But this: shell-like

Not this: trolllike
But this: troll-like

Preventing Misused Hyphens

514 *Generally, don't use a hyphen after a prefix unless (1) the solid form might be confusing (e.g., "anti-intellectual"), (2) the primary word is capitalized (e.g., "non-European citizen"), (3) the prefix is part of a noun phrase (e.g., "non-contract-law doctrine"), or (4) the unhyphenated form has a different meaning (e.g., "prejudicial" vs. "pre-judicial").*

> *Not this:* The sound of his old Chevy lurching down the road was as un-mistakable as smoker's cough.
> *But this:* The sound of his old Chevy lurching down the road was as unmistakable as smoker's cough.

> *Not this:* Having chest hair was considered a pre-condition for making it on the Varsity.
> *But this:* Having chest hair was considered a precondition for making it on the Varsity.

> *Not this:* Public Health officials urged college students to wash their hands frequently with anti-bacterial soap.
> *But this:* Public Health officials urged college students to wash their hands frequently with antibacterial soap.

515 *Don't use a hyphen (or even a pair of hyphens) in place of an em-dash.*

> *Not this:* In the summer it was too hot to sit outside scheming - all plans had to be made inside.
> *But this:* In the summer it was too hot to sit outside scheming—all plans had to be made inside.

> *Not this:* Her grandmother would have been pleased--she being a stringently upright woman--but she had died four years earlier.
> *But this:* Her grandmother would have been pleased—she being a stringently upright woman—but she had died four years earlier.

516   *Don't use a hyphen in a two-word adjective phrase formed with an "-ly" adverb and a participial adjective.*

> *Not this:* federally-recognized tribe
> *But this:* federally recognized tribe

> *Not this:* publicly-traded company
> *But this:* publicly traded company

> *Not this:* widely-held view
> *But this:* widely held view

> *Not this:* mildly-disconcerting errors
> *But this:* mildly disconcerting errors

> *But:*   not-so-widely-held view

517   *Don't use a hyphen in a phrasal verb.*

> *Not this:* Please set-up the tables.
> *But this:* Please set up the tables.

> *Not this:* We should back-off.
> *But this:* We should back off.

The Apostrophe

3 Uses, 2 Misuses

> *The apostrophe (') is an above-the-line symbol that marks the omission of a letter or syllable—or (rarely) that removes a visual ambiguity that might otherwise appear in a plural.*

Using Apostrophes

518 *Use an apostrophe to indicate the possessive case.*

- By a miracle, my grandmother's silver mirror was never touched. (Isabel Allende)
- He sat down and ate the boiled oats with cinnamon bark and goat's milk. (Paul Bowles)
- If the fathers ate sour grapes, are the children's teeth set on edge? (F. L. Lucas)
- The Dickenses' house is the one nearest the railing. (Susan M. Rossi-Wilcox)
- Julian Mack, a lover of fine food, once commented that when you went to the Brandeises' for dinner you had to eat beforehand and then again afterward. (Nelson L. Dawson)

519 *Use an apostrophe to mark the omission of one or more letters from a word, especially in a contraction or to signal dialectal speech.*

- I'd always assumed that this preemptive "you're welcome" required a much busier—and ruder—setting than the sleepy Maple Syrup state [Vermont]. (Philip Galanes)
- But even if you win the rat race, you're still a rat. (Donald McCullough)
- Spenser wasn't much into subtlety. (John Bemelmans Marciano)
- There was a pause, and then one of those creamy West Country voices drawled, "Aw, don' 'ee worry. Us'n'll beat they!" (Sir William Slim)

520   *Use an apostrophe to form the plural of lowercase letters, capital letters when necessary to avoid a miscue, symbols, single-digit numerals, lowercase abbreviations, and capitalized abbreviations with periods.*

- Amazingly, the printing we all learned in school—known also as *manuscript writing,* and often called *ball and stick* from the way the *b*'s, *d*'s, and other letters are formed—has been around for less than a hundred years. (Kitty Burns Florey)
- The half-filled bookshelf is also half empty, of course, with books leaning left and right to form M's, N's, V's, and W's to fill the voids between clusters of vertical and not-so-vertical I's. (Henry Petroski)
- The 75s spoke with piercing shriek over the fields as the French entered the territory that had once been theirs. (Barbara W. Tuchman)

Preventing Misused Apostrophes

521   *Generally, don't use an apostrophe to form a plural (but dot your i's and cross your t's).*

Not this: I think he was born in the early 1980's.[1]
But this: I think he was born in the early 1980s.

Not this: *The Stevenson's weren't home.
But this: The Stevensons weren't home.

Not this: *The Weatherly's have gone on vacation.
But this: The Weatherlys have gone on vacation.

Not this: *The Hughes' are invited over.
But this: The Hugheses are invited over.

522   *Don't drop obligatory apostrophes.*

Not this: He gave *two weeks notice.
But this: He gave two weeks' notice.

Not this: It was one *oclock when the women went to bed.
But this: It was one o'clock when the women went to bed.

---

1   Formerly common, this form is now avoided in preference to a decade reference with no apostrophe.

Quotation Marks

7 Uses, 2 Misuses

*Quotation marks are paired notations (" " on first occur-
rence in AmE, ' ' in BrE) placed at the beginning and end
of a quoted word or passage, of a word or phrase referred to
as such, or of a definition. A quotation within a quotation
normally has single instead of double marks (or, in BrE,
double instead of single). It was formerly common to place
an initial quotation mark at the beginning of each line
quoted, but today the usual practice is to repeat it only at
the beginning of each new paragraph.*

Using Quotation Marks

523 *Use quotation marks when you're quoting a word, phrase, or any passage
of 50 or fewer words. (Set off a longer quotation by indenting it on both
sides.)*

- She told him that she "adored" vaudeville. (Sinclair Lewis)
- The twentieth century, as we know, has frequently been called
  "the century of the child." (Havelock Ellis)
- "Good morning, Linda," Mother said. "You've torn your sleeve."
  (William Faulkner)
- "Three feet, sir," replied Johnson, screwing up his eyes against
  the glare of the newly risen sun. (Richard Woodman)
- Darwin concluded that all domestic breeds of horses stem from
  a single wild species "of a dun color and more or less striped,"
  to which modern descendants "occasionally revert." (J. Frank
  Dobie)

524 *Use quotation marks when (1) referring to a word as a word or a phrase
as a phrase (although italics are better if you do this frequently); or (2)
providing a definition.*

- To call Randolph "the American Burke" is no great exaggeration.
  (Russell Kirk)
- "Poor little" and "poor old," I must explain, were among his
  favorite epithets. (Peter Quennell)
- "To devour a book" has long been a fashionable cliché but
  nothing more. (Harry C. Bauer)

- "Junk science," which has become a fashionable pejorative in recent years, does not always mean what a reasonable person would expect it to mean. (Susan Jacoby)

525 *Use quotation marks when you mean "so-called" or "self-styled," or even "so-called-but-not-really."*

> Though I realize that my analogy may not be completely valid, it nonetheless seems perfectly reasonable to me to say that anyone who can negotiate the complexities of getting around efficiently in a place such as Los Angeles certainly has the native intelligence to learn to punctuate. . . . The whole question is one of motivation.
> —W. Ross Winterowd
> *Contemporary Rhetoric*

- Adams called himself "a constructive anarchist." (Michael Kammen)
- In 1967, the "normality" of the Barrow gang and their individual aspirations toward respectability are the craziest things about them. (Pauline Kael)
- We got glimpses of women in politics and in such "men's sports" as boxing, football, and hockey. (Vermout Royster)
- U.S. military authorities are avoiding anything in the nature of a "body count" for Operation Desert Storm. (Christopher Hitchens)
- The most valuable real estate in the Hill Country was in its leading "city," Fredericksburg. (Robert A. Caro)
- We are as silly as the people in Garrison Keillor's fictional heartland, where *all* the children are claimed to be "above average." (William A. Henry III)
- The "positive evaluation" of *passio* in the mystical ecstasy of love must also be considered with caution. (Erich Auerbach)

526 *Quotation marks are traditionally used for titles of short-format works, such as songs, short stories, poems, articles, and essays, and for those of constituent elements of larger works, such as book chapters and television episodes. But styles vary. Be consistent in using a house style or a standard style manual.*

- He's the definition of a line I used in "Vertigo": *A feeling is much stronger than a thought.* (Bono, referring to Daniel Lanois)
- He took over the starring part in every family gathering, warbling such favorites as "Rose Marie" or "Three Little Words" while his sister Olive accompanied him on the piano. (T. Harry Williams)

527 *Use single quotation marks for quoted words within a quotation. (The convention in BrE is to begin with single quotation marks and to use double marks for quoted words within a quotation.)*

- "That ended amicably, with her singing, by request, 'Don't Stand There on the Coconut Mat.'" (James Thurber)
- Another undertaking has been Edward Allen's tax exams: "After the CFA, I said I was never going to do any exams ever again," but duty intervened: "It's always valuable to have a different approach. We sat down and thought, 'How can we better serve and get closer to our clients?' And as tax is important to clients it's important for me as an adviser." (Giulia Cambieri and Alex Matchett)

528 *Use quotation marks to signal a word or phrase used idiomatically—in a way that might otherwise be misread.*

- Publicity for the American writer is of the "personality" kind: a photograph in *Harper's Bazaar*, bland television appearances . . . the writer as minor movie star, and as unheeded. (Gore Vidal)
- "Just plain" Republicans are the second most critical of the media, but they are never, or hardly ever, uniformly antimedia. (Barry Sussman)

529 *Place quotation marks correctly in relation to other punctuation: (1) commas and periods go inside (in AmE); (2) colons and semicolons go outside; and (3) question marks and exclamation marks go either inside or outside, depending on whether they're part of the quoted matter.*

- To counter what she called a "crisis of meaning," she called for what would amount to a new politics of kindness. (Bob Woodward)
- "This obviously is not a tax-reform bill," summarized Ways and Means Chairman Al Ullman. "It is an economic tax package." (Robert L. Bartley)
- His spouse, charmingly attired in frilly negligee, poised behind him with a silver coffee pot, inquired, "More coffee, dear?" (Jerome Beatty Jr.)
- Humphrey cocks his head and gazes up the tall recruit's nostrils. "Your hygiene is unsatisfactory. Did you shave? No discipline. NO DISCIPLINE!" (Thomas E. Ricks)
- "If wisdom be in suffering," he argues, why should not soldiers "let the foes quietly cut their throats"? (Donald A. Stauffer)

Preventing Misused Quotation Marks

530 *Don't use quotation marks for a phrasal adjective.*

> *Not this:* We now have a plethora of "long distance" services.
> *But this:* We now have a plethora of long-distance services.

> *Not this:* The "so-so" scholar might have secured tenure by
> courtesy in his first or second post.
> *But this:* The so-so scholar might have secured tenure by courtesy
> in his first or second post.

531 *Don't use quotation marks merely to emphasize a word or to acknowledge its informality, because doing so looks amateurish and can easily be misunderstood as marking sarcasm.*

> *Not this:* His remarks seemed "snarky."
> *But this:* His remarks seemed snarky.

> *Not this:* I don't know what can be "done" about it.
> *But this:* I don't know what can be done about it.

> *Not this:* We offer all types of "hors d'oeuvres."
> *But this:* We offer all types of hors d'oeuvres.

> *Not this:* On these terms, a person's daily "earthly" activities are
> stripped of ethical and social values.
> *But this:* On these terms, a person's daily earthly activities are
> stripped of ethical and social values. (Consider deleting
> *earthly.*)

The Question Mark

1 Use, 1 Misuse

A question mark (?) appears at the end of an interrogative sentence, usually to signal that it is seeking a response.

Using Question Marks

532 *Use a question mark after a direct question.*

- "What do you seek here, Stephen?" said she. (Nathaniel Hawthorne)
- But what, then, was the usual height of the upper stage? (C. Walter Hodges)
- Is a service to the public or one's country worth one's life if it becomes necessary to give it, to accomplish the end sought? (Margaret Truman)
- Could Leonardo have been content with such a commonplace pose? (Kenneth Clark)

Preventing Misused Question Marks

533 *Don't use a question mark after an indirect question.*

Not this: He wondered whether he could make it?
But this: He wondered whether he could make it.

Not this: I asked why that was so?
But this: I asked why that was so.

Not this: He reflected on why it was he couldn't win in actual competition?
But this: He reflected on why it was he couldn't win in actual competition.

The Exclamation Mark

1 Use, 1 Misuse

> *An exclamation mark (or exclamation point) (!) appears at the end of an interjection or exclamation to signal its character.*

Using Exclamation Marks

534 *Use an exclamation mark after an exclamatory word, phrase, or sentence—especially when quoting someone else.*

- How earnestly did she then wish that her former opinions had been more reasonable, her expressions more moderate! (Jane Austen)
- Hot dog! Go, Mama! (Lorraine Hansberry)
- Oh, thank God, the synagogue is still here! (Paddy Chayefsky)
- "Wretch!" cried the widow. (Ambrose Bierce)
- Some readers are saying right now as they read these lines: "Oh, phooey! *Flattery! Bear oil!* I've tried that stuff." (Dale Carnegie)

Preventing Misused Exclamation Marks

535 *Generally, don't use an exclamation mark to express your own surprise or amazement.*

Not this: During his testimony, the expert witness for the defense claimed the dumping was having a negligible impact on the wetlands. Outrageous!

But this: During his testimony, the expert witness for the defense had the audacity to claim that the dumping was having a negligible impact on the wetlands.

Not this: Without warning, the dogcatcher walked straight up to the constable and smacked him!

But this: Without warning, the dogcatcher walked straight up to the constable and smacked him.

The Period

4 Uses, 1 Misuse

A period (.) is a dot placed after every complete declarative sentence and after most abbreviations. It is identical to the decimal marker.

Using Periods

536 ***Use a period to end a sentence that is neither a question nor an exclamation.***

- Wendell began to cry. (Eudora Welty)
- Alix was indeed an enigma. (Louis Auchincloss)
- The examiner showed a row of unusually mutilated teeth. (Saul Bellow)

> No iron spike can pierce a human heart as icily as a period in the right place.
> —Isaac Babel
> "Guy de Maupassant"

- Against my cheek I felt the patter of sand driving from nowhere to nowhere across the wastes. (J. M. Coetzee)

537 ***Use a period to indicate an abbreviated name or title.*** [The salutary trend, though, is to omit periods with acronyms and initialisms—hence *BBC* would be usual today in the final bulleted example.]

- I never recovered from the shock of that moment when I was pulled out of the security of Mr. Holmes's stern classroom. (Azar Nafisi)
- The central character, Mrs. Alving, is not simply a *raisonneuse*, mouthing the author's opinions, but also a tragic protagonist whose suffering demonstrates the hollowness of even the most emancipated opinions when not backed with radical acts. (Robert Brustein)
- I had seen my sisters' scapulars and knew that the bit of cloth at the end had a picture of the Virgin or St. Joseph on it. (Rudolfo Anaya)
- The B.B.C. is not an institution whose function is to annoy. (Harold Nicolson)

538 *Put the period outside parentheses or brackets that enclose only part of a sentence, but inside parentheses or brackets that enclose a sentence.*

- Rumsfeld is here employing the old con known as *ignoratio elenchi* ("ignorance of the issue," perhaps better translated in this case as "ignoring the issue"). (Thomas Cathcart and Daniel Klein)
- Next day he talked to the inventor of a spaceship who was planning a voyage to the moon (this was the 1920s). (J. B. McGeachy)
- If the problem was successfully solved, then the solver got the reward. (The money was the incentive.) (Jonah Lehrer)
- He has bid us "quit ourselves like men." (On his lips quotations from the Bible, from *The Times*, seem equally magnificent.) (Virginia Woolf)

539 *Use a period to show a decimal place in a numeral.*

- The statistics as of 1989 are extremely reassuring: 1,700 births—1.5 percent cesareans; 4.8 percent transported to the hospital; .5 percent forceps. (Jessica Mitford)
- The researchers placed a 3.3-foot-high foam obstacle in the middle of the room and handed each couple a large pillow. (Richard Wiseman)
- Average estimated lost productivity per person per day due to interruptions, based on a 40-hour workweek: 2.1 hours. (Dave Crenshaw)

Preventing Misused Periods

540 *If a sentence ends with an abbreviation, don't put an additional period after the abbreviation.*

Not this: Other positive effects bear upon cooperation, higher pay, etc..

But this: Other positive effects bear upon cooperation, higher pay, etc.

Brackets

3 Uses, 1 Misuse

Brackets ([ ]) are pairs of squared marks that enclose any part of a text to be separated or distinguished from the rest. They are also used in place of parentheses that would appear in a passage already placed within parentheses.

Using Brackets

541 *Use a pair of brackets in a quotation to enclose an editorial comment, correction, explanation, interpolation, substitution, or translation that was not in the original text.*

- In another essay he wrote: "What Mr. [D. H.] Lawrence's art stands most desperately in need of is a shower bath of vital ideas." (Evelyn Waugh referring to an essay by his father, Arthur Waugh)
- As she could never write him an entirely agreeable letter, she had to finish with: "You are old [he was forty-nine], you have no children, you are unhealthy." (Nancy Mitford)
- Why didn't it [*Conquistador*] ring your bell? (Archibald MacLeish in a letter to H. Phelps Putnam [with editor's interpolation])
- Rather than a sovereign entity, the conscious mind is a partially sighted servant of a dominant, child-obsessed will-to-life: "[The intellect] does not penetrate into the secret workshop of the will's decisions." (Alain de Botton, quoting Arthur Schopenhauer)

542 *Use a pair of brackets for parenthetical material that appears within material already within parentheses.*

- Proust had a debilitating assessment of his own qualities ("I certainly think less of myself than Antoine [his butler] does of himself"). (Alain de Botton)

543 *Use a pair of brackets (if desired) to insert the citation of a source, as in a footnote.*

- For the details of this affair, see principally the Legislative Documents, 22d Congress, 2d session, no. 30. [Senate, "Presidential Message with Proclamations, Proceedings, and Documents, on Measures of South Carolina and General Government on Nullification," 22d Cong., 2d sess., 1832–33, Sen. Doc., serial 230.] (Alexis de Tocqueville [editors' footnoted citation])

Preventing Misused Brackets

544 *Don't use brackets in place of ellipsis dots when one or more words have been deleted without any replacement language.*

Not this: All [ ] have to contribute to this mighty work.
But this: All . . . have to contribute to this mighty work.

Not this: The first form of religion had been infra-intellectual, [ ] the second was supra-intellectual.
But this: The first form of religion had been infra-intellectual, . . . the second was supra-intellectual.

The Slash (Virgule)

5 Uses, 1 Misuse

> *A slash (/), also known as a* virgule *or* solidus, *divides alternatives, fractions, months and days, and similar elements.*

Using Slashes

545   *Use a slash to separate alternatives (but remember to avoid "and/or"!).*

- The fourth line might look as if it has the antithesis that we are used to ("shoot"/"be shot," and so on). (Christopher Ricks)
- And as she bends to shake each one's hand, I glance down at her pad on the coffee table and read the notes she has jotted: *Trauma/dictatorship/family bonds strong/mother devoted.* (Julia Alvarez)
- You may have been the recipient of a comment in the vein of "I think I just saw/read/heard/ate something that you created/wrote/composed/cooked." (Henry Alford)
- My metaphors, speaking gear versus writing gear or uttering versus constructing, imply a binary, either/or choice. (Peter Elbow) [An en-dash is also permissible here: *either–or choice.*]

546   *Use a slash to separate the numerator from the denominator in a fraction.*

- If the elasticity of demand is, say, 1/4, it means that a 1 percent reduction in output will bring a 4 percent increase in price. (Mancur Olson)
- 3/4 cup walnuts, toasted and finely chopped. (Irma S. Rombauer)
- Never mind all that: like the old Ivory Soap ads, *99 and 44/100 percent pure—it floats!* (Barbara Herrnstein Smith)

547   *In informal writing, use a slash to separate the elements in a date.*

- This was just after 9/11, when the cynicism and shallowness that had been beaten through the lifeblood of the city was interpreted as unnecessary cruelty, and it was all at once tacky to wish for anything other than world peace. (Candace Bushnell)

548 *In informal writing, use a slash as a shorthand signal for "per."*

- Your travel allowance will be $75/day.
- The industry is now losing workers at the rate of 1,000/week.
- We have a minimum of $20/bet.

549 *Use a slash to indicate separate lines of poetry or of a song.*

- To be excessively controlled by sexual reinforcement is to be "infatuated," and the etymology of the word was memorialized by Kipling in two famous lines: "A fool there was and he made his prayer . . . / To a rag, a bone, and a hank of hair." (B. F. Skinner)
- Say, did you ever hear that old song of Kurt Weill's from *Knickerbocker Holiday*: "When lovely Venus lies beside / Her lord and master Mars / They mutually profit / By their scars"? (Kurth Sprague)
- One of the most arresting places in the entire passage, for the sensitive reader, has this kind of mixed diction for its chief distinction: *we have done but greenly, / In hugger-mugger to inter him.* (John Crowe Ransom)

Preventing Misused Slashes

550 *Don't use a slash when a hyphen or en-dash would suffice.*

Not this: On July 4/5, 1968, celebrations in the nation's capital were hot, violent affairs.

But this: On July 4–5, 1968, celebrations in the nation's capital were hot, violent affairs.

Not this: The historic evening of December 31, 1999/January 1, 2000, will be remembered forever as monumentally uneventful.

But this: The historic evening of December 31, 1999–January 1, 2000, will be remembered forever as monumentally uneventful.

Bullets

1 Use

A bullet (•) is a ball-like mark that demarcates text, especially each of a series of listed items.

551 **Use bullets to mark a series of listed items that are of a more or less equal ranking, especially to draw the reader's attention and make reading easier by breaking out items into discrete chunks.**

Every community needs to ask these questions:

- Does it have first-rate people on its school board, and are they broadly representative of the community?
- Does the board have open lines of communication to the school administration, to the teachers and to the entire community?
- Is it getting the information it needs to make responsible decisions, both short- and long-range?
- Does it have effective liaison with allied community programs: with the departments of health and welfare, with housing, private industry, transportation, and total city planning?
- Is it doing what a board should do—setting the policy for a strong administrator responsible to it—or is it wasting its time by dabbling in administrative details?

(John Gardner)

In airplane travel, small infringements can affect the well-being of many. Helpful behavior includes:

- Organizing one's hand baggage before boarding in such a way as to make it possible to slip into one's seat with it and then distribute it overhead and underfoot, rather than standing in the aisle to do so while several hundred people pile behind you.
- Taking no more than one's share of the amenities—pillows, blankets—and of storage space, and less of that, if possible.
- Cooperating in exchanging seats with people who want to sit together.

- Spending as little time in the bathrooms as possible, for which Miss Manners will give special dispensation to do moderated grooming at one's seat.
- Staying out of the aisles and out of the way of moving service carts.
- Not begrudging moving to let those in one's row out when they deem it necessary for whatever reason.
- Controlling one's children so that they refrain from such voluntary actions as kicking the backs of the seats in front of them and endowing them with strong constitutions so that they do not indulge in involuntary unpleasant actions, as referred to above.

(Judith Martin)

You may feel your presence at home, in the office, or at a party will be less than well received, given the amount of garlic you have just consumed at a particular meal. Any one of the following actions might help you deal with the problem, to everyone's relief:

- Chew and swallow some fresh parsley.
- Rub a piece of lemon over your tongue and the insides of your mouth.
- Chew a few coffee beans.
- Take some antacid.
- Use some mints.

(Letitia Baldridge)

Ellipsis Dots

5 Uses, 2 Misuses

> *Ellipsis dots (. . .), typographically identical with periods, are sets of three marks indicating an omission or suppression of words. When a fourth dot appears, it is inevitably a period—and best thought of that way instead of as a fourth ellipsis dot.*

Using Ellipsis Dots

552 *Use three ellipsis dots to show that an unfinished sentence trails off.*

- They, they themselves, have created their own lives, not in that half-conscious, underground, interior way that we all do, but manifestly, out there in their own land: they are alive; they breathe the breath of their own houses . . . (Christopher Alexander, at chapter's end)
- But—oh, Rosalind! Rosalind! . . . (F. Scott Fitzgerald, at paragraph's end)
- Not at all, your excellency; on the contrary . . . I . . . (Ivan Turgenev, at the end of an uncompleted statement)

553 *Use three ellipsis dots to signal rumination, musing, or hesitant continuation of a thought.*

- He could close his eyes and try to believe that all that mattered was that *he* knew his work was great . . . and that other artists respected it . . . and that history would surely record his achievements . . . but deep down he knew he was lying to himself. (Tom Wolfe)
- I had never in my life done anything like it; I had made something, no matter how bad it was; and it was mine . . . Now, to whom could I show it? (Richard Wright)
- After all my lectures . . . after the infamous green binge-drinking chart . . . after expelling the dinosaur from our home . . . here I was queuing up like a hardened beer bonger! (Chris Volkmann and Toren Volkmann)
- And yet . . . and yet. There was something wrong. (Elizabeth Ironside)

554 *Use three ellipsis dots to signal that you've omitted one or more words within a sentence that you're quoting.*

- It would help, too, to remember the words of Hobbes: "For words are wise men's counters, they do but reckon with them; but they are the money of fools that value them ... by authority." (Richard Mitchell)
- Othello's foil of course is Iago, about whose imagery and speech there hangs, as recent commentators have pointed out, a constructed air, essentially suited to one who, as W. H. Clemen has said, "seeks to poison ... others with his images." (Maynard Mack)
- In the *Phaedrus* Plato speaks of the two halves as a team of two horses driven by a charioteer: "The right-hand horse is upright and cleanly made and has a lofty neck and an aquiline nose: his color is white ... he is a lover of honesty and modesty and temperance, and the follower of true glory." (Stephen Potter)

555 *Use four dots—three ellipsis dots plus a period—when you've omitted one or more words at the end of a sentence. (A space goes before the first ellipsis dot.)*

- I stepped to the edge of the stage in the school auditorium and began, in a carefully rehearsed singsong, "I *saw* the *spires* of *Ox*ford / As *I* was *passing* by . . . ." (Brendan Gill)
- Having enumerated the principal classes of missing documents, [Geoffrey Scott] wrote: "That the existing elements now exist is improbable . . . . Further discoveries ... even in this realm of miracles, even in this realm of miracles, can hardly be looked for." (Richard D. Altick)

556 *Use four dots—a period plus three ellipsis dots—when you've omitted material following a sentence but the quotation continues. (No space goes before the first dot [the period].)*

- The reasons for Sainte-Beuve's failings as a critic are not difficult to discover. "We judge a work of art," said Lawrence, "by its effect on our sincere and vital emotion and nothing else. . . . A critic must be able to *feel* the impact of a work of art in all its complexity and all its force." (Martin Turnell, quoting D. H. Lawrence)

- Lear weaves Gloucester into his brilliant synthesis of the world and of the play: "Your eyes are in a heavy case, your purse in a light. You see how the world goes. . . . A man may see how the world goes with no eyes." (Robert B. Heilman, quoting Shakespeare)

- "There was a time when I really did love books," [Orwell] wrote, "loved the sight and smell and feel of them, I mean, at least if they were fifty or more years old. Nothing pleased me quite so much as to buy a job lot of them for a shilling at a country auction. . . . But as soon as I went to work in the bookshop I stopped buying books." (Anne Fadiman, quoting George Orwell)

Preventing Misused Ellipsis Dots

557 *Don't use ellipsis dots without the equivalent of a letter space between each pair, and don't allow the string of dots to be split between consecutive lines.*

Not this: Tomé has explained that this overreliance on technology "is regressive; it … makes us evolve in a direction that would ultimately see us morph into sensationless semimachines."

But this: Tomé has explained that this overreliance on technology "is regressive; it . . . makes us evolve in a direction that would ultimately see us morph into sensationless semimachines."

Not this: As Basbanes once lamented quite eloquently: "The 'cases' in which books are bound are produced nowadays by machine, and the human binder merely needs to know . . . before he starts just how many are needed."

But this: As Basbanes once lamented quite eloquently: "The 'cases' in which books are bound are produced nowadays by machine, and the human binder merely needs to know . . . before he starts just how many are needed."

558   *Don't begin a quotation with ellipsis dots.*

    Not this: Tate attests to this fact in his preface to his *Selected Poems*: "... that, as a poet, I have never had any original experience, and that, as a poet, my concern is the experience that I hope the reader will have in reading the poem."

    But this: Tate attests to this fact in his preface to his *Selected Poems*: "As a poet, I have never had any original experience, and ... as a poet, my concern is the experience that I hope the reader will have in reading the poem."

abbreviation, *n.* A shortened form of a word or phrase, such as *pl.* for *plural* or *sc.* for *scilicet.*

ablaut, *n.* The change of a vowel in cognate words, esp. as a result of inflection {stink–stank–stunk} {slink–slunk–slunk} {strike–struck–struck–stricken}.

absolute construction. A phrase that is grammatically independent of the rest of the sentence {the race having ended, many spectators rushed onto the field}. It typically consists of a noun or pronoun followed by a nonfinite verb or an adjective phrase {his arm in a sling, he kept bumping his neighbor}. When the phrase begins with a pronoun in the nominative case, an absolute construction is often called a *nominative absolute* {she having finally arrived, we were all relieved} {the horse having been broken, we rode it}.

abstract noun. See **noun.**

accent. 1. The emphasis or stress given to a syllable or word when it is spoken. **2.** An identifiable way of pronouncing a given language within a specific region or social class. **3.** Same as **diacritical mark.**

acceptability. The extent to which an expression or grammatical construction is considered unobjectionable by the speakers of a language, esp. by standard speakers.—**acceptable,** *adj.*

accidence. 1. The part of grammar dealing with how words vary to express differences in case (e.g., *I gave a book; give me a book*), number (e.g., *one person called; two people called*), voice (e.g., *the car hit a tree; the tree was hit by a car*), etc.; specif., a subset of etymology treating the inflections of words. **2.** The specific inflections, esp. suffixes and prefixes, used to distinguish grammatical categories and relationships. For example, the suffix *-ed* often shows that a verb is in the past tense (as in *jog–jogged*), and the prefix *uni-* indicates that there is only one of something (as in *unicycle*).—Also termed *inflectional morphology.* **3.** A usu. small book explaining the rudiments of the aspect of grammar dealing with differences in case.

accusative case. See *objective case* under **case.**

acronym /ak-rə-nim/. A word formed from initial letters (e.g., *NASA, POTUS*) or syllables (e.g., *defcon, radar*) of words in a phrase and pronounced as a single word. An acronym is traditionally distinguished from an initialism (e.g., *HIV, CIA*), in which the individual letters are given in sequence. See § 425. Cf. **initialism.**—**acronymic,** *adj.*

action verb. See **verb.**

active voice. The voice formed either by the simple inflected forms of a transitive verb with auxiliaries other than *be* or by adding the present participle to a *be*-verb {Billy chased Johnny} {the dog can't find the bone} {some people resent that epithet}. See **voice.** Cf. **passive voice.**

additive coordinating conjunction. See *copulative conjunction* under **conjunction.**

adfix. *Rare.* A prefix or suffix. This term is distinguished from *affix* because it does not include infixes.

adjectival /aj-ek-tɪ-vəl/, *adj.* Of, relating to, or consisting of an adjective or of a phrase or clause functioning as an adjective.

adjective /aj-ek-tiv/, *n.* A type of word or phrase whose main function is to describe or limit a noun element, usu. by expressing an attribute or quality or by describing a property or state. Many adjectives have a distinguishing suffix such as *-able* {connectable}, *-al* {traditional}, *-ary* {hereditary}, *-en* {leaden}, *-ful* {useful}, *-ible* {reducible}, *-ic* {pedantic}, *-ish* {childish}, *-ive* {reflective}, *-less* {meaningless}, *-like* {crustlike}, *-ous* {pretentious}, *-some* {winsome}, and *-y* {foggy}. When a phrase functions as an adjective, it is called a *phrasal adjective* or *compound modifier.* See § 131.

▸ **appositive adjective.** A postpositive adjective or adjective phrase that is set off by commas or dashes {the process, long and arduous, was hardly worth the time it took} {the travelers—exhausted, hungry, and haggard—finally saw their ordeal end}. Poetry aside, appositive adjectives most commonly appear in pairs or triads. Although they may resemble predicate adjectives, appositive adjectives differ in this respect: they could be transplanted before the noun element they modify with essentially the same sense.

▸ **attribute adjective.** See *predicate adjective.*

▸ **attributive adjective.** An adjective that, like almost all others, precedes the noun that it modifies {a popular book}—as contrasted with a *predicate adjective* or an *appositive adjective.*—Also termed *prepositive adjective.*

▸ **central adjective.** An adjective that (like most) can serve as either an attributive adjective {a tall boy} or a predicate adjective {the boy is tall}. Cf. *peripheral adjective.*

▸ **common adjective.** A generic adjective, usu. one not derived from a proper noun, customarily spelled in lowercase. Even an adjective that derives from a proper noun may become common {a stygian demeanor—*stygian* deriving from the mythical River Styx}.

▸ **comparative adjective.** An adjective in the intermediate degree of comparison {worse} {better}.

▶ **compound adjective.** An adjective made up of two or more words—whether as a single word {cutthroat} {dryasdust} {straitlaced} {upbeat} or hyphenated as a phrasal adjective {an after-dinner talk} {a not-for-profit company} {a down-in-the-mouth expression} {a back-of-the-envelope calculation}.

▶ **coordinate adjective.** One of a series of adjectives of equal rank and allied sense modifying the same noun {her goal was an ethical, corruption-free administration}.

▶ **definitive adjective.** See *limiting adjective.*

▶ **demonstrative adjective.** An adjective that points to things, persons, or ideas in a general way {this bookend belongs at the end of that row} {those enrollees haven't paid for this course}. Cf. *demonstrative pronoun* under **pronoun.**

▶ **descriptive adjective.** An adjective that identifies some quality of the noun element it modifies {the prickly needles startled the weary explorer when he backed into them}.—Also termed *qualifying adjective.*

▶ **gradable adjective.** An adjective capable of taking both the comparative and superlative inflections {small–smaller–smallest}.

▶ **indefinite adjective.** An adjective that limits the meaning of the noun element without indicating a definite number or quantity—the most frequent examples being *all, any, each, either, few, less, many, much, neither, several,* and *some* {some faculty members support the measure} {all the issues have been addressed}. Although *all* might not seem indefinite, it is called an *indefinite adjective* because two, two thousand, or two million (etc.) might be involved.

▶ **interrogative adjective.** An adjective that introduces a direct or indirect question while modifying a noun element in the question {which team won?} {Paul asked what steps we should take}.

▶ **limiting adjective.** An adjective that defines or restricts the meaning of its noun element, including articles {the book}, pronominal adjectives {her book}, and numeric adjectives {five books}.—Also termed *definitive adjective.*

▶ **numeric adjective.** An adjective that indicates number or rank {three finalists are contending for first prize}.—Also termed *numerical adjective; numeral adjective.*

▶ **participial adjective.** An adjective made from an inflected verb; specif., a present participle or past participle functioning as an adjective {boiling water} {the wrecked car}.—Also termed *verbal adjective.*

▶ **peripheral adjective.** An adjective that can function attributively or predicatively but not in both ways {utter stupidity} {outright bigotry} {she is asleep} {I'm loath to agree}. Cf. *central adjective.*

▶ **personal adjective.** A personal pronoun in the possessive case used to modify a noun element {our true friends are our champions} {your mailbox is full}.

▶ **phrasal adjective.** A phrase preceding a noun element and functioning adjectivally as a unit, and therefore usu. taking one or more internal hyphens in modifying a noun. Unless the phrasal adjective is a proper noun or a foreign phrase, it is hyphenated {a seat-of-the-pants approach}.—Also termed (less precisely) *compound modifier.*

▶ **positive adjective.** An adjective in the simple uncompared degree {bad} {good}.

▶ **possessive adjective.** A possessive-case form of a noun or pronoun that indicates source, possession, ownership, or the like {I saw your marginal comments in my book} {his arguments about your position seemed fair}.

▶ **postpositive adjective.** An adjective that immediately follows the noun it modifies; specif., an adjective that flouts normal English word order by following the noun it modifies, usu. because the phrase in which it appears is of Romance origin {attorney general} {battle royal} {femme fatale} {postmaster general}.—Also termed *postpositive modifier.*

▶ **predicate adjective.** An adjective or adjective phrase functioning either as a subjective complement {the handbook is thorough} or as an objective complement {he painted the walls red}. A predicate adjective is one type of subjective complement. Either way, the predicate adjective completes the sense of the predicate. A few adjectives can be only predicate adjectives, never attributive adjectives (e.g., *he is asleep*).—Also termed *predicate adjectival; predicate attribute; subjective adjective; attribute adjective.*

▶ **prepositive adjective.** See *attributive adjective.*

▶ **pronominal adjective.** **1.** A possessive pronoun functioning adjectivally {all test-takers must sign their affidavits} {the glory is yours}. **2.** Any pronoun that functions as an adjective {any candy} {each person} {which kind of pet?}.—Also termed *adjective pronoun.*

▶ **proper adjective.** An adjective derived from a proper noun and, not having become generic, is capitalized {American folkways} {Euclidean geometry} {Greek philosophy}.

▶ **qualifying adjective.** See *descriptive adjective.*

▶ **relative adjective.** An adjective that relates one clause to another, as by introducing a subordinate adjective or noun clause or by modifying a noun element in the clause it introduces {she is someone whose opinion carries great weight} {order whatever materials you need}.

▶ **simple adjective.** An adjective that isn't a compound {big} {small} {tall} {short}.

▶ **subjective adjective.** See *predicate adjective.*

▶ **superlative adjective.** An adjective in the extreme degree of comparison {worst} {best}.

▶ **verbal adjective.** See *participial adjective.*

adjective clause. See **clause.**

adjective cluster. A single-word adjective and its adverbial modifiers {a thoroughly familiar proposition} {an utterly incompetent mechanic}.

adjective–noun agreement. See **agreement.**

adjective phrase. See **phrase.**

adjective pronoun. See *pronominal adjective* under **adjective.**

adjunct /aj-ənkt/. **1.** A word or phrase—typically an adjective, adverb, or complement—added to define, limit, qualify, or modify other words. An adjunct normally adds information about the time, place, manner, purpose, result, or other characteristic of a state or event {he played golf with rented clubs} {she slowed down, which was smart}. **2.** A subordinate or optional element whose removal from a sentence does not affect the grammatical structure—as with the vocative *Joan* in the statement *Joan, you're right.*

adnoun. 1. *Obs.* An adjective. **2.** An adjective that is used as a noun {the poor and the meek}.

adverb /ad-vərb/. A word that modifies or describes a word or phrase other than a noun or pronoun, or sometimes an entire clause, usu. to say when, where, or how something happens. An adverb may appear with a verb (e.g., in *we fly frequently,* the word *frequently* modifies the verb *fly*), an adjective (e.g., in *the painting looks quite old,* the word *quite* modifies the adjective *old*), another adverb (e.g., in *she patted the dog very gingerly,* the word *very* modifies the adverb *gingerly*), a preposition (e.g., in *I went home just before the rain,* the word *just* modifies the preposition *before*), or a conjunction (e.g., in *he disappeared precisely when he was needed,* the word *precisely* modifies the conjunction *when*). An adverb may also qualify a clause or a sentence (e.g., in *frankly, your excuse is unbelievable,* the word *frankly* modifies the entire clause). Many adverbs (but hardly all) have an *-ly* suffix. But not all words with an *-ly* suffix are adverbs—some are adjectives (e.g., *kingly*). See § 212.

▶ **adverb of manner.** See *manner adverb.*

▶ **compound adverb.** An adverb formed from two or more words combined {nowhere} {somewhere} {whenever} {wherever}.

▶ **conjunctive adverb.** An adverb that indicates a logical relationship between two clauses (e.g., *however, moreover, nevertheless, therefore, whenever*). Unlike a conjunction, a conjunctive adverb has considerable freedom of movement or position in the second of the conjoined elements.—Also termed *adverbial conjunction; connective adverb; half conjunction; illative conjunction; introductory adverb; transitional adverb.*

▶ **connective adverb.** See *conjunctive adverb.*

▶ **degree adverb.** An adverb that describes the degree to which a principal verb's action is performed {barely} {thoroughly} {entirely} {relatively}.

▶ **exclamatory adverb.** An adverb that introduces an exclamation {how kind of you to invite me!}.

▶ **flat adverb.** An adverb without the adverbial suffix *-ly* {he doubtless malingered} {therefore, we stayed behind} {they played fast and loose with the facts}.—Also termed *adverbial.*

▶ **independent adverb.** See *sentence adverb.*

▶ **intensifying adverb.** See **intensifier.**

▶ **interrogative adverb.** An adverb that introduces a direct or indirect question {how should I approach the subject?} {she asked where the rare-book room is}.

▶ **introductory adverb.** See *conjunctive adverb.*

▶ **manner adverb.** An adverb that describes how or in what manner something is done {slowly} {lazily} {posthaste}.—Also termed *adverb of manner.*

▶ **phrasal adverb.** See *adverbial phrase* under **phrase.**

▶ **relative adverb.** An adverb that joins (that is, "relates") a dependent clause to an independent clause {he stopped at a place where few people had been before} {work stops when the 5:30 bell rings} {we know why the imprints differ}.

▶ **sentence adverb.** An adverb that modifies an entire clause or sentence, not just one word or phrase in the sentence {undoubtedly you'll still need some cash}.—Also termed *sentence modifier; independent adverb; transitional adverb.*

▶ **simple adverb.** Any adverb that isn't a compound adverb {now} {then} {this} {where}.

▶ **transitional adverb. 1.** See *conjunctive adverb.* **2.** See *sentence adverb.*

adverb clause. See *adverbial clause* under **clause.**

adverbial, *adj.* Of, relating to, or consisting of an adverb or a phrase or clause functioning as an adverb.

adverbial, *n.* **1.** A word, phrase, or clause that functions as an adverb, often as a means of expressing time (*when; after the meal*), manner (*how; with a worried expression*), or place (*there; where they first met in Portland*). **2.** See *flat adverb* under **adverb.**

adverbial clause. See **clause.**

adverbial conjunction. See *conjunctive adverb* under **adverb.**

adverbial noun. See **adverbial objective.**

adverbial objective. A noun element that functions as an adverb or adverbial phrase {he was sent home} {he discovered his error the hard way}.—Also termed *adverbial noun.*

adverbial phrase. See **phrase.**

adverb of manner. See *manner adverb* under **adverb.**

adverb phrase. See *adverbial phrase* under **phrase.**

adversative clause. See **clause.**

adversative conjunction. See **conjunction.**

affix /af-iks/. A prefix, suffix, or infix; specif., a bound morpheme that can be added to a word's base or stem. Most affixes in English are either prefixes (e.g., *non-, pre-, sub-*) or suffixes (e.g., *-er, -ment, -ness*).—**affixation,** *n.*

▸ **derivational affix.** An affix that changes a word from one part of speech to another. Examples are *-al* {coincidental}, *be-* {befriend}, *-ful* {hopeful}, *-ion* {subjection}, *-ness* {goodness}, and *-ous* {hazardous}.

▸ **inflectional affix.** A grammatical affix that attaches to a word to mark it as a particular part of speech—examples being the plural *-s* added to pluralize a noun, the past-tense *-ed* added to a verb, and the prefix *en-* to make a verb {enlarge}.

agent. The doer that performs the action in a clause.

agentless passive. See *short passive voice* under **passive voice.**

agent noun. See **noun.**

agglutination /ə-gloot-ə-nay-shən/. The combination of simple words or root words into compounds, without change of form or meaning.—**agglutinative,** *n.*

agreement. Grammatical and logical relationship between one word in a phrase, clause, or sentence and another word, dictating gender, number, person, or any other grammatical property. The three kinds of agreement are (1) subject–verb, (2) pronoun–antecedent, and (3) adjective–noun.—Also termed *concord.*

▸ **adjective–noun agreement.** The singular–plural agreement between a demonstrative adjective and its noun {this book} {these books} {that paper} {those papers}.

▸ **pronoun–antecedent agreement.** Grammatical agreement in person, number, and gender between an antecedent and its pronoun {Derrick must call his mother} {Ayoka must call her mother} {Ayoka and Derrick must call their mothers}.

▸ **subject–verb agreement.** The singular–plural agreement between a subject and its verb {a scout with a clipboard was in the stands} {a mother and her son paid their respects}.

alliteration /ə-li-tə-**ray**-shən/. The use of words that begin with or contain the same sound, esp. produced by the same letter or letters {Phil fretted through his fateful finals}.—**alliterative,** *adj.*

alphabetism. See **initialism.**

alternative question. See **question.**

ambiguity, *n.* Uncertainty or inexactness of linguistic meaning, esp. as a result of a polysemous word or phrase, or else unclear modification of a syntactic construction.—**ambiguous,** *adj.*

ambisyllabic, *adj.* Of, relating to, or involving a consonant that may belong to either the preceding or the following syllable (as with the *-t-* in *falter* or *waiter*).

> It is hard to give any kind of language instruction to students who lack the conceptual framework provided by the terms of basic grammar.
> —David Mulroy
> *The War Against Grammar*

ambitransitive verb. See *ergative verb* under **verb.**

amelioration. A word's usu. gradual acquisition of positive connotations or associations.—Also termed *appreciation.*

Americanism. An expression that either had its origins in North America or is felt to be typical mostly of AmE.

analytic comparative. See *periphrastic comparative* under **comparative.**

analytic language /an-ə-**lit**-ik/. A language that expresses the modification of word meanings by syntax, with particles and auxiliaries, and not much by inflection. Cf. **synthetic language.**

anaphora /ə-**naf**-ə-rə/, *n.* **1.** *Grammar.* The use of a word that refers to or replaces a word used earlier in a sentence {I want to and so do they} (*do* is anaphoric for *want*). **2.** *Rhetoric.* The repetition of a word or phrase at the outset of successive clauses {I came; I saw; I conquered}.—**anaphoric,** *adj.*—**anaphor,** *n.*

anaphoric pronoun. See **pronoun.**

anaptyxis. See **epenthesis.**

Anglo-Saxon. See **Old English.**

animate noun. See **noun.**

anomalous verb. See *irregular verb* under **verb.**

antecedent /an-ti-**seed**-ənt/. A noun element to which a personal or relative pronoun refers {when Mother got home, she gave us cookies} {she was instructed what to do, and she should have known all about it}.

anticipatory reference. See **cataphora.**

anticipatory subject. See **subject.**

antonym /an-tə-nim/. A word whose meaning is opposite that of another (e.g., *hot* is an antonym of *cold*; *short* is an antonym of *tall*).—**antonymous,** *adj.*—**antonymy** /an-**ton**-ə-mee/, *n.*

> ▶ **binary antonyms.** A pair of antonyms that are incompatible and that, between them, exhaust all the possibilities {true–false} {dead–alive}.

> ▶ **gradable antonyms.** A pair of antonyms that admit a range of possibilities between the concepts denoted by them {hot–cold} {good–bad}.

aphaeresis /ə-**fer**-ə-səs/. The dropping of one or more syllables or sounds at the beginning of a word (e.g., *raccoon→coon, telephone→phone, opossum→possum, esquire→squire, advantage→vantage*).—**aphaeretic,** *adj.*

aphesis /af-ə-səs/. The gradual dropping of a word's initial unstressed vowel (as in *acute→cute* and *especial→special*). This is a species of aphaeresis.—**aphetic,** *adj.*

apocope /ə-**pok**-ə-pee/. The dropping of one or more of a word's last letters, syllables, or sounds. For instance, *ad* derives from *advertisement, cinema* from *cinematograph, drunk* from *drunken,* and *oft* from *often.* In speech, *jus'* for *just* is an instance of apocope.—Also termed *apocopation.*

apodosis /ə-**pod**-ə-səs/. The main clause in a conditional sentence. In the sentence *If he doesn't pass this exam, he'll have to repeat the course,* the apodosis is *he'll have to repeat the course.*—Also termed *consequent.* Cf. *conditional clause* under **clause.**

apposition. The relation between two or more nouns or noun elements denoting the same person or thing when (1) all are in the same subject or predicate {my daughter Alexandra likes writing} or (2) one is in attributive or complementary relation {this is another fine mess}.

appositional compound. See **compound (1).**

appositional phrase. See **appositive.**

appositive /ə-**poz**-ə-tiv/. A word, phrase, or clause that identifies with greater particularity the noun element that immediately precedes it; esp., a noun element that refers to a person or thing by a different name, usu. an explanatory word or phrase that narrows a more general phrase or proper name {my adviser,

Dr. Moreland, advised against this subject for my junior research paper}. An appositive is usually a restated noun element—though not always. See §§ 40, 311, 359, 489.—Also termed (when it's a phrase) *appositional phrase.*

▸ **nonrestrictive appositive.** An appositive that merely elaborates or explains, so that it might be omitted from the sentence without seriously detracting from its meaning {my history teacher, Ms. Bergerac, asked us to read parts of Barzun's *From Dawn to Decadence*}. A nonrestrictive appositive is normally set off from the rest of the sentence with punctuation.—Also termed *loose appositive; nonessential appositive.*

▸ **restrictive appositive.** An appositive that is needed to identify or limit the words preceding it {David Foster Wallace's book *Consider the Lobster* is among his finest work}.—Also termed *close appositive; essential appositive.*

appositive adjective. See **adjective.**

appositive clause. See **clause.**

appositive phrase. See **phrase.**

appreciation. See **amelioration.**

archaism /**ahr**-kay-iz-əm/. An antiquated word, phrase, or style that has fallen out of ordinary usage.—**archaic,** *adj.*

argot /**ahr**-gət *or* **ahr**-goh/. The slang or jargon of a particular class or group.

article. A limiting adjective that idiomatically introduces most of the nouns or noun phrases in the language (*a, an, the*).

▸ **definite article.** The word *the,* which introduces both singular and plural nouns and often (but not always) indicates a specific person, place, thing, or idea. It is more specific in meaning than the two indefinite articles.

▸ **indefinite article.** The word *a* or *an,* which introduces singular nouns and noun phrases only and does not indicate any specific person, place, thing, or idea. The article *a* precedes a word that begins with a consonant sound {a violin} {a euphonium}; the article *an* precedes a word that begins with a vowel sound {an oboe} {an FBI agent}.

▸ **zero article.** An instance in which a noun is not preceded by an article {diet soda might be bad for people}.

aspect. A grammatical form or category of a verb relating the time of an action to the status of an event, rather than denoting only the time of the event (past, present, or future). Aspect correlates with features such as inception, duration, repetition, and completion.

▸ **continuous aspect.** See *progressive aspect.*

▸ **imperfect aspect.** The aspect denoting that an action is incomplete at a given point in time {you can't still be hunting for your glasses}.—Also termed *progressive aspect.*

▸ **perfect aspect.** The aspect denoting that an action is complete; a past participle shows that the action is over {Marjorie has collected seven witness statements}.

▸ **progressive aspect. 1.** The aspect denoting that an action is ongoing {Noor is swimming laps}. **2.** See *imperfect aspect.* See *progressive tense* under **tense.**— Also termed *continuous aspect.*

asserting verb. See *linking verb* under **verb.**

assertive. See **declarative.**

assimilation /ə-sim-ə-**lay**-shən/. The change of a speech sound because of another sound next to it (as when *grandpa*, with its three medial consonants, is pronounced /**gram**-pə/). Cf. **dissimilation.**—**assimilative,** *adj.*

assonance /**as**-ə-nən[t]s/. A rhyme or near-rhyme; esp., the repetition of identical or similar vowel sounds, often including imperfect rhymes {the rain in Spain stays mainly in the plain} {full fathom five thy father lies}. Cf. **consonance.**

asterisk. A star-shaped typographical symbol (*) used for various purposes in different disciplines. Common uses include indicating footnotes and censoring profanity. In this book, the asterisk (when used at the front of a word or phrase) indicates a deviation from well-edited English.

asyndetic coordination. See **coordination.**

asyndeton /ə-**sin**-də-ton/. The omission of conjunctions between coordinate words or clauses, esp. for brevity or style (as when *and* is omitted between the last two items in a list of three or more).—Also termed *parataxis.* Cf. **syndeton & polysyndeton.**—**asyndetic,** *adj.*

attribute adjective. See *predicate adjective* under **adjective.**

attribute complement. See *subjective complement* under **complement.**

attribute noun. 1. See *predicate noun* (1) under **noun. 2.** See **predicate nominative.**

attribute pronoun. 1. See **pronoun. 2.** See **predicate nominative.**

attributive, *adj.* **1.** (Of an adjective) directly preceding a noun {remarkable performance}. **2.** (Of a noun) being used in an adjectival sense directly before another noun {nurse practitioner}.

attributive adjective. See **adjective.**

attributive noun. See **noun.**

auxiliary verb /awg-**zil**-yə-ree/. A special kind of verb that is used with another (principal) verb to form a verb phrase that indicates mood, tense, voice, aspect, negation, or interrogativeness {must you study for the exam?} {I will go to the store} {the show was interrupted}. The most commonly used auxiliaries are *be, can, do, have, may, must, ought, shall,* and *will.*—Also termed *helping verb; helper.*—Often shortened to *auxiliary.* See *principal verb* under **verb.**

▸ **dummy auxiliary verb.** The auxiliary verb *do,* which merely stands in as an auxiliary without specific meaning because the construction requires an auxiliary but all others would be inappropriate {I don't know} {Bill does} {did Sheila go?}.—Also termed *pro-verb; empty auxiliary verb.*

▸ **modal auxiliary verb.** An auxiliary verb used to indicate such things as ability, necessity, obligation, permission, possibility, probability, or willingness. Among the modal auxiliaries—so called because they express the *mood* of the verb—are *can, could, dare, may, might, must, need, ought, shall, should, will,* and *would.*—Also shortened to *modal verb; modal auxiliary; modal.* See **mood** & **double modal.**

▸ **semi-auxiliary verb.** A verb phrase (or part of one) that functions much like an auxiliary verb—examples being *be able to* {see whether you're able to write something for us}, *be about to* {I'm about to go}, *be supposed to* {we're supposed to be there}, and *have to* {we have to go!}.

back-formation. A word formed by subtracting part of a longer word with which it is thought to be cognate—as with *peddle* from *peddler* (back-formed in the 16th century), **administrate* from *administration* (*administer* is the age-old, preferred verb), or **conversate* from *conversation* (*converse* is the age-old, preferred verb).

backshifting. The changing of a verb's tense to match the tense of indirect or reported speech, as in "Emily said she couldn't wait to get going" when in fact she said, "I can't wait to get going."—**backshift,** *vb.*

bad grammar. See **grammar.**

bare infinitive. See **infinitive.**

base. See **stem.**

being verb. See *linking verb* under **verb.**

be-**verb.** See **verb.**

binary antonyms. See **antonym.**

blend. See *portmanteau word* under **word.**

borrowing, *n.* **1.** The practice or an instance of making a word phrase by imitating a word or phrase from another language, or else by importing it wholesale. **2.** An expression so derived.

bounded noun. See **noun.**

bound morpheme. See **morpheme.**

branching diagram. See **tree diagram.**

Briticism. An expression that is peculiar to or most strongly associated with BrE.— Also termed *Britishism*.

broad reference. A construction in which a pronoun is thought to refer to an entire idea instead of to some identifiable antecedent {he was perpetually overconfi- dent; this in the end caused the disillusionment of friends who saw he couldn't measure up}.—Also termed *broad construction*.

calque. See **loan translation.**

cardinal number. See **number.**

case. One of a set of suffixes and word forms by which a language differenti- ates the roles of the participants in a sentence. In Modern English, inflectional forms affect nouns and pronouns. In Old English, they affect nouns, pronouns, articles, and adjectives. Modern English nouns now have two case forms (*dog* [nominative/objective], *dog's* [possessive]) and English pronouns three (*she* [nominative], *her* [objective/possessive], *hers* [absolute possessive]).

▶ **accusative case.** See *objective case.*

▶ **common case.** The form of an English noun listed in the dictionary and used in all constructions not requiring the possessive case {man} {woman} {dog} {cat}.

▶ **genitive case.** See *possessive case.*

▶ **nominative case.** The case of a pronoun that is the subject of a finite verb {I am happy} {we are the champions}.—Also termed *subjective case; subject case.*

▶ **objective case.** The case of a pronoun that is the object of either a finite verb {the bodyguards threw him to the ground} or a preposition {please keep this between you and me}.—Also termed *accusative case.*

NOMINATIVE	OBJECTIVE
I	me
he	him
she	her
we	us
they	them
who	whom

▶ **oblique case.** Any case other than the nominative—in other words, for nouns generally the possessive case; for personal pronouns and the relative/inter- rogative pronoun *who*, the possessive or objective case.

▶ **possessive case.** The case of a noun or pronoun denoting possession, origin, or the like. A noun in the possessive case is formed by adding -'s to a singular or to an irregular plural {Bill's} {women's}, and only an apostrophe to a regular plural {the Joneses' house}. See **genitive.**—Also termed *genitive case.*

▸ **subjective case.** See *nominative case.*

catachresis /kat-ə-**kree**-səs/. The incorrect use of a word for a similar-looking or -sounding word (e.g., *cachet* for *cache; corollary* for *correlation; tantamount* for *paramount*). Cf. **solecism; vulgarism.**—**catachrestic,** *adj.*

cataphora. A forward reference in a text, as when a pronoun precedes the noun for which it is a substitute {if he needs help, Neal will surely call us}.—Also termed *anticipatory reference.*—**cataphoric,** *adj.*

central adjective. See **adjective.**

clang association. The misuse of a word as a result of either idiosyncratic or widespread confusion by speakers and writers as a result of a similar-sounding word with which it is erroneously connected in their minds—sometimes resulting, finally, in semantic shift. See **semantic contamination.** Cf. **overgeneralization.**

class dialect. See **dialect.**

clausal, *adj.* Of, relating to, or involving a clause.

clause. A grammatical unit that contains a subject, a finite verb, and any complements that the verb requires. A clause has many or all of the basic ingredients of a complete sentence.—Also termed *predication.* Cf. **sentence; phrase.**

▸ **adjective clause.** A dependent clause that functions adjectivally by modifying a noun element in an independent clause {the game that everyone watched was disappointing}.

▸ **adverbial clause.** A dependent proposition in a complex sentence; specif., a dependent clause that modifies a verb, an adjective, or an adverb in an independent clause {she wrapped the dustjacket in a protective cover when she got home} {I will call you when I arrive}.—Also termed *adverb clause.*

▸ **adversative clause.** A clause expressing an idea that contrasts with another clause in the sentence {while I admire his chutzpah, it sometimes gets him into trouble}.

▸ **appositive clause.** A clause used in apposition {the question whether he will attend is an interesting one} {the idea that bad guys always get their just deserts runs throughout the entire television series}.

▸ **comment clause.** A clause by which a speaker or writer expresses his or her attitude about what is being said or how it is being said {I think} {to be sure} {we can only hope} {as you may know}. Comment clauses may be adverbial clauses {at the risk of repeating myself, ...}, relative clauses {what is even stranger, ...}, infinitive clauses {to put it another way, . . .}, present-participial clauses {generally speaking, . . .}, or past-participial clauses {stated otherwise, . . .}.

▸ **comparative clause.** A clause that expresses a comparison with respect to some standard {my three-pointer was longer than Al's [was]}.

▸ **complement clause.** A subordinate clause that functions as either (1) the direct object of a verb such as *believe, know, say, tell, think,* or *understand* {I think that it will work}, or (2) the complement of a noun or adjective {the staffers were troubled by the gossip that the board might replace the CEO} {we were happy that the Thanksgiving holiday brought everyone together}.

▸ **concessive clause.** An adverbial clause that opposes the idea of the main clause {although he is a good actor, he is hardly great}.

▸ **conditional clause.** An adverbial clause stating a condition, typically introduced by *if, should,* or *unless* {if you call me, I will come} {unless you call, I won't be going}.—Also termed *protasis.* Cf. **apodosis.**

▸ **confirmation clause.** See *tag question* under **question.**

▸ **contact clause.** A clause that opens with an implied relative pronoun (such as a whiz-deletion)—that is, a relative clause without a relative pronoun {all the people I asked said they would help}.

▸ **coordinate clause.** An independent clause in a compound sentence.

▸ **dependent clause.** A clause that functions as a single part of speech so that it cannot stand as a well-formed sentence. A dependent clause may function as subject {that you say so worries me}, object {ask whoever needs some help to come see me}, complement {the scores are what I had hoped for}, or an adverbial clause {call me when you're next in town}. A dependent clause may also function as only part of a clause element, as when it is the object of a preposition {so much depends on where you live}.—Also termed *subordinate clause.*

▸ **elliptical clause.** A clause in which a grammatically necessary part has been omitted but is supplied by the listener or reader and is therefore fully understood; a clause that is grammatically incomplete in the literal sense but is clear in meaning because the implicit words are supplied by the reader or listener {I'm not as gung-ho as she [is]} {while [you are] packing your things, don't forget to include your vitamins} {why [should we] not try again tomorrow?} {if [it is] possible, we should try again tomorrow}. Omission of the bracketed words in these examples makes the clauses elliptical. See **ellipsis (1).**

▸ **embedded clause.** A clause that has been subordinated to another clause {the team that I want to join isn't listed}.

▸ **essential clause.** See *restrictive clause.*

▶ **finite clause.** A clause whose principal verb is finite.

▶ **independent clause.** A clause that can stand by itself as a well-formed sentence (and sometimes does) because it contains both a subject and a predicate and does not, taken as a whole, function only as a noun, an adjective, or an adverb {the dog barked} {the air-conditioning stopped as soon as the temperature topped 100° F} {the police arrived, and all was well}.—Also termed *main clause; principal clause.*

▶ **limiting clause.** See *restrictive clause.*

▶ **main clause.** See *independent clause.*

▶ **matrix clause.** A clause into which another clause has been embedded. In the sentence *The fact that you took two hours longer will affect your grade,* the matrix clause is *The fact will affect your grade;* the embedded clause is *that you took two hours longer.*

▶ **nominal clause.** See *noun clause.*

▶ **nonrestrictive clause.** An adjective clause that is informative but is not essential to the meaning of a statement {the editor, who liked your manuscript, will send a letter} {the house, which has been fully refurbished, is now admired as a marvel of architecture}.—Also termed *nonessential clause; nonlimiting clause.*

▶ **noun clause.** A dependent clause that functions as a noun element.—Also termed *substantive clause; nominal clause.*

▶ **passive clause.** A clause in which the recipient of the action of the main verb is expressed as the subject {Jack was kicked} {nobody expected that Jack would be kicked}. See **passive voice.**

▶ **principal clause.** See *independent clause.*

▶ **relative clause.** A subordinate clause that modifies a noun element; specif., a clause occurring in a complex sentence, being introduced by a relative pronoun (*that, which, who*), having a subject and predicate of its own, and referring to, describing, or limiting an antecedent {the man who greeted us wasn't Bill's uncle}.

▶ **restrictive clause.** A clause that is an essential modifier that defines or identifies by limiting the meaning of a noun element {we offer loans to people who have good credit} {the building that I mentioned last week has been completed}.—Also termed *essential clause; limiting clause.*

▶ **sentential relative clause.** A relative clause that, through broad reference, is attached not to an identifiable antecedent but to the entire idea of the main clause {Gardea was early for the tree-trimming, which meant that the yard workers would be able to work uninterrupted}.

▶ **subject clause.** A noun clause functioning as the subject of a sentence {that you called so often cheered me up}.

▶ **subordinate clause.** See *dependent clause.*

▶ **substantive clause.** See *noun clause.*

▶ *that*-**clause.** A noun clause that is introduced by the subordinate conjunction *that* and includes a tensed verb or a modal verb {that we managed to swim ashore is incredible} {I understand that he couldn't get there on time}.

cleft sentence. See **sentence.**

clipped form. A word formed by shortening a longer expression (as with *fax* from *facsimile*, *fridge* from *refrigerator*, *lab* from *laboratory*, or *tux* from *tuxedo*).

clipping, *n.* **1.** The forming of a word or name by abbreviating an existing word or name (e.g., *fan* [= a devotee] from *fanatic*, *bus* from *omnibus*, or *lab* from *laboratory*). **2.** The practice or an instance of speaking in a precise, rapid, staccato manner.

clitic. See *bound morpheme* under **morpheme.**

close appositive. See *restrictive appositive* under **appositive.**

closed syllable. See **syllable.**

closed word class. See **word class.**

cognate, *adj.* (Of words) deriving from a common source.

cognate /**kog**-nayt/, *n.* A word or phrase that is connected to another by common derivation from the same source—that is, their etymologies are related.

cognate object. See **object.**

cohesion, *n.* A unified effect within a discourse, achieved by a combination of relevance of topics covered, orderly movement from one to the next, and the deft use of transitional words.—**cohesive,** *adj.*

collective noun. See **noun.**

collocation /kol-ə-**kay**-shən/. A characteristic or traditional combination of words, as in idioms or in prepositions commonly paired with verbs.—**collocate,** *vb.*

command. See **directive.**

comma splice. The erroneous joining of two independent clauses with a comma, as opposed to a comma plus a coordinating conjunction or a semicolon. One of the most frequent comma splices occurs when *however* (a conjunctive adverb) is used as if it were a full-fledged conjunction—e.g., **I didn't want to go, however, Jack persuaded me to,* in which *however* should be either replaced by *but* or preceded by a semicolon.—Also termed *run-on sentence; run-together sentence.*

comment clause. See **clause.**

common adjective. See **adjective.**

common case. See **case.**

common gender. See **gender.**

common noun. See **noun.**

comparative /kəm-pa-rə-tiv/, *adj. & n.* An adjective or adverb whose form has been changed to indicate a greater or lesser degree {bolder} {swifter}. See **comparison (1)** & **degree.** Cf. **positive** & **superlative.**

▸ **analytic comparative.** See *periphrastic comparative.*

▸ **double comparative.** A grammatical fault in which the comparative degree is indicated twice—redundantly {this detergent is *more better than that one}.

▸ **periphrastic comparative** /per-i-**fras**-tik/. A comparative formed by using an auxiliary word or words (esp. *more*) to serve the function of inflection. For example, in the phrase *more difficult*, the adverb *more* serves the same function as the *-er* suffix in *harder*. See §§ 126, 131.—Also termed *analytic comparative.*

▸ **synthetic comparative.** An inflected comparative formed by adding *-er* to the positive form of the adjective or adverb {faster} {lamer}.

comparative adjective. See **adjective.**

comparative clause. See **clause.**

comparison. 1. In grammar, the inflection of adjectives or adverbs to indicate differences of degree in quality. The three degrees of comparison are the positive {good} {smooth}, the comparative {better} {smoother}, and the superlative {best} {smoothest}. With most words affected by comparison, the comparative and superlative are most commonly expressed by adding *-er* or *-est* to the positive form, or (especially with words of more than two syllables) by preceding the positive form by *more, most, less,* or *least.* See **positive, comparative** & **superlative. 2.** In rhetoric, the setting forth of points of similarity or contrast between one thing and another.

complement. A word or phrase (other than the principal verb or verb phrase and any adverb that modifies it) by which a predicate is completed (e.g., *the point* in the sentence *they couldn't resolve the point;* or *of no use* in *it was of no use*). Complements may include direct objects, indirect objects, subjective complements, and objective complements.—Also termed *completer.*

▸ **attribute complement.** See *subjective complement.*

▸ **inner complement.** The first of two complements after a transitive verb—either an indirect object {you gave me permission} or a direct object {we considered the event a success}, depending on the sentence pattern.

▶ **objective complement.** A noun or adjective that follows the direct object of a verb and completes the action the verb denotes {you make me angry [the object *me* needs the adjective *angry* to complete the sense of *make*]} {students elected Kim president [the object *Kim* needs the noun *president* to complete the sense of *elected*]}. Verbs that take an objective complement usually carry the sense of transforming (e.g., *leave*; *render*) or regarding (e.g., *consider*; *deem*).—Also termed *complementary object*; *object complement*; *objective predicate*; *predicate objective*; *factitive complement*; *factitive object*; *objective attribute*.

▶ **outer complement.** The second of two complements after a transitive verb— either a direct object {she gave me the book} or an objective complement {his colleagues considered him a sage}.

▶ **predicate complement.** See *subjective complement*.

▶ **subjective complement.** A predicate adjective {he is happy} or predicate nominative {she is an optimist}.—Also termed *attribute complement*; *subject complement*; *predicate complement*.

▶ ***that*-complement.** A *that*-clause functioning as a complement {he believes that Martians will soon be invading Earth}.

complementary infinitive. See **infinitive.**

complementary object. See *objective complement* under **complement.**

complement clause. See **clause.**

complete predicate. See **predicate.**

completer. See **complement.**

complete sentence. See **sentence.**

complete subject. See **subject.**

complete verb. See **verb.**

complex preposition. See **preposition.**

complex sentence. See **sentence.**

compound, *n.* **1.** A word made up of two or more existing words joined together {bellhop} {blackbird} {housekeeper} {steamship}.—Also termed *compound word*.

▶ **appositional compound.** A compound whose constituents contribute equally to the meaning {bittersweet} {student-teacher} {blue-green}.

▶ **endocentric compound.** A compound whose head bears its literal sense, as with *blackbird* or *bluebird*. Cf. *exocentric compound*.

▶ **exocentric compound.** A metaphorical compound such as *mouthpiece* (= lawyer) or *redeye* (an overnight flight), which does not literally denote what it seems to describe. Another example is *loudmouth*, which denotes a person, not a mouth. Cf. *endocentric compound*.

▶ **neoclassical compound.** A compound whose parts derive from Latin or Greek {Anglophile} {homophobia} {xenophobe}.

2. Less commonly, a short sequence of words that function more or less like a unit {below-the-belt} {blue-green} {bus stop} {hand-washing} {tractor-trailer}.

compound adjective. See **adjective.**

compound adverb. See **adverb.**

compound-complex sentence. See **sentence.**

compound conjunction. See **conjunction.**

compounding, *n.* The act, the practice, or an instance of forming a word by combining at least two elements that otherwise occur as independent words {Chinese-American} {headhunter} {motorcycle} {tugboat}. Compounding is not the same as affixation, which involves morphemes that do not have the status of individual words.

compound modifier. See *phrasal adjective* under **adjective.**

compound noun. See **noun.**

compound objects. See **object.**

compound personal pronoun. See *personal pronoun* under **pronoun.**

compound predicate. See **predicate.**

compound preposition. See **preposition.**

compound pronoun. See **pronoun.**

compound sentence. See **sentence.**

compound subject. See **subject.**

compound tense. See **tense.**

compound word. See **compound.**

concessive clause. See **clause.**

concord. See **agreement.**

concord of proximity. See **false attraction.**

concrete noun. See **noun.**

conditional clause. See **clause.**

conditional sentence. See **sentence.**

confirmation clause. See *tag question* under **question.**

conjugation /kon-jə-**gay**-shən/. **1.** A change in the form of a verb to indicate tense, voice, mood, number, or person. **2.** A list of verb inflections, such as *like–likes–liked–liked; hang–hangs–hung–hung.* **3.** The classification of verbs according to these types of inflections as being either weak (*like*) or strong (*hang*). See *regular verb* & *irregular verb* under **verb.**—**conjugational,** *adj.*

conjunction /kon-**jənk**-shən/. A word that connects words {scarlet or blue}, clauses {the first plate remained intact, but the second one broke}, or sentences {They accomplished their objectives. And they did rejoice.}.—**conjunctive,** *adj.*

▸ **additive coordinating conjunction.** See *copulative conjunction.*

▸ **adverbial conjunction.** See *conjunctive adverb* under **adverb.**

▸ **adversative conjunction.** A conjunction that denotes a contrast or comparison; the second clause (also called the *adversative clause*) usu. qualifies the first clause {it was 104 degrees in the shade at the time of the wedding, yet the bride looked cool and calm} {I'll attend the meeting on Tuesday, but my partner is unavailable until Thursday morning}.—Also termed *contrasting coordinating conjunction.*

▸ **compound conjunction.** An adverb formed from two or more words combined {although} {because} {notwithstanding}.

▸ **contrasting coordinating conjunction.** See *adversative conjunction.*

▸ **coordinating conjunction.** A conjunction that unites equal items (e.g., *and, but, or, nor, for*).—Also termed *coordinator.*

▸ **copulative conjunction.** A conjunction that denotes addition; the second clause adds a related fact to the first clause {the last flight out for the night was canceled, and all the hotel rooms were booked}.—Also termed *additive coordinating conjunction.*

▸ **correlative conjunctions.** A pair of corresponding conjunctions that commonly frame syntactically matching parts as coordinate structures {both–and} {either–or} {neither–nor} {not only–but also}. —Also termed *correlating conjunctions.*—Often shortened to *correlatives.* See **correlative,** *n.*

▸ **disjunctive conjunction.** A conjunction that denotes separation or alternatives {you can go to the zoo or the park tomorrow} {please wear the new raincoat; otherwise, the water will soak through your dress}.—Also termed *separative coordinating conjunction.*

▸ **final conjunction.** A conjunction that denotes inferences or consequences {his son threw 12 strikeouts; as a result, the team won the playoff game} {I paid the extra fee so that we'll have covered parking}.—Also termed *illative coordinating conjunction.*

▸ **half conjunction.** See *conjunctive adverb* under **adverb.**

▸ **illative conjunction.** See *conjunctive adverb* under **adverb.**

▸ **illative coordinating conjunction.** See *final conjunction.*

▸ **phrasal conjunction.** A combination of two or more words serving as a conjunction {he stood on a chair so that he could reach the top shelf}. Among the most common examples are *as if, as though, inasmuch as, insofar as, provided that,* and *so that.*

▸ **separative coordinating conjunction.** See *disjunctive conjunction.*

▸ **simple conjunction.** A one-word conjunction, such as *and, but, if, nor, or, so, yet.*

▸ **subordinating conjunction.** A conjunction that creates a dependent clause to be attached to an independent clause (e.g., *after, although, as if, as though, because, if, since, when, where, while*) {we'll see you when we get back} {if you need help, call tech support}.—Also termed *subordinator.*

conjunctive adverb. See **adverb.**

connecting verb. See *linking verb* under **verb.**

connective. A word or group of words that joins or shows the relationship between words, phrases, or clauses {college students and other protesters sat on the lawn outside Batts Auditorium}. Connectives include conjunctions, prepositions, relative pronouns, conjunctive adverbs, relative adjectives, and relative adverbs.

connective adverb. See *conjunctive adverb* under **adverb.**

connotation. The feeling or idea that a word carries in addition to its literal or principal meaning. For instance, the adjective *notorious* means "well known," but it has negative connotations {a notorious thief}. Cf. **denotation.**—**connote,** *vb.*

consequent. See **apodosis.**

consonance. The correspondence between nearby consonant sounds, esp. the pleasant repetition of like sounds as in rhyming. Cf. **assonance.**

consonant /kon[t]-sə-nənt/. **1.** A speech sound that is articulated by partial or complete obstruction of the vocal tract. **2.** A letter that represents such a sound. Cf. **vowel.**—**consonantal,** *adj.*

constituent, *n.* A word or group of words constituting part of a larger grammatical construction {students who study are smart}.

▸ **immediate constituent.** A constituent of a constituent {students who study are smart}. The immediate constituents of the complete subject *students who* *study* are *students*, the simple subject, and *who study*, an adjective clause modifying *students*. The immediate constituents of that relative clause (*who study*) are the relative pronoun *who* (the subject) and the verb *study*. The predicate *are smart* consists of the immediate constituents *are* (a linking verb) and *smart* (a predicate adjective). To be immediate constituents, words must form a definite grammatical unit—hence not *students who* or *study are*.

constructio ad sensum. See **synesis**.

construction. 1. A group of words having grammatical significance; esp., a syntactic arrangement of two or more constituents {faulty construction}. **2.** Interpretation {statutory construction}.

contact clause. See **clause**.

content word. See **word**.

continuous aspect. See *progressive aspect* under **aspect**.

continuous tense. See *progressive tense* under **tense**.

contraction. A word formed by shortening and compounding two or more words and eliding some elements {I'm} {we've} {you'll} {he's} {she'd}. *Goodbye* is a contraction of *God be with ye*.

contrasting coordinating conjunction. See *adversative conjunction* under **conjunction**.

conversion. The use of a word in a different part of speech from its usual one, without a change of form {don't father-in-law me!} {take a listen}.—Also termed *functional shift; zero derivation*.

coordinate, *adj.* (Of a word, phrase, or clause) being one of two that are equal in rank and fulfill identical functions; (of a grammatical element) having equal syntactic standing {coordinate adjectives}.

coordinate, *n.* One of two or more words, phrases, or clauses that are equal in rank and fulfill identical functions; one of two or more grammatical elements of equal syntactic standing.

coordinate adjective. See **adjective**.

coordinate clause. See **clause**.

coordinate objects. See *compound objects* under **object**.

coordinate subjects. See *compound subject* under **subject**.

coordinate verbs. See **verb**.

coordinating conjunction. See **conjunction**.

coordination. The grammatical or syntactic linking of parallel elements in a sentence, usu. by a conjunction, thereby giving them the same status in the sentence.

For example, the coordination in *are you driving or flying?* is shown by the *or* that links the participles *driving* and *flying.* Cf. **subordination.**

▸ **asyndetic coordination.** Coordination that involves no use of a coordinating conjunction {we went to Melbourne, Sydney, Perth}. See **asyndeton.**

▸ **correlative coordination.** Coordination that involves the use of such strings as *both–and, not only–but also, either–or,* or *neither–nor.*

▸ **polysyndetic coordination.** Coordination that involves the use of a repeated coordinating conjunction {we went to Melbourne and Sydney and Perth}. See **polysyndeton.**

▸ **syndetic coordination.** Coordination that involves the use of a coordinating conjunction (*and* or *or*) {we went to Melbourne, Sydney, and Perth}. See **syndeton.**

coordinator. See *coordinating conjunction* under **conjunction.**

copula /kop-yə-lə/. See *linking verb* under **verb.**

copular, *adj.* Of, relating to, or involving a linking verb (copula).

copular verb. See *linking verb* under **verb.**

copulative conjunction. See **conjunction.**

copulative verb. See *linking verb* under **verb.**

correlating conjunctions. See *correlative conjunctions* under **conjunction.**

correlative /kə-rel-ə-tiv/, *adj.* (Of a pair of words or phrases) having reciprocal or corresponding functions and typically being used together (but not side by side) in a sentence. Conjunctions are often correlative. Common examples are *both–and, either–or,* and *not only–but also.* See § 266.

correlative, *n.* One of a pair of conjunctions, adverbs, or conjunction–adverb combinations that join coordinate elements in a sentence to achieve balance. Among the most frequently used correlatives are these:

- as–as
- both–and
- either–or
- neither–nor
- not only–but also
- whether–or

—Also termed *correlative conjunction; correlating conjunction.*

correlative conjunctions. See **conjunction.**

correlative coordination. See **coordination.**

count noun. See **noun.**

dangler. A participle, participial phrase, or infinitive phrase that is not syntactically connected to the noun that, logically, it should modify {pawing the ground, the matador anticipated the bull's charge}. In that example, the action of the introductory phrase *pawing the ground* wants to attach to the closest noun (*matador* rather than *bull*)—and *bull* doesn't even appear in the sentence except in the possessive form. Less commonly than participial phrases, infinitive phrases can also dangle {to enroll in these seminars, an extra fee will be necessary [a fee cannot enroll]}. See §§ 121, 150, 159–60.—Also termed *dangling modifier.*

declarative /di-kla-rə-tiv/, *adj.* Of, relating to, or involving a sentence in which the speaker makes a statement {our company had a profitable quarter}, as opposed to asking a question or giving an order. Most sentences are declarative.—Also termed *assertive.*—**declaration,** *n.*

declarative sentence. See **sentence.**

declarative yes–no question. See **question.**

declension /də-klen-shən/. **1.** The change in the form of a noun or pronoun to show case, number, or gender. **2.** A catalogue of inflections in a noun, pronoun, or adjective (as in *woman–woman's–women–women's* or *he–him–his*). **3.** The classification according to such inflections, as in *girl* regular, *woman* irregular.—**decline,** *vb.*

deep structure. See **structure.**

defective /di-fek-tiv/, *adj.* Lacking one or more of the inflected forms that are normal for a class of words. Most modal verbs, for example, do not have present- or past-participial forms (e.g., *beware*). Some lack infinitive forms (e.g., *may*).

defective verb. See **verb.**

deferred preposition. See *stranded preposition* under **preposition.**

deferred subject. See *delayed subject* under **subject.**

definite article. See **article.**

definiteness. A distinction in specificity or particularity marked by an article (definite or indefinite) so as to convey whether a noun is known to the listener or reader already {the painting was soon sold} or is being introduced for the first time {a painting was soon sold}. See **article.**

definite noun. See **noun.**

definitive adjective. See *limiting adjective* under **adjective.**

degree. A step on the scale of comparison for gradable adjectives and adverbs. There are three degrees of comparison, in ascending order: positive (*early*), comparative (*earlier*), and superlative (*earliest*). See **positive, comparative & superlative.**

degree adverb. See **adverb.**

deixis /dɪk-sis/. The function that pointing words such as *the* or demonstrative pronouns have in specifying what is being referred to in a given discourse.—**deictic**, *adj.*

delayed subject. See **subject.**

demonstrative /di-**mon**-strə-tiv/, *adj.* (Of a word) pointing at the person or thing speaking, addressed, or referred to, esp. by way of indicating something's position in relation to the speaker {the book} {that cat}.

demonstrative adjective. See **adjective.**

demonstrative pronoun. See **pronoun.**

denominalized verb. See *denominal verb* under **verb.**

denominal verb. See **verb.**

denotation. The central meaning of a word, stripped of emotive associations. Cf. **connotation.**—**denotative**, *adj.*—**denote**, *vb.*

dental preterite. See *regular verb* under **verb.**

deontic, *adj.* Of, relating to, or consisting of the use of a modal verb to express necessity, obligation, possibility, etc. {must I sit down?} {you may now leave} {they should certainly tell him}.

dependent clause. See **clause.**

derivation /der-ə-**vay**-shən/. **1.** The formation of a word by adding an affix to another word, such as *broaden* from *broad*, *reinforce* from *enforce*, and *womanly* from *woman*. **2.** See **etymology (2).**—**derivative**, *adj. & n.*—**derive**, *vb.*

▸ **zero derivation.** See **conversion.**

derivational affix. See **affix.**

derivational suffix. See **suffix.**

descriptive adjective. See **adjective.**

descriptive grammar. See **grammar.**

descriptive possessive. See **possessive.**

descriptivism /di-**skrip**-ti-vi-zəm/. An approach to language study that forswears value judgments in deciding what is "correct" or "incorrect," effective or ineffective, and instead describes how people use the language without ever passing judgment on the forms they use. Cf. **prescriptivism.**—**descriptivist**, *adj. & n.*

> I have long felt that the virtuous claim of many academics to be *descriptive*—to keep account of linguistic fact but to withhold evaluation—is a comfortable evasion, a defection from responsibility.
> —Walter Nash
> *An Uncommon Tongue: The Uses and Resources of English*

determiner. A word that (1) indicates that one of the words occurring soon after it is a noun and (2) serves as one means of identifying a word as a noun. Examples are articles (*a, an, the*); the possessive forms of nouns and pronouns (*Bill's, my, our, your, his, her, its, their*); indefinite adjectives (*all, any, both, each, either, every, few, less, little, many, more, most, much, neither, no, several, some, that, these, this, those, what, whatever, which, whichever*); and numerals (*one, two, three,* etc.).— Also termed *noun indicator*.

diacritical mark /dɪ-ə-**krit**-i-kəl/. An orthographical character that indicates a special phonetic quality for a given character.—Also termed *accent*.

diaeresis /dɪ-**er**-ə-sis/. **1.** A mark [¨] over the second of two adjacent vowels, signaling that the marked vowel is treated as a second syllable, as in *Zoë*. Cf. **umlaut**. **2.** The division of a sound into two syllables, esp. by separating two vowels in a diphthong. For example, a diaeresis occurs when *medieval* is pronounced /med-i-**ee**-vəl/ (separating the *-ie-* into two vowel sounds) rather than /med-**ee**-vəl/ (keeping the *-ie-* as one vowel).—Also spelled *dieresis*. Cf. **synaeresis**.

dialect /dɪ-ə-lekt/. A linguistic variety routinely spoken by an identifiable group of native speakers, usu. categorizable by region (e.g., New England), class (e.g., middle), ethnic group (e.g., Black English), or occupation (e.g., engineering). A dialect is identifiable by its grammar and vocabulary.—**dialectal,** *adj.*

▸ **class dialect.** A dialect used by a particular social group, esp. as reflecting a more or less well-defined stratum of society according to educational level.— Also termed *social dialect*.

▸ **regional dialect.** A dialect used in a particular geographic area.

▸ **social dialect.** See *class dialect*.

diction. 1. Vocabulary or choice of words, esp. in poetry; the selection of words, esp. as regards meaning and contextual appropriateness. Diction can be simple, abstruse, heightened, low, pedantic, colloquial, voguish, archaic, etc. **2.** Distinct enunciation, as of a public speaker or actor.

dieresis. See **diaeresis**.

differentiation. The linguistic process by which similar words, usu. those having a common etymology, gradually diverge in meaning, each taking on a distinct sense or senses.

digraph, *n.* A combination of two letters to represent a single sound (as with *-ch-* in *chic*). Cf. **ligature**.

diminutive. A suffix that denotes smallness (e.g., the *-ella* in *novella,* the *-ette* in *luncheonette,* or the *-ule* in *granule*). By extension, diminutives may also connote fondness (e.g., the *-kins* in *lambkins*), subordinate rank or age (e.g., the *-ling* in *underling* or *sapling*), or inferiority (e.g., the *-aster* in *poetaster*).

diphthong /dif-thong/. A combination of two vowel sounds in one syllable; specif., a vowel sound in a single syllable that glides from one quality to another because the speech organs move from one position to another during the articulation, as in *high* and *out*.—**diphthongal,** *adj.*

direct address. 1. The use of the second person (*you*) in speaking straight to a listener or writing straight to the reader {you may well wonder just why you can't get that rate of return in this market}. **2.** The use of the vocative {Mr. President, we appreciate your time and effort}.

direct discourse. See **discourse** (1).

directive, *n.* A statement using the imperative mood of a verb.—Also termed *command.*

direct object. See **object.**

direct question. See **question.**

direct speech. See *direct discourse* under **discourse** (1).

discourse. 1. Continuous expression or exchange of ideas; connected communication of thought.

▸ **direct discourse.** A statement that reports and expressly quotes the verbatim words of a speaker {she said, "Please send my regards"}. Direct discourse normally appears within quotation marks.—Also termed *direct speech; oratio recta; oratio directa.*

▸ **indirect discourse.** A statement that reports another's words without quoting, either as a paraphrase or as a verbatim rendering but without quotation marks {she asked me to send her regards}.—Also termed *indirect speech; oratio obliqua.*

2. A formal disquisition, treatise, lecture, or sermon. **3.** The power of analytically consecutive thought; esp., the ability to deduce conclusions from the successive consideration of factual and rule-based premises. **4.** The human faculty or ability to communicate one's mental states to other minds by means of language.

disjunctive /dis-jəng[k]-tiv/, *adj.* Denoting an alternative, a choice, a contrast, or opposition. The conjunction *or* is the most frequent word performing a disjunctive function (sometimes with its correlative conjunction *either*). *Neither–nor* are also disjunctive words.—**disjunctive,** *n.*

disjunctive conjunction. See **conjunction.**

dissimilation. A change in a sound to make it unlike another nearby sound. An example is seen in the change from the Old French *cinnamome* to the English *cinnamon*, or from Old French *berfrey* to *belfry* in English. Cf. **assimilation.**

ditransitive verb. See **verb.**

double comparative. See **comparative.**

double genitive. See *double possessive* under **possessive.**

double modal. A nonstandard verb-phrase construction in which two modal auxiliary verbs appear in succession {*had ought} {*might could} {*ought to could}. In Standard English, only one modal verb appears in a verb phrase.

double negative. A statement in which two negatives are unnecessarily used {*I didn't say nothing}—as opposed to using only one negating term {I said nothing} {I didn't say anything}.

double possessive. See **possessive.**

double subject. See **subject.**

double superlative. See **superlative.**

doublet /dəb-lət/. **1.** A word differing in form or meaning from another word that derives from a common source (e.g., *chief* and *chef, frail* and *fragile*). **2.** A synonymic doubling of terms characteristic of the rhetorical and oratorical style of Middle English. Examples are *all and sundry, fit and proper,* and *total and entire.*

drift. The increasing tendency of speakers of a given language to use a particular form, structure, or word choice—esp. one not traditionally considered part of the standard language.

d-structure. See *deep structure* under **structure.**

dummy auxiliary verb. See **auxiliary verb.**

dummy word. See **expletive** (1).

dynamic verb. See **verb.**

dysphemism /dis-fə-miz-əm/. **1.** A disagreeable word or phrase that is substituted for a neutral or even positive one (e.g., *sawbones* for *surgeon*). **2.** The use of such a word or phrase. Cf. **euphemism.**—**dysphemistic,** *adj.*

Early Modern English. The English language used from about 1500 to about 1700.

echo utterance. A question or exclamation that mirrors another speaker's sentence {"John missed the opening." "He missed what?"} {"Sit there." "Sit where?"} {"What a wonderful gift." "What a wonderful gift, indeed!"}—Sometimes shortened to *echo.*—Also termed *echo question.*—**echoic,** *adj.*

elision /i-lizh-ən/. **1.** The omission or suppression of a syllable or sound, esp. to improve the sound and flow of a writing, as in *o'er the ramparts we watch* or *e'en now the raven haunts me.* **2.** The omission of a word, sentence, or passage from a text, usu. for some particular purpose.—**elide,** *vb.*

ellipsis /i-**lip**-səs *or* ee-/. **1.** The omission of a sound, syllable, word, phrase, or clause; esp., the shortening of a clause or phrase by the omission of one or more words that can be easily understood from the context or from the reader's common sense. Speakers and writers often use an ellipsis to avoid repetition (e.g., in *if I can lift that weight, anybody can*, a second occurrence of *lift that weight* after *anybody can* is understood even though the predicate in the main clause is incomplete). Cf. **recoverability. 2.** Collectively, the three period-dots that mark a writer's omission of one or more words from a quoted passage.—**elliptical**, *adj.*

elliptical clause. See **clause.**

embedded clause. See **clause.**

embedded question. See **question.**

emphatic pronoun. See *intensive pronoun* under **pronoun.**

emphatic verb. See **verb.**

empty auxiliary verb. See *dummy auxiliary verb* under **auxiliary verb.**

enclitic /en-**klit**-ik/, *n.* A compound that is formed when a word that follows another is pronounced with so little emphasis that it is usu. combined with the preceding word. This occurs, for example, when *can not* becomes *cannot* (*not* is the enclitic element), or when a contraction is compounded from a word and an informal part (such as *n't* in *couldn't*). Cf. *bound morpheme* under **morpheme.**

endocentric compound. See **compound.**

epenthesis /i-**pen**[t]-thə-səs *or* ee-/. The addition of a sound or an unetymological letter into a word. For example, the -*b*- in *thimble* has no etymological basis, but the letter began appearing in the 15th century, perhaps because of *thimble's* similarity to *humble* and *nimble*. A modern example is **preventative* (for *preventive*). When the additional sound is that of a vowel—as when *athlete* is erroneously pronounced /**ath**-ə-leet/ instead of /**ath**-leet/, or *film* is pronounced /**fil**-əm/ instead of /film/—the technical name is *anaptyxis*.—**epenthetic**, *adj.*

eponym /**ep**-ə-nim/. **1.** A person, real or imaginary, after whom an event, invention, etc., is named (e.g., Louis Pasteur, the French chemist and bacteriologist, is the eponym for *pasteurize* and *pasteurization*). **2.** A word derived from a proper name (the word *boycott*, for example, comes from Captain C. C. Boycott [1832–97], an English landlord who was stigmatized by his Irish tenants in 1880 for raising rents).—**eponymous**, *adj.*

ergative verb. See **verb.**

essential appositive. See *restrictive appositive* under **appositive.**

essential clause. See *restrictive clause* under **clause.**

etymological sense. The meaning of a word at an earlier time in its history, esp. when it then bore a literal meaning but has since taken on extended meanings.

etymology /et-ə-**mol**-i-jee/. **1.** The study of word origins. **2.** The origin and history of a word or of words generally.—Also termed (in sense 2) *derivation*.

etymon /**et**-i-mon/, *n.* **1.** A word or morpheme from which a word or words are formed, esp. in another language. For example, the Greek *oktopous* is the etymon of the English word *octopus*. **2.** A word's original or fundamental sense.

euphemism /**yoo**-fə-miz-əm/. **1.** A soft or relatively unobjectionable word or phrase used in place of a harsh or objectionable one; a terminological replacement for a word or phrase that has lost prestige or has become subject to a taboo. **2.** The use of such a word or phrase. **3.** The process by which such replacements occur in language. Cf. **dysphemism.**—**euphemistic,** *adj.*

euphony /**yoo**-fə-nee/. The prose quality of sounding pleasant; agreeableness to the ear.—**euphonious,** *adj.*

euphuism /**yoof**-yə-wi-zəm/. A convoluted, artificial, embellished style of speaking or writing.—**euphuistic,** *adj.*

exclamation. A sentence that conveys or purports to convey a fairly strong emotion {oh, dear!} {we thought he was a scoundrel!} {what a fine mess you've made of this!}.—Also termed *exclamatory sentence.*—**exclamatory,** *adj.*

exclamatory adverb. See **adverb.**

exclamatory question. See **question.**

exclamatory sentence. See **exclamation.**

existential sentence. See **sentence.**

exocentric compound. See **compound.**

expanded tense. See **tense.**

expletive /eks-**plə**-tiv/. **1.** A word or phrase that pads or supports a sentence but does not add to the sense. *It* and *there* are commonly used as expletives {it looks like rain} {there is an interesting letter in the newspaper}. When *it* is used in this way, it is sometimes called the "nonreferential *it.*" Likewise, *there* used not in reference to a place is sometimes called the "nonreferential *there.*"—Also termed *dummy word* (more particularly "expletive *it*" and "expletive *there*"). **2.** A swearword {damn!}.—**expletive,** *adj.*

extraposition. The placement of a clause outside its normal position in the sentence, as by using an expletive—e.g., *why you came doesn't matter* when it becomes *it doesn't matter why you came.*—**extrapositioning,** *n.*

factitive complement. See *objective complement* under **complement.**

factitive object. See *objective complement* under **complement.**

factitive verb. See **verb.**

false attraction. A mismatching in the number of a verb with its subject caused by the intervention (between the two) of another noun of a different number {the number of students are [read *is*] increasing} {the interests of each child is [read *are*] best served by the appointment of a guardian}.—Also termed (less judgmentally) *concord of proximity.*

feminine gender. See **gender.**

figurative language. An expression or reference in which the words aren't to be taken literally because they involve a metaphor, usu. to add beauty or force. See **figure of speech.**

figure of speech. An expression in which language is manipulated for rhetorical effect. Specific categories into which figures of speech fall include anticlimax, antithesis, climax, euphemism, hyperbole, litotes, metonymy, and synecdoche.

filler. A more or less meaningless brief utterance, such as *um, like,* or *you know,* that commonly appears in speech just before a peak of information {that house looks like—you know—a mansion} {that was, like, a mansion}. Fillers allow the speaker to formulate the coming material and signal to the hearer that the speaker will continue talking (that is, that the hearer's turn to reply hasn't yet come). Fillers are widely condemned when they become so numerous in speech as to be noticeable. But a competent user of the language edits them out automatically. Unless they are frequent or habitual enough to become distracting, the hearer tends not to notice them.

final conjunction. See **conjunction.**

finite clause. See **clause.**

finite verb. See **verb.**

flat adverb. See **adverb.**

folk etymology. 1. The alteration, in popular usage, of an unfamiliar word to a more familiar form (as with *crayfish,* which derives from the French *crevisse* [crab] but was changed to the unrelated *-fish*). **2.** A popular misconception about the origin of a word (e.g., the false notion that *posh* derives from "port outward, starboard home").

form class. See **part of speech.**

formulaic subjunctive. See **subjunctive,** *n.*

form word. See *function word* under **word.**

fragment. A group of words that, although written as a sentence, doesn't constitute a grammatically complete sentence {We took a break for lunch at noon.

*Because we were hungry.}.—Also termed *sentence fragment*; *fragmentary sentence*; *period fault*.

free morpheme. See **morpheme.**

fronting. See **inversion.**

full sentence. See **sentence.**

full verb. See *lexical verb* under **verb.**

function. The grammatical role that a word or group of words plays in a sentence. For example, an adjective's function is to modify a noun element; a preposition's function is to relate its object to some other word in the sentence; and an adverb's function is to modify a verb, adjective, or other adverb.

functional change. See **functional variation.**

functional morpheme. See *function word* under **word.**

functional shift. 1. See **conversion. 2.** See **functional variation.**

functional variation. The ability of a word or phrase to be used in different parts of speech without a change of form.—Also termed *functional shift*; *shift*; *functional change*. Cf. **conversion.**

function word. See **word.**

fused participle. A gerund used after a noun element that would more properly be a possessive adjective. In *the author having full rights to the work means you must ask the author for permission*, the participle *having* is fused with the preceding noun to form the subject *the author having*. Traditional grammarians prefer *the author's having full rights to the work means . . . .* See § 158.

future-perfect tense. See **tense.**

future tense. See **tense.**

Garner's Law of Loanwords. The principle that the more arcane or technical a loanword is, the more likely it is to retain a foreign plural, diacritical marks, and italics, and that the more common it becomes, the more likely it is to lose them. Corollary: if the loanword becomes widespread, it typically loses italics first, diacritical marks second, and a foreign plural last.

gender /jen-dər/. **1.** A system of dividing nouns and pronouns into sets according to their morphology regardless of the characteristics of the things denoted, so that in Spanish *un vestido* (= a dress) is masculine and *una cartera* (= a purse) is feminine. Some languages also have the neuter and common genders. **2.** A property indicating the sex or sexlessness of something denoted by a noun or pronoun, or described by an adjective. In English, only a few words reflect a referent's sex. Among them are the pronouns *he* and *she*, nouns such as *bull* and *heifer, fiancé* and *fiancée*, and adjectives such as *distrait* and *distraite* (although the feminine forms of adjectives are rapidly disappearing).

▸ **common gender.** The gender of a noun element that names a person or animal without indicating sex {adviser} {author} {orator} {postal carrier}.—Also termed *indefinite gender.*

▸ **feminine gender.** The gender of a noun or pronoun indicating female sex {sister} {mother} {aunt} {she} {her}.

▸ **indefinite gender.** See *common gender.*

▸ **masculine gender.** The gender of a noun or pronoun indicating male sex {brother} {father} {uncle} {he} {him}.

▸ **neuter gender.** The gender of a noun or pronoun indicating absence of sex {it} {airplane} {seat} {engraving} {book}.

generalization. The broadening of a word's meaning over time. For example, *pigeon* originally referred to a young dove but now refers to any bird of the whole family. Cf. **specialization.**

generic, *adj.* (Of an expression) referring to an entire class or kind and not just to one or several specific individuals. Context typically determines whether a term is being used generically {the cockatoo is an Australian parrot} or specifically {the cockatoo escaped from its cage}.

genitive /jen-ə-tiv/, *n.* The case used to show a thing's source {the car's exhaust}, a trait or characteristic {women's intuition}, or possession or ownership {our new house}. In English, the genitive case is identical to the possessive case. With animate nouns, the genitive is generally indicated through inflection—the addition of *-'s* for a singular {boy's} or *-s'* for a plural {boys'}. With inanimate nouns, the *of*-genitive is most common {the purpose of the remark}. See **possessive.**

▸ **genitive of measure.** A possessive used idiomatically to indicate time, distance, or value, as a shorter form than an *of*-genitive would produce—so that *time of two weeks* becomes *two weeks' time* {an hour's labor} {a day's journey} {a month's notice} {a dollar's worth}.

▸ **genitive of origin.** A possessive used to indicate source instead of possession {Teuscher's chocolates} {Shakespeare's sonnets}.

▸ **group genitive.** A genitive construction in which the possessive *'s* is added to the end of a full noun phrase instead of to the head {my mother-in-law's dress}. Many such constructions are faulty {*the man down the street's car} {the Duchess of York's son}.

▸ **independent genitive.** See *independent possessive* under **possessive.**

▸ *of*-genitive. An *of*-construction by which the idea of possession, ownership, quantity, or close relationship is indicated {the plays of Shakespeare} {the role of the publisher} {the roar of the lion} {a bushel of corn}.—Also termed *periphrastic genitive; periphrastic possessive; phrasal genitive.*

▸ **partitive genitive.** An *of*-genitive used in expressing a quantity {a gallon of milk} {a cupful of sugar} {a pint of beer}.

▸ **periphrastic genitive.** See *of-genitive.*

▸ **phrasal genitive.** See *of-genitive.*

genitive case. See *possessive case* under **case.**

gerund /jer-ənd/. A present participle (ending in -*ing*) used as a noun. A gerund may be another verb's subject {traveling makes me tired}, another verb's object {I enjoy your singing}, a noun complement {my hobby is collecting stamps}, or a preposition's object {the storm prevented me from attending}.—Also termed *verbal noun.* Cf. **participle.**

▸ **perfect gerund.** A gerund form that indicates completed action {I regret having gone there} {she remembers having been seen by him}.—Also termed *present-perfect gerund.*

▸ **present gerund.** A gerund that suggests timelessness, that is, connoting past, present, future, or continuing action or status {walking through museums is a great pleasure} {being ignored can be a huge annoyance}.

▸ **present-perfect gerund.** See *perfect gerund.*

gerund phrase. See **phrase.**

get-passive. A passive-voice construction consisting of the verb *get* plus a past participle (as opposed to the more frequent *be* plus a past participle) {he got rejected}.

good grammar. See **grammar.**

gradable, *adj.* (Of an adjective or adverb) capable of being sorted into a series of degrees, such as positive, comparative, and superlative.

gradable adjective. See **adjective.**

gradable antonyms. See **antonym.**

grammar /gram-ər/. **1.** A language's structure and system for oral and written communication; specif., a conventional system of rules by which the speakers of a language form the expressions that belong to the language. **2.** The set of rules and notions about the standard use of a language. **3.** The field of linguistics concerned with a language's morphology and syntax, and sometimes also with phonology and semantics. **4.** The study of how a given language operates, esp. in its standard form.

▸ **bad grammar.** The use of a construction, inflectional form, or dialectal idiom not in accord with the accepted usage of educated people. Examples are double negatives {I don't have no money}, stigmatized words {I ain't got no money}, violations in agreement {we was there}, incorrect cases {me and John went to see Sally and he} {please give it to Sally or I}, and catachreses {if I had of went there, I would of seen it}.

▸ **descriptive grammar.** The synchronic study of how speakers (and, to a much lesser extent, writers) actually use a given language, with a decided agnosticism about whether any given grammatical construction might be preferable to another.

▸ **good grammar.** The use of constructions, inflectional forms, and idioms that are conventional among educated people.

▸ **historical grammar.** The diachronic study of a given language, the development of its grammatical constructions and concepts, and the evolution of its syntax and word forms.

▸ **prescriptive grammar.** The study of how speakers and (esp.) writers of a standard language can use it most effectively. Ideally, a prescriptive approach is based on a sound knowledge of how native speakers of the language actually use it—or else the approach is of little value.

grammatical, *adj.* **1.** Of, relating to, or involving grammar. **2.** In accord with the traditional rules of grammar, rightly understood. Cf. **lexical.**

grammatical category. See **part of speech.**

grammatical function. 1. The type of role that a given word performs in a sentence, as fitted into a known category. **2.** A category for which some words are inflected, such as case, gender, number, definiteness, person, tense, mood, and aspect. See **function.**

grammatical morpheme. See *bound morpheme* under **morpheme.**

group genitive. See **genitive.**

group possessive. See **possessive.**

group preposition. See *phrasal preposition* under **preposition.**

group verbal. See **verbal,** *n.*

half conjunction. See *conjunctive adverb* under **adverb.**

hapax legomenon /**hap**-aks lə-**gom**-ə-nən/, *n.* **1.** A word or phrase found only once in the written record of a language. **2.** A word or phrase found only once in the work of a particular author.

haplology /ha-**plo**-lə-jee/. The contraction of a word by omitting an internal sound or syllable that is identical or similar to another (as with the pronunciation "deteriate" for *deteriorate*, "meterology" for *meteorology*, or "prob'ly" for *probably*).—**haplologic,** *adj.*

head. 1. The key word in a grammatical unit; esp., the grammatically central word in a particular phrase {large red-brick house} {played furiously}. **2.** The main constituent of a compound word, the other constituents being its modifiers {armchair} {newspaper}. **3.** The notional (principal) verb in a verb phrase {has been considered}.

helper. See **auxiliary verb.**

helping verb. See **auxiliary verb.**

heteronym. 1. A word that is spelled like another word but has a different meaning and is pronounced differently. For instance, *lead* can mean "to guide" (/leed/) or "a metallic element" (/led/). Similarly, *alternate* can mean "the next choice" (/**awl**-tər-nit/) or "to switch back and forth" (/**awl**-tər-nayt/). **2.** A phrase referring to a thing that is called by an entirely different name in a different geographical area. For example, an apple coated with hardened red sugar syrup is called a "candy apple" in New York and a "taffy apple" in Pennsylvania. **3.** A word that has the same meaning as another but is not written similarly and has a different origin. *Bucket* and *pail*, for instance, refer to the same object, but *bucket* derives from Anglo-Norman, while the precise origin of *pail* is unknown— though it may derive from Old French.—**heteronymous,** *adj.*

historical grammar. See **grammar.**

historical-present tense. See **tense.**

homograph /**ho**-mə-graf *or* **hoh**-/. A word that is spelled the same as another but is pronounced differently (e.g., *minute* [*n.*] /**min**-ət/ vs. *minute* [*adj.*] /mɪ-n[**y**]oot/).—**homographic,** *adj.*

homonym /**hom**-ə-nim *or* **hoh**-mə-/. **1.** A word that is spelled and pronounced the same as another word but has a different meaning and usu. a different origin (e.g., *riverbank, savings bank*). **2.** A word that has the same pronunciation as another word but is spelled differently and has a different meaning, such as *taut–taught, tea–tee,* and *there–their–they're.*—Also termed (in sense 2) *homophone.*

homophone /**hom**-ə-fohn *or* **hoh**-mə-/. **1.** A word that sounds like another but is spelled differently (e.g., *there, their,* and *they're* are homophones). —Also termed *homonym.* **2.** A letter or combination of letters denoting the same sound as a dissimilar letter or set of letters. For example, *-ea-* and *-ie-* have the same sound in *tear* and *tier,* the short *-e-* and *-ea-* sound alike in *led* and *lead,* the *-au-* in *taut* sounds like the *-augh-* in *taught,* and the *-e-* in *vinegar* sounds like the *-u-* in *dug.*

hybrid /**hɪ**-brid/. A word whose elements have roots in more than one language. For instance, *automobile* derives partly from the Greek *autos,* partly from the Latin *mobilis.*

hypallage /hɪ-**pal**-ə-jee/. A figure of speech in which the proper subject is displaced by what would logically be the object (if it were named directly), as in *a careless cigarette* (it's not the cigarette that's careless but the smoker) or *educated speech* (it's not the speech that's educated but the speaker).

hypercorrection. The erroneous use of a word or form resulting from a misdirected effort to use what is believed to be a grammatically correct form (e.g., saying *I* when the objective case *me* is called for, as in **between you and I* instead of *between you and me*).

hyphaeresis /hɪ-**fer**-ə-sis/. The omission of a syllable or sound from within a word (as when *over* is made *o'er* or *heaven* is made *heav'n*).—Also termed *syncope*. See **syncope.**

hyponym. A narrowed synonym—that is, a word that denotes one type of a broader genus denoted by a more general synonym. Hence *scarlet* is a hyponym of *red*, *bedroom* is a hyponym of *room*, and *noun* is a hyponym of *word*. Cf. **superordinate.**

hypotaxis /hɪ-poh-**tak**-sis/. The subordinate relationship that a dependent clause has with an independent clause.—**hypotactic,** *adj.*

idiolect /**id**-ee-ə-lekt/. The language traits of a particular person, influenced by many conditions such as age, sex, geographic area, and level of education.

idiom. 1. An expression characteristic of a particular culture and language; a group of words that bear a peculiar sense in a specific language {to put up with} {to bring about} {to come by [= obtain]} {to set about [= begin]}. **2.** Loosely, a language or dialect used by a specific group of people {the Spanish idiom}. See **modal idiom.**—**idiomatic,** *adj.*

illative conjunction. See *conjunctive adverb* under **adverb.**

illative coordinating conjunction. See *final conjunction* under **conjunction.**

illeism /**il**-ee-iz-əm/. The act or an instance of referring to oneself in the third person, as by using one's own name {let me tell you what Bob thinks [Bob is speaking]} or by using a third-person pronoun {he thinks this problem has no easy solution [Bob is still speaking]}. Often thought to be silly or pretentious in Modern English, illeism is sometimes used in self-mockery.

illiteracy. 1. Traditionally, a serious departure from Standard English committed only by uneducated people {*he done real good} {*it don't make me no nevermind}. **2.** Inability to read and write. **3.** More broadly, lack of education; esp., ignorance of literature. See **vulgarism.**—**illiterate,** *adj.*

immediate constituent. See **constituent.**

imperative /im-**per**-ə-tiv/, *adj.* (Of verbs) expressing a command {come here}, prohibition {don't touch that}, request {help me a minute}, warning {stay out or else!}, or the like. An imperative is normally a clause lacking an express subject and beginning with an uninflected verb. Cf. **subjunctive, interrogative** & **indicative.**

▸ **vocative imperative.** An imperative that begins or ends with an address form {Hyuk, get over here!}.

imperative mood. See **mood.**

imperative sentence. See **sentence.**

imperfect aspect. See **aspect.**

impersonal pronoun. See *indefinite pronoun* under **pronoun.**

impersonal sentence. See **sentence.**

inanimate noun. See **noun.**

inclusive *we.* A plural first-person pronoun that is intended to include the reader or listener in the statement.

incomplete sentence. See **sentence.**

indefinite adjective. See **adjective.**

indefinite article. See **article.**

indefinite gender. See *common gender* under **gender.**

indefinite noun. See **noun.**

indefinite pronoun. See **pronoun.**

independent adverb. See *sentence adverb* under **adverb.**

independent clause. See **clause.**

independent element. A word, phrase, or clause outside the grammatical structure of the sentence in which it appears, as when it is a nominative of address, an interjection, a sentence adverb, a transitional term, or an absolute construction.

independent genitive. See *independent possessive* under **possessive.**

independent possessive. See **possessive.**

indicative /in-**dik**-ə-tiv/, *adj.* (Of a verb) expressing a plain statement—as contrasted with the terms *subjunctive, imperative,* and *interrogative.* Cf. **subjunctive, imperative** & **interrogative.**

indicative mood. See **mood.**

indicator. See **marker.**

indirect discourse. See **discourse** (1).

indirect object. See **object.**

indirect question. See **question.**

indirect speech. See *indirect discourse* under **discourse** (1).

infinitive /in-**fin**-ə-tiv/, *n.* A verb's uninflected form, almost always preceded by *to*, that is not affected by voice, tense, person, or number but that may take objects and adverbs. For instance, in *the teacher started to grade the exams, started* is a finite verb that is limited by the singular noun *teacher,* the past tense, and the indicative mood, but the infinitive *to grade* is wholly unaffected. An infinitive can also readily function as a noun (as in *to dream is to create*). An infinitive is also called a *nonfinite verb* or an *infinitive verb.*—**infinitival** /in-fin-i-**tɪ**-vəl/, *adj.*

▸ **bare infinitive.** An infinitive in which *to* is omitted. This type almost always follows an auxiliary verb {Rupert would enjoy this view}, although *ought* is an exception {that ought to do the job} and a bare infinitive may follow the verbs *dare* and *help* {he dared not do it} {I helped look after the baby}. A bare infinitive is also used frequently in dependent clauses {we watched Edward wash his car}.—Also termed *plain infinitive; pure infinitive; simple infinitive; present stem; unmarked infinitive.*

▸ **complementary infinitive.** An infinitive that completes the sense of the predicate verb but is neither an objective nor a subjective complement {we are to sing tomorrow}.

▸ **marked infinitive.** An infinitive in which the word *to* is included. *To* is sometimes called the "mark" or "sign" of the infinitive.

▸ **perfect infinitive.** An infinitive that indicates action that has occurred before that of the principal verb {he is known to have been a member of that gang} {the manuscript seems to have been edited recently}.—Also termed *present-perfect infinitive.*

▸ **plain infinitive.** See *bare infinitive.*

▸ **present infinitive.** An infinitive suggesting action simultaneous with or later than that of the principal verb {to know her is to like her} {her not-so-secret ambition was to become president} {we asked him to play with us again next week}.

▸ **present-perfect infinitive.** See *perfect infinitive.*

▸ **pure infinitive.** See *bare infinitive.*

▸ **simple infinitive.** See *bare infinitive.*

▸ **split infinitive.** An infinitive in which one or more words are inserted between *to* and the verb (e.g., *to constantly demand* instead of *to demand constantly*). See § 148.

▶ **unmarked infinitive.** See *bare infinitive*.

infinitive phrase. See **phrase**.

infinitive verb. See **infinitive**.

infix /in-fiks/, *n.* **1.** A sound element, such as a letter or syllable, inserted within a word. In a string of suffixes, as in *cleanliness* where *-ly* and *-ness* are both suffixes, some grammarians treat all but the last-added syllable as infixes. Otherwise, infixes are comparatively rare in English. **2.** A word inserted between the parts of a compound word, often typical of slang (e.g., *some-damn-where, absobloo-dylutely*).—**infixation**, *n.*

inflect, *vb.* To change the ending of (a word) to express varying grammatical function. Whereas Latin is a highly inflected language, English is little inflected.

inflected possessive. See **possessive**.

inflection /in-**flek**-shən/. **1.** A grammatical change in a word's form, through declension (e.g., *woman–woman's, women–women's*), conjugation (e.g., *drive–drove–driven*), or comparison (e.g., *big–bigger–biggest*). **2.** The act of inflecting words.—Also spelled *inflexion*.—**inflectional**, *adj.*

▶ **irregular inflection.** An inflection that does not follow strict morphological rules and is therefore anomalous, as with the plurals for *man* and *woman* or the past tense and past participle of *go*.

▶ **regular inflection.** An inflection that follows strict morphological rules, as with the plurals for *cat* and *dog* or the past tense for *beg*.

inflectional affix. See **affix**.

inflectional morphology /in-**flek**-shə-nəl mor-**fol**-ə-jee/. See **accidence** (2).

inflectional suffix. See **suffix**.

inflexion. See **inflection**.

initialism /i-**nish**-ə-li-zəm/. A word or abbreviation that is (1) formed from the initial letters of other words or syllables and (2) pronounced by sounding out the letters individually {FBI} {VP}.—Also termed *alphabetism*. Cf. **acronym**.

inner complement. See **complement**.

intensifier. An adverb that cannot modify a verb but that always modifies either an adjective {he worked very hard} or an adverb {she swam quite fast}, usu. by strengthening the characteristic described—though *rather* and *somewhat* can moderate the characteristic. Examples are *rather, quite,* and *very.* See § 220.—Also termed *intensifying adverb.*

intensifying adverb. See **intensifier**.

intensifying pronoun. See *intensive pronoun* under **pronoun**.

intensive pronoun. See **pronoun.**

interjection /in-tər-**jek**-shən/. A word or group of words that are grammatically independent of a sentence and that convey an exclamation, usu. with a mild to strong but always sudden emotion {oh!} {ouch!} {hurray!}.

interrogative /in-tə-**rog**-ə-tiv/, *adj.* Expressing a question (as in *who is making that awful noise?* or *why didn't the mail come today?*). Cf. **subjunctive, imperative** & **indicative.**

interrogative, *n.* A question. See *interrogative sentence* under **sentence.**

interrogative adjective. See **adjective.**

interrogative adverb. See **adverb.**

interrogative pronoun. See **pronoun.**

interrogative sentence. See **sentence.**

interrupter. Any parenthetical matter, such as an aside, that breaks one main thought of the sentence {we listened closely to the (ahem) maestro} {Bill, however, had a different view} {in *Lamie v. United States Tr.,* 540 U.S. 526 (2004), Justice Scalia noted his rejection of legislative history as bearing on his vote}.

intonation. The pitch variation of speech; spoken melody.

intonation pattern. The rhythmic pattern of natural speech, including stressed syllables, pitches, and pauses.

intransitive verb. See **verb.**

introductory adverb. See *conjunctive adverb* under **adverb.**

intrusive *r.* An unetymological *r*-sound added in some dialects between a word ending in a vowel and another word that begins with one {the idear is to make a little money}.

intrusive schwa. The insertion of a schwa sound by epenthesis in some dialects, as with the standard two-syllable *athlete* mispronounced /**ath**-ə-leet/ or the one-syllable *film* mispronounced /**fil**-əm/. See **epenthesis.**

invariable noun. See **noun.**

inversion. The changing of words from their ordinary positions within a sentence; esp., a sentence arrangement that puts all or part of the predicate before the subject {up the hill came Jack}.—Also termed (when the movement is to the beginning of a sentence) *fronting.*

irregular, *adj.* (Of a word or phrase) not conforming to the usual rules of grammatical formation. For example, an irregular noun forms its plural in some way other than adding -*s* or -*es* (e.g., *woman* becomes *women; phenomenon* becomes *phenomena*). Cf. **regular.**

irregular inflection. See **inflection.**

irregular plural. See **plural.**

irregular verb. See **verb.**

irreversible binomial. A set phrase consisting of two coordinated elements whose order cannot be switched while maintaining standard idiom {spaghetti and meatballs} {cup and saucer} {fish and chips}.

joint possessive. See *group possessive* under **possessive.**

language, *n.* **1.** A particular system of conventional signs by which human beings communicate. **2.** The ability of human beings to communicate through such a system.

learned loanword. See **loanword.**

lexeme. A unit in the vocabulary or lexicon of a language, whether it is a single word {paper}, part of a word {auto-} {non-}, a phrase {pass the buck} {keel over}, or a clipping {bus} {flu}.—**lexemic,** *adj.*

lexical, *adj.* **1.** Of, relating to, or involving a word or words. **2.** Of, relating to, or involving the vocabulary of a language. **3.** Of, relating to, or involving a dictionary. Cf. **grammatical.**

lexical category. See **part of speech.**

lexical morpheme. 1. See *free morpheme* under **morpheme. 2.** See *content word* under **word.**

lexical verb. See **verb.**

lexicology /lek-si-**kol**-ə-jee/. The study of the derivation and meaning of words in a language.—**lexicological,** *adj.*

lexicon /lek-si-kən/. **1.** The vocabulary of an individual, of those who speak a common language, of a branch of knowledge, or of a language. **2.** A dictionary. **3.** The mental dictionary that speakers of a language unconsciously acquire as they learn a language.

lexis, *n.* The semantic units of a language (morphemes, words, and idioms).

ligature, *n.* A written symbol (such as æ or œ) made from two letters that are visually linked. Cf. **digraph.**

limiting adjective. See **adjective.**

linguistic genotype. See *deep structure* under **structure.**

linguistic phenotype. See *surface structure* under **structure.**

linguistics. The systematic study of language and its structure, including morphology, syntax, phonetics, semantics, sociolinguistics, dialectology, psycholinguistics, lexicography, computational studies, and applied linguistics.

linking verb. See **verb**.

loan translation. An expression made by translating a foreign word or (more typically) phrase into the host language.—Also termed *calque*.

loanword. A word borrowed from a foreign language and naturalized.

> ▸ **learned loanword** /lər-nəd/. A bookish foreignism used in educated circles and typically retaining some of its foreignness, as by being italicized and preserving one or more characteristics of the originating language, such as pronunciation, diacritical marks, inflections, and sense-associations {*Festschrift–Festschriften*} {*bête noire*} {prolegomenon–prolegomena}. See **Garner's Law of Loanwords**.

local possessive. See **possessive**.

long passive voice. See **passive voice**.

long syllable. See **syllable**.

loose appositive. See *nonrestrictive appositive* under **appositive**.

macron /**may**-kron/. In some pronunciation systems, the long straight line placed over long vowels to show that they are to be so pronounced /lī-**bā**-shən/.

main clause. See *independent clause* under **clause**.

main verb. See **verb**.

major sentence. See *complete sentence* under **sentence**.

majuscule, *n*. A capital letter.

malapropism /**mal**-ə-prop-iz-əm/. The misuse of a word or phrase that produces a humorous effect.

mandative subjunctive. See **subjunctive**, *n*.

manner adverb. See **adverb**.

marked infinitive. See **infinitive**.

marker. A word that identifies a particular grammatical element that follows it. Hence determiners are noun markers; auxiliaries are markers of principal verbs; prepositions are phrase markers; relative pronouns are clause markers, as are subordinating conjunctions; and interrogative words such as *how, what, where, who,* and *why* are question markers.—Also termed *indicator*.

> ▸ **plural marker.** An adjective or indefinite pronoun that indicates more than one, such as *two, few, several,* and *both*.—Also termed *plural indicator*.

> ▸ **portion marker.** An adjective or indefinite pronoun that indicates an amount of a thing, such as *half, much,* or *little*.—Also termed *portion indicator*.

▶ **singular marker.** An adjective or indefinite pronoun that indicates only one: *each, one, anyone, someone,* etc.—Also termed *singular indicator.*

masculine gender. See **gender.**

mass noun. See **noun.**

material noun. See *mass noun* under **noun.**

matrix clause. See **clause.**

melioration /meel-yə-**ray**-shən *or* mee-lee-ə-/. The elevation of a word's meaning or the improvement of its connotations. Cf. **pejoration (1).**—**meliorative,** *adj.*

metaphor /**met**-ə-fohr *or* -fər/. A figure of speech in which one thing is called by the name of something else (e.g., *welcome to my modest Taj Mahal*) or is said to be that other thing (e.g., *life is a cabaret*); an implicit comparison. Cf. **simile.**

metathesis /mə-**tath**-ə-səs/. The transposition of successive sounds or letters in a word (e.g., pronouncing *comfortable* /kəmf-tər-bəl/ instead of /kəm-fər-tə-bəl/, or misspelling *chipotle* as **chipolte.*—**metathetic,** *adj.*

metonymy /mə-**ton**-ə-mee/. Substitution of an attribute or other suggestive word for a name (e.g., referring to the president as *the White House* or rich people as *moneybags*).—**metonymic,** *adj.*

Middle English. The English language used from about 1100 to 1500.

middle verb. See **verb.**

minor sentence. See *incomplete sentence* under **sentence.**

misplaced modifier. See **modifier.**

modal, *n.* See *modal auxiliary verb* under **auxiliary verb.**

▶ **double modal.** See **double modal.**

modal auxiliary verb. See **auxiliary verb.**

modal idiom. An expression that behaves somewhat like a modal auxiliary verb; specif., a form such as *had better* {we'd better leave}, *would rather* {she would rather not go}, *are to be* {we're to be there at eight o'clock}, and *have go to* or *have to* {we have to stay here}. See **idiom.**

modality. See **mood.**

modal tense. See *potential tense* under **tense.**

mode. See **mood.**

Modern English. The English language in use since about 1500.

modificand. A word, phrase, or clause modified by another word, phrase, or clause.

modification structure. See **structure.**

modifier. A word or group of words that describes, limits, or qualifies the meaning of another word or group of words; esp., an adjective or adverb, or its equivalent in the form of a phrase or clause.

▶ **compound modifier.** See *phrasal adjective* under **adjective.**

▶ **dangling modifier.** See **dangler.**

▶ **misplaced modifier.** A modifier so placed that it appears to modify some word other than the one that it was probably or obviously intended to modify {dirty men's golf shoes littered the bag room} {I saw the Statue of Liberty flying into Newark} {once disfavored, English teachers now approve of an occasional split infinitive—if it is essentially unavoidable}.

▶ **postpositive modifier.** See *postpositive adjective* under **adjective.**

▶ **resumptive modifier.** A sentence-ending modifier that repeats a word or idea from the main clause and elaborates or qualifies it {Twain attacked representative government with a fierce humor, fierce because in Congress he could see how men of sawdust and solder could make a democratic-republican government a corruption and an absurdity}.

▶ **sentence modifier.** See *sentence adverb* under **adverb.**

▶ **squinting modifier.** A modifier ill-advisedly placed so that it might modify either the element preceding it or the element following it {the marble that was damaged today is being discounted} {she pledged during the summer to help in our fundraising efforts}.—Also termed *squinting construction.*

▶ **summative modifier.** A modifier that wraps up the idea in the main clause by bringing it to a conclusion {the taxpayers' initiative was to lower property taxes—an idea long thought to be unworkable} {imagine having your own actions in any given situation universalized for all of humankind—a version of Kant's categorical imperative}.

monophthong /**mon**-əf-thong/. A single vowel sound, as in *cat, sit, sleet.*

monotransitive verb. See **verb.**

mood. A conjugational category that shows something about the speaker's attitude toward the action, as by expressing a fact, a command, a wish, an assumption, a desirability, or a possibility (e.g., *he writes* [factual attitude = indicative mood]; *if he wrote* [conditional attitude = subjunctive mood]; and *write!* [directing attitude = imperative mood]).—Also termed *mode; modality.*

▶ **imperative mood.** The mood used in expressing a command {go to your places!}, making a request {please call me next week}, or giving directions {open carefully and fold the flaps back}.

▶ **indicative mood.** The mood used in making statements of fact or opinion and in asking questions.

▶ **subjunctive mood.** Traditionally speaking, the mood used in expressing (1) conditional statements that are contrary to fact or contain a strong element of doubt {if I were Harry, I'd . . .}, (2) wishes or prayers {I wish I were in that position}, (3) motions, resolutions, demands, recommendations, commands, or requests involving *that*-clauses {I demand that he remove the fence immediately}, and (4) archaically, concessions {though this be incorrect, all must consider it}.

morpheme. The smallest meaningful unit into which a word can be divided {un-mean-ing-ful-ly} {anti-dis-establish-ment-arian-ism}.—**morphemic,** *adj.*

▶ **bound morpheme.** A morpheme that never occurs except by being attached to another morpheme {dogs} {disheveled}.—Also termed *clitic; grammatical morpheme.*

▶ **free morpheme.** A morpheme that can occur by itself, esp. as a stand-alone word in a sentence {the} {notebook} {stationery}.—Also termed *lexical morpheme.*

▶ **functional morpheme.** See *function word* under **word.**

▶ **lexical morpheme. 1.** See *free morpheme.* **2.** See *content word* under **word.**

morphology /mor-fo-lə-jee/. **1.** The study of internal word structures and of word formation in a language, esp. as regards inflection, derivation, and compounding. **2.** The means by which words are formed in a language. See **word formation.**

▶ **inflectional morphology.** See **accidence (2).**

multiword verb. See *phrasal verb* under **verb.**

mutation plural. See **plural.**

negation. The introduction of a negative—esp. *not, -n't,* or *un-* —into a construction.

negative, *adj.* (Of a clause or sentence) expressing the absence or nonexistence of some thing or condition {they weren't cold}, or else the falsity of a proposition {that was not a sincere letter}.

negative cleft sentence. See **sentence.**

negative question. See **question.**

neoclassical compound. See **compound.**

neologism /nee-ol-ə-jiz-əm/, *n.* A newly coined word.—**neologistic,** *adj.*

neologizing, *n.* The creation of new words, esp. when not based on existing morphemes.—**neologize** /nee-ol-ə-jɪz/, *vb.*

neuter gender. See **gender.**

nominal, *adj.* Of, relating to, or involving a noun element.

nominal, *n.* A noun, noun phrase, or noun clause—that is, a *noun element.*

▶ **predicate nominal.** See **predicate nominative.**

nominal clause. See *noun clause* under **clause.**

nominal element. See **noun element.**

nominalization. 1. The conversion into a noun of a word or phrase that is not ordinarily a noun, esp. by suffixation {prioritization} {eloquentness}. **2.** A word so converted. In sense 2, when the word displaces a verb, a nominalization is also termed a *zombie noun* (e.g., *protect* is replaced by the phrase *provide protection to*—*protection* being the zombie noun).—**nominalize,** *vb.*

nominal phrase. See *noun phrase* under **phrase.**

nominative, *adj.* (Of a pronoun [or, not quite correctly, the noun]) being the subject of a sentence.—Also termed *subjective.*

nominative, *n.* The case of a pronoun that functions as the subject of a sentence.

nominative absolute. See **absolute construction.**

nominative case. See **case.**

nominative of address. See **vocative,** *n.*

nonaction verb. See *stative verb* under **verb.**

noncount noun. See **noun.**

nonessential appositive. See *nonrestrictive appositive* under **appositive.**

nonessential clause. See *nonrestrictive clause* under **clause.**

nonfinite verb. See **verb** & **infinitive.**

nonlimiting clause. See *nonrestrictive clause* under **clause.**

nonreferential *it.* See **expletive** (1).

nonreferential *there.* See **expletive** (1).

nonrestrictive, *adj.* (Of the modifier of a noun element) supplying additional information that is omissible. Cf. **restrictive.**

nonrestrictive appositive. See **appositive.**

nonrestrictive clause. See **clause.**

nonsentence. 1. A group of words not constituting a grammatically complete sentence {the boy down the street}. Cf. *full sentence* under **sentence. 2.** See *verbless sentence* under **sentence.**

notional concord. See **synesis.**

notional passive. A construction that contains a passive idea even though it lacks a passive-voice verb, esp. through the use of an ergative verb {your book will ship [= be shipped] on Tuesday}.

notional verb. See *principal verb* under **verb.**

noun /nown/. A word that names a thing, whether tangible or intangible; the part of speech that denotes thingness and can serve as the subject of a sentence. There are several ways to classify nouns: common vs. proper, count vs. mass, and abstract vs. concrete.

▸ **abstract noun.** A noun that names an idea, quality, condition, or action that cannot be physiologically sensed (e.g., *administration, courage, fear, husbandry, inertia, intelligence, profundity, tenderness, truth, warfare*).

▸ **adverbial noun.** See **adverbial objective.**

▸ **agent noun.** A noun that denotes someone or something that performs the action of a verb. Agent nouns typically end in *-er* {employer} {worker} or *-or* {illustrator} {sculptor}. Cf. *recipient noun.*

▸ **animate noun.** A noun that denotes a living thing {boy} {girl} {bull} {cow}.

▸ **attribute noun.** See *predicate noun* (1).

▸ **attributive noun.** A noun placed immediately before another noun and used adjectivally to denote a characteristic of it (e.g., *dawn patrol, harvest moon, newspaper reporter*). The noun used attributively functions as an adjective.—Also termed *noun adjunct.*

▸ **bounded noun.** A noun that in the singular is ordinarily preceded by an article or other determiner {ball, hall, mall, wall}.

▸ **collective noun.** The name of a group considered as a unit, as with *club, faculty, flock, herd, party, team.*

▸ **common noun.** A noun that informally names a generic class or type of person, place, or thing (e.g., *apple, chair, desk, engineer, highway*). It is capitalized only if it is the first word in a sentence.

▸ **compound noun.** A noun formed from two or more words combined—usu. written as a single word {deskbook} {football} {typescript}, but also sometimes as a hyphenated word {father-in-law} {case-in-chief} or as a noun phrase consisting of separate words {credit card} {editor in chief} {ice cream}.

▸ **concrete noun.** The name of a person, place, or thing perceivable by one or more of the senses {cologne} {fence} {films} {Kansas City} {pianist} {screwdriver}.

▸ **count noun.** A common noun that names something that comes in discrete, countable units {car} {hammer}, whether or not the noun has an explicit plural form to contrast with a singular {buffalo} {fish}.—Also termed *countable noun.*

▸ **definite noun.** A count noun that, being preceded by a definite article, refers to a particular referent or set of referents {the cow} {the cattle}.

▸ **inanimate noun.** A noun that denotes something that isn't living {bag} {cart} {orthodoxy}.

▸ **indefinite noun.** A count noun that, being preceded by an indefinite article or a zero article, refers to no particular thing or set of things {a cow} {cattle}.

▸ **invariable noun.** A noun that either is always singular {New York is a great city} or does not change its form when functioning as a plural as opposed to a singular because it is either always singular {linguistics is fun} or always plural {the scissors are on the table}.

▸ **mass noun.** A common noun that names unsegmented material in an undifferentiated body, pile, heap, or load; esp., a noun denoting something that does not come in countable units and that does not ordinarily accept an indefinite article or a plural inflection (e.g., *equipment, robustness*).—Also termed *noncount noun; material noun.*

▸ **material noun.** See *mass noun.*

▸ **noncount noun.** A common noun referring to an entity that neither can be counted nor can vary for number {milk} {salt} {air}.—Also termed *uncountable noun; mass noun.*

▸ **partitive noun.** A noun that when coupled with the preposition *of* creates a countable expression from a mass noun—examples being *bit* and *piece* {a bit of luck} {a piece of bad news}.—Also termed *noun of partition.*

▸ **predicate noun. 1.** A noun, noun phrase, or pronoun functioning as a subjective complement {Caroline is a lawyer}.—Also termed *attribute noun; predicate pronoun.* **2.** A noun functioning as an objective complement {they elected her chair}.

▸ **proper noun.** A noun that is the formal or official name of a specific person, place, or thing (e.g., *Paul McNamara, Buckingham Palace, the Hope Diamond*) and that is always capitalized, regardless of how it is used. A common noun may become a proper noun (e.g., *the ballpark* becomes *the Ballpark in Arlington*). Sometimes a proper noun may become a common noun (e.g., *sandwich* gets its name from its supposed inventor, the Earl of Sandwich).—Also termed *proper name.*

▸ **recipient noun.** A noun that denotes a person who receives some thing or action, or one for whom something is done. Cf. *agent noun.*

▸ **simple noun.** A noun not made by compounding {house} {paper} {vision}.

▸ **verbal noun.** See **gerund.**

▸ **zombie noun.** An abstract noun that obscures the agent of the action it denotes—esp. one ending in *-ion, -ence, -ance, -ity,* or *-ment.*—Also termed *nominalization.*

noun adjunct. See *attributive noun* under **noun.**

noun-banging. The unfortunate stylistic tendency to use several attributive nouns at once {the Department of Defense strategy defense tactic apologists argue otherwise}.

noun clause. See **clause.**

noun cluster. A noun and all its modifiers {the antiquarian books held at the HRC are invaluable [the noun *books* is modified by the article *the,* the attributive adjective *antiquarian,* and the relative clause (with a whiz-deletion) *held at the HRC*]}.

noun element. A noun, pronoun, noun phrase, or noun clause.—Also termed *substantive; nominal; nominal element.*

noun group. A construction that consists of a noun preceded by one or more single-word modifiers {he threw out his battered green canvas fishing hat}.

noun indicator. See **determiner.**

noun phrase. See **phrase.**

number. 1. The quality of a word as being (in Modern English) either singular or plural, as reflected in declension (e.g., *I–we*), conjugation (e.g., *say–says*), and agreement between different parts of speech (e.g., *this book–these books*). **2.** One of a series of symbols or words used in arranging or classifying quantities; esp., a numeral.—Also termed (in sense 2) *numeral.*

▸ **cardinal number.** A number as it is used in counting {one, two, three}.

▸ **ordinal number.** A numerical adjective used to indicate order {first, second, third}.

▸ **plural number.** The form of a noun, pronoun, or verb indicating that a reference is to more than one {the flowers are pleasingly varied} {they bloom throughout the cold months}.

▸ **singular number.** The form of a noun, pronoun, or verb indicating that a reference is to only one {the prospective hire is most promising} {someone texted me last night}.

numeral. See **number (2).**

numeral adjective. See *numeric adjective* under **adjective.**

numeric adjective. See **adjective.**

numerical adjective. See *numeric adjective* under **adjective.**

object. A noun element that either (1) is acted on by or receives the action of a verb, or (2) is the main noun in a prepositional phrase. An object does not control the inflection of a verb. Cf. **subject.**—**objective,** *adj.*

▸ **cognate object.** An object that is closely related etymologically to the verb of which it is an object {he drank a stiff drink} {she built a great building} {she died a good death}.

▸ **complementary object.** See *objective complement* under **complement.**

▸ **compound objects.** Two or more objects that are recipients of the action of one transitive verb {we traveled over mountains, lakes, and plains}.—Also termed *coordinate objects.*

▸ **direct object.** A noun element that denotes a thing or person that is necessarily involved in the action of a transitive verb and that completes the meaning of the predicate. The direct object is essential to the sentence's meaning; the sentence does not make sense if the transitive verb lacks a direct object {I lit a match}. In that example, *I lit* would make no sense without the direct object *a match.* In other sentences the meaning would change {I burned the soup}. That example would make sense without the direct object, *the soup,* but the sense would be quite different.—Also termed *object accusative; patient.*

▸ **indirect object.** A noun element that identifies a person or thing that is affected by a transitive verb, usu. as the recipient of the action but not immediately involved in the action; the first object after a ditransitive verb {bake your sister a cake}. In that example, the act of baking affects *your sister* (she will get a cake), but she is not what is baked, so *a cake* is the direct object and *your sister* is an indirect object. If the indirect object were excluded, the sentence would still make sense {bake a cake}. An indirect object can always be replaced by a prepositional phrase {bake a cake for your sister}. An indirect object always precedes the direct object—and normally it occurs only in a sentence having a direct object.

▸ **object of a gerund.** The noun element that receives the action of a gerund {teaching the seminar will be great fun} {we enjoyed hosting the party}.

▸ **object of an infinitive.** The noun element that receives the action of an infinitive {to admire her is inevitable} {the committee was formed specifically to investigate allegations}.

▸ **object of a preposition.** A noun element related to the grammatical structure of a sentence by a preposition {we'll be gone by midnight} {her daughter traveled with her} {I'm the guest of a friend}.

▸ **oblique object.** The object of a preposition {he hid under the stairs}.

object accusative. See *direct object* under **object.**

object complement. See complement.

objective /ob-jek-tiv/, n. See *objective case* under case.

objective attribute. See *objective complement* under complement.

objective case. See case.

objective complement. See complement.

objective predicate. See *objective complement* under complement.

object of a gerund. See object.

object of an infinitive. See object.

object of a preposition. See object.

oblique case. See case.

oblique object. See object.

of-genitive. See genitive.

Old English. The Anglo-Saxon language, used in England from around AD 450 to 1100.—Also termed *Anglo-Saxon.*

onomatopoeia /o-nə-mat-ə-**pee**-ə/. The effect of matching the sound to the sense of a word or phrase. Some words are formed by imitating the sound associated with the intended meaning, such as *buzz, cock-a-doodle-doo,* and *pop.*

open syllable. See syllable.

open word class. See word class.

oratio directa; oratio recta. See *direct discourse* under discourse (1).

oratio obliqua. See *indirect discourse* under discourse (1).

ordinal number. See number.

orthoepy /or-thə-we-pee *or* or-**thoh**-ə-pee/. 1. The study of the customary pronunciation of words, esp. what is considered correct. 2. The accepted or correct pronunciation of words.—**orthoepist,** *n.*

orthography /or-**thog**-rə-fee/. 1. The system for writing the words or sounds of a particular language. 2. The art of spelling words properly.—**orthographer,** *n.*

orthology /or-**thol**-ə-jee/. The art of using words properly.—**orthological,** *adj.*

outer complement. See complement.

overgeneralization. The creation of a nonstandard linguistic form by false analogy. Cf. clang association.

oxymoron. A figure of speech that is or seems to be a contradiction in terms (e.g., *jumbo shrimp; explicit allusion*). —**oxymoronic,** *adj.*

paradigm, *n.* A set of linguistic items that form mutually exclusive choices in particular syntactic roles; esp., a roster of conjugations or declensions that show a word in all its inflectional forms.—**paradigmatic** /pa-rə-dig-**mat**-ik/, *adj.*

parallelism, *n.* The use of successive grammatical constructions that correspond in structure, sound, meaning, etc.; the use of coordinate parts having the same grammatical form {she typed accurately, answered calls professionally, and presented herself impeccably}.—Also termed *parallel structure.*—**parallel,** *adj.*

parallel structure. See **parallelism.**

parataxis /pair-ə-**tak**-sis/. See **asyndeton.**

parenthetical element. A word or group of words that suspends the flow of a sentence to provide a transition, additional information, an aside, or some other interpolated idea.

parse, *vb.* To explain the construction of a sentence by describing the grammatical relationships within it; esp., to diagram a sentence according to the traditional Reed–Kellogg system.

participial adjective. See **adjective.**

participial phrase. See **phrase.**

participial verb. See **verb.**

participle. A verb form that may be used as either a verb or an adjective. Cf. **gerund.**—**participial,** *adj.*

▸ **past participle.** The inflected form of a verb (marked by an -*ed* ending in regular verbs) used to indicate action that has already occurred {canceled by one network, the show was picked up by a rival network} {the canceled show was picked up by a rival network}. A past participle may be used to express either the perfect tense (with the auxiliary *have*) {we have arrived} or the passive voice (with the auxiliary *be*) {he is expected to arrive any day now}.

▸ **perfect participle.** A past participle when used with *having* (in the active voice) {having learned from Harvey Penick, I will never be complacent} or *having been* (in the passive voice) {having been taught by Harvey Penick, I will never be complacent}.

▸ **present participle.** The inflected form of a verb (marked by an -*ing* ending in regular verbs) used to indicate action that is occurring {running past a stream, we saw an otter} {a young otter was playing in the running water}.

▸ **present-perfect participle.** The past participle when paired with the auxiliary *having* (in the active voice) {having considered your proposal, we are happy to accept it} or the auxiliaries *having been* (in the passive voice) {having been passed over last time, I hope I'll get the promotion this time}.

particle /pahr-ti-kəl/. A word or wordlike element that cannot be inflected, has little meaning, and serves other functions, usu. as an affix or part of a phrasal verb; specif., a small word (or an affix) that does not fit into any clear word class. In English, particles include prepositions used in phrasal verbs (as in *take in, take off, take over*, and *take up*); a few spatial adverbs (such as *aback, ahead, aside, away, back, in front*); prefixes such as *un-* (as in *pleasant–unpleasant*); and suffixes such as *-ness* (as in *good–goodness*).

partitive genitive. See **genitive.**

partitive noun. See **noun.**

part of speech. One of a class of words grouped according to function within a sentence and their inflectional characteristics. Traditionally, there are eight parts of speech in English: nouns, pronouns, adjectives, verbs, adverbs, prepositions, conjunctions, and interjections. Some grammarians add a ninth (articles).—Also termed *lexical category; grammatical category; word class; form class.*

passive clause. See **clause.**

passive voice. The voice formed with a *be*-verb and a past participle {the hamster was named Bernie} {he is being appointed secretary} {the theory has been accepted for centuries}. In the passive voice, the subject of the sentence does not perform the action of the predicate but is acted on, often by the object of a *by*-phrase {the role of Martha was played by Elizabeth Taylor}. See **voice.** Cf. **active voice.**

▸ **long passive voice.** A passive-voice construction in which the actor is specified in a prepositional phrase beginning with *by* {the book was read by Derek Jacobi}.

▸ **short passive voice.** A passive-voice construction in which the actor is omitted from the predicate {the book was read}.—Also termed *agentless passive; truncated passive.*

past participle. See **participle.**

past-perfect tense. See **tense.**

past subjunctive. See **subjunctive,** *n.*

past tense. See **tense.**

patient. See *direct object* under **object.**

pejoration /pee-jə-**ray**-shən *or* pej-ə-/. **1.** The depreciation, dilution, or erosion of a word's meaning; esp., a word's gradual acquisition of negative connotations or sometimes even denotations. For example, in Old English, the word *silly* meant "happy" or "blessed." In Middle English, the meaning changed to "innocent," then "feeble-minded" or "ignorant." Today it means "foolish." Cf.

melioration. 2. The depreciation of a word by adding a negative affix such as -*aster*. For example, a *poet* is merely one who writes verse; the word denotes nothing about quality. But a *poetaster* is a poet who produces trash.

perfect aspect. See **aspect.**

perfect gerund. See **gerund.**

perfect infinitive. See **infinitive.**

perfect participle. See **participle.**

perfect tense. 1. See *compound tense* under **tense. 2.** See *present-perfect tense* under tense. **3.** See *past-perfect tense* under **tense.**

period fault. See **fragment.**

peripheral adjective. See **adjective.**

periphrasis /pə-**rif**-rə-səs/. **1.** Circumlocution; roundabout wording, as when a cook is called *a practitioner of the culinary arts*. **2.** The use of a function word (e.g., *more, less*) instead of an inflection, esp. to express degrees of comparison (e.g., *more stupid* is the periphrastic alternative to *stupider*).—**periphrastic,** *adj.*

periphrastic comparative. See **comparative.**

periphrastic genitive. See *of-genitive* under **genitive.**

periphrastic modal. Any one of a set of complex modal verbs, such as *be able to* or *be about to.*

periphrastic possessive. See *of-genitive* under **genitive.**

periphrastic superlative. See **superlative.**

person. A category of declension (*I, you, he, she, it, we, you, they*) and conjugation (*am, are, is*) that specifies the person speaking (first person), spoken to (second person), or spoken about (third person).

personal adjective. See **adjective.**

personal pronoun. See **pronoun.**

phatic exchange. A rudimentary, superficial conversation made only for general purposes of social interaction and not for literal meaning. {Hello. How are you? Just fine, thanks. And you? Fine. Have a good day.}.

phoneme /**foh**-neem/. A language's smallest distinct sound unit that can distinguish two words; specif., the basic unit of a language's sound system as it can be varied or arranged in vocal expression. It can be a single letter, such as a vowel or consonant. The vowels *a, i,* and *o* produce very different sounds in *tap, tip,* and *top.* The consonants *b, d, p,* and *t* also distinguish words: *tab, tad, tap, tat.* Cf. **morpheme.**—**phonemic,** *adj.*

phrasal adjective. See **adjective.**

phrasal adverb. See *adverbial phrase* under **phrase.**

phrasal conjunction. See **conjunction.**

phrasal genitive. See *of-genitive* under **genitive.**

phrasal preposition. See **preposition.**

phrasal prepositional verb. See **verb.**

phrasal pronoun. See **pronoun.**

phrasal verb. See **verb.**

phrase. 1. A grammatical unit of two or more words that do not include a related subject and predicate and that do function together as a single part of speech in a sentence {Rob, a big-animal veterinarian, loves to browse used-book stores [the phrases *big-animal* and *used-book* function as adjectives modifying *veterinarian* and *stores*, respectively]}. A phrase may contain a subordinate clause {Dad sold the big house that I grew up in [the phrase *the big house that I grew up in* contains the clause *that I grew up in*, functioning as an adjective modifying *house*; but the full phrase serves a single grammatical function in the sentence: a noun that is the direct object of the verb *sold*]}. Some typical simple phrases: *might be expected; could be seen; ran down the street; all the king's horses; very excited; over the counter; not very compelling.* **2.** In some newer grammars, the smallest syntactic unit, which is usu. (though not necessarily) more than one word.—**phrasal,** *adj.*

▸ **adjective phrase.** Any phrase that modifies a noun element—often a prepositional phrase {the shell on the beach was one I'd never seen}, a participial phrase {the man living down the street was wandering in the woods}, or an infinitive phrase {the last person to leave the room should tidy up}. Traditionally, *phrasal adjective* refers to a prepositive modifier {an on-the-fly lunch}, whereas *adjective phrase* refers to a postpositive modifier {lunch on the fly}.

▸ **adverbial phrase.** A phrase that functions as an adverb {he hung 68 portraits on the wall} {she called to extend her condolences}. It differs from an adverbial clause only because it lacks a subject and predicate.—Also termed *adverb phrase; phrasal adverb.*

▸ **appositional phrase.** See **appositive.**

▸ **appositive phrase.** A phrase used in apposition {she kept her promise to visit daily}.

▸ **gerund phrase.** A phrase that consists of a gerund, its object, and any modifiers that may be present {playing two rounds of golf in one day made him happy}; a noun phrase in which a gerund is the head {building houses is her main occupation} {my job was filing papers}.

▸ **infinitive phrase.** A phrase in which an infinitive is the head; specif., the full infinitive (with *to* expressed), together with any object and modifiers that may be present {to sail the North Sea in his sailboat has long been his monomaniacal goal}. An infinitive phrase may function as an adjective phrase {her desire to shorten the story left the characters underdeveloped}, an adverbial phrase {he did his own laundry to economize}, or a noun phrase {there is nothing better than to help others}.

▸ **noun phrase.** A phrase that functions as a noun. Transformational grammarians tend to refer to individual nouns as noun phrases.—Also termed *nominal phrase; substantive phrase.*

▸ **participial phrase.** A phrase consisting of a participle together with any modifiers or complements, as well as any modifiers that might belong to the complement {a soloist singing quickly could finish the piece in under 60 seconds} {the music stands placed near the choir-room entrance have been damaged}. A participial phrase may be either an adjective phrase (as in the preceding examples) or an absolute phrase {generally speaking, band students do quite well academically}.

▸ **prepositional phrase.** A phrase consisting of a preposition, its object, and any modifiers or connectives that may be present.

▸ **set phrase.** A phrase that is fossilized in form and meaning, such as *on bended knee* (*bended* is the old past form of *bend*; now the only acceptable past form, apart from that idiom, is *bent*).

▸ **substantive phrase.** See *noun phrase.*

▸ **verb phrase. 1.** Two or more words functioning together as the verb within a clause {must have thought} {would have voted}. **2.** In transformational grammar, one or more words performing this function.—Also termed *verb cluster.*

phrase marker. See **tree diagram.**

phrase-structure tree. See **tree diagram.**

pied-piping. See **preposition-stranding.**

plain infinitive. See *bare infinitive* under **infinitive.**

pluperfect. See *past-perfect tense* under **tense.**

plural, *adj.* Denoting more than one of a thing.

plural, *n.* The form of a noun indicating more than one of a thing.

▸ **irregular plural.** A plural that is formed in some way other than by adding *-s* or *-es* {women} {phyla}.

▶ **mutation plural.** An irregular plural in which the contrast between the singular and the plural forms consists of a simple vowel alteration {foot–feet} {goose–geese}.—Also termed *umlaut plural.*

▶ **regular plural.** A plural that is formed in the normal way by adding *-s* or *-es* {tables} {hands}.

▶ **umlaut plural.** See *mutation plural.*

▶ **uninflected plural.** A plural that is identical in form with its singular {deer} {fish [although *fishes* is permissible for a few individual ichthyic animals]} {moose} {swine}.—Also termed *zero plural.*

▶ **weak plural.** A plural consisting of a base plus *-en* {brethren} {children} {oxen}. Only a few such forms survive in Modern English.

▶ **zero plural.** See *uninflected plural.*

plural indicator. See *plural marker* under **marker.**

plural marker. See **marker.**

plural number. See **number.**

point of view. The speaker's or writer's attitude vis-à-vis the reader as evident from pronouns (first person, second person, third person).

polar question. See *yes–no question* under **question.**

polysemous /po-lee-**seem**-əs/ *adj.* (Of a word) having more than one sense, usu. many senses (e.g., *bank* can mean "a financial institution," "the earth beside a river," or "a billiard shot that bounces off the edge of the table").—**polysemy,** *n.*

polysyndetic coordination. See **coordination.**

polysyndeton /pol-ee-**sin**-də-ton/. The repeated—and sometimes repetitive—use of conjunctions in a series of words, phrases, or clauses {we will keep our hopes alive and we will keep pursuing our goals and we will win in the end}. Cf. **syndeton** & **asyndeton.**—**polysyndetic** /pol-ee-sin-**det**-ik/, *adj.*

portion indicator. See *portion marker* under **marker.**

portion marker. See **marker.**

portmanteau word. See **word.**

positive, *adj.* & *n.* The lowest degree of comparison for gradable adjectives and adverbs. The positive is the ordinary condition of such a word (e.g., *smart* is positive, *smarter* is comparative, and *smartest* is superlative). For both adjectives and adverbs, the positive merely expresses quality without comparison to any other thing. See **degree.** Cf. **comparative** & **superlative.**

positive adjective. See **adjective.**

positive question. See **question.**

possessive /pə-**zes**-iv/, *n.* The case used to show possession, ownership, or close relationship. In English, most nouns form the possessive by adding -'s to the singular and irregular plural forms, and an apostrophe alone to regular plural forms. But the term *possessive* also embraces words such as *mine, yours, ours,* and *theirs,* as well as *my, your, our,* and *their.* See §§ 71–72, 98, 518. See **genitive.**

▸ **descriptive possessive.** The possessive form of a noun used in a way that describes (so that it functions as a descriptive adjective) {men's restroom} {children's pool} {heroin's victims}.

▸ **double possessive.** The idiomatic combination of an inflected possessive and a periphrastic possessive {a friend of Alexandra's} {a relative of Father's}.—Also termed *double genitive; postgenitive.*

▸ **group possessive.** A possessive construction in which two or more words are considered as a unit and therefore take a single -'s {several of Rodgers and Hammerstein's musicals are masterpieces} {let's go to Neil and Tasca's house}.—Also termed *joint possessive.*

▸ **independent possessive.** A possessive that has a noun elided after it because the context makes the meaning obvious {my little brother is taller than Jane's}.—Also termed *independent genitive.*

▸ **inflected possessive.** A possessive ending in -'s or -s', used most commonly for nouns that refer to people and that indicate ownership or source {John's house} {Sally's ideas}.

▸ **joint possessive.** See *group possessive.*

▸ **local possessive.** A possessive used for denoting a business or similar establishment {McDonald's} {Schlotzsky's} {St. James's}.

▸ **periphrastic possessive.** See *of-genitive* under **genitive.**

possessive adjective. See **adjective.**

possessive case. See **case.**

possessive pronoun. See **pronoun.**

postgenitive. See *double possessive* under **possessive.**

postpositive /pohs[t]-**poz**-i-tiv/, *adj. & n.* A word or particle that is placed after or suffixed to another word. Postpositives include adjectives {accounts receivable} {battle royal} and prepositions used in phrasal verbs {settle down} {step out}. Cf. **prepositive.**

postpositive adjective. See **adjective.**

postpositive modifier. See *postpositive adjective* under **adjective.**

potential tense. See **tense.**

pragmatics, *n.* The study of meaning as it derives from context; esp., the analysis of language as it relates to human users and their behavior.—**pragmatic,** *adj.*

predicate. The part of a clause that begins with a finite verb; the core part of a clause minus the subject.

> ▸ **complete predicate.** The finite verb of a clause with all its modifiers, objects, and associated complements {she called her broker, who was in Venice Beach at the time}.—Also termed *verb cluster.*

> ▸ **compound predicate.** Collectively, two or more finite verbs joined by a coordinating conjunction and having the same subject {she relaxed and watched TV} {he grilled steaks but didn't enjoy it}.

> ▸ **simple predicate.** The finite verb of a clause, whether independent or dependent {she called her broker, who was in Venice Beach at the time}.

predicate adjectival. See *predicate adjective* under **adjective.**

predicate adjective. See **adjective.**

predicate attribute. See *predicate adjective* under **adjective.**

predicate complement. See *subjective complement* under **complement.**

predicate nominal. See **predicate nominative.**

predicate nominative. A pronoun (or noun) that follows a linking verb (in traditional syntax) and refers to the subject {this is he} {you are a saint} A *predicate nominative* is one type of subjective complement.—Also termed *subjective noun; subjective pronoun; attribute noun; attribute pronoun; predicate noun; predicate nominal; predicate pronoun; predicate substantive.* See *subjective complement* under **complement.**

predicate noun. **1.** See **noun. 2.** See **predicate nominative.**

predicate objective. See *objective complement* under **complement.**

predicate pronoun. 1. See *predicate noun* (1) under **noun. 2.** See **predicate nominative.**

predicate substantive. See **predicate nominative.**

predicate verb. See **verb.**

predicating verb. See *action verb* under **verb.**

predication. See **clause.**

predicative, *adj.* (Of an adjective) occurring after a linking verb {Billy is rowdy} {the mood became cheery} or after an object {she painted the walk blue}.

prefix /**pree**-fiks/. An element, such as a letter, number, syllable, or word, placed at the beginning of a word to alter or qualify the meaning. For instance, a prefix may distinguish word classes (such as the verb *sleep* and the adjective *asleep*), denote an opposite (such as *nondairy–dairy*), or denote a distinction (such as between *bicycle* and *tricycle*). Among the most common prefixes are *con-, dis-, ex-, in-, non-, post-, pre-,* and *un-.* Cf. **suffix.**—**prefixation,** *n.*

preposition /prep-ə-**zish**-ən/. A word or phrase that shows a relationship between its object and another part of the sentence (such as between the nouns in *the devil is in the details*). The preposition's object is usually a noun or pronoun, which is always in the objective case (e.g., in *that sounds good to me*, the pronoun *me* is the object of the preposition *to*, so it is in the objective case). Although the preposition usually appears immediately before its object, it can also follow it {we have a serious problem to talk about}. (See § 249.) Prepositions frequently serve as particles in phrasal verbs. See **particle.**—**prepositional,** *adj.*

> The legitimacy of the prepositional ending in literary English must be uncompromisingly maintained.
> —H. W. Fowler
> *A Dictionary of Modern English Usage*

▸ **complex preposition.** A phrasal preposition that indicates more than one relationship between the antecedent and the preposition's object {as of} {from between} {out from under}. See *phrasal preposition.*

▸ **compound preposition. 1.** A preposition consisting of two or more words written as one {within} {without}. **2.** See *phrasal preposition.*

▸ **deferred preposition.** See *stranded preposition.*

▸ **group preposition.** See *phrasal preposition.*

▸ **phrasal preposition.** A preposition made up of two or more words and used as a single prepositional unit (e.g., *according to; along with; as regards; because of; by means of; contrary to; in accordance with; in front of; in place of; in respect of; on account of; regardless of; together with; with regard to*).—Also termed *group preposition; complex preposition; compound preposition.*

▸ **simple preposition.** A preposition not made through compounding (*down, in, on, out, up,* etc.).

▸ **stranded preposition.** A preposition that is not directly followed by its object {what are you calling about?} {what do you need a screwdriver for?}.—Also termed *terminal preposition; deferred preposition.*

▸ **terminal preposition.** See *stranded preposition.*

prepositional phrase. See **phrase.**

prepositional verb. See *phrasal verb* under **verb.**

preposition-stranding. The act or practice of putting a preposition at the end of a sentence or clause.—Also termed *pied-piping.*

prepositive, *adj.* (Of a particle, phrase, word, etc.) placed before or attached to the front of a word or stem (e.g., *quasi-scientific, absolutely wonderful, very questionable premise*). Cf. **postpositive.**

prepositive, *n.* A word or particle that is placed before or attached to the front of a word.

prepositive adjective. See *attributive adjective* under **adjective.**

prescriptive grammar. See **grammar.**

prescriptivism /pree-**skrip**-ti-viz-əm/. An approach to language study that embraces the role of value judgments in deciding what is linguistically effective or ineffective, better or worse, and therefore guides people in a didactic manner toward mastering a standard language. At its best, prescriptivism is grounded in empirical evidence such as the ngrams displayed in chapter 4. At its worst, it amounts to ill-informed, off-the-cuff pronouncements by people without an understanding of linguistic study. Cf. **descriptivism.—prescriptivist,** *adj.* & *n.*

> It is a travesty of the history of grammar to represent prescriptivism as relying invariably or typically on dubious criteria. It is no less a travesty of reasoning to argue against it that there is only one correct interpretation of correctness (that being, needless to say, the linguist's).
> —Roy Harris
> *The Language Machine*

present gerund. See **gerund.**

present infinitive. See **infinitive.**

present participle. See **participle.**

present-perfect gerund. See *perfect gerund* under **gerund.**

present-perfect infinitive. See *perfect infinitive* under **infinitive.**

present-perfect participle. See **participle.**

present-perfect tense. See **tense.**

present stem. See *bare infinitive* under **infinitive.**

present subjunctive. See **subjunctive,** *n.*

present tense. See **tense.**

preterit. See *past tense* under **tense.**

preterite. See *past tense* under **tense.**

primary stress. See **stress.**

primary verb. See **verb.**

principal clause. See *independent clause* under **clause.**

principal part. Any one of the three verb forms from which almost all verbs are formed—namely, the present stem (or simple infinitive) {ring}, the first person of the past tense {rang}, and the past participle {rung}. Only the defective verbs *may, can, must, ought, shall,* and *will* don't have all the principal parts. Regular verbs have only two distinct forms for the three {careen–careened–careened} {play–played–played} {state–stated–stated}. As for irregular verbs, some have three distinct forms {go–went–gone} {sing–sang–sung}, others have identical forms for both past forms {bring–brought–brought} {sell–sold–sold}, still others are distinct only in past tense {come–came–come} {run–ran–run}, and a few are the same in all three forms {cut–cut–cut} {hit–hit–hit}.

principal verb. See **verb.**

privative /priv-ə-tiv/, *adj.* Expressing the idea that some quality has been subtracted, lost, or negated, or is absent. Common privative affixes are *a-* {amoral}, *-less* {useless}, *non-* {nondisposable}, and *un-* {unknown}.

progressive aspect. See **aspect.**

progressive tense. See **tense.**

pronominal adjective. See **adjective.**

pronoun /proh-nown/. A word that can substitute for a noun element, whether that element is expressed or understood. When its antecedent is clear, use of a pronoun avoids awkward repetition.—**pronominal** /proh-nom-i-nəl/, *adj.*

▶ **adjective pronoun.** See *pronominal adjective* under **adjective.**

▶ **anaphoric pronoun.** A pronoun that has an antecedent. Almost all properly used pronouns in English are anaphoric.

▶ **attribute pronoun.** A pronoun functioning as a subjective complement {this is he}.

▶ **compound pronoun.** A pronoun that consists of two or more words written as one {nobody} {myself} {someone} {whoever} {whosoever}.

▶ **demonstrative pronoun.** The pronoun *this, that, these,* or *those* when used by itself as a noun element {this will be fun} {those are my favorites}. Cf. *demonstrative adjective* under **adjective.**

▶ **impersonal pronoun.** See *indefinite pronoun.*

▶ **indefinite pronoun.** A pronoun that doesn't refer to a definite person or thing {anyone} {anybody} {someone} {one} {somebody}.—Also termed *impersonal pronoun.*

▶ **intensive pronoun.** Any one of several compound personal pronouns ending in *-self* or *-selves* and functioning as an appositive modifier for emphasis {I did it myself} {you yourself said so} {the CEO himself gave me a tour of the C-suites}.—Also termed *intensifying pronoun; emphatic pronoun.*

▸ **interrogative pronoun.** A pronoun that introduces a direct or indirect question in which the pronoun serves as a noun element {who placed that call?} {we all wondered what we would do}.

▸ **personal pronoun.** A pronoun that refers to a specific person or thing; specif., a pronoun used for a speaker (first person: *I* or *we*), someone spoken to (second person: *you*), or someone or something spoken of (third person: *he, she, it,* or *they*). A personal pronoun formed with *-self* or *-selves* {ourselves} {yourself} is termed a *compound personal pronoun.*

▸ **phrasal pronoun.** A pronoun that consists of two words written separately {each other} {one another}.

▸ **possessive pronoun.** A pronoun in the possessive case—namely, *my, mine, your, yours, his, her, hers, our, ours, their, theirs,* or *whose.*

▸ **predicate pronoun.** 1. See *predicate noun* (1) under **noun.** 2. See **predicate nominative.**

▸ **reciprocal pronoun.** A pronoun phrase that expresses mutuality of relationship—the two examples in English being *each other* and *one another.*

▸ **reflexive pronoun.** Any one of several compound personal pronouns ending in *-self* or *-selves* and functioning as a direct object, a subjective complement, or the object of a preposition, gerund, or infinitive:
- Direct object: Jane hurt herself.
- Indirect object: Give yourself plenty of leeway.
- Subjective complement: Bob is himself again.
- Object of a preposition: We saved some water for ourselves.
- Object of a gerund: Bill's praising himself was unseemly.
- Object of an infinitive: They wanted to make themselves available.

The reflexive pronouns are *myself, ourselves, yourself, yourselves, himself, herself, themselves, itself,* and *oneself.*

▸ **relative pronoun.** A pronoun that introduces a subordinate clause and relates it to the main clause. Common relative pronouns include *what, which, who,* and *that. Who* is the only relative pronoun that changes form when it changes case: *who* (nominative: *who wants the last piece of cake?*), *whom* (objective: *an informant whom we cannot identify*), and *whose* (possessive: *whose notes did you borrow?*). See §§ 80–93, 192.

▸ **resumptive pronoun.** A grammatical fault in which a pronoun subsumed with a relative clause is inappropriately included at the end of the clause {sometimes you will receive gifts that you don't like them}.

▸ **simple pronoun.** A pronoun that has always consisted of a single word {I} {you} {he} {she} {they}.

pronoun–antecedent agreement. See **agreement.**

pronunciation. 1. The way words are said; the act or an instance of saying words or syllables aloud. **2.** The study of how words or syllables are correctly said aloud according to the standard of educated speakers.

▸ **retarded pronunciation.** An unusually old-fashioned pronunciation.

▸ **spelling pronunciation.** A pronunciation or mispronunciation that is influenced by or derived from a word's spelling, such as by sounding the traditionally silent -t- in *often*, the silent -l- in *salmon*, or the silent -mp- in *comptroller* /kən-**troh**-lər/.

proper adjective. See **adjective.**

proper name. See *proper noun* under **noun.**

proper noun. See **noun.**

prosody /**pros**-ə-dee/, *n.* **1.** The study of the accent, quality, and quantity of syllables, esp. in metrical composition such as verse. **2.** The meaningful variation of pitch, volume, speed, and rhythm of speech.—**prosodic** /prə-**sod**-ik/, *adj.*

protasis /**prah**-tə-səs/. See *conditional clause* under **clause.**

pro-verb. See *dummy auxiliary verb* under **auxiliary verb.**

pseudo-transitive verb. See **verb.**

pure infinitive. See *bare infinitive* under **infinitive.**

purism, *n.* **1.** The belief that a language has an absolute, immutable standard of correctness. Self-described "purists" are often stunningly ill-informed about grammar and usage. **2.** *Archaic.* The belief that the foreign element in a language is highly undesirable—e.g., that Anglo-Saxon compounds (*agenbite*, for example) are preferable to words of non-English origin (*remorse*).—**purist,** *adj. & n.*

qualifying adjective. See *descriptive adjective* under **adjective.**

question. An interrogative sentence calling for an answer; a request for information.

▸ **alternative question.** A question that offers the choice of two or more options {is your favorite reading fiction or nonfiction?} {would you prefer sausage or bacon—and if sausage, link or patty?}.

▸ **declarative yes–no question.** A reduced yes–no question phrased as a sentence {you own Norwegian elkhounds?}.

▸ **direct question.** An interrogative sentence that poses a straightforward query {may I take a day off?}.

▸ **echo question.** See **echo utterance.**

▸ **embedded question.** A question that appears in indirect discourse {I asked whether he thought he was up to the trip}.

▸ **exclamatory question.** A sentence that structurally resembles a question but is used as an exclamation, usu. to express a strong feeling while seeking the listener's or reader's assent {wasn't that hailstorm scary!} {was she ever angry!}.

▸ **indirect question.** A declarative sentence that includes but does not pose a query {he asked whether he might take a day off}. In this type of sentence, the question is placed in a subordinate clause {I want to know where Ollie hid my Christmas present [instead of *where did Ollie hide my Christmas present?*]}.

▸ **negative question.** A question phrased with a negating word {will we never go?}.

▸ **polar question.** See *yes–no question.*

▸ **positive question.** A question phrased without negation {when will we go?}.

▸ **rhetorical question.** An interrogative sentence that does not invite an answer, usu. because the answer is obvious or the speaker clearly does not expect one (e.g., a comment such as *have you ever seen so much traffic?* is often rhetorical).

▸ **tag question.** A question that follows and mirrors a statement, the purpose being to seek (or purport to seek) assent; a follow-on clause asking for confirmation of the idea in the preceding clause {it's a pretty day, isn't it?} {that wasn't so bad, was it?}.—Also termed *confirmation clause.*

▸ *wh-* **question.** A question beginning with *who, what, when, where, why,* or even (by common acceptance) *how.*

▸ **yes–no question.** A question that is directly answerable in either the affirmative or the negative, even though a fuller response may be appropriate.—Also termed *polar question.*

recipient noun. See **noun.**

reciprocal pronoun. See **pronoun.**

recoverability. The ability of a listener or reader to infer exactly which words have been left out from an elliptical expression {he asked whether I could go with him, but I said I couldn't [go with him]} {you like? [do you like this?]} {[the] government [is] to bail out banks}. Cf. **ellipsis (1).**—**recoverable,** *adj.*

▸ **situational recoverability.** Inferability of the full form of a sentence by virtue of the circumstance in which it appears {don't want to go}.

▸ **structural recoverability.** Inferability of the full form of a sentence by virtue of the reader's or listener's linguistic knowledge {5,000 to be hired}.

▶ **textual recoverability.** Inferability of the full form of a sentence by virtue of considering the rest of the text, esp. the rest of the sentence {Sandra consulted two books and Jenny five articles}.

redundancy, *n.* The use of words that could be omitted with no loss in meaning and usu. with a gain in both clarity and force; linguistic superfluity.

redundant subject. See *double subject* under **subject.**

reduplication. The formation of a word through rhymed, highly alliterative syllables {hurly-burly} {mishmash} {zigzag}.—**reduplicative,** *adj.*

Reed–Kellogg diagram. A traditional sentence diagram developed in the 19th century and illustrated in §§ 339–64.

referent. Something to which a word or symbol refers. The referent of *stool,* in the ordinary sense, is the three- or four-legged object on which a person can sit. In the sentence *I saw the musical and liked it,* the referent of *it* might be considered either the antecedent (the phrase *the musical*) or the musical production itself.

reflexive, *n.* **1.** A part of speech used for emphasis by repetition. A reflexive pronoun mirrors the subject and ends in either *-self* or *-selves.* It often follows the subject immediately {the thought itself is unimportant}. But it may also follow the verb {Sarah painted the room herself}. (See *reflexive pronoun* under **pronoun.**) A reflexive verb has a reflexive pronoun as its object {Esteban worked himself into a panic}. **2.** Any construction in which two words or noun phrases are understood to have the same referent.

reflexive pronoun. See **pronoun.**

reflexive verb. See **verb.**

regional dialect. See **dialect.**

register, *n.* A variety of language usu. classifiable on a spectrum of formal–informal and used for particular purposes in particular circumstances.

regular, *adj.* (Of a word or phrase) conforming to the usual rules of grammatical formation. For example, a regular noun forms its plural by adding *-s* or *-es* (e.g., *pot* becomes *pots; fox* becomes *foxes*). Cf. **irregular.**

regular inflection. See **inflection.**

regular plural. See **plural.**

regular verb. See **verb.**

relative adjective. See **adjective.**

relative adverb. See **adverb.**

relative clause. See **clause.**

relative pronoun. See **pronoun.**

restrictive, *adj.* (Of the modifier of a noun element) adding information that more positively identifies the referent. For example, in *the tents that are on aisle 3 are on sale,* the clause *that are on aisle 3* is restrictive because it identifies which tents are on sale—tents on other aisles may not be. Similarly in *the senator–songwriter Orrin Hatch will perform,* the name *Orrin Hatch* specifically identifies which senator–songwriter is being referred to, so it is a restrictive appositive. Restrictive modifiers are never set off from the rest of the sentence by commas. Cf. **nonrestrictive.**

restrictive appositive. See **appositive.**

restrictive clause. See **clause.**

resumptive modifier. See **modifier.**

resumptive pronoun. See **pronoun.**

retarded pronunciation. See **pronunciation.**

retronym. A word or phrase invented to denote what was originally a genus term but has now become just one more species in a larger genus (e.g., *solid-core door* came to describe what all old doors used to be until the advent of the *hollow-core door*).

rhetorical question. See **question.**

root. The irreducible base of a word—the part left behind after all affixes have been stripped away (e.g., *form* is the root of *performances*). Cf. **stem.**

run-on sentence. 1. See **sentence. 2.** See **comma splice.**

run-together sentence. See **comma splice.**

schwa /shwah/. A short indeterminate vowel represented as [ə] (an inverted backward *e*), sounded as in the first syllable of *about* or the final syllable of *schadenfreude.* See **intrusive schwa.**

semantic contamination. A change in meaning that occurs through the influence of a similar-sounding word. See **clang association.**

semantics. 1. The study of the significance of words and the development of their meanings. **2.** Meaning in language.—**semantic,** *adj.*

semantic shift. A change in a word's meaning; specif., the gradual transfer of a word's denotations from one set of referents to another.

semi-auxiliary verb. See **auxiliary verb.**

sensory verb. See **verb.**

sentence. A grammatical unit that conveys a complete thought, that consists of a subject and predicate, either of which may be express or understood, and for which the rules of grammar do not control the order in which it is placed in relation to other units; esp., a stretch of words beginning with a capital letter and ending with terminal punctuation (a period, question mark, or exclamation mark). For example, grammatical rules govern the placement of *it, here,* and *bring* in forming a sentence: *bring it here!* (understood subject [you], verb, object, adverb). But grammar does not govern where to place that sentence in a paragraph. A sentence is made up of one or more clauses.—**sentential,** *adj.*

▶ **cleft sentence.** A syntactic variant in which an *it*-clause, a *what*-clause, or a similar clause changes the focus by adding two or three words (such as *it, was,* and *who; there, are,* and *that;* or *what* and *is*) {it was he who was responsible} {there are many reasons that underlie our decision} {what we need is more ingenuity}. Most often a cleft sentence begins with the expletive *it* and a *be*-verb {it was the building code that caused her so many headaches} {it was the goalie who won outstanding player}. A cleft sentence is also called an "*it*-cleft" when it has an *it*-clause or a "*wh*-cleft" when the first clause begins with a *wh*-word.—Often shortened to *cleft.*

▶ **complete sentence.** Another term for *sentence* as defined above in the main entry.—Also termed *major sentence.* Cf. *incomplete sentence.*

▶ **complex sentence.** A sentence consisting of an independent clause and at least one subordinate clause {because we're celebrating, I'll bring champagne [*because we're celebrating* is a subordinate clause because it cannot stand on its own; *I'll bring champagne* is the independent (main) clause]}.

▶ **compound-complex sentence.** A sentence consisting of two or more independent clauses and at least one subordinate clause {I don't know if he'll be allowed to watch the football game, but he hasn't finished those chores that he was assigned}.

▶ **compound sentence.** A sentence consisting of two or more independent clauses connected by a coordinating conjunction {the moon has risen, and the air is getting cold} or a semicolon {the moon has risen; the air is getting cold}.

▶ **conditional sentence.** A sentence expressing the relation of condition to conclusion between its subordinate and main clauses. Several types of conditional sentences are past neutral (e.g., *if he won, he was lucky*), past contrary to fact (e.g., *had he won, he would have been lucky*), present neutral (e.g., *if he is winning, he is lucky*), present contrary to fact (e.g., *if he were winning, he would be lucky*), future less vivid (e.g., *if he should win, he would be lucky*), and future more vivid (e.g., *if he wins, he will be lucky*). See **apodosis** & *conditional clause* under **clause.**

▶ **declarative sentence.** A sentence that takes the form of a simple statement (as contrasted with a command, a question, or an exclamation).

▶ **exclamatory sentence.** See **exclamation.**

▶ **existential sentence.** A sentence that expresses the existence of something by using the expletive *there* plus a *be*-verb {there are many rare animals at the National Zoo}.

▶ **fragmentary sentence.** See **fragment.**

▶ **full sentence.** A sentence in which the subject and verb are expressly stated. Cf. **nonsentence.**

▶ **imperative sentence.** A sentence expressing a command {close the door!}, making a request {please let me know}, or giving directions {check to see that all bolts are tight}.

▶ **impersonal sentence.** A sentence in which the main actor's identity is kept unmentioned, as with the use of a truncated passive {mistakes were made}, an expletive {it's hard to say}, or gerunds and infinitives {sleeping well is important} {to wine and dine is of limited value in this business}.

> Many single words or self-contained groups of words, of any size, may perform the work of a sentence; e.g. Speaking; Thanks; Down! Sh!; Out with it!; Farewell; Goodbye; What?; Murder!; Nonsense!; Splendid! "Yes" and "no" are long-established sentence-words; they are *equivalent* to sentences; e.g. "Will you come?"—"Yes" (= I will come).
> —C. T. Onions
> *Modern English Syntax*

▶ **incomplete sentence.** A statement that is not grammatically complete {nothing of that sort} {nonsense} {when I can}.—Also termed *minor sentence.* Cf. *complete sentence.*

▶ **interrogative sentence.** A sentence that poses a direct question {how many people live here?} {what will this cost me?}. By contrast, a sentence containing an indirect question {she asked me where the main campus is} is considered a declarative sentence.—Also termed *interrogative.*

▶ **major sentence.** See *complete sentence.*

▶ **minor sentence.** See *incomplete sentence.*

▶ **negative cleft sentence.** A cleft sentence that creates or implies a contrast by negating the opening clause {it was not he who was responsible [someone else was responsible]} {there are not many reasons that underlie our decision [there are only a few]} {what we do not need is more ingenuity [we need something else]}. See *cleft sentence.*

▶ **run-on sentence.** 1. A grammatical fault whereby independent clauses are fused together without any proper link such as a conjunction or appropriate punctuation {we need to leave soon we might be late} {I want that book it looks interesting}. In these examples, the statements consist of two independent clauses; in the absence of a conjunction between the independent clauses, a semicolon is needed after *soon* in the first example and after *book* in the second. **2.** Loosely—and improperly, from a grammarian's standpoint—a sentence that is awfully long.

▸ **simple sentence.** A sentence containing one principal clause and no dependent clauses.

▸ **verbless sentence.** A group of words conveying meaning even though the statement contains no finite verb {nonsense!} {what claptrap!} {heavens to Betsy!} {scones, anyone?} {what else?}.—Also termed *nonsentence*.

sentence adverb. See **adverb**.

sentence fragment. See **fragment**.

sentence modifier. See *sentence adverb* under **adverb**.

sentential relative clause. See **clause**.

separative coordinating conjunction. See *disjunctive conjunction* under **conjunction**.

sequence of tenses. The order of tenses that a language requires or allows in combined sentences or in a succession of clauses {if I had been there, I would have contributed [where the conditional past perfect is followed by the conditional perfect]}. See **backshifting**.

set phrase. See **phrase**.

shift. 1. A faulty grammatical construction in which an unwarranted change occurs in number {civics is my favorite class, and they are important for participating in society}, person {one must be careful with your technique}, mood {if you go, you would see}, tense {Hamlet then fights Laertes and died}, or subject and voice {I carried the boxes downstairs, and then they were set on the dais}. **2.** See **functional variation**.

short passive voice. See **passive voice**.

simile /sim-ə-lee/. A figure of speech in which two things of different kinds are explicitly compared using the word *like* or *as* (e.g., *the humidity made the air as sticky as molasses*). Cf. **metaphor**.

simple. 1. (Of a sentence) consisting of one independent clause and no dependent clauses. **2.** (Of a sentence element) consisting of one part not compounded with any other elements. **3.** (Of a tense) formed by a verb without an auxiliary (e.g., *walks* rather than *is walking*).

simple adjective. See **adjective**.

simple adverb. See **adverb**.

simple conjunction. See **conjunction**.

simple infinitive. See *bare infinitive* under **infinitive.**

simple noun. See **noun.**

simple-past tense. See *past tense* under **tense.**

simple predicate. See **predicate.**

simple preposition. See **preposition.**

simple pronoun. See **pronoun.**

simple sentence. See **sentence.**

simple subject. See **subject.**

simple tense. See **tense.**

singular, *adj.* Denoting one of a thing or a mass of indivisible stuff; not plural {bell-man} {excuse} {receptionist} {snowball} {sugar}.

singular indicator. See *singular marker* under **marker.**

singular marker. See **marker.**

singular number. See **number.**

situational recoverability. See **recoverability.**

slang, *n.* A purposely undignified form of expression that marks its user as being part of a particular in-group, usu. of some youthful or antiestablishment bent.

social dialect. See *class dialect* under **dialect.**

solecism /sol-ə-siz-əm/, *n.* **1.** A grammatical or syntactic error, often a gross mistake; the use of a nonstandard grammatical form {look at them golf balls!} {they's a-floatin'!}. **2.** Figuratively, a social impropriety.—**solecistic,** *adj.*

specialization. The narrowing of a word's meaning over time. For example, *molest* long meant "to interfere with (a person), usu. but not always with bad intent." Today the word's primary sense is "to sexually assault, esp. a child." Cf. **generalization.**

> As teachers and students of standard English, we must do whatever we can (1) to make sure that demands for its use are not arbitrary but functionally justified, (2) to make sure that the standard dialect is accessible to all the people, not just the privileged minority, and (3) to make sure that those intelligent *young* people who through no fault of their own either cannot or will not learn the standard dialect are not denied economic opportunity and social acceptance.
> —James Sledd
> "Something About Language and Social Class"

spelling, *n.* The representation of words by written letters.

spelling pronunciation. See **pronunciation.**

spelling reform. Any suggestion or campaign to change the methods of English spelling to make it more nearly reflect pronunciation.

split infinitive. See **infinitive.**

squinting construction. See *squinting modifier* under **modifier.**

squinting modifier. See **modifier.**

s-structure. See *surface structure* under **structure.**

Standard English. The type of English traditionally used by educated people of the recent past; specif., a prestigious variety of the language taught in traditional grammars, customarily used in schools and universities, and used for public affairs throughout the nation.

Standard Written English. The refined Standard English found in writing that has been professionally edited or that more or less meets that standard.

statement. 1. The act of saying or writing something. **2.** A verbal presentation, esp. a formal or precise one. **3.** Something that is said or written.

stative verb. See **verb.**

stem. A basic word or part of a word that can be combined with prefixes, suffixes, or both to derive other words. For instance, the basic noun *thought* can take the prefix *un-* and the suffix *-ful* to derive the adjective *unthoughtful,* and the additional suffix *-ness* to derive the noun *unthoughtfulness.*—Also termed *word-stem; base.* Cf. **root.**

stranded preposition. See **preposition.**

stress, *n.* The vocal emphasis placed on a word or a particular syllable, usu. by raising the voice, changing the pitch, drawing out the sounds, or a combination; esp., the relative intensity with which vowels are pronounced.

▸ **primary stress.** The most prominent stress in a word or phrase.

strong verb. See *irregular verb* under **verb.**

structural recoverability. See **recoverability.**

structure. The arrangement of individual parts of speech into an utterance.

▸ **deep structure.** In transformational grammar, the underlying form of a sentence, bearing its essential meaning; specif., the abstract structure of a sentence from which its actual structure (or surface structure) may be derived by transformation. In scientific terms, it would be the "linguistic genotype."—Sometimes abbreviated *d-structure.*

▸ **modification structure.** A head together with all its modifiers {the man who lives down the street and likes to walk at night with a miner's cap has gone missing}.

▸ **surface structure.** In transformational grammar, the form of a sentence that appears after it has been subjected to transformations. In scientific terms, it would be the "linguistic phenotype."—Sometimes abbreviated *s-structure*.

structure word. See *function word* under **word**.

subject. The noun element that (1) performs the first syntactic function in a basic sentence and (2) controls the number of the verb. It usually identifies the thing that brings about the action, state, or condition in the predicate (in the active voice) or receives the action, state, or condition (in the passive voice). In yes–no questions, it is inverted with the auxiliary verb. Cf. **object**.—**subjective**, *adj*.

▸ **anticipatory subject.** A subject that has been inverted with its verb, which must anticipate it. A delayed subject is one type of anticipatory subject. See *delayed subject*.

▸ **complete subject.** The simple subject of a finite verb along with all its modifying elements {huge tomes lined the walls} {the golf course that we played last week was recently redesigned}.

▸ **compound subject.** Collectively, two or more noun elements that are subjects of the same verb {Sam and Siobhan arrived together} {what they want and what they need may be different things altogether}. Individually, the two or more noun elements are called *coordinate subjects*.

▸ **coordinate subject.** See *compound subject*.

▸ **deferred subject.** See *delayed subject*.

▸ **delayed subject.** The subject that appears after the verb in a sentence that begins with an expletive {here comes the judge} {there will be flowers at the altar}.—Also termed *deferred subject; anticipatory subject*.

▸ **double subject.** A construction in which both a pronoun and its antecedent are used as the subject of the same verb—a violation of Standard English characteristic of children's speech and certain dialects. Oddly, this construction is considered faulty in spoken English only when the antecedent and the pronoun are delivered in rapid succession {my sister she's a cheerleader} {my father he's a mechanic}, whereas a pause makes a difference in acceptability as Standard English {my sister—she's a cheerleader} {my father—he's a mechanic}.—Also termed *redundant subject*.

▸ **redundant subject.** See *double subject*.

▸ **simple subject.** The noun element that identifies the person, place, thing, or idea about whom or which a statement is made—that is, the complete subject minus any modifiers {the tennis courts that we played on yesterday were state-of-the-art [*courts* is the simple subject of the main clause, with the

▶ **past subjunctive.** A subjunctive form that conveys present or future meaning by using a past tense, esp. *were* {if I were in Cincinnati, I'd go see her} {if they were urged they would nevertheless decline}.—Also termed *were-subjunctive.*

▶ **present subjunctive.** A subjunctive that conveys present or future action by using the word *be* {I suggest that he be promoted} {we insist that all Ebola victims be quarantined}.

▶ *were-***subjunctive.** See **past subjunctive.**

subjunctive mood. See **mood.**

subordinate clause. See *dependent clause* under **clause.**

subordinating conjunction. See **conjunction.**

subordination. The combining of simple sentences into a complex sentence by using a dependent clause and an independent clause. Cf. **coordination.**

▶ **upside-down subordination.** A faulty construction in which a more important idea appears in a subordinate clause and a less important idea appears in the principal clause {the planes flew for four straight hours, finally falling to the ground in a fiery crash when they ran out of fuel}. In that example, timing is in the main clause, perishing in the subordinate. Better phrasing matches the grammar of the sentence with its meaning {after flying four straight hours, the planes finally ran out of fuel and fell to the ground in a fiery crash}. Note that the original emphasized *fuel* by putting it in the final position (the most important) in the sentence; the revision emphasizes *fiery crash*, which is surely the most important idea: it is now in a principal clause in the most emphatic position.

subordinator. See *subordinating conjunction* under **conjunction.**

substantive. See **noun element.**

substantive clause. See *noun clause* under **clause.**

substantive phrase. See *noun phrase* under **phrase.**

suffix /sǝf-iks/. An affix attached to the end of a word-stem, either by derivation (e.g., *fill–filler*) or by inflection (e.g., *fill–filled*). Common suffixes include *-able, -ation, -ful, -fy, -ing, -itis, -ly,* and *-ness.* Cf. **prefix.**—**suffixation,** *n.*

▶ **derivational suffix.** A suffix that reliably produces a noun {-ion}, verb {-ize}, or adjective {-ous}.

▶ **inflectional suffix.** A suffix that marks (but does not itself produce) a particular part of speech (as with the past-tense *-ed* or the comparative *-er*).

summative modifier. See **modifier.**

superlative /sǝ-pǝr-lǝ-tiv/, *adj. & n.* The highest of three degrees of comparison for gradable adjectives and adverbs, showing that one thing has more of a quality than any of the other things to which it is compared. A superlative adjective or adverb is usually signaled by an -*est* suffix or by *most* or *least*. A superlative adjective compares a specified quality possessed by at least three things and denotes the quality's extreme amount or intensity (e.g., *that was the best movie Spielberg ever made*). A superlative adverb compares a specified action or condition common to at least three things (e.g., *he is the most talented player on the baseball team*); it might also be used loosely for emphasis instead of comparison (e.g., *because the presentation was very important, Belle prepared most diligently*). See **degree**. Cf. **comparative** & **positive**.

▶ **double superlative.** A grammatical fault in which the superlative degree is indicated twice—redundantly {*Rudolph is the most wisest person I know}.

▶ **periphrastic superlative.** A superlative formed by using an auxiliary word or words to serve the function of inflection {least qualified} {most accomplished}.

▶ **synthetic superlative.** An inflective superlative formed by adding -*est* to the positive form of the adjective or adverb {fastest} {lamest}.

superlative adjective. See **adjective**.

superordinate, *n.* A genus-term—that is, a word whose meaning embraces that of several more-specific terms. Hence *blue* is a superordinate of *azure, room* is (for most normal senses) a superordinate of *kitchen,* and *word* is a superordinate of *verb.*—Also termed **hypernym.** Cf. **hyponym.**

suppletion /sə-**plee**-shən/, *n.* An inflection change involving a complete replacement of the underlying word {be–am} {go–went} {good–best}.

surface structure. See **structure**.

suspended prepositional construction. A grammatical construction in which two or more prepositions have the same subject {I disagreed with but did not overtly object to the opinions he espoused} {we assented to and even expressed appreciation for the plan to acquire new conference tables}.

syllable. 1. A pronunciational unit that has only one vowel sound, which may or may not be flanked by consonants, and forms part or all of a word (e.g., *a* has one syllable, *table* /**tay**-bəl/ two, *furniture* /**fər**-ni-chər/ three, and so on). **2.** The smallest possible utterance or writing, often used figuratively (as in *I'd never have whispered a syllable if an innocent person hadn't been accused*).—**syllabic,** *adj.*

▶ **closed syllable.** A syllable ending with a consonant.

▶ **long syllable.** A syllable with a long vowel or else a short vowel followed by two or more consonants.

▶ **open syllable.** A syllable ending with a vowel.

syllepsis /sə-**lep**-səs/. **1.** A construction in which one part of speech, often a verb, applies to two things in different ways (e.g., *while trying to teach the children to bake, I ran out of flour and patience*). **2.** See **zeugma** (1). —**sylleptic,** *adj.*

synaeresis /sə-**nair**-ə-səs/. The contraction of two syllables or vowels into one, or into a diphthong (e.g., *you all* becomes, in Southern speech, *y'all*); *al Qaeda* /ahl kah-**ee**-də/ becomes, in English, /ahl **kɪ**-də/; *lien* /**lee**-ən/ becomes /leen/). Cf. **diaeresis** (2).

synaloepha /sin-ə-**lee**-fə/. The contraction of two syllables into one, seen most frequently in old poetry, often where a word's terminal vowel may flow into the immediately following word's identical initial vowel (e.g., *th'elements* for *the elements*).—Also spelled *synalepha*.

syncopation. See **syncope**.

syncope /**sin**[g]-kə-pee/. The omission of a sound from the interior of a word; specif., the elision of one or more letters, syllables, or sounds in the middle of a word (e.g., *ne'er* for *never*, *probably* in two syllables instead of three, *subsidiary* in four syllables instead of five, *meteorologist* in five syllables instead of six).—Also termed *syncopation*. See **hyphaeresis**.

syndetic coordination. See **coordination**.

syndeton /**sin**-di-ton/. A construction in which the parts are joined by conjunctions or phrases. Cf. **asyndeton** & **polysyndeton**.—**syndetic,** *adj.*

synecdoche /sə-**nek**-də-kee/. A figure of speech in which a less inclusive term is used to mean a more inclusive term, esp. a part of something for the whole thing. For example, *hands* may refer to workers, or *eyes* to proofreaders.

synesis /**sin**-ə-səs/. A construction in which the syntax is governed by meaning and not by strict grammar (as in *a multitude of complaints await the new mayor*, in which the grammatically singular *multitude* has a plural sense and takes a plural verb). The number of the verb is determined by the sense of the sentence rather than the grammatical number of the true subject.—Also termed *notional concord*; *constructio ad sensum*. See §§ 10–13, 186; p. 120.

synonym. 1. Most strictly, a word that bears a sense virtually identical with that of another in the same language {cocktail–mixed drink} {face–mien–visage}. **2.** More broadly, any one of two or more words (within the same language) bearing the same general sense, but each possessing also other senses and idiomatic uses not shared by the others {snake–serpent} {reddish–rubicund} {happy–joyful–joyous} {homicide–murder}. Cf. **hyponym**.—**synonymy** /si-**non**-i-mee/, *n.*—**synonymous,** *adj.*

syntax /sin-taks/. **1.** The rules governing the arrangement of words and phrases to form sentences. **2.** The arrangement itself. **3.** The study of a language's rules that affect how words and phrases are arranged.—**syntactic,** *adj.*

synthetic comparative. See **comparative.**

synthetic language /sin-**thet**-ik/. A language that expresses grammatical structure by inflecting words rather than using additional, auxiliary words. Cf. **analytic language.**

synthetic superlative. See **superlative.**

taboo. A tacit social convention by which a subject or word is prohibited in normal discourse.

tag question. See **question.**

tautology /taw-**tol**-ə-jee/, *n.* Unintentional repetition; the saying of the same thing more than once, usu. in different words {his firstborn child was a girl} {abandoned by all, he stood by himself and meditated in the solitude of one who was without companion}.—**tautological,** *adj.*

tense. A verb quality that expresses the time of action—past, present, or future.

▶ **compound tense.** A tense that is compounded by using a form as an auxiliary—that is, the present perfect {have left}, past perfect {had left}, future perfect {will have left}, or any progressive {is leaving}.—Also termed *perfect tense.* See §§ 176–78.

▶ **continuous tense.** See *progressive tense.*

▶ **expanded tense.** A tense that requires additional words for its expression; esp., any one of the progressive tenses. See *progressive tense.* See § 179.

▶ **future-perfect tense.** The tense indicating that an act, state, or condition is expected to have been completed before some other future act or time {the deadline will have expired by midnight}. The future perfect is formed by using *will have* with the verb's past participle (e.g., *will have seen*). For more on tense, see § 176.

▶ **future tense.** The tense indicating that an act, state, or condition is likely or certain to occur {we will arrive safely} or will be started or completed at some time after the statement {Harry is going to begin his first year at West Texas A&M in August}. Some grammarians and linguists contend that English lacks a distinct future tense because it does not use inflection but relies on *will* (or, rarely, *shall*) plus an infinitive, or a present-tense verb plus an adverb of time to express expectations, promises, predictions, and the like. Essentially, these grammarians distinguish between *tense* (form) and *time* (meaning). But in the popular mind, the future tense still exists. See §§ 175, 178.

▶ **historical-present tense.** The present tense used (1) in a statement that is permanently true {Aristotle remains the ancient philosopher with the broadest influence on modern thought}, (2) in a narrative about the past that, as a matter of mannerism, is cast as now occurring {he then walks into the bar, asks what year it is, and upon being told 1880, takes out his pistol and begins shooting}, or (3) in a plot summary {Hamlet first confronts the ghost in act I, scene iv}. See p. 95.

▶ **modal tense.** See *potential tense.*

▶ **past-perfect tense.** The tense indicating that an act, state, or condition was completed before another specified past time or past action. It is formed by using *had* with the principal verb's past participle {before we could say anything, he had slammed the door}.—Also termed *pluperfect tense.*—Often shortened to *past perfect; pluperfect.* See § 177.

▶ **past tense.** The tense indicating that an act, state, or condition was completed or ended at some time before a statement's frame of reference {Pamela danced all night}. This tense is also used to express many subjunctive statements. There is no time element because what is expressed in subjunctive has not yet occurred and may never occur {if I typed faster, I could finish my term paper sooner}.—Also termed *preterit; preterite; simple-past tense.* See § 174.

▶ **perfect tense. 1.** See *compound tense.* **2.** See *present-perfect tense.* See § 176.

▶ **pluperfect tense.** See *past-perfect tense.*

▶ **potential tense.** A term sometimes used for any tense form that includes *can, could, may,* or *might* {I could read that book if I wanted to} {it might rain today}.—Also termed *modal tense.*

▶ **present-perfect tense.** The tense indicating that an act, state, or condition was completed in the indefinite past or continues up to the present. The present-perfect tense is formed by using *have* or *has* with the principal verb's past participle (e.g., *have tossed; has argued*) {I have swept the patio} {the wind has blown more leaves on it already}. The present-perfect tense differs from the past tense in that the past tense indicates a more specific or a more remote time in the past.—Sometimes shortened to *perfect tense.* See § 176.

▶ **present tense.** The tense indicating a current action, state, or condition {Arnold teaches English} {we drive there routinely}. The action, state, or condition may be ongoing {Amy is writing her master's thesis}. See § 173.

▶ **preterit tense.** See *past tense.*

▶ **progressive tense.** An expanded tense form that shows action continuing or progressing. More modernly, grammarians tend to separate *progressive aspect* from any notion of tense.—Also termed *continuous tense.* See § 179.

▶ **simple-past tense.** See *past tense.*

▶ **simple tense.** A tense that does not involve any compounding of the verb with an auxiliary—that is, present tense {sees} or past tense {saw}. See §§ 173–74.

terminal preposition. See *stranded preposition* under **preposition.**

textual recoverability. See **recoverability.**

that-**clause.** See **clause.**

that-**complement.** See **complement.**

tmesis /[tə-]**mee**-səs/. A figure of speech by which a compound word is broken apart and one or more words are inserted between the parts (e.g., *what person soever*).

tone. 1. The style or manner of somebody's use of language, either in speech or in writing; the method of address. **2.** The musical pitch or intonation of an utterance.

transformation. A grammatical operation or rule that changes one linguistic structure into another. Transformations may add, subtract, replace, or rearrange elements within a string.—**transformational,** *adj.*

transitional adverb. 1. See *conjunctive adverb* under **adverb. 2.** See *sentence adverb* under **adverb.**

transitive, *adj.* (Of a verb) taking a direct object—and therefore typically followed by a noun element.

transitive verb. See **verb.**

tree diagram. In transformational grammar, a diagram that depicts the structure of a sentence.—Also termed *branching diagram; phrase marker; phrase-structure tree.*

truncated passive. See *short passive voice* under **passive voice.**

umlaut. 1. In some languages, such as German, the change of one vowel to another, esp. as a result of the partial assimilation to a succeeding sound; vowel mutation. **2.** A diaeresis in German used to indicate umlaut. Cf. **diaeresis (1).**

umlaut plural. See *mutation plural* under **plural.**

uncountable noun. See *noncount noun* under **noun.**

understood subject. See **subject.**

ungrammatical, *adj.* **1.** Not in accord with traditional notions of Standard Written English. **2.** (In linguistics) of, relating to, or consisting of a form or arrangement that the language does not allow. Cf. **grammatical.**

uninflected plural. See **plural.**

unmarked infinitive. See *bare infinitive* under **infinitive.**

unmarked word. A word that lacks a semantic limitation present in semantic sub-types (e.g., *sheep* is unmarked for sex whereas *ram* and *ewe* are both marked, and so is *lamb* for age).

upside-down subordination. See **subordination.**

usage. 1. The established, customary ways of using language; the traditional meanings and uses of words and idioms. Hence it is possible to speak of standard and nonstandard usage. **2.** A particular expression or collocation in speech or writing.

variant. An alternative form or version of a standard thing. For instance, the word *archaeology* is frequently spelled *archeology*, a variant spelling recorded in many dictionaries.

verb. A word that denotes the performance or occurrence of an action (such as *throw, leap, drive*) or denotes a state of being or condition (such as *dream, consider, fear*). A verb is traditionally considered the only part of speech that can stand alone (the subject is understood) and form a sentence, usually a command {stop!} {look!} {listen!}.

▸ **action verb.** Any transitive or intransitive verb—in contrast to a linking verb {the teacher presented several awards} {the horse galloped}.—Also termed *predicating verb; dynamic verb.*

▸ **ambitransitive verb.** See *ergative verb.*

▸ **anomalous verb.** See *irregular verb.*

▸ **asserting verb.** See *linking verb.*

▸ **auxiliary verb.** See **auxiliary verb.**

▸ **being verb.** See *linking verb.*

▸ *be*-**verb.** A linking verb consisting of an inflected or uninflected form of the verb *to be* (*is, are, was, were, been, being, be,* and *am*).

▸ **complete verb. 1.** A verb phrase {they have been known to do things like that}. **2.** The notional verb in a verb phrase {they have been known to do things like that}. **3.** Any finite verb other than a linking verb {like} {write} {skate}. On the reasons for avoiding this phrase, see § 145.

▸ **connecting verb.** See *linking verb.*

▸ **coordinate verbs.** Two or more verbs joined in a compound predicate {she sat down and ordered her dinner} {he protested but found no relief}.

▸ **copular verb.** See *linking verb.*

▸ **copulative verb.** See *linking verb.*

▸ **defective verb.** A verb that lacks one or more principal parts so that it can't be fully conjugated. *Can* and *may,* for example, lack participial and infinitive forms. And the verbs *must* and *ought* can't make past-tense, participial, or infinitive forms.

▸ **denominal verb.** A verb that has been derived from a noun {contact me next week} {we need to prioritize these agenda items}.—Also termed *denominalized verb*.

▸ **ditransitive verb.** A transitive verb that takes both a direct object and an indirect object {the chef cooked us a feast}. In that example, *cooked* behaves as a ditransitive verb with the direct object *feast* and the indirect object *us*. An indirect object can be substituted by a *for-* or *to-*phrase {the chef cooked a feast for us} {let me give some advice to you}. Cf. *monotransitive verb*.

▸ **dummy auxiliary verb.** See **auxiliary verb**.

▸ **dynamic verb.** A verb that expresses action that an agent (the subject) can perform.—Also termed *action verb*.

▸ **emphatic verb.** An expanded form of a verb consisting of the appropriate form of *do* plus the present stem of the principal verb {we do plan to board the plane in a moment} {I do hope that all turns out well}.

▸ **ergative verb** /ər-gə-tiv/. A verb that can be used transitively {Chuck closed the window} or intransitively {the window closed}. See § 139.—Also termed *ambitransitive verb*.

▸ **factitive verb. 1.** A verb that is followed by a direct object and an objective complement, used in such a way that the verb brings about a change in its object. Among the common factitive verbs are *appoint, choose, designate, elect, keep, make, name,* and *render* {we elected Gary president} {the cashier's incompetence made customers upset} {flooding rendered the building uninhabitable}. **2.** Any verb capable of taking both a direct object and an objective complement. Under this broader definition, all the verbs listed in sense 1 would be included plus such verbs as *call, consider, find, imagine, judge, prove,* and *think* {we considered him a virtuoso} {they proved him wrong}.

▸ **finite verb** /fī-nit/. A verb's inflected form showing voice, mood, tense, person, or number and not preceded by *to*; esp., a verb form marked for either present or past tense. A finite verb can serve as the principal verb of a sentence or clause. The inflection limits the verb {we played basketball till dark [the verb *played* is limited by the indicative mood and past tense]}. Cf. **infinitive**.

▸ **full verb.** See *lexical verb*.

▸ **helping verb.** See **auxiliary verb**.

▸ **infinitive verb.** See **infinitive**.

▶ **intransitive verb.** A verb that takes a subject but not a direct object because it is capable of making a complete statement without the aid of an object {we soon left} {they came and went as they pleased}.—Also termed *verb of complete predication.*

▶ **irregular verb.** A verb that is inflected (1) by internal vowel change but not by affixation, (2) by no change at all, or (3) by radically changing in the past-tense and past-participial forms, which are not predictable from the root. For example, the root verbs *begin* and *shrink* might suggest that irregular verbs with an *-i-* take an *-a-* in the past tense and a *-u-* in the participle (e.g., *begin–began–begun, shrink–shrank–shrunk*). But the pattern doesn't apply universally (e.g., *bring–brought–brought*). Some irregular verbs do not change at all (e.g., *cast–cast–cast*). And a few verbs, such as *be* and *go,* change radically (i.e., *be–was–been, go–went–gone*). Only about 165 verbs currently used in English are irregular verbs.—Also termed *strong verb; anomalous verb.* Cf. *regular verb.*

▶ **lexical verb.** A verb with semantic content; specif., any verb other than an auxiliary verb.—Also termed *full verb.* See *principal verb.*

▶ **linking verb.** A connecting verb, esp. a form of *be,* that links the subject of a sentence with an adjective or complement (e.g., *Shannon is happy today* or *Marlon is a teacher*). Other verbs besides *be*—*appear, become, feel, seem,* and *taste,* to name a few—can function as linking verbs (e.g., *Linda soon grew restless*).—Also termed *connecting verb; copula; copulative verb; copular verb; being verb; asserting verb.*

▶ **main verb.** The final verb in a clause; esp., a verb that is not auxiliary {we will soon be returning to the airport}. See *principal verb.*

▶ **middle verb.** A verb that is neither intransitive nor fully transitive because it cannot ordinarily be used in a passive-voice construction (e.g., *fit, have, resemble, suit*).

▶ **modal auxiliary verb.** See *modal auxiliary verb* under **auxiliary verb.**

▶ **monotransitive verb.** A transitive verb with a single object; specif., within a verb phrase, the verb that expresses the action, state, or relation—and doesn't function as an auxiliary verb. Cf. *ditransitive verb.*

▶ **multiword verb.** See *phrasal verb.*

▶ **nonaction verb.** See *stative verb.*

▶ **nonfinite verb.** A verb form not marked for tense—that is, either an infinitive {to dive} or a participle {diving}. See **infinitive.**

▶ **notional verb.** See *principal verb.*

▶ **participial verb.** A participle that functions not as an adjective but as a verb {the trip tired me}.

▶ **phrasal prepositional verb.** A verb–particle–prepositional combination that functions as a verb {get away with} {put up with}.

▶ **phrasal verb.** A verb made up of more than one word, often a verb and a preposition acting as an adverbial particle (e.g., *knock out, point out, put off, put up with, stand aside*).—Also termed *multiword verb; prepositional verb; verb–adverb combination*.

▶ **predicate verb.** The finite verb that functions as the head of a predicate {we watched as she ascended the hill}.

▶ **predicating verb.** See *action verb*.

▶ **prepositional verb.** See *phrasal verb*.

▶ **primary verb.** A verb that can function as either a principal verb or an auxiliary verb. There are three primary verbs: (1) *be* {she is cheerful [principal]} {she is becoming more cheerful [auxiliary]}; (2) *have* {he has frostbite [principal]} {he has been frostbitten several times [auxiliary]}; and (3) *do* {you do the math [principal]} {they do need fuel badly! [auxiliary]}.

▶ **principal verb.** Within a verb phrase, the verb that expresses the action, state, or relation—and doesn't function as an auxiliary verb. If combined with another verb, it expresses the main thought of the combination (e.g., *a lion is roaring*).—Also termed *lexical verb; main verb; notional verb*. Cf. **auxiliary verb**.

▶ **pro-verb.** See *dummy auxiliary verb* under **auxiliary verb**.

▶ **pseudo-transitive verb.** A verb that takes a direct object but cannot be made into a passive-voice construction {he has a good temperament [not *a good temperament is had by him*]}.

▶ **reflexive verb.** The principal verb that precedes a reflexive pronoun {he acquitted himself with honor}.

▶ **regular verb.** A verb that is inflected by affixation and has predictable past-tense and past-participial forms. For example, the general rule for verb inflection is to add an -*ed* ending (dropping a silent -*e*, if necessary) to form the past and participle (e.g., *walk–walked–walked, reap–reaped–reaped*). Linguists call this the *dental preterite*. Most verbs in English are regular.—Also termed *weak verb*. Cf. *irregular verb*.

▶ **semi-auxiliary verb.** See **auxiliary verb**.

▶ **sensory verb.** A verb that pertains to one of the senses (*feel, look, smell, sound, taste*). They are often linking verbs {that felt great} {sounds good!} {it tastes sour}, but some of them can be transitive {he smelled the sour milk} {she sounded the alarm} or intransitive {the refrigerator smells!} {the water tastes of gasoline}.

▸ **stative verb.** A verb that expresses a state or condition instead of an activity or event—examples being *be* and *know* (as opposed to *throw* or *usurp*).—Also termed *nonaction verb*.

▸ **strong verb.** See *irregular verb*.

▸ **transitive verb.** A verb that takes a direct object {we saw the car}. It is sometimes called a *verb of incomplete predication* because it needs the object to complete its meaning.

▸ **verb of complete predication.** See *intransitive verb*.

▸ **verb of incomplete predication.** See *transitive verb*.

▸ **weak verb.** See *regular verb*.

verb–adverb combination. See *phrasal verb* under **verb.**

verbal, *adj.* **1.** Of or relating to a verbal. **2.** Of or relating to a verb.

verbal, *n.* **1.** One of the three verb forms—namely, gerunds, infinitives, and participles—that function as a noun or modifier rather than as a verb.

▸ **group verbal.** A phrase made up of more than one verbal {trying to decide is what always stalls us}.

2. In some grammars, the verb element (whether a single verb or a verb phrase) within a clause.

verbal adjective. See *participial adjective* under **adjective.**

verbalist, *n.* **1.** A critic of words; one who deals with words, esp. as a profession. **2.** Someone who prizes words over ideas and linguistic form over substance.

verbal noun. See **gerund.**

verbarian, *n.* A word-coiner; neologist.

verb cluster. 1. See *verb phrase* (sense 1 or 2) under **phrase. 2.** See *complete predicate* under **predicate.**

verb group. A verb phrase that has an adverb contained within it {will soon be going} {cannot be readily seen} {will more than double}.

verbless sentence. See **sentence.**

verb of complete predication. See *intransitive verb* under **verb.**

verb of incomplete predication. See *transitive verb* under **verb.**

verbomaniac, *n.* Someone who obsesses about words; one who is excessively preoccupied with words and their etymology, meaning, and use, almost to the exclusion of the things they represent.

verb phrase. See **phrase.**

vocabulary. 1. The word-stock of a language. **2.** The (much more limited) word-stock of an individual.—**vocabularian,** *n.*

vocative /vah-kə-tiv/, *adj.* (Of words, esp. nouns and pronouns) used to address someone or something directly. In some languages, vocative words have special forms, but not in English. The term is still used for the *vocative O* {O Canada}.

vocative, *n.* **1.** The use of the name or abstraction being addressed directly {Mrs. Robinson, do you really mean to do this?} {Frank, I appreciate your candor}. **2.** The name or abstraction so used.—Also termed *nominative of address.*

vocative imperative. See **imperative.**

vogue word. A faddish term (e.g., *awesome*).

voice. 1. A quality of a transitive verb showing whether the subject acts (active voice) or is acted on (passive voice); in other words, whether the subject performs or receives the action of the verb. Compare *the car is towing the trailer* (active voice: the car is acting) with *the trailer is being towed by the car* (passive voice: the trailer is receiving). See **active voice** & **passive voice. 2.** A sound produced by vibration of the vocal cords and used to pronounce vowels and some consonants.

vowel, *n.* **1.** A spoken sound produced without interrupting the airflow and without audible friction. **2.** Broadly, the most prominent sound in a syllable. **3.** A letter that represents such a sound, usu. *a, e, i, o, u.* Cf. **consonant.**

vulgarism. 1. A word or phrase widely thought to be offensive to good taste or indicative of lack of culture or refinement, esp. because it is coarse or scatological. **2.** Any violation of good usage. Cf. **illiteracy; catachresis; solecism.**

weak plural. See **plural.**

weak verb. See *regular verb* under **verb.**

were-**subjunctive.** See *past subjunctive* under **subjunctive,** *n.*

whiz-deletion. The reduction of a relative clause by omitting the relative pronoun and the *be*-verb (e.g., *who is*—hence *whiz*) {the person [who is] sitting there happens to be my cousin}.

wh- **question.** See **question.**

word. The smallest complete unit that can be uttered and understood alone and can be used alongside similar units to make up a sentence. It is typically identifiable as an item listed separately in a reliable dictionary. In print, a word has a space on each side to set it off.

▶ **compound word.** See **compound.**

▶ **content word.** A noun, verb, adjective, or adverb—that is, a word that conveys semantic significance as opposed to signaling syntactic relationships (as function words do).—Also termed *lexical morpheme.*

▶ **function word.** A word that is more important for the part it plays in the structure of the sentence than for its semantic content. Examples are articles, prepositions, conjunctions, auxiliaries, interjections, *more* and *most* used in comparisons, *to* as part of the infinitive (traditionally viewed as a preposition), and the expletives *there* and *it.*—Also termed *structure word; form word; functional morpheme.*

▶ **portmanteau word** /pohrt-man-toh/. A word formed by combining parts of two existing words, such as *motel* (from *motor* and *hotel*) or *brunch* (from *breakfast* and *lunch*).—Also termed *blend.* See p. 219.

▶ **superordinate word.** See **superordinate.**

▶ **unmarked word.** See **unmarked word.**

word class. A group of words with the same or similar syntactic qualities and grammatical categories. Modern linguists often use this term in preference to *part of speech.* See **part of speech.**

▶ **closed word class.** A verbal type whose members can be exhaustively listed or recognized—examples being pronouns, auxiliary verbs, and irregular verbs.—Often shortened to *closed class.*

▶ **open word class.** A verbal type whose members cannot be exhaustively listed or recognized, such as nouns, verbs, and adjectives.

word formation. The study or practice of building words from roots and affixes. See **morphology.**

word order. The sequencing of words, esp. as a signal of grammatical structure.

word-stem. See **stem.**

yes–no question. See **question.**

zero article. See **article.**

zero derivation. See **conversion.**

zero plural. See *uninflected plural* under **plural.**

zeugma /zoog-mə/. **1.** A construction in which one part of speech applies to two things but matches only one for number, gender, etc. {neither the sisters nor the brother is available just now}. **2.** See **syllepsis (1).**

zombie noun. See **noun.**

Sources for Inset Quotations

Epigraphs on Frontispiece

John of Salisbury (ca. 1120–80), *The Metalogicon of John of Salisbury: A Twelfth-Century Defense of the Verbal and Logical Arts of the Trivium*, trans. D. D. McGarry (Berkeley: Univ. of California Press, 1955), 1.13, quoted in *Medieval Grammar and Rhetoric: Language Arts and Literary Theory, AD 300–1475*, ed. Rita Copeland and Ineke Sluiter (Oxford: Oxford Univ. Press, 2009), 493.

L. A. G. Strong, *English for Pleasure* (London: Methuen, 1941), 2.

Ayn Rand, *The Art of Nonfiction: A Guide for Writers and Readers*, ed. Robert Mayhew (New York: Plume, 2001), 101 [reconstructed from lectures delivered in 1969].

V. Louise Higgins, "Approaching Usage in the Classroom" (1960), in *Readings in Applied English Linguistics*, ed. Harold Byron Allen, 2nd ed. (New York: Appleton-Century-Crofts, 1964), 335.

Page 1: I. A. Richards, *The Philosophy of Rhetoric* (New York: Oxford Univ. Press, 1936), 52.

Page 3: Bertrand Evans, "Grammar and Writing," in *A Linguistics Reader*, ed. Graham Wilson (New York: Harper and Row, 1967), 112.

Page 5: Simeon Potter, *Our Language*, rev. ed. (Baltimore: Penguin Books, 1966), 7.

Page 14: W. Nelson Francis, "Revolution in Grammar" (1954), in *Readings in Applied English Linguistics*, ed. Harold Byron Allen, 2nd ed. (New York: Appleton-Century-Crofts, 1964), 77.

Page 23: Noah Webster, *A Grammatical Institute of the English Language*, 5th Conn. ed. (Hartford, CT: Hudson and Goodwin, 1796), 3.

Page 36: Patricia T. O'Conner, *Woe Is I: The Grammarphobe's Guide to Better English in Plain English*, 2nd ed. (New York: Riverhead, 2003), 1.

Page 43: William Cobbett, *A Grammar of the English Language: In a Series of Letters* (New York: Printed for author by Clayton and Kingsland, 1818), 9.

Page 71: Donald Hall, *Writing Well*, 4th ed. (Boston: Little, Brown, 1982), 83.

Page 82: W. F. Bolton, *The Language of 1984: Orwell's English and Ours* (Knoxville: Univ. of Tennessee Press, 1984), 52.

Page 90: Lucille Vaughan Payne, *The Lively Art of Writing* (Chicago: Follett, 1965), 101.

Page 97: W. P. Jowett, *Chatting About English* (London: Longmans, Green, 1945), 140.

Page 127: John R. Trimble, *Writing with Style: Conversations on the Art of Writing*, 2nd ed. (Upper Saddle River, NJ: Prentice Hall, 2000), 77.

Page 135: W. P. Jowett, *Chatting About English* (London: Longmans, Green, 1945), 184.

Page 137: George Frederick Genung, *The Working Principles of Grammar* (Springfield, MA: Home Correspondence School, 1922), 184.

Page 142: Richard Burton, *Why Do You Talk like That? Not to Mention: Why Do You Write That Way?* (Indianapolis: Bobbs-Merrill, 1929), 186–87.

Page 144: Lester S. King, *Why Not Say It Clearly: A Guide to Scientific Writing* (Boston: Little, Brown, 1978), 34.

Page 159: Louis Foley, *Beneath the Crust of Words* (Columbus: Ohio State Univ. Press, 1928), 131.

Page 165: Barbara Tuchman, *Practicing History: Selected Essays* (New York: Alfred A. Knopf, 1981), 4.

Page 175: Sheridan Baker, *The Practical Stylist*, 8th ed. (New York: Longman, 1998), 101.

Page 181: Gertrude Stein, "Poetry and Grammar" (1935), in *Perspectives on Style*, ed. Frederick Candelaria (Boston: Allyn and Bacon, 1968), 46.

Page 182: Wayne C. Booth, "The Rhetorical Stance" (1963), in *Contemporary Rhetoric: A Conceptual Background with Readings*, ed. W. Ross Winterowd (New York: Harcourt Brace Jovanovich, 1975), 79.

Page 195: James Sledd, "Syntactic Strictures" (1961), in *Readings in Applied English Linguistics*, ed. Harold Byron Allen, 2nd ed. (New York: Appleton-Century-Crofts, 1964), 420.

Page 205: Joan Didion, "Why I Write" (1976), in *The Living Language: A Reader*, ed. Linda A. Morris et al. (San Diego: Harcourt Brace Jovanovich, 1984), 400.

Page 215: Simeon Potter, *Modern Linguistics*, 2nd ed. (London: Deutsch, 1967), 90–91.

Page 225: Peter Farb, *Word Play: What Happens When People Talk* (1974; repr., New York: Alfred A. Knopf, 1975), 84.

Page 226: Max Black, *The Labyrinth of Language* (New York: Praeger, 1968), 73.

Page 231: David Foster Wallace, "Authority and American Usage," in *Consider the Lobster and Other Essays* (Boston: Little, Brown, 2005), 97–98.

Page 239: Thomas R. Lounsbury, *History of the English Language*, rev. ed. (New York: H. Holt, 1907), 187.

Page 242: Sidney Greenbaum, *Good English and the Grammarian* (London: Longman, 1988), 33–34.

Page 251: Adam Gowans Whyte, *An Anthology of Errors* (London: Chaterson, 1947), ix–x.

Page 256: William Dwight Whitney, *The Life and Growth of Language* (1875; repr., New York: Dover, 1979), 34.

Page 257: Margaret Schlauch, *The Gift of Tongues* (1943; repr., London: Allen and Unwin, 1960), 261.

Page 258: Marcus Aurelius, *Meditations*, trans. Maxwell Staniforth (Baltimore: Penguin Books, 1964), 37 (1.10).

Page 262: Mark Twain, "Fenimore Cooper's Literary Offenses" (1895), in *A Reader for Writers: A Critical Anthology of Prose Readings*, ed. William Targ (New York: McGraw-Hill, 1951), 248.

Page 263: Paul Roberts, "The Relation of Linguistics to the Teaching of English," in *A Linguistics Reader*, ed. Graham Wilson (New York: Harper and Row, 1967), 33–34.

Page 265: Wilson Follett, *Modern American Usage: A Guide* (New York: Hill and Wang, 1966), 12.

Page 267: Konstantin Fedin, "Notebook," in Maxim Gorky et al., *On the Art and Craft of Writing*, trans. Alex Miller (Moscow: Progress, 1972), 261.

Page 279: Edward N. Teall, *Putting Words to Work: A Lively Guide to Correct and Vigorous English* (New York: D. Appleton-Century, 1940), 4.

Page 281: Wallace L. Anderson and Norman C. Stageberg, eds., *Introductory Readings on Language*, 3rd ed. (New York: Holt, Rinehart, and Winston, 1970), 127.

Page 283: Henry Bradley, *The Making of English* (1904; repr., New York: Macmillan, 1951), 74.

Page 284: R. L. Trask, *Language: The Basics* (London: Routledge, 1995), 79.

Page 285: A. P. Herbert, *What a Word!* (London: Methuen, 1935), 2.

Page 288: George Carlin, *Brain Droppings* (New York: Hyperion, 1997), 115.

Page 289: Henry Alexander, *The Story of Our Language* (Toronto: Thomas Nelson and Sons, 1940), 16.

Page 293: Sidney Greenbaum, *Good English and the Grammarian* (London: Longman, 1988), ix.

Page 296: Richard Grant White, *Every-Day English* (Boston: Houghton, Mifflin, 1880), xxiii.

Page 299: William H. C. Propp, introduction to *Exodus 1–18: A New Translation with Introduction and Commentary*, Anchor Bible 2 (New York: Doubleday, 1999), 40.

Page 302: M. Alderton Pink, *Craftsmanship in Writing* (London: Macmillan, 1960), 55.

Page 304: Henry Bett, *Some Secrets of Style* (London: Allen and Unwin, 1932), 93.

Page 307: S. I. Hayakawa, *Symbol, Status, and Personality* (New York: Harcourt, Brace, and World, 1963), 17.

Page 313: Henry Bradley, *The Making of English* (1904; repr., New York: Macmillan, 1951), 18.

Page 314: Otto Jespersen, *Growth and Structure of the English Language*, 9th ed. (1938; repr., Chicago: Univ. of Chicago Press, 1982), 13.

Page 315: Henry Bett, *Some Secrets of Style* (London: Allen and Unwin, 1932), 93.

Page 317: Mortimer Adler, "How to Read a Dictionary" (1941), in *Weigh the Word*, ed. Charles B. Jennings et al. (New York: Harper, 1957), 189.

Page 323: Konstantin Fedin, "Notebook," in Maxim Gorky et al., *On the Art and Craft of Writing*, trans. Alex Miller (Moscow: Progress, 1972), 257.

Page 327: Maxine Hairston, *Successful Writing*, 2nd ed. (New York: W. W. Norton, 1986), 125.

Page 345: Pico Iyer, "In Praise of the Humble Comma," in *About Language: A Reader for Writers*, ed. William H. Roberts and Gregoire Turgeon, 2nd ed. (Boston: Houghton Mifflin, 1989), 58.

Page 351: G. H. Vallins, *Good English: How to Write It* (London: Pan Books, 1951), 103.

Page 354: Reginald O. Kapp, *The Presentation of Technical Information* (London: Constable, 1948), 16.

simple predicate *were*; *we* is the simple subject of a relative clause, with the corresponding simple predicate *played*]}.

▸ **subject of an infinitive.** A noun element that precedes an infinitive in an infinitive phrase {the participants asked her to make the presentation} {for him to have stayed silent seems anomalous}. As in those examples, if the subject of the infinitive is a pronoun, it is inevitably in the objective case.

▸ **understood subject.** The pronoun *you* when it is only implicit (not expressly stated) as the subject of a verb in the imperative mood {[you] don't go in that room!}.

subject case. See *nominative case* under **case.**

subject clause. See **clause.**

subjective. See **nominative,** *adj.*

subjective adjective. See *predicate adjective* under **adjective.**

subjective case. See *nominative case* under **case.**

subjective complement. See **complement.**

subjective noun. See **predicate nominative.**

subjective pronoun. See **predicate nominative.**

subject of an infinitive. See **subject.**

subject–verb agreement. See **agreement.**

subjunctive /səb-jən[g]k-tiv/, *adj.* (Of a verb) expressing a contrary-to-fact assumption {if I were you}, a supposition {if I were to go, I'd be late}, a wish {I wish I were better!}, a demand or command {I insist that you be there}, a suggestion or proposal {I suggested that she think about it more carefully}, or a statement of necessity {it's necessary that we all be there}. Cf. **imperative, interrogative** & **indicative.** See §§ 167–71; pp. 103–5, 109–11, 114–15.

subjunctive, *n.* A verb mood that expresses a contrary-to-fact assumption, a supposition, a wish, a demand or command, a suggestion or proposal, or a statement of necessity.

▸ **formulaic subjunctive.** An idiom or set phrase that contains a subjunctive verb {would that it were so!} {come what may, we'll be there} {be it noted that she wasn't even present}.

▸ **mandative subjunctive.** A subjunctive verb used in expressing a demand, proposal, resolution, or other attitude of requirement or obligation {I demand that you be there} {I propose that he wait until all the bids are in}. The mandative subjunctive is much more prevalent in AmE than in BrE.

Page 371: T. S. Eliot, quoted in *Good Advice on Writing: Writers Past and Present on How to Write Well*, ed. William Safire and Leonard Safir (New York: Simon and Schuster, 1992), 214.

Page 375: Karen Elizabeth Gordon, *The New Well-Tempered Sentence: A Punctuation Handbook for the Innocent, the Eager, and the Doomed*, rev. ed. (New York: Ticknor and Fields, 1993), ix.

Page 383: W. Ross Winterowd, *Contemporary Rhetoric: A Conceptual Background with Readings* (New York: Harcourt Brace Jovanovich, 1975), 23.

Page 388: Isaac Babel, "Guy de Maupassant" (1932), in *The Complete Works of Isaac Babel*, trans. Peter W. Constantine (New York: W. W. Norton, 2002), 681.

Page 408: David Mulroy, *The War Against Grammar* (Portsmouth, NH: Boynton/Cook, 2003), 3.

Page 426: Walter Nash, *An Uncommon Tongue: The Uses and Resources of English* (London: Routledge, 1992), 31.

Page 462: H. W. Fowler, *A Dictionary of Modern English Usage* (Oxford: Oxford Univ. Press, 1926), 458.

Page 463: Roy Harris, *The Language Machine* (Ithaca, NY: Cornell Univ. Press, 1987), 127.

Page 471: C. T. Onions, *Modern English Syntax*, rev. B. D. H. Miller, new ed. (London: Routledge, 1971), 1.

Page 473: James Sledd, "Something About Language and Social Class," in *The Legacy of Language: A Tribute to Charlton Laird*, ed. Phillip C. Boardman (Reno: Univ. of Nevada Press, 1987), 98–99.

Select Bibliography

English Grammar

Aarts, Bas. *Oxford Modern English Grammar.* Oxford: Oxford Univ. Press, 2011.

Biber, Douglas, Stig Johansson, Geoffrey Leech, Susan Conrad, and Edward Finegan. *Longman Grammar of Spoken and Written English.* Harlow, Essex, UK: Pearson Education, 1999.

Brown, Goold. *The Grammar of English Grammars.* 10th ed. New York: William Wood, 1851.

Chalker, Sylvia, and Edmund S. C. Weiner. *The Oxford Dictionary of English Grammar.* Oxford: Clarendon, 1994.

Crystal, David. *Making Sense of Grammar.* Harlow, Essex, UK: Pearson Education, 2004.

Curme, George O. *English Grammar.* New York: Barnes and Noble Books, 1947.

———. *English Syntax.* Boston: D. C. Heath, 1931.

———. *Parts of Speech and Accidence.* New York: D. C. Heath, 1935.

Fernald, James C. *English Grammar Simplified.* Rev. ed. Cedric Gale. New York: Barnes and Noble, 1963.

Good, C. Edward. *A Grammar Book for You and I (Oops, Me!).* Sterling, VA: Capital Books, 2002.

Greenbaum, Sidney. *The Oxford English Grammar.* Oxford: Oxford Univ. Press, 1996.

Huddleston, Rodney D., and Geoffrey K. Pullum. *The Cambridge Grammar of the English Language.* Cambridge: Cambridge Univ. Press, 2002.

Hurford, James R. *Grammar: A Student's Guide.* Cambridge: Cambridge Univ. Press, 1994.

Jespersen, Otto. *Essentials of English Grammar.* New York: Holt, 1933. Reprint, Tuscaloosa: Univ. of Alabama Press, 1964.

Kittredge, George Lyman, and Frank Edgar Farley. *An Advanced English Grammar.* Boston: Ginn, 1913.

Opdycke, John B. *Harper's English Grammar.* Rev. Stewart Benedict. New York: Harper and Row, 1965.

Quirk, Randolph, et al. *A Comprehensive Grammar of the English Language.* London: Longmans, 1985.

Sledd, James. *A Short Introduction to English Grammar.* Chicago: Scott, Foresman, 1959.

Zandvoort, R. W. *A Handbook of English Grammar.* 3rd ed. Englewood Cliffs, NJ: Prentice-Hall, 1966.

Transformational Grammar

Bach, Emmon. *An Introduction to Transformational Grammars.* New York: Holt, Rinehart and Winston, 1964.

Jacobs, Roderick A., and Peter S. Rosenbaum. *English Transformational Grammar.* Waltham, MA: Xerox College, 1968.

Liles, Bruce L. *An Introductory Transformational Grammar.* Englewood Cliffs, NJ: Prentice-Hall, 1971.

Malmstrom, Jean, and Constance Weaver. *Transgrammar: English Structure, Style, and Dialects.* Glenview, IL: Scott, Foresman, 1973.

Palmatier, Robert A. *A Glossary for English Transformational Grammar.* New York: Appleton-Century-Crofts, 1972.

Radford, Andrew. *Transformational Grammar: A First Course.* Cambridge: Cambridge Univ. Press, 1988.

Thomas, Owen. *Transformational Grammar and the Teacher of English.* New York: Holt, Rinehart and Winston, 1965.

English Usage

Bernstein, Theodore M. *The Careful Writer: A Modern Guide to English Usage.* New York: Atheneum, 1965.

Burchfield, R. W. *The New Fowler's Modern English Usage.* Oxford: Oxford Univ. Press, 2004.

Copperud, Roy H. *American Usage and Style: The Consensus.* New York: Van Nostrand Reinhold, 1980.

Evans, Bergen, and Cornelia Evans. *A Dictionary of Contemporary American Usage.* New York: Random House, 1957.

Follett, Wilson. *Modern American Usage: A Guide.* Rev. Erik Wensberg. Rev. ed. New York: Hill and Wang, 1998.

Fowler, H. W. *A Dictionary of Modern English Usage*. Oxford: Oxford Univ. Press, 1926. Rev. Ernest Gowers. 2nd ed. New York: Oxford Univ. Press, 1965.

Fowler, H. W., and F. G. Fowler. *The King's English*. Oxford: Clarendon, 1906. 3rd ed. Oxford: Clarendon, 1934.

Garner, Bryan A. *Garner's Dictionary of Legal Usage*. 3rd ed. New York: Oxford Univ. Press, 2011.

———. *Garner's Modern English Usage*. 4th ed. New York: Oxford Univ. Press, 2016.

Lamberts, J. J. *A Short Introduction to English Usage*. New York: McGraw-Hill, 1972.

Merriam-Webster's Concise Dictionary of English Usage. Springfield, MA: Merriam-Webster, 2002.

Norris, Mary. *Between You and Me: Confessions of a Comma Queen*. New York: W. W. Norton, 2015.

O'Conner, Patricia. *Woe Is I: The Grammarphobe's Guide to Better English in Plain English*. 2nd ed. New York: Riverhead, 2003.

Partridge, Eric. *Usage and Abusage: A Guide to Good English*. 1942. Rev. Janet Whitcut. New ed. New York: W. W. Norton, 1994.

Peters, Pam. *The Cambridge Guide to English Usage*. Cambridge: Cambridge Univ. Press, 2004.

Swan, Michael. *Practical English Usage*. 3rd ed. Oxford: Oxford Univ. Press, 2005.

Wallraff, Barbara. *Word Court*. New York: Harcourt, 2000.

———. *Your Own Words*. New York: Counterpoint, 2004.

Walsh, Bill. *The Elephants of Style*. New York: McGraw-Hill, 2004.

———. *Lapsing into a Comma*. Chicago: Contemporary Books, 2000.

———. *Yes, I Could Care Less: How to Be a Language Snob without Being a Jerk*. New York: St. Martin's Griffin, 2013.

Grammatical Pedagogy

Alston, R. C. *English Grammars Written in English*. London: E. J. Arnold and Sons, 1965.

Braddock, Richard Reed. *Research in Written Composition*. Champaign, IL: National Council of Teachers of English, 1963.

Carr, Jean Ferguson, Stephen L. Carr, and Lucille M. Schultz. *Archives of Instruction: Nineteenth-Century Rhetorics, Readers, and Composition Books in the United States*. Carbondale: Southern Illinois Univ. Press, 2005.

Chubb, Percival. *The Teaching of English in the Elementary and the Secondary School*. New York: Macmillan, 1910.

Connors, Robert J. *Composition—Rhetoric: Backgrounds, Theory, and Pedagogy*. Pittsburgh: Univ. of Pittsburgh Press, 1997.

Copeland, Rita, and Ineke Sluiter, eds. *Medieval Grammar and Rhetoric: Language Arts and Literary Theory, AD 300–1475*. New York: Oxford Univ. Press, 2009.

Crowley, Sharon. *Composition in the University*. Pittsburgh: Univ. of Pittsburgh Press, 1998.

Dalton-Puffer, Christiane, Dieter Kastovsky, Nikolaus Ritt, and Herbert Schendl, eds. *Syntax, Style and Grammatical Norms: English from 1500–2000*. Bern: Peter Lang, 2006.

DeBoar, John J., Walter V. Kaulfers, and Helen Rand Miller. *Teaching Secondary English*. New York: McGraw-Hill, 1951.

Gneuss, Helmut. *English Language Scholarship: A Survey and Bibliography from the Beginnings to the End of the Nineteenth Century*. Binghamton, NY: Center for Medieval and Early Renaissance Studies, 1996.

Görlach, Manfred. *An Annotated Bibliography of 19th-Century Grammars of English*. Amsterdam: John Benjamins, 1998.

———. *English in Nineteenth-Century England: An Introduction*. Cambridge: Cambridge Univ. Press, 1999.

Hunter, Susan, and Ray Wallace, eds. *The Place of Grammar in Writing Instruction*. Portsmouth, NH: Boynton/Cook, 1995.

Lyman, Rollo LaVerne. *English Grammar in American Schools before 1850*. Washington, DC: Government Printing Office, 1922.

Michael, Ian. *English Grammatical Categories and the Tradition to 1800*. Cambridge: Cambridge Univ. Press, 1970.

————. *The Teaching of English from the Sixteenth Century to 1870.* Cambridge: Cambridge Univ. Press, 1987.

Mulroy, David. *The War Against Grammar.* Portsmouth, NH: Boynton/Cook, 2003.

Pooley, Robert C. *Teaching English Grammar.* New York: Appleton-Century-Crofts, 1957.

Wright, Laura, ed. *The Development of Standard English 1300–1800: Theories, Descriptions, Conflicts.* Cambridge: Cambridge Univ. Press, 2000.

The English Language

Alexander, Henry. *The Story of Our Language.* Toronto: Thomas Nelson and Sons, 1940. Rev. ed. Garden City, NY: Dolphin Books, 1962.

Allen, Harold Byron, ed. *Readings in Applied English Linguistics.* 2nd ed. New York: Appleton-Century-Crofts, 1964.

Baugh, Albert C., and Thomas Cable. *A History of the English Language.* 5th ed. Englewood Cliffs, NJ: Prentice-Hall, 2001.

Bryant, Margaret M. *Modern English and Its Heritage.* 2nd ed. New York: Macmillan, 1962.

Burchfield, Robert W. *The English Language.* Oxford: Oxford Univ. Press, 1985.

————. *Unlocking the English Language.* New York: Hill and Wang, 1991.

Crystal, David. *The Cambridge Encyclopedia of the English Language.* 2nd ed. Cambridge: Cambridge Univ. Press, 2003.

————. *The English Language.* London: Penguin Books, 1988.

Flexner, Stuart Berg, and Anne H. Soukhanov. *Speaking Freely: A Guided Tour of American English.* New York: Oxford Univ. Press, 1997.

Garner, Bryan A. *Garner on Language and Writing.* Chicago: American Bar Association, 2009.

Jespersen, Otto. *Growth and Structure of the English Language.* 9th ed. 1938. Reprint, Chicago: Univ. of Chicago Press, 1982.

Krapp, George Philip. *Modern English: Its Growth and Present Use.* 1909. Reprint, New York: Frederick Ungar, 1966. 2nd ed. Edited by Albert H. Marckwardt. New York: Charles Scribner's Sons, 1969.

McArthur, Tom, ed. *The Oxford Companion to the English Language.* Oxford: Oxford Univ. Press, 1992.

McKnight, George H. *English Words and Their Background.* New York: D. Appleton, 1925. Reprint, New York: Gordian, 1969.

———. *Modern English in the Making.* New York: D. Appleton, 1928. Reprinted as *The Evolution of the English Language.* New York: Dover, 1968.

Mencken, H. L. *The American Language.* Edited by Raven I. McDavid Jr. Abr. ed. New York: Alfred A. Knopf, 1963.

Potter, Simeon. *Our Language.* 1950. Rev. ed. Baltimore: Penguin Books, 1966.

Pyles, Thomas, and John Algeo. *The Origins and Development of the English Language.* 6th ed. New York: Wadsworth, 2009.

Smith, Logan Pearsall. *The English Language.* 3rd ed. London: Oxford Univ. Press, 1966.

Strong, L. A. G. *English for Pleasure.* London: Methuen, 1941.

Plain English

Eagleson, Robert D., Gloria Jones, and Sue Hassall. *Writing in Plain English.* Canberra: Australian Government Publishing Service, 1990.

Flesch, Rudolf. *The Art of Plain Talk.* New York: Harper and Bros., 1946.

Gowers, Ernest. *The Complete Plain Words.* Revised by Sidney Greenbaum and Janet Whitcut. 1st Am. ed. Boston: D. R. Godine, 2002. Revised by Rebecca Gowers. New ed. London: Particular Books, 2014.

Gunning, Robert. *The Technique of Clear Writing.* Rev. ed. New York: McGraw-Hill, 1968.

Lauchman, Richard. *Plain Style: Techniques for Simple, Concise, Emphatic Business Writing.* New York: AMACOM, 1993.

Steinberg, Erwin R., ed. *Plain Language: Principles and Practice.* Detroit: Wayne State Univ. Press, 1991.

Style Manuals

The Associated Press Stylebook and Briefing on Media Law. Edited by Darrell Christian, Sally Jacobsen, and David Minthorn. 2013 ed. New York: Basic Books, 2013.

The Chicago Manual of Style. 16th ed. Chicago: Univ. of Chicago Press, 2010.

Garner, Bryan A. *The Redbook: A Manual on Legal Style.* 3rd ed. St. Paul: West, 2013.

Sabin, William A. *The Gregg Reference Manual: A Manual of Style, Grammar, Usage, and Formatting.* Tribute ed. New York: McGraw-Hill, 2011.

English-Language Dictionaries
(New versions of most issued periodically.)

The American Heritage Dictionary of the English Language.

The Concise Oxford Dictionary.

Merriam-Webster's Collegiate Dictionary.

The New Oxford American Dictionary.

The New Shorter Oxford English Dictionary.

The Oxford American Dictionary and Thesaurus.

The Oxford English Dictionary. 2nd ed. 20 vols. Oxford: Clarendon, 1989. Additions 1993–97, edited by John Simpson and Edmund Weiner. 3rd ed. 2000–present, edited by Michael Proffitt. *OED Online.* Oxford University Press <http://dictionary.oed.com>.

The Random House Dictionary of the English Language.

Webster's New International Dictionary of the English Language. 2nd ed. Springfield, MA: Merriam, 1934.

Webster's New World College Dictionary.

Webster's Third New International Dictionary of the English Language.

Etymology

Ayto, John. *Dictionary of Word Origins.* New York: Arcade, 1990.

Barnhart, Robert K., ed. *The Barnhart Dictionary of Etymology.* Bronx: H. W. Wilson, 1988.

The Concise Oxford Dictionary of English Etymology. Edited by T. F. Hoad. Oxford: Clarendon, 1986.

Hendrickson, Robert. *The Encyclopedia of Word and Phrase Origins.* 4th ed. New York: Facts on File, 2008.

The Merriam-Webster New Book of Word Histories. Springfield, MA: Merriam-Webster, 1991.

The Oxford Dictionary of English Etymology. Ed. C. T. Onions, with G. W. S. Friedrichsen and R. W. Burchfield. Oxford: Clarendon, 1966.

Partridge, Eric. *Origins: A Short Etymological Dictionary of Modern English.* 4th ed. London: Routledge and Kegan Paul, 1966.

Rawson, Hugh. *Devious Derivations.* New York: Crown Trade Paperbacks, 1994.

Room, Adrian. *Dictionary of True Etymologies*. London: Routledge, 1986.

Skeat, Walter W. *An Etymological Dictionary of the English Language*. 4th ed. Oxford: Clarendon Press, 1910.

Weekley, Ernest. *Etymological Dictionary of Modern English*. New York: Dutton, 1921. Reprint, 2 vols. New York: Dover, 1967.

Punctuation

Brittain, Robert. *A Pocket Guide to Correct Punctuation*. 3rd ed. Hauppage, NY: Barron's, 1997.

Capon, Rene J. *The Associated Press Guide to Punctuation*. Cambridge, MA: Basic Books, 2003.

Carey, G. V. *Mind the Stop: A Brief Guide to Punctuation with a Note on Proof-Correction*. Rev. ed. Harmondsworth, UK: Penguin, 1971.

Gordon, Karen E. *The New Well-Tempered Sentence: A Punctuation Handbook for the Innocent, the Eager, and the Doomed*. Rev. and exp. ed. New York: Ticknor and Fields, 1993.

Partridge, Eric. *You Have a Point There: A Guide to Punctuation and Its Allies*. London: Routledge and Kegan Paul, 1953. Reprint, 1978.

Paxson, William C. *The Mentor Guide to Punctuation*. New York: New American Library, 1986.

Shaw, Harry. *Punctuate It Right!* New York: Barnes and Noble, 1963.

Literary Terms

Abrams, M. H. *A Glossary of Literary Terms*. 9th ed. Boston: Wadsworth, 2005.

Baldick, Chris. *The Concise Oxford Dictionary of Literary Terms*. Oxford: Oxford Univ. Press, 1990.

Barnet, Sylvan, Morton Berman, and William Burto. *A Dictionary of Literary Terms*. Boston: Little, Brown, 1960.

Cuddon, J. A. *The Penguin Dictionary of Literary Terms and Literary Theory*. 4th ed. London: Penguin, 1999.

Farnsworth, Ward. *Farnsworth's Classical English Rhetoric*. Boston: David R. Godine, 2011.

Frye, Northrup, Sheridan Baker, George Perkins, and Barbara M. Perkins. *The Harper Handbook to Literature*. New York: Longman, 1997.

Garner, Bryan A. "Glossary of Grammatical, Rhetorical, and Other Language-Related Terms." In *Garner's Modern English Usage*, pp. 985–1036. 4th ed. New York: Oxford Univ. Press, 2016.

Lanham, Richard A. *A Handlist of Rhetorical Terms: A Guide for Students of English Literature*. 2nd ed. Berkeley: Univ. of California Press, 1991.

The New Princeton Encyclopedia of Poetry and Poetics. Edited by Alex Preminger and T. V. F. Brogan. New York: MJF Books, 1993.

Quinn, Edward. *A Dictionary of Literary and Thematic Terms*. New York: Facts on File, 1999.

Acknowledgments

A book like this one couldn't materialize without the contributions of many friends and allies. I'm especially grateful to my own collegiate teachers of grammar: our close family friend the late Pat Sullivan of West Texas A&M University, and both Thomas Cable and the late John W. Velz of the University of Texas at Austin. My de facto godfather, the noted Chaucerian Alan M. F. Gunn of Texas Tech University, aroused my interest in grammar when I was young and encouraged it through the time when I started writing professionally about English philology nearly 40 years ago.

My parents, of course, were responsible for much of this early exposure to English professors and for the almost-nonstop commentary on the English language in the Garner household. Little did they know . . . or perhaps somehow they did.

Some debts are more immediately related to the book. Garrett Kiely and Mary Laur of the University of Chicago Press encouraged me to expand my chapter 5 of *The Chicago Manual of Style* into this stand-alone book—and gave useful advice as the manuscript took shape. Their outside reviewers of the manuscript—John Hoarty, John McIntyre, Elizabeth Metzger, Alison Parker, and David Yerkes—made many valuable suggestions. I'm grateful to Shmuel Gerber for reading and commenting on an early draft. Ruth Goring of the University of Chicago Press and Karen Magnuson of Portland, Oregon, each copyedited the final manuscript with acumen and punctilio.

The book's ultimate form and focus were influenced by my informal panel of local educators—namely, David Brown of St. Mark's School of Texas; Monica Cochran and Megan Griffin of Ursuline Academy of Dallas; Gary M. Nied of Cistercian Preparatory School; and Katherine Downey, Jennifer Boulanger, and Jennifer McEachern of the Hockaday School. In one of our sessions, Marie Sidonie of St. Paul also made helpful suggestions.

As always, my colleagues at LawProse proved enormously helpful: I'm grateful to Jeff Newman, Tiger Jackson, Becky R. McDaniel, and Ryden McComas Anderson for the relentless pains they took to ensure the accuracy and reliability of the book. In particular, Jeff Newman—a typesetter as well as a splendid lawyer and editor—made possible the many diagrams and graphic elements, including ngrams, that appear throughout. I am fortunate to have a team as dedicated and as professional as Jeff, Tiger, Becky, and Ryden.

The book is dedicated to my wife Karolyne, our general counsel at LawProse Inc., who similarly helped on various aspects of the book, such as collecting exemplars of punctuation marks from major writers for part 5. She makes home life and work life a great pleasure. For a writer or anyone else, that's priceless.

—B.A.G.
Dallas, Texas
22 Jan. 2016

Word Index

Asterisk (*) denotes an invariably inferior form.

a, 20–21, 22, 61, 62, 228
aberration, 329
abhor, 229
abhorrence, 329
abhorrent, 329
abide, 74, 329
ability, 228
abjure, 228–29
abound, 329
about, 129, 130, 139, 140, 229, 240, 283–84, 286
above, 130, 139, 143
abridgment, 229
abrogate, 229
absolute, 68
absolve, 329
absolved, 329
abstain, 329
abstruse, 298
abut, 329
accede, 329
accept, 229
acceptance, 229
acceptation, 229
access, 229–30
accommodate, 329
accompanied, 329
accompany, 329
accord, 230, 329
accordance, 230, 329
according to, 140
account, 329
accountable, 329
accuse, 230, 329
acknowledgment, 230
acquainted, 329
acquiesce, 230, 329
acquit, 329
across, 129, 139
act, 81, 215, 330
actual fact, in, 230
actually, 230

acuity, 230
acumen, 230
acute, 230
ad, 217
adapt, 232, 330
addendum; addenda, 231
addicted, 231, 330
additionally, 237
adduce, 231
adept, 330
adequate, 68, 231, 330
adhere, 330
adherence, 231, 330
adhesion, 231, 330
adjacent, 330
adjure, 228–29
adjust, 330
administration; administer; *administrate, 217
administrator; administratrix, 271
admission, 231–32
admit, 330
admittance, 231–32
adopt, 232
adopted, 232
adoptive, 232
adult, 284
adverse, 232, 330
advert, 330
advice, 232
advise, 232
adviser; advisor, 232
advisory, 232
affect, 232–33, 282
affiliate, 330
affirmative, in the, 233
afflict, 284, 330
affront, 268
after, 129, 130, 133, 139, 148, 149, 194, 233, 273, 316
*after having [+ past participle], 233
afterward, 129, 233, 320

afterwards, 320
afterword, 233
against, 139, 295
*aged —— years old, 233
agenda, 28, 233–34
agendas, 234
agendum, 233
aggravate, 234
agree, 330
aid, 234
aide, 234
*ain't, 234
airplane, 216
albeit, 148
alga; algae, 27
alibi, 234
alight, 74
alike, 129
all, 60, 234, 299
alleged(ly), 234
allow, 330
all ready, 235
all right, 235
all together, 236
allude, 235
allusion, 235
almost, 129
alongside (of), 139, 140, 235
along with, 120, 140
a lot; *alot, 235
already, 235
*alright, 235
also, 129, 147
altar, 236
alter, 236
alternate, 236, 330
alternative, 236
although, 146, 148, 166, 188, 236, 298, 322
altogether, 129, 236
alum, 236
alumna; alumnae, 27, 236
alumnus; alumni, 27, 28, 236
always, 129, 130, 135, 249
am, 73, 112–15, 121, 170
am able, 85
amend; amendment, 236
amiable, 236

amicable, 236
amid; amidst, 244
am not, 83, 170
*amn't, 83
among; amongst, 244
amount, 236
an, 20–21, 61, 62, 228
analogous, 330
anchor; anchorperson, 327
and, 39, 40, 69, 116, 117–18, 120, 146, 147, 148, 150, 151, 152, 237, 296, 347, 348
*and etc., 270
and/or, 237
and so forth, 350
and the like, 350
anecdotal, 237
anecdote, 237
angry, 292, 330
annoy, 234
another, 42, 50, 56, 60
answer, 330
antagonism, 330
antagonistic, 330
antepenultimate, 303
anticipate, 237
antidisestablishmentarianism, 214
antidote, 237
antipathy, 330
anxious, 237, 330
any, 22, 42, 56, 60, 173, 237–38
anybody, 40, 56, 118, 173, 327
any one, 237–38
anyone, 40, 55, 56, 118, 173, 237–38, 322
anyone who, 322
any place; *anyplace, 238
anything, 56, 173
anyway; *anyways, 238
anywhere, 129, 130, 173, 238
apart from, 140
*apparati, 238
apparatus(es), 28, 238
appear, 72, 81–82, 135
appendix; appendixes; appendices, 238
appertain, 304
apply, 330
appoint, 164
appraise, 239

appreciate, 239
apprise, 239, 330
approve, 239
approximately, 229
apropos, 330
apt, 239
are, 9, 73, 112–15, 121, 178
area, 239, 314
aren't, 84, 170
argue, 73, 330
arise, 74
around, 129, 139
arrive, 72
arrogate, 229
as, 37, 133, 139, 143–44, 146, 148, 149, 256, 270, 291
as a consequence, 147
as against, 140
as a result, 147
as–as, 45, 67, 147
as between, 140
as compared with, 140
as distinct from, 140
as distinguished from, 140
as far as, 140, 148, 239
as for, 239
aside from, 140
as if, 133, 143–44, 148, 291
as is, 239–40
"as is" basis, on an, 240
ask, 330
as long as, 148
as much as, 148
*as of yet, 241
as opposed to, 140
*as per, 240
as regards, 140
assault, 240
assemblage, 240
assembly, 240
assent, 240
as–so, 176
associated with, 283
as soon as, 188
as such, 240
assuming, 141
assumption, 240

assure, 269
as though, 146, 148
as to, 140, 240
as touching, 140
as well as, 120, 148, 241
*as yet, 241
at, 139, 187
athlete, 217
at present, 241
attach, 72
attain, 241
attend, 330
attendee; attender, 33
at the cost of, 140
at the hands of, 140
at the instance of, 140
at the point of, 140
at the present time, 241
at the risk of, 140
at the time that/when, 241
at this time, 241
attributable to, 267
attribute, 330
auger, 241
augur; augury, 241
author; authoress, 327
avenge, 241
averse, 232, 330
avocation, 241
awake, 74
away, 129
a while, 241–42
awhile, 241–42

bacillus; bacilli, 27
backward(s), 320
bacterium; bacteria, 27, 242
bade, 74
badge, 330
badger, 330
bail, 242
*baited breath, 243
balance, 330
bale, 242
ban, 330
banish, 330
bank, 330

bar, 330
barbecue; *barbeque; *Bar-B-Q, 242
barely, 68, 132, 169, 172
bargain, 330
barge, 330
barring, 141, 149
barter, 330
base, 242, 330
based, 242, 330
based on, 242
basis; bases, 27, 242–43
basketball, 216
bated breath, 243
battery, 240
battle royal, 199
be, 30, 45, 73, 74, 81, 83, 90–92, 93, 98,
    112–15, 135, 163, 174, 179, 186, 190,
    201, 202, 207, 211
be able to, 122
bear, 74, 246
beat, 74
because, 146, 148, 194, 243, 248, 267, 283,
    313, 330
because of, 140, 267
beckon, 330
become, 75, 81, 135, 186, 275
becoming, 330
beeline, 330
been, 73, 112–15
befall, 75
before, 130, 133, 139, 148, 149, 187, 188,
    306, 307
beg, 330
beget, 75
beggar, 243
begin, 73, 75
*begs belief/description, 243
beg the question, 243
beguile, 330
behalf, 243, 330
behave, 330
behind, 143
behold, 75
beholden, 330
being, 73, 98, 112–15
believe, 272
belong, 72, 330

below, 129, 130, 139, 143
bemused, 243
bend, 75
beneath, 139
beneficence, 244
benefit, 330
benevolence, 244
bereave, 75
bereft, 330
beseech, 75
beset, 75, 330
beside, 244
besides, 244
bespeak, 75
bestow, 330
bet, 73, 75
betray, 330
betrayed, 330
better, 244
between, 140, 244–45
between him and me; *between him and
    I, 8–9
between you and me; *between you and I,
    42, 244–45
beyond, 129
bi-, 245–46
biannual, 246
bias, 330
biased, 330
biceps; bicep; bicepses; bicipites, 246
bid, 74, 75, 85, 330
bidden, 74
biennial, 246
bigoted, 330
bigotry, 330
billion, 246
bind, 73, 75
binding, 330
bite, 73, 75
bittersweet, 215
biweekly, 245
blackboard, 215
blame, 330
blaspheme, 330
blasphemy, 330
blatant, 246
bleed, 75, 330

blend, 330
block, 72
blossom, 330
blow, 75
blunder, 330
bode, 241
body politic, 199
bombastic, 246
bona fide, 246
bona fides, 246
bond, 331
boo-boo, 218
boogie-woogie, 218
boohoo, 218
border, 331
bored, 68, 331
bork, 219
born, 246, 331
borne, 246, 331
borrow, 72
both, 56, 60
both–and, 147, 176, 247
boundaries, 302
boy, 216
boycott, 331
brace, 331
breach, 247
break, 75, 331
breakdown, 216
break Priscian's head, 14
breech, 247
breed, 75
brighten, 213
bring, 75, 163, 247
bristle, 331
broadcast, 74, 75, 247
*broadcasted, 247
browbeat, 75
browse, 331
brush, 331
budget, 331
build, 75
bunch of, 20
burn, 75, 247
burned, 247
burn out; burnout, 82
burnt, 247

burst, 75
bus, 216
but, 143, 146, 147, 150, 151, 173, 237, 247, 347
butt, 331
buy, 72, 75, 163, 331
by, 91, 129, 139, 143, 145, 207, 247
by contrast with, 140
by means of, 140, 247
by reason of, 140, 248
by way of, 140

cablecast, 74
cache, 248
cachet, 248
cactus; cacti, 27, 248
cactuses, 248
cahoots, 331
cajoled, 331
call, 73, 99–105, 257
can, 83, 121–22, 170, 248
candelabrum; candelabra; *candelabras, 248
cannon, 248
cannot, 170, 248
can not only–but also, 248
canon, 248
can't, 84, 170, 248
*can't hardly, 278
capability, 228
capable, 331
capacity, 228, 331
capital, 248
capitalize, 331
capitol, 248
capitulate, 331
carat, 249
care, 331
careen, 249
career, 249
careful, 331
careless, 331
caret, 249
cars, 19
case, 249
cast, 75
catch, 75
cause, 331

caused, 331
cause(s) célèbre(s), 249
caution, 331
cautious, 331
celebrated, 331
cellphone, 219
censer, 249–50
censor, 249–50
censure, 250, 331
center, 331
*center around, 250
center on, 250
certainty, 250
certitude, 250
chafe, 331
chagrined, 331
chair; chairperson, 250, 327
chairman; chairwoman, 250
chaise(s) longue(s); *chaise lounge, 251
chance, 331
characteristic, 331
characterize, 331
characterized, 331
charge, 73, 230, 331
chase, 331
chastise; *chastize, 251
cheap(en)(ed), 213
cheat, 331
check, 331
cherub; cherubim, 27, 251
cherubs, 251
chide, 331
chief, 68
child, 284
childish, 251
childlike, 251
china, 20
choose, 75, 164
chord, 251
chortle, 331
chute, 217
circumstances, 251–52
citation, 252
cite, 252
citizen, 252
claim, 331
clamor, 331

class, 252
classic, 252
classical, 252
clean, 252
cleanse, 252
cleave, 75, 252
cleaved, 252
cleft, 252
clench, 253
climate; climatic, 253
climax; climactic, 253
clinch, 253
cling, 75, 331
clock, 23
close, 72, 129, 253
*close proximity, 253
closure, 253
clothe, 75
cloture, 253
clove(n), 252
cluster, 331
coalesce, 331
coax, 331
coeducational; coed, 216
coequal, 331
coerce, 331
cognizant, 331
cohabit, 253
*cohabitate, 217, 253
cohabitation, 253
cohesion, 331
cohort, 253
coin (a phrase/word), 253
coincide, 331
coincidental, 331
coleslaw; *coldslaw, 254
collaborate, 254, 331
collaboration, 70
collaborative, 70
collapse, 72
collectibles, 70
college, 254
collegial; colleague, 254
collegiate; college, 254
collide, 331
collude, 331
collusion, 331

colonization, 215
combine, 214
come, 72, 75
comfort, 331
commendable, 254
commendatory, 254
commensurate, 331
comment, 284, 331
commiserate, 331
commit, 331
common, 254
commonweal, 254
commonwealth, 254
commune, 331
communion, 331
comp, 216
compare, 254, 331
compare with/to, 254
compatible, 331
compel(led), 254
compendious, 254
compete, 331
competitive, 331
complacent, 255, 331
complaisant, 255
complement; complementary, 255, 331
complete, 68
*completely decimated, 261
compliant, 255
compliment; complimentary, 255, 332
comply, 332
comport, 332
compose, 255
composed (of), 255, 332
composition, 216
compress, 332
comprise, 255, 283
*comprised of, 255
compromise, 332
conceive, 332
concept, 255
conception, 255
concerning, 141, 286
concord, 332
concur, 332
concurrence, 332
condemn, 332

condition, 305
condole; condolence, 255–56
conducive, 332
confer, 332
conference, 332
confidant, 256
confidante, 256
confide, 332
confidence, 332
confident, 256
conflict, 332
conform, 332
conformance, 332
confuse, 332
confusion, 332
congruence, 332
congruent, 256, 332
congruous, 256
connected, 332
connivance, 332
connive, 332
connote, 256
consent, 240
consequent, 256
consequently, 147
consider, 73, 256, 332
considerate, 332
consideration, 332
considering, 141, 149
consist, 256–57, 332
consistent, 332
consist of/in, 255, 256–57
console; consolation, 255–56
consonant, 332
conspire, 332
constrain, 332
constraint, 332
construe, 332
construed, 332
consult, 332
consultant, 332
contact, 229, 257
contagious, 257
contaminate, 332
contemporaneous, 257, 332
contemporary, 257, 332
contempt, 332

contemptible, 257
contemptuous, 257
contend, 332
content, 257
contents, 257
contiguous, 332
contingent, 332
continual, 257–58
continuous, 257–58
contract, 332
contrary (to), 140, 332
contrast, 332
contravene, 258
contribute, 332
control, 332
controvert, 258
convenient, 332
conversant, 332
convict, 332
convince, 304, 332
co-op, 216
cooperative, 216
coordinate, 332
coordination, 332
copter, 216
copyright(ed), 258
cord, 251
core, 258
corollary, 258
corporal, 258
corporeal, 258
corps, 258
correlate, 332
correlation, 258, 332
correspond, 332
correspondence, 332
corrigendum; corrigenda, 27
corroborate, 254
cost, 75, 202
couch potatoes, 219
cough, 72
could, 121–22, 248
could have; could've; *could of, 258
couldn't, 84
couldn't care less; *could care less, 258–59
councillor, 259
counselor/counsellor, 259

count, 332
couple, 20, 259, 332
court-martial, 259–60
credible, 260
credit, 332
creditable, 260
credulous, 260
creep, 75, 260
creep(ed) out, 260
crept, 260
crevasse, 260
crevice, 260
criminal, 321
crisis; crises, 27
*criterias, 260
criterion; criteria, 27, 28, 260
crow, 75
crusade, 332
cry, 72
culminate, 332
cure, 332, 333
current, 260
currently, 241, 260
cut, 72, 75

dabble, 333
dally, 333
damp, 260
dampen, 260
dare, 85, 124
darken, 213
datum; data, 27, 28, 261
dawdle, 333
deadly, 261
deal, 75, 333
deathly, 261
debar, 333
debate, 333
debut, 229
deceptively, 261
decide, 263, 333
decide whether/if, 263
decimate, 261
deduce, 231, 333
deduct, 333
deduction, 333
deep, 129

defamation, 261
default, 333
defer, 333
deference, 333
deferential, 333
defiant, 333
definite, 261–62
definitive, 261–62
defrauded, 333
defuse, 262
degenerate, 333
delegate, 310
deliberate, 262, 333
deliberative, 262
delight, 333
delighted, 333
*delimitate, 217
delve, 333
demonstrate, 333
denote, 256
denounce, 262
dental, 214
dentist, 214
dentition, 214
denture, 214
depend, 262, 333
dependant, 262
dependent, 231, 262, 333
depend on, 262
depict, 333
deprecate(d), 262–63
deprive, 333
derisive, 263
derisory, 263
derive, 333
derogate, 333
derogatory, 333
described, 333
deserts, 263
desideratum; desiderata, 27
design, 255
designated, 333
designation, 333
desist, 333
despair, 333
desperate, 333
despite, 140, 166, 263, 298

despondent, 333
desserts, 263
destitute, 333
destructive, 333
determine, 263
determine whether/if, 263
detract, 265, 333
detriment, 333
deviate, 333
device, 263
devise, 263
devoid, 68, 333
devolve, 333
devoted, 333
devotee, 333
devotion, 333
dice, 263
dictate, 333
did, 125, 169–70
die, 263, 267, 333
differ, 333
difference, 333
different, 263–64, 333
different from/than/to, 263–64
differentiate, 333
differently (than), 263, 333
differ from/with, 264
diffuse, 262
dig, 75
digress, 333
digression, 333
diphtheria, 264
diphthong, 264
disabuse, 333
disappear, 72
*disassociate, 265
disbar, 333
disburse, 264
disc, 265
discomfit(ed); discomfiture, 264
discomfort, 264
discourage, 333
discouraged, 333
discover, 35
discredit, 333
discreet, 264
discrete, 264

discriminate, 333
discriminating, 264–65
discrimination, 264–65
discriminatory, 264–65
disdain, 333
disdainful, 333
disgruntled, 333
disinterested, 265
disk, 265
disloyal, 333
disloyalty, 333
disorganized, 265
dispense, 333
disperse, 264
displaced, 333
displeased, 333
dispose, 334
disposition, 334
dispossessed, 334
dispute, 334
disqualify, 334
disregard, 334
dissent, 334
dissimilar, 334
dissociate, 265, 334
distaste, 334
distinctive, 265
distinguish, 334
distinguishable, 265
distinguished, 265, 334
distract, 265
distraught, 334
distressed, 334
dive(d); dove, 75, 265–66
diverge, 334
diverted, 334
divested, 334
divide, 334
divided, 334
DNA, 219
do, 37, 75, 83, 125, 126, 158, 169–70
do away with, 82
doctrinaire, 266
doctrinal, 266
does, 125
dominant, 305, 334
dominate, 305–6, 334

dominion, 334
done, 125
don't, 84
doom, 334
doomed, 334
dote, 334
doubt, 73
doubtfully, 266
doubtless; *doubtlessly, 129, 266
doubt that/whether/if, 266
dove, 265–66
dovetail, 334
down, 129, 139, 143
downward(s), 266, 320
draft, 73
drag, 266
dragged, 266
drank, 266
draw, 76, 284
drawing, 217
dread, 73
dream, 76, 266
dreamed; dreamt, 74, 266
drink, 73, 76, 266
drip, 334
drive, 73, 76
drown, 266
drowned, 266
drug, 266
drunk, 266, 267
drunkard, 267
drunken, 267
dual, 267
due, 334
duel, 267
due to, 267
due to the fact that, 267
dumb, 267
dun, 334
during, 139, 141
dwarf(s); *dwarves, 267
dwell, 76
dye, 267
dyeing, 87, 267
dying, 87, 267

each, 39, 40, 42, 56, 60, 118, 267
each other, 36, 42, 50, 267
eager, 67, 237
ear, 334
early, 130
earmark, 334
eat, 76
eatable, 268
economic, 267–68
economical, 267–68
ecstatic, 334
edible, 268
educate, 334
education, 334
effect, 232–33
effective, 334
effete, 268
effrontery, 268
e.g., 270, 281
either, 40, 42, 56, 60, 147, 268, 296
either–or, 39, 121, 147, 151, 176, 193
eject, 214
elated, 334
elect, 164
elemental, 268
elementary, 268
elements, 302
elicit, 268
eligible, 334
else, 57, 147, 148
elude, 235
e-mail, 257
embark, 334
embarrass, 278
embody, 334
emend; emendation, 236
emerge, 334
emigrant, 282
emigrate, 282, 334
émigré, 282, 334
eminent, 268
emotional, 268
emotive, 268
empathize, 334
empathy, 269
emphatic, 334
employ, 334

enamored, 334
encouraged, 334
encroach, 334
encumbered, 334
endemic, 270
endorse, 239
endow, 334
endowed, 334
enervate, 269
enforce, 334
enjoin, 334
enjoy, 73
enlarge, 334
enlighten, 213
enormity, 269
enormousness, 269
enough, 231
enquire; enquiry, 285
ensure, 269, 334
enter, 334
*enthused, 270
enthusiastic, 270, 334
entice, 334
entire, 67, 68
entitle, 334
entrap, 334
entrapment, 334
entrust, 334
enumerable, 270
envious, 334
envision, 334
envy, 287
epidemic, 270
equal, 334
*equally as, 270
equate, 334
equidistant, 334
equivalent, 334
equivocal, 334
ere, 133
erratum; errata, 27
escalate, 334
escape, 334
espresso, 270
establish, 215
estimate, 229
estrange, 334

estrangement, 334
et al.; *et alii*, 270, 350
etc.; *et cetera*, 270, 350
etch, 334
ethics, 118
even, 129
event, 271
eventuality, 271
every, 39, 60, 118
everybody, 40, 56, 118, 271
every day, 271
everyday, 271
every one, 271
everyone, 40, 50, 56, 118, 271
*everyplace, 271
everything, 56
everywhere, 130, 271
evoke, 271
evolve, 334
exam, 217
exasperate, 234
exasperated, 334
except, 140, 148, 173, 229
exceptionable, 271
exceptional, 271
excerpt, 334
exclusive (of), 140, 335
excuse, 234
executor; executrix, 271
exempli gratia, 281
exile, 335
exist, 72, 73
exonerate, 335
expand, 335
expect, 237
explicit, 271
export, 335
*expresso, 270
expropriate, 335
expunge, 335
extolled, 335
extradite, 335

facility, 335
facsimile transmission, 271
fact that, due to the, 267
fact that, the, 271

fail, 215
fall, 72, 76
false, 68
family, 217
famous, 335
far, 129
farther, 129, 271
fascinated, 335
fascination, 335
fashion, 335
fast, 129
fasten, 335
fast results, 33–34
fatal, 68
fault, 335
favor, 335
favorite, 68
fax(es), 271–72
faze, 272
feed, 76
feel, 76, 81–82, 85, 135, 272
feel bad; *feel badly, 135, 272
female, 326
feud, 335
few, 19, 20, 60, 169, 172
fewer, 66, 290
fiction, 272
fictional, 272
fictitious, 272
fictive, 272
fidget, 335
fight, 76
filch, 335
file, 72
filet(s), 27
filet(s) mignon(s), 27
fill, 335
*filtrate, 217
final, 68
finalize, 272
finally, 288
find, 76, 335
finicky, 335
finish, 272
firefighter, 328
first(ly), 272, 288
fish(es), 272

fit, 76, 202, 272–73
fitted, 272–73
fix, 72
fixation, 335
flagrant, 246
flair, 273, 335
flammable, 273
flare, 273
flare up, to; flare-up, a, 82
flaunt, 273
flee, 76, 335
fleshly, 273
fleshy, 273
flimflam, 218
flinch, 335
fling, 76
flirt, 335
floodlight, 76
flounder, 273
flout, 273
flu, 216
fly, 73, 76
following, 273
fond, 335
fondness, 335
foolishly, 130
for, 139, 147, 148, 284, 285, 347
forage, 335
forbear, 76, 274
forbid, 76, 335
force, 335
forebear, 274
forecast, 76
foreclose, 335
forego, 274
foregone conclusion, 274
foresee, 76
foretell, 76
foreword, 274
for example, 142, 270
for fear of, 140
forget, 76
forgive, 76
forgo, 274
for instance, 142
formally, 274
former, 274

formerly, 274
for purposes of, 140
forsake, 76
forswear, 76
for the sake of, 140
fortify, 335
fortuitous, 274
fortunate, 274, 335
fortunately, 318
forward, 130, 320
forwards, 320
founder, 273
fraternize, 335
fraught, 335
free, 335
free rein; *free reign, 274
freeze, 76
French, 70
fret, 335
fridge, 216
from, 139, 264, 265
from among, 140
from between, 140
from–to, 374
froufrou, 218
frugal, 335
fulminate, 335
fulsome, 274
fume, 335
fun; *funner; *funnest, 274
fungus; fungi, 28
furious, 335
furnish, 335
furniture, 29
further, 129, 237, 271
furthermore, 237
future, in the near, 274

gainsay, 76
gallop, 72
gamut, 335
gantlet, 275
gantlope, 275
gasp, 335
gauntlet, 275
generally, 135
generous, 335

genial, 335
gentle, 335
gentleman, 275
get, 76, 81, 90, 163, 275
get rid of, 82
gibe, 275, 335
gild, 277
give, 72, 76, 163
given, 335
glare, 335
glisten, 335
glitter, 335
gloat, 335
go, 76, 81, 275
goes, 239
gone, 275
good, 152
gourmand, 276
gourmet, 276
graduate, 276, 335
graffito; graffiti, 276
grapple, 335
grateful, 276, 335
gratified, 276, 335
gravitate, 335
greater, 66
grieve, 335
grievous; *grievious, 276
grind, 76
gripe, 335
grisly, 276
grizzly, 276
grounded, 335
grounds, 302
grow, 72, 76, 81, 186
grudge, 335
guard, 335
guarded, 335
guess, 229
guidelines, 302
guild, 277

habit, 335
hack, 335
had, 97, 125
had been, 94
had better, 244

haggle, 335
hail, 277, 335
*hairbrained, 278
hale, 277, 335
half, 277
hammer, 335
hamstring, 76
handful, 277
handheld device, 219
handy, 335
hang, 76
hangar, 277
hanged, 277–78
hanger, 277
hangry, 219
hanker, 335
happen, 72, 335
harass, 278
hard, 129
hardened, 335
hardly, 132, 169, 172, 278
harebrained, 278
hark back; *harken back; *hearken back, 278
harm, 306
harp, 335
has, 97, 125
hasn't, 170
hassle, 335
hate, 73
have, 37, 76, 83, 84, 97, 125–26, 201, 202,
    278
have got, 126, 278
have to, 123, 124
he, 38, 40, 42, 46, 47, 50, 278, 324, 327
healthful, 278
healthy, 278
he and I, 9
hear, 76, 85, 135
*hearken back, 278
heave, 76
hedge, 336
heedful, 336
heedless, 336
hegemony, 336
helicopter, 216
help, 85, 152, 278
helter-skelter, 218

hence, 147
he or she, 47, 278, 326
her, 38, 44, 47, 48, 59
here, 35, 119, 129, 130
hereafter, 129
here and now, 35
hers, 47, 48, 279
herself, 48, 49
*he/she, 278, 324
hesitate, 336
hesitation, 336
hew, 76
hide, 76, 105–11
high, 129
highly, 131
him, 38, 40, 46, 48
*him and I, 9
him or her, 47
himself, 48, 49
himself or herself, 47
hinder, 336
hindrance, 336
hinge, 336
his, 40, 46, 47, 48, 59
his or her, 47
historic, 279
historical, 228, 279
hit, 72, 76
hoard, 279
hobnob, 218, 336
Hobson's choice; *Hobbesian choice, 279
hocus pocus, 218
hodgepodge, 218
hoi polloi, 279–80
hoity-toity, 279
hold, 77
holdover, 336
hold up, 82
holocaust, 280
home, 136
home in, 280
homesickness, 218
homicide, 295–96
homogeneous; *homogenous, 280
*hone in, 280
honoree, 32–33
hopefully, 266, 280

horde, 279
horses, 19
host, 229
hostile, 336
hostility, 336
hover, 336
how, 129, 131–32, 149, 157, 158, 187, 189
however, 127, 151, 247
huddle, 336
humanitarian, 281
humankind, 293
humdrum, 218
hung, 277–78
hunger, 336
hurly-burly, 218
hurt, 77, 306
hurtle, 336
husband, 34

I, 37, 38, 42, 43, 50, 281, 296, 304
I'd, 84
idea, 255
ideal, 68, 281
identical, 336
identify, 336
id est, 281
idiot, 152
idolize, 336
I'd've, 84
idyllic; idyll, 281
i.e., 281
if, 93, 94, 146, 148, 166, 188, 189, 194, 249, 263, 271, 281, 325
if–then, 147, 176
ignoramus(es); *ignorami, 282
ignorance, 336
ignorant, 336
ilk, 282
ill, 129
illegal, 321
illegible, 282
illicit, 268, 321
illude, 235
imagine, 73
imbued, 336
immediately, 130
immigrant, 282, 336

immigrate, 282, 336
imminent, 268
immune, 336
immunize, 336
impact, 282
impatience, 336
impeachment, 282
impel(led), 254
impinge, 336
implication, 284
implicit, 271, 336
imply, 73, 225, 283
import, 336
important(ly), 283
importune, 336
impose, 336
impossible, 67, 68
impracticable, 283
impractical, 283
impregnate, 336
impress, 336
impressed, 336
impression, 336
impute, 336
in, 129, 130, 139, 143
in accordance with, 140
in addition (to), 120, 140, 237
in any event, 142
in apposition with/to, 140
inasmuch as, 146, 148, 283
inaugurate, 336
in a word, 142
in back, 130
Inc., 356
in case (of), 140, 146, 249
incidence, 283
incident, 283
incidental, 336
include, 283, 336
inclusive, 336
in comparison with, 140
incompatible, 336
incompetence, 336
incongruent, 336
incongruous, 256, 336
in connection with, 140, 283–84
in consideration of, 140

inconsistent, 336
in contrast to, 140
in contrast with, 140
incorporate, 336
incredible, 284
incredulous, 284
inculcate, 284, 336
incumbent, 336
indeed, 129, 152
independence, 336
independent, 336
indicate, 284
indifferent, 336
indigenous, 336
indignant, 336
individual, 284
indoctrinate, 284
induce, 231
induct, 336
indulge, 336
indulgent, 336
in every case, 249
inevitable, 68
in excess of, 284
infatuation, 336
infected, 284
infectious, 257
infer, 225, 283, 336
inference, 284
infested, 284
infiltrate, 336
infiltration, 336
infinite, 68
inflammable, 273
inflict, 284, 336
influence, 282, 336
influenza, 216
inform, 336
information, 19, 28
informed, 336
infringe, 336
infringement, 336
in front (of), 130, 140
infuse, 336
ingenious, 285
ingenuous, 285
ingratiate, 336

in here, 130
inhere, 336
inherent, 285, 336
inimical, 336
initiate, 336
inject, 336
inlay, 77
in most cases, 249
innate, 285, 336
innervate, 269
innocent, 285
innumerable, 270
inoculate, 336
in order that, 148
in order to/for, 285
in place of, 140
in preparing for, 306
in proximity, 253
input, 77, 285, 336
inquire, 285, 337–38
inquiry, 285
inquisitive, 337
*in regards to, 286
in regard to, 140, 286
in relation to, 140
in respect of, 140
in respect to, 140
inroad, 337
inseparable, 337
inset, 77
inside, 130, 140, 299
insidious, 286
insight, 337
insist, 337
insofar as, 140
in spite of, 140, 263, 298
instance, 283
instead of, 140
instill, 337
insulate, 337
insure, 269, 337
intense, 286
intensely, 286
intensive, 286
intensive care, 286
intent, 337
intention, 337

intently, 286
inter, 286
intercede, 337
interest, 337
interested, 68
interject, 337
interlace, 337
interment, 286
in terms of, 140
intern, 286
internal, 214
internecine, 287
internment, 286
*interpretate, 217
interweave, 77
in the affirmative, 233
in the case of, 141
in the circumstances, 251
in the event that, 271
in the interest of, 141
in the last analysis, 142
in the long run, 142
in the matter of, 141
in the near future, 274
in the negative, 233
in the process of, 307
in the way of, 141
into, 139, 216, 284
intrude, 337
inveigh, 287, 337
inveigle, 287, 337
invidious, 286
in view of, 141
invoke, 271
*irregardless, 225, 287
irrespective (of), 141, 287
irrevocable, 68
irritate, 234
is, 73, 84, 112–15, 312
is composed of, 255
*is comprised of, 255
is concerned, 239
it, 37, 38, 42, 46–47, 48, 89–90, 173–74,
    178–79, 287, 327
itch, 214
it'd, 84
it is I, 45, 287

it is me, 45, 164, 287
it's, 48, 287
its, 47, 48, 59, 287
itself, 48, 49

jealous, 337
jealousy, 287
jibe, 275, 337
jiggery-pokery, 218
jive, 275
join, 337
journalists, 28
Jr., 356
judgment, 288
jump, 73, 337
junior, 337
jurisdiction, 337
just, 129
just deserts; *just desserts, 263
justified, 337
juxtaposed, 337

karat, 249
keep, 77
kick, 72
kid, 337
kindness, 337
kind(s), 50, 288
knack, 337
kneel, 77
knickknack, 218
know, 73, 77
knowledgeable, 337
known, 337
kowtow, 218
kudos; *kudo, 288, 337

label, 337
labor-intensive, 286
lacking, 337
laden, 337
lady, 275, 288, 326
laid, 288–89
lain, 288–89
lament, 337
languish, 337
lap, 337

lapse, 337
largely, 67
larva; larvae, 28
laser, 219
lash, 337
last(ly), 288
latch, 337
late, 129, 130
later, 316
latter, 274
laudable, 288
laudatory, 288
laugh, 72
lavish, 337
lawbook, 216
lax, 337
lay, 77, 288–89
leach, 289
lead, 77, 289
leaf, 337
lean(ed); *leant, 289
leap(ed); leapt, 77, 289
learn(ed); learnt, 74, 77, 289
lease, 289
least, 67, 134
leave, 77
led, 289
leech, 289
leer, 337
leery, 337
lend; lent, 77, 289–90
lenient, 337
less, 22, 60, 66, 67, 129, 133, 290
lessee, 33
lest, 290
let, 77, 85, 158, 289
level, 337
liable, 337
liaison, 337
libel, 261
liberate, 337
liberties, 337
lice, 27
licence, 290
license, 290
lie, 77, 81, 288–89
life-and-death; *life-or-death, 290–91

lift, 72, 73
light, 77, 291
lighted, 291
lightning, 291
like, 37, 139, 143–44, 291
likely, 239
liken, 337
likeness, 337
limited, 337
limits, 302
linger, 337
lit, 291
literally, 292
little, 68, 129, 169, 172
loan, 289–90
loath, 292
loathe, 292
loathsome; *loathesome, 292
lock, 337
long, 129
look, 81, 135, 214
loose, 292
loosen, 292
lose, 77, 292
lot, 20, 116, 199
lots, 313
loud, 129
louse(s); lice, 27
low, 129
Ltd., 356
lull, 337
lure, 337
lurk, 337
luxuriant, 292
luxurious, 292

mad, 292, 337
made, 337
magnanimous, 337
mail carrier, 328
main, 68
mainstream, 34
majority, 21, 116, 292–93
majuscule, 294
make, 72, 77, 85, 164, 284
maleficent, 293
malevolent, 293

malice, 337
malodorous, 298–99
maltreatment, 295
man, 26, 275, 284
maneuver, 337
man-hour(s); *men-hours, 26
manifest, 68
mankind, 293
man-of-war; men-of-war; *man-of-wars, 26
manservant, 26
manslaughter, 295–96
mantel, 293
mantle, 293
manual, 214
many, 60, 298, 313
marred, 337
marriage, 293, 337
married, 337
marry, 337
martyr, 337
martyred, 337
marvel, 337
masterful, 293
masterly; *masterlily, 293
masterpiece, 218
mastery, 337
math, 216
mathematics, 216
may, 83, 122, 201, 248, 293–94, 312
maybe, 127
me, 38, 50, 152, 281, 296
mean, 77
means of, by, 140, 247
meant, 337
medal, 294
meddle, 294, 337
medium; media, 28, 294
mediums, 294
meet, 77
*meet(ed) out, 294
memorandum; memoranda, 28, 294
memorandums, 294
*men-hours, 26
men-of-war, 26
menservants, 26
merge, 337
mesh, 337

metal, 294
mete out, 294
meter/metre, 294
meticulous, 337
mettle, 294
might, 122, 293–94
migrate, 337
militate, 295, 338
mill, 338
mindful, 338
mine, 47, 48
mini, 294
*miniscule, 294
minister, 338
minuscule, 294
miscast, 77
mischievous; *mischievious, 295
misdeal, 77
mishear, 77
mislay, 77
mislead, 77
misread, 77
misspell(ed); misspelt, 77, 295
misspend, 77
mistake, 77
mistreatment, 295
misunderstand, 77
mitigate, 295, 338
*mitigate against, 295
modern, 257
modify, 214
moot, 295
more, 66, 67, 127, 133
more important(ly), 283
moreover, 147, 237
more perfect, 67
more than, 284, 301
most, 66, 67, 127, 134, 292
move, 72
mow, 77
much, 22, 60, 68, 127, 129, 295
mulct, 338
multitude, 116
murder, 295–96
muse, 338
must, 83, 96, 122–23, 125, 201, 312
mute, 267, 295

mutiny, 338
mutual, 254
my, 47, 48, 59
myriad, 116
myself, 48, 49, 50, 296

nail, 338
naive, 338
name, 72
namely, 130
nap, 72
NATO, 218
naturalist, 296
naturist, 296
nauseated, 296
nauseating, 296
nauseous, 296
navicert, 217
near, 129
near future, in the, 274
necessary, 296, 338
necessitous, 296
necessity, 338
need, 73, 85, 124, 338
negative, in the, 233
neglectful, 338
negligent, 338
negotiate, 338
neither, 40, 56, 60, 147, 169, 171, 268, 296
neither–nor, 39, 121, 147, 171, 176, 296
nerve-racking; *nerve-wracking, 297
nestle, 338
never, 129, 132, 135, 169, 171, 177
nevertheless, 146, 147, 297
newcomer, 338
next to, 141
niggardly, 338
niggle, 338
no, 39, 60, 132, 169, 171, 172, 179, 233
nobody, 40, 56, 118, 169, 171
noisome, 297
no less than, 147
nominate, 338
none, 42, 56, 60, 169, 171, 297
nonetheless, 297
nonflammable, 273
nonplussed; *nonplused, 297

no one, 36, 40, 50, 56, 118, 169, 171
nor, 39, 40, 116, 147, 169, 171, 296, 347
normality; *normalcy, 297
not, 83, 84, 123, 125, 127, 129, 132, 169–71,
    172, 173, 179
notable, 298
noteworthy, 298
not guilty, 285
nothing, 169, 171
noticeable, 298
not only–but also, 147, 176, 193
notorious, 338
notwithstanding, 141, 146, 298
now, 35, 129, 130, 149, 241, 306
nowadays, 241
nowhere, 129, 169, 171
number, 20, 116, 236
number of, 21
numerous, 298

O, 153
oats, 29
object, 338
obligation, 338
obligatory, 338
oblivious, 338
observance, 298, 338
observant, 338
observation, 298, 338
obsessed, 338
obsession, 338
obstinate, 338
obtain, 241, 275
obtrude, 338
obtuse, 298
occur, 72
octopus(es); *octopi, 298
odds, 338
*odiferous, 299
odious, 298–99, 338
odoriferous, 298–99
odorous, 298–99
of, 20–21, 22, 30, 31–32, 47, 116, 139, 144,
    145, 187, 199, 234, 239, 259, 277, 283,
    299, 301
off, 128, 129, 139, 143, 299, 338
offend, 338

offended, 338
offensive, 338
offer, 72, 338
officer, 299
official, 299
officious, 299
often, 130, 135, 299
oftentimes, 299
of that/what/which/whom, 54–55
oh, 153
omen, 338
omnibus, 216
on, 130, 139, 140, 143, 262, 299, 300
on a . . . basis, 242–43
on account of, 141
on an "as is" basis, 240
on behalf of, 141
once, 148, 188
one, 30, 40, 48, 54, 56, 57, 60, 299–300, 325
one another, 36, 42, 50, 267
one of the few, 54
one of those who/that, 22, 30, 54, 119,
    299–300
oneself, 48, 56, 300
*one's self, 300
online training, 219
only, 68, 137–38
on the part of, 141
on to, 300
onto, 140, 300
oops, 152
open, 72, 338
operate, 338
ophthalmology, 264
opposite, 140, 338
opposition, 338
oppress, 300
or, 39, 40, 116, 118, 121, 146, 147, 148, 151,
    237, 296, 300, 347
oral, 321
oration, 303
ordeal, 338
ordinance, 300
ordnance, 300
orient, 300–301
orientate, 300–301
or not, whether, 322

or–or both, 237
oscillate, 338
other, 56, 60, 147, 148
otherwise, 130, 147, 148
ouch, 152
ought, 83, 85, 123–24, 301
oughtn't, 84
our, 47, 48, 59
ours, 47, 48, 301
*ourself, 301
ourselves, 48, 49, 301
oust, 338
out, 129
outbid, 77
outdo, 77
outgrow, 77
outlet, 338
out of, 139, 141
out of regard for, 141
out of respect for, 141
output, 77, 301
outrun, 77, 216
outsell, 77
outshine, 77
outside, 299, 301
over, 284, 301
over-, 301
overbid, 78
overcome, 78, 338
overdo, 78
overdraw, 78
overeat, 78
overfly, 78
overgrown, 338
overhang, 78
overhear, 78
overlay, 78
overlie, 78
*overly, 301
overpay, 78
override, 78
overrun, 78
oversee, 78
overshoot, 78
oversleep, 78
overtake, 78
overthrow, 78

owed to, 267
owing, 338
owing to, 141, 267

pacifiers, 215
pair(s), 22, 301
palate, 301
pale, 338
palette, 301
pall, 338
pallet, 301
panacea, 338
pandemic, 270
pander, 338
panic, 338
parallel, 338
parameters, 302
paramount, 68, 338
paranoid, 338
parity, 338
parlay, 338
parley, 338
part, 338
partake, 78, 338
partake in/of, 302
partial, 338
partially, 302
partly, 302
pass, 302
passed, 302
past, 302
pastime, 302
patterned, 338
pay, 78
peaceable, 302
peaceful, 302
peak, 302
peculiar, 338
pedal, 302
peddle, 302
peek, 302
penchant, 338
pendant, 303
pendent, 303
peninsula, 303
penultimate, 303
people, 29, 303

peoples, 29
per, 240
perceive, 338
perceptible, 338
perceptive, 338
perfect, 68
perhaps, 129
period (of time), 303
peripheral, 338
periphery, 338
permeate, 338
permeated, 338
permit, 338
peroration, 303
perpendicular, 338
perpetrate, 303
perpetual, 68
perpetuate, 303
persecution, 338
persevere, 339
persist, 339
person, 29, 284, 327
personally, 303–4
persons, 29, 303
person that/who, 318–19
perspective, 304
persuade, 304, 339
persuaded, 339
pertain, 304
pertaining, 339
pertinent, 339
perturbed, 339
pervaded, 339
phase, 272
phenomenon; phenomena, 28, 304
phylum; phyla, 28
piece, 22
pilfer, 339
pine, 339
pique, 302
piqued, 339
pitiable, 304
pitiful, 304
plane, 216
pleaded, 305
please, 92, 127
pleased, 68

*pled, 305
plenty; plentiful, 58
plethora, 305
plot, 339
plow, 339
plunge, 339
plus, 140
podcast, 219
polar; polarize; polarization, 215
pole, 215
police officer, 328
politics, 118
pompom, 305
pompon, 305
ponder, 339
pooh-pooh, 218
poor, 35
pop music, 217
populace, 305
populous, 305
pore, 305, 339
possibility, 271
possible, 68, 305
possibly, 127, 259
postmortem, 70
posture, 339
pour, 305
powwow, 218
pox, 339
practicable, 305
practical, 305
preach, 339
precede; *preceed, 305
precedence, 305, 339
precedent, 339
precipitate, 305
precipitous, 305
precise, 339
preclude, 339
precondition, 305
precursor, 339
predestined, 339
predicate, 339
predilection, 339
predisposed, 339
predominant, 305–6
predominate, 305–6, 339

preeminent, 339
preface, 274, 339
prefer, 73
preferable, 68, 339
preference, 339
prefix, 339
pregnant, 67, 339
prejudice, 306, 339
prejudiced, 339
prejudicial, 339
preliminary to, 306
preoccupied, 339
preparatory, 339
prepare, 339
prerequisite, 305, 339
prerogative, 306
prescribe, 307
present, 339
present, at, 241
presently, 306
present time, at the, 241
preside, 339
presumption, 240
pretext, 339
prevail, 339
prevent, 339
preventive; *preventative, 217, 306
*previous to, 306
principal, 68, 307
principle, 307
principled, 307
*prior to, 141, 307
probable, 239
probably, 239
proceed, 305
proceeds, 339
process of, in the, 307
proclivity, 339
procure, 275
prod, 339
prodigal, 339
proficient, 339
profit, 339
program, 255
prohibit, 339
prohibition, 339
prolegomenon; prolegomena, 28

prologue, 339
propaganda(s), 307
propensity, 339
proper, 67
prophecy, 307
prophesy; *prophesize, 307
propinquity, 339
propitious, 339
proscribe, 307
prospective, 304
prostate, 307
prostate/prostatic cancer, 34
prostrate, 307
protect, 339
protective, 339
protest, 339
protrude, 307
protuberance, 307
prove, 81, 308
proved, 308
proven, 308
provide, 339
provided, 141, 149
provided that, 146
provoke, 339
proximity, 253
psst, 152
punch, 72
punctilious, 339
punish, 339
punishable, 339
purge, 339
purposefully, 308
purposely, 308
push, 73
put, 78
puzzle, 339
puzzling, 339

quake, 339
qualified, 339
qualify, 339
qualms, 339
quandary, 339
quarrel, 339, 340
question (of/as to) whether, 308
quibble, 340

quick, 129, 308
quickly, 130, 152, 308
quit, 78
quite, 67, 68, 127, 129
quiver, 340
quotation, 308–9
quote, 235, 308–9

rack, 309
radar, 219
radiant, 340
rage, 340
rail, 340
railroad, 340
raise, 309, 340
raised, 340
rally, 340
ram, 340
rant, 340
rarely, 130, 135, 169, 172
rate, 340
rather, 127, 129, 148
rationalization, 340
rave, 340
raze, 309
react, 340
read, 78
real, 67
really, 127
realtor, 217
reason, 309, 340
reasonable, 340
reason . . . is that; *reason . . . is because, 309
reason of, by, 140, 248
reason why/that, 309
rebuild, 78
recast, 78
recede, 340
receptive, 340
reciprocate, 340
reciprocity, 340
reckon, 340
recoil, 340
recompense, 340
reconcile, 340
reconciliation, 340
recourse, 340

recur, 309
redbird, 216
redeem, 340
redo, 78
redolent, 340
redound, 340
reek, 323
refer, 235, 340
reference, 235, 309–10
referral, 309–10
refrain, 310
refrigerator, 216
refute, 310
regale, 340
regard, 340
regarding, 141, 149, 286
regardless, 225, 287, 340
regardless of, 141
regret, 340
regretful; regretfully, 310
regrettable; regrettably, 310
rehear, 78
reign, 310
rein, 310
reject, 72
rejoice, 340
related to, 283
relation, 340
relations, 340
relationship, 340
relegate, 310, 340
relieve, 340
relieved, 340
reluctant, 311
remain, 72, 81
remake, 78
remarkable, 340
remember, 340
remembrance, 340
reminisce, 340
reminiscent, 340
rend, 78, 340
render, 164
renege, 340
renounce, 262
renowned, 340
reoccur, 309

repay, 78
repellent, 310
repent, 340
repentance, 340
repetitious, 310
repetitive, 310
replace, 316, 340
replaced, 340
replacement, 340
replete, 340
representative, 340
repress, 300
reprisal, 340
reprove, 340
repugnance, 340
repugnant, 340
repulsive, 310
request, 340
require, 229
reread, 78
rerun, 78
resell, 78
resemblance, 340
resemble, 202
resentment, 340
reservations, 340
reset, 78
resign, 340
resit, 78
resolute, 340
respect, 340
respecting, 141
respite, 340
rest (up), 82
restaurateur; *restauranteur, 225, 311
restful, 311
restive, 311
restrain, 310, 340
restraint, 340
result, 271, 340
resulting, 340
retake, 78
retell, 78
reticent, 311, 341
retire, 341
retroactive, 341
revel, 341

revelation, 341
revenge, 241, 341
*revolute, 217
revolve (around), 250, 341
revulsion, 341
reward, 341
rewrite, 78
rid, 78
ride, 71, 78
riffraff, 218
rifle, 341
right, 67, 129
ring, 79
ripe, 341
ripen, 341
rise, 72, 79
roam, 341
rob, 311, 341
role, 311
roll, 311
rpm, 219
ruminate, 341
run, 79
rundown, 216
run the gauntlet/gantlet, 275

sacrilege; sacrilegious, 311
safe, 341
salesperson, 327
salt, 19
sanction, 341
sanctuary, 341
sandwich, 20
sank, 313
satiate, 341
satisfaction, 341
satisfied, 68, 341
saw, 79
say, 79, 284
scarcely, 132, 169, 172, 278
scared, 341
scavenge, 341
schism, 341
schooled, 341
scissors, 22, 29
scoff, 341
scourge, 341

scream, 341
screen, 341
scuba, 218–19
seasonable, 311–12
seasonal, 311–12
secede, 341
second(ly), 272, 288
secure, 341
see, 79, 85
seek, 79
seem, 73, 81, 135, 186
segregate, 341
seldom, 130, 135, 169, 172
self-deprecating; self-depreciating, 262
selfie, 219
self-restraint, 310
self-styled, 383
sell, 79
semblance, 214
semi-, 245–46
semiannual, 246
semiweekly, 245
send, 79, 163
sensible, 341
sensitive, 341
sensor, 249–50
sensual, 312
sensuous, 312
sentimental, 341
separate, 341
seraph; seraphim, 28
serve, 341
set, 79
settle, 341
several, 60
sew, 73, 79
sewage, 312
sewer, 312
sewerage, 312
shake, 79
shall, 83, 96, 97, 123, 170–71, 312
shall not, 170–71
shame, 341
shan't, 170–71
share, 341
sharp, 129
*(s)he, 278

*s/he, 47, 278, 324, 327
she, 38, 42, 44, 50, 327
shear, 79, 312
shed, 79
she'd've, 84
sheer, 312
sherbet; *sherbert, 312
shield, 341
shine(d); shone, 79, 313
ship, 72
shiver, 341
shoe, 79
shone, 313
shoot, 79
shopaholic, 219
shortly, 274
should, 123–24, 166, 301
should've, 84
shout, 73
show, 79, 284
shriek, 341
shrink, 79, 341
shrive, 79
shrug, 341
shudder, 341
shut, 79
shuttle, 341
shy, 341
sift, 341
sight, 313
significance, 341
significant, 341
similar, 341
similarity, 341
simple, 313
simplistic, 313
simulcast, 74
simultaneous, 341
since, 129, 133, 140, 148, 149, 283, 313
sing, 79
singeing, 87
singing, 87
singular, 68
sink, 79, 313
sit, 79, 81
sitcom, 217
site, 252, 313

skeptical, 341
sketch, 73
skillful, 341
skulduggery; skullduggery, 313
slacks, 29
slander, 261
slanted, 341
slave, 341
slay, 79, 314
sleep, 72, 79, 341
slew, 313–14
slide, 79
sling, 79
slink, 79
slit, 79
slough, 313–14
slow(ed), 216
slow(er); slowest, 216
slow(ly), 129, 314
*slue, 313–14
smash, 72
smell, 79, 81–82, 135, 314, 341
smelled, 314
smelly, 299
smelt, 314
smile, 72, 341
smite, 79
smitten, 341
sneak(ed); *snuck, 314
sneeze, 72
snuggle, 341
so, 67, 129, 147, 149, 150, 347
so–as, 147
so-called, 383
so far, 241
soften, 213
*solicitate, 217
solicitous, 341
solicitude, 341
solidarity, 341
somber, 67
some, 19, 22, 56, 60, 173, 199
somebody, 40, 56, 118, 173
somehow, 129
someone, 40, 56, 118, 173, 327
something, 173, 217
somewhat, 127, 129

somewhere, 129, 173
soon, 129, 130, 274, 306
sore, 341
sorry, 341
sort(s), 50, 314
so that, 131, 146, 147, 148
so then, 147
sought, 341
sound, 81–82
sow, 79
space, 314
spaghetti, 29
spat, 79, 315, 341
speak, 79, 214
speaking, 149
speaking of, 141
speculate, 341
speculator, 341
speed, 79
spell(ed); spelt, 74, 79, 314
spend, 79
spill(ed); spilt, 79, 314
spin, 79
spit(ted); spat, 79, 315
split, 80
spoil(ed); spoilt, 80, 315
spread, 80
spring; sprang; sprung, 80, 315
spy, 341
squeeze, 341
Sr., 356
stadiums, 28
stanch, 315
stand, 80
standing, 341
standpoint, 218
standstill, 216
staple, 72
started, 342
state, 254, 284
stationary, 68, 315
stationer, 315
stationery, 315
staunch, 315
stave, 80
stay, 72, 81
steadfast(ly), 129

steal, 80, 311
stern, 342
stick, 80
stiffen, 213
stigma, 342
stigmatize, 342
still, 129, 147, 241
stimulus; stimuli, 28
sting, 80
stink, 80
stint, 342
stir, 342
stirfry, 216
stock, 342
stoical, 342
storm, 342
straight, 129, 315–16
strains credibility; *strains credulity, 260
strait, 315–16
straitjacket; *straightjacket, 316
stratagem, 316
*stratas, 316
strategy, 316
stratum; strata, 28, 316
stray, 342
streak, 342
streaked, 342
stream, 342
strength, 213
strew, 80
strewn, 342
stricken, 342
strict, 342
stride, 80
strife, 342
strike, 80, 342
string, 80
strive, 80, 342
struggle, 342
study, 342
stumble, 342
style; stylish, 58
subject, 252
sublet, 80
submit, 342
subordinate, 342
subscribe, 342

subsequent, 256
subsequently, 316
*subsequent to, 141, 316
subsidiary, 342
subsidy, 342
subsist, 342
substitute, 316, 342
succeed, 71, 342
such, 56, 59, 240, 316
such as, 270, 291
such that, 131, 148
suffer, 73, 342
sufficient, 68, 231
suggest, 284
suit, 202
suitable, 342
suited, 342
summon, 342
sunglasses, 22
sunk, 313
supersede; *supercede, 317
superstitious, 342
supervision, 342
supplement, 342
supplementary, 342
supply, 342
supposing, 149
supposing that, 146
susceptible, 342
suspect, 342
suspicion, 342
suspicious, 342
swam, 317
swear, 80
sweep, 80
swim, 80, 317
swimming, 35
swing, 80, 342
swum, 317
sympathetic, 342
sympathize, 342
sympathy, 269, 342
synchronize, 342
synchronous, 342
synonymous, 342
systematic, 317
systemic, 317

tactics, 316
take, 72, 80, 247
taken, 342
tally, 342
tantalizing, 317
tantamount, 342
tap, 342
taste, 73, 81–82, 135, 186, 342
taunt, 342
teach, 80, 163
tear, 80, 342
tease, 342
teem, 342
tell, 80, 163, 232
tenacious, 214
tend, 342
tendency, 342
tender, 342
terms, 342
testator; testatrix, 327
testify, 342
text(ed), 317
than, 45, 143, 146, 148, 318
than I, 143
thankful, 342
thankfully, 318
thank goodness, 318
than me, 143
that, 22, 37, 42, 49–50, 52, 53, 54, 55, 59,
    139, 148, 166, 168, 178, 187, 189, 194,
    271, 316, 318–19
that's him, 164
that which, 54
thaw, 319
the, 21, 22, 59, 61, 63, 116, 316
their, 40, 47, 48, 59, 319, 327
theirs, 47, 319
them, 38, 47, 48, 327
*themself, 47, 319
themselves, 47, 48, 49, 319
then, 129
there, 38, 48, 89–90, 119, 129, 173–75, 178,
    319
therefor, 319
therefore, 131, 147, 240, 319
there're, 84
there's, 84

these, 49–50, 59, 316
*these kind of, 288
*these sort of, 314
they, 38, 42, 46, 47, 50, 259, 324, 327
they're, 48, 319
think, 80, 164, 272
third(ly), 272
thirst, 342
this, 37, 42, 49–50, 59, 316
this is he; *this is him, 45
those, 49–50, 59, 316
though, 146, 148, 166, 236
thought, 255
threshold, 319
through, 129, 140, 151
throughout, 140
throw, 80
throw down the gauntlet, 275
thrust, 80
thus, 129, 131, 147, 319
*thusly, 129, 319
'til, 319
till, 133, 319
timber, 319
timbre, 319
time, 303
time, at this, 241
time period, 303
time that/when, at the, 241
timid, 343
tinge, 343
tinged, 343
tinker, 343
titillating, 317
to, 84–85, 123, 127, 135, 139, 140, 185,
    189–90, 203–4, 278, 285, 300, 301
toast, 343
today, 130, 241
together with, 120
tolerance, 320, 343
tolerant, 320
toleration, 320
tomorrow, 130
tonight, 130
too, 127, 129, 131
toothpick, 216
torpid, 320

tortious, 320
tortuous, 320
torturous, 320
total, 116
tough, 343
tout, 343
toward, 139, 140, 320
towards, 320
toy, 343
trade, 343
traffic, 343
transcript, 320
transcription, 320
transpire, 320
tread, 80
treat, 343
tremble, 343
trillion, 246
triumphal, 320
triumphant, 320
trouble, 343
trust, 343
try and/to, 320
turbid, 320
turgid, 320
turn, 81

ugh, 152
ultimate, 68, 303
umbrage, 343
unanimous, 68
unavoidable, 68
unawares, 129
unbeatable, 343
unbecoming, 343
unbiased, 343
unbroken, 68
unburden, 343
uncomfortable, 343
uncooperative, 343
undaunted, 343
under, 129, 139
underbid, 80
undercut, 80
undergo, 80
underlie, 80
underneath, 140

underpay, 80
undersell, 80
understand, 73, 80
undertake, 80
under the circumstances, 251
underwrite, 80
undo, 80
undoubtedly, 266
unduly, 301
unequal, 343
unexceptionable, 321
unexceptional, 321
unfaithful, 343
unfamiliar, 343
unfazed, 272
unfeeling, 343
unfortunately, 310
unfreeze, 80
uniform, 68, 343
uniformity, 343
unify, 343
uninterested, 265
unique, 67, 68, 321, 343
universal, 68
unjustified, 343
unlawful, 321
unless, 146, 148, 166
unlucky; unluckier, 66
unmindful, 343
unmisgivingly, 213
unorganized, 265
unpalatable, 343
*unphased, 272
unpopular, 343
unreadable, 282
unsparing, 343
unsteady; unsteadier, 66
unstinting, 343
unsuitable, 343
unsuited, 343
*unthaw, 319
until, 133, 139, 140, 148, 149, 307, 319
unused, 343
unwind, 80
up, 128, 129, 140, 143
upbraid, 343
uphold, 80

*upmost, 321
upon, 130, 262, 299
upset, 81, 343
up to, 141
upward(s), 320
us, 37, 38
use, 72, 321
used, 343
usually, 249
utilize, 321
utmost, 321
uxorial, 214

vacillate, 343
value, 343
vanish, 72, 343
variance, 343
variation, 343
variety, 343
vary, 343
venal, 321
vengeance, 241
venial, 321
verbal, 321
verge, 343
versatile, 343
very, 67, 68, 129, 131, 295
very much, 68
vest, 343
vested, 343
vexed, 343
vie, 343
visualize, 343
vocation, 241
void, 68, 343
voluminous, 254
voter awareness, 34

wade, 343
wage, 343
wait, 343
waive, 321
waiver, 343
wake, 81
walk, 73
wangle, 323
want, 343

wanted, 343
wanting, 343
war, 343
was, 21, 73, 112–15, 178
wash, 73, 217
wasn't, 84
watch, 73, 343
wave, 321
waver, 343
wax, 81
we, 37, 38, 42, 46, 50
weak, 343
weakened, 343
weakness, 344
wean, 344
wear, 81
weave, 81
webinar, 219
wed, 81
wedding, 293
weep, 81, 344
weigh, 202, 344
well, 129, 152
went, 275
were, 21, 73, 93–94, 112–15
wet, 81
what, 38, 42, 51, 52, 54, 55, 148, 149, 157,
    158, 178–79, 189
whatever, 55, 187
Whatever!, 259
wheat, 29
when, 129, 131–32, 133, 148, 149, 157, 187,
    188, 189, 194, 241
whence, 133
whenever, 129, 188
where, 119, 129, 131–32, 133, 148, 149, 157,
    187, 188, 189, 194
whereas, 322
where–there, 147, 176
wherever, 129
whether, 148, 263, 281, 322
whether or not, 322
whew, 152
which, 38, 42, 51, 52, 53, 54, 55, 139, 157,
    166, 168, 189, 194, 318–19
whichever, 55, 187
while, 133, 148, 322

whitewash, 216
whither, 133
who, 22, 23, 30, 38, 42, 51, 52, 53, 54, 55, 60,
    157, 166, 168, 178, 187, 194, 299–300,
    322, 325
whoever, 38, 50, 55–56, 322
whoever's, 322
who is, 166
whole, 68
whom, 38, 51, 52, 55, 139, 187, 322
whomever, 38, 55–56, 322
who're, 84
who's, 48, 322
whose, 48, 51, 52, 55, 187, 189, 322
whosever, 322
why, 129, 131–32, 148, 149, 152, 157, 187,
    189, 194
wide, 129
will, 83, 96, 123, 124, 170, 312
will have, 97
will not, 170
willy-nilly, 218
win, 81
wince, 344
wind, 81
with, 140, 149–50, 247, 264, 284
with a view to, 141
withdraw, 81
withhold, 81, 319
within, 130
without, 140, 148
without regard to, 141
with reference to, 141
with regard to, 140, 141
with respect to, 141
withstand, 81
with the view of, 141
wizard, 344
woman, 26, 284, 288, 326

*(wo)man, 327
wonder, 344
won't, 170
work, 323
workers' compensation; workmen's
    compensation, 322–23
workroom, 216
worm, 344
worse, 129
worthy, 344
would, 124, 201
wouldn't, 170
would've, 84
wrack, 309
wrangle, 323, 344
wreak, 323
wreaked, 323
wrest, 344
wring, 81
write, 81, 163, 257
wrong, 67, 129, 323
wrongful, 323
wrought, 323

yearn, 344
yes, 132, 233
yet, 129, 147, 241, 347
yield, 344
you, 37, 38, 42, 43, 46
your, 47, 48, 59, 323
you're, 48, 323
yours, 47, 48
yourself; yourselves, 48, 49

zeal, 344
zealous, 344
zeros, 26
zigzag, 218

General Index

Aarts, Bas, 5n21, 327n5, 497
abbreviation, 61, 62, 218–19, 388–89, 401
ABC's of Languages and Linguistics, The
    (Hayes), 18n46
ablaut, 73, 401
About Language (W. Roberts & Turgeon,
    eds.), 494
Abraham Lincoln, The Prairie Years
    (Sandburg), 6n24, 6n25
Abrams, M. H., 504
absolute construction, 192, 401
abstract noun, 19, 23, 449
*Abstract of the First Principles of English
    Grammar, An* (Hutchins), 16n26
accent, 401
acceptability, 401
accidence, 213, 401
Accidence, The (Devis), 16n21
Accidence Will Happen (Kamm), 42n3
accusative case, 30, 413
accusative function, 30
acronym, 62, 218–19, 388, 401
action verb, 483, 484
active voice, 85, 86, 89, 90–92, 97–98, 145,
    184, 210–11, 402
additive coordinating conjunction, 147, 421
address, punctuating, 349
adfix, 214, 402
adjectival, 141, 165, 402
adjective, 58–70
    absolute, 66
    adverb, distinguished from, 65, 128
    agreement with noun, 59, 407
    articles functioning as, 61–63
    appositive, 64, 402
    attribute, 404
    attributive, 58, 64, 402
    be-verb as part of, 112
    central, 402
    common, 66, 402
    comparative, 66–67, 402
    compound, 60, 403

compound modifier, 62–63, 69, 402, 404
coordinate, 69, 348, 356, 403
dangling participle, 65
date functioning as, 10, 63
defined, 58, 402
definitive, 403
degrees, 66–68
demonstrative, 59, 403
descriptive, 31, 58, 63, 403
distributive, 60
double comparative, 67, 418
double superlative, 67, 478
exclamatory, 152
functioning as other parts of speech, 70
gradable, 66–68, 403
indefinite, 22, 60, 403
interrogative, 59, 403
irregular, 67
limiting, 47, 58, 61–63, 403
linking verb with, 64–65
misused, 70
noncomparable, 67–68
noun functioning as, 33–34
numeric, 58–59, 403
other parts of speech functioning as, 70
participial, 65, 67, 68, 87, 295, 379, 403
participle, distinguished from, 65
peripheral, 403
periphrastic comparative, 66, 133, 418
periphrastic superlative, 66, 134, 478
personal, 404
phrasal, 60, 64, 69–70, 375–76, 385, 404,
    457
place names functioning as, 60
position, 64–65
positive, 66, 404
possessive, 59, 404
possessive functioning as, 37
possessive with, 64
postpositive, 64, 199, 404
predicate, 58, 64–65, 181, 186, 202, 404
predicative, 58, 461

adjective (*cont.*)
  prepositive, 402
  pronominal, 60, 404
  pronoun with, 64
  proper, 60, 404
  punctuating, 63, 69–70
  qualifying, 60, 403
  qualitative, 58
  quantitative, 58–59
  relative, 52, 60, 404
  relative pronoun functioning as, 52
  simple, 405
  subjective, 404
  suffixes, 58, 65, 66–67
  superlative, 66–67, 405
  synthetic comparative, 66, 418
  synthetic superlative, 66, 478
  types, 58–60, 68–70
  verbal, 403
  verb functioning as, 85
adjective clause, 187, 414
adjective cluster, 134, 405
adjective–noun agreement, 59, 407
adjective phrase, 64, 171, 379, 457
adjective pronoun, 42, 404
adjunct, 58, 127, 163, 405
Adler, Mortimer, 317, 494
adnoun, 70, 405
Advanced English Grammar, An (Kittredge &
    Farley), 3n10, 497
Advanced Lessons in English Grammar
    (Maxwell), 2n8
adverb, 127–38
  adjective, distinguished from, 65, 128
  affirmative, 132
  auxiliary verb with, 135
  be-verb with, 135
  cause, of, 131
  comparative, 133
  compound, 130, 405
  conjunction, distinguished from, 149
  conjunction functioning as, 149
  conjunctive, 131, 133, 151, 406
  conjunctive relative, 148–49
  connective, 133, 406
  consequence, of, 131
  consequential, 131

defined, 127, 405
degree, of, 131, 406
degrees, 133–34
double, 129
exclamatory, 132, 152, 406
flat, 128–29, 406
focusing, 137–38
functions, 127, 135–36, 143
independent, 406
intensifying, 127, 441
interrogative, 131–32, 149, 406
intransitive verb with, 135
introductory, 406
irregular, 134
linking verb with, 135
location, of, 130–31
locative, 130–31
manner, of, 130, 131, 204, 406
modal, 127
modifying nonverb, 134
modifying sentence, 127, 192, 406
negating, 169, 171, 172
negative, 83, 132
noncomparable, 134
noun functioning as, 34
number, of, 131
numeric, 131
parallel pairs, 176
particle, 128
periphrastic comparative, 133, 418
periphrastic superlative, 134, 478
phrasal, 130, 457
place, of, 130–31, 174–75
position in sentence, 134–38
positive, 133
prepositional, 128
prepositional phrase, replacing, 144
preposition functioning as, 82, 128, 143
reason, of, 131
relative, 132, 406
sentence, 127, 192, 406
simple, 128–29, 203–4, 406
standard, 128–29
suffixes, 128, 131, 133–34
superlative, 133–34, 477–78
synthetic comparative, 133, 418
synthetic superlative, 134, 478

there as, 174–75
time, of, 130
transitional, 406
types, 130–33
verb functioning as, 85
verb phrase, within, 83, 135–36
adverb clause, 414
adverbial, 406, 407
  identifying as sentence element, 164
  infinitive with, 85, 135
  linking verb with, 81–82
  position in verb phrase, 135
  prepositional phrase functioning as, 71,
    130, 164, 204
  suffix, 128
  transformational grammar, 203–5
adverbial clause, 136–37, 165, 166, 188, 414
adverbial conjunction, 148–49, 406
adverbial noun, 407
adverbial objective, 34, 136, 407
adverbial phrase, 68, 131, 136, 141, 457
adverb phrase, 457
adversative clause, 147, 414, 421
adversative conjunction, 137, 147, 150, 421
affirmative adverb, 132
affixation, 214–15, 407
  derivational, 215, 407
  inflectional, 215, 407
  negation, 169, 172
  See also adfix; infix; prefix; suffix
agent, 407
agentless passive, 455
agent noun, 32–33, 449
agglutination, 216, 407
agreement, 407
  adjective–noun, 59, 407
  pronoun–antecedent, 20, 21, 38–42, 44,
    52, 408
  subject–verb, 20, 95, 115–17, 118–20, 121,
    408
  See also concord
Aiken, Janet Rankin, 3
Aitchison, James, 18n48
Alcott, Louisa May, 370
Alexander, Caleb, 16
Alexander, Christopher, 396
Alexander, Henry, 289, 494, 501

Alford, Henry, 392
Algeo, John, 502
Allen, Harold Byron, vii, 491, 492, 501
Allen, Robert L., 7n27
Allende, Isabel, 358, 380
alliteration, 408
alphabetism, 441
Alston, R. C., 500
alternative question, 157, 466
Altick, Richard D., 397
Alvarez, Julia, 392
ambient *it*, 174
ambiguity, 33–34, 36, 53, 59, 84, 89, 137–38,
    141, 168, 171, 173, 207–10, 408
ambisyllabic, 408
ambitransitive verb, 72, 484
Ambrose, Stephen, 366
amelioration, 408
American Grammar (J. Brown), 17
American Grammar, The (Ross), 17
*American Heritage Dictionary of the English
    Language, The*, 225, 503
Americanism, 408
American Language, The (Mencken), 502
American Usage and Style (Copperud), 498
ampersand, 348
analytic comparative, 418
analytic language, 157, 160, 408
Analyzing Grammar (Kroeger), 18n46
anaphora, 36, 408
anaphoric ellipsis, 167–68
anaphoric pronoun, 36, 464
anaptyxis, 430
Anaya, Rudolfo, 388
Anderson, Wallace L., 281, 493
Angelou, Maya, 366
Anglo-Saxon, 453
animate noun, 449
*Annotated Bibliography of 19th-Century
    Grammars of English, An* (Görlach), 500
anomalous verb, 485
antecedent, 36–40, 49–50, 52, 53, 54,
    118–19, 325, 327, 409
  agreement with pronoun, 20, 21, 38–42,
    44, 52, 408
Anthology of Errors, An (Whyte), 251, 493
anticipatory *it*, 174

anticipatory reference, 37, 414
anticipatory subject, 119, 475
antonym, 409
    binary, 409
    gradable, 409
aphaeresis, 217, 409
aphesis, 409
apocopation, 409
apocope, 217, 409
apodosis, 166, 409
apostrophe, 380–81
    contractions, 48, 380
    defined, 380
    genitive, 23, 31–32, 50 (*see also*
        apostrophe: possessive)
    obligatory, 381
    plurals, 25, 381
    possessive, 23, 31–32, 47–48, 50, 380
    -*s*, with, 25, 381
    uses and misuses, 380–81
apposition, 33, 409
appositional compound, 419
appositional phrase, 409–10
appositive
    close, 410
    defined, 33, 192, 409–10
    diagramming, 192
    essential, 410
    gerund phrase functioning as, 88
    loose, 410
    nonessential, 410
    nonrestrictive, 33, 410
    placement in sentence, 64
    pronouns, with, 38, 41
    punctuation of, 33, 348, 355
    restrictive, 33, 355, 410
appositive adjective, 64, 402
appositive clause, 166, 414
appositive phrase, 192, 457
appreciation, 408
"Approaching Usage in the Classroom"
    (Higgins), vii, 491
archaism, 410
Archives of Instruction (J. Carr, S. Carr &
    Schultz), 500
argot, 410
Armstrong, Karen, 377

Ars Grammatica (Donatus), 13
article, 61–63
    choosing which to use, 62
    coordinate nouns with, 62
    defined, 61, 410
    definite, 61–63, 116, 198, 325, 410
    demonstrative value of, 62–63
    indefinite, 20–21, 22, 61–62, 198, 228,
        325, 410
    omitted, 63
    pronoun substitute, 63
    proper name with, 61
    zero, 63, 410
Art of Nonfiction, The (Rand), vii, 491
Art of Plain Talk, The (Flesch), 502
Ash, John, 15n14
aspect, 94–95, 410
    continuous, 94–95, 411
    imperfect, 94–95, 411
    perfect, 94–95, 411 (*see also* perfect tense)
    progressive, 94–95, 97–98, 411, 481 (*see
        also* progressive tense)
asserting verb, 485
assertive, 425
assimilation, 411
Associated Press Guide to Punctuation, The
    (Capon), 504
*Associated Press Stylebook and Briefing on
    Media Law, The*, 31, 502
assonance, 411
asterisk, 411
asyndetic coordination, 424
asyndeton, 411
attribute adjective, 404
attribute complement, 419
attribute noun, 450, 461
attribute pronoun, 45, 461, 464
attributive, 411
attributive adjective, 58, 64, 402
attributive noun, 33–34, 449
Auchincloss, Louis, 388
Auerbach, Erich, 383
Aurelius, Marcus, 258, 493
Austen, Jane, 387
"Authority and American Usage" (D.
    Wallace), 231, 493

auxiliary verb, 121–26
  adverb with, 135
  contractions, 83–84, 169–70
  defined, 83, 121, 411–12
  dummy, 125, 412
  empty, 412
  interrogative sentence, in, 83
  modal (*see* modal auxiliary verb)
  not with, 169–70
  parallelism, 177
  semi-auxiliary, 412
  transformational grammar, 201–2
  verb phrase, in, 83–84, 135
Ayto, John, 503

Babel, Isaac, 388, 495
Bach, Emmon, 498
back-formation, 217, 412
backshifting, 98–99, 166, 412
bad grammar, 14, 258, 435–36
Baker, Sheridan, 175, 492, 504
Balch, William S., 17
Baldick, Chris, 504
Baldridge, Letitia, 395
bare infinitive, 189–90, 440
Barker, Isaac, 14n8
Barnet, Sylvan, 504
Barnhart, Robert K., 503
Barnhart Dictionary of Etymology, The
  (Barnhart, ed.), 503
Barrie, J. M., 371
Bartley, Robert L., 384
Barzun, Jacques, 370
base, 474
Bateson, F. W., 347
Bauer, Harry C., 382
Bauer, Laurie, 18n52
Baugh, Albert C., 501
Beatty, Jerome, Jr., 384
being verb, 485
Belloc, Hilaire, 361
Bellow, Saul, 388
Beneath the Crust of Words (Foley), 159, 492
Benedict, Stewart, 497
Berger, John, 367
Berman, Morton, 504
Bernstein, Theodore M., 498

Bett, Henry, 304, 315, 494
Between You and Me (M. Norris), 499
be-verb
  adjective or noun, as part of, 112
  adverbs with, 135
  cleft sentence, in, 178–79
  conjugation, 112–15
  contracted, 84
  defined, 81, 483
  passive voice, 90–91, 98, 207, 211
  progressive aspect, 91–92, 98
  subjective complement, 163, 186
  transformational grammar, 201, 202, 207,
    211
  whiz-deletion, 90–91
  See also linking verb
bias-free language, 324–28
  gender-neutral language, 44, 47, 278,
    324–28
  labels, 328
  personal characteristics, 328
  problematic suffixes, 327–28
  pronouns, 324–27
  traits, 328
  types of bias, 324
  writer's credibility, 324, 328
Biber, Douglas, 245n1, 497
Bierce, Ambrose, 387
binary antonyms, 409
Bingham, Caleb, 16
Black, Max, 226, 493
blend, 489
Boardman, Phillip C., 495
Bolton, W. F., 82, 491
Bono (Paul David Hewson), 383
Booth, Wayne C., ii, 182, 492
borrowing, 412
Bosworth, Sheila, 375
bounded noun, 449
bound morpheme, 214, 447
Bowles, Paul, 380
brackets, 390–91
  citation, 391
  defined, 390
  ellipsis dots, displacing, 391
  other punctuation, with, 389, 390, 391
  parentheses, within, 390

brackets (*cont.*)
   quotations, in, 390
Bradbury, Ray, 349
Braddock, Richard Reed, 500
Bradley, Henry, 283, 313, 493, 494
Brain Droppings (Carlin), 288, 493
branching diagram, 482
Brief Grammar of Modern Written English, A
   (Gray), 18n42
Briticism, Britishism, 413
Brittain, Robert, 504
broad construction, 413
broad reference, 37, 413
Brogan, T. V. F., 505
Brown, Goold, 2, 497
Brown, James, 17
Brustein, Robert, 388
Bryant, Margaret M., 501
Buckley, William F., 370
bullets, 177–78, 394–95
Bunyan, John, 313
Burchfield, Robert W., 1n1, 5, 18n49, 498,
   501, 503
Burgess, Anthony, 365
Burnett, Frances Hodgson, 370
Burnham, James, 362
Burr, Aaron, 17
Burto, William, 504
Burton, Richard, 142, 492
Bushnell, Candace, 392
Butler, Noble, 17n41

Cable, Thomas, 501, 507
calque, 218, 444
Cambieri, Giulia, 384
*Cambridge Encyclopedia of the English
   Language, The* (Crystal), 501
*Cambridge Grammar of the English Language,
   The* (Huddleston & Pullum), 8n29,
   18n47, 245n2, 497
Cambridge Guide to English Usage, The
   (Peters), 499
Candelaria, Frederick, 492
capitalization, 19–20, 43, 60, 153, 364
Capon, Rene J., 504
cardinal number, 58–59, 198, 451
Careful Writer, The (Bernstein), 498

Carey, G. V., 504
Carlin, George, 288, 493
Carnegie, Dale, 387
Carnes, Mark, 2n2, 367
Caro, Robert A., 383
Carr, Jean Ferguson, 500
Carr, Stephen L., 500
case, 29–32
   accusative, 30, 413
   common, 29–30, 413
   defined, 23, 29, 41, 413
   genitive (*see* genitive)
   inflection, 23
   nominative, 29–30, 41–42, 43, 44–45, 413
   noun, 23, 29–32
   objective, 41–42, 43, 143, 413
   oblique, 413
   possessive (*see* possessive)
   pronoun, 23, 38, 41, 42, 43, 44–45, 52–53,
      143, 164
   subjective, 413
   See also function
catachresis, 223, 292, 414
cataphora, 37, 414
cataphoric ellipsis, 167–68
Cathcart, Thomas, 389
Cather, Willa, 365
Cecil, Henry, 366
central adjective, 402
Chalker, Sylvia, 497
Chandler, Raymond, 351, 370
changes in meaning. *See* meaning, changes
   in
Chatting About English (Jowett), 97, 135, 492
Chaucer, Geoffrey, 32, 313
Chayefsky, Paddy, 387
Cheever, Susan, 370
Chicago Manual of Style, The, 10–11, 366,
   502, 507
Chomsky, Noam, 4, 195
Christian, Darrell, 502
Christie, Agatha, 363
Chubb, Percival, 3n14, 500
Churchill, Winston, 142, 182, 357
Circles of Gomer, The (R. Jones), 16n20
clang association, 414
Clark, John, 14

Clark, Kenneth, 386
class dialect, 4, 257, 427
clausal, 414
clause, 165–66
  adjective, 187, 414
  adverbial, 136–37, 165, 166, 188, 414
  adversative, 147, 414, 421
  apodosis, 409
  appositive, 166, 414
  comment, 414–15
  comparative, 415
  complement, 415
  complex sentence, 159
  compound-complex sentence, 159
  concessive, 415
  conditional, 166, 415
  confirmation, 467
  contact, 165–66, 415
  coordinate, 159, 415
  defined, 165, 414
  dependent, 90, 133, 136, 159, 165, 194, 358, 415
  diagramming, 187–89
  ellipsis with, 167–68
  elliptical, 415
  embedded, 415
  essential, 416
  finite, 416
  gerund, 191–92
  hypothetical conditional, 99, 166
  independent, 52, 89–90, 133, 136, 159, 165, 183, 416
  limiting, 416
  main, 132, 166–68, 416
  matrix, 416
  nominal, 416
  nonessential, 416
  nonlimiting, 416
  nonrestrictive, 187, 416
  noun, 188–89, 416
  passive, 416
  principal, 416
  protasis, 166, 415
  relative, 52–54, 165–66, 168–69, 416
  remote relative, 53–54
  restrictive, 187, 355, 416
  sentential relative, 416

simple sentence, 159, 472
subject, 178–79, 417
subordinate, 132, 136, 165, 168, 187, 188, 189, 194, 347, 415
substantive, 416
that-clause, 417
types of, 165–66
whiz-deletion, 91, 165–66, 168–69, 179, 488
cleft sentence, 178–80
  be-verb in, 178–79
  defined, 178–79, 470
  functions, 179–80
  negative, 179, 471
  relative pronoun, 178–79
  types, 179
  whiz-deletion, 179
Clinton, Bill, 376
clipped form, 217, 417
clipping, 217, 417
clitic, 447
close appositive, 410
closed syllable, 478
closed word class, 74, 489
Coar, Thomas, 16
Cobbett, William, 43, 491
Coetzee, J. M., 388
cognate, 417
cognate object, 71, 452
Cohen, Cathy J., 350
cohesion, 417
collective noun, 19, 20–21, 22, 39, 116, 449
collocation, 417
colon, 361–64
  capitalization with, 364
  citations, 363
  defined, 361
  linking clauses or phrases, 361
  lists, 361–62, 364
  quotation, 362–63, 364
  quotation marks, with, 384
  salutation, 363
  time, 363
Columbian Accidence, The (Gurney), 16n32
Comly, John, 16
comma, 347–56
  addresses, 349

comma (*cont.*)
  adjectives, 69, 356
  adverb, 352
  ampersand, 348
  appositive, 33, 348
  compound predicate, 352–53
  dates, 63, 349
  defined, 347
  direct question, 350
  independent clauses, 347, 353
  interjections, 152–53
  introductions, 347
  lists, 350, 358
  misused, 351–56
  nonrestrictive element, 348, 351
  numbers, 349
  parenthesis, 368
  place-names, 60
  quotation, 349, 352
  quotation marks, with, 384
  restrictive phrase, 355
  salutation, 351, 363
  semicolon, displaced by, 359, 360
  sentence-starting conjunction, 354
  serial, 348
  speech, direct and indirect, 349
  splice, 281, 353, 417
  subject and verb, 351
  subordinate clause, 347
  suffixes following names, 356
  transitions, 347
  verb and object, 351–52
  vocative, 350
Commager, Henry Steele, 348
command, 92, 158, 428
comma splice, 281, 353, 417
comment clause, 414–15
common adjective, 66, 402
common case, 29–30, 413
common gender, 40, 433–34
common noun, 19, 20, 24, 449
*Common-School Grammar of the English
    Language, A* (Kerl), 2n7
Commonsense Grammar (Aiken), 3n12
comparative, 418
  analytic, 418
  double, 67, 418

  periphrastic, 66, 133, 418
  suffix, 215
  synthetic, 66, 133, 418
comparative adjective, 66–67, 402
comparative adverb, 133
comparative clause, 415
comparison, 67, 133–34, 136–37, 147, 148,
    216, 418
"Compendious English Grammar, A"
    (Dyche), 15n10
complement
  attribute, 419
  defined, 418
  diagramming, 185, 186
  factitive, 419
  identifying in sentence, 163–64
  inner, 164, 418
  object, 419
  objective, 85, 88, 163–64, 185, 419
  objective attribute, 419
  outer, 164, 419
  predicate, 85, 419
  subjective, 81, 88, 162, 163–64, 183, 184,
      186, 419
  that-complement, 419
complementary infinitive, 85, 440
complementary object, 419
complement clause, 415
Complete Plain Words, The (E. Gowers), 502
complete predicate, 84, 162, 461
completer, 418
complete sentence, 470
complete subject, 162, 475
complete verb, 84, 483
Complete Works of Isaac Babel, The
    (Constantine, trans.), 495
complex preposition, 140–41, 462
complex sentence, 159, 165, 194, 470
compositional compound word, 215–16
Composition in the University (Crowley), 500
Composition—Rhetoric (Connors), 500
compound, 215–16, 217, 419–20
  appositional, 419
  compositional, 215–16
  conjunction, 146, 421
  endocentric, 419
  exocentric, 420

indefinite pronoun, 56
neoclassical, 420
noncompositional, 215–16
compound adjective, 60, 403
compound adverb, 130, 405
compound-complex sentence, 159, 194, 470
compounding, 215–16, 420
compound modifier, 62–63, 69, 402, 404
compound noun, 20, 26–27, 31, 69, 199, 376, 449
compound object, 41, 452
compound personal pronoun, 48–49, 465
compound predicate, 159, 352–53, 461
compound preposition, 139–40, 462
compound pronoun, 48–49, 55, 464
compound relative pronoun, 55
compound subject, 41, 117–18, 120, 475
compound tense, 97, 480
compound word. *See* compound
Comprehensive Grammar of the English Language, A (Quirk), 18n50, 498
concessive clause, 415
Concise Oxford Dictionary, The, 503
Concise Oxford Dictionary of English Etymology, The (Hoad, ed.), 503
Concise Oxford Dictionary of Literary Terms, The (Baldick), 504
concord, 407
  notional, 21, 116, 479
  proximity, of, 432
  See also agreement
concrete noun, 19, 22–23, 449
conditional clause, 166, 415
conditional sentence, 166, 470
confirmation clause, 467
conjugation, 421
  progressive, 91–92
  to be, of, 112–15
  to call, of, 99–105
  to hide, of, 105–11
conjunction, 146–51
  additive coordinating, 147, 421
  adverb, distinguished from, 149
  adverbial, 148–49, 406
  adversative, 137, 147, 150, 421
  beginning sentence with, 150–51
  compound, 146, 421

contrasting coordinating, 147, 421
coordinating, 146, 147, 151, 169, 347, 421–22
copulative, 147, 421
correlating, 421
correlative, 146–47, 171, 176, 193, 421
defined, 146, 421–22
diagramming, 193
disguised, 149
disjunctive, 117, 118, 146, 147, 151, 421
expletive, 149
final, 147, 421–22
half, 406
illative, 406
illative coordinating, 147, 421–22
interrogative adverbial, 149
negation, 169, 171
number of verb, 151
parallelism, 146–47, 176
participial preposition, distinguished from, 149
participle functioning as, 149
phrasal, 146, 422
pronoun with, 146
relative adverbial, 149
separative coordinating, 147, 421
simple, 146, 422
subordinating, 141, 146–48, 161, 165, 187, 188, 194, 243, 422
conjunctive adverb, 131, 133, 151, 406
conjunctive compound subject, 117–18
conjunctive phrase, 148
connecting verb, 81–82, 485
connective, 120, 146, 165–66, 422
connective adverb, 133, 406
Connors, Robert J., 500
connotation, 422
Conrad, Susan, 497
consequent, 409
consequential adverb, 131
Consider the Lobster and Other Essays (D. Wallace), 493
consonance, 422
consonant, 422
Constantine, Peter W., 495
constituent, 161–62, 422
  defined, 422

constituent (*cont.*)
immediate, 161–62, 422–23
sentence element, 161–62
constructio ad sensum, 479
construction, 423
contact clause, 165–66, 415
Contemporary Rhetoric (Winterowd), 383, 492, 495
content word, 61, 98, 489
continuous aspect, 94–95, 411
continuous tense, 94, 97–98, 481
contraction, 48, 83, 84, 170, 380, 423
contrasting coordinating conjunction, 147, 421
conversion, 33–35, 70, 82, 216, 423
coordinate, 332, 421
coordinate adjective, 69, 348, 356, 403
coordinate clause, 159, 415
coordinated pronouns, 245
coordinate noun, 62
coordinate objects, 452
coordinate subjects, 475
coordinate verbs, 159, 483
coordinating conjunction, 146, 147, 151, 169, 347, 421–22
coordination, 175–76, 357, 423–24
asyndetic, 424
correlative, 424
polysyndetic, 424
syndetic, 424
coordinator, 421
Copeland, Rita, 13n2, 14n3, 491, 500
Copperud, Roy H., 498
copula, 81, 485
copular, 424
copular verb, 485
copulative conjunction, 147, 421
copulative verb, 485
correlating conjunctions, 421
correlative, 182, 266, 424
correlative conjunctions, 146–47, 171, 176, 193, 421
correlative coordination, 424
countable noun, 22–23, 449–50
count noun, 19, 20, 22–23, 28, 57, 449–50
Cousins, Norman, 369
Coward, Noel, 351

Craftsmanship in Writing (Pink), 302, 494
Crane, Hart, 348
Crane, Stephen, 347
Crenshaw, Dave, 389
Crombie, Alexander, 16
Cronin, Helena, 375
Crowley, Sharon, 500
Crystal, David, 497, 501
Cuddon, J. A., 504
Curme, George O., 3, 497

Dalton-Puffer, Christiane, 500
dangler, 65, 85–86, 89–90, 141, 242, 424–25
dangling modifier, 424–25
dashes, 64, 152–53, 318, 353, 358, 361, 369–74, 377, 378, 392, 393, 402. *See also* em-dash; en-dash
date
functioning as descriptive adjective, 10, 63
punctuating, 63, 349, 392
Davies, Hugh Sykes, 345n1
Dawson, Nelson L., 380
DeBoar, John J., 500
de Botton, Alain, 390
decimal point, 388, 389
declarative, 157, 179, 388, 425
declarative sentence, 157, 179, 388, 470
declarative yes–no question, 157, 466
declension, 9, 23, 238, 282, 425
deep structure, 205, 209–10, 474
defective, 122–23, 425
defective verb, 122, 483–84
deferred preposition, 462
deferred subject, 475
definite article, 61–63, 116, 198, 325, 410
definiteness, 425
definite noun, 450
definitive adjective, 403
degree, 425
adjectives, of, 66–68
adverbs, of, 133–34
comparative (*see* comparative)
positive (*see* positive)
superlative (*see* superlative)
degree adverb, 131, 406
deictic pronoun, 49

deixis, 98, 426
delayed subject, 119, 475
demonstrative, 62–63, 426
demonstrative adjective, 59, 403
demonstrative pronoun, 37, 42, 49–50, 198, 464
denominalized verb, 484
denominal verb, 34, 217, 484
denotation, 426
dental preterite, 486
deontic, 426
dependent clause, 90, 133, 136, 159, 165, 194, 358, 415
derivation, 214, 426, 431
derivational affix, 215, 407
derivational suffix, 215, 477
descriptive adjective, 31, 58, 63, 403
descriptive grammar, 196, 436
descriptive possessive, 30–31, 460
descriptivism, 426
determiner, 19, 20, 22, 198–99, 426–27
de Tocqueville, Alexis, 391
Development of Standard English 1300–1800, The (L. Wright, ed.), 501
Devious Derivations (Rawson), 503
Devis, Ellin, 16
diacritical mark, 427
diaeresis, 427
diagramming sentences, 181–94
    appositives, 192
    benefits and uses of, 181–82
    clauses, 187–89
    complements, 185, 186
    conjunctions, 193
    constituent elements and, 162
    criticized, 3, 182
    gerunds, 191–92
    how-to, traditional, 183–94
    infinitives, 189–90
    modifiers, 186
    objects, 184–85
    participles, 190–91
    predicate, 183, 184
    prepositional phrases, 187
    subject, 184
    verbs, 189–92

dialect, 1, 223, 427
    class, 4, 257, 427
    regional, 223, 427
    social, 427
dialectal speech, 380
Dickens, Charles, 370
Dickinson, Patric, 358
diction, 207, 258, 393, 427
dictionaries, 225, 443, 503
Dictionary of Contemporary American Usage, A (Bergen Evans & C. Evans), 498
Dictionary of English Grammar (Aitchison), 18n48
Dictionary of Linguistics (Pei & Gaynor), 18n46
Dictionary of Literary and Thematic Terms, A (Quinn), 505
Dictionary of Literary Terms, A (Barnet, Berman & Burto), 502
Dictionary of Modern English Usage, A (Fowler), 318, 462, 495, 499
Dictionary of True Etymologies (Room), 504
Dictionary of Word Origins (Ayto), 503
Didion, Joan, 205, 492
dieresis, 427
differentiation, 427
digraph, 427
Dilworth, Thomas, 14n8
diminutive, 427
Dionysios Thrax, 13–14
diphthong, 264, 428
direct address, 37–38, 92, 153, 192–93, 428
direct discourse, 98, 428
directive, 158, 428
direct question, 131, 350, 364, 386, 466
direct speech, 98, 349, 428
discourse, 98, 428
    direct, 98, 428
    indirect, 98–99, 428
disjunctive, 428
disjunctive compound subject, 117
disjunctive conjunction, 117, 118, 146, 147, 151, 421
dissimilation, 428
ditransitive verb, 484
Dobie, J. Frank, 382
Donatus, Aelius, 13–14

double adverb, 129
double comparative, 67, 418
double genitive, 32, 460
double modal, 429
double negative, 132, 172–73, 429, 436
double possessive, 32, 47, 460
double subject, 475
double superlative, 67, 478
doublet, 429
Doyle, Sir Arthur Conan, 371
drift, 429
Dryden, John, 280
d-structure, 474
dummy auxiliary verb, 125, 412
dummy *it*, 174
dummy subject, 119
dummy word, 431
Duncan, Daniel, 14n8
Dyche, Thomas, 15
dynamic verb, 72–73, 483, 484
dysphemism, 429

Eagleson, Robert D., 40n2, 502
Early Modern English, 429
echo question, 429
echo utterance, 429
editorial *we*, 46
Ehrenreich, Barbara, 349
Elbow, Peter, 392
elements, grammatical. *See* grammatical
  elements
Elements of English Grammar, The (Ussher),
  16n18
Elements of Style, The (Strunk & E. B.
  White), 31
Elephants of Style, The (Walsh), 499
Eliot, T. S., 365, 371, 495
elision, 10, 429
ellipsis, 167–68, 430
  anaphoric, 167–68
  cataphoric, 167–68
  whiz-deletion, 91, 165–66, 168–69, 179,
    488
ellipsis dots, 396–99
  brackets, displaced by, 391
  defined, 396, 430
  form, 398

omissions, 397–98
  quotations, 397–98, 399
  signals, 396
elliptical clause, 415
Ellis, Havelock, 382
Ellison, Ralph, 347
Eloquent President, The (Ronald White),
  6n26
embedded clause, 415
embedded question, 467
em-dash, 369–72
  afterthoughts, 370
  defined, 369
  hyphen, displaced by, 378
  insertions, 369
  interruption, 152–53, 370–71
  introducing list or specification, 370
  no more than two in a sentence, 371
  other punctuation, with, 372
  setting off, 369–70
emphatic pronoun, 464–65
emphatic verb, 125, 484
empty auxiliary verb, 412
empty *it*, 174
enclitic, 430
Encyclopædia of English Grammar (Hall),
  18n41
Encyclopedia of Word and Phrase Origins, The
  (Hendrickson), 503
en-dash, 373–74, 393
endocentric compound, 419
*English Accidence, Being the Grounds of Our
  Mother Tongue, The* (Anonymous),
  15n13
English for Pleasure (Strong), vii, 491, 502
English Grammar (Curme), 497
English Grammar (Gardiner), 16n31
English Grammar (Murray), 2
English Grammar, for Schools (Lindsay),
  17n41
English Grammar, The (Jonson), 14n4, 14n5,
  14n6, 15n13
*English Grammar Adapted to Different
  Classes of Learners* (Murray), 16n19
*English Grammar in American Schools before
  1850* (Lyman), 500

English Grammar in Familiar Lectures (Kirkham), 6
English Grammar Made Easy to the Teacher and Pupil (Comly), 16n34
English Grammars and English Grammar (R. Allen), 7n27
English Grammar Showing the Nature and Grounds of the English Language, An (Barker), 14n8
English Grammar Simplified (Fernald), 497
English Grammars Written in English (Alston), 500
"English Grammar Writing" (Linn), 5n21
English Grammatical Categories and the Tradition to 1800 (Michael), 500
English in Nineteenth-Century England (Görlach), 500
English Language, The (Burchfield), 501
English Language, The (Crystal), 501
English Language, The (L. Smith), 502
English Language Scholarship (Gneuss), 500
English Syntax (Curme), 497
English Transformational Grammar (Jacobs & Rosenbaum), 498
English Words and Their Background (McKnight), 501
Entick, John, 15
epenthesis, 217, 430
eponym, 20, 430
Epstein, Jacob, 359
Epstein, Joseph, 376
ergative verb, 72, 484
Essay Towards an English Grammar, An (Fell), 16n17
Essay Towards a Practical English Grammar, An (Greenwood), 14n7
essential appositive, 410
essential clause, 416
Essentials of English Grammar (Jespersen), 3n11, 497
Etymological Dictionary of Modern English (Weekley), 504
Etymological Dictionary of the English Language, An (Skeat), 504
etymological sense, 431
etymology, 431

Etymology and Syntax of the English Language, The (Crombie), 16n33
etymon, 431
euphemism, 431
euphony, 25, 151, 285, 329, 431
euphuism, 431
Evans, Bergen, 498
Evans, Bertrand, 3, 491
Evans, Cornelia, 498
Every-Day English (Richard White), 296, 494
Evolution of the English Language, The (McKnight), 502
exclamation, 7, 92, 132, 152, 158, 167
exclamation mark, 152, 157, 367, 368, 384, 387
exclamatory adverb, 132, 152, 406
exclamatory question, 158, 467
exclamatory sentence, 431
existential sentence, 471
exocentric compound, 420
Exodus 1–18 (Introduction) (Propp), 299, 494
expanded tense, 98, 480
expletive, 38, 46, 119, 149, 173–75, 178–79, 431
expletive conjunction, 149
expletive *it*, 38, 46, 173–74, 178–79
expletive pronoun, 38, 46
expletive *there*, 38, 119, 173–75
expressions of multitude, 20–21, 116
expressions of partition, 21–22
extraposition, 431

factitive complement, 419
factitive object, 419
factitive verb, 164, 484
Fadiman, Anne, 398
false attraction, 432
Farb, Peter, 225, 492
Farley, Frank Edgar, 3, 497
Farnsworth, Ward, 504
Farnsworth's Classical English Rhetoric (Farnsworth), 504
Faulkner, William, 382
Fedin, Konstantin, 267, 323, 493, 494
Fell, John, 16

feminine gender, 24, 40, 44, 47, 236, 256, 271, 327, 434
"Fenimore Cooper's Literary Offenses" (Twain), 262, 493
Fenn, Lady Eleanor, 16
Fernald, James C., 497
Fey, Tina, 363
figurative language, 432
figure of speech, 37, 44, 432
filler, 239, 432
final conjunction, 147, 421–22
Finegan, Edward, 497
finite clause, 416
finite verb, 41, 84, 85, 116, 162, 165, 484
First Lessons in English Grammar (Kerl), 2n7
Fisher, Anne, 15
Fitzgerald, F. Scott, 396
flat adverb, 128–29, 406
Fleming, Ian, 351
Flesch, Rudolf, 502
Flexner, Stuart Berg, 501
Florey, Kitty Burns, 381
focusing adverb, 137–38
Foley, Louis, 159, 492
folk etymology, 432
Follett, Wilson, 265, 493, 498
form class, 455
formulaic subjunctive, 476
form word, 489
Forster, E. M., 363
Fowler, F. G., 499
Fowler, H. W., 318, 462, 495, 499
Fowler's Modern English Usage, 225
fragment, 432–33
fragmentary sentence, 432–33
Francis, W. Nelson, 14, 491
Frazee, Bradford, 17n41
free morpheme, 214, 447
Friedrichsen, G. W. S., 503
Fries, Charles Carpenter, 3–4, 5
fronting, 442
Frye, Northrup, 504
full sentence, 471
full verb, 124–25, 485
function
    accusative, 30
    defined, 29, 433
    nominative, 29–30
    objective, 30
    subjective, 29–30
functional morpheme, 489
functional shift (variation), 70, 423, 433. *See also* conversion
function word, 489
fused participle, 88–89, 433
future-perfect progressive, 98
future-perfect tense, 86, 94, 97, 480
future tense, 94, 96, 480

Galanes, Philip, 380
Gandhi, Mohandas K., 366–67
Gardiner, Jane, 16
Gardner, Erle Stanley, 348
Gardner, John, 394
Garner on Language and Writing, 170n1, 501
Garner's Dictionary of Legal Usage, 312n3, 499
Garner's Law of Loanwords, 433
Garner's Modern English Usage, 42, 225, 318n4, 499, 505
Gaynor, Frank, 18n46
gender
    common, 40, 433–34
    defined, 24, 433–34
    determining, 44
    expressing, 44
    feminine, 24, 40, 44, 47, 236, 256, 271, 327, 434
    indefinite, 57, 434
    masculine, 24, 44, 46, 47, 324, 434
    neuter, 434
    noun, 24
    pronoun, 38, 40–41, 42, 44, 46, 47, 52, 57
    suffixes, 24, 326, 327–28
gender neutrality, 44, 47, 278, 324–28
generalization, 434
generative grammar, 195
generative grammarians, 4
generative-transformational grammar, 195
generative-transformational theory, 195
generic, 19, 47, 57, 278, 324, 434
genitive
    apostrophe, 23, 31–32, 50
    case, 23, 30–32

contrasted with possessive, 30–31
defined, 30–31, 434
descriptive-possessive function, 30–31, 460
double, 32, 460
functions, 30–31
group, 434
group and joint possessive, 32, 460
independent, 460
inflected, 23, 31–32, 50
measure, of, 434
names, 32
of-form, 31–32, 435
origin, of, 434
partitive, 21–22, 435
periphrastic, 435
phrasal, 435
plural, 31
postgenitive, 460
prepositional phrase, replacing, 145
pronouns, 43, 44, 50, 54–55
See also possessive
Genung, George Frederick, 137, 492
Gershwin, Ira, 350
gerund, 87–90
dangling, 89–90
defined, 87, 191–92, 435
diagramming, 191–92
functions, 35, 87–88
fused participle, 88–89, 433
infinitive substitute, 87
modifiers, 88
object of, 452
participle, distinguished from, 88
perfect, 435
present, 435
present-perfect, 435
gerund clause, 191–92
gerund phrase, 88, 191–92, 457
get-passive, 275, 435
Gift of Tongues, The (Schlauch), 257, 493
Gill, Brendan, 397
Ginsburg, Ruth Bader, 367
glossary, 8, 10, 401–89
Glossary for English Transformational Grammar, A (Palmatier), 498

"Glossary of Grammatical, Rhetorical, and Other Language-Related Terms" (Garner), 505
Glossary of Literary Terms, A (Abrams), 504
Gneuss, Helmut, 500
Goldberg, Natalie, 376
Good, C. Edward, 497
Good Advice on Writing (Safire & Safir, eds.), 371, 495
Good English (Vallins), 351, 494
Good English and the Grammarian (Greenbaum), 242, 293, 493, 494
good grammar, 4, 436
Google ngrams, 8–10, 225–27
Gordon, Karen Elizabeth, 375, 495, 504
Gorky, Maxim, 493, 494
Görlach, Manfred, 500
Gorrell, Robert M., 18n43
Gowers, Ernest, 499, 502
Gowers, Rebecca, 502
gradable, 66, 435
gradable adjective, 66–68, 403
gradable antonyms, 409
Graded Lessons in English (Kellogg & Reed), 181
grammar
acceptability, 401
bad, 14, 258, 435–36
campaign against traditional, 3–5
defined, 1–2, 7, 435
descriptive, 196, 436
good, 4, 436
historical, 436
importance of, vii, 5–7
linguists' views of, 4–5
popularity and decline, 2–5
prescriptive, 436
preventive, 40, 52, 121, 227
transformational, 4, 195–211
usage, contrasted with, 223
Grammar (Hurford), 7n28, 497
"Grammar and Writing" (Evans), 3, 491
Grammar Book for You and I (Oops, Me!), A (Good), 497
Grammar of English Grammars (G. Brown), 2, 497

Grammar of the English Language, A
  (Cobbett), 43, 491
Grammar of the English Language, A (Hart),
  2n4
Grammar of the English Language, The
  (Curme), 3n13
Grammar of the English Tongue, A (Coar),
  16n28
Grammar Without Tears (Davies), 345n1
grammatical, 436
grammatical category, 455
grammatical elements
  adverbial element, 164
  constituent (*see* constituent)
  identifying, 162–64
  independent element, 439
  nonrestrictive element, 348, 351
  noun element, 451
  parenthetical element, 454 (*see also*
    interrupter)
  placement within sentences, 160–61
  quantifying elements, 20–21
grammatical function, 436
*Grammatical Institute of the English
  Language, A* (Webster), 17n36, 23, 491
Grammatical Institutes (Ash), 15n14
*Grammatical Introduction to the English
  Tongue, A* (Entick), 15n9
grammatical morpheme, 447
*Grammatical System of the English Language,
  A* (Caleb Alexander), 16n27
Grass, Günter, 377
Graves, Robert, 370
Gray, Ernest W., 18n42
Greenbaum, Sidney, 18n48, 18n49, 242,
  293, 493, 494, 497, 502
Greene, Graham, 349
Greene, Samuel Stillman, 18n41
Greenwood, James, 14
Gregg Reference Manual, The (Sabin), 502
Grisham, John, 377
group genitive, 434
group possessive, 32, 460
group preposition, 462
group verbal, 88, 487
Growth and Structure of the English Language
  (Jespersen), 314, 494, 501

Gunning, Robert, 502
Gurney, David, 16
"Guy de Maupassant" (Babel), 388, 495

Hairston, Maxine, 327, 494
Haley, J. Evetts, 349
half conjunction, 406
Hall, Donald, 71, 491
Hall, William, 18n41
Hammett, Dashiell, 349
Handbook of English Grammar, A
  (Zandvoort), 498
Handbook of English Linguistics, The (Aarts
  & McMahon, eds.), 5n21
Handlist of Rhetorical Terms, A (Lanham),
  505
Hanff, Helene, 363
Hannon, William Morgan, 350
Hansberry, Lorraine, 387
hapax legomenon, 436
haplology, 436
Hardy, Thomas, 357
Harper Handbook to Literature, The (Frye et
  al.), 504
Harper's English Grammar (Opdycke), 497
Harris, James, 15
Harris, Roy, 463, 495
Harrison, Ralph, 16
Harrold, E., 16
Hart, John Seely, 2
Harvey, Paul, 2n2
Harvey, Thomas N., 2
Hassall, Sue, 502
Hawthorne, Nathaniel, 386
Hayakawa, S. I., 307, 494
Hayes, Curtis W., 18n46
Haynes, David, 376
head, 26–27
Heath, Chip, 366
Heath, Dan, 366
Heilman, Robert B., 398
helper, 411–12
helping verb, 121, 411–12
Hemingway, Ernest, 349
Hendrickson, Robert, 503
Henry, William A., III, 383
Herbert, A. P., 285, 493

Hermes, or A Philosophical Inquiry Concerning Universal Grammar (J. Harris), 15n12
heteronym, 437
Higgins, V. Louise, vii, 491
Higher Lessons in English (Kellogg & Reed), 181
historical grammar, 436
historical-present tense, 95, 481
History of the English Language, A (Baugh & Cable), 501
History of the English Language (Lounsbury), 239, 493
Hitchens, Christopher, 364, 383
Hoad, T. F., 503
Hobbes, Thomas, 279, 363
Hobson, Thomas, 279
Hodges, C. Walter, 386
homograph, 437
homonym, 437
homophone, 437
"How to Read a Dictionary" (Adler), 317, 494
Huddleston, Rodney D., 8n29, 18n47, 245n2, 497
Hunter, Susan, 500
Hurford, James R., 7n28, 497
Hutchins, John, 16
Huxley, Aldous, 350, 365
hybrid, 437
hypallage, 438
hypercorrection, 238, 244, 438
hypernym, 478
hyphaeresis, 217, 438
hyphen, 375–79
    accentuation, 377
    adjective phrase, 379
    compound nouns, 26, 376
    defined, 375
    em-dash, displacing, 378
    en-dash, displacing, 373
    fractions, 376
    names, in, 377
    noun phrases, 376
    numbers, 377
    phonetic uses, 377
    phrasal adjectives, 60, 69–70, 375

phrasal verb, 82, 379
    prefix, with, 378
    proper names, 377
    separation, 377
    slash, displaced by, 393
    suffix, with, 377–78
    suspensive, 69, 376
hyponym, 438
hypotaxis, 438

Ibsen, Henrik, 363
idiolect, 438
idioms, prepositional, 329–44
illative conjunction, 406
illative coordinating conjunction, 147, 421–22
illeism, 438
illiteracy, 438
immediate constituent, 161–62, 422–23
imperative, 439
    mood, 92, 158, 177, 325, 446
    vocative, 439
imperative sentence, 158, 172, 471
imperfect aspect, 94–95, 411
impersonal pronoun, 464
impersonal sentence, 471
Improved Grammar of the English Language, An (Frazee), 17n41
Improved Grammar of the English Language, An (Webster), 17n37
inanimate noun, 450
inclusive *we*, 439
incomplete sentence, 471
indefinite adjective, 22, 60, 403
indefinite article, 20–21, 22, 61–62, 198, 228, 325, 410
indefinite gender, 57, 434
indefinite noun, 450
indefinite pronoun, 42, 46–47, 48–49, 56–57, 118, 197, 327, 464
independent adverb, 406
independent clause, 52, 89–90, 133, 136, 159, 165, 183, 416
independent element, 439
independent genitive, 460
independent possessive, 47, 460

indicative, 439
  mood, 92–93, 94, 447
indicator, 444–45
indirect discourse, 98–99, 428
indirect object, 161, 163, 185, 452
indirect question, 131, 148, 149, 386, 467
indirect speech, 98–99, 349, 428
infinitive, 84–86
  adverbial with, 85, 135
  bare, 189–90, 440
  complementary, 85, 440
  dangling, 85–86
  defined, 84–85, 440
  diagramming, 189–90
  gerund, substitute for, 87
  marked, 440
  object of, 452
  perfect, 440
  plain, 440
  present, 440
  pure, 440
  simple, 440
  split, 85, 135–36, 203, 440
  subject of, 476
  unmarked, 440
  uses of, 85
infinitive phrase, 85–86, 189–90, 458
infix, 214–15, 217, 441
inflect, 441
inflected genitive, 23, 31–32, 50
inflected possessive, 31, 460
inflection, 213, 441
  case, 23
  genitive, 23, 31–32, 50
  irregular verbs, 73–81, 441
  regular verbs, 73, 441
  syntax, contrasted with, 157, 160
  verb properties, reflecting, 90 (see also conjugation)
inflectional affix, 215, 407
inflectional morphology, 213, 401
inflectional suffix, 215, 477
inflexion. See inflection
initialism, 218–19, 228, 441
inner complement, 164, 418
"In Praise of the Humble Comma" (Iyer), 345, 494

intensifier, 127, 441
intensifying adverb, 127, 441
intensifying pronoun, 464–65
interjection, 152–53, 158, 192, 387, 442
interrogative, 442
interrogative adjective, 59, 403
interrogative adverb, 131–32, 149, 406
interrogative marker, 444
interrogative pronoun, 38, 42, 51, 52–53, 189, 465
interrogative sentence, 55, 83–84, 157–58, 172, 206, 386, 471
interrupter, 152–53, 442
intonation, 138, 442
intonation pattern, 442
intransitive verb, 71–72, 81–82, 135, 202, 485
Introduction to Transformational Grammars, An (Bach), 498
introductory adverb, 406
introductory *it*, 174
introductory phrase, comma with, 347
Introductory Readings on Language (Anderson & Stageberg, eds.), 281, 493
Introductory Transformational Grammar, An (Liles), 498
intrusive *r*, 442
intrusive schwa, 442
invariable noun, 450
inversion, 29–30, 119, 157–58, 161, 442
Invisible Giants (Carnes, ed.), 2n2
Ironside, Elizabeth, 396
irregular, 442
irregular adjective, 67
irregular adverb, 134
irregular inflection, 441
irregular plural, 27–28, 458
irregular verb, 73–81, 86–87, 96, 485
irreversible binomial, 445
Iyer, Pico, 345, 494

Jacobs, Roderick A., 498
Jacobsen, Sally, 502
Jacoby, Susan, 383
Jain, Sanjay, 376
Jennings, Charles B., 494
Jespersen, Otto, 3, 314, 494, 497, 501

Johansson, Stig, 497
John of Salisbury, vii, 491
Johnson, Samuel, 363
joint possessive, 32, 460
Jones, Gloria, 502
Jones, Rowland, 16
Jonson, Ben, 14, 15
Jowett, W. P., 97, 135, 492
Joyce, James, 361

Kael, Pauline, 383
Kahneman, Daniel, 373
Kamm, Oliver, 8n29, 42n3
Kammen, Michael, 383
Kapp, Reginald O., 354, 494
Kastovsky, Dieter, 500
Kaulfers, Walter V., 500
Kearn, Graham C., 350
Kellogg, Brainerd, 181, 182, 207, 454, 468
Kennedy, David M., 349
Ker, W. P., 368
Kerl, Simon, 2
Kesey, Ken, 377
King, Lester S., 144, 492
King, Martin Luther, Jr., 350
King's English, The (H. Fowler & F. Fowler), 499
Kirk, Russell, 382
Kirkham, Samuel, 6
Kittredge, George Lyman, 3, 497
Klein, Daniel, 389
Kline, Michael J., 349
Klopfer, Peter H., 350
Knight, Dame Laura, 358
Kolln, Martha, 18n50
Krapp, George Philip, 501
Kroeger, Paul, 18n46
Krutch, Joseph Wood, 375

Labyrinth of Language, The (Black), 226, 493
Laird, Charlton, 18n43, 495
Lamberts, J. J., 499
Landon, Brooks, 358
language, 443
Language (Trask), 96n4, 284, 493
Language Machine, The (R. Harris), 462, 495
Language of 1984, The (Bolton), 82, 491

Lanham, Richard A., 505
Lapsing into a Comma (Walsh), 499
Lauchman, Richard, 502
learned loanword, 444
Lectures on Language (Balch), 17n39
Leech, Geoffrey, 497
Legacy of Language, The (Boardman, ed.), 495
Legal Writing in Plain English (Garner), 312n3
Lehrer, Jonah, 389
Lemann, Thomas B., 373
Levine, Bruce, 364
Lewis, Anthony, 364
Lewis, C. S., 376
Lewis, Sinclair, 382
lexeme, 443
lexical, 445
lexical category, 455
lexical morpheme, 447, 489
lexical verb, 485, 486
lexicology, 443
lexicon, 443
lexis, 443
Life and Growth of Language, The (Whitney), 256, 493
ligature, 443
Liles, Bruce L., 498
limiting adjective, 47, 58, 61–63, 403
limiting clause, 416
Lincoln, Abraham, 6
"Lindley Murray" (Garner), 2n2
Lindsay, John, 17n41
linguistics, 443
Linguistics Reader, A (G. Wilson, ed.), 491, 493
Linguistics Student's Handbook, The (Bauer), 18n52
linguists
    structural, 4
    views on grammar, 4–5
linking verb, 81–82, 485
    adjective with, 64–65
    adverb with, 135
    adverbial with, 81–82
    be-verb (see be-verb)
    passive voice and, 81

linking verb (*cont.*)
    pronoun case, 45
Linn, Andrew, 5n21
list
    bullets, 177–78, 394–95
    parallelism, 177–78
    punctuating, 350, 358, 361–62, 364,
       367–68, 370, 394–95
Lively Art of Writing, The (Payne), 90, 492
Living Language, The (Morris, ed.), 492
Livingstone, Sir Richard, 357
Lloyd, Charles Allen, 150
loan translation, 218, 444
loanword, 444
    Garner's Law of, 433
    learned, 444
Loberger, Gordon J., 18n45
local possessive, 460
locative adverb, 130–31
London Review of Books (C. Ricks), 5n19
Long, Ralph Bernard, 18n44
long dash. *See* em-dash
Longman Grammar of Spoken and Written
    English (Biber), 245n1, 497
long passive voice, 91, 145, 455
long syllable, 478
loose appositive, 410
Lounsbury, Thomas R., 239, 493
Lowth, Robert, 16
Lucas, F. L., 380
Lyman, Rollo LaVerne, 500

Macaulay, Thomas Babington, 351
Macdonald, Dwight, 373
Mack, Maynard, 397
Mackintosh, Duncan, 16
MacLeish, Archibald, 350, 390
macron, 444
Mailer, Norman, 376
main clause, 132, 166–68, 416
main verb, 97–98, 135, 181, 184, 189, 190,
    485, 486
major sentence, 470
majuscule, 444
Making of English, The (Bradley), 283, 313,
    493, 494
Making Sense of Grammar (Crystal), 497

malapropism, 444
Malmstrom, Jean, 498
mandative subjunctive, 476
manner adverb, 130, 131, 204, 406
Marciano, John Bemelmans, 380
Marckwardt, Albert H., 501
marked infinitive, 440
marker, 444–45
    plural, 444
    portion, 444
    singular, 445
Martin, Judith, 395
masculine gender, 24, 44, 46, 47, 324, 434
mass noun, 19, 20–21, 22–23, 28, 29, 116,
    118, 450
Matchett, Alex, 384
material noun, 450
matrix clause, 416
Maugham, W. Somerset, 347
Maxwell, William H., 2
Mayhew, Robert, vii, 491
McAleer, Andrew, 366
McArthur, Tom, 501
McCullough, Donald, 380
McDavid, Raven I., Jr., 502
McGarry, D. D., 491
McGeachy, J. B., 389
McKnight, George H., 501, 502
McMahon, April, 5n21
McMurtry, Larry, 370
meaning, changes in
    clang association, 414
    conversion, 33–35, 70, 82, 216, 423
    differentiation, 427
    drift, 429
    etymological sense, 431
    generalization, 434
    melioration, 445
    pejoration, 455–56
    semantic contamination, 469
Medieval Grammar and Rhetoric (Copeland
    & Sluiter, eds.), 13n2, 14n3, 491, 500
Meditations (Aurelius), 258, 493
melioration, 445
Mencken, H. L., 357, 502
Mentor Guide to Punctuation, The (Paxson),
    504

Merriam-Webster New Book of Word Histories, The, 503

Merriam-Webster's Collegiate Dictionary, 225, 503

Merriam-Webster's Concise Dictionary of English Usage, 499

Metalogicon of John of Salisbury, The (McGarry, trans.), 491

metaphor, 445

metathesis, 445

metonymy, 445

Michael, Ian, 17n40, 500, 501

Michener, James, 362

Middle English, 160, 172–73, 445

middle verb, 202–3, 485

Miller, Alex, 493, 494

Miller, B. D. H., 495

Miller, Helen Rand, 500

Miller, Henry, 369

Mind the Stop (Carey), 504

minor sentence, 471

Minthorn, David, 502

misplaced modifier, 89, 168, 446

Mitchell, Margaret, 348

Mitchell, Richard, 397

Mitford, Jessica, 389

Mitford, Nancy, 390

modal, 121, 412

modal adverb, 127

modal auxiliary verb, 121–24
  defined, 121, 412
  double, 429
  periphrastic, 456

modal idiom, 445

modality, 446

modal tense, 481

mode, 92, 446

Modern American Usage (Follett), 265, 493, 498

Modern English, 38, 40, 143, 445

Modern English (Krapp), 501

Modern English and Its Heritage (Bryant), 501

Modern English Handbook (Gorrell & Laird), 18n43

Modern English in the Making (McKnight), 502

Modern English Syntax (Onions), 471, 495

Modern Linguistics (Simeon Potter), 215, 492

modificand, 445

modification structure, 474

modifier
  compound, 62–63, 69, 402, 404
  dangling, 424–25
  defined, 186, 446
  diagramming, 186
  gerund, 88
  misplaced, 89, 168, 446
  participle, 88–89
  postpositive, 404
  resumptive, 446
  sentence, 197, 406
  squinting, 446
  summative, 446
  transformational grammar, 199

Monaghan, Charles, 2n3

monophthong, 446

monotransitive verb, 485

mood, 92–94
  defined, 92, 446
  expressing a state contrary to fact, 92–93, 94
  expressing facts, 92
  imperative, 92, 158, 177, 325, 446 (*see also* imperative)
  indicative, 92–93, 94, 447 (*see also* indicative)
  past-perfect subjunctive, 94
  past-tense subjunctive, 93–94, 477
  present-tense subjunctive, 93, 477
  referring to past, 94
  referring to present or future, 93
  subjunctive, 92–94, 97, 447 (*see also* subjunctive)

morpheme, 213–15, 447
  bound, 214, 447
  free, 214, 447
  functional, 489
  grammatical, 447
  lexical, 447, 489

morphology, 213–19, 447
  inflectional, 213, 401

Morris, Linda A., 492

Mother's Grammar, The (Fenn), 16n25

Muir, Frank, 348
Mulroy, David, 5, 13n1, 408, 495, 501
multitude, expressions of, 20–21, 116
multiword verb, 486
Murray, Lindley, 2, 3, 16
Murrays of Murray Hill, The (Monaghan), 2n3
mutation plural, 459

Nabokov, Vladimir, 357
Nafisi, Azar, 388
Nash, Walter, 426, 495
negation, 169–73
  affixes, 169, 172
  conjunctions, 169, 171
  contractions, 170
  defined, 169, 447
  double negative, 132, 172–73, 429
  negating adverb, 169, 171, 172
  negating pronoun, 171
  neither, 172
  no, 172
  nor, 172
  not, 83, 169–71
  prefixes, 172
  statement, 172
  suffixes, 172
  types of, 169
  verb phrases, 83–84
  without plainly negative elements, 173
negative, 447
negative, double, 132, 172–73, 429, 436
negative adverb, 83, 132
negative cleft sentence, 179, 471
negative particle, 162, 169, 172, 173
negative question, 172, 467
neoclassical compound, 420
neologisms, 220, 447
neologizing, 447
neuter gender, 434
New English Grammar, A (Duncan), 14n8
New English Grammar, A (Sweet), 3n9
New Fowler's Modern English Usage, The (Burchfield), 18n49, 498
New General English Dictionary, A, 15n10
New Guide to the English Tongue in Five Parts, A (Dilworth), 14n8

New Oxford American Dictionary, The, 503
New Princeton Encyclopedia of Poetry and Poetics, The (Preminger & Brogan, eds.), 505
New Shorter Oxford English Dictionary, The, 503
New Well-Tempered Sentence, The (Gordon), 375, 495, 504
ngrams, 8–10, 225–27
Nicolson, Harold, 388
Nizer, Louis, 368
nominal, 448, 451
  predicate, 461
nominal clause, 416
nominal element, 451
nominalization, 144, 448, 451
nominal phrase, 458
nominative, 25, 29–30, 448
nominative absolute, 401
nominative case, 29–30, 41–42, 43, 44–45, 413
nominative function, 29–30
nominative of address, 488
nonaction verb, 487
noncomparable adjective, 67–68
noncomparable adverb, 134
noncompositional compound word, 215–16
noncount noun, 22, 450
nonessential appositive, 410
nonessential clause, 416
nonfinite verb, 86, 440, 485
nonlimiting clause, 416
nonreferential *it*, 174, 431
nonreferential *there*, 431
nonrestrictive, 448
nonrestrictive appositive, 33, 410
nonrestrictive clause, 187, 416
nonsentence, 448, 472
nonstandard, 67
Norris, Frank, 348
Norris, Mary, 499
"Notebook" (Fedin), 267, 323, 493, 494
notional accord, 116
notional concord, 21, 116, 479
notional passive, 449
notional verb, 486

noun, 19–35
    abstract, 19, 23, 449
    adjective functioning as, 70
    adverbial, 407
    agent, 32–33, 449
    agreement with adjective, 59, 407
    animate, 449
    appositive, 33
    attribute, 450, 461
    attributive, 33–34, 449
    be-verb as part of, 112
    bounded, 449
    case, 23, 29–32
    collective, 19, 20–21, 22, 39, 116, 449
    common, 19, 20, 24, 449
    compound, 20, 26–27, 31, 69, 199, 376,
        449
    concrete, 19, 22–23, 449
    contractions with, 84
    coordinate, 62
    count, 19, 20, 22–23, 28, 57, 449–50
    declension, 9, 23, 238, 282, 425
    defined, 19, 449
    definite, 450
    exclamatory, 152
    functioning as adjective, 33–34
    functioning as adverb, 34
    functioning as verb, 34
    gender, 24
    inanimate, 450
    indefinite, 450
    invariable, 450
    mass, 19, 20–21, 22–23, 28, 29, 116, 118,
        450
    material, 450
    multitude, 20–21
    nominalization, 144, 448, 451
    noncount, 22, 450
    nonnaturalized, 28
    noun element, 451
    noun-equivalent, 19
    number, 23–24
    of-phrase, in, 21–22
    participle functioning as (*see* gerund)
    partition, of, 450
    partitive, 21–22, 450
    person, 24–25

    plural (*see* plurals)
    possessive, 30–32
    predicate, 120, 450, 461
    proper, 19–20, 25, 29, 31, 197, 450
    properties, 23–25
    recipient, 32–33, 450
    simple, 450
    uncountable, 450
    verbal, 85, 435
    verb functioning as, 85
    zombie, 144, 448, 451
noun adjunct, 449
noun-banging, 451
noun clause, 188–89, 416
noun cluster, 451
noun element, 451
noun-equivalent, 19
noun group, 451
noun indicator, 426–27
noun phrase, 64, 162, 184, 196, 197–200,
        204, 205, 376, 378, 458
number, 23–24, 38–39, 115–21, 198, 451
    cardinal, 58–59, 198, 451
    noun, 23–24
    ordinal, 58–59, 131, 198, 451
    plural (*see* plurals)
    pronoun, 38, 39, 42, 44, 52
    singular, 451
    verb (*see* verb number)
numeral, 451
numeral adjective, 403
numeric adjective, 58–59, 403
numeric adverb, 131
numerical adjective, 403

object
    cognate, 71, 452
    complementary, 419
    compound, 41, 452
    coordinate, 452
    defined, 163, 452
    diagramming, 184–85
    direct, 163, 184–85, 452
    factitive, 419
    gerund, of, 452
    identifying in predicate, 163
    indirect, 161, 163, 185, 452

object (*cont.*)
  infinitive, of, 452
  oblique, 139, 452
  passive voice, role in, 184, 203
  placement in sentence, 160–61
  preposition, of, 30, 43, 44–45, 90, 139, 187, 204, 211, 452
object accusative, 452
object complement, 419
objective attribute, 419
objective case, 41–42, 43, 143, 413
objective complement, 85, 88, 163–64, 185, 419
objective function, 30
objective predicate, 419
objective pronoun, 43, 44–45
oblique case, 413
oblique object, 139, 452
O'Brian, Patrick, 349
Ocampo, Victoria, 350
O'Conner, Patricia T., 36, 491, 499
of-genitive, 31–32, 435
of-phrase, 21–22, 31, 116
O'Hara, John, 377
Old English, 75, 160, 453
Olson, Mancur, 392
O'Neill, Eugene, 348, 377
Onions, C. T., 471, 495, 503
onomatopoeia, 453
On the Art and Craft of Writing (Gorky et al.), 493, 494
Opdycke, John B., 497
open syllable, 478
open word class, 489
Orage, A. R., 348
oratio directa, 428
oratio obliqua, 428
oratio recta, 428
ordinal number, 58–59, 131, 198, 451
Origins (Partridge), 503
Origins and Development of the English Language, The (Pyles & Algeo), 502
orthoepy, 453
orthography, 453
orthology, 453
Orwell, George, 347, 398
Our Language (Simeon Potter), 5, 491, 502

outer complement, 164, 419
overgeneralization, 453
Oxford American Dictionary and Thesaurus, The, 503
Oxford Companion to English Literature, The (P. Harvey), 2n2
Oxford Companion to the English Language, The (McArthur, ed.), 501
Oxford Dictionary of English Etymology, The (Onions, Friedrichsen & Burchfield, eds.), 503
Oxford Dictionary of English Grammar, The (Chalker & Weiner), 497
Oxford English Dictionary, The, 1, 5, 503
Oxford English Grammar, The (Greenbaum), 18n49, 497
Oxford Modern English Grammar (Aarts), 327n5, 497
Oxford University Press, 225
oxymoron, 453

Palmatier, Robert A., 498
paradigm, 454
parallelism, 175–78
  adverb pairs, 176
  auxiliary verbs, 177
  conjunctions, 146–47, 176
  defined, 175, 454
  directives, 177
  ellipsis, 167–68
  listed items, 177–78
  prepositional phrases, 176
parallel structure, 454
parataxis, 411
parentheses, 365–68
  brackets within, 390
  citation, 367
  clarifying, 366–67
  defined, 365
  enclosing aside, 368
  interjection, 152–53
  introducing, 366–67
  lists, 367–68
  minimizing effect, 365
  other punctuation, with, 367–68, 389, 390
  setting off element, 365
  traditional diagramming, use in, 192

transformational grammar, use in, 196, 200, 204
parenthetical element, 454. *See also* interrupter
Parkinson, C. Northcote, 366
parse, 454
partial conversion, 216
participial adjective, 65, 67, 68, 87, 295, 379, 403
participial phrase, 65, 87–90, 170, 190–91, 458
participial verb, 486
participle, 86–90
  adjective, distinguished from, 65
  alternative forms, 74
  considered part of speech, 13, 15n10, 16, 17
  dangling, 65, 89–90
  defined, 86, 190–91, 454
  diagramming, 190–91
  forming, 86–87, 95–96, 215
  functioning as adjective, 65, 67, 68, 87, 88–89, 295, 379, 403
  functioning as conjunction, 149
  functioning as noun (*see* gerund)
  functioning as preposition, 141, 149
  fused, 88–89, 433
  gerund (*see* gerund)
  gerund, distinguished from, 88
  modifiers, 88–89
  not with, 170
  passive voice, in, 90–92, 207
  past (*see* past participle)
  perfect, 86, 97, 454
  perfect aspect, forming, 97
  perfect-progressive, 86
  present (*see* present participle)
  present-perfect, 454
  progressive aspect, forming, 97–98
  suffixes, 215
particle, 15n9, 15n11, 82–83, 127, 128, 184, 455
  negative, 162, 169, 172, 173
particle adverb, 128
partition, expressions of, 21–22
partitive genitive, 21–22, 435
partitive noun, 21–22, 450

Partridge, Eric, 499, 503, 504
parts of speech, 13–153
  approaches to classifying, 13–18
  See also conversion; function
Parts of Speech and Accidence (Curme), 497
passive clause, 416
passive voice, 90–92, 455
  agentless passive, 455
  be-verbs and, 90–91, 98, 207, 211
  dangler, producing, 89
  get-passive, 275, 435
  infinitive, followed by, 85
  linking verbs and, 81
  long, 91, 145, 455
  notional passive, 449
  participles, forming with, 90–92, 112, 207
  progressive aspect, 98
  short, 91, 455
  subject and object, roles of, 184, 203
  transformational grammar, 207, 210–11
  transforming to/from active voice, 207
  transitive vs. intransitive verbs, 202
  truncated passive, 455
past participle
  alternative forms, 74
  defined, 86, 454
  diagramming, 190–91
  forming, 87, 95–96, 215
  functioning as adjective, 68
  ngrams and, 227
  passive voice, forming, 90–91, 92, 112
  perfect aspect, forming, 97
  progressive aspect, forming, 98
  suffix, 215
past-perfect tense, 94, 97, 98, 481
past subjunctive, 93–94, 477
past tense, 73–74, 86, 93–96, 190, 481
patient, 452
Paxson, William C., 504
Payne, Lucille Vaughan, 90, 492
"Pedant, The" (Kamm), 8n29
Pei, Mario, 18n46
pejoration, 455–56
Penguin Dictionary of Literary Terms and Literary Theory, The (Cuddon), 504
perfect aspect, 94–95, 411. *See also* perfect tense

perfect gerund, 435
perfect infinitive, 440
perfect participle, 86, 97, 454
perfect tense, 94–95, 97, 190, 480, 481
period, 384, 388–89, 396, 397
period fault, 433
peripheral adjective, 403
periphrasis, 456
periphrastic comparative, 66, 133, 418
periphrastic genitive, 435
periphrastic modal, 456
periphrastic possessive, 435
periphrastic superlative, 66, 134, 478
Perkins, Barbara M., 504
Perkins, George, 504
person
    agreement, pronoun–antecedent, 39–40, 52, 408
    agreement, subject–verb, 95, 116, 121, 408
    defined, 24–25, 456
    indirect discourse, shifts in, 98
    nouns, 25–25
    pronouns, 38, 42–43
    shall and *will*, with, 96–97
    transformational grammar, 200
    verbs, 90, 95–96, 98, 115–16, 121, 456
personal adjective, 404
personal pronoun, 38, 41, 42–49, 52, 121, 197, 325–26, 465
personification, 44
Perspectives on Style (Candelaria, ed.), 492
Peters, Pam, 499
Petroski, Henry, 381
phatic exchange, 456
Philosophy of Grammar, The (Jespersen), 3n11
Philosophy of Rhetoric, The (Richards), 1, 491
phoneme, 456
phrasal adjective, 60, 64, 69–70, 375–76, 385, 404, 457
phrasal adverb, 130, 457
phrasal conjunction, 146, 422
phrasal genitive, 435
phrasal preposition, 140–41, 462
phrasal prepositional verb, 486
phrasal pronoun, 36, 50, 465

phrasal verb, 82–84, 128, 142, 184, 379, 486
phrase
    adjective, 64, 171, 379, 457
    adverbial, 68, 131, 136, 141, 457
    appositional, 409–10
    appositive, 192, 457
    conjunctive, 148
    defined, 457
    gerund, 88, 191–92, 457
    infinitive, 85–86, 189–90, 458
    nominal, 458
    noun, 64, 162, 184, 196, 197–200, 204, 205, 376, 378, 458
    of-phrase, 21–22, 31, 116
    participial, 65, 87–90, 170, 190–91, 458
    prepositional (*see* prepositional phrase)
    set, 458
    simple, 457
    substantive, 458
    verb, 83–84, 86, 132, 135–36, 174, 196–97, 200–202, 458
phrase marker, 482
phrase-structure tree, 482
pied-piping, 142, 462
Pilgrim's Progress (Bunyan), 313
Pink, M. Alderton, 302, 494
Pinneo, Timothy Stone, 18n41
Pinneo's Analytical Grammar of the English Language (Pinneo), 18n41
Place of Grammar in Writing Instruction, The (Hunter & R. Wallace, eds.), 500
plain infinitive, 440
Plain Language (Steinberg, ed.), 502
Plain, Rational Essay on English Grammar, A (Mackintosh), 16n29
Plain Style (Lauchman), 502
Plain Writing Act of 2010, 362
Plotkin, Fred, 366
pluperfect tense, 97, 481
plural indicator, 444
plural marker, 444
plurals, 25–29
    apostrophes and, 25, 381
    borrowed, 27–28
    compound subject, in, 118
    defined, 451
    expressions of multitude, 20–21

expressions of partition, 21–22
foreign (*see* plurals: borrowed)
forming, 25–29
genitive, 31
irregular, 27–28, 458
loanwords (*see* plurals: borrowed)
mutation, 459
possessive, 31, 32
pronoun, 43, 46
proper noun, 25, 29
regular, 25–26, 459
singular sense, 28–29, 118
suffix, 215
umlaut, 459
uninflected, 459
weak, 459
zero, 459
Pocket Guide to Correct Punctuation, A
    (Brittain), 504
Poe, Edgar Allan, 364
"Poetry and Grammar" (Stein), 181, 492
point of view, 91, 459
polar question, 467
polysemous, 459
polysyndetic coordination, 424
polysyndeton, 459
Pooley, Robert C., 3n15, 501
portion indicator, 444
portion marker, 444
portmanteau word, 219, 489
positive, 459
positive adjective, 66, 404
positive adverb, 133
positive question, 172, 467
possessive
    adjective position, 64
    apostrophe, 23, 31–32, 47–48, 50, 380
    case, 30–32, 41, 380, 413–14
    contractions, compared with, 48, 84
    dangling participle with, 65
    defined, 30–31, 460
    descriptive, 30–31, 460
    double, 32, 47, 460
    functioning as adjective, 37
    fused participles and, 89
    genitive, contrasted with, 30–31
    group, 32, 460

indefinite pronouns, 57
independent, 47, 460
inflected, 31, 215, 460
joint, 32, 460
local, 460
noun, 30–32
periphrastic, 435
plural, 31, 32
reflexive pronouns, 48
relative pronouns, 55
singular, 31
suffix, 215
transformational grammar, 200
    See also genitive
possessive adjective, 59, 404
possessive pronoun, 38, 47–48, 59, 63, 64,
    143, 465
postgenitive, 460
postpositive, 460
postpositive adjective, 64, 199, 404
postpositive modifier, 404
potential tense, 481
Potter, Simeon, 5, 215, 491, 492, 502
Potter, Stephen, 397
Practical English Usage (Swan), 499
Practical Grammar of the English Language, A
    (Butler), 17n41
Practical Grammar of the English Language, A
    (T. Harvey), 2n6
Practical New Grammar, A (Fisher), 15n11
Practical Stylist, The (Baker), 175, 492
Practicing History (Tuchman), 165, 492
pragmatics, 461
predicate
    complete, 84, 162, 461
    components of, 161–64
    compound, 159, 352–53, 461
    defined, 30, 162, 184, 461
    diagramming, 183, 184
    effect of expletive on, 174
    effect of prepositional phrase on, 142
    identifying, 162
    simple, 161–62, 200, 461
    transformational grammar, 196–97, 200
predicate adjectival, 404
predicate adjective, 58, 64–65, 181, 186,
    202, 404

predicate attribute, 404
predicate complement, 85, 419
predicate nominal, 461
predicate nominative, 30, 45, 181, 186, 202, 461
predicate noun, 120, 450, 461
predicate objective, 419
predicate pronoun, 450, 461
predicate substantive, 461
predicate verb, 486
predicating verb, 483
predication, 414
predicative, 58, 461
prefix, 172, 214, 216, 378, 461–62
Preminger, Alex, 505
preposition, 139–45
    clashing, 142
    complex, 140–41, 462
    compound, 139–40, 462
    deferred, 462
    defined, 139, 462
    functioning as adverb, 82, 128, 143
    functions, 139, 143
    group, 462
    noun conversion, omission for, 34
    object of, 30, 43, 44–45, 90, 139, 187, 204, 211, 452
    oblique object of, 139, 452 (see also preposition: object of)
    other parts of speech, distinguished from, 143, 149
    other parts of speech functioning as, 89, 143
    participial, 141, 149
    phrasal, 140–41, 462
    phrasal verb, in, 82–83, 142 (see also particle)
    placement, 139, 176
    prepositional phrase (see prepositional phrase)
    reducing use of, 144–45
    sentence-ending, 142, 150
    simple, 139–40, 462
    stranded, 51, 142, 462
    terminal, 142, 462
    types, 139–41
prepositional adverb, 128. See also particle

prepositional idioms, 329–44
prepositional phrase, 141–45
    controlling pronoun case, 43, 44–45, 143
    defined, 141, 187, 458
    diagramming, 187
    elliptical, 142
    functioning as adverbial, 71, 130, 164, 204
    functions, 141
    intransitive verb with, 71
    object of, 30, 43, 44–45, 90, 139, 187, 204, 211, 452
    parallelism, 176
    passive voice, in, 91, 145, 211 (see also long passive voice)
    phrasal verbs and, 82–83, 142 (see also particle)
    placement, 141–42
    reducing use of, 144–45
    replacing, 130, 144–45
    transformational grammar, 204
    verb number, and, 118, 119, 120, 142
prepositional verb, 486
preposition-stranding, 142, 462
prepositive, 463
prepositive adjective, 402
prescriptive grammar, 436
prescriptivism, 463
Presentation of Technical Information, The (Kapp), 354, 494
present gerund, 435
present infinitive, 440
present participle
    defined, 86, 454
    diagramming, 190–91
    forming, 86–87, 215
    functioning as adjective, 68
    gerund, distinguished from, 88–89, 191
    progressive aspect, forming, 91–92, 97–98, 112
    suffix, 215
present-perfect gerund, 435
present-perfect infinitive, 440
present-perfect participle, 454
present-perfect tense, 94, 95, 97, 481
present stem, 86, 440
present subjunctive, 93, 477
present tense, 93, 94, 95, 99, 481

preterit, preterite, 481
preventive grammar, 40, 52, 121, 227
Priestley, J. B., 376
Priestley, Joseph, 15, 17
primary stress, 474
primary verb, 486
principal clause, 416
principal part, 86, 464
principal verb, 83–84, 85, 86, 92, 112, 121,
    125, 126, 135, 200, 201, 202–3, 486
principle of recoverability, 167, 467
Priscian, 14
Pritchett, V. S., 348
privative, 172, 464
Proffitt, Michael, 503
progressive aspect, 94–95, 97–98, 411. *See
    also* progressive tense
Progressive English Grammar, The (Weld),
    2n5
progressive tense, 73, 94–95, 97–98, 191,
    481
pronominal adjective, 60, 404
pronoun, 36–57
  adjective, 42, 404
  agreement with antecedent, 20, 21,
    38–42, 44, 52, 408
  anaphoric, 36, 464
  antecedent of, 36–40, 49–50, 52, 53, 54,
    118–19, 325, 327, 409
  appositives, 38, 41
  article as substitute for, 63
  attribute, 45, 461, 464
  capitalizing, 43
  case, 23, 38, 41, 42, 43, 44–45, 52–53,
    143, 164
  classes, 42
  colloquial objective, 45
  colloquial *they*, 38, 40, 47
  comparative construction, in, 45
  compound, 48–49, 55, 56, 464, 465
  compound personal, 48–49, 465
  compound relative, 55
  contraction with, 84
  coordinated, 245
  defined, 36, 464
  deictic, 49
  demonstrative, 37, 42, 49–50, 198, 464

distributive, 56
editorial *we*, 46
emphatic, 464–65
exclamatory, 152
expletive, 38, 46
feminine, 44, 47, 434
first-person, 37, 38, 43, 281
form, 42
functions, 42, 55–57
gender, 38, 40–41, 42, 44, 46, 47, 52, 57
gender-neutral language and, 44, 47, 278,
    324–28
genitive, 43, 44, 50, 54–55
imperatives, 38, 92
impersonal, 464
indefinite, 42, 46–47, 48–49, 56–57, 118,
    197, 327, 464
indeterminate, 46
intensifying, 464–65
intensive, 48–49, 464–65
interrogative, 38, 42, 51, 52–53, 189, 465
linking verb, case after, 45
masculine, 44, 46, 47, 324, 434
misused, 41–42
negating, 171
neuter, 327, 434
nominative, 43, 44, 45
number, 38, 39, 42, 44, 52
objective, 43, 44–45
person, 38, 42–43
personal, 38, 41, 42–49, 52, 121, 197,
    325–26, 465
phrasal, 36, 50, 465
plural, 43, 46
possessive, 38, 47–48, 59, 63, 64, 143, 465
predicate, 450, 461
prepositional phrase, in, 43, 44–45, 143
properties, 38–42
reciprocal, 42, 50, 465
referent, 51, 468
reflexive, 43, 48–49, 50, 465
relative, 38, 42, 52–56, 60, 118, 139,
    165–66, 168, 179, 325, 465
resumptive, 465
second-person, 37, 38, 42, 43, 465
simple, 50, 466
singular *they*, 47

pronoun (*cont.*)
  subjective, 461
  third-person, 38, 42, 43, 44, 47, 327
  traditional singular, 40
pronoun–antecedent agreement, 20, 21,
    38–42, 44, 52, 408
pronunciation, 466
  assimilation, 411
  diphthong, 264, 428
  dissimilation, 428
  epenthesis, 217, 430
  haplology, 436
  hyphaeresis, 217, 438
  intonation pattern, 442
  intrusive *r*, 442
  intrusive schwa, 442
  metathesis, 445
  orthoepy, 453
  stress, 474
  syllable, 478
  synaeresis, 479
  synaloepha, 479
  syncope, 217, 479
  retarded, 466
  spelling, 466
proper adjective, 60, 404
proper name, 26, 31, 60, 61, 70, 377, 450
proper noun, 19–20, 25, 29, 31, 197, 450
prop *it*, 174
Propp, William H. C., 299, 494
prosody, 466
protasis, 166, 415
Proulx, Annie, 375
pro-verb, 412
pseudo-transitive verb, 486
Pullum, Geoffrey K., 8n29, 18n47, 245n2,
    497
Punctuate It Right! (H. Shaw), 504
punctuation, 345–99
pure infinitive, 440
purism, 466
Putting Words to Work (Teall), 279, 493
Pyles, Thomas, 502
Pynchon, Thomas, 370

Quack This Way, vi, 11n30
qualifying adjective, 60, 403

quantifying elements, 20–21
Queen, Ellery, 376
Quennell, Peter, 382
question
  alternative, 157, 466
  declarative yes–no, 157, 466
  defined, 157, 466
  direct, 131, 350, 364, 386, 466
  echo, 429
  ellipsis, 167
  embedded, 467
  exclamatory, 158, 467
  indirect, 131, 148, 149, 386, 467
  negative, 172, 467
  polar, 467
  positive, 172, 467
  punctuating, 386
  rhetorical, 158, 467
  sentence pattern, 160, 161
  tag, 157–58, 467
  types of, 157–58
  wh- question, 157, 467
  yes–no, 125, 157–58, 466, 467
question mark, 157, 367, 368, 372, 384, 386
Quinn, Edward, 505
Quirk, Randolph, 18n48, 18n50, 498
quotation
  brackets in, 390
  colon introducing, 362–63, 364
  comma introducing, 349, 352
  ellipsis dots indicating omission, 397–98,
    399
  indenting, 382
  nonoriginal content, 390
  omitted words, 397–98
  parenthetical material, 390–91
  punctuating, 352, 382, 387, 390, 397–98
quotation marks, 382–85
  American style, 382, 384
  British style, 382, 384
  defined, 382
  definitions, with, 382–83
  idiomatic usage, 384
  misplaced emphasis, 385
  other punctuation, with, 384
  phrasal adjectives, 385
  quoted words, 382, 384

reference, 382–83
sarcasm, 385
"so-called," 383
title, 383

Radford, Andrew, 498
Rand, Ayn, vii, 347, 491
Randall, Henry S., 351
Random House Dictionary of the English Language, The, 225, 503
Ransom, John Crowe, 393
Rawson, Hugh, 503
Reader for Writers, A (Targ, ed.), 493
Readings in Applied English Linguistics (Allen, ed.), vii, 491, 492, 501
recipient noun, 32–33, 450
reciprocal pronoun, 42, 50, 465
recoverability, 167, 467
　situational, 467
　structural, 467
　textual, 468
Redbook, The (Garner), vi, 362, 502
redundancy, 468
redundant subject, 475
reduplication, 218, 468
Reed, Alonzo, 181, 182, 207, 454, 468
Reed–Kellogg diagram, 181–94, 207, 468
referent, 51, 468
reflexive, 468
reflexive pronoun, 43, 48–49, 50, 465
reflexive verb, 486
regional dialect, 223, 427
register, 468
regular, 468
regular inflection, 441
regular plural, 25–26, 459
regular verb, 73–74, 86, 87, 95–96, 99–105, 486
"Relation of Linguistics to the Teaching of English, The" (P. Roberts), 263, 493
relative adjective, 52, 60, 404
relative adverb, 132, 406
relative clause, 52–54, 165–66, 168–69, 416
relative-clause reduction, 168–69. *See also* whiz-deletion
relative pronoun, 38, 42, 52–56, 60, 118, 139, 165–66, 168, 179, 325, 465

repetition, avoiding, 36, 125, 167
reported speech, 98–99, 124, 412
Research in Written Composition (Braddock), 500
restrictive, 469
restrictive appositive, 33, 355, 410
restrictive clause, 187, 355, 416
resumptive modifier, 446
resumptive pronoun, 465
retarded pronunciation, 466
retronym, 469
"Revolution in Grammar" (Francis), 14, 491
rhetorical question, 158, 467
"Rhetorical Stance, The" (Booth), 182, 492
Richards, I. A., 1, 491
Ricks, Christopher, 5, 392
Ricks, Thomas E., 384
Ritt, Nikolaus, 500
Roberts, Paul, 263, 493
Roberts, William H., 494
Robertson, James I., Jr., 363
Rogers, Will, 223
Rombauer, Irma S., 392
Room, Adrian, 504
Roosevelt, Theodore, 363
root, 84–85, 469
Rosenbaum, Peter S., 498
Ross, Robert, 17
Rossi-Wilcox, Susan M., 380
Rowan, Carl T., 349
Rowling, J. K., 376
Royster, Vermout, 383
Rudiments of English Grammar (Harrison), 16n22
Rudiments of English Grammar (Priestley), 15
run-on sentence, 417, 471–72
run-together sentence, 417

Sabin, William A., 502
Sackville-West, V., 357
Safir, Leonard, 371, 495
Safire, William, 371, 495
Salisbury, John of, vii, 491
salutation, 351, 359, 363
Sandburg, Carl, 6n24, 6n25, 350, 375
Schendl, Herbert, 500

Schlauch, Margaret, 257, 493
Schultz, Lucille M., 500
schwa, 469
    intrusive, 442
Scribes J. Legal Writing, 40n2
semantic contamination, 469
semantics, 469
semantic shift, 469
semi-auxiliary verb, 412
semicolon, 357–60
    comma, displacing, 359, 360
    defined, 357
    list, 358
    old-fashioned style, 358–59
    quotation marks, with, 384
    salutation, misused in, 359
    sentences, closely connected, 357
    series, 358
sensory verb, 486–87
sentence
    basic SVO structure of, 160–61
    clause (*see* clause)
    cleft (*see* cleft sentence)
    commands, 158, 167
    complete, 470
    complex, 159, 165, 194, 470
    compound, 159, 193, 470
    compound-complex, 159, 194, 470
    conditional, 166, 470
    constituent elements (*see* constituent)
    declarative, 157, 179, 388, 470
    defined, 469–70
    diagramming (*see* diagramming
        sentences)
    directive, 158, 177, 428
    elliptical, 71, 167
    exclamatory, 431
    existential, 471
    fragmentary, 432–33
    full, 471
    identifying elements of, 162–64
    imperative, 158, 172, 471
    impersonal, 471
    incomplete, 471
    interrogative, 55, 83–84, 157–58, 172,
        206, 386, 471
    inversion in, 157–58

    major, 470
    minor, 471
    negation (*see* negation)
    negative cleft, 179, 471
    nonsentence, 448, 472
    patterns, 160–64
    placement of elements in, 160–61
    run-on, 417, 471–72
    run-together, 417
    simple, 159, 472
    transformational grammar, 196–97
    verbless, 472
sentence adverb, 127, 192, 406
sentence fragment, 432–33
sentence modifier, 197, 406
sentence patterns, 160–64
sentences, diagramming. *See* diagramming
    sentences
sentential relative clause, 416
separative coordinating conjunction, 147,
    421
sequence of tenses, 99, 472
set phrase, 458
Shakespeare, William, 245, 398
Shattuck, Roger, 347
Shaw, George Bernard, 348
Shaw, Harry, 504
Sheed, Wilfrid, 348
shift, 472
    functional, 423, 433
    semantic, 469
Short but Comprehensive Grammar, A
    (Staniford), 16n30
short dash. *See* en-dash
Short Introduction to English Grammar, A
    (Harrold), 16n24
Short Introduction to English Grammar, A
    (Lowth), 16n16
Short Introduction to English Grammar, A
    (Sledd), 18n51, 498
Short Introduction to English Usage, A
    (Lamberts), 499
sibilant, 25, 32, 48
simile, 472
Simon, John, 361
simple, 472
simple adjective, 405

simple adverb, 128–29, 203–4, 406
simple conjunction, 146, 422
simple infinitive, 440
simple noun, 450
simple past tense, 481
simple phrase, 457
simple predicate, 161–62, 200, 461
simple preposition, 139–40, 462
simple pronoun, 50, 466
simple sentence, 159, 472
simple statement, 470
simple subject, 161–62, 475–76
simple tense, 482
Simpson, John, 503
Singer, Isaac Bashevis, 370
singular, 473
singular indicator, 445
singular marker, 445
singular number, 451
"Singular Use of *They*, A" (Eagleson), 40n2
situational recoverability, 467
Sitwell, Sacheverell, 359
Skeat, Walter W., 504
Skinner, B. F., 393
slang, 70, 214, 217, 473
slash, 392–93
    date, 392
    defined, 392
    other punctuation, displacing, 393
    per, 393
    separation, 392, 393
Sledd, James, 18n51, 195, 473, 492, 495, 498
Slim, Sir William, 380
Sluiter, Ineke, 13n2, 14n3, 491, 500
Smith, Barbara Herrnstein, 392
Smith, Hallett, 368
Smith, Logan Pearsall, 502
Snow, C. P., 361
social dialect, 427
solecism, 473
Some Secrets of Style (Bett), 304, 315, 494
"Something About Language and Social
    Class" (Sledd), 473, 495
Soukhanov, Anne H., 501
Sowell, Thomas, 366
Spark, Muriel, 361
Speaking Freely (Flexner & Soukhanov), 501

specialization, 473
speech
    colloquial, 167
    dialectal, 380
    direct, 98, 349, 428
    figure of, 37, 44, 432
    indirect, 98–99, 349, 428
    informal, 128
    parts of (*see* parts of speech)
    reported, 98–99, 124, 412
spelling, 473
spelling pronunciation, 466
spelling reform, 473
split infinitive, 85, 135–36, 440
Sprague, Kurth, 393
squinting construction, 446
squinting modifier, 446
s-structure, 475
Stageberg, Norman C., 281, 493
Standard English, 474. *See also* Standard
    Written English
Standard Written English, 4, 7, 8–10, 11, 28,
    37, 42, 223, 225–27, 474
Staniford, Daniel, 16
Staniforth, Maxwell, 493
statement, 474
stative verb, 72–73, 487
Stauffer, Donald A., 384
Stein, Gertrude, 181, 492
Steinbeck, John, 370
Steinberg, Erwin R., 502
stem, 84, 86–87, 92, 95, 96, 112, 121, 122,
    123, 124, 213, 214–15, 474
Stevenson, Robert Louis, 358
Story of Our Language, The (H. Alexander),
    289, 494, 501
stranded preposition, 51, 142, 462
Street, Harry, 367
stress, 474
    primary, 474
Strong, L. A. G., vii, 491, 502
strong verb, 73, 485
structural recoverability, 467
structure, 474
    deep, 205, 209–10, 474
    modification, 474
    parallel, 454

structure (*cont.*)
  surface, 205, 208–9, 475
  SVO, 160–61
structure word, 489
Strunk, William, Jr., 31
subject
  agreement with verb, 20, 95, 115–17, 118–20, 121, 408
  anticipatory, 119, 475
  complete, 162, 475
  compound, 41, 117–18, 120, 475
  conjunctive compound, 117–18
  coordinate, 475
  deferred, 475
  defined, 184, 475
  delayed, 119, 475
  diagramming, 184
  disjunctive compound, 117
  double, 475
  dummy, 119
  functions, 162
  identifying in sentence, 162
  infinitive, of, 476
  passive voice, role in, 184–203
  placement in sentence, 160–61
  redundant, 475
  simple, 161–62, 475–76
  understood, 476
subject case, 413
subject clause, 178–79, 417
subject complement, 419
subjective, 448
subjective adjective, 404
subjective case, 413
subjective complement, 81, 88, 162, 163–64, 183, 184, 186, 419
subjective function, 29–30
subjective noun, 461
subjective pronoun, 461
subject–verb agreement, 20, 95, 115–17, 118–20, 121, 408
subjunctive, 122, 476–77
  formulaic, 476
  mandative, 476
  mood, 92–94, 97, 447
  past, 93–94, 477
  past-perfect, 94

  present, 93, 477
  were-subjunctive, 477
subordinate clause, 132, 136, 165, 168, 187, 188, 189, 194, 347, 415
subordinating conjunction, 141, 146–48, 161, 165, 187, 188, 194, 243, 422
subordination, 165, 477
  upside-down, 477
subordinator, 422
substantive, 451
substantive clause, 416
substantive phrase, 458
Successful Writing (Hairston), 327, 494
suffix
  adjectives, 58, 65, 66–67
  adverbs, 128, 131, 133–34
  conversion, 216
  defined, 477
  derivational, 215, 477
  -ee/-er/-or, 32
  -ever, 55
  gendered, 24, 326, 327–28
  inflectional, 215, 477
  -less/-like, 377–78
  names, following, 356
  negative, 172
  -self/-selves, 48
  suspensive hyphen, 376
  verbs, 73–74, 215
  word formation, 213, 214–15, 216
summative modifier, 446
Summerson, John, 369
superlative, 477–78
  double, 67, 478
  periphrastic, 66, 134, 478
  suffix, 215
  synthetic, 66, 134, 478
superlative adjective, 66–67, 405
superlative adverb, 133–34, 477–78
superordinate, 478
superstitions, 142, 150
suppletion, 478
surface structure, 205, 208–9, 475
suspended prepositional construction, 478
Sussman, Barry, 384
SVO sentence structure, 160–61
Swan, Michael, 499

Sweet, Henry, 3
Swinburne, Algernon Charles, 369
syllable, 478
   closed, 478
   long, 478
   open, 478
syllepsis, 479
Symbol, Status, and Personality (Hayakawa),
   307, 494
synaeresis, 479
synaloepha, 479
syncopation, 479
syncope, 217, 479
syndetic coordination, 424
syndeton, 479
synecdoche, 479
synesis, 116, 120, 479
synonym, 479
"Syntactic Strictures" (Sledd), 195, 492
Syntactic Structures (Chomsky), 4n18
syntax, 155–211
   clause (*see* clause)
   collective nouns, 19, 20–21, 22, 29, 39,
      116, 449
   coordination (*see* coordination)
   defined, 157, 480
   directive, 157, 158, 177, 428
   exclamation, 92, 132, 152, 157, 158, 167,
      431
   expression of multitude, 20–21
   generally, 7
   inflection, contrasted with, 157, 160
   inverted, 30, 55–56, 119, 158
   negation of (*see* negation)
   parallelism (*see* parallelism)
   question (*see* question)
   sentence (*see* sentence)
   sentence patterns, 160–64
   statement, 157–58, 160, 169, 172–73, 257,
      474
   word order, 160, 489
Syntax, Style and Grammatical Norms
   (Dalton-Puffer et al., eds.), 500
synthetic comparative, 66, 133, 418
synthetic language, 160, 480
synthetic superlative, 66, 134, 478

System of English Grammar, The (Long),
   18n44

taboo, 480
tag question, 157–58, 467
Targ, William, 493
Taub-Dix, Bonnie, 350
tautology, 480
Teaching English Grammar (Pooley), 3n15,
   501
*Teaching of English from the Sixteenth
   Century to 1870, The* (Michael), 17n40,
   501
*Teaching of English in the Elementary and the
   Secondary School, The* (Chubb), 3n14,
   500
Teaching of the English Language (Fries), 3–4
Teaching Secondary English (DeBoar,
   Kaulfers & Helen Miller), 500
Teachout, Terry, 377
Teall, Edward N., 279, 493
Technique of Clear Writing, The (Gunning),
   502
Téknē Grammatiké (or *The Grammatical Art*)
   (Dionysios Thrax), 13
tense, 94–115
   compound, 97, 480
   continuous, 94, 97–98, 481
   defined, 94–95, 480
   doubled consonants, 95–96
   effects of backshifting, 98–99
   expanded, 98, 480
   forming, 95–98
   future, 94, 96, 480
   future-perfect, 86, 94, 97, 480
   historical-present, 95, 481
   imperfect, 94
   modal, 481
   past, 73–74, 86, 93–96, 190, 481
   past indicative, 87, 95–96
   past-perfect, 94, 97, 98, 481
   past-progressive, 73, 98
   perfect, 94–95, 97, 190, 480, 481
   pluperfect, 97, 481
   potential, 481
   present, 93, 94, 95, 99, 481
   present indicative, 95

tense (*cont.*)
  present-perfect, 94, 95, 97, 481
  present-progressive, 73, 98
  preterit, 481
  progressive, 73, 94–95, 97–98, 191, 481
  sequence of, 99, 472
  simple, 482
  suffixes, 215
terminal preposition, 142, 462
textual recoverability, 468
that-clause, 417
that-complement, 419
Thomas, Owen, 498
Thrax, Dionysios, 13–14
Thurber, James, 384
Times (London), 8n29, 389
tmesis, 214–15, 217, 482
tone, 38, 130, 152, 158, 281, 322, 482
transformation, 205–7, 482
transformational-generative grammar, 195
transformational grammar, 4, 195–211
  active voice, 210–11
  adverbials, 203–5
  ambiguity, 208–10
  auxiliary, 201–2
  be-verb, 201, 202, 207, 211
  deep structure, 205, 209–10, 474
  defined, 4, 195
  determiners, 198–99
  lexical ambiguity, 207–8
  middle verb, 202–3
  modifier, 199
  noun phrase, 197–200
  number, 200
  passive voice, 207, 210–11
  person, 200
  possession, 200
  prearticle, 199
  predicate, 196–97, 200
  prepositional phrase, 204
  principal verb, 202–3
  rules of, 196–207
  sentence basics, 196–97
  surface structure, 205, 208–10, 474
  surface transformation, 205–7
  symbols for rules, 196
  terminology, 195

  tree diagram, 195, 196, 200, 207, 209, 482
  verb phrase, 200–202
Transformational Grammar (Radford), 498
Transformational Grammar and the Teacher of English (Thomas), 498
Transgrammar (Malmstrom & Weaver), 498
transitive, 71–72, 482
transitive verb, 30, 71–72, 85, 86, 90, 92, 163, 164, 181, 202–3, 204, 486, 487
Trask, R. L., 96n4, 284, 493
Treatise on the Structure of the English Language, A (S. Greene), 18n41
tree diagram, 195, 196, 200, 207, 209, 482
Trilling, Lionel, 363
Trimble, John R., 127, 492
Truman, Margaret, 373, 386
truncated passive, 455
Tuchman, Barbara, 165, 381, 492
Turgenev, Ivan, 396
Turgeon, Gregoire, 494
Turkle, Sherry, 350
Turnell, Martin, 397
Twain, Mark, 262, 369, 493

umlaut, 482
umlaut plural, 459
Uncommon Tongue, An (Nash), 426, 495
uncountable noun, 450
Understanding English Grammar (Kolln), 18n50
understood subject, 476
ungrammatical, 482
uninflected plural, 459
University Grammar of English, A (Quirk & Greenbaum), 18n48
Unlocking the English Language (Burchfield), 1n1, 5n20, 501
unmarked infinitive, 440
unmarked word, 483
Updike, John, 361
upside-down subordination, 477
usage, 221–344
  big data in assessing, 8–10, 225–27
  defined, 483
  dictionaries and, 225
  empiricism, 8–10, 225–27
  good vs. common, 225

Google ngrams, 8–10, 225–27
grammar, contrasted with, 223
overview, 8
Usage and Abusage (Partridge), 499
Ussher, George Neville, 16

vagueness, 34, 91, 283, 284
Vallins, G. H., 351, 494
variant, 483
verb, 71–126
    action, 483, 484
    adjective functioning as, 70
    agreement with subject, 20, 95, 115–17,
        118–20, 121, 408
    ambitransitive, 72, 484
    anomalous, 485
    asserting, 485
    auxiliary (*see* auxiliary verb)
    being, 485
    be-verb (*see* *be*-verb)
    complementary infinitive, 85, 440
    complete, 84, 483
    complete predication, of, 485
    conjugation (*see* conjugation)
    connecting, 81–82, 485
    contractions, 83, 84, 380, 423
    coordinate, 159, 483
    copula, 81–82, 485
    copular, 485
    copulative, 485
    dangling gerund, 65, 89–90
    dangling infinitive, 85–86
    defective, 122, 483–84
    defined, 483
    denominal, 34, 217, 484
    diagramming, 189–92
    ditransitive, 484
    dynamic, 72–73, 483, 484
    emphatic, 125, 484
    ergative, 72, 484
    exclamatory, 152
    factitive, 164, 484
    finite, 41, 84, 85, 116, 162, 165, 484
    full, 124–25, 485
    function, 71
    functioning as other parts of speech, 85,
        88

    gerund (*see* gerund)
    helping, 121, 411–12
    identifying in predicate, 163
    infinitive (*see* infinitive)
    inflection, 73–81, 90, 441
    intransitive, 71–72, 81–82, 135, 202, 485
    irregular, 73–81, 86–87, 96, 485
    lexical, 485, 486
    linking (*see* linking verb)
    main, 97–98, 135, 181, 184, 189, 190, 485,
        486
    middle, 202–3, 485
    modal auxiliary (*see* modal auxiliary verb)
    monotransitive, 485
    mood (*see* mood)
    multiword, 486
    negating verb phrase, 83–84
    nonaction, 487
    noncount, 22, 450
    nonfinite, 86, 440, 485
    notional, 486
    noun functioning as, 34
    number (*see* verb number)
    participial, 486
    participle (*see* participle)
    person, 90, 95–96, 98, 115–16, 121, 456
    phrasal, 82–84, 128, 142, 184, 379, 486
    phrasal prepositional, 486
    placement in sentence, 160–61
    predicate, 486
    predicating, 483
    prepositional, 486
    primary, 486
    principal, 83–84, 85, 86, 92, 112, 121,
        125, 126, 135, 200, 201, 202–3, 486
    properties, 90–121
    pro-verb, 412
    pseudo-transitive, 486
    reflexive, 486
    regular, 73–74, 86, 87, 95–96, 99–105,
        486
    root, 84–85, 469
    sensory, 486–87
    split infinitive, 85, 135–36, 203, 440
    splitting verb phrase, 83–84, 135
    stative, 72–73, 487

verb (*cont.*)
  stem, 84, 86–87, 92, 95, 96, 112, 121, 122,
    123, 124, 213, 214–15, 474
  strong, 73, 485
  suffixes, 73–74, 215
  tense (*see* tense)
  transitive, 30, 71–72, 85, 86, 90, 92, 163,
    164, 181, 202–3, 204, 486, 487
  voice (*see* voice)
  weak, 73, 486
  zombie nouns and, 144
verb–adverb combination, 216, 486
verbal, 88, 200–203, 206–7, 487
  group, 88, 487
verbal adjective, 403
verbalist, 487
verbal noun, 85, 435
verbarian, 487
verb cluster, 458
verb group, 487
verbless sentence, 472
verb number, 115–21
  agreement with subject, 115–17, 118–20,
    121, 408
  compound subjects, 117–18
  connectives and conjunctions, 120, 121
  determining, 118
  effect of conjunction on, 151
  expletive, with, 119
  gerund, infinitive, or clause as subject,
    with, 117
  inversion, 118
  nouns with plural form but singular sense,
    118
  prepositional phrase and, 118, 119, 120,
    142
verbomaniac, 488
verb phrase, 83–84, 86, 132, 135–36, 174,
  196–97, 200–202, 458
Vidal, Gore, 384
virgule. *See* slash
vocabulary, 10, 160, 488
vocative, 192, 350, 488
vocative imperative, 439
voice, 90–92, 488
  active, 85, 86, 89, 90–92, 97–98, 145, 184,
    210–11, 402

passive (*see* passive voice)
Volkmann, Chris, 396
Volkmann, Toren, 396
vowel, 26, 62, 67, 73, 95, 128, 217, 218, 228,
  488
vulgarism, 488

Waite, Alice Vinton, 14n4
Wallace, David Foster, 11n30, 231, 375, 493
Wallace, Ray, 500
Wallraff, Barbara, 499
Walsh, Bill, 499
War Against Grammar, The (Mulroy), 5,
  13n1, 408, 495, 501
Warfel, Harry C., 5
Waugh, Evelyn, 363, 390
weak plural, 459
weak verb, 73, 486
Weaver, Constance, 498
Webster, Noah, 17, 23, 491
*Webster's New International Dictionary of the
  English Language*, 503
Webster's New World College Dictionary, 225,
  503
*Webster's New World English Grammar
  Handbook* (Loberger & Welsh), 18n45
*Webster's Third New International Dictionary
  of the English Language*, 503
Weekley, Ernest, 504
Weigh the Word (Jennings et al., eds.), 494
Weiner, Edmund S. C., 497, 503
Weld, Allen Hayden, 2, 17n41
Weld's English Grammar (Weld), 17n41
Wells, H. G., 373, 376
Welsh, Kate Shoup, 18n45
Welty, Eudora, 388
Wensberg, Erik, 498
were-subjunctive, 477
We Who Speak English (Lloyd), 150n5
Wharton, Edith, 361
What a Word! (Herbert), 285, 493
Whitcut, Janet, 499, 502
White, E. B., 31, 358, 363
White, Richard Grant, 296, 494
White, Ronald C., Jr., 6n26
White, Theodore H., 347
Whitman, Walt, 350

Whitney, William Dwight, 256, 493
whiz-deletion, 91, 165–66, 168–69, 179, 488
Who Killed Grammar? (Warfel), 5
wh- question, 157, 467
Why Do You Talk like That? (Burton), 142, 492
"Why I Write" (Didion), 205, 492
Why Not Say It Clearly (King), 144, 492
Whyte, Adam Gowans, 251, 493
Wilde, Oscar, 348
Williams, T. Harry, 383
Williams, Tennessee, 350
Wills, Garry, 369
Wilson, Edmund, 369
Wilson, Graham, 491, 493
Winterowd, W. Ross, 383, 490, 493
Wiseman, Richard, 389
Woe Is I (O'Conner), 36, 491, 499
Wolfe, Tom, 396
Woodman, Richard, 382
Woodward, Bob, 384
Woolf, Virginia, 370, 389
Woollcott, Alexander, 350, 351
word
    compound (*see* compound)
    content, 61, 98, 489
    defined, 488–89
    dummy, 431
    form, 489
    function, 489
    portmanteau, 219, 489
    structure, 489
    superordinate, 489
    unmarked, 483
word class, 489
    closed, 74, 489
    open, 489
Word Court (Wallraff), 499
word formation, 213–19
    accidence, 213, 401
    acronyms, 218–19, 401
    affixation (*see* affixation)
    agglutination, 216, 407
    aphaeresis, 217, 409
    aphesis, 409
    apocope, 217, 409
    apothegm, 217

back-formations, 217, 412
    changing part of speech, 216
    clipping, 216–17, 417
    compounding, 215–16, 420
    defined, 213, 489
    dissimilation, 428
    elongation, 217
    epenthesis, 217, 430
    hyphaeresis, 217, 438
    infixes, 214–15, 217, 441
    initialisms, 219, 441
    loan translation, 218, 444
    morphemes, 213–15, 447
    morphology (*see* morphology)
    neologisms, 219, 447
    prefixes, 213–14, 461–62
    reduplication, 218, 468
    stem, 214, 215, 474
    suffixes (*see* suffix)
    syncope, 217, 479
    tmesis, 214–15, 217, 482
word order, importance of, 160, 489
Word Play (Farb), 225, 492
word-stem, 474
Working Principles of Grammar, The (Genung), 137, 492
Wright, Laura, 501
Wright, Richard, 396
Writing in Plain English (Eagleson, G. Jones & Hassall), 502
Writing Well (D. Hall), 71, 491
Writing with Style (Trimble), 127, 492

Yes, I Could Care Less (Walsh), 499
yes–no question, 125, 157–58, 466, 467
You Have a Point There (Partridge), 504
Young Lady's Accidence, The (Bingham), 16n23
Your Own Words (Wallraff), 499

Zandvoort, R. W., 498
zero article, 63, 410
zero derivation, 423
zero plural, 459
zeugma, 489
zombie noun, 144, 448, 451

Pronunciation Guide

ə *for all the vowel sounds in*
burden, circus, function, putt

a *as in* fact, plat

ah *as in* balm, father

ahr *as in* bar, start

air *as in* flare, lair

aw *as in* law, paw

ay *as in* page, same

b *as in* balk, rob

ch *as in* chief, breach

d *as in* debt, docket

e *as in* leg, tenant

ee *as in* plea, legal

eer *as in* mere, tier

er *as in* merit, stationery

f *as in* father, off

g *as in* go, fog

h *as in* hearsay, hold

hw *as in* whereas, while

i *as in* risk, intent

ɪ *as in* crime, idle

j *as in* jury, judge

k *as in* kidnap, flak

l *as in* lawyer, trial

m *as in* motion, malice

n *as in* notice, negate

n for a nasalized
Francophone *n*
(as in *embonpoint*)

ng *as in* long, ring

o *as in* contract, loss

oh *as in* oath, impose

oo *as in* rule, school

oor *as in* lure, tour

or *as in* board, court

ow *as in* allow, oust

oy *as in* join, ploy

p *as in* perjury, prize

r *as in* revolt, terror

s *as in* sanction, pace

sh *as in* sheriff, flash

t *as in* intent, term

th *as in* theory, theft

<u>th</u> *as in* there, whether

uu *as in* took, pull

uur *as in* insurance, plural

v *as in* vague, waiver

w *as in* warranty, willful

y *as in* year, yield

z *as in* zoning, maze

zh *as in* measure, vision